Individual and Conflict in Greek Ethics

INDIVIDUAL AND CONFLICT IN GREEK ETHICS

Nicholas White

CLARENDON PRESS · OXFORD
2002

OXFORD

UNIVERSITY PRESS

Great Clarendon Street, Oxford OX2 6DP

Oxford University Press is a department of the University of Oxford.
It furthers the University's objective of excellence in research, scholarship,
and education by publishing worldwide in

Oxford New York

Auckland Bangkok Buenos Aires Cape Town Chennai
Dar es Salaam Delhi Hong Kong Istanbul Karachi Kolkata
Kuala Lumpur Madrid Melbourne Mexico City Mumbai Nairobi
São Paulo Shanghai Singapore Taipei Tokyo Toronto

with an associated company in Berlin

Oxford is a registered trade mark of Oxford University Press
in the UK and in certain other countries

Published in the United States
by Oxford University Press Inc., New York

© Nicholas White 2002

British Library Cataloguing in Publication Data

Data available

Library of Congress Cataloging in Publication Data

White, Nicholas P., 1942–
Individual and conflict in Greek ethics / Nicholas White.
p. cm.
Includes bibliographical references and index.
1. Ethics—Greece. 2. Ethics—History. I. Title.
BJ161 .W47 2002   170´.938—dc21   2001052063

ISBN 0–19–825059–2

1 3 5 7 9 10 8 6 4 2

Typeset by Invisible Ink
Printed in Great Britain
on acid-free paper by
Biddles Ltd.,
Guildford & King's Lynn

FOR J. R. W., O. L. W., AND A. C. W.

Acknowledgements

I do not merely follow custom when I say that more people have contributed to the writing of this book than I can thank properly. A number of people read a very early draft, which was faulty enough to try their patience sorely. If the present version is better, that is because of them. Here I thank especially Julia Annas, the late William Frankena, and David Velleman. Others also had a look at the manuscript later, some of them anonymously. I am grateful for their suggestions.

Many audiences at various universities, including students in courses at the University of Michigan, the University of Utah, and the University of California at Irvine, have had the main ideas of the book inflicted on them, and they too have my thanks. So, too, do partners in numerous conversations whose comments and reactions have been helpful. I am notably indebted to audiences at the University of Hamburg, where I lectured on some of this material in 1999—without, I would add, convincing all of my colleagues there of all of the interpretations that I espoused. Helpful criticism there, especially by Dorothea Frede and Ulrich Steinvorth, has in all of these cases led to what I hope are substantial improvements.

I am especially indebted, too, to the many scholars who have produced the large amount of good work on ancient ethics that has appeared during recent decades. This work is gradually freeing itself from the misapprehensions for which I here criticize standard interpretations. The present book is in many ways simply a consolidation of the progress that has already been made—though of course I cannot pretend, assume, or probably even hope that those who are responsible for that progress will accept all of the things that I have, as I see it, built upon what they have said and shown.

I should add that I have been unable to take adequate account of all of the material that has been written on this subject. In particular, much new material has been written since I conceived this project and set down its main ideas. When one is in this position, one thus tries weakly to play Achilles to the constantly growing tortoise of advancing scholarship. An attempt to take account of all of the work that could reasonably be cited would probably have postponed the appearance of this book forever.

For help in the writing of this book my main debt is to William Frankena, and also to his memory. Beginning in about 1974 he sat patiently through our weekly discussions of Greek ethics. My overall views about the subject were by that time largely formed, but many of the improvements and refinements introduced since then, and since the early eighties when those views had become more definite, have been due to his steady probing. I am sure that if he were alive today he would disagree with a good deal of what I say, but the hope of saying things that would have convinced him, or at least would have struck him as reasonable and plausible, still seems to me an extremely good guide for thinking about these matters.

I give warm thanks, too, to Angela Blackburn for her extraordinary editorial assistance, and to D. Kenneth Brown for help with indexing and proofreading. Both have saved me from many errors.

It goes without saying that I thank Morton White for all he has done for me over the years, philosophically and paternally, and equally Lucia Perry White in as many ways. Also the acronymous dedicatees, for more than (I think) they can realize. And obviously, for so much, Christine Chwaszcza.

Contents

Introduction

This book is not a history of Greek ethics. Nor is it a history of the reception of Greek ethics or of the use of it by recent philosophers. Indeed, it is not intended as a *history of* anything at all. Rather, it is intended as something like a prolegomenon to a history of Greek ethics—a piece of ground-clearing. For reasons that will emerge, I think ground-clearing is required by the way in which the history of these matters has been treated over the last two centuries. Accordingly, this book examines, among other things, some factors that, by oversimplifying of our conception of Greek ethical thinking, have made it difficult for us to conceive or write the history of Greek ethics as it should be conceived and written. Most of these difficulties have been of two types. First, we have had a mistaken view of the overall course of Greek ethics pressed upon us. Second, we have been induced to generalize much too freely about Greek ethics, and to think that there is an outlook on ethics that was adopted by 'the Greeks' as opposed to us moderns, whereas there is scarcely any such thing at all.

Since this is not a history of Greek ethics, I have not attempted to treat all of the issues or figures that such a history should treat, nor have I given exhaustive treatments even of those figures whom I have discussed. I have emphasized certain aspects of the historiography of Greek ethics of the last two hundred years, but I have not written a history of that either. Occasionally, as in the chapter on Hellenistic ethics, I have covered some standard material in an introductory manner. My purpose in such cases, however, is to set the stage for the particular issues that I treat, in the interests of readers who are unfamiliar with the relevant figures; my aim is not to give a survey of the relevant material or period.

The main point of the book is as follows. It opposes the thesis that Greek ethical thinkers pursued their ideas mainly by presupposing, or with a view to establishing or defending, a harmony or consistency of worthwhile human aims or goods. This thesis, though it is often espoused or simply taken for granted, seems to me false. Rather, the Greeks were every bit as troubled by the difficulty of discovering such a consistency as moderns are, and by no means confident that it could be done. They did not take for granted that no conflicts between goods could exist. It is accordingly mistaken to see a sharp contrast in this area between 'the ancient' and 'the modern'.

In particular, the Greeks realized, just as clearly as modern thinkers, the extreme difficulty of reconciling an individual's own happiness with a concern for the happiness of others and conformity to ethical norms. Greek philosophers were not prey to illusions about any easy such harmony. The 'Classical' philosophers—Socrates, Plato,

and Aristotle—did not presuppose or even believe that such consistency grew directly out of the ethical thinking of their culture. Earlier writers had been at least as sceptical about the matter. Later thinkers, in the 'Hellenistic' schools of Stoicism and
Epicureanism, were prepared to try to introduce systematic consistency into practical
deliberation, but they recognized that in order to do so they had to depart radically
from ordinary ways of thinking.

Because this book to a large extent aims to clear the ground for something further,
large stretches are devoted to a purely negative project: arguing against interpretations of Greek ethics which have been widespread and influential. I have aimed, however, to replace those ideas with elements of a more positive picture of what Greek
ethics was. That picture shows Greek ethics as diverse and multifariously motivated,
not a uniform whole to be contrasted with modern ethics. One Greek view of ethics is
often as different from another Greek view as it is from any modern view. Thematic
unity of a history of Greek ethics can look as if it comes cheap, but the price is a distortion of the subject matter.

I hope that the plan of this book will convince people of the importance, when one
investigates the history of philosophy, of paying attention both to the past historiography of philosophy and to the philosophical debates that have shaped it. People
who write about a historical period of philosophy, if they have anything interesting
to say about it, are inescapably influenced by the philosophical atmosphere of their
own time. There is no way to talk significantly about historical issues without breath-
ing the philosophical atmosphere around one. Historians of philosophy, moreover,
are always reacting to earlier scholars, who had been in their turn influenced by the
philosophical thoughts of their own time and normally, too, by earlier historical
writing. It is a myth to think that one learns about philosophy purely by studying its
history rather than the other way around. One begins where one is, as Peirce saw;
then, with a clear focus on one's present location, one tries to find out how one got
there.

Trying to write about the history of Greek ethics, in particular, makes little sense
unless one thinks about the philosophical issues as best one can in one's own terms, and
also about the philosophical motivations that moved earlier writers on the history of
Greek ethics. It goes without saying that one must then study the texts as con-
scientiously as one can, so as to try to minimize anachronisms in one's own interpretation.

I have tried to write a book that will interest readers beyond the circle of those who
study ancient philosophy—without, however, aiming simply for a popular audience.
I may thus have fallen between the various stools. Certainly I have made concessions
at some points—though by no means always. Sometimes I have indulged in brisk
summaries, because I thought many readers likely to be unfamiliar with the relevant
material. Sometimes, too, I have used readily available translations without much

comment, even though certain points of interpretation that they incorporate might well have been discussed in critical detail. At other times, however, I have lingered over issues that seemed important to my main theme, and have often included quotations of passages that seemed to be worth presenting to the reader fairly fully. I hope that the seeming inconsistency is not too obtrusive.

Chapter 1

THE IDEA OF HELLENIC
HARMONY

I. Motivations of Philosophical Historiography

1. Philosophical Motivations of Philosophical Historiography

People who study the past are hardly ever motivated by historical curiosity alone. For better or worse, most human beings who think about earlier times do so because of some concern about the present and future. There does perhaps exist in some individuals a form of curiosity directed merely at how things used to be. Some people seem, after all, to wonder quite idly what's down the road or on the other side of the mountain. I suppose that it is possible also to wonder idly what happened before now. But the fact that idle curiosity exists does not mean that it very often operates by itself. In general, when people ask questions about what happened, their main reason for doing so originates from further questions in their minds about what is happening now or will happen later, and about what they wish to see happen or want to cause to happen.

The foregoing is only a rough generalization about how people are normally motivated. It is unlikely to be a necessary truth or to show an essential feature of our nature. It simply describes how things in fact are.

What I have said is not intended to be a sweeping claim about historical objectivity. My point is not that there is no such thing. Nor, for that matter, do I claim that our concern for the present and the future always or necessarily distorts what we believe about the past. Perhaps it does, and perhaps it does not. Perhaps our interest in what is happening now and will happen later sometimes leaves our thinking about the past completely neutral and unbiased. Or perhaps it never does. Either view is compatible with the idea that thoughts about the past are almost always influenced significantly by beliefs and attitudes about the present and future. That point should be uncontroversial enough to begin from.

To be sure, historians of ideas sometimes try hard to disentangle their thinking from the ideas that are current in their own day. For example, about one hundred years ago it was proclaimed by Victor Brochard that the history of philosophy had finally achieved its own autonomous status, and was no longer the servant of philosophy.[1] Brochard had a point. It does not, however, contradict what I am saying. His point was simply that the historian of philosophy is not obliged to treat earlier ideas merely as anticipations of what people think now. That is true. In fact, historians can even recognize that earlier thinkers were concerned with quite different issues from the ones that now seem important.

Even so, hardly any work in the history of ideas is free from the influence of present or recent thought. Even writers who are naive about the ideas of their own time are almost always influenced by what they themselves regard as important philosophical questions, and the intellectual atmosphere surrounding them helps determine what those questions are.

2. Philosophical Motivations of the Historiography of Greek Thought

What holds for the history of ideas in general holds likewise in this case for the history of Greek thought. I doubt that anyone has ever investigated those ideas without being actively concerned about what bearing the investigation ought to have on the thought of his own time and place. Even when Greeks are presented to us within an ostensibly antique tableau, they are always also simultaneously playing a modern role on a modern stage.

Causes of this state of affairs are obvious enough. Greek thinkers propounded many ideas that are central to philosophical debates now. To describe Greek thought is often to describe some issue that is still alive. Furthermore, the Greeks' position at the chronological beginning of the Western philosophical tradition has appeared to many to lend their thinking a special status—that of having been there first. Thus many people feel that an idea is more authoritative if an ancient Greek had it.

Others, however, have the opposite reaction. From their perspective, the fact that a thought originated in Greek antiquity gives rise to suspicion. Being old can seem to connote being out of date. The fact that an idea was first conceived long ago by a well-known thinker can appear to suggest not that it is good, but that it is merely entrenched. Old thoughts often seem worth clearing away, and the debunking of a thought seems all the more significant if the thought is ancient.

This same division of opinion appears when we examine the particular topic of this book, the issue of conflict and harmony in practical deliberation concerning one's own happiness and considerations of a broader sort, especially those involving various

---

[1] Brochard 1901: 1; see also the reply by Sertillanges 1901, as well as Gauthier and Jolif 1970: i. 292 and ii. 569.

ethical norms and the good of others, the treatment of this issue by the Greeks, and the interpretation and use of Greek thought by modern thinkers. Modern reactions to Greek ideas about it, moreover, exhibit the intellectual motivations that drive the main modern responses to what the Greeks said. Some of these responses are crude and can be painted with a broad brush. Others are more scholarly, nuanced, and detailed. Even these, however, are heavily influenced by the broader and simpler tendencies visible in modern reactions to Greek thought, and tend to align themselves with one or the other of them, or at least be influenced by them to some notable extent.

It therefore makes sense to set the stage with a broad presentation—extended, but by no means complete—of some main ways in which thinkers over the last two centuries have responded to Greek ethical thought as they interpreted it.

II. Historiographical Themes: Modern Fragmentation and Ancient Harmony

1. Modern Fragmentation and Disharmony

Words like 'disharmony' and 'fragmentation' have been widely used to characterize the period of the last two hundred years or so. Although a variety of different meanings have been attached to these terms, there is a palpable kinship among them. Two centuries ago, Friedrich Schiller said that the modern state is 'an ingenious clockwork, in which out of the piecing together of innumerable but lifeless parts, a mechanical kind of collective life ensued'. The modern individual, on the other hand, is described by Schiller this way:

> Forever chained to just a single little fragment of the whole, man develops into nothing but a fragment himself; forever in his ear the monotonous sound of the wheel that he turns, he never develops the harmony of his being, and instead of putting the stamp of humanity on his own nature, he becomes just an imprint of his occupation, his specialized knowledge.[2]

Schiller's thought is that the political institutions in which we live form a complex totality, in which each one of us is confined to just a small role. In such a role only a small part of an individual's nature is allowed expression. The full range of capacities is suppressed, and human life is stunted.

If we try to embrace all of the facets of the totality of what goes on around us, Schiller's thought continues, we find ourselves pulled apart into numerous pieces. The complexity of modern life is too great for a single human being to encompass. Walter Pater, writing a century later than Schiller, fixes his attention on a related

---

[2] Schiller 1967: Letter VI, sec. 7 (I have slightly altered the translation by Wilkinson and Willoughby). On the continuation of this theme in Hegel and Marx, see Kain 1982.

matter, 'the problem of unity with ourselves'. This problem, he says, strikes us 'of the modern world, with its conflicting claims, its entangled interests, distracted by so many sorrows, with many preoccupations, so bewildering an experience'.[3]

The general theme of modern fragmentation is still a commonplace now. A version of it is applied, for instance, by Alasdair MacIntyre:

> What we possess . . . are the fragments of a conceptual scheme, parts which now lack those contexts from which their significance derived. We possess indeed simulacra of morality, we continue to use many of the key expressions. But we have—very largely, if not entirely—lost our comprehension, both theoretical and practical, of morality.[4]

A general sense of disunity, then, is said to attach to the modern world, to our view of it, to our theories about it, and to our motivations in response to it.[5] To writers like Schiller, Pater, MacIntyre, and many others, the modern world presents itself as too complex to be comprehended within a single view. Our experience of it, as well as our attempts to find a way of coping with it, turn out to be disunified in a damaging way. As Schiller saw things, the only feasible alternative is to bind oneself to only one part of it. But if one does that, one's capacities are straitjacketed, and the 'ingenious clockwork', with all its complexity and disharmony, goes on heedless.

2. Hellenic Eudaimonism

The contrast between ancient harmony and modern fragmentation finds expression in the historiography of Greek ethics. The best way to introduce the matter is to focus on the Greek word *eudaimonia*. It can be translated in a number of ways. Possible translations include 'happiness' and 'well-being', and in addition one can say that to speak of *eudaimonia* is to speak of one's 'good'.[6] I shall use these three expressions interchangeably.

Helping themselves to the term *eudaimonia*, most modern writers maintain that Greek ethics is 'eudaimonist'.[7] The meaning of this contention, however, varies from writer to writer. Many use the term loosely, to suggest either that Greek ethics somehow stresses the notion of happiness, or else merely that Greek treatments of ethics often begin by focusing on it. In addition the suggestion can also be that a Greek philosopher, as he begins his reflections, feels constrained to make his philosophical

---

[3] Pater 1980: 182.

[4] MacIntyre 1981: 2.

[5] See generally on this theme, Larmore 1987: passim, as well as Taylor 1989: passim and esp. e.g. 510.

[6] 'Flourishing' is also sometimes offered as an equivalent. At times it is appropriate, but it also has its drawbacks, both as a translation and as a designation of what *eudaimonia* was taken to be. See Kraut 1979.

[7] This has been a standard view since the time of Kant, as we shall see; it has also been reflected throughout this century by scholars of ancient philosophy; see e.g. Brochard 1901: 3–4.

results conform reasonably closely, in particular, to the concept of *eudaimonia* that he finds in ordinary Greek thought.[8]

Nevertheless, the ascription of eudaimonism to the Greeks usually connotes something yet further, and must do so if the ascription is to have the philosophical importance that has been claimed for it.[9] It usually indicates not just something about the starting point or expected results of philosophical investigation, but something more definite about the content of the ethical position that is ascribed to Greek thinkers.

A more definite and substantial idea of what Greek eudaimonism can amount to is given by Henry Sidgwick:

[I]n the whole ethical controversy of ancient Greece . . . it was assumed on all sides that a rational individual would make the pursuit of his own good his supreme aim.[10]

Sidgwick here formulates a straightforward version of what many philosophers and historians of philosophy suppose to be characteristic of ancient as opposed to modern ethics. Sharpening Sidgwick's point still a little further, let us take eudaimonism to be the view that an individual human being has a single ultimate rational aim, in the sense of the one thing that is rationally aimed at for its own sake rather than because of its contribution (causal or other) to some further aim, and that this aim is that individual's happiness or good or well-being.[11] The word 'rational' here carries no special meaning: it indicates merely what one is well advised to aim at when everything relevant is taken into account.[12]

Divergent versions of eudaimonism will differ as to what they take an individual's happiness to be, but there is good reason to apply the label principally to this thesis

---

[8] The notion of an 'entry point' into philosophical discussion is used by Annas 1993; see also Cottingham 1991: 812–13. Striker 1996: 170 uses the expression 'starting point' without explanation, and employs the term 'eudaimonism' in a way that resembles Annas's; likewise Cooper's usage in his 1996: 261–2. Brink 1997: 124 begins by explaining 'eudaimonist' by saying that it involves the belief that 'an agent's practical reasoning should be regulated by a correct conception of his own happiness or *eudaimonia*'. This seems a fairly weak condition. However, Brink then goes on to say that 'eudaimonism implies that if practical virtues are to be worth acting on then they must be beneficial to the agent'. This is stronger, though not strong enough to exclude serious deliberative conflicts between one's happiness and other considerations.

[9] It is customary to maintain—I am uncertain how correctly—that Kant coined the term 'eudaimonism'—or rather, 'Eudämonismus'. He associated it with the word 'Glückseligkeitslehre' (see Gauthier and Jolif 1970: i. 290).

[10] Sidgwick 1931: 198; see also his 1907: 91–2, and compare Urmson 1988: 90.

[11] It is true that Sidgwick probably had something weaker in mind when he said that the Greeks regarded one's *eudaimonia* as the 'supreme' aim. This statement leaves room, perhaps, for a plurality of aims, of which *eudaimonia* is in some way the weightiest. Some version of this idea could be true enough. However, whenever Sidgwick discusses Greek ethics in further detail, he does not cite any other aim in Greek ethics that might be placed alongside *eudaimonia*, and consistently treats *eudaimonia* as the only one adopted by it.

[12] See Chapter 2, sec. VII. 1.

about what an individual's final rational or worthwhile aim is.[13] We could, to be sure, use the word 'eudaimonism' for something less definite than a particular thesis, or for some thesis less definite than this one. To do that, however, would be to risk an undesirable looseness that would undermine the most interesting philosophical purpose of many ascriptions of eudaimonism to Greek thinkers. This purpose is to mark a supposed difference between Greek and modern ethics concerning the structure of rational deliberation.

A great deal hinges philosophically on whether happiness is claimed to be merely an important or salient aim or, instead and much more strongly, the unique thing aimed at for itself. If it is the former, then there is plenty of leeway to pursue other aims in particular cases. Implicit in many of even the more casual attributions of eudaimonism to the Greeks, however, is the idea that they took aims other than one's wellbeing to be of little or no account, and did not believe, moreover, that any rival aims could lead a reasonable person, or perhaps anyone at all, in other directions than towards his happiness.

This is an important issue philosophically as well as historically. Those who think that Greek ethics is eudaimonist almost invariably have in mind the thought that because it is so, it either does not admit or else greatly mitigates, by contrast with typically modern ethical thought, conflict between the aim of happiness and any other consideration. A looser use of the term 'eudaimonism' would allow us to call the Greeks eudaimonists even while we say that according to them, conflicts between one's own happiness and other aims can break out freely. That has not been the normal way of bringing them under this term.[14]

Let us here make use of two broad and simple paradigms of philosophers who reject Greek ethics and those who admire it. According to the former, its principal defect is its failure to recognize the importance, for our deliberations about how to live and act, of other considerations independent of one's own happiness. To its admirers, on the other hand, its virtue lies precisely in the fact that because it rejects the idea of an aim rivalling one's happiness, it makes possible a more unitary and harmonious account of deliberation and practical reason than does any position holding that a person must sometimes decide, for instance, whether to pursue his own well-being or to conform to ethical norms or further the well-being of others.

---

[13] Another way of expressing the same idea is to say that practical rationality amounts simply to what used to be called 'prudence'—before that word came to mean merely the same as 'caution'. I shall not use that term here.

[14] Thus I think it would be misguided to think that I am focusing on an over-narrow or over-strict use of the word 'eudaimonism'. The point of the use is to preserve what have been, historically and philosophically, the important implications of using it. There are, of course, other issues that can be taken as the focus when one compares ancient and modern ethics; for an example, see Schneewind 1996.

3. Modern Deliberative Dualism and Ancient Eudaimonist Deliberative Monism

The view that Greek ethics is eudaimonist is intimately connected with the wider claim that Greek thought generally exhibits a substantially greater degree of deliberative consistency than does modern ethics. A further part of Sidgwick's picture of Greek ethics involves this contrast:

[I]n Greek [ethics] generally, but one regulative and governing faculty is recognized under the name of reason; in the modern ethical view, when it has worked itself clear, there are found to be two.[15]

The 'regulative faculty' that Sidgwick takes to be recognized by ancient ethics is of course one that pursues one's *eudaimonia*. Sidgwick calls this 'egoistic reason'. The other faculty, which when added to the first one yields the modern view, is labelled by Sidgwick 'universal reason'. According to him and many others as well, the modern conception of deliberation equips it with two distinct and independent fundamental aims by which to govern itself, not merely one. Its conception of rational deliberation is taken to be dualist where the Greek conception appeared to be monist.

The second term of this dualism is designated in various ways. Under a common kantian view it is often designated by the word 'morality', which is typically associated with altruistic considerations concerning the well-being of other people and also with what can broadly be called ethical norms. For the present, we can allow the dualism to remain thus vaguely specified. The term 'morality', for its part, has a serious disadvantage: the variability of its usage. For that reason I generally avoid employing it in the framing of any important issues. I shall steer clear of it, on the whole, except when problems linked with it are explicitly in play.[16]

Admirers of Greek ethics have often regarded the dualism to which Sidgwick points as a serious flaw in the modern ethical outlook. Because—so it is supposed—there are now held to be two (at least) fundamentally distinct and independent types of deliberative consideration rather than only one, practical thinking does not have a single star by which to steer itself. Therefore a new type of conflict arises that was not, according to this account, present in Greek ethics. For if the advancing of one's well-being should ever conflict with or exclude the pursuit of the second aim that is posited by modern ethics, then the person who takes both of these aims seriously will be

[15] Sidgwick 1931: 198. Sidgwick here seems to give Joseph Butler the main credit for 'working the dualism clear', but see Frankena 1992.

[16] Sidgwick uses the word, but with a special connotation; see Frankena 1992. In Sidgwick's usage, any system of norms that is regarded by a person as overriding all others counts as that person's morality. Thus according to this terminology eudaimonism was the Greeks' morality. Others use the term without this connotation of overridingness. See Chapter 2, sec. IV. 3.

pulled in two opposite directions. Modern ethics is thus contrasted with the harmony and unity of ancient eudaimonism with its single fundamental aim.

4. Norms of Deliberation

Observe that the issue in this context is not psychological dualism or conflict. The chief pertinent claim is not that moderns are in fact torn by conflicting desires whereas ancients were not—though that contention can be a corollary of some versions of a thesis that will figure here. The main question is how we *should* or *should reasonably* deliberate, not how we do deliberate. Probably the way we should deliberate is to some extent a function of how we do, or at least a function of our psychological make-up—though according to some philosophical views it is not. Although issues of psychology bear on some of the questions to be discussed here, they do so only in a secondary way. The reader should not look here, therefore, for a general treatment of Greek psychology.

The main point of contact between psychological questions about how we do deliberate and (if you will) normative questions about how we should deliberate is this: the answer to the latter question sets an optimum for answers to the former. If rational deliberation cannot avoid conflict of aims, for instance, then as long as we are not blind to relevant considerations, the best actual deliberation that we can hope for will contain conflict too. If on the other hand we can show that reasonable thinking about our aims can be fully consistent, we can at least hope that, in the best of human circumstances, our actual deliberations may be so too.

According to some ways of comparing ancient and modern ethical outlooks, then, the former presents an ideal of how we should deliberate that is more encouraging, and gives us hope that we may be able actually to be relatively little subject to opposing pulls when we think about what to do, while the latter outlook seems to condemn us to unavoidable fragmentation of practical reason.

5. Literary Themes in England: Pater, Arnold, and Swinburne

During the two centuries through which moderns have frequently complained of this sense of fragmentation, Classical Greek culture has appeared to many to be a model of unified order, serenity, and harmony. The thought starts in eighteenth-century Germany, but it follows a continuous line through the Victorian age in Britain and on into modern British and American philosophical writings.[17]

Here is how Pater goes on, after the words that I quoted a short while ago, to invoke the Greeks:

---

[17] See in general Jenkyns 1980 and Turner 1981, with Arnold 1994: 42, 43.

Certainly, for us of the modern world, with its conflicting claims, its entangled interests, distracted by so many sorrows, with many preoccupations, so bewildering an experience, the problem of unity with ourselves, in blitheness and repose, is far harder than it was for the Greek within the simple terms of antique life.

And then,

Breadth, centrality, with blitheness and repose, are the marks of Hellenic culture. Is such a culture a lost art? . . . Can we bring down that idea into the gaudy, perplexed light of modern life?[18]

Matthew Arnold spoke for this same view of the Greeks. In *Culture and Anarchy*, he credits them with having expressed, through the word *euphyia*, the polar opposite of the modern Philistinism that he wished to attack:

exactly the notion of perfection as culture brings us to conceive it: a harmonious perfection, a perfection in which the characters of beauty and intelligence are both present, which unites 'the two noblest things', . . . sweetness and light.

Greece, said Arnold, shows us 'the idea of beauty, harmony, and complete human perfection'.[19]

In Germany, this admiration for Greece had sometimes been linked to a rejection of Christianity or at least some aspects of it.[20] The same association was also familiar in Britain.[21] This association was as much a matter of cultural allegiance as it was of religious belief. Socrates, for instance, appeared as a person of 'agnostic reasonableness'. He seemed to exhibit a way in which a person could have 'religious emotion without the religion . . . [or] the stubborn lumps of dogma and the unyielding claims of revelation'.[22] Here the Greeks are the representatives of rationality, set against the irrational claims of Christian revelation.

Some nineteenth-century British thinkers could regard the Greek outlook as superior to Christianity without introducing a contrast between the rationality of the former and the irrationalism of the latter. Some writers, for instance, felt that Christianity was cold and unappealing compared to the warmth of Greece. Hence the words that Swinburne puts into the mouth of the Roman emperor, Julian the Apostate, who rejected Christianity and attempted to take his empire back to

---

[18] Pater 1980: 18, 19.

[19] The phrase 'sweetness and light' is quoted by Arnold from Jonathan Swift, *The Battle of the Books* (see Arnold 1994: 29–48, 161). Arnold did not maintain, it should be noted, that the Greeks always exemplified these characteristics or their combination. Also, there is reason not to take Arnold's view, influential as it was, as fully typical of Victorian views of Greece; see Turner 1981: 9, 14, 61–2.

[20] See Hatfield 1964: esp. chs. 8, 10.

[21] See Jenkyns 1980: esp. 69–73, 241–53. Greek thought was also, of course, often invoked by Christians too.

[22] These are the words of Jenkyns 1980: 230.

paganism. Swinburne shows him conceding to Jesus, with regret, that the pagan cause could not win:

> Thou hast conquered, O pale Galilean; the world has grown grey from thy
> breath;
> We have drunken of things Lethean, and fed on the fullness of death.
> Laurel is green for a season, and love is sweet for a day;
> But love grows bitter with treason, and laurel outlives not May.
> Sleep, shall we sleep after all? for the world is not sweet in the end;
> For the old faiths loosen and fall, the new years ruin and rend.[23]

6. German Origins: Winckelmann

It was the German scholar Johann Joachim Winckelmann who first painted this kind of portrait of the Greeks. His idea for it emerged from his study of Greek art and especially Greek sculpture. Far from being confined to art historians and Classical scholars, however, Winckelmann's thinking set off a wave of enthusiasm for Hellenism that spread to literature, philosophy, and on into the general culture of Europe.

The mood that prevailed in Greek sculpture, as Winckelmann saw it, was one of harmony and tranquillity: 'The universal, dominant characteristic of Greek masterpieces . . . is noble simplicity and serene greatness in the pose as well as in the expression.' Winckelmann did not, however, limit his description to Greek sculpture or even to fine art. He also applied it to literature and especially to Greek philosophical thinking: 'The noble simplicity and serene greatness of Greek statues is the true characteristic of Greek literature of the best period, the writings of the Socratic school.'[24]

Winckelmann pressed this idea as far as he could. He even took it to the point of claiming—'with a perversity so astounding that it amounts almost to genius'[25]—that one of the most famous pieces of ancient sculpture, the statue of Laocoon struggling to free himself and his sons from two huge snakes, was a manifestation of precisely this serenity. Nowadays it is hard to see how anyone who had seen the statue, or even a copy of it (which was all that Winckelmann had available to him), could even entertain such a thought (though it is only fair to add that Winckelmann later changed his interpretation).[26] More recent writers have strained for an explanation of Winckelmann's reaction to the statue. He was 'in a trance', says one historian, 'and

---

[23] Swinburne 1970: 72–3, from the 'Hymn to Proserpine' (1866). Swinburne here alludes to the story according to which the last words of the emperor were, in reference to Jesus, 'Vicisti, Galilaee': 'Thou hast conquered, Galilean.'

[24] Winckelmann 1755, quoted in Butler 1935. As far as I can tell, Winckelmann meant the so-called 'Socratic school' to be Socrates, Plato, and Aristotle.

[25] Jenkyns 1980: 13.

[26] See Hatfield 1964: 22, 26.

like many another clairvoyant, he was uttering truths which did not apply to the object before him, but were associated with it in his mind'.[27] But it is not just Winckelmann's acceptance of this idea that needs explaining. The idea took hold, and came to dominate most people's impression of Greek culture. Thenceforth many thinkers took it to be an unassailable commonplace, the only natural way of summing up the Greek outlook.

When we look back at Winckelmann's reaction to the Laocoon, therefore, we see much more than merely a strange misapprehension or an inexplicable delusion. One is tempted to say that Winckelmann and his followers were determined to find harmony and serenity in Greek culture no matter what, because they so urgently needed it to set against the disharmony that they saw and felt in the modern world. Stereotypes can sometimes be inevitable, even in spite of contrary evidence right in front of one's nose.

7. *Schiller and Others*

From the start, as I have said, Winckelmann's view of Greece was hugely influential. It has gone on to have a decisive effect on innumerable thinkers, including many who have been quite unaware of its origins. Winckelmann created 'a literary revolution . . . in the magic name of Greece'.[28] His ideas found a receptive audience in late eighteenth-century Germany, and were passed along further by Humboldt, Schiller, Hölderlin, and others. They found expression, to give a notable example, in Schiller's famous poem, 'The Gods of Greece', of which a part runs:

> What time the happy world was guided,
> Ye Gods, by your indulgent hand,
> When over happy men presided
> Fair beings born of Fable-land, . . .
> . . . .
> For then were Heroes, Gods, and Mortals
> United in the bonds of love;
> Equal in Amathusian portals,
> Men bowed with those who rule above.
> . . . .
> All sceptic gloom and dulness vanished
> Where your inspiring cult was known;
> Untuneful souls were rightly banished,
> And glad contentment ruled alone.
> The Beauty for itself was treasured;
> No need your godlike joys to rein

---

[27] Butler 1935: 47; see also Hatfield 1964: 9, and Boyle 1991: i. 28–9.
[28] Butler 1935: 48.

> While blushing Nymphs and graces measured
> The Limits of your happy chain.
>
> . . . .
>
> Those buds have all untimely perished
> Before the scathing Northern blast
> Farewell, ye Gods, so dearly cherished;
> Ye pass away that One may last.[29]

The same nostalgia for 'Greece, blessed land, the house of all the immortals' was expressed even more fervidly by Hölderlin:

> Then, o then, you joys of Athens, you deeds done at Sparta,
> You delicious springtime in Grecian lands! When our autumn
> Comes, when you all, grown mature, you genii known in the ancient
> World return—and, look, the year's consummation approaches—
> Then may the feast-day preserve you also, great era long ended,
> May the people look towards Hellas and thanksgiving, weeping,
> Make the proud day of their triumph gentle with solemn remembrance![30]

---

[29] Trans., somewhat unhappily, Forster and Pinkerton (Schiller 1902). The original runs:

> Da ihr noch die schöne Welt regieret,
> An der Freude leichtem Gängelband
> Seliger Geschlechter noch geführet,
> Schoene Wesen aus dem Fabelland!
> . . . .
> Zwischen Menschen, Göttern und Heroen
> Knüpfte Amor einen schönen Bund,
> Sterbliche mit Göttern und Heroen
> Huldigten in Amathunt.
> . . . .
> Finstrer Ernst und trauriges Entsagen
> War aus eurem heitern Dienst verbannt,
> Glücklich sollten alle Herzen schlagen,
> Denn euch war der Glückliche verwandt.
> Damals war nichts heilig als das Schöne,
> Keiner Freude schämte sich der Gott,
> Wo die keusch errötende Kamöne,
> Wo die Grazie gebot.
> . . . .
> Alle jene Bluten sind gefallen
> Von des Nordes schauerlichem Wehn,
> Einen zu bereichern unter allen,
> Musste diese Götterwelt vergehn.

[30] From 'The Archipelago', trans. Hamburger (Hölderlin 1994: 217–35, at 233; cf. also 'Bread and Wine', pp. 263–73 of that edition). Hölderlin's novel *Hyperion* is probably the *locus classicus* for the expression of such sentiments.

The attitude expressed in these poems came to typify a dominant modern European attitude towards ancient Greek culture.

The influential part of Schiller's picture of Greece remained his image of its serenity and concord. The last lines of 'The Gods of Greece', in particular, show not merely nostalgia for Greek antiquity, with its harmony of human and divine beings, but also regret both at the coming of Christianity, and at the particular philosophical form in which Schiller sees it embodied.[31] He finds it dominated by the spirit of kantian ethics—'the scathing Northern blast' plainly blows not out of Galilee but from Germany and in particular from Kant's Königsberg, as we shall see. Through Schiller and others, including Hegel, this outlook on Greece, as the source of an alternative to kantianism, was to have a decisive influence not only in Germany but in Britain and America as well.[32]

Schiller's view was typical of his time and place. August Wilhelm Schlegel was another German spokesman for the same attitude. The Greek ideal, he said, was 'perfect concord and proportion of all powers, natural harmony'. Moderns, on the other hand, have come to a consciousness of an inner bipartite division, which makes such an ideal impossible.[33] Like Schiller, Schlegel drew a contrast between the Greek spirit and modernity, especially as manifested in romanticism. For Schlegel, as A. O. Lovejoy says, '[a] recognized characteristic of the "romantic" was ethical dualism, a conviction that there are in man's constitution two natures ceaselessly at war'.[34] Schlegel contrasted this dualism directly with the harmony that he associated with Greek culture. 'The poetry of the ancients was that of possession; ours is that of longing.'[35] Novalis could describe the ancient Greek scene like this: 'Life, an unending many-coloured festival of the children of heaven and of the dwellers of earth, rushed like a springtime down through the centuries.'[36]

Not everyone fell under the same magical Hellenic spell. Schiller himself was not always unambivalently enthusiastic about the Greeks. His attitude was nuanced, and it tended also to fluctuate.[37] Nor, for that matter, was the German view of the Greeks

---

[31] See Hatfield 1964: ch. 8.

[32] See Ewen 1932: esp. 70–1, on the influence of Schiller's view of the Greeks on Coleridge.

[33] '[V]ollkommene Eintracht und Ebenmass aller Kräfte, natürliche Harmonie': Schlegel 1966: 26.

[34] Lovejoy 1948: 247.

[35] Schlegel 1966: 25.

[36] '[E]in ewig buntes Fest der Himmelskinder und der Erdbewohner': Novalis 1960: sec. 5 (my translation). Novalis's attitude is complex. He associates the Greeks with sunlight and serenity, but at the same time he welcomes the night that he takes as the representative of Christianity.

[37] See Hatfield 1964: ch. 8. One should especially not leave out of account Schiller's epigram, 'Die höchste Harmonie':

> Oedipus reisst die Augen sich aus, Jokasta erhenkt sich,
> Beide schuldlos; das Stück hat sich harmonisch gelöst.

('Oedipus tears his eyes out, Jocasta hangs herself./ Both guiltlessly; The play ends harmoniously.' Hatfield 1964: 141, 263.)

unanimous. Not all writers regarded Greece as a symbol of harmony, serenity, and repose. Goethe, to take the pre-eminent example, always kept Hellenomania at a distance.[38] Moreover, many German writers saw what Nietzsche was later to call the 'Dionysiac' side of Greek culture: a sense of turmoil and a propensity to irrationalism.[39] Nevertheless, these very exceptions make it all the more striking that the other, harmonizing view has so dominated the modern idea of Greece.

8. Hellenism and Christianity

Thus the Hellenic ideal tended strongly to be regarded still as an ideal of rationality, of harmony consisting in reasoned order. Moreover, it was not just a superficial rationality, a forcible imposition of structure upon a resistant, seething, chaotic mass underneath. Rather, harmony prevails—the thought is, or the metaphor governing it—because the fact that the parts of one's self that are not themselves somehow contained within reason fit effortlessly into the pattern that reason endorses. Admiration for Greek rationality is equivalent to admiration for a condition in which a person governs his life by a consistent notion of well-being, and is not torn by conflicting considerations or ideals.

Pater took Greek sculpture to represent 'types' that are abstracted from detail. 'Works produced under this law', he says, 'are really characterized by Hellenic generality or breadth . . . It keeps passion always below that degree of intensity at which it must necessarily be transitory, never winding up the features to one note of anger, or desire, or surprise.'[40] Pater does not think that Greek art represents passion as pent up by the person experiencing it. He thinks that passion is shown falling of its own accord within measured limits.

Schiller sometimes goes even further in describing this harmony. On his view, the idea is not just that passion unresistingly falls into a pattern determined by reason. He thinks that together reason and passion actively determine, in unison, what the pattern shall be:

What [man] is meant to be is neither [an animal void of reason nor an animal endowed with reason]; he is meant to be a human being. Nature is not meant to rule him exclusively, nor reason to rule him conditionally. Both of these systems of rule are meant to coexist, in perfect independence of each other, and yet in perfect concord.[41]

The outline of what these thinkers were striving for is unmistakable. It is the idea that somehow human motivations and human personality are to be free of inner conflict.

---

[38] See Hatfield 1964: 100ff.

[39] See Hatfield 1964: 12 and passim. For Nietzsche' own influence on views about Greece, which ran against the current that I am describing, see Aschheim 1992: 66.

[40] Pater 1980: 172.   [41] Schiller 1967: Letter XXIV, sec. 8.

What they attribute to Greek culture is an unhindered conception of this condition, and some considerable ability to put it into practice.

This condition of rational, harmonious structure was taken to be the hallmark of the superiority of the Greek condition to what has come since. Though in many respects a very different sort of thinker from Schiller and Pater, John Stuart Mill believed that precisely because of the rationalist bent of the Greeks, Plato must be a better moral teacher than Christ could ever be:

Christ did not argue about virtue, but commanded it; Plato, when he argues about it, argues for the most part inconclusively, but he resembles Christ in the love which he inspires for it, and in the stern resolution never to swerve from it.[42]

Here the difference between Greek harmonious rationality and the Christian attitude, as Mill sees them, appears as the difference between reasoned argument and unexplained command. Mill plainly regards the former as less strained than the latter.

9. *Schiller and Herder: The Harmonious* Polis

When moderns have associated harmony with Hellenism, the association has not been a matter only of style or mood. It has also focused on a particular institution. From the start, admirers of the Greeks have linked the ideal that they saw exemplified in Greek culture with the characteristically Greek form of life, the *polis*. When Schiller spoke about the 'ingenious clockwork' of the modern state, he contrasted it with '[t]he polypoid character of the Greek states, in which every individual enjoyed an independent existence but could, when need arose, grow into the whole organism'.[43] The emphasis on the *polis* was not peripheral to this reaction to the Greeks. The unity of the Greek *polis*, Schiller thought, was itself the cause of the fact that an individual Greek could unite all good human qualities:

What individual modern could sally forth and engage, man against man, with an individual Athenian for the prize of humanity? ... Whence this disadvantage among individuals ...? Why was the individual Greek qualified to be the representative of his age, and why can no single modern venture as much?

Schiller's answer is that the increase of knowledge and the increasingly complex machinery of the state—the ingenious clockwork—have forced us to be specialized. The Greeks, he took it, suffered no such fate.

A related view of the unity of the Greek *polis* had also already been propounded by Johann Gottfried von Herder. In his *Ideen zur Philosophie der Geschichte der Menschheit*, he attributed the magnificence of Greek architecture and sculpture to the

---

[42] Mill 1834, in Mill 1965: 77.
[43] Schiller 1967: Letter VI, sec.7.

fact that the members of the *polis* were willing to work for the common good. Harking back to Winckelmann, he said,

This common spirit, of doing everything at least to appearances for the whole, was the soul of the Greek state. This is what Winckelmann doubtless meant when he glorified the free Greek republics as the golden age of art. For splendour and greatness were not dispersed, as in modern times; rather they were fused as the concern of the state.[44]

As Herder and Schiller saw matters, the unity exhibited by the Greek *polis* also makes possible a corresponding unity of the individual. If the city is not broken into a mass of clashing interests, then one and the same person can represent all of its virtues. Any individual, moreover, can set out to advance both its good and his own well-being without being subject to conflicting pulls.

III. More Recent Responses among Classicists to the Theme of Hellenic Harmony

1. Wilamowitz's Scepticism

Nowadays we have become used to revisionism about practically everything. Accordingly, we might well have expected the spell of Hellenic harmony to have been dissipated or debunked. In some quarters it has been. Historians have pretty well ceased to portray ancient Greece as politically harmonious, and now often stress the prevalence of strife and discord in Greek society, both between city-states and within the typical *polis* itself.[45] By the same token, it is also rare nowadays to treat Greek society—as was done persistently during the Victorian period and for some time after it—as an edifying model of civic concord that modern statecraft should imitate.

In fact, the debunking of edifying myths by Classical scholars began a long time ago. Perhaps the most influential German Classical scholar of modern times, Ulrich von Wilamowitz-Moellendorf, said,

That antiquity which was supposed to be an absolutely compulsory model for art and life was a serious danger to both, if only because it was a hallucination. A century of historical

---

[44] Herder 1989: III. 13. iii. 3:

Dieser Gemeingeist, alles wenigstens dem Scheine nach für das Ganze zu tun, war die Seele der griechischen Staaten, den ohne Zweifel auch Winkelmann [sic] meinte, wenn er die Freiheit der griechischen Republiken als das goldne Zeitalter der Kunst pries. Pracht und Grösse nämlich waren in ihnen nicht so verteilt, wie in den neueren Zeiten, sondern flossen in dem zusammen, was den Staat anging.

[45] See, for instance, Ehrenberg 1969: 89–92, and Ste Croix 1981. Ehrenberg, however, sometimes lapses into what I would call a hegelian belief in the harmony of the good of the *polis* with the good of the individual citizen (see e.g. Ehrenberg 1969: 91).

research has rid us of it . . . [H]istorical science had to destroy the belief in such an abstract ideal, because a golden age lies as little behind us as before us.[46]

This tough-minded scholarly approach to ancient thought has to a fair extent counteracted the starry-eyed admiration for the Greeks of less disciplined thinkers who were looking for a refuge from what they saw as the perils of the modern world.

Historians of philosophy, too, have by now moved beyond the notion that they must singlemindedly either reject or embrace Greek ethics. They see far more complexity, too, in ancient eudaimonism than did earlier thinkers who dismissed it or looked to it as a panacea for modern fragmentation.

2. Nietzsche, Dodds, and Others: The Irrational Breakdown of Harmony

One might have thought that this more sceptical, accurate, and scholarly picture of the Greeks would have won the day quickly, and that the idealization of the Greeks would by now have been dead. The striking fact is, however, that the old picture of ancient Greek thought, as a scheme governed by concord and serenity, has continued to show extraordinary vigour in spite of the warnings against it by Wilamowitz and others.

Often the question has been divided. A division has been posited between an earlier period, in which there was supposedly little sign of deliberative harmony, and a later, Classical period during which harmony is said to have prevailed. Often the thought is that a Classical idea of harmony eventually dominated, settling in to quiet an earlier rude Archaic discord. More often than not, however, the rest of the story is told in such a way as to present a subsequent irrationalist breakdown of harmony after the Classical period was over.

One index of the strength of the theme of Hellenic harmony can be found in the fact that it has survived an attack on it by Friedrich Nietzsche—who has otherwise had an almost irresistible impact on modern ways of looking at Greek antiquity. The reason is clear. Although Nietzsche stressed an irrationalist, 'Dionysiac' element of Greek culture, he located it not at the central, Classical period of Greek thought but in Archaic times. Rather than denying that the notion of harmony dominated the Classical period of Greece to which it had been assigned, Nietzsche looked instead to the earlier, Archaic period for thinking more congenial to his own outlook, to Heraclitus and the warrior heroes of the Homeric epics. As a result, Nietzsche left the standard picture of Classical Greece largely intact.[47]

---

[46] Wilamowitz-Moellendorf 1913: 114. See also ibid. 126–31.

[47] Something very similar can be said of Bernard Williams's recent study (1993), which owes much both to Nietzsche's views and to his strategy. In this book, Williams looks to Aeschylus and Thucydides for the Greek ideas he wants, and leaves Classical figures in the hands of other interpreters. On another way of

Much the same can be said of later attempts to focus on the same side of Greek culture that Nietzsche emphasized, even when they were produced by historians and Classicists of the highest calibre. In 1951, E. R. Dodds published his influential book, *The Greeks and the Irrational*. There he aimed to dispel the standard belief that the Classical Greek outlook was almost uniformly rational, in a sense that he took to exclude fundamental conflict. Dodds's rejection of this belief was not by any means greeted as a platitude. Nor did he expect it to be taken so. On the contrary, he describes the impetus that led to the book this way:

Some years ago I was in the British Museum looking at the Parthenon sculptures when a young man came up to me and said with a worried air, 'I know it's an awful thing to confess, but this Greek stuff doesn't move me one bit.' I said that was very interesting: could he define at all the reasons for his lack of response? He reflected for a minute or two. Then he said, 'Well, it's all so terribly rational, if you know what I mean.' I thought I did know. The young man was only saying what has been said more articulately by Roger Fry and others. To a generation whose sensibilities have been trained on African and Aztec art, and on the work of such men as Modigliani and Henry Moore, the art of the Greeks, and Greek culture in general, is apt to appear lacking in the awareness of mystery and in the ability to penetrate to the deeper, less conscious levels of human experience.[48]

Like Winckelmann looking at the Laocoon long before, the young man observing the Parthenon sculptures saw in them not an art in which reason needs to restrain an irrational part of the self that struggles against it, but an art in which moderation is effortless and no forcible restraint of a recalcitrant opponent is required.

Not surprisingly, Dodds thought that this way of thinking about the Greeks was prevalent and important enough to require a sustained response: 'This fragment of conversation stuck in my head and set me thinking. Were the Greeks in fact quite so blind to the importance of non-rational factors in man's experience and behaviour as is commonly assumed by their apologists and their critics? That is the question out of which this book grew.' Thus *The Greeks and the Irrational* insists on aspects of Greek life that were not rational, and Dodds demonstrates that Greek literature offers depictions of intense conflicts within the human personality.

In spite of all this, however, the startling fact about Dodds's book is not how far he moves his readers away from the attitude of the young man in the British Museum, but how much of that same attitude to the Classical period he allows them to retain. Dodds himself moves only a short way in the direction in which he points. For him the Classical period in Greece, down to near the end of the fourth century BCE, is still a period of 'rationalism'. It is even the start of 'an age when Greek rationalism appeared

---

carving up Greek intellectual history so as to leave the notion of Hellenic harmony standing, see further below, sec. VII.

[48] Dodds 1951: 1.

to be on the verge of final triumph'.[49] Dodds thought that much of what is best in Hellenism does indeed exhibit precisely that rationality without signficant opposition. His story of the weakening of Greek influence, in favour of Roman and ultimately Christian influence, is essentially a story of Greek rationality in decline.[50] He insists that Greek thought had room for irrationality, though unlike Nietzsche he places it at the later rather than the earlier end of the Greek chronology. Like Nietzsche, however, he believes that during its central historical period, the Greek outlook is typified by a rationality not subject to disharmony or conflict.

In light of these facts, it is less surprising that recent views of Greek ethics have been occluded, at least in the popular perception, by the same serene nimbus that exhibited itself in Winckelmann and others like him. When modern writers have wanted to find Greek models for what they regard as the decadence of modern society, their impulse has not often been to abandon the idealization of the Classical period. Instead they find the model for their own circumstances in the idea of the decline of Greece in its later stages. Looking back in 1938, for instance, Louis MacNeice compared England to the Athens of Hellenistic and Roman times:

> And Athens became a mere university city . . .
> And for a thousand years they went on talking,
> Making such apt remarks,
> A race no longer of heroes but of professors
> And crooked businessmen and secretaries and clerks.[51]

This way of thinking about Greek history persists today, too, as part of a general pattern. Thus Isaiah Berlin wrote:

It seems to me a historical fact that whenever rationalism goes far enough there often tends to occur some kind of emotional resistance, a 'backlash', which springs from that which is irrational in man. This took place in Greece in the fourth and third centuries B.C.E., when the great Socratic schools produced their magnificent rationalistic systems: seldom . . . did mystery religions, occultism, irrationalism, mysticisms of all kinds flourish so richly.[52]

The idealization of Classical Greece becomes embedded, first, within the Romans' story of their own hegemony, and later within a historical generalization. But the idealization itself has in many minds stayed intact throughout.

In this way, Dodds naturally felt the impulse to regard failure of rationality as something that during the Classical period was *creeping into* the Greek outlook, only later to dominate it. He did not wish to think of the potential for disharmony and conflict as something already fully present. Certainly Classicists in the Nietzschean

---

[49] Dodds 1951: 236.
[50] Dodds, in Plato 1959: 195, 236ff., 247ff.
[51] MacNeice 1946: sec. ix.   [52] Berlin 1991b: 34–5.

tradition had thought otherwise.[53] But Dodds's view, and the fact that it seemed as strikingly new as it did when it appeared, showed how strong the idea remained, even into the middle of the twentieth century, that the Greek mind was governed by a largely effortless consistency of rational human motivation.

IV. Some Philosophers' Responses to Greek Ethics

1. The Kantian and Hegelian Views of Eudaimonist Monism

Despite the fact that most philosophers and scholars of ancient philosophy in recent times have neither the nostalgic temperament nor the edifying purpose of some of the thinkers whom I have discussed, nevertheless the pictures of Greek ethics that many of them have and convey are unavoidably influenced by the general intellectual background against which they do their work. To a striking extent, philosophical and scholarly discussions of Greek ethics retain, even to the present day, the imprint of the ideas that I have described.

The reason for this fact is, I believe, quite simple. Greek ethics for the last two centuries has been caught up in modern philosophical debates. The role of Greek ethics in those debates has had a major impact on the way in which it has been interpreted over this period. The debate crystallized around discussion of Kant's ethics and ethical views similar to his, and especially around opposition to them on the part of thinkers like Schiller and Hegel. Both of these figures appealed to Greek ethics for ideas that they believed would serve them in opposing the kind of position that Kant represented. They were supported in this tendency by the fact that Kant himself had self-consciously turned his face away from Greek ethics and eudaimonism as he thought of it. What more natural way to oppose him than to invoke the very figures whose influence he had so noticeably rejected?

In broad outline, the result was a picture of Greek ethics, as a whole, as a eudaimonist form of deliberative monism. It was monist by virtue of believing that there exists a single rational human aim; it was eudaimonist by virtue of taking this aim to be the individual's happiness. Even though *eudaimonia* was frequently held to contain a plurality of parts—distinct activities or states of which a happy life would consist— nevertheless those parts were conceived of by Greek thinkers, the belief was, as combinable somehow into a whole. It was not uncommon, in addition, to think of this whole as relatively if not wholly free from internal conflict, or at least to have been intended by Greek thinkers to be so. For a chief purpose of this line of interpretation was to provide a way of counteracting the 'fragmentation' that was regarded as such a deplorable feature of modern life and thinking.

---

[53] Nietzsche's influence is discussed below; see also Hatfield 1964: 12.

This picture of Greek ethics, we should bear in mind, both reflected and further encouraged the supposition that Greek ethics is in important respects homogeneous, especially during the Classical period which is regarded as typical of Hellenism in general. Thus over the last two centuries we find it often presupposed that there is a single outlook on this or that issue that is characteristic of 'the Greeks'.

Because the two most influential responses to Greek ethics arose from debates over kantian ethics, and because Hegel has in the ensuing time come to appear the major philosophical spokesman for the relevant opposition to kantian views, it is useful for mnemonic purposes to speak of two broad ways of thinking of Greek ethics and its philosophical significance, the 'kantian' and the 'hegelian'. Neither Kant nor Hegel originated these tendencies or articulated them in this form. Nevertheless, the historical importance of their influence crystallized these two ways of responding to Greek thinking. It became common for subsequent people's attitudes towards the Greeks to vary in accordance, at least approximately, with whether or not their sympathies were with, or against, the one philosopher or the other. These two tendencies have remained discernible even in recent work on ancient philosophy by scholars who do not think of themselves as particularly kantian or hegelian overall.

2. Kantian Anti-Hellenism and Hegelian Hellenism

The kantian response is built around the philosophical judgement that eudaimonism is untenable. It says that the Greeks' failure to recognize this fact notwithstanding, certain aims are worth pursuing quite independently of their bearing on one's own well-being. Thus kantians in this sense think that rational deliberation cannot be focused on one's happiness alone. Either practical reason must aim at something else entirely (as Kant himself believed), or else (as Sidgwick feared) it must somehow direct itself at two distinct and independent ultimate aims, happiness and something else—with the possibility that these two aims might conceivably end up conflicting with each other. Thus there is a dualism, which potentially confronts an individual's well-being with considerations of a broader sort, usually having to do, as I have said, with the well-being of others and conformity to ethical standards or norms.[54] For a kantian-minded interpreter, it is a deficiency of Greek ethics to be eudaimonist in the sense stipulated here.

On the other side, the advocates of the hegelian response attempt to defend what they take to be the central feature of Greek ethical thought. They maintain that—granted, of course, an adequate conception of happiness—eudaimonism can be upheld. An adequate conception of happiness, the most extreme version of this view

---

[54] This is linked with the fact that kantian ethical theories tend to try to define the notion of duty and morality independently of the notion of non-moral goodness (see Frankena 1973a: passim, and Trianosky 1990: 339).

contends, will show it to be a single, harmonious aim under which seemingly or potentially conflicting aims can in the end be reconciled. More moderate versions maintain that even if complete harmony cannot be achieved, the concept of *eudaimonia* can be employed to mitigate significantly the deliberative conflicts that a dualist scheme seems potentially to impose.

The 'kantian' and 'hegelian' interpretations form distinct ways of ascribing eudaimonism to the Greeks. Philosophically, the important difference is that the kantian response is essentially unsympathetic to Greek ethics, while the hegelian response is favourable to it. Nevertheless, they are also strongly similar to each other in crucial respects. Indeed, each in some ways even reinforces the other. Both are prepared to see a strong contrast between Greek views and kantian ethical doctrines. In particular, in that connection, both picture the Greeks as eudaimonists, though they have two different opinions about exactly what *eudaimonia* is—a fact that is not unconnected with their divergent assessments of the merits of eudaimonism.

Among recent students of Greek ethics, hegelian-style interpretations are far more common than kantian ones. This fact is by no means surprising. The kantian response encourages us to regard the Greeks as philosophical primitives who believed in the harmony of practical reason only because they were naively unaware of distinct and independent considerations arising from morality as Kant understood it.

The hegelian response, on the other hand, is much more sympathetic to what it takes to be the main thrust of Greek thought, and consequently tends more to encourage the study of it. It appeals to thinkers who hope that the study of Greek antiquity can confer some direct benefit on modern thought. In addition, the hegelian response is also much more closely similar to, and hence supported by, the enthusiastic reactions to Greek culture on the part of influential non-philosophers from Winckelmann onwards. One might well expect an interest in Greek ethics to go along with a propensity to believe that it has something philosophically valuable to offer. That is what one finds, even though scholarly treatments are far more qualified and nuanced than the crudely enthusiastic idea of Hellenic harmony that one encounters in less careful writers.

V. The Kantian Response

1. The Dualism of Duty and Inclination

It is something of an irony that Kant should play any role at all in the history of modern reactions to Greek ethics, inasmuch as he devotes virtually no energy at all to discussing it—so patently inadequate does he take it to be.[55] His importance to the

---

[55] It is noteworthy, for instance, that Kant's explicit references to Greek philosophers in *Religion within the Limits of Reason Alone*, for instance, deal mainly with topics other than central ethical ones. It is hard

historiography of Greek ethics consists almost entirely in the ways in which his opponents used Greek thinking to attack his doctrines. But before I can fully describe the use of Greek thought against him, I should note some features of his own philosophical position, and also about the way in which it leads to the kantian response to Greek ethics.

Kant draws a sharp distinction between 'moral duty' and 'inclination'. Inclinations are, roughly, a person's desires and other similar motivations to action, which are associated by Kant mainly with sensation. Kant holds that duty, as articulated in the Categorical Imperative, is endorsed by 'practical reason'. Customarily he thinks of the motivation to do one's duty as something quite different from a desire or inclination, namely, 'respect for the moral law'. A person's own happiness, on the other hand, Kant maintains, is either a disorganized and unrationalizable jumble of satisfactions of multifarious inclinations, or else an aggregation of them that possesses little if any coherence and cannot be dignified by the term 'reason'.[56]

Sometimes, of course, a person will have an inclination to do something that, as a matter of purely contingent fact, is also prescribed by duty. Even in such a case, however, the fact that a person has that inclination, according to Kant, has nothing to do with the action's being either obligatory or rational. In the *Critique of Practical Reason*, Kant writes:

The essential point in all determination of the will through the moral law is this: as a free will, and thus not only without cooperating with sensuous impulses but even rejecting all of them and checking all inclinations so far as they could be antagonistic to the law, it is determined merely by the law.[57]

This familiar kantian idea entails something that is absolutely central to the whole issue of 'fragmentation' and the unity of deliberation.[58]

In effect, Kant thus seems to be denying that the condition of a person in whom reason respects the law is made better, in any relevant sense, if the person's inclinations coincide with reason. Because inclinations themselves lie outside of the province of

---

not to take his silence on Greek thought as a studied neglect, expressive of a belief that the Greeks' views, at least for his purposes, did not need to be taken very seriously. Nevertheless, a case can be made for the contention that Kant's ethical views were in fact influenced, partly by way of reaction, by Greek ethics; see Reich 1939.

[56] Kant 1981: 390: 'Men can make no definite and certain concept of the sum of satisfaction of all inclinations which goes under the name of happiness.' Cf. Kant 1956: 25–6.

[57] See also Kant 1956: 71–90. The passage quoted (trans. Beck) occurs at 72. As Paton points out (1947: 49), desires play a role in moral motivation, but they may not be, as he puts it, 'the determining factor'.

[58] I here leave aside, as irrelevant to present matters, another significant element of this part of Kant's view, namely, the notion that rational thinking must be determined independently of empirical considerations. There is an important connection between this epistemological issue and the one that I am discussing. See Kant 1956: 70–2.

reason, and because happiness is a matter of inclinations alone, the reconciling of the aim of happiness with rational respect for the moral law is not a desideratum of which reason need take account when it determines what is one's duty. It is true that Kant often writes so as to acknowledge such a rational desideratum, when he says, for instance, that one must rationally suppose that one's moral actions will be followed by happiness.[59] Nevertheless, Kant's readers could be forgiven for supposing, as, for example, Schiller plainly did, that according to his doctrine, whether or not the Categorical Imperative and one's inclinations recommend the same course or not is of no rational moment. Small wonder that these opponents of Kant's sought to articulate a view that would make clear how this opposition might be lessened.

Not, of course, that Kant was the first to maintain the possibility of a conflict between duty and inclination, for instance, or between respect for morality and the desire for one's own happiness. Already in Joseph Butler, to mention just one example, one finds (as Sidgwick later stressed) full awareness of the notion that a person can have duties that are important to perform quite regardless of the contribution to his own happiness that might be made by fulfilling them.[60] Nevertheless, Kant enunciated this idea with a forcefulness that was unique, and that provoked an equally significant counterreaction. Largely because Kant had so conspicuously ignored Greek ethics, anti-kantian thinkers quickly seized on it as a source of material to be used against him.

2. The Kantian Opposition to Monistic Eudaimonist Ethical Motivation

In a further way, too, Kant minimizes the importance of an action's being acquiesced in or supported by inclination. He holds that if a person is moved wholly by inclination to perform an act that would also be recommended by reason, then he is doing the right thing from the wrong motivation, so that his action has no moral worth. Thus if we attempt to justify a particular action or outcome by citing an inclination to do or attain it, Kant believes, we fail entirely, and not merely partially, to produce thereby a genuine rational justification of the action. Accordingly, a person who thinks that he is rationally justifying something by citing some inclination of his in its favour is in error about what rational justification amounts to. Citing an inclination to do something is strictly irrelevant to showing that it is endorsed by reason, Kant believes, and a right-minded philosopher must recognize the difference.

But—says the kantian response—Greek writers on ethics were quite unaware of this difference. Greek ethics aims ultimately at a person's own happiness alone, and acknowledges no other considerations possessing independent force. Because of being thus truncated and one-sided, Greek belief in a harmony of practical aims is

---

[59] Kant 1956: 25, 113–14.
[60] See esp. Butler 1726: Sermon XI.

unfounded and naive. Moreover, the response continues, Greek thinkers both demonstrate and also compound this mistake by continually attempting to justify right action by arguing that it causes a person to be happy. This fact itself shows, the response asserts, that on the Greek view the only ground for any course of action is the belief that it will lead to happiness; and that fact in turn dramatizes the Greeks' misguided idea that one's happiness is the only ultimate aim.

This criticism of Greek ethics, for example of Plato's *Republic* and Aristotle's *Nicomachean Ethics*, has long been standard in the writings of kantian-minded interpreters.[61] Those who construe the *Republic* in this way—as I do not[62]—have supposed that Plato never entertains even the remotest suspicion that there could conceivably be any way rationally to persuade a person to be just otherwise than by arguing that justice has happiness as a consequence.[63] Not only is Plato a eudaimonist, they think, but he is also a crude eudaimonist, on whom it never dawns that a person might have any other important ultimate goal than his own well-being. Here, then, would be an indication, according to the kantian response, of how little examination the Greeks had given to questions about the nature of rational deliberation.

The same fact also is often taken as an indication of what is stigmatized as the essentially 'egoist' and 'selfish' character of the Greek ethics. Sometimes this is viewed as a manifestation of its failure to attain the level of selflessness and charity ascribed to Christianity and its ethical outlook. But even without this religious element, the criticism of Greek ethics for being unduly self-regarding is one to which its admirers, as we shall see later, have often felt called upon to reply.

On the foregoing basis, criticism is sometimes levelled at Greek ethics for not only not having the requisite conceptions, but also, as a result, for not having subjected them to philosophical scrutiny. Thus if the Greeks did not have the notion of moral obligation, for instance, their writings must also fail to exhibit any reflections on or analysis of that concept. Obviously one should not normally blame someone for failing to investigate a notion that he did not possess. Nevertheless, the absence of treatments of the idea of obligation, or morality, or respect for the moral law, and so forth, must seem to partisans of these notions to be a deficiency, and also a reason to regard Greek ethics as comparatively uninteresting. So it seemed to Kant, evidently, and to others who share his views. That fact has left the study of the subject more or less open, as I have already remarked, to people who find more in it to applaud.

3. The Sense of an Unavoidable Dualism in Kantian Ethics

Kant held that some actions are unconditionally required of a person regardless of whether he is himself benefited by doing them. To do justice to this idea, Kant

---

[61] See, for instance, Prichard 1928, Foster 1937, and Adkins 1960: 2–3.   [62] See Chapter 5.
[63] See esp. Prichard 1928.

believed, we must recognize the existence of a rational motivation, respect for the moral law, that stands over against inclination, and to which any thought of, or desire for, one's happiness is strictly irrelevant.

The salient element of this doctrine that Kant's opponents could not accept was his picture of a human being as divided into two potentially conflicting elements, one moved by respect for the law of reason, and the other following inclinations towards happiness. These opponents believed that the inclinations that Kant had placed outside reason were far too important a part of a human being to be relegated to a place outside the sphere of deliberation that is genuinely rational or reasonable in some substantial sense. They wanted, that is, a concept of practical rationality according to which a person could be said to deliberate rationally only if he took into account more than the moral considerations to which Kant had restricted the title 'reason'. They believed that an agent must reckon, *rationally*, with the inclinations aiming at happiness that, they held, are an integral part of what a human being ought to be concerned about. Whether it was fair to Kant to criticize him in this way is not the issue; probably it was not. The point is that many of his critics did reply to him in this way, and that that reply had a strong influence on views about Greek ethics.

Some of Kant's critics focused not just on his suggestion that reason does not include adequate regard for inclinations, but they also reacted to the fact that he regarded a human being as possessing both reason and inclination, which could be opposed to each other, and thus as having a 'double nature'.[64] The task that many of Kant's opponents set themselves was to develop a notion of practical reason, or some functional equivalent thereof, that would bring a wide range of considerations into, as it were, a single forum in which their various claims could be dealt with.

Not surprisingly, this thought led not only to the suggestion that all of these considerations could be examined by, so to speak, the same faculty, but also to the hope that they might all somehow be reconciled. The ultimate goal, at its most ambitious, was to develop a broad notion of practical reason that would allow Kant's opponents to uphold the compatibility of *all* aims—particularly those implicated in Kant's treatment of duty and inclination—that might plausibly be held to be important to a human being. Many of these hopes were made to rest on the Greek notion of *eudaimonia*. The harmony and concord that Winckelmann and others had associated with Greek culture afforded a possibility of a way in which Greek philosophy could, if suitably expounded, counteract the feared modern disharmony of rational human aims, and perhaps even establish that those aims are consistent.

---

[64] See e.g. Broad 1930: 135–9.

VI. Schiller's Reaction

1. Schiller's Efforts at Dualist Harmony

Friedrich Schiller went part of the way towards this goal. He was one of the earliest writers to express reservations about Kant's account of human deliberation and motivation. He frequently criticized Kant's views on this issue, notably in the essay 'On Grace and Dignity' ('Über Anmut und Würde') and in the *Letters on the Aesthetic Education of Man*. As Schiller saw matters, Kant's sharp separation of reason and inclination was in and of itself problematical.[65] Schiller believed that that separation made for damaging conflict within our concept of a human being, a conflict that would make it look as though any internal coherence of outlook or aim impossible. Furthermore, Schiller held that Kant's willlingness to grant unqualified deliberative priority to reason would—in addition to leaving only an inadequate place for the aesthetic faculty and responses that Schiller valued very highly—also deny rightful status to the inclinations and therefore also to the aim of happiness.

Even though on this score Schiller found Kant's thinking unacceptably dualistic, he did not go so far as to reject Kant's views completely.[66] For one thing, Schiller had no reservations about Kant's notion of morality. Nor did Schiller urge that people act on inclination alone, as many Romantic thinkers did. What he objected to was Kant's way of setting morality against inclination, and intimating that a sense of duty is so often a sense of happiness sacrificed.

For the same reason, Schiller also objects to Kant's manner of formulating the conclusions of rational deliberation. In a move that I shall explore in detail later,[67] Schiller criticizes Kant's notion that reason and duty are to be expressed in the form of an 'imperative' or command. Echoing an idea that had already been expressed by Kant, Schiller says that a command is a manifestation of a need to overcome resistance. However, in a fully admirable person—what Schiller called a 'fair soul', a *schöne Seele*[68]—no resistance to reason will be present. For such a person, therefore, standards of morality need not be framed in imperative form.[69]

The idea of a 'fair soul' is Schiller's attempt to respond directly to the dualism that he sees in Kant. In a fair soul, Schiller maintains, the inclinations and reason are not opposed to each other, nor is one in any sense authoritative vis-à-vis the other:[70] 'Both

---

[65] For a discussion of Schiller's criticisms of Kant and replies to them, see Reiner 1983: esp. 28–49.

[66] See Reiner 1983 and Hatfield 1964: 131.

[67] See Chapter 3.

[68] See Schiller 1961.

[69] Schiller 1967: Letter XXIV, sec. 7, and Schiller 1961; see also Chapter 3 below.

[70] See also Schiller 1961, esp. the later parts, and also Reiner 1983: 29–35. (Schiller denied that any actual human being could achieve full such harmony.)

of these systems of rule are meant to coexist, in perfect independence of each other, and yet in perfect concord.'[71]

Further,

Man not only is permitted to but ought to reconcile desire and duty; he ought to obey his reason with joy. A sensuous nature was wedded to his spiritual nature, not so that he might throw it off as a burden or shuck it off as a coarse shell, but so that he might unite it intimately with his higher self . . . [S]o long as the moral spirit uses coercion, the natural drives are bound to possess force to oppose it.[72]

We can entertain, Schiller thus contends, the idea of a possible state of a human being—not some imaginary ideal, but an actual human being—in whom there is no conflict between reason and inclination.

In all of his thinking on these matters, Schiller regarded himself not as breaking new ground, but as essentially following the lines already laid down by the Greeks— by which Schiller meant the Greeks of the Classical period:

The Greeks put us to shame, not only by a simplicity to which our age is a stranger; they are at the same time our rivals, indeed often our models, in those very excellences with which we are wont to console ourselves for the unnaturalness of our manners.[73]

Although Schiller acknowledged limitations on the level of knowledge which the Greeks had been able to attain,[74] he believed that Greek thought and culture showed how a view of humanity diverging from Kant's could be powerfully articulated and elaborated in both art and philosophy, and could form the basis of an ideal of life free from internal conflict.

2. The Strategy of Aesthetic Reconciliation

The fact that Schiller's ideas have had relatively limited influence on philosophers, especially in the English-speaking world, is due mainly to the fact that he does not develop them fully enough or with sufficient sharpness, but the general thrust of his criticism is powerful. Kant seemed to Schiller to force into a region beyond reason's ambit many considerations—those associated with inclinations—that a human being could not in fact properly disregard in his practical deliberations. In effect, Kant

---

[71] Schiller 1967: Letter XXIV, sec. 8.

[72] Schiller 1961: 464–5 (my translation). The full German runs as follows (emphasis in the original):

und der Mensch *darf* nicht nur, sondern *soll* Lust und Pflicht in Verbindung bringen; er soll seiner Vernunft mit Freude gehorchen. Nicht um sie wie eine Last wegzuwerfen oder wie eine grobe Hülle von sich abzustreifen, nein, um sie aufs innigste mit seinem höheren Selbst zu vereinbaren, ist seiner reinen Geisternatur eine sinnliche beigestellt . . . [D]enn solange der sittliche Geist noch *Gewalt* anwendet, so muss der Naturbetrieb ihm noch *Macht* entgegenzusetzen haben.

[73] Schiller 1967: Letter VI, sec. 2.   [74] See Schiller 1967: Letter VI, secs. 4 and 11.

seemed to have won a freedom from conflict within practical reason by simply gerrymandering out of reason's district all of the considerations that might clash with
morality as he construed it.

In different terms, Schiller's thought is that the condition of a person in whom
inclination and reason are in harmony is *superior* to the condition of someone in whom
they conflict. Moreover, this kind of superiority, Schiller believed, is one that properly should be taken account of by something deserving the title of reason. In other
words, it seemed to Schiller *rational*, in some overarching sense of that term, to prefer
a state in which reason and inclinations are consistent to a state in which they are not.

The difficulty confronting Schiller was consequently twofold. For a philosopher
adopting his stance in opposition to Kant, the first matter on the agenda must be to
show that the various considerations of reason and inclination are indeed consistent.
The second item would be to demonstrate that reason recommends aspiring to such a
condition.

On the first issue, Schiller's view is that such a harmonious state is possible, and he
goes to great lengths in the *Letters on the Aesthetic Education of Man* to insist that it can
be established by the development of the aesthetic faculty. On the second point,
Schiller says less. He does seemingly commit himself to the claim that a person rationally ought to bring reason and inclination into accord with one another. I have
already indicated that in Kant's view there is no ground for making the latter assertion. From Kant's standpoint, it is problematic to talk of a rational dictate to coordinate reason and inclination. In his view, rational motivation is nothing other than
respect for the moral law. Whether one's inclinations coincide therewith is an empirical contingency. And the idea of adjusting reason and inclination to each other by
some sort of compromise would leave these problems unresolved. It therefore does
not appear that a kantian justification can be found for the obligation that Schiller
tries to invoke.

Schiller's critique was forceful, but it left gaps waiting to be filled by subsequent
thinkers. Especially unsettled was Schiller's basis for the belief that a way could be
found to harmonize reason and inclination. Hegel attempted to make good this lack,
and like Schiller he too believed that the best source of ideas for this purpose lay in
Greek thought.

VII. The Hegelian Response

1. The Ambition to Eliminate the Dualism

The account of Greek practical philosophy that Hegel inspired was squarely in a tradition that had already been established by Winckelmann, Herder, Hölderlin,
Schiller, and others. Hegel developed it, however, in a sweepingly ambitious fashion,

so that it was able to constitute a distinctive approach to Greek ethics, and to continue to be so up to the present day. It consists of two parts. One is an interpretation of Greek ethics, that is, a complex of historical claims about what were its theses and its main preoccupations. The other is a way of using it to address modern philosophical problems, especially as they appeared after the work of Kant.

The hegelian response—to reiterate: I speak here of a general way of approaching Greek ideas that was influenced by Hegel, rather than of the details of his actual views—attempts to show, in a more robust way than had Schiller, why the aim of the individual's own happiness should be regarded as consistent with the kinds of moral considerations that both Kant and Schiller had thought of under the rubrics of rationality and morality. Thus the hegelian response strives to restore the idea of a single aim of practical reason, and to vindicate a monist conception of practical reason as a form of eudaimonism.

Hegel's reaction to Kant was far more radical than Schiller's. Whereas Schiller acknowledged Kant's dualism of reason and inclination but tried to paper it over, Hegel attempted to demonstrate that it did not really exist at all. Schiller had maintained that a human being would be best off if the recommendations of reason and the urgings of inclination were consistent, and that such a condition was rationally to be sought. Hegel went further, by trying to argue that the dualism presupposed by both Kant and Schiller was entirely misconceived.

What Hegel hoped to learn from the Greeks was likewise less superficial than what Schiller had derived from them. According to Schiller's account, the Greeks had favoured and admired a harmony of reason and inclination, made possible by their aesthetic outlook. Hegel, on the other hand, hoped to show that the Greek concept of *eudaimonia*, as manifested during the Classical period, was the key by which the elements of the seeming dualism could be joined together.

This effort in turn involved a special account of Greek eudaimonism. In making a particular use of *eudaimonia*, as they construed it, that is, by employing it to respond to problems arising from the threat of deliberative dualism emerging from Kant, advocates of the hegelian response presumed that Greek thinkers themselves had, whether unselfconsciously or explicitly, developed their eudaimonistic thinking for that very same purpose. This meant not only that hegelian interpreters tended to ascribe eudaimonist views to the Greeks when the occasion offered itself, but also that they presupposed that whenever Greek thinkers said eudaimonist-sounding things, their true significance must have been to express a harmony of rational human aims.

Under the hegelian response, two different accounts are possible of how the Greeks came to adopt such a concept of happiness. One view, which appears in Hegel and is the more common of the two, says that the Greeks possessed their concept unselfconsciously and without philosophical reflection. According to the other account, the Greeks, or at least some of their philosophers, developed the concept with the purpose, more or less explicit, of establishing a harmony of human aims. Either way the result was the same: the enlistment of the Greeks into the anti-kantian, anti-dualist project.

2. The Widening of the Concept of Happiness

The fundamental feature of the hegelian response is this: it denies the existence of a genuine dualism of deliberative considerations, and thus tries to eliminate it from our conceptual repertoire. Rather than there being two distinct and independent overall rational aims, it contends, there is really only one. According to this view, the kantian outlook suffers from a kind of conceptual double vision by manufacturing a dualism, and with it a threat of more conflict than ever need have been entertained.

A complex interplay of various questions is involved in the disagreement over whether there can be a conflict between an individual's happiness and such seemingly broader considerations as the happiness of others and conformity to ethical norms. Everything depends on both how happiness is conceived, in the case of oneself and of others,[75] and also on which other considerations are recognized to be relevant.

One thrust of the hegelian criticism of Kant, for instance, is to say that Kant construed the individual's happiness too narrowly, and that if it is conceived in a properly broad way, the considerations of ethics that might seem to work against it are actually incorporated into it. Any considerations that are vitally important for a person to attend to, the thought is, must be counted as related to his well-being. It is an excessively narrow conception of what one's well-being must consist in—that is, a conception that makes it out to be entirely self-confined—that leads, the hegelian view suggests, to the idea of this opposition. And once we allow a wider conception of the individual's good, it concludes, we shall be able to resolve or mitigate the conflicts that it engenders, but without ignoring other-regarding and ethical considerations, and without adopting an egoist stance.[76]

3. Some Terminology

Let us fix some terminology to help us articulate these issues. I use the term 'self-confined' for those states or aims that are within an individual. Obviously this notion

---

[75] There is always a danger of definitional circularity when one specifies the happiness of individual in a way that includes the happiness of others, but I shall ignore this issue in what follows, as not germane to the questions that concern me.

[76] Certainly Hegel had no intention of adopting an egoist position, and also opposed many of the individualist tendencies of romanticism. See Wood 1991: 201, 216; Gray 1941: 40, 53. Wood associates romanticism with individualism (xiii–xiv, 202–3), whereas Larmore 1987 connects it with anti-individualism (98–9, 107–8). This just goes to show that, as one would expect, there are (at least) two kinds of romanticism. See Lovejoy 1948b. Lovejoy also observes that there are two sorts of individualism, one characteristic of the enlightenment and the other of romanticism (1948c: 82).

has its unclarities, but it will do for our purposes. It is contrasted with what is 'outside' the individual or 'external' to him or simply 'non-self-confined'.

Another useful distinction contrasts aims that are counted, by a particular view, as part of the individual's well-being and those that are beyond it. Let us say that the aims and considerations that a view places within a person's happiness are 'self-regarding' according to that view, and that the others are 'non-self-regarding' or, for short, 'broader'. Because different philosophical views adopt different accounts of what well-being is, this distinction must be thought of as relative to the particular view under discussion. A typical hedonist holds that one's happiness consists solely of pleasant experiences. Someone else may hold that it includes in part the well-being of one's society.[77] For the latter philosopher, the well-being of society is a self-regarding consideration, whereas for the hedonist it is not.

Plainly these two distinctions do not coincide. The main point of a hegelian construal of happiness, indeed, is to allow that external or non-self-confined aims can be self-regarding, because they can themselves be parts or constituents of an individual's own well-being, even though they have to do with other people or with other things lying outside that individual himself. According to the usual hegelian view, an important deficiency of a kantian view may be to refuse to recognize this point. We shall see how this disagreement plays itself out in interpretations of Greek ethics.

The self-regarding and self-confined may both be thought of as embraced by a broader category, the *self-referential*. A self-referential aim is, roughly, an aim that must be specified by reference to oneself. An example would be the well-being of one's own city. This aim is not self-confined in any normal sense. Moreover, on some accounts of one's happiness, such as hedonism, it is not self-regarding either. Nevertheless, it is defined by a relation to oneself. As such it is not completely non-self-referential or, as the term is sometimes used, 'absolute'. This is the kind of aim that makes for what C. D. Broad called 'self-referential altruism', that is, an aim or motivation directed at the well-being of someone other than oneself but specified by relation to oneself.[78]

Self-referentiality may appear to be a matter merely of how an aim is referred to rather than of what it really is. Nevertheless in this case labels may be important. Someone may in a hegelian vein say, for instance, that the happiness of even all other people is a part of one's own well-being, and perhaps add that this is because they are all one's fellow creatures. But some kantian-minded thinkers are still liable to reply that what makes the well-being of other people a rational consideration is that it is a universal or impartial concern, *not* that it is part of *one's* well-being, and indeed not that it has any connection with oneself.[79] To the kantian, there is something question-

---

[77] Below I shall use the term 'pluralist' to label this type of view.
[78] See Broad 1942 and 1952.
[79] This general line of thought can be found in e.g. Nagel 1986: chs. 8–10, as well as Nagel 1970.

able about the invocation, in rational deliberation, of a relation to oneself as such, no matter how all-embracing it may be.

As a result of this last-mentioned issue, it becomes important to ask whether the Greeks possessed a notion of a non-self-referential goodness, or a non-self-referentially expressible reason for action. There is a widespread tendency, not always fully articulated, to think of the Greeks as not possessing such a notion, but instead as thinking that the only valid practical consideration must involve some relation of a state of affairs to oneself, as one's own *eudaimonia* or the well-being of oneself as a human being. In what follows I shall argue that they did indeed have, and use, such a non-self-referential concept.

4. Fusionist and Inclusivist Strategies

Historically the hegelian strategy has been pursued in two ways, which I shall call 'fusionism' and 'inclusivism'. Both have figured in the historiography of Greek ethical thought. The fusionist version says that, initial appearances notwithstanding, there is really no difference at all between the individual's own good, on the one hand, and, on the other hand, such matters as the good of others and conformity to ethical standards.[80] Rather, these seemingly distinct aims are—as can be seen when they are properly understood—in fact *identical*. The concept of identity that is in play here is problematic, but this view presupposes that it can be adequately comprehended. Indeed, this version of the hegelian position holds that the appearance of a distinction, and thus of the possibility of conflict, is the very dualistic mistake that this notion of identity is devised to reveal. The other, more complex, articulation of the hegelian view, inclusivism, employs not the notion of identity but the notion of inclusion or parthood. This view maintains that an individual's well-being in some sense includes, as parts or constituents or components, the well-being of others and one's own conformity to ethical standards. Inclusivism seems the less radical of the two positions, at least on the surface, and perhaps for that reason is the more commonly employed for the interpretation of Greek ethics.[81]

Differences between fusionism and inclusivism aside, their common purpose is evident. Both propose to develop an account of human well-being under which it can be shown to incorporate conformity to ethical norms and concern for the good of other people. The purpose is to try to mitigate the conflicts that are thought to arise

[80] Thus there can be different types of fusionism, depending on the particular view that is adopted about what the good of others and appropriate ethical standards actually are. Something analogous applies, of course, to inclusivism too.

[81] Roughly this notion of 'inclusion' is explicit in Aristotle; in modern scholarship one finds it in, for instance, Hardie 1965, Ackrill 1980, and Cooper 1975: 131–2.

from, in particular, the kind of dualism that appears in kantian thinking between one's happiness and ethical or moral considerations.

5. Adjudication, Elimination, and Evaluative Holism

The fusionist idea that one's well-being consists solely of one's adherence to ethical standards, or the like, is radical enough to have been advocated by only a few philosophers, including, as we shall see later, the Stoics.[82] Fusionism eliminates conflict in one fell swoop by denying that there are any distinct things between which such conflict could arise. Nevertheless, it seems to run counter to the common conviction that worthwhile aims are plural—though some monist accounts of aims, such as quantitative hedonism, accept fusionism despite this fact; and likewise most interpreters of Classical Greek ethics, in particular, have found an inclusivist account of Greek views more plausible.

But the inclusivist strategy is more problematic. Consider its simplest form, which says merely that conformity to ethical norms and action for the well-being of others are 'parts' of an individual's well-being. To say this, however, is not necessarily to demonstrate, or even to assert, that the two are fully consistent, any more than to say that Quebec is a part of Canada is to say that the interests of the former coincide with those of the latter. In general, the good of one part of a thing can conflict with the good of second part, and if the good of the whole turns out to be generated mainly by the good of the former part, then it will conflict with the good of the latter. So if there is a clash between one's happiness and one's obligation, expanding the boundaries of the *expression* 'happiness' so that it includes the fulfilment of one's obligations is nothing but a mere relabelling. Some inclusivists, however, have been attentive to this fact, among them not only Mill but also some recent interpreters of the Greeks. We shall need to consider this matter more closely when we come to particular applications of it to Greek ethics.[83]

There are a number of ways in which to go beyond simple inclusivism so as to use the concept of happiness to try to lessen deliberative conflict. One is to say that the concept includes an assignment of priorities, to determine which aims must give way to others. This is a reasonable enough idea, but it does not suit the purposes of the inclusivist or more generally the hegelian responses.

The reason for this is that the chief goal of these accounts is not, as we might put it, to *adjudicate* deliberative conflicts but rather to *eliminate* or at least *mitigate* them. The rough idea of Hellenic harmony is that Greek ethics simply gets rid of the kind of oppositions that Kant's doctrine and others like it generate—as opposed to simply telling us which, from among what are acknowledged to be two distinct worthwhile

---

[82] See Chapter 7, sec. IV.

[83] See further Chapter 2, sec. VII with Chapter 6, sec. IV, and White 1994a and 1999b.

options that cannot both be attained, to choose. Kant, after all, does something like that. He tells us that reason follows morality, not inclination, not that there really is no difference between them. On the other hand, hegelian responses to Greek ethics look to it for much more deepgoing solutions to deliberative problems than that. They tell us that the conflicts are either unreal or much less severe than they looked initially.

Elimination or mitigation of conflict thus involves saying that it *does not really arise*, or arises to a significantly lesser degree than appears. One way to develop this idea is to say that when we consider what well-being really is, and what the reasonable ethical standards really amount to, we shall see that any initial impression that they collide turns out to be an illusion. There are various ways to try to do this.

One way is by rejecting the distinction between self-confined and external aims, or between aims that are self-regarding and those that are broader. In that case, though there may still be conflicts, they will not be classified as, so to speak, self–other oppositions. This strategy, too, might be thought to be merely a kind of relabelling, like simple inclusivism, of an opposition that would remain in place. Nevertheless, the strategy would give the opposition a different character, and might make it appear less severe, at least by some standards.

A more sweeping strategy can be used against all deliberative oppositions as such. Conflicts arise when aims that are incompatible are both conceived of as worthwhile or rational taken one by one. A person believes that it would be worthwhile to do one thing, and that it would be worthwhile to do another; then he sees that one cannot do both. The problem does not arise if one always evaluates options only in the full light of attention to the question of their compatibility with other options. In that case, one does not conclude that something is worthwhile *until* one sees whether it fits with everything else that one will deem worthwhile, and one tries to decide on the *whole package* of aims together.

The result of this line of thought is a kind of *evaluative holism*. Under the extreme version, the only thing to be evaluated is the whole complex of aims. Each component aim itself is thought of as having only *contributive* value, that is, value arising from its contribution to the overall value of the whole.[84] (A common political application of this idea is obviously the view, sometimes called 'totalitarianism', that the value of individual citizens' lives is not intrinsic, but rather is simply the contribution that they make to the community viewed 'as an organic whole'.)[85] Whether this is a viable conception is debatable: arguably we are incapable of evaluating complex wholes without some genuine evaluation of their components. In any case, some philosophers have

---

[84] On this notion of contributive value, see Lewis 1946. There are inherent difficulties in the assignment of contributive value because of the difficulty of assigning responsibility for a resultant condition to each among many of the factors involved in generating it. Nothing that I say here depends on solving these difficulties.

[85] On this well-known theme, see e.g. Berlin 1991b: 31

espoused forms of evaluative holism. The Stoics are among them, as we shall see, and they used this strategy, along with fusionism, as an extreme way of arguing that deliberative oppositions in fact do not exist.

Evaluative holism need not, however, take such a radical form, and need not claim to eliminate conflict altogether. Milder forms can attempt merely to mitigate oppositions, not to establish complete harmony. This can be done—though again the viability of the idea is subject to debate—by saying that a thing may both have contributive value and at the same time also be intrinsically worthwhile, or valuable in its own right. Under such a scheme there can be conflict between two aims, and the need to sacrifice one partially for the sake of the other can be regarded as a genuine loss, but at the same time satisfaction can be taken in some compromise arrangement that includes at least some of each of them. I shall argue later that Aristotle adopted a view of this sort, though he placed far more emphasis—standard interpretations to the contrary—on the conflict than on the reconciliation.[86]

6. Moralität and Sittlichkeit

As described so far, the hegelian response to Greek ethics directs its attention principally to explaining the notion of happiness. At the same time, however, we could equally well focus our attention on other aspects of this same outlook. Hegel himself, as well as many of those influenced by him, also wished to recast another one of the notions that seemed to be opposed to individual good. This notion was *morality*. Kant himself had appropriated the word 'morality', or *Moralität*, for his own particular way of articulating his conception of duty as he contrasted it with inclination and happiness. Hegel wished to supplant Kant's notion by a quite different one, which he labelled *Sittlichkeit*.[87]

Kant conceives of *Moralität* as binding upon all rational beings as such, and so upon all humanity. Hegel moves away from this conception. On his view, *Sittlichkeit* does not represent universal moral obligations under which a rational being as such falls. Rather, the *Sittlichkeit* that Hegel holds relevant to a given person consists in the norms and obligations that operate in a particular historical community of which the person is actually a part.

In Hegel's opinion, this normative notion is superior to the kantian notion of morality, in large part because it was easier, Hegel thought, to see how considerations of *Sittlichkeit* could stand in harmony with the notion of individual good that he had

---

[86] I shall pursue all of these issues further below, esp. in Chapter 2, sec VII. On Aristotle, see Chapter 6, esp. sec. IX.

[87] Kant himself had used both terms for his notion; Hegel granted him the one and appropriated the other. For discussion, see Bubner 1986 and Kuhlmann 1986b.

articulated. His notion of individual good and his notion of *Sittlichkeit* were made to fit each other, each designed as part of an attempt to show that, when they are both properly understood, an individual's well-being and broader considerations coincide, and that the latter really is not in any important sense broader than the former at all.

This is the way, viewed from this angle, in which the hegelian approach hopes to achieve the additional advantage over dualistic or kantian positions of positing a single end of rational deliberation and simultaneously avoiding, it hopes, the idea that altruistic and ethical considerations are somehow alien to the individual's concern for his own well-being. The kantian position, hegelians hold, makes *Sittlichkeit* appear to be an outside force that hems the individual in. Moreover it also seems to some to be misguided in its insistence that a person's reason must sometimes rationally choose to sacrifice his own good.

7. *The Harmonious Hegelian* Polis

The hegelian response was committed to paying far more attention to the institutions of Greek society than the kantian response ever did. Like Herder and others, Hegel took as the focus of his own account of the Greek outlook the institution of the *polis*. Recognizing that a Greek citizen's role in the *polis* was in many ways the focus of his life, Hegel held that it was through this institution that Hellenic thought had effected a fusion of individual and social good.

Hegel begins with the idea that in the period between about 492 and 431 BCE, the Greeks—and especially the Athenians—took the individual to be in an important sense wholly bound up with the *polis*. For the Greeks, he held, the norms to which an individual is to conform needed to be given to him by the community (in the modern age, it could be the state) of which he is a part. Hegel himself endorses this idea:

[A] consistent 'doctrine of duties' can be nothing except the serial exposition of the relationships which are necessitated by the Idea of freedom, and are therefore realized across their whole extent, that is, in some state.[88]

In the Greek case, as Hegel sees it, the customs of one's own *polis* are the whole expression of what one can take as the norms that one accepts and by which one abides:

The interests of the community may ... continue to be entrusted to the will and resolve of the citizens—and this must be the basis of the Greek constitution; for no principle has as yet manifested itself, which can contravene such choice conditioned by custom, and hinder its realizing itself in action. The Democratic Constitution is here the only possible one: *the citizens are still unconscious of particular interests*, and therefore of a corrupting element.[89]

[88] Hegel 1965: sec. 148, trans. Knox with revisions by Taylor, as given in Taylor 1979: 375.
[89] Hegel 1991: 252; cf. 253, 255. Compare Hegel 1955: ii. 98–9, 99–100, 114; and Hegel 1965: secs. 142–9, which exhibit both inclusivist and fusionist lines of thought. See also Gray 1941: 44–5, 61–3.

This is the core of Hegel's interpretation of Greek ethics. As Hegel understood them, the Classical Greeks did not possess a conception of the individual's good or self-interest as potentially in conflict with his *polis*. Under such an interpretation, the individual's good is conceived as being so closely bound up with his own *polis* that it is not really distinct from it.[90] As Charles Taylor explains Hegel's view,

> Hegel's notion of *Sittlichkeit* is in part a rendering of that expressive unity which his whole generation saw in the Greek *polis* where—it was believed—men had seen the collective life of their city as the essence and meaning of their own lives, had sought their glory in its public life, their rewards in power and reputation within it, and immortality in its memory.[91]

Quite aside from its status as an interpretation of Hegel's own thinking, Taylor's remarks exemplify the picture of Greek ethics that became widespread through Hegel's influence.

The idea is sometimes carried to the point of declaring an essential connection between the individual and the community, and then arguing on that basis for a coincidence of their goods. One reasons somewhat as follows: if a citizen takes his whole life and everything valuable in it to be in some sense defined by his relation to his *polis*, or if he believes that he could not exist detached from it, then it follows that he sees his good and that of the *polis* to be identical or necessarily consistent with each other.

Hegel thought he found in Classical Athens not merely the development of the *concept* of the *polis* as I have just described it, but also its *exemplification*. This, too, he thought he found in Periclean Athens. By the end of the fifth century, he believed, and in fact after the Peloponnesian War began in 431 BCE, the harmony of the *polis* departed from Greek life. Still, he thought that even then the ideal of the *polis* lived on in the Greeks' memory as a pattern by which they believed that social life actually might be lived. And the idea of the harmony of the *polis* can easily be thought to implicate, as it tends to in Hegel, a harmony of all important human aims.

Hegel's invocation of what he took to be events in Greek political history is not for him merely a marginal theme but an integral part of his philosophical thinking. When he turned his attention to the Greeks, he did not claim to be describing Hellenic ideas in abstraction from the practical world of politics. He was not, he thought, merely conveying a remote philosophical ideal, but instead a thought that he claimed had actually been put into practice and lived.

---

[90] Hegel 1955: ii. 98–9, 112–13, 209. Cf. Taylor 1979: 379–80, 383–8; Gray 1941: 59–60. Perhaps one should add that this is so only under certain conditions, i.e., given that the *polis* in question is a genuine community; see Wood 1991: ch. 11, esp. 202–8.

[91] Taylor 1979: 378. Taylor's explanation of *Sittlichkeit* (376) is contrasted with *Moralität*, which is Hegel's word for the notion of morality that he finds in Kant. Under a quite common interpretation of Hegel, this notion would implicate him in a kind of localism or relativism in ethics, and he would be committed to supposing that a person was bound to accept whatever norms were laid down by his society. Against that interpretation, see Wood 1991: 202–8.

Ever since, this fact has lent added prestige to the hegelian use of Greek philosophical ethics. This supposition—that a harmony of individual and social goods was,
at some particular time and place, actually put into practice—has made the idea seem
much more plausible, as a truly workable piece of political philosophy, than it would
have been if it had been advanced merely as a product of the academic imagination.

Most Greek historians would now deny that any Greek society or *polis* ever really
did exhibit the degree of concord and unity that Hegel attributed to Periclean
Athens.[92] Nonetheless, much of the appeal of the philosophical notion of Hellenic
harmony, over the years and up to the present day, is owed to the belief that that harmony is more than a theoretician's dream, and to the conviction that its defenders can
actually point to a setting, even if only one in the distant past, in which it found its realization. To some extent, that is, the fact that there actually were Greek city-states, and
that they are believed to have fit the hegelian pattern, has fostered the hope that the
consistency of rational human aims might be not merely a goal of remote theoretical
yearning but more genuinely attainable.

8. The Hegelian Aims of Plato and Aristotle

Although Hegel's account of Greek eudaimonism is itself a self-consciously philosophical account, the view that it ascribes to the Hellenic mind is, according to Hegel,
an unreflective and unselfconscious one. Hegel did not believe that the Greeks were
in a position to articulate the view explicitly as he himself had.[93] He says that in a
democratically constituted *polis* such as Athens, '[t]he Democratic Constitution is
here the only possible one: the citizens *are still unconscious of* particular interests, and
therefore of a corrupting element'.[94] This seems to suggest that in such conditions,
people are in a state of conceptual innocence. That is, in some degree they do not possess the concepts necessary to formulate a conflict or even a distinction between their
own good and the good of their community.[95] In such a condition, seemingly, the 'cor-

---

[92] See, just for example, Ehrenberg 1969: 91.

[93] The Greeks' failure to perfect the idea was caused by their failure fully to develop the idea of the
individual; see Taylor 1979: 378; Wood 1991; Apel 1986: 219–20. The influence of Hegel's invocation of the
Greeks is of course demonstrated by the association of Plato and Hegel in Karl Popper's well-known attack
on both in Popper 1950.

[94] Hegel 1991: 252.

[95] Sometimes certain features of the Greek language are adduced to support such a view, for example
the fact that the terms *eu prattein* and *eupragia* can be used to mean to mean 'do well' in the sense either of
'be happy' or of 'act (ethically) well', and is also sometimes ambiguous (e.g. see perhaps Plato, *Euthydemus*
278e–282a). By itself such evidence is utterly inconclusive, though people often rely on it. It is no more
plausible to say that the term *eupragia* by itself shows a failure to distinguish the two notions than it is to say
that because English speakers use 'snow' to cover many different formations, they are incapable of distin-
guishing them when they need to. Any decent skier can understand the point; see Quammen 1998.

rupting' notion of their own 'subjective', private good, as distinct from the well-being of the *polis*, is simply not present to their minds. Their unreflective way of thinking presents to them a notion of good in which there is no bifurcation of 'my good' and 'the good of the *polis*'.[96]

Observe that the notion that Hegel seems to have in mind under the label 'the *polis*' is really tantamount to that of the *polis* that is *mine*, that is, the one of which *I* am a citizen. This fact engages disagreement from more kantian-minded philosophers, a disagreement that arises from their tendency, noted above, to think that rational or genuinely weighty considerations cannot be essentially defined by some relation to oneself, but must rather be formulable in impartial or universal terms.

As Hegel recognized, there is more to the story of ethics in the Classical period than purely unselfconscious identification of citizen with his *polis*. Plato and Aristotle do not simply express unreflectively an unbifurcated notion of good that is embodied in their community. Rather, we find explicit and extensive discussions in works like Plato's *Republic* of the question whether justice is advantageous for the person who possesses it. That question arises in that work precisely because in Book I, Thrasymachus is made to contend explicitly and emphatically that, precisely because being just is not in one's own interest, justice is a foolish trait to possess and to cultivate. That shows that the issue had become a matter of dispute in Plato's time.

In view of this obvious fact, Hegel attempts to construct an explanation of how a society, which at one stage was unconscious of a distinction between the good of the individual and the good of the *polis*, could have shifted to a condition in which open and self-conscious discussions of the relation between the two took place. He attributes the discovery of the question, and perhaps of the notion of 'subjective' individual good necessary to formulate it, to the intellectual activity, in the latter part of the fifth century BCE, of Socrates and the so-called Sophists.[97]

The hegelian account assigns to Plato and Aristotle, then, the task of restoring to Greek thought its lost innocence. That is, they would strive to demonstrate that the two considerations, of individual good and ethical and social value, which had somehow seemed to come apart under the influence of Socrates and the Sophists, really are not separable in the way that they had been made to appear to be. This would not be

---

[96] See also Chapter 4, secs. I–II.

[97] Hegel 1991: 252, 268–71. MacIntyre follows Hegel pretty closely on this point; see MacIntyre 1988: 74. He suggests that in this period it became possible to conceive of aiming for what he calls the 'goods of effectiveness' independently of what he calls the 'goods of excellence' (32, 35). Roughly, this means that it became possible to satisfy desires for things like money and power independently of achieving the excellence intrinsic to a particular sort of activity. This led, he says, to a situation in which competition raged over the goods of effectiveness, which the Sophists advised people on how to win (32–46). Like Hegel's story, this story seems to presuppose that people were to some degree attracted by the goods of effectiveness to begin with. Cf. n. 99.

an easy philosophical task. Showing that a distinction that seems to exist really does not exist risks looking like trying to restore unity to Humpty Dumpty.[98] But the hegelian will reply that the distinction was never really made in the first place, or that it was all along really a distinction without a difference, and moreover that human society can function best without it.[99]

The hegelian line of interpretation thus typically looks to Classical Greek philosophy for two points. Plato, for example, is confronted by a Thrasymachus who purports to draw the disfavoured distinction, and to claim that it generates a conflict. Plato must then hope to demonstrate that Thrasymachus's distinction is misguided, in a way that will make sense to Thrasymachus and those who agree with him— including, if possible, his modern dualist heirs.[100] At the same time, Plato needs to present a society that functions without the distinction. This Plato supposedly does in his description of the ideal *polis*.[101] On this interpretation, the people who inhabit the *polis* are intended to live in the state of innocence that prevailed before the disfavoured distinction was foisted upon them by the Sophists and Socrates.[102]

There is an obvious parallel between what Hegel was trying to do and the project that he attributed to the Classical Greek philosophers. They were trying to oppose the Sophists in the same way as the hegelian view, for its part, was attempting to combat both individualism and kantianism in ethics, and particularly the deliberative dualism that they both seemed to espouse. Both of these latter two lines of thought insisted on a distinction between the good of the individual and some sort of broader considerations which might or might not be worthy of being followed. These interpreters thus pictured the Classical Greek philosophers as agreeing with their own position, and as working against the same sorts of dualist adversaries.

[98] See Chapter 2, sec. I.

[99] MacIntyre's way is to say that Plato urges the importance of the 'goods of excellence' (cf. n. 97), and their superior claim to be thought of as genuine goods, against the 'goods of effectiveness' (1988: 68, 74–7). Underlying this account is the idea that in Plato's view, it is striving for the latter goods, not the former, that produces conflict, both among different individuals and between the individual and the *polis*. Plato's opponents of course will reply that the goods of excellence can perfectly well generate conflict too; see Adkins 1960: 277–8: 'two sculptors cannot carve a statue from a piece of stone big enough for only one of them, nor two doctors amputate the same limb.'

[100] It is sometime contended (see e.g. MacIntyre 1988: 74–7) that there is no common ground between Plato and Thrasymachus, and that Plato's argument in the *Republic* is not and cannot be designed to convince Thrasymachus or someone with his views. That Plato did not see matters this way appears to me to be clear from his attempt in *Rep.* IX to demonstrate that the tyrant's desires undercut his own satisfaction because of the frustration that is supposedly consequent upon them (see esp. 576b–580a with White 1979b: 25–8, 223–4).

[101] And esp. in such passages as *Rep.* 412c–e; see Hegel 1991: ii. 93.

[102] Compare Popper 1950: 21–4, 157–64. In many respects Popper much exaggerates the extent to which Plato aims to depict an earlier golden age. What Popper is reacting to, however, is the feature of the hegelian reading that I am describing here.

9. *The Non-Hegelian Socrates*

Not all Classical Greek philosophers were so pictured, however. An exception, according to some but not all hegelian-minded thinkers, was Socrates. Rather than picturing him as joined with Plato and Aristotle in the attempt to restore harmony, Hegel himself regarded Socrates as allied with Sophists in contributing to its breakdown. Socrates' contribution, Hegel thought, was the value that he attached to the concern for his own soul, together with the historical fact of Socrates' having set himself against his *polis*, Athens, and so having been put to death by it and his fellow citizens.

This way of looking at Socrates runs in some ways counter to two important elements of his own thinking. These elements, surprisingly enough, support the idea of deliberative harmony and work against the notion that rational considerations might clash. Here I have in mind a famous pair of Socratic doctrines, the thesis that someone who knows what is good to do will not fail to do it, and the claim of the so-called unity of the virtues.

Although the doctrine of the unity of the virtues as we find it in Plato's *Protagoras*, for example, is not completely unambiguous, it holds at the very least that acting in accordance with one virtue is fully consistent with acting in accordance with every other. Some of the evidence suggests that the doctrine goes even farther than this, to the point of asserting that each virtue is actually identical with every other.[103] Be that as it may, however, the position certainly rules out the possibility that possessing or acting upon one virtue might preclude having or manifesting another, or that a person might ever be in a quandary as to which virtue to exhibit.

By itself, the unity of the virtues would not rule out all possibility that a rational person might encounter a conflict in his aims. It excludes only the possibility of clashes among the virtues themselves. In particular, the unity of the virtues would not eliminate the possibility that the cultivation of virtue might be irreconcilable with the pursuit of one's own happiness. That possibility, however, might seem to be denied, or close to it, by the other Socratic doctrine mentioned above. This thesis says that knowledge of what is good is by itself a sufficient condition for aiming to do it. Given that the virtues are good, the conclusion seems to be that a person who knows what is good to do from a non-self-regarding standpoint could not be led away from doing it by the consideration of his own well-being.

In view of the ease with which this line of thought can be ascribed to Socrates, it is remarkable that Hegel did not make such a use of Socratic thinking. By way of explanation one can only say that the countervailing considerations—Socrates' idea of the care of one's soul and the fact of his execution by Athens—weighed more strongly in Hegel's assessment of Socrates' significance. For Hegel, Socrates was pre-eminently

---

[103] Examples of the extensive literature on this question include Penner 1973 and Vlastos 1991.

an originator of 'subjectivity', and in particular of the notion of an individual's conception of his own good as distinct from that of his *polis*.[104] He therefore was not from Hegel's standpoint a promising enlistee in the campaign for a Hellenic harmony of rational aims, but instead an agent of its dissolution.

VIII. Nietzsche and his Influence

1. Nietzsche's Rejection of Harmony

In the modern historiography of Greek ethical philosophy, the kantian and hegelian responses are the ones that have exerted the most influence. That fact should seem surprising, as I have already noted, to anyone who recognizes the importance of Nietzsche for the development of modern thinking about Greece, especially inasmuch as in *The Birth of Tragedy* he strove to overthrow the notion that ancient Greece was a land of serenity and concord. Nevertheless this is the case. In the context of the present discussion, Nietzsche is a marginal figure. Although his account of the Greeks has been followed by some more recent thinkers, he failed in general to loosen the hold of the idea that Classical Greek ethics is substantially different from modern ethics, and that in some way it exemplified a harmony and unity of motivation that modern ethics lacks. Indeed, he did not in all ways let go of that idea himself.

There is a straightforward explanation of this state of affairs. Nietzsche did not enter into a discussion of the differences between ancient and modern philosophical writers on ethics. The simple reason for this is that he did not believe in the difference. He thought that both ancient and modern ethics were more or less the same. He attacked the notion of morality which he saw embodied in Christianity and the modern European ethical views that grew out of it. Unlike advocates of the kantian interpretation, however, he did not think that philosophers such as Plato and Aristotle offered anything better or even different.

Indeed, Nietzsche did not interpret Classical Greek ethics as eudaimonistic. Instead, he took Greek practical philosophy from Socrates onward to be scarcely distinguishable from the kind of modern Christian moral thinking that he despised. He believed that Socrates marked the beginning of the decadence that was accelerated by Christianity and brought to a contemptible nadir by the anaemic egalitarianism of modern Europe. For he thought that the mainstream of Greek ethics represented the morality of the herd, bent on suppressing the gifts of splendid individuals.[105]

The kinds of harmony that thinkers like Herder, Schiller, and Hegel found in Classical Greece did not interest Nietzsche. He had no use for Schiller's idea that obedience to duty is an instance of concord. The type of human being that Nietzsche

---

[104] See esp. Hegel 1991: 250–3, 269–71. [105] Nietzsche 1966b: e.g. secs. 190, 202.

regarded as admirable was, he thought, above both the possibility of such a harmony and also the need for it.[106]

The reason for this seems to be that in Nietzsche's view the kind of conflict that Kant's position on moral psychology seemed to generate was of no importance, because Nietzsche attached little importance to either of the poles of the dualism. On the one side was morality, which Nietzsche for the most part disdained—both *Moralität* and *Sittlichkeit*. On the other side was inclination, which Nietzsche, not without justification, tended to think of in terms of an unimportant and unimpressive kind of pleasure, which he thought was characteristically of concern only to inferior people. If neither of these considerations was of much significance to him, he had no reason to be overly exercised about any clash that might occur between them.

Nor, therefore, was Nietzsche eager to focus attention on an interpretation of Greek ethics that gave an important place to such a dualism. From his standpoint, Greek philosophy would have appeared all the better if he had thought that it avoided the kantian notions of morality, duty, and a rationality that underwrote them. By the same token, he could have regarded it as no great achievement to have harmonized morality with its counterweight in Kant, namely, individual happiness as merely the satisfaction of the inclinations. If that had been all that the Greeks had accomplished, it would in his eyes have seemed no good ground for glorifying them. For this reason, neither schillerian nor hegelian interpretations could have held any appeal for him.

2. Nietzschean Nostalgia

Not that Nietzsche was free himself from nostalgia for a Greek ideal. The focus of his admiration for Hellenism, however, was quite different from that of earlier eighteenth- and nineteenth-century thinkers. It was not associated with Greek philosophical ethics of the Classical period. Rather, he was nostalgic for a still earlier period of Greek thought, namely the Archaic, heroic, and Presocratic elements of Greek culture, represented for him by Homeric heroes and a few Sophistic figures, like the character Callicles in Plato's *Gorgias*,[107] as well as the cosmological strife embodied in the thought of Heraclitus. Nietzsche regarded this early era of Greek culture, unlike the period from Socrates on, as a time when the kind of bold self-assertion that he admired was unencumbered by the scruples of 'slave morality'.[108]

---

[106] Due qualification perhaps needs to be entered here. Arguably *The Birth of Tragedy* exhibits a sense of the importance of community that contrasts with the seeming individualism of other, later works, at least in the view of some interpreters; see Aschheim 1992: 41, 60. Nevertheless, this communitarianism has little to do with the kind of deliberative monism that the kantian or hegelian responses ascribe to Greek ethics.

[107] On the relation between Callicles and Nietzsche, see Dodds 1959: 387–91.

[108] See e.g. Nietzsche 1996b: esp. Pt. 9.

In spite of these facts, it is significant that even Nietzsche's vision of the Greeks did not deny an important place to the concept of harmony. On the contrary, in this respect he remained within the tradition of Hellenic nostalgia that went back to Winckelmann. Nietzsche's account of Heraclitus insists—just as one would expect from the nature of its subject—on the centrality of the idea of conflict between opposites. At the same time, however, Heraclitean conflicts are, according to Nietzsche, bound up together in a harmony:

Everything that happens, happens in accordance with this strife [of opposites], and it is just in the strife that eternal justice is revealed. It is a wonderful idea, welling up from the purest springs of Hellenism, the idea that strife embodies the everlasting sovereignty of strict justice, bound to everlasting laws.

Here it appears that according to Nietzsche the conflicts are still present in the structure that embraces them. The harmony does not remove them but somehow merely consists of them. Farther on, however, he invokes the notion of harmony explicitly:

Do guilt, injustice, contradiction and suffering exist in this world? They do, proclaims Heraclitus, but only for the limited human mind, which sees things apart but not connected, not for the con-tuitive god. For him all contradictions run into harmony.

However, this divine view of things is not, according to Nietzsche, accessible to human beings:

Insofar as [simple-minded man] shares, of necessity, in fire, he has a plus of rationality; insofar as he consists of water and earth, his reason is in a bad way.[109]

Thus even the conflict-hungry Nietzsche sees even the conflict-obsessed Heraclitus as representing a characteristically Hellenic harmony in the world.

Nonetheless, this is not a harmony that enters into human affairs. Heraclitus's aim is not to exhibit how conflicts among people can be resolved or shown to be nonexistent. Nietzsche even sees conflict in Heraclitus as a principle responsible for the existence of the *polis*. Strife bound by justice 'is the contest-idea of the Greek individual and the Greek state, taken from the gymnasium and the palaestra, from the artist's *agon*, from the contest between political parties and between cities'.[110] This is far from Hegel's idea of the *polis* as the place in which conflicts are erased or transcended through a concord of individual and social good.

3. *The Weakness of Nietzsche's Influence*

Given these facts about Nietzsche's attitudes, it would be impossible for him to take part in the discussion of Hellenism that is relevant to the topics at issue here, and his

---

[109] Nietzsche 1962: 55, 61, 63.   [110] Ibid. 55.

influence in this area could be only indirect. Though he retained something of an idea of Hellenic harmony, his version of it had little to do with the harmony of individual good with broader considerations. The problems raised by that dualism simply did not much affect his thinking about Greek culture. The overall effect of Nietzsche's thinking was to bypass the discussion that had been begun between kantian and hegelian interpretations of Greek ethics. Those two ways of looking at the Greeks, and of focusing on the Classical period, continued as before, each claiming its own adherents and together, as will emerge in the next chapter, dominating twentieth-century discussions of Greek ethics.

Chapter 2

DELIBERATIVE CONFLICT: SOME RECENT PHILOSOPHICAL CONCEPTS

I. The Kantian and Hegelian Responses
Early in the Twentieth Century

1. The Continuation of the Kantian and Hegelian Responses

The historiographical material of the previous chapter forms the background against which contemporary discussions of Greek ethics take place. Most important twentieth-century treatments of Greek ethical ideas are influenced to some extent by the issues thus far described. In these treatments something is almost always at stake philosophically concerning eudaimonism and possibility of conflicts among rational aims.

The purpose of the present chapter is to carry into the twentieth century the story that was begun in the previous chapter, in such a way as to show how the ideas that motivated earlier discussions of Greek ethics continue to make their influence felt in recent writings on it. In particular, I shall explain why it makes sense to focus in one and the same discussion on issues concerning both eudaimonism and also deliberative conflict and consistency. The reason, as I shall explain, is that many of the other ideas that are brought nowadays into discussions of Greek ethics are very largely motivated by precisely these problems together, even in cases where those links are not made explicit.

The kantian and hegelian retain a strong influence, in spite of the ever-increasing historical sophistication of writings on Greek ethics. Very recent responses to Greek ethics have often been more detailed and nuanced than earlier ones, and most of the former have contained less in the way of crude attempts to appropriate ancient ideas for contemporary philosophical or polemical purposes. Nevertheless, many of the underlying interpretative motivations persist in subtler forms. It is often still easy, for instance, to see the old kantian and hegelian responses and their accompanying interpretations simply taken for granted as commonplaces, with less than sufficient attention to the evidence for, or against, them. Most notably, there remains a strong tendency for more or less anti-kantian thinkers to try to trace their philosophical ideas back to the Greeks, especially by presuming not only that Greek ethics was essentially eudaimonist, but also that it deployed the concept for the particular purpose of mitigating or eliminating the kind of deliberative conflicts that these interpreters object to in Kant and his followers. This way of thinking gives rise, then, to a corresponding view of what is supposed to be the characteristic difference between ancient and modern approaches to ethics.

To treat these matters seriously we must have the relevant philosophical concepts in view. If our purpose here were to give a purely historical or even antiquarian description of Greek thinking, we could be content with cursory explanations of those concepts. But because we are investigating the roles played by appeals to the Greeks in some philosophical arguments that have become more and more complex over time, we need to be a little more thorough. In later sections of this chapter, therefore, I shall spend some time explaining the relevant arguments, and the ways in which certain Greek notions are supposed to figure in them.

2. Sidgwick and Prichard

During most of the first half of the twentieth century, the kantian response to Greek ethics prevailed in the English-speaking world. This was a period in which much ethical thought in general dwelt on kantian themes, such as the nature of moral obligation and the conflict between duty and interest. On the whole the kantian tenor of the philosophical discussion was then reflected in the way in which most philosophers read the Greeks: as thinkers who had not attained a full comprehension of the overall structure of ethical problems, because they had allegedly not freed themselves from the eudaimonist outlook that Kant had so firmly rejected.

Sidgwick's account of Greek ethics was one of the most influential kantian-style interpretations. I have already cited his claim that 'in the whole ethical controversy of ancient Greece . . . it was assumed on all sides that a rational individual would make the pursuit of his own good his supreme aim.'[1] Sidgwick also contends that Greek ethics identifies, as he puts it, practical reason with egoistic reason or self-love:

[I]n Greek moral philosophy generally, but one regulative and governing faculty is recognized under the name of reason; in the modern ethical view, when it has worked itself clear,

---

[1] Sidgwick 1907: 91–2, or 1931: 198; cf. Urmson 1988: 91: 'All ancient philosophers . . . subscribed to the view that all men desire above all their own wellbeing.'

there are found to be two, —Universal Reason and Egoistic Reason, or Conscience and Self-love.[2]

Like Kant, moreover, Sidgwick believes that in making this identification, the Greeks had left out something crucial. Sidgwick himself adheres to the 'the modern ethical view', and therefore thinks that the Greeks simply ignored one of the two important rival conceptions of practical reason.

Other interpreters of Greek ethics went even further in criticizing the Greeks for leaving fundamental practical considerations out of account. One prominent such interpreter was H. A. Prichard. Prichard took important parts of Greek ethics to be straightforwardly hedonist.[3] He thought that the Greeks held that one's ultimate good is simply one's pleasure, or happiness as identified with pleasure. It also appeared that on Prichard's type of interpretation, Greek views were in a straightforward way egoist, precisely because they did not take due account of moral considerations conceived to be independent of a person's own happiness. Accordingly, philosophers such as G. C. Field and William Frankena regarded Greek ethical views as forms of egoism.[4]

The view that Prichard ascribes to Plato does not of itself imply that an individual's good and the well-being of the community must necessarily be at odds with each other. Moreover, Prichard was well aware of the contention that in the *Republic* Plato had tried to show that a person can advance the one if and only if he advances the other. Prichard denied, however, that Plato's attempt to show this had come close to being successful. That is, Prichard thought that Plato in fact adopted a concept of a person's happiness under which it would almost certainly fail to coincide with the good of his *polis*. That separates Prichard's interpretation from interpretations of the hegelian type, whose whole point is precisely to maintain that given the Greek conception of these two things they really must go together, and indeed need not really be two things at all.

3. Sidgwick's Account of the Transition from Ancient to Modern

Sidgwick did more than merely declare that there is a difference between ancient and modern ways of approaching ethics. He also constructed an account of how the transition from ancient Greek monism to modern dualism took place.[5] Like many others

---

[2] Sidgwick 1931: 198. Sidgwick gives Joseph Butler the credit for 'working the view clear', as Sidgwick puts it. See, however, Frankena 1992.

[3] See Prichard 1968: 208–9 (on Plato), and 1968a (on Aristotle).

[4] For instance, Field interprets Aristotle as quite straightforwardly a defender of a form of egoism, and Frankena also says that his position may be an egoistic one. See Field 1932: 108–10; Frankena 1965: 34, 37.

[5] For an outline of Sidgwick's own account, see Frankena 1973a in tandem with Sidgwick 1931: ch. 24.

since, he believed that the transition was fairly straightforward.[6] The ancient idea of
regarding one's own happiness as an ultimate rational aim was not discarded. On the
contrary, it continued to be taken very seriously. Against it, however, there appeared
a rival candidate for the role of the guiding aim of practical deliberation. This was the
idea of an ultimate aim, conceived as additional to and independent of the aim of one's
own well-being. This general picture of how modern ethics developed out of ancient
ethics, it is fair to say, is now pretty standard, even among philosophers who are
unsympathetic to what they see as modern dualism and would prefer to adopt a eudaimonist position.

This new aim, putatively independent of one's well-being, is variously conceived
and variously labelled—for example, as 'right' or 'duty' or 'morality'. Many people
maintain that Christianity was responsible for this development. Others hold that the
Stoics started it.[7] Still others think of it as having arisen, at least in its distinctive modern form, in the seventeenth century.[8] In any event, the important feature of the supposed transition is that the new, non-eudaimonist aim was eventually conceived of as
not deriving its force from any contribution to the old one. That is, the weight of the
new aim in determining what a person is to do was thought not to depend on its somehow advancing the person's own well-being. Rather, the new aim was felt to possess a
rational force all its own.

4. Hegelian and Non-Hegelian Inclusivist Thinking: Green and Mill

In the process by which the hegelian response or elements of it were passed down to
present-day Anglo-American philosophers, the most important intermediaries were
British figures of the Victorian period. They include a number of neo-hegelian
philosophers, who found the notion of Hellenic harmony congenial. In Britain, views
of this type were advocated by philosophers with hegelian sympathies such as T. H.
Green, Bernard Bosanquet, and F. H. Bradley. As part of his interpretation of
Aristotle, Green says:

[T]he idea of a true good as for oneself . . . is ultimately or in principle an idea of satisfaction
for a self that abides and contemplates itself as abiding, but which can only so contemplate
itself in identification with some sort of society.[9]

Outside the sphere of strictly philosophical writers, moreover, an interest in Hegel's
philosophy in tandem with ancient thought was closely bound up with a more gener-

---

[6] It is, however, only a part of a more complex transition; see the description and critique of Sidgwick's
story in Frankena 1993: 264–9.

[7] See Frankena 1993, and above, Chapter 1, sec. I. 2.

[8] See Darwall 1995: 2.

[9] Green 1883: sec. 236.

al nostalgia for Greek culture which burgeoned during the Victorian period in Britain, and generated debates in France as well.[10] Idealization of the Greeks manifested itself both inside and outside philosophy, uniting poets like Shelley with scholars like Benjamin Jowett.[11]

In the case of a thinker like Green, the influence of Hegel was direct. In addition, however, we see in recent interpretations of Greek ethics a complex mixture of ideas and arguments that are due not only to Hegel but also to the British philosophers Joseph Butler and John Stuart Mill. I shall now briefly sketch this combination.

Inclusivism appears already in Butler, along with the notion that 'self-love' is a higher-order aim, directed at the achievement of one's other aims. At one point in his well-known argument for the thesis that not all things that one desires are desired for the sake of one's own happiness, Butler says that

happiness *consists in* the gratification of certain affections, appetites, passions, with objects which are by nature adapted to them.

He maintains further that

[l]ove of our neighbor is one of those affections in whose gratification happiness *consists*.[12]

This is a clear statement of an inclusivist position.[13]

In his essay *Utilitarianism*, Mill espouses a thesis that is superficially similar but that leads him far beyond what Butler says. Mill upholds the eudaimonist thesis that everyone's sole aim is happiness. He then says that 'the *ingredients* of happiness are very various', and goes to assert that a plurality of things are 'desired as *part* of happiness'. He then goes on to maintain that virtue, which includes benevolence, is one of these ingredients.[14] He then attempts to infer, from this inclusivist thesis, not only the

---

[10] See the exchange between Brochard 1901 and Sertillanges 1901, both under the title 'La Morale ancienne et la morale moderne'. Brochard represents something like what I call the hegelian viewpoint, while Sertillanges, though not a kantian, falls on the kantian side of my distinction, as does Gauthier later.

[11] Jenkyns 1980: ch. 10; note esp. 247–8.

[12] Butler 1726: Sermon XI, sec. 16 (my emphasis), with sec. 9.

[13] In rough outline, Butler's reasoning runs as follows. He argues, first of all, that the desire for one's own happiness could not be one's *only* desire. For if a desire for one's own happiness amounts to a higher-order desire for one's desires to be satisfied (as Butler controversially assumes), then it seems to presuppose the existence of particular substantive desires, since otherwise the desire for one's desires to be satisfied will have nothing definite to be concerned with. Next Butler points out that we do in fact have particular substantive desires (e.g. for food). Moreover, he observes, the desire for the happiness of other people is also a desire that most of us have. But if the desire for one's happiness is a desire that one's desires be satisfied, and if among one's desires is benevolence, then the desire for one's own happiness turns out to be a desire for, *in part*, the happiness of others Butler thus concludes that there is no 'peculiar contrariety' between self-love and benevolence.

[14] Mill 1871: ch. 4. The use of the notion of inclusion in these contexts becomes pretty normal subsequently. See e.g. Bradley 1927: 81, 219ff., where an inclusivist conception is espoused, though not a harmonizing one (228).

claim that virtue is a part of happiness, but also the claim that aiming for virtue is fully consistent with aiming at virtue *for its own sake*.[15] Mill has an important strategic reason for wishing to make this latter claim. He does so in order to reply to opponents of his Utilitarianism. They, he thinks, will object to Utilitarianism that if happiness is everyone's sole end, then we cannot aim at virtue for itself, but must rather aim at it only in order to be happy. So from the statement that virtue is a part of happiness, Mill infers the following:

> *In being desired for its own sake* [a thing] is . . . *desired as a part of happiness.* The person is made, or he thinks he would be made, happy by its mere possession; and is made unhappy by failure to obtain it.

Mill then concludes:

> It results from the preceding consideration that there is in reality *nothing desired except happiness.* Whatever is desired otherwise than as a means to some end beyond itself, and ultimately to happiness, is desired as itself a part of happiness, and is not desired for itself until it has become so.[16]

This argument, Mill hopes, will meet his opponents' objection.

5. Inclusivist Background in Butler

It will be helpful to pause for a moment to see in this argument both that Mill goes beyond Butler, and that by doing so he commits a fallacy by taking for granted that if virtue is a part of happiness, then it must be at least to some degree consistent with other parts thereof.

The crucial point is this. Mill completely ignores the fact that as an aim, virtue might very well conflict seriously with some *other* aim that was *also* a part of happiness. In that case it would be extremely misleading, to put it mildly, to assert that a person who desired virtue would *eo ipso* be desiring virtue as a part of happiness. For unless it had already been shown that the other aim was not more important to one's happiness than virtue, the aim of virtue could amount in those circumstances to a *diminution* of one's happiness by leading one to pursue or attain the other aim less than one might. Mill's explicit purpose here is of course not to establish a complete harmony of worthwhile aims. Nevertheless, his argument requires him to move in that direction by in effect *presupposing* that, in contending that virtue is a part of happiness, he may simply take it for granted that there is no very substantial or problematic conflict between seeking to be virtuous and seeking to be happy.

---

[15] Cf. Field 1932: 89–90.

[16] Mill 1871: ch. 4, with my emphasis. A similar idea can be found in Butler's eleventh sermon. On the use of this idea in the interpretation of Greek ethics, see esp. Chapter 6, sec. IV. 3.

Butler's conclusion, on the other hand, is argumentatively more cautious than Mill's. Butler does not try to demonstrate that there is no conflict at all between self-love and benevolence, or even that the conflict is minimal. Rather, he argues that there *need* be no conflict between self-love and benevolence *in the case of* someone who is by luck so constituted and circumstanced that his benevolent desires are fairly well consistent with the satisfaction of his other, more self-confined desires. Someone in different circumstances, however, might not have such a harmonious set of desires. Moreover, if his self-confined desires outweigh his benevolent desires, then his happiness may be secured only by *not* being benevolent.

Butler appreciates this fact fully. He is normally careful not to say that there is '*no* contrariety' between benevolence and self-love. Rather, he states, circumspectly, only that 'there is no *peculiar* contrariety between self-love and benevolence, no *greater* competition between these *than between any other* particular affections and self-love'.[17] That is, he is plainly aware that there can be conflicts between happiness and its component parts, because there can be conflicts within happiness between one part and another. His purpose is to argue merely that, contrary to a commonly held opinion, benevolence is *intrinsically* no *more* liable to conflict with one's happiness than any other of its component aims is.[18]

In some recent readings of Greek ethics we see a coming together of influences from both Butler and Mill on the one hand and Hegel and the British hegelians on the other. These readings combine inclusivist ideas with portrayals of Plato and Aristotle as endeavouring, in part through those ideas, to mitigate deliberative conflicts. A case in point is the work of Terence Irwin, who in the course of giving an inclusivist interpretation that construes both Plato and Aristotle as trying to establish that individual happiness and ethical considerations are consistent, acknowledges both the ideas of Mill and Butler and also the influence of Green.[19] Quite apart from the question whether such interpretations fall into the mistake that Mill commits, the point here is simply that all of these lines of thought have recently been brought to bear, by important scholarly work, on Greek ethical writings.[20]

The influence, direct and indirect, of important elements of the hegelian response

---

[17] Butler 1726: Sermon XI, with my emphasis.

[18] I do not here assert that Butler's argument for this contention is entirely cogent, but only that he does not fall into the same error as Mill and other incautious inclusivists. (Mill's mistake is due ultimately to his failure to take happiness, as Butler in effect does, as the satisfaction of a higher-order desire, namely, the desire that one's other desires be satisfied.)

[19] See Irwin 1977: 341, and Irwin 1992.

[20] In Chapter 6, sec. IV, it will emerge that in attempting to defend Aristotle against the charge of advocating a 'substantively egoist' position, Williams makes a mistaken assumption similar to Mill's. See White 1999a for discussion of Irwin's interpretation of Plato, which imputes to Plato an inclusivist strategy—though a more complex one than the one that I have described here—for arguing that 'duty and interest' do not conflict (see Irwin 1995: 301 with 314).

thus persists. This is not to say that all heirs to the hegelian interpretative tradition adopt the extreme claim that the Greeks established, or even tried to establish, that all worthwhile goods stand in complete harmony. Many scholars would maintain at most merely that the Greeks moved or tried to move in that direction. Nevertheless, even when all due qualifications and nuances are taken into account, it remains true that many historians of philosophy believe that the Greeks either explicitly adopted strategies for dealing with deliberative conflicts that it is fair to associate with the kinds of anti-kantian efforts that I have described so far, or else had the material for such strategies at their fingertips. These readings of Greek ethics include fusionist and especially inclusivist ideas—though these are not always clearly distinguished from one another.[21] These ideas are in turn very often associated with the view that a proper understanding of the concept of *eudaimonia* can, rather than merely adjudicating oppositions, actually eliminate them, that is, show that they either are illusory or else are far less severe than they appear to be.

II. Moore's Non-Eudaimonist Reading of Plato

Although kantian and hegelian interpretations of Greek ethics dominated the field during the period that I am treating, there also appeared on the margins of the discussion another sort of account that takes a quite different, non-eudaimonist direction. In his *Principia Ethica* of 1903, which helped shape British and American ethical philosophy for the next half-century and more, G. E. Moore attributed to Plato a position that he himself favoured, and that was incompatible with eudaimonism as it was understood by both kantian and hegelian interpreters.[22]

According to Moore, the notion of 'my good' or 'what is good for me' can amount to nothing except the notion of 'what is both good—in an absolute, non-relative sense—and is also mine'. Moore in fact goes so far as to deny that there can be an intelligible person-relative notion of 'good' at all. On his view, the putative notion of a thing's being 'something that is good for me but not good for you' does not even make sense—unless, again, it comes simply to the same as 'something that is good, which I have and you do not'. Moore is thus disputing—on what he thought were Platonic grounds—something that most people take for granted, that a notion of person-relative goodness is perfectly intelligible.

On this basis, then, Moore argues that egoism in the relevant sense involves a contradiction. Moore's argument is intensely problematic and difficult to follow, and there is no reason to rehearse it here. The relevant feature for our purposes is his con-

---

[21] A tendency to conflate the two can be seen, for instance, in Sandel 1982: 62–5.
[22] Moore 1903: 97–105; the reference to Plato occurs on 98.

clusion, which he explicitly contrasts with Sidgwick's view.[23] Moore claims that there can be no such thing as taking 'one's own good' as one's sole ultimate rational end. The only possible rational end is, he says, '*the* good', conceived as in no way person-relative. Therefore, he held, there can be no intelligible doctrine such as Sidgwick and others supposed Greek eudaimonism to be.

Furthermore, Moore maintained that Plato himself had endorsed this position. Indeed, Moore said, it had, 'perhaps, been more clearly perceived by Plato than by any other moralist'. As a result, Moore cannot have supposed that Plato was a eudaimonist in Sidgwick's sense. Indeed, Moore plainly attributes to Plato an explicit rejection of eudaimonism in this sense.

In spite of the enormous influence that Moore's views on ethics enjoyed during the ensuing decades, the influence of his interpretation of Plato was extremely modest.[24] Although Moore was strongly affected by Plato's ethics, he put almost no effort— much less effort than had Sidgwick—into expounding and justifying his way of read-ing Plato as a piece of history of philosophy. This fact is unfortunate, because, as will emerge in due course, Moore's interpretation of Plato is in important respects correct. Nevertheless, philosophical interpreters of Greek ethics did not treat it as a live option. The field was left almost entirely to the kantian and especially to the hegelian accounts.

III. More Recent Philosophical Views of Greek Ethics

1. Recent Anti-Kantian Views of Greek Ethics

Philosophical debates of the last couple of decades have seen a revival of interest in Greek ethics which has had a strongly hegelian and distinctly anti-kantian flavor. True, some interpreters have in recent years attempted to interpret Aristotle, in par-ticular, as himself holding views very similar to Kant's. It remains to be seen how influential this line of interpretation will become.[25] But however that may be, the fact remains that because Kant found little in Greek philosophy to interest him, and because Greek ethics has appeared from the standard Kantian perspective to be

---

[23] Moore must have known that he was also opposing Hegel's interpretation of Plato. Moore had after all been a follower of Hegel in his earlier days, and it is hard to believe that he could have been ignorant of the accounts of Greek ethics that were espoused by Hegel and hegelians. Moreover, that Moore was a seri-ous reader of Plato can be seen not only from his *Principia Ethica* itself, but also, it would appear, from R. G. Bury's 1897 commentary on the *Philebus*, p. vii. (The history of Moore's interest in Plato has not, so far as I know, been investigated, but it would be worth trying to find out whether Moore's interpretation of Plato was influenced in any degree by his abandonment of Hegelianism, or vice versa.)

[24] One can see some faint and partial traces of it in, for example, Annas 1981: 331–4.

[25] Examples are Korsgaard 1996 and, to a lesser extent, McDowell 1996.

primitive and misguided, the field has been left clear, on the whole, for Kant's opponents to make use of Greek thought in mounting their attacks against him. Thus to a great extent Hellenism in ethics has continued to be closely tied to anti-kantianism. This trend has been encouraged, no doubt, by a propensity of 'communitarian' thinkers to hearken back to Hegel and also to make use of what they have taken to be Greek notions of community, especially as manifested in the concept of the *polis*.[26]

Another anti-kantian use of Greek thinking is also evident in writings about the 'ethics of virtue', by philosophers like G. E. M. Anscombe and Philippa Foot. According to this line of thought, there is a sharp contrast to be drawn between an *ethics of virtue* and and *ethics of duty*, so that notions of virtue derived from Greek ethics appear as an alternative to Kant's reliance on the notion of moral obligation, against which thinkers of this type often raise vigorous objections.[27] Such a use of Greek themes is directly anti-kantian without being much influenced by hegelian thinking, but its similarity to the hegelian response is nonetheless palpable.

In this continuation of the hegelian interpretative tradition the idea of Hellenic harmony comes to the fore. Instructive examples of this tendency can be found in the writings of Alasdair MacIntyre, Michael Sandel, and Charles Taylor. MacIntyre, for instance, whose views on these matters follow those of Hegel extremely closely, places a great deal of emphasis on the familiar idea of the contrast between modern and premodern philosophy (though under the latter heading he invokes not only the Greeks but also the medievals).[28] He says:

> from an Aristotelian point of view a modern liberal political society can appear only as a collection of citizens of nowhere ... That they lack the bond of friendship is of course bound up with the self-avowed moral pluralism of such liberal societies. They have abandoned the moral unity of Aristotelianism.

In the seventeenth and eighteenth centuries, he says, human beings came to be thought to be

> in some dangerous measure egoistic by nature ... whereas in premodern periods [by which MacIntyre means 'the ancient and medieval world'] one thought that my good as a man is one and the same as the good of those others with whom I am bound up in human community.[29]

Here, echoing the hegelian version of the thought, is the voice of nostalgia for Greek ethics, and an attempt to use it to help us repair fragmentation and restore unity.

---

[26] See Chapter 4.   [27] On this theme, see further Chapter 3.

[28] In the contrast between the ancient and the modern, the Middle Ages have at times been put with the former and at other times assigned to the latter. See Lovejoy 1948d: 205–6. On Hegel's attitude towards medieval feudal society, see Wood 1991: 203.

[29] MacIntyre 1981: 147, 213. For critical reaction to this sort of view compare Larmore 1987: ch. 2 and pp. 97, 102, 105.

2. Hegelian and Nietzschean Themes in Williams and Others

I have already indicated that even in Nietzsche, philosophically opposed though he was to the whole notion of a harmony of human aims, the historical thesis that the Greeks of the Classical era embraced that ideal remained strong. This is precisely the reason why, as I emphasized, Nietzsche took a dim view of Classical Greek thought and sought his own intellectual forebears in the earlier, Archaic period. He ceded Plato and Aristotle to the hegelian interpretation, and then sought to find his own views in earlier Greeks. The difference between him and hegelian readers is that whereas they believed that Plato and Aristotle were trying to restore the deliberative harmony that had been disrupted by the Sophists, Nietzsche took them to be reacting instead against pre-Classical thinking in a moralistic way. And whereas Hegel took Plato and Aristotle to represent the truly Hellenic outlook, Nietzsche sometimes saw them as deplorably anticipating the anaemic ethics of Christianity.[30]

Another twentieth-century instance of the type of reading of Aristotle, as someone attempting to establish deliberative harmony, can be found in a quite different quarter, in René Antoine Gauthier's French commentary on Aristotle's *Ethics*.[31] In the end, Gauthier believes, ethics for Aristotle is 'the reduction of a dualism to unity'. Aristotle is motivated, says Gauthier, by the fact that 'we feel in ourselves two elements struggling, the combat between which tears us apart'. Aristotle's aim, like Plato's, is according to Gauthier to show us the way out of this struggle, to the peace that we long for.

Another reader of Classical Greek ethics who sees it as striving for deliberative consistency is Bernard Williams. He is far from being a believer in deliberative harmony himself.[32] In many ways a philosophical follower of Nietzsche and Berlin, he questions the idea that there can ever be full consistency among an individual's worthwhile aims, or that we should welcome such a state of affairs.[33] Like Nietzsche, moreover, Williams attributes to pre-Classical Greek thinkers a rejection of the attainability of this kind of harmony. Thucydides and Sophocles, he maintains, 'leave us with no . . . sense . . . that the universe or history or the structure of human reason

---

[30] See e.g. the preface to *Beyond Good and Evil* (Nietzsche 1966b: 2), 'Christianity is Platonism for the "People"'.

[31] Gauthier and Jolif 1970: i. 297–9.

[32] Indeed, in the more recent 1993, Williams is philosophically even less sympathetic to ideals of harmony than he is in 1985, and less partial, too, to Greek ethics of the Classical period, especially Aristotle's.

[33] At the same time, however, he criticizes Nietzsche for not realizing that 'we need a politics, in the sense of a coherent set of opinions about the ways in which power should be exercised in modern societies, with what limitations and to what ends' (1993: 10–11). It is unclear to what extent such a 'politics' might end up requiring, in order to attain 'coherence', a harmonization of aims much like the one that Williams thinks Aristotle hoped for but that he seems to reject, or indeed, much like the kind that many partisans of modern morality seek (see White 1994b). The same questions arise at other points in Williams's writings, for instance, in 1981b, esp. at 30–2.

can, when properly understood, yield a pattern that makes sense of human life and aspirations'. On the contrary, Williams says, these writers present us with 'human beings . . . dealing sensibly, foolishly, sometimes catastrophically, sometimes nobly, with a world that is only partially intelligible to human agency and in itself is not necessarily well adjusted to ethical aspirations'.[34]

These pre-Classical thinkers, Williams believes, recognize that what is valuable in human life can be destroyed by contingencies that are beyond an individual's control. The result of ethically good action cannot be expected to be the kind of reward that people want. For that reason, it will generally be irrational for a human being to hope that his aims—both the aim of ethically good action and the desires for reward from it—can be satisfied together.[35] The attitude adopted by thinkers of the Classical period, according to Williams, was quite different. They went astray in assuming all too easily that there might be no fundamental obstacle to the joint satisfaction of all human aspirations. They espoused the position, he says, that 'what is of highest value, what matters most, [is] entirely under the self's control'.[36] To say this was to take an important step in the direction of the conclusion that all of our important aims are rationally reconcilable with each other.

And indeed Williams agrees fully with both Hegel and Nietzsche in holding that the Greeks of the Classical era took for granted that a harmony of rational human aims is possible—especially a harmony of individual and social considerations (which it is easy to assimilate to a harmony of all considerations whatsoever).[37] In this period, Williams says, 'there is not a rift between a world of public "moral rules" and of private personal ideals', and in a way remarkably reminiscent of Hegel, he ascribes to the thought of this period an 'inability to separate questions of how one should relate to others and to society from questions of what life it is worth leading and of what one basically wants'.[38]

Williams's reading of Aristotle follows the same pattern as his account of Classical thought in general:

Aristotle saw a certain kind of ethical, cultural, and indeed political life as a harmonious culmination of human potentialities, recoverable from an absolute understanding of nature.

On Aristotle's view, Williams continues,

---

[34] Williams 1993: 163–4.

[35] Williams 1981b: 33–4. The theme is developed by Nussbaum 1986.

[36] Williams 1981e: 252.

[37] The assimilation is not logically obligatory. That seems clear. On the other hand, a full harmony follows from a harmony of individual and social considerations on the assumption, which is dubious but easy to fall into, that within a society all human considerations are represented.

[38] Williams 1981e: 251.

[the] perfection [of the virtuous agent can] be displayed harmoniously, so that the development of ... ethical capacities will fit with other forms of human excellence. Aristotle's theory means that when the agent reflects ... on all his needs and capacities, he will find no conflict with his ethical dispositions.[39]

Williams's picture of what the Greeks of the Classical period were trying to do shows how very much life there is, even now, in the belief that Greek ethics was principally an effort to establish that worthwhile human aims are in harmony with each other.[40]

The same belief is a latent presupposition of Williams's defence of Greek eudaimonism against the kantian accusation, already mentioned, that it is a form of egoism. Williams replies to this charge by contending that Greek eudaimonism is merely 'formally' but not 'substantively' egoist.[41] The idea is that although the Greeks take a person's sole aim to be his happiness, nevertheless happiness is so understood as to include such aims as the well-being of others and conformity to ethical norms, as well as one's own self-confined goods. This, as I have indicated already, is an element of the hegelian type of view that I have called 'inclusivist'.[42]

As Williams deploys this idea, it contains no explicit assumption that the component aims of happiness must be consistent with each other. Nevertheless, some degree of consistency among them is plainly presupposed, and indeed must be presupposed. If it were not presupposed, then in order to determine that Greek eudaimonism truly is *not* a form of substantive egoism, one would need to argue that when one seeks happiness, one will not seek the self-confined parts of it to the exclusion of the external parts. For if no argument for this thesis is given, then we shall not have excluded the possibility, once again, that in fact the seeking of one's happiness might after all exclude the good of others. Williams, however, gives no such argument, nor even alludes to the need for it. Evidently, then, he takes for granted some tendency on the part of the Greeks to assume that happiness contains no pervasive oppositions within happiness itself. We shall have occasion to return to this theme later.[43]

3. Disharmony and Harmony in Further Recent Work on Greek Ethics

Similar ideas continue to appear in philosophically informed scholarly treatments of Greek ethics. I shall not attempt to catalogue them nor to demonstrate which represent the statistical preponderance of opinion. It is evident that numerous scholars of

---

[39] Williams 1985: 52. In a similar vein Nussbaum 1994: 480 speaks of 'the Aristotelian, who so wants all of life to fit harmoniously together' (though for an indication that she holds a different view, see Chapter 7, sec. V. 3).

[40] See also Nehamas 1994: 45.

[41] Williams 1985: 32, 49–52; see also Annas 1993: 127.

[42] See Chapter 1, sec. VII. 4.

[43] For the terminology, see Chapter 1, sec. VII; for the theme, see Chapter 6, sec. IV.

Greek philosophy think of some degree of harmony of deliberative considerations to be an aim or a presupposition of Greek ethics.

Not that there are no exceptions. Recently Martha Nussbaum and Michael Stocker have focused on Aristotle, and have argued that he acknowledges the existence of deliberative conflicts within ethical virtue. These are in many ways welcome moves in the right direction.[44] Nevertheless, they represent, it seems to me, more or less isolated exceptions to the general pattern which, as I have said, has prevailed for over two centuries now.

It will suffice here to cite a few examples of the recent continuation to the pattern. One is Julia Annas's contention that

[a]ncient [ethical] theories . . . are based on the assumption that ethical beliefs can in fact be unified.[45]

Another example is Irwin's view, shared by many interpreters of both kantian and hegelian types, that Plato's aim in pursuing the idea that justice is a part of happiness is to establish that there is 'no conflict between duty and interest'. 'If he cannot defend this view,' Irwin states, 'he leaves a serious gap in the main argument of the *Republic*.'[46] Similarly, many have offered much the same defence as Williams of Greek ethics against the charge of being egoist.[47] By and large these efforts consist in arguing, along the lines of the inclusivist hegelian interpretation, that because the ancient notion of a person's well-being includes both altruistic activity and conformity to ethical standards, the effort to achieve one's own well-being need not be egoistic in any objectionable way.[48]

Often, too, the idea of a harmonious conception of *eudaimonia* creeps into recent interpretations without its being clear how far the notion of harmony is to be pushed. For example, John Cooper says that in Aristotle's view, '[t]he set of interests and desires which is given to [the virtuous man] in the character he has attained is . . . a consistent and harmonious whole', and that '[a]ll the different types of desires and interests he has can be harmoniously satisfied'.[49] Evidently the idea is at work here, as in the

[44] See Nussbaum 1986 and Stocker 1990. For discussion of their readings of Aristotle, see Chapter 6, sec. V.

[45] Annas 1993: 444 with 4–5. See also ibid. 28, where she says that, although the ancients were aware of ethical conflicts, they did not think it the point of ethical theories to solve them, but rather thought that an ethical theory should be constructed in outline first, and that then conflicts should somehow be dealt with in (as I take it) a kind of mopping-up operation.

[46] Irwin 1995: 301. On this theme in Irwin see further White 1999a.

[47] See Ackrill 1980; Annas 1992b: 137; Cooper 1975: 115–33; Irwin 1977: 300–1; along with White 1994a: 61–2

[48] See Ackrill 1981: 135–41; as well as Irwin 1988: chs. 17–18, esp. secs. 199–204, 208–17, and Irwin 1985: 370–1.

[49] Cooper 1975: 132, 131; cf. 95–7.

works of many scholars of Greek philosophy, that desires that in most people normally conflict will in the good man somehow not do so, and that seems to suggest, at the very least, a complete harmony and freedom from deliberative opposition.

Moreover, in spite of the reservations about this suggestion that one finds in works by specialists on Greek philosophy, non-specialists are still liable to assume that the Greeks as a group, or at least the Classical Greeks, were harmonizing eudaimonists. This is so in spite of the fact that most philosophers would acknowledge freely that to be a eudaimonist is not necessarily to be a eudaimonist who believes that the aims that go to make up happiness are all consistent with each other. Among philosophers at large there is still plenty of life left in the tradition of reading the Greeks as eudaimonists with a strong belief that the constituents of happiness are mutually consistent, and that this consistency is built into the very concept of *eudaimonia*.[50]

IV. The Importance of Deliberative Conflict: Morality

1. The Pervasiveness of the Issue of Conflict

So far in this chapter I have looked at the way in which a belief that Greek ethics was eudaimonist, and in conjunction therewith a tendency to believe that it aimed at deliberative harmony of rational aims, has been a regular feature of modern thinking. However, that is certainly not the only philosophical theme that has played a role in modern treatments of Greek ethical thought, and other contrasts have been drawn between ancient and modern ethics than the ones that I have mentioned. Why attend so much, then, to questions about deliberative conflict and deliberative monism and dualism? Before continuing, I need to say something to justify putting the spotlight on these particular questions.

Let me mention three of the other contrasts and explain in turn why I have not focused on each of them. The first contrast revolves around the notion of *morality*; the contention is that that notion is an invention of modern times which was alien to Greek ways of thinking. The second arises from the claim that, whereas modern ethics is typically an ethics of *duty*, ancient ethics was an ethics of *virtue*. A third contrast emerges from the thesis that Greek thought does more justice than modern thought to the role that *contingency* plays in ethical evaluation and deliberation.

My point about each of these contrasts—whether they be real or merely alleged— will be the same. Although each possesses philosophical interest on its own, nevertheless they all derive much of their importance, historical and philosophical, from their respective connections to issues of deliberative conflict. For in every case the relevant

---

[50] For a representative example of the tendency to assume that, according to Plato and Aristotle, personal and impartial considerations can be 'harmoniously' realized, see Ashford 2000: 426.

contrast is regarded as significant mainly because it shows how Greek ethics is free from a problem of conflict to which modern ethics is subject. Sometimes this aspect of the matter is highlighted by modern thinkers, sometimes not. Nevertheless, the issue of conflict always plays some role, even in recent scholarly work that is on the whole fairly free of the kind of nostalgic hegelian thinking that most strongly stresses Hellenic harmony. Thus there is a systematic reason, in addition to the historiographical tradition associated with the theme of Hellenic harmony, for focusing on problems of deliberative consistency and conflict.

2. The Slippery Term 'Morality'

I shall begin with the issue concerning the concept of morality. This issue is in these contexts probably the most frequently mentioned. One often hears the historical claim that morality—whether the notion, or the institution, or both—was unknown to the Greeks and was discovered or created in the modern era, and that this fact marks a crucial difference between the two periods.[51] It is also claimed that the modern sense of the term 'morality' is different from any ancient meaning of any term. As a philosophical matter, some philosophers have suggested that we should abandon the term 'morality,' and the notion that it expresses, and return instead to something else which is more like what the Greeks possessed.[52] It might therefore be proposed that we should examine ancient and modern ethics chiefly by asking whether this claimed contrast really holds.

At least two thoughts militate against this suggestion. The first is a trivial but irksome matter of terminology. Even within fairly recent ethics, the term 'morality' has been employed in a bewildering variety of ways, and there has been both confusion and also explicit debate about what meaning is best attached to it.[53] I do not think that these debates have come to a satisfactory conclusion, and moreover confusion often reigns unchecked. Sometimes philosophers who discuss 'morality' presuppose without further ado that the term is synonymous with 'morality as explicated by Kant', or 'morality as explicated by Utilitarians', or the like. Such an explicit presupposition

---

[51] See e.g. Brochard 1901 and Anscombe 1958, as well as Darwall 1995: 1–4. In both writers an anti-kantian aim is prominent; see Gauthier and Jolif 1970: i. 290–4. Annas has in many writings (esp. 1992a, 1993, 1996) opposed the idea that the ancients did not have the concept of morality. A great deal depends on which issues one thinks of as saliently hinging on whether we say that they did or did not; for a viewpoint at variance with Annas's, see Schneewind 1996. It seems to me that both Annas and Schneewind could be right in what they say.

[52] See Anscombe 1958 and Williams 1985, e.g. 181. Williams normally likes to use the term 'ethics' for the kind of normative discussion that he favours. His choice of terminology is in some ways reminiscent of Hegel's preference for the word *Sittlichkeit* over Kant's term *Moralität*; cf. Chapter 1, sec. VII. 6. I here prefer 'ethics' to 'morality', so as to be as neutral on these issues as I can be.

[53] For one important ambiguity in uses of the term, see Mackie 1977: 106.

would, to be sure, make for some terminological clarification. However, it makes for excessive narrowness to take 'morality' to cover merely, say, what we find in Kant and the British Utilitarians, since one would thereby exclude, for instance, important ethical intuitionists like W. D. Ross and A. C. Ewing, as well as more recent anti-kantian and anti-utilitarian developments in ethics. The term 'morality' belongs to a wide variety of thinkers, however large Kant, Bentham, and Mill may loom among them.

A second reason not to focus on the term 'morality' is that philosophical criticisms of morality have been levelled at many different aspects of it. Thinkers who believe that what they call 'morality' should be rejected may, even if they subsume the same thing under the word, have different reasons for rejecting it, and these reasons arise from different features of it. Thus these critics of morality, while agreeing about what its characteristics are, disagree about which of them are the objectionable ones. As a result, there is sometimes unclarity or uncertainty about precisely which issues about 'morality' are the significant ones.[54] If we had enough time we could perhaps sort through this matter here. For present purposes, however, it does not seem worthwhile to try to fix on a definite meaning for the term. Instead let us try to move ahead as well as we can without doing so.[55]

I shall argue, instead, for a thesis that does not depend on sharpening the notion of morality or even using the term, if one chooses to avoid it. When philosophers have asked whether the Greeks possessed the institution or concept of morality, their chief concern, I contend, has been the bearing of that question on the very issues about deliberative conflict on which I concentrate in this book. In other words, questions about deliberative dualism are what motivate questions about whether the Greeks had such a thing as morality, not the other way around.

This thesis seems to me to be confirmed by, among other things, an examination of the kantian and hegelian responses and their relations to each other. To those who adopt the kantian response, the Greeks' alleged ignorance or neglect of the notion of morality is claimed to arise mainly from their obliviousness to the possibility of a rational aim besides one's own happiness. Furthermore, the same claim is accepted by those hegelian-minded philosophers who congratulate the Greeks on having gotten along without morality and its dualist tendencies. Moreover, even those philosophers

---

[54] For a perspective on the situation, along with discussion of a number of views about what morality is and does, see Frankena 1980a and 1980b, along with the various views expressed by Anscombe 1958, Foot 1978d, Tugendhat 1992, Williams 1985, and Miller 1992.

[55] Some writers on Greek ethics employ the term 'morality' and its cognates in a relatively loose way (see e.g. Striker 1996: 178, 256). This practice need not be problematic for some purposes, but it does not help us much when we discuss the ways in which Greek ideas have been brought to bear on problems that have been formulated in a modern context—as are most of the problems figuring in the present book. For a discussion of whether it is appropriate to use the term 'morality' to apply to ancient ethics, see Annas 1992a (pp. 130-2 intersect with the issues that I focus on here).

who are not closely or explicitly aligned with either the hegelian or the kantian response tend, I maintain, to accord to the issue of conflict between happiness and other possible aims a significant place in their interpretative thinking about the Greeks. The following remarks will be useful as an indication of what I have in mind, and will help prepare the ground for subsequent discussion.

3. Criticisms of Morality

As a point of departure, consider some of the objections that have been raised against the notion or the institution of morality, and the corresponding reasons for commending the Greeks for, allegedly, not possessing it. Chief among these objections are some that adduce features commonly ascribed to morality, especially by people who have reservations about it. Among these features the following four are especially significant: *overridingness*, *imperativity*, *impartiality*, and *impersonality*.

Never mind whether these are as a matter of fact features of morality as it should be construed. As I have intimated, that term is employed to designate too many different things for such an issue to be open to decisive adjudication. The point, rather, is this: regardless of whether we ought to say that morality really does possess these characteristics, the motivation for regarding them as *defects* of morality arises primarily from the sense that they contribute to conflicts and, in particular, conflicts that morality is alleged to precipitate between the individual's good and the norms that morality imposes.

The idea that morality *overrides* or takes precedence over all other deliberative considerations is a common theme among both proponents and opponents of morality. Among the opponents, this theme is closely connected with the suggestion that morality has, as Anscombe puts it, a special 'mesmerizing' force, which makes it outbid all other considerations.[56]

Bernard Williams focuses on a special way in which morality, he maintains, is held to be overriding, and which clearly leads to conflicts between practical considerations. Morality, Williams claims, contains a special clause that asserts its own superiority to other viewpoints, and disapproves of applying and taking seriously the evaluations that those viewpoints deliver. 'The morality system', he says, 'is closed in on itself and must consider it an indecent misunderstanding to apply . . . any values other than those of morality itself.'[57] It is obvious that conflicts will arise if morality is such as

---

[56] See Anscombe 1958 and also Williams 1981d. A related idea is discussed in Larmore 1996: 11–12, namely, that morality is binding on all regardless of their views of the good.

[57] Williams 1985: 195. The indicated gap contains the words 'to the system', but I think that Williams clearly attributes to morality the generalization that is expressed by the formulation that results when those words are omitted.

Williams holds it to be, as long as there exist any other evaluative viewpoints beside morality itself. For morality will in some sense deny their point or legitimacy.

Among the considerations over which morality is said to take precedence it is the individual's own happiness, as well as other considerations closely related to it, that invariably take on paramount significance.[58] The idea of overridingness, that is, arises with urgency only in connection with the supposition, common to many people, that morality can clash with a person's effort to attain well-being. Plainly this idea is at work in Kant as well as others. Equally plainly it is responsible for much criticism of kantian thinking, from the side of philosophers who find kantian conceptions of morality restrictive, or too restrictive, of the individual's happiness. It is taken to be obvious that morality can conflict with one's happiness; the idea that morality is overriding is then brought in to adjudicate the conflict in favour of morality and to the detriment of the individual's well-being.

The next feature of morality that is often singled out for criticism is the tendency of moral norms to be expressed in *imperative* language. By 'imperative language' I mean, roughly, language that conveys a command or the overtone of one. Here what is at issue is the seeming fact that moral norms often restrict the happiness of whoever adheres to them. Philosophers have often maintained that a norm is appropriately expressed as a command or imperative only in a special sort of circumstance, namely, when the people to whom the norm is directed may be expected to resist what it recommends. The thought commonly is that moral standards should be framed as imperatives precisely because they constrain, and are resisted by, most people's efforts to advance their own happiness.[59] As we shall see later, what drives the kantian use of imperatives in morality, as well as anti-kantian objections to them, is the notion that morality can clash signficantly with one's happiness.[60]

A common view, which only seems to oppose what I have just maintained, is that the appropriateness of framing moral norms as imperatives arises simply from their overridingness, that is, what makes it acceptable to say 'Do X!' in the imperative mode can only be the fact that doing X takes precedence over all other considerations. It might therefore be contended, in opposition to what I am claiming, that the use of imperatives in moral language has nothing to do with a tendency of morality to work against one's well-being, but rather arises simply from the claim of morality to be overriding in some special 'mesmerizing' way. In response, it seems to me that the original reason for trying to attach mesmerizing force to moral norms, and also for casting them in imperative terms, is simply the fact that such force is felt to be

---

[58] The 'other considerations' in question include notably the ones that Williams, in 1981b and elsewhere, calls an individual's 'projects'. Like 'happiness', the phrase 'one's projects' can of course subsume considerations that are not self-confined.

[59] This matter is treated in Chapter 3.

[60] See e.g. Williams 1985: 180–2, 184, and compare Taylor 1989: 89–90.

necessary if they are to have a chance of persuading someone to act against what he perceives as his well-being.[61]

Third on the list is *impartiality*. The propensity of moral norms to work against the happiness of individuals, at least under many conditions, can be accounted for by the fact that moral norms are impartial. The significant point here is that these norms often do not take special account of one's well-being, nor of the well-being of particular people who are related to oneself in a special way. If morality permitted an individual to favor the people and projects to which he is closely attached then, it is felt, morality would not restrict one's efforts towards happiness in the way that it does.[62]

Fourth, if morality is not merely impartial but *impersonal*—perhaps in the sense of not being constructed principally to fulfil human needs or the like at all, but of being rather some absolute imperative or divine directive, which is not based on facts about humans—then there would be all the more reason to expect morality to clash with individuals' aims. If morality is impersonal in the sense that it is not intrinsically constituted so as to respond to the needs and aspirations, and so forth, of human beings, then one would obviously expect it to be in danger of clashing with human well-being in general. The danger of such clashes, then, would be the reason why an impersonal conception of morality would occasion suspicion and opposition.

The conclusion is evident. In all of these four ways, it seems that an interest in whether or not the Greeks possessed the notion or institution of morality is intimately connected with and importantly motivated by the question whether Greek ethics avoided or obviated deliberative conflicts. That is, the likelihood of a conflict between morality and an individual's happiness is central not only to the standard critiques of morality on all counts, but also to the belief that the Greeks did well not to have it.

V. The Importance of Deliberative Conflict: The Ethics of Virtue

1. The Distinction between the Ethics of Virtue and the Ethics of Duty

Another contrast that is often drawn between ancient and modern ethics concerns the notion of virtue, and a difference that is often alleged between virtue and duty. As understood here, 'virtue' may be taken to be either moral virtue, narrowly construed, or virtue in some wider sense.

One often finds it maintained that whereas modern ethics, or modern moral philosophy, is an 'ethics of duty', Classical Greek ethics is rather an 'ethics of virtue'.[63]

---

[61] This seems obviously to be what drives Kant's use of imperatives: see below, Chapter 3. What other countervailing considerations could make such force seem to have a point? Considerations of aesthetics or etiquette? Hardly.

[62] See Williams 1985: 14–15, 19–20; Slote 1990: esp. 434–9.

[63] Most recently see e.g. Hursthouse 1999: 1, 8, 13, and passim.

Closely related to this contention we also frequently hear it said that in contrast to modern ethics, which focuses chiefly on the evaluation of actions, Greek ethics was concerned principally to describe and evaluate a person's traits or character. The connection usually made between these two theses is that the word 'duty', after all, refers to actions, whereas the term 'virtue' seems principally to apply to persons or to their traits, which go together to make up what we call a person's character. This way of contrasting ancient and modern ethics is typically associated with a criticism of modern ethics and a correspondingly favourable attitude towards its ancient counterpart.

It is possible to complain with some justification that the contrast between an ethics of virtue and an ethics of duty is not sharp, in part because the distinction between virtues and duties, or between virtue concepts and duty concepts, is itself unclear. It is not infrequently stated, for example, that such-and-such a virtue 'demands' or 'requires' a particular action.[64] The occurrence of this sort of statement surely makes for difficulty in contrasting the two sorts of ethics sharply with each other, since one naturally associates talk of demands and requirements, which has an imperative overtone, with the notion of duty and even with the notion of moral duty.[65] That means that it may be hard to differentiate sharply between virtue concepts and duty concepts.

But even if one can make that differentiation, there is still an additional unclarity about determining whether an ethical view is an ethics of duty or an ethics of virtue. Most ethical outlooks make some use of both types of notions. Thus the mere use of expressions standing for virtues does not turn an ethical position into an ethics of virtue; nor does the use of words like 'should' or 'ought' or 'duty' turn a view into an ethics of duty as ordinarily understood. Rather, an ethics of duty is an ethics in which a notion of duty has some special importance as compared with notions of virtue; and likewise, *mutatis mutandis*, for an ethics of virtue. But what sort of special importance is required? Usage varies on this point. Fortunately, present purposes do not require us to precisify these matters—though later I shall have occasion to try to be, in certain respects, a bit more meticulous about it.[66]

2. Virtue and Freedom from Conflict

But now let me turn to the main point here, which is that the aim of showing that ancient ethics is freer from conflict, and particularly from a conflict between one's well-being and some broader consideration such as ethical norms, contributes

---

[64] See e.g. Foot 1978b: 53, 54. See Hursthouse 1999: 4–5 on the inadvisability of putting much stress on the classification, and Trianosky 1990: 340 on the difficulty of drawing the distinction in spite of the professions of some philosophers to be adopting the one type of theory or the other.

[65] On this theme, see further Chapter 3.

[66] When I deal, that is, with imperative and attractive notions in Chapter 3.

substantially to the effort to show that ancient ethics is, unlike characteristically modern ethics, an ethics of virtue.

Although I shall indeed argue later that it is mistaken from the start to contrast Greek ethics and modern ethics by saying that the former is an ethics of virtue whereas the latter is an ethics of duty—at least insofar as an ethics of duty must primarily rely on imperative notions—the present question concerns not that argument, but rather a factor that I think has substantially motivated its advocates to advance it.[67] That factor is the belief, to repeat, that the concept of virtue is less likely to implicate a conflict between deliberative considerations than is the concept of duty. Duty—so runs the reasoning behind the claim that an ethics of duty involves conflict—is mainly a 'moral' notion. Moreover, it carries an overtly imperative connotation, by calling up the image of someone's being commanded to do or not to do something or other. Consequently, the thought of duty suggests some resistance, on the part of a person who is commanded, towards the command that is issued to him—that is, of a less than completely cooperative and harmonious relationship between him and whatever is doing the commanding.

The same line of thought is suggested by two other quite plain contrasts between the concept of virtue and that of duty. In the first place, while it seems quite possible to defend the view that it is part of the concept of what we call a 'virtue' that a virtue must benefit its possessor, no one could defensibly maintain the analogue of this thesis with regard to duty. That is, no one could plausibly advance the thesis that part of what one says when one calls something a duty is that it benefits the one who does it. On the other side, it was possible for Kant to hold that it is part of the concept of duty that any benefit that might be gained by doing one's duty cannot be part of the reason for doing it. No one could ever maintain, by analogy, that it is part of the concept of virtue that a person could not wish to acquire a virtue on the ground that he would benefit by so doing. In light of these facts, it is hard to see how the idea of an ethics of virtue could fail, under normal circumstances, to carry less of a suggestion of such conflict than does the idea of an ethics of duty.

Modern philosophers who commend the notion of virtue as superior to duty as a tool for ethical thought have indeed offered a variety of reasons for so doing. By singling out one of them for special attention, I do not mean to deny the importance of the others. I wish merely to urge that one of the important ones is the idea that, as compared with the notion of duty, the notion of virtue does not carry the suggestion of conflict, or not as strongly, and particularly the suggestion of a conflict between the individual's well-being and ethical norms. Let me give a couple of examples of this idea.

In the first place, it is sometimes held that a trait cannot properly be called a virtue at all unless it benefits its possessor, at least in general.[68] Thus Foot has written:

---

[67] See Chapter 3.

[68] This view was advocated by Foot 1978c: 126, though she later retracted it in 1978d: 159–60, 168.

In the *Republic* it is assumed that if justice is not a good to the just man, moralists who recommend it as a virtue are perpetrating a fraud. Agreeing with this, I shall be asked where exactly the fraud comes in; where the untruth that justice is profitable to the individual is supposed to be told.[69]

My present point concerns, not Foot's reading of Plato,[70] but rather her view about what it is for a trait to be a virtue. A virtue, she maintains, must benefit its possessor, whereas a moral duty, many moralists would hold, need not do so. It would follow that an interpretation of Greek ethics that takes it to be an ethics of virtue could be seen as capable of ascribing to the Greeks a more harmonious account of human deliberative aims than might be found in an ethics of duty of the modern type.[71]

Secondly, even philosophers who do not assert such a tight connection between virtue and a person's own good often maintain, in the spirit of Hume, that, as Michael Slote puts it, '[o]ur common understanding of what it is to be or exemplify a virtue … is unburdened with agent-sacrificing moral connotation', and that therefore 'virtue theory gains an important superiority over the familiar sort of moral view that employs terms like "right", "wrong", and "morally good"'.[72]

In such ways as these, the hope of mitigating the potential conflict between ethical norms and happiness encourages some to take a favourable attitude towards the ethics of virtue, and to try to work towards what one might call a harmonizing ethics of virtue.

VI. The Importance of Deliberative Conflict: Contingency

1. Contingency and Morality

In addition to morality and virtue, a third notion is also sometimes nowadays held to play a role in the contrast between Greek ethical views and ours. That notion is contingency—to use the term introduced into recent discussion by Bernard Williams. Taking up a Nietzschean idea, Williams has contended that Greek ethics, especially in its Archaic phase, was alive to the role of contingency in ethics. By contrast, Williams holds, modern ethics ignores or reduces the extent to which important assessments of human affairs, including ethical considerations, should be said to be subject to contingency.[73]

---

[69] Foot 1978c: 126.

[70] The interpretation that I shall propose in Chapter 5 is sharply at variance with hers.

[71] See also Hursthouse 1999: esp. chs. 9 and 11.

[72] Slote 1990: 436–7, and 1992: esp. chs. 1 and 8; in a vaguely similar vein, see Taylor 1989: 79–80.

[73] See Williams 1981c as well as 1985: 195–7; and 1993: 163–4.

When he talks of 'contingency', Williams means, very briefly, the following.[74] When one tries to determine whether someone's action is justified, whether in prospect or in retrospect, one is tempted, by our standard conception of morality, to try to leave out of account all those features of the action that were brought about by factors lying outside the agent's control. These factors include both the past factors that determined, independently of the agent himself, that he would be as he is, and also those further factors that subsequently produced consequences of the action that were not part of what the agent intended. All of these factors are included under the label 'contingency' or, sometimes, 'luck'.[75]

Williams's chief philosophical contention is that the modern notion of morality is mistaken in trying to isolate those features of an action that are not due to luck in this sense, and in trying to evaluate the action, and the person who performs it, by reference to those features. First, Williams thinks that the distinction cannot reasonably be drawn. Second, he maintains that by any reasonable standard, contingent features of an action can be relevant to the most important evaluations of it—contrary to the modern moralist's claim that only non-contingent features are relevant to the most important, moral, evaluations.

Although Williams does not normally frame these issues concerning contingency by reference to the idea of conflict, nevertheless that idea plays a significant role in his thinking. According to him, the world cannot be counted on to respond to our efforts at moral action by rewarding them. Rather, it often greets those efforts with results

---

[74] See esp. Williams 1981b. A notion of contingency is also treated by Nussbaum 1986, but her treatment seems to me so to confuse two quite different issues that its relevance to the present matter is compromised (see White 1988b).

[75] In terms of the traditional debate about moral responsibility and free will, these are factors for which the agent is not responsible because he did not choose them or did not choose them freely. One way of thinking about Williams's view is this (1981b): it is an affirmation of the standard claim that everything relevant to the assessment of what an agent does is decisively determined by factors for which he is not responsible, so that there is no room left for traditional assignments of 'moral' responsibility and moral evaluations of actions (as actions for which the agent is morally responsible). Unlike most 'hard determinists', however, Williams does not say that every feature of every action is completely determined by factors outside the agent's control. Instead he seems to claim merely that every feature of an agent's actions that is relevant to assessment is so substantially influenced by such factors that one cannot isolate those features for which the agent can himself be held fully responsible. Thus there is nothing isolable that can be assigned to the agent's own account, as 'moral' evaluation tries to do. In addition, Williams introduces a second idea. He is not concerned to deny, as traditional hard determinists do, that a person is morally responsible for anything at all. Rather, he aims mainly to deny the defensibility of the *distinction* (which is a standard part of the normal conception of morality as he interprets it) between those features of an action that enter into the moral evaluation of it and of the person who does it and those features that do not do so. In other words, he thinks it a mistake to try to isolate, in the way that morality does, the features of an action for which the performer of it is morally responsible from those which, because they are contingent, he is not thus responsible. Moreover, he thinks that some features for which the agent plainly is not responsible in any clear sense are relevant to the assessment of the action and of the agent for doing it, or for trying to do it.

that one finds undesirable. These results include pain and suffering, and also the failure of one's project as a result of factors beyond one's control.

Such a situation might seem to be best characterized as simply bad luck, an unfortunate and undesirable lack of 'fit' between one's moral aims and the world's response—and this is the aspect of the matter that Williams emphasizes. However, we are dealing here also with a conflict between different aims, in the broad sense in which I use that term.[76] We undertake morally praiseworthy activities, as we think, but we find that they bring us undesirable or undesired results. With dismay we must realize, accordingly, that the world will not allow us successfully to aim both at moral action and at the results that we would like or find choiceworthy. The things that we want to happen cannot happen all together.

According to Williams, modern moralists react to this state of affairs by maintaining that morality and its evaluations override other considerations in a special way. Moralists deny that non-moral values should be accorded any genuine importance when those values conflict with moral judgements themselves, or even that they should be used retrospectively in giving any serious evaluation of one's decisions and actions. Williams thus thinks of morality as making a second-order claim to its own priority over all other evaluations.[77] Morality not only issues its evaluations; it is also given the function of serving as referee, to adjudicate the rival claims of its evaluations as against other, non-moral ones. Morality says, so to speak, that its own evaluations take priority over others.[78] This gives us a hypothetical conflict, built into the concept of morality, between morality and other values. Morality says that its values take precedence over others, whenever its values and other values cannot be attained together.

However, there is an additional way in which, according to Williams, morality generates conflicts. These further conflicts are not merely thus hypothetical or dependent on accidental facts about whether moral and other values can in fact be attained together. Here the notion of contingency enters directly into the verdict that morality gives about other values. 'The ideal of morality', says Williams, 'is a value, moral value, that transcends luck.' He goes on:

The value must, however, be supreme. It will be no good if moral value is merely a consolation prize you get if you are not in worldly terms happy or talented or good-humored or loved. It has to be what ultimately matters.[79]

The words of this paragraph express, according to Williams, the position that morality itself takes. For Williams thinks it a conceptual truth that morality asserts the

---

[76] See sec. VI. 1. [77] See above, sec. IV. 3.
[78] Note the parallel argument that Plato makes concerning reason at *Rep.* IX. 580–3, and that Mill also makes in 1871: ch. 4.
[79] Williams 1985: 195.

intrinsic unimportance of values that attach to a person simply by luck, as compared with the kind of value, moral value, that in Williams's phrase 'transcends luck'.

As a result, morality must *necessarily* come into direct conflict with any viewpoint that generates any evaluations of the non-moral, luck-entangled kind. Morality says, so to speak, that merely by virtue of the fact that non-moral values are contingent in Williams's sense,[80] they are, strictly speaking, not really worth attending to. Accordingly, the moral view says that a person's moral aspirations cannot coexist with significant positive evaluations of other sorts. Morality thus tries, according to Williams, to place under a cloud the whole practice of making non-moral evaluations and taking them seriously.

2. *Contingency and Conflict in Ancient and Modern Ethics*

We come now to Williams's contention about ancient and modern ethics. Williams sees a difference between the two. He suggests that 'the ancient world was better off, and asked more fruitful questions, than most modern moral philosophy'. He continues, 'Although it had its own limiting concerns, such as the desire to reduce life's exposure to luck, it was typically less obsessional than modern philosophy, less determined to impose rationality through reductive theory'.[81] Williams thus grants that some ancients tried to distinguish between the contingent and non-contingent features of an action and tried to limit the extent to which a person might suffer from bad contingent consequences of actions. This aim, he thinks, brings the ancients far too close to the mistake made by modern moral thinking. For these ancient thinkers tried, Williams maintains, to develop conceptions of human well-being for which this contingency will not obtain.

Modern moralists, however, have gone even further, in Williams's view. In reaction to their disappointment over the fact that moral aspirations are not reliably rewarded by other things that people value, moralists distort the notion of an adequate reward so as to reduce the gap. That is, they insist on regarding as good, in the important sense, only what is guaranteed to follow non-contingently upon moral high-mindedness.[82] Bad luck and good luck both become irrelevant. The belief that moral virtue is its own reward, and that nothing else could be a significant reward, is an extreme instance of this strategy.

However, the price that modern moral views pay for adopting this strategy is, precisely, their implausible assertion that contingent things, simply by being contingent, cannot possess any value that really counts. The result, as already explained, is that

---

[80] This sense is discussed by Williams, esp. in his 1981d.   [81] Williams 1985: 197.

[82] Williams seems to see this tendency in Plato's and Aristotle's efforts, as he construes them, to show that justice or moral virtue, respectively, must lead to happiness, not contingently but necessarily. It will become clear in Chapters 5 and 6 that I disagree with Williams's interpretations in substantial ways.

they bring about an inevitable conflict between themselves and other evaluative viewpoints. For these viewpoints prize those values, while morality condemns or disregards them precisely because of their contingent character.[83] Thus, once again, the generation of a conflict is laid at the door of a modern conception of morality.

VII. Aims and Conflicts

1. More Terminology

In what terms, then, shall we discuss the issues of conflict and consistency in rational deliberation? It will be useful to bring some terminological and conceptual points directly into view.

One point should be kept in mind throughout. In order to describe various interpretations of Greek ethics and to discuss them together, I shall need to adopt language adequate to express an equally wide variety of concepts and philosophical presuppositions that have figured in those interpretations. Sometimes that requires considerable terminological flexibility and even looseness, as well as a willingness to operate with concepts which I would not employ on my own behalf, and to which the reader might object on philosophical grounds. I shall try to keep that circumstance from unduly stretching the fabric of my own argument.

Because I am concerned with a very broad class of deliberative conflicts, I use the term 'aim' in an extremely wide sense—wider than that of the word 'goal', which for its part I normally mean a result for whose sake an action or process is carried out or to which it is supposed to lead causally. An aim in my sense is anything that is desired or valued or regarded as worthwhile, even if it is not explicitly sought or planned for. An aim can include, for instance, an activity engaged in or valued for its own sake and not for the sake of any result that will ensue or is intended. I often use the word 'consideration' almost equivalently and equally broadly, to stand for anything that can be taken up or cited in making decisions or retrospectively rationalizing or justifying them—or, alternatively, to stand for a thought or linguistic expression in which a thing of that sort figures or is cited.[84]

---

[83] As noted, Williams himself is not an opponent of the idea that goods may come into conflict with each other. On the contrary, he takes over precisely that view from Berlin and defends it (see esp. Williams 1981a, and also Taylor 1985 and 1989: ch. 3 and pp. 503, 518).

[84] I use the word 'consideration' here much as does Foot 1978a. There is much about the notions mentioned here that could easily use clarification. As they stand, however, they should serve present purposes well enough. It is not here implied that all good things are thought of as the attainment of actual aims, since things may be discovered to be valuable or worthwhile even if one has not previously known of them and thus has not aimed at them. Nevertheless, when we consider practical deliberation we are necessarily focusing on things that the deliberator brings to mind in advance. For the most part, therefore, I shall talk in those terms.

I shall also use terms like 'conflict', 'opposition', and 'dualism' in a quite free way. Roughly, a dualism is for my purposes a distinction between aims or the like, whereas a conflict or opposition involves cases in which those aims are inconsistent in the sense that they cannot both be pursued together or—a very important type of case—cannot both be pursued fully or adequately. For most practical purposes we care about practical dualisms only when they actually break out into conflicts.

The issue of conflict that I treat has to do with the possibility of conflict among 'rational' aims—whether there can be, that is, conflicts among *rational* aims, which are genuine goods, and whether the Greeks believed that there can be.[85]

By the word 'rational' here I do not intend to call up any very precise notion—one associated, say, with decision theory or traditional philosophical rationalism or the like. Nor do I invoke the views of any particular philosopher, such as Kant or Hume. No more do I intend any special contrast between rationality and some definite other thing, such as emotion or desire. The terms 'rational' and 'practical reason' here point only to something very vague, namely, whatever, according to the particular thinker under discussion at a given juncture, is the way in which it is advisable to think in order to arrive at decisions about what to do, what kind of person to be, or how to live life.

I talk of an individual's 'well-being' or 'happiness' and of 'one's good' in an analogously schematic way. I have not tried to specify what someone's well-being consists in, nor need I do so. The goal is, I repeat, to make my usage wide enough to accommodate the full range of views on this matter that appear within both ancient Greek ethics and the various interpretations thereof, without gerrymandering any relevant positions out of my account.

In particular, in order to reflect what is said both within Greek ethics itself and in long-standing discussions of it, we must often think of *eudaimonia* in a 'pluralist' fashion, so to speak, as a complex or composite condition made up of 'parts' or 'constituents'. These parts are the respective attainments of a plurality of aims or conditions that are valued or taken to be worthwhile. Such parts may either be given in a list or else, alternatively, be thought of as put together in some complex structure that needs to be described in a more complex way.[86]

On the whole—though with certain notable exceptions[87]—Greek ethics, especially in the Classical period, thinks of these aims as they are ordinarily presented to an individual in everyday life, rather than as having already been regimented within some philosophical scheme or systematic description. The aims appear as separate

---

[85]   This question is frequently discussed by Berlin, for instance at many points in his 1991a, and is rightly regarded by Gray 1996 as central to his work.

[86]   Ackrill 1980, for instance, notes the existence of these interpretative alternatives.

[87]   These are mainly the monist hedonism of Epicurus (see Chapter 7), and perhaps in his precursors such as Democritus and Eudoxus, as well as the account of pleasure in Plato's *Protagoras*.

from each other, not simply as falling under some common heading, and they often appear to require reconciliation or strenuous efforts to coordinate them with each other so that they do not clash. This conception is not at all unknown to modern ethics. For instance, Joseph Butler and, sometimes, John Stuart Mill employ a notion of happiness as something that has parts; and the same notion is often borrowed from them and used in clarifying Greek thinking about *eudaimonia*.[88]

2. Conflicts of Aims

Obviously aims may conflict with each other in the loose sense of not being realizable together. Direct logical or physical incompatibilities may exist between them, or oppositions may be generated by the fact that human beings are inevitably subject to limitations of time, energy, and other resources, so that one cannot necessarily pursue all of one's aims, or at least not fully or adequately. Everyone is aware that our lives are too short and our capacities are too limited for the realization of all available options, and that to some extent we have to adjust each of our aims to each of our other aims, and sometimes must eschew highly valued aims altogether.[89]

Greek philosophers were vividly aware of this fact, though many of their interpreters neglect it.[90] Moreover, some ancients, including Plato and Aristotle, accord it a determinative role in their ethical doctrines.[91] The distinction between a man and a god—that is, between a mortal and an immortal—was always present to the minds of Greek thinkers as chiefly the distinction of a being with limited and a being with unlimited opportunities and resources. This contrast plays a role in Greek ethics that is easy to pass over in a modern secular milieu. Nevertheless, the Greeks were always alive to the fact that a good human life has room for much less than is contained in the best conceivable life.

Because we all know that some aims conflict with others, we feel called upon to arrange or coordinate the activities and states that we conceive of as parts of happiness.[92] Thus we make plans.[93] Sometimes plans cover the whole of one's life. The

---

[88] See Butler 1726: Sermon XI, and Mill 1871: ch. 4. This notion of happiness in Mill seems to coexist uneasily, as is often observed, with a more straightforwardly hedonist notion, but here only the former is pertinent. For the use of Mill's (sometimes) inclusivist ideas in interpreting ancient ethics see esp. Irwin 1977: 341; Irwin also adopts essentially the same strategy in his 1988 and 1995.

[89] The philosophical problems associated with this idea are very considerable. Two relevant recent discussions are Bratman 1987 and Millgram 1997.

[90] Exceptions include Cooper 1980: 332 and 338 n. 18, Nussbaum 1986: ch. 2 passim, and Sherman 1989: 127; the last two both briefly note the existence of such conflicts.

[91] See Chapters 5 and 6.

[92] In Plato's *Gorgias*, the character Callicles is made to try to deny this and is duly refuted; see e.g. White 1985a and Irwin 1995: ch. 8, esp. 114–18.

[93] See esp. Bratman 1987.

Greeks paid attention to such extended plans.[94] Perhaps surprisingly, they tended to think of such plans not as dynamic or evolving over time, but as static, as made during youth and then simply followed out.[95] Greek philosophical discussions do not deal in any substantial way with questions about how a life plan might rationally be revised at later stages, that is, with the diachronic reorganization of a plan of life. Thus Plato in *Republic* IX and Aristotle in *Nicomachean Ethics* I and *Eudemian Ethics* I ask simply which the best life is—one devoted to money or to statecraft or to something else. That is, they thought that a philosopher should enable a person to decide what plan to adopt at or near the start of adult life—or to choose for his son, let us say—not show how to re-examine or revise plans as life goes along. Plato recognizes that plans and lifestyles can differ from one generation to the next—the father is frugal, the son is profligate— and that is a manifestation of a kind of adaptability. We see little sign, however, of a recognition of planned flexibility within an individual life.[96]

3. Adjudication, Elimination, and Holism Again

When we work on the assumption that some Greek views of happiness are 'pluralist', we think of happiness as being made up of a plurality of distinguishable parts or com- ponent activities and states.[97] For most purposes we have to assume, in addition, that this pluralism is irreducible—that a person's various aims cannot all be said to be tan- tamount to, for example, quantities of pleasure or some other single thing. This plu- ralism means, in addition, that we cannot think that free trade-offs among components of *eudaimonia* are possible, that is, that the benefit of doing one thing and the benefit of doing another are mutually exchangeable. (I shall here leave aside the question whether we should express this idea by saying either that goods are 'fungi- ble' or that they are 'commensurable'.)

Recall the distinction that I drew earlier between the strategy of adjudicating con- flicts and that of mitigating or eliminating them.[98] The *adjudicative* strategy involves

---

[94] See e.g. Hardie 1965, Nussbaum 1986: 6, 51, and passim, and Annas 1993: esp. 27–46.

[95] One exception is the way in which Plato's philosopher-rulers, after they reach an understanding of what the Good is, come to have an altered, broader perspective on the grounds for making choices (cf. Chapter 5). However, Plato is envisaging this process as determinable and predictable, and thus as being settlable, in advance. See further Chapter 5, sec. VII, and Chapter 6, sec. IX. 1.

[96] This is perhaps a negative aspect of the oft-noted fact—see e.g. Annas 1993—that the Greeks tend- ed strongly to evaluate a human life as a whole.

[97] Some aims are of a 'second (or higher) order': they have to do with other aims. The Greeks were aware of this fact. Plato in the *Republic* thinks of reason as having aims to control appetites, and Aristotle thinks of practical wisdom (phronêsis) in a similar way.

[98] See Chapter 1, sec. VII. 5 and Stocker 1990. The distinction here is much the same as one suggested in passing by Becker 1990–1: 134. Important related issues are also discussed by Larmore 1996 and the con- tributors to Chang 1997.

trying to settle disputes by turning them over, so to speak, to a higher court of appeal for a decision. The presupposition underlying this approach is that the disputes do indeed exist. The model is that of the law court, from which the several parties exit in disagreement still, but willing nevertheless to abide by a common verdict about what to do. The other, *eliminative* or *mitigative* type of conception is intended to show, respectively, that the initial impression of conflict is wholly or partly illusory, and thus that there really never was a conflict to be settled in the first place. This would be like showing two parties to a dispute, who thought they had a bone of contention between them, that their seemingly divergent cases were fully compatible after all, or, more fancifully, that the disputants were after all identical.[99]

As I have already pointed out, this latter, eliminativist model is the one that is employed, in effect, by hegelian thinking as I have conceived it.[100] In the present context, *mutatis mutandis*, the 'inclusivist' and 'fusionist' positions described earlier can both be thought of as eliminative. The kantian outlook, on the other hand, is adjudicative: it should be thought of as presenting us with a dispute that needs settling, which Kant himself tries to do by—to put it very roughly—siding with reason against inclination. Moreover, it is the latter model that is generally ascribed to the Greeks, both by kantian interpreters and by those who welcome it themselves on hegelian terms.

It is obvious enough that a steadfastly pluralist conception of goods will normally be resistant to an eliminative strategy. As long as someone retains the sense that each of various goods has its own importance, and is not simply fungible vis-à-vis others, he will find it difficult to accept the idea that when circumstances keep those several goods from being realizable together, the appearance of a conflict between them is illusory.[101]

Another implication of the conception of happiness as consisting genuinely of parts is significant for the notion of what it is to have a more or less harmonious conception of happiness. This implication is the idea that one's failure to attain one part, even if it is accompanied by a gain with respect to another, will often be felt as an *uncompensated* or not fully compensated *loss*. If someone gains in political stature but the well-being of his family suffers, for example, then no matter how great the gain on the former side may be, he may still think that he has lost something, and indeed something important in its own right. He will not, that is, think it reasonable to look

---

[99] Sometimes there is room for disagreement or uncertainty about whether a given strategy is eliminative or adjudicative. The position with regard to moral conflicts that is adopted by Hare 1981, for instance (see esp. ch. 2), seems to me to be eliminativist, though one might try to classify it as adjudicative.

[100] Remember, once again, how relatively small is my interest in presenting the actual views of Hegel.

[101] By the same token, a systematizing view such as quantitative hedonism is in effect a way of implementing an eliminative strategy. The importance of this fact will be highlighted in the discussion of Epicureanism in Chapter 7.

at the whole ledger and see that the loss may be compensated by the gain. Nor, for that matter, will he necessarily see the gain as vitiated by the loss. The two entries in the ledger will each have their own salience. From a theoretical standpoint that is an inelegance and, some would say, worse. Still, it seems to be a fact of our experience.[102] Indeed it seems to be implicated in the notion of a plurality of parts of well-being. If there were a way of trading off each part of happiness against the other without loss, then there would be no need to think of them as distinct parts. They would all be manifestations of a single underlying aim.

It seems evident that to the extent that one hopes to mitigate the sense that aims conflict, one must be able to lessen the sense of loss that can come from pursuing one aim at the expense of pursuit of another. The sense of loss is associated with the idea that one has, as I have put it, adjudicated between the two considerations, but that they both retain their force. If there is to be less sense of loss, or none at all, that must be because one takes the conflict between the considerations to be significantly less than it appeared or to be for some reason, after all, nonexistent.[103]

This strategy can be implemented, as I have said, through the adoption of a *holist* view of value. Holism may come in degrees. At the extreme is the position that the parts of happiness have no intrinsic value at all, but that their value arises only from their contributions (insofar as they can be identified) to the value of the whole. Under such a view, one does not suffer by the lesser pursuit of one aim in order to pursue a second aim to such an extent that it contributes to the maximum value of one's whole life. This would be a *perfect harmony* of aims. I shall argue eventually that this is the conception of goodness that the Stoics try to articulate extensively, but that in Greek ethics before them, and especially in the Classical period, it is very little pursued or developed.

One might, however, conceive of each component of one's well-being as possessing some value intrinsically on its own, even as one *also* simultaneously regards the whole

---

[102] It is comparable to one of the phenomena that gives rise to so-called 'moral dilemmas' and 'tragic dilemmas'. See e.g. Williams 1973a: sec. 5, as well as Nussbaum 1986: ch. 2, Williams 1993: 164, Sinnott-Armstrong 1988, Stocker 1990, and Hursthouse 1999: ch. 3. On related issues in Nietzsche, see Nehamas 1985: 42–3; for a discussion of related issues in drama, see Benjamin 1928: ch. 2. Although the notions of moral and tragic dilemma are not my topic here, they are closely related to the matters under discussion. Usually such dilemmas are conceived of as involving conflicts of right and wrong or obligation, whereas the issue here has to do with oppositions of good or wellbeing. Stocker 1990 explores these issues, rightly emphasizing the importance of 'double-counting' for the notion of a dilemma of this type. The present issues are closer to, though not identical with, those involving what Gert and Sinnott-Armstrong call 'ideals' as opposed to 'requirements' (see Gert 1988: ch. 8 and Sinnott-Armstrong 1988: 11–15).

[103] It might be suggested that the present issue is responded to by the idea of a progressive adjustment of one's conception of happiness, in the ways described, for instance, by Annas 1993: 27–46, 439–46, and Irwin 1995: 202. This, however, is a separate matter. The present issue is not how we adjust aims to each other by a procedure that seems reasonable, but whether, or to what extent, we think of something as having, at the end of the process, been lost.

arrangement of parts as valuable as well. This is a little like regarding one colour in a painting as especially attractive, and more attractive than some of the others, while also believing that the painting as a whole also gains by the combining of different colours, even those that one finds less attractive on their own than one's favourite colour in it. There is a kind of schizophrenia at work here: one simultaneously judges the combination and also the individual colours that are combined.[104] Arguably we do the same when we think of well-being: the parts are valued separately, and likewise also their combination in some pattern.[105] Perhaps this double conception is problematic from an ideally rational viewpoint. For it can leave us in doubt about whether a basis exists for a single, all-in evaluation or justification of action. Should one act simply to further the global good of the whole, or is one also to be influenced by the intrinsic values of the parts? That is not clear. But if this is a problematic conception, it is one that people often try to live with. I shall argue, too, that it is to be found in Aristotle.

4. Harmonizing Strategies

The main topic of this book is not deliberative conflict per se, but conflict of particular sort, having to do with an individual's good on the one hand and considerations thought of as falling beyond it. I must say enough about what this distinction amounts to so that I can clarify the outlines of Greek views and the uses that have been made of them.

I have taken for granted the viability of the distinctions between *self-confined* and *external* aims, and between *self-regarding* and *broader* aims. I have in effect also assumed that we can make sense of the notion of the good 'of' an individual, and likewise of 'his' well-being or happiness.[106] None of these distinctions is easy to draw clearly, and I shall not try to meet any of the difficulties here.

I have in addition mentioned the difficulties raised by what C. D. Broad labelled 'self-referential altruism'.[107] This is a matter of wishing to further the happiness of other people because they bear a special relation *to oneself*. These people are in an obvious sense not identical with oneself. On the other hand, it seems misleading to say that an intention to help them is a case of altruism *tout court*, because the intention is in some sense conditional upon their connection or relation to oneself. We might press the flat question whether their happiness is a component of one's own, or not. A more

---

[104] See Stocker 1990.

[105] I believe that we think of a 'well-rounded' person in this way: we esteem a combination of activities, while recognizing that the person could have done certain things better for not having done so many.

[106] Some philosophers, notably G. E. Moore (see his 1903: 96–109) and Donald Regan deny that the notion of 'good for' makes sense, or try to call it into doubt, but it seems to me that the notion does make sense more or less as it stands, and I shall proceed on that assumption.

[107] See Broad 1942, and for a related issue see Sandel 1982: 62.

'communitarian' outlook might say yes, while a more 'individualist' view says no. How do we decide? This is a problem that raises its head repeatedly in the history of Greek philosophy and modern reactions to it, but is not easy to solve straight-forwardly.

Furthermore, as we have seen, it is possible to deny that the distinction between self-regarding and broader considerations is a real one. For instance, we might con-tend that every consideration bears on oneself in some way, however remote, and that all considerations related to oneself also have some connection with other people. By the same token we might also reject the other distinction, namely, between the self-confined and the external. In these ways a hegelian-minded thinker may deny that there can ever be a conflict between one's own good and anything else, on the ground that there is no such distinction at all for the conflict to arise from. And indeed the Stoics appear, I shall urge, to have adopted just such a position.[108] The strength of that position would be increased by the difficulty of finding a satisfactory and agreed-upon way of showing how the distinction is to be drawn.

Thus at least one important strand of deliberative monism—a version of which seems to be present at times in Hegel himself—rejects the whole way of framing the issue that I have just now been employing. According to such a hegelian view, an understanding of an individual's well-being, and thus of the contribution to it of any of its constituents, will emerge only after a long period of historical social develop-ment, but is by no means available to us now. Only by comprehending the ultimate condition of society, and the place of individuals in it, will we be able to say just what place any particular constituent aim or activity may have in a person's happiness.[109]

The question whether this is so or not is, indeed, one of the major philosophical issues in the philosophical background that animates this book. Still, in order to broach this question, we have to formulate it. That requires making at least provi-sional use of a notional contrast between what is contained in an individual's good and what lies beyond it. Provisional use of the contrast does not seem illegitimate in gen-eral. Even Kant—for what this fact is worth—can maintain that happiness is deserved by someone who wills to do his duty, even while he also sometimes denies that there is any clear conception of happiness that we could possess.[110] I take it, there-

---

[108] See Chapter 7, sec. IV.

[109] For a convenient brief summary of this aspect of Hegel's view, thus interpreted, see Sidgwick 1931: 278–9.

[110] Kant says that the idea of one's happiness is a 'fluctuating' one, which is incapable of being clarified sufficiently to determine action. He thinks that the aim of happiness is a kind of aggregation of one's dif-ferent inclinations, but that the idea of such an aggregation is intrinsically unclear. Therefore, he thinks, it is incapable of consistently determining what we do. People have, Kant says,

the strongest and deepest inclination toward happiness, because just in this idea are all inclinations combined into a sum total. But the precept of happiness is often so constituted as greatly to interfere

fore, that my expository use of the contrast should not be regarded as begging any questions against those who believe it to be misguided.[111]

We may close this discussion with one remark that will help us understand certain instances in which we shall wish to distinguish one person's good and another's, at least in the course of discussing Greek thinkers.

Intuitively it appears that some goods, like some aims, are *competitive*: there is not enough to go around for everyone to be completely adequately supplied. Hegelian and other such views attempt to counteract this feeling by philosophical arguments against the possibility of genuine conflict, and by adducing such fellow feeling as human beings may possess. And indeed perhaps the notion of 'competitiveness' tacitly takes for granted the notion of an individual's good that we are trying to understand. If so, I think that it does so in an intuitively illuminating way. At any rate, insofar as we are prepared at the start of our thinking to regard some aims and goods as rather obviously competitive, to that extent we shall obviously think of the good of one individual as distinct from the good of others, and may hold that an individual might conceivably take considerations into account that lie outside his own well-being. For the purposes of this book I shall assume that we can at least provisionally understand these notions. The questions to be raised concern whether, or to what extent, they play a role in Greek ethics.

with some inclinations, and yet men *cannot form any definite and certain concept of* the sum of satisfaction of all inclinations that is called happiness.

He goes on:

Hence there is no wonder that a single inclination which is determinate both as to what it promises and as to the time within which it can be satisfied may outweigh *a fluctuating idea*. (1981: sec. 399)

Thus, he thinks, a single particular inclination will in general be able to influence a person more than an indefinite and uncertain idea of the aggregate of one's various inclinations taken together. But that does not prevent him, in the *Critique of Practical Reason* (1956: 206–15), from maintaining that we must believe that we deserve to be happy.

[111] In his 1982, for instance, Sandel in effect charges Rawls with a kind of begging of certain questions in favour of an individualist view and against a communitarian one (see esp. 154–61). I take myself here not to fall into such begging of questions, either philosophically or historically.

Chapter 3

IMPERATIVES IN GREEK
ETHICS

I. The Rejection of Imperativity

1. The Imperative Mood

One of the main reasons why so many modern interpretations of Greek ethics have gone astray, I say, arises from the way in which ancient ethics has been used in modern debates, and particularly in reactions against kantian thinking. This factor has led to the prominence of a few stereotypes in our picture of Greek ethics. These present to us alleged aspects of Greek ethics that we then take to be indicative of the entire structure. One of these aspects has to do with the supposed role of the city-state or *polis* in Greek thought. This has led to many misconceptions of Greek politics and ethics, which I shall discuss later.[1]

The other aspect, which I shall treat in the present chapter, is a matter of tone and language. It has to do with the way in which Greek ethical thinking is, supposedly, formulated. According to a now well-established account, the tone of Greek ethics is quite different from the tone of modern ethics, and this difference in tone is the result of the kind of language in which the two outlooks are respectively couched, which in turn reflects different conceptions of what ethics is. Thus Annas says, citing Bradley:

Ancient ethics is . . . not based on . . . 'the notion that morality is a life harassed and persecuted everywhere by "imperatives" and disagreeable duties, and that without these you have not got morality.' Its leading notions are not those of obligation, duty and rule-following; instead of these 'imperative' notions it uses 'attractive' notions like those of goodness and worth.[2]

I want to focus for a while on this issue. I shall deal with it primarily as a matter of tone, language and—in two senses, grammatical and stylistic—mood. I believe that on the

---

[1] In Chapter 4.
[2] Annas 1993: 4. The quotation comes from Bradley 1927: 215.

whole this way of contrasting ancient and modern ethics is a misconception which often screens readers off from a clear view of what Greek ethical writings say and do. In this chapter, I shall present some grounds for putting this conception aside, then, so that we can look more clearsightedly at the content, as well as the style, of Greek thinking.

2. Schiller and Sidgwick on Moral Laws and Imperatives

One of the reasons why Friedrich Schiller admired Greek thought is apparent from his essay, *On the Aesthetic Education of Man*. In a criticism directed against the way in which the idea of duty presents itself to moderns, he says:

Even what is most sacred in man, the moral law, when it first makes its appearance in the life of sense . . ., since its voice is . . . inhibitory and against the interest of his animal self-love, . . . is bound to seem like something external to himself . . . He persuades himself to regard the concepts of right and wrong as statutes introduced by some will, not as something valid in themselves for all eternity.[3]

According to Schiller, a defect of modern thinking is that it represents ethical norms as deliverances of the 'moral law'. This notion, like that of duty, seems to him indicative of a less than wholehearted allegiance to the norm. It suggests a standard felt as generated and imposed from outside the individual. The Greeks, Schiller thought, looked at ethical matters differently.

The notion of 'moral law' against which Schiller directs his criticism contains two components: morality and law. These are usually treated together, and sometimes are even confused. Nevertheless, they are plainly distinct. Not all laws are moral laws, and not all expressions of moral norms take the form of laws. For example, it is possible to speak of somebody as morally good. It is therefore necessary to treat the two components separately, and to ask what Schiller's criticism is of each. Here I shall concern myself chiefly with the imperativity that is often associated most closely with the notion of a law, but also appears in other, related concepts.

Like others who have thought along the same lines, Schiller aims his criticism at a very broad target. He does not, for instance, object specifically to law or the legal system in the literal sense as an institution of government or the like. Instead, he is concerned with a general way in which norms or standards are sometimes formulated. This is the sort of formulation for which Sidgwick employs the label 'imperative'. In the first instance, imperative language includes grammatically overt commands. In addition, however, it includes many other linguistic expressions that are closely linked to imperatives, like 'ought', 'must', 'duty', 'obligation', and 'law'. All of these have in common that in one way or another, they convey a sense of someone's being either

---

[3] Schiller 1967: Letter XXIV, sec. 7.

commanded to do something or commanded not to do something, that is, forbidden to do it.[4]

Many modern philosophers have objected to the use of imperative notions in ethical discourse. Their objections often lead to views that are designed to minimize or avoid their use. Certainly the feelings that generate these protests are easy to understand. Imperative expressions tend to make people feel badgered. Lists of 'Dos and 'Don'ts' tend to antagonize us. Rhetorically it often seems expedient to say, 'It would be good not to do that', instead of 'Don't do that', or 'You ought not to do that', or 'You are forbidden to do that', or even the milder but still imperatival 'You shouldn't do that'.[5] A fundamental reason for misgivings about imperative formulations of norms is brought out by this fact. The misgivings are focused on the use of the psychology of imperativity to convey standards by which a person might be expected to govern his life.

From this fact it is easy to see that, although many people tend to run the two issues together, criticism of the use of *imperative* notions in ethics is not the same as criticism of *morality* per se. It can be objected against morality that it must be couched, or is most naturally couched, in imperative form. It can also be objected that although moral norms are often expressed as imperatives, the arguments supporting those norms cannot justify the particular urgency and stringency that imperative language tends to convey. Both of these objections are often raised.[6] Both of them presuppose, however, that there is something problematical about the use of imperative language itself as a way of formulating the body of norms by which people are expected to govern themselves. And some philosophers have thought just that.

Schiller's suggestion, with which many writers since have concurred, is that imperative formulations are characteristic of modern morality. He maintained that Greek thought was free of this feature. This idea is emphasized by Sidgwick, too, even though he does not agree with Schiller's unfavourable attitude towards imperative formulations. Sidgwick maintains that there is a difference between 'the Greek view of ethics, in which the notions of Good and Virtue were taken as fundamental, [and] the modern view in which ethics is conceived as primarily a study of the "moral code"'. Sidgwick explains the shift from the one view to the other as mainly the result of Christianity and its Jewish antecedents:

[E]ven if the notion of law had been more prominent than it was in ancient ethical thought, it could never have led to a juridical . . . treatment of morality. In Christianity, on the other

---

[4] In saying this I am not giving a definition of imperativity (as a definition, what I just offered is obviously circular). The class of expression in question and the sense that they convey are obvious enough for present purposes.

[5] Anscombe notes, in sec. 35 of 1963, that 'should' is 'a rather light word'. That is true, though the same cannot be said, as we shall have occasion to note below, for Aristotle's *dei*, which which she seems to equate 'should'.   [6] Chapter 2, sec. IV. 3.

hand, we early find that the method of moralists determining right conduct is to a great extent analogous to that of jurists interpreting a code . . . This juridical method descended naturally from the Jewish theocracy, which was universalized in Christendom.[7]

In speaking here of a 'code', Sidgwick is alluding to two things. One is a particular manner, which he takes to be typical both of legal systems and of modern ethics, of applying general attitudes or standards to particular cases. This matter is not at issue here.[8] The other part of Sidgwick's contrast concerns imperative notions. Like Schiller, he regards the use of these as a hallmark of modern ethics, which distinguishes it from its Greek predecessor.[9]

3. Objections to the Mood of Imperatives, and to the People who Respond to Them

What is at stake in the contention that Greek and modern ethics differ in this way? The answer to this question emerges when we consider why a good many modern philosophers have followed Schiller in objecting to certain uses of imperative language in ethics. We can start with Bernard Williams's statement: 'It is a mistake of morality to try to make everything into obligations.'[10] Consider first the fact that the concept of obligation is quite straightforwardly imperatival, and that its imperativity seems to be part of what Williams holds against it. Likewise, one of the counts brought against morality has been that, according to its critics, it uses a bogus air of *authority* that is lent to its claims by its appropriation of imperative language. For instance, Philippa Foot takes a dim view of Kant's idea that 'moral rules . . . are categorical commands'. She says: 'Kant's argument that moral rules have a peculiar and dignified status depends wholly upon his attempt to link moral action with rationality through the mere concept of the form of law and the principle of universalizability.'[11] Of the phrase 'morally ought', G. E. M. Anscombe says flatly: 'It would be most reasonable to drop it.' 'This word "ought"', she says, '[has] become a word of mere mesmeric force.'[12] This kind of objection to imperatives, furthermore, is not confined to the contemporary context of discussion. The same criticism of imperatives had also been made early in this century by Victor Brochard, urging us to abandon the chiefly

---

[7] Sidgwick 1931: 97–8, 111–13.

[8] It is a large topic unto itself within legal philosophy. Sidgwick is in effect espousing the controversial view that a legal system should be regarded as a system of 'rules'. In controversies of the present day, this notion connotes more than mere imperativity. See e.g. Hart 1961 and MacCormick 1978. Moreover, within the notion of a 'system of rules' are contained two further constituents, the notion of a rule and also the notion of a system thereof. As will be observed below, sec. V, the Greeks at times think of rules without thinking of them as being arranged in a system.

[9] Thus see also Sidgwick 1907: 105–6.

[10] Williams 1985: 180.

[11] Foot 1978d: 172; cf. 166, 171. See also Brochard 1901 (see also below, n. 63).

[12] Anscombe 1958: 8.

imperative moral formulations of Kant, and to recapture some of the non-imperative thinking that he ascribed to the Greeks.[13]

Opposition to this employment of imperatives sometimes extends beyond the sphere of language and the notions expressed by it. Some philosophers are unimpressed by, hostile to, or even contemptuous of the kinds of *people* who are obedient to commands. These same philosophers often also find something objectionable about what might be called the mood that imperativity creates. Nietzsche disdains 'slave morality', 'the imperative of herd timidity', and 'the fair, modest, submissive, conforming mentality'. He sarcastically imagines Kant expressing the thought that 'what deserves respect in me is that I can obey'.[14] In a somewhat similar vein, Bernard Williams speaks disparagingly of the 'intimidating structure that morality has made out of the idea of obligation'.[15] One is reminded of the words that Schiller in 1781 put into the mouth of the character Moor in *The Robbers*:

I am supposed to lace my body in a corset, and strait-jacket my will with laws. The law has cramped the flight of eagles to a snail's pace. The law never yet made a great man, but freedom will breed a giant, a colossus.[16]

4. Commands without a Commander

I have remarked that imperatives can seem objectionable merely because of their tone, and also because they carry the undertone of a command or prohibition. Other objections have a slightly different focus. For instance, one argument against certain uses of imperatives, particularly in a moral theory, says that they generate a false appearance that a command has been issued when really there has been no actual command at all, or else that these uses arise from 'a confusion of the philosophical viewpoint and the viewpoint of religion or theology'.[17]

Sometimes, of course, the intent behind an imperative word like 'ought' is to indicate that a command actually *has* been given. Many religious views, in particular, have based ethical standards on divine law, and have then in turn based divine law on divine commandment. 'You ought not to kill' can certainly sometimes convey the thought that someone has commanded something, namely, 'Thou shalt not kill'; and often that is much of what is meant.[18]

On the other hand, during the last two centuries the notion of obligation has large-

---

[13] Brochard 1901.   [14] Nietzsche 1966b: secs. 260, 201, 187.

[15] Williams 1985: 182.

[16] Schiller 1979: 36. (Note the difference in the character Moor's attitude towards law in his last speeches in the play.)

[17] Brochard 1901: 7: 'une confusion entre le point de vue philosophique et le point de vue religieux ou théologique'.

[18] It seems to me that Sidgwick is correct, however, in denying that this is all of what is meant; see his 1907: 313.

ly been secularized and is often part of a completely atheistic outlook. Sometimes a doctrine will employ the idea of an ethical command but will assign the function of issuing the commands not to a deity, but to some other sort of entity such as a society or state or the laws of some such institution; or else the command can be held to arise somehow from some primal social contract, real or hypothetical.

Often, however, the language of moral 'oughts' and obligations and laws, together with its suggestion of commands, is used in the absence of any idea that any actual commanding has taken place. It is this fact that has attracted the criticism that I am now discussing. This criticism has been directed very sharply against Kant's notion of the so-called categorical imperative. As Kant expounds it, this type of imperative seems to involve the idea of a command, but not the idea of any commander. But does such a notion make sense? Some opponents of Kant have found it absurd. Anscombe says the phrase 'morally ought' 'has no reasonable sense outside of a law conception of ethics'.[19] 'What . . . does it mean to say', Foot also asks, 'that moral rules are commands?' And she continues:

In the first place they are not commands at all, neither commands of men nor commands or God . . . What we actually have are rules of conduct adopted by certain societies and individuals . . .; and Kant is saying that these rules are universally valid. But when we put it this way, in terms of rules, the difficulty of understanding the notion of universal validity is apparent. (It can no longer mean that everyone is commanded, which shows that there is some point in denying Kant the picturesque language of commands.)[20]

5. Imperatives and Conflicting Motivations

Yet further objections have been raised against Kant's use of imperativity. When we look at the remarks of Schiller that were quoted at the beginning of this chapter, we can easily see that one of his criticisms of imperatives—not just in morality but in any kind of ethical discourse at all—is provoked by the impression, which imperatives convey, of emanating from something alien to a person and imposed from outside him. The Kantian may reply that Kant's kind of imperatives are issued by the person to himself, and therefore are not external. But an objection is brought against this idea too. If a person 'internalizes' the imperative, perhaps in the sense that he himself endorses its content and its imperative force, then—the objection is—there arises a feeling that one's self is fragmented. That is, one has the sense of being divided into two parts, the part that is being commanded and the part that is doing the commanding.

Sympathizing as he does with important features of Kant's position, Schiller tries

---

[19] Anscombe 1958: 8. She thinks that '[t]o have a law conception of ethics is to hold that what is needed for conformity with the virtues . . . is required by divine law' (5).

[20] Foot 1978d: 171.

to find a way out. He calls on a special kind of outlook or consideration, which he identifies as the 'aesthetic', whose function is 'to cast toils of grace over the mind', so that '[d]uty, stern voice of necessity, must moderate the censorious tone of its precepts'.

> Taste alone fosters harmony in society, because it fosters harmony in the individual . . . All other forms of perception divide man . . .; only the aesthetic mode of perception makes of him a whole.[21]

Schiller thus held that commands and the language suggestive of them are best put aside. The only purpose of framing moral standards in the form of commands, he thought, was that in cases in which the self is not harmonious, even standards that one accepts face recalcitrance from a part of oneself, so that the imperative formulation is required to overcome this recalcitrance. The censorious tone of the precepts of duty is 'only justified by the resistance that they encounter'.

Kant's readers often take him to be so attached to imperative formulations that he would find Schiller's view on this matter uncongenial. It therefore needs to be stressed that Kant agrees with Schiller's idea that imperativity arises from resistance to moral commands. Kant is widely criticized for having been the champion of imperative notions, but he himself stressed that under ideal conditions imperative terms would not be needed to express moral standards at all:

> All imperatives are expressed by an *ought* and thereby indicate the relation of an objective law of reason to a will that is not necessarily determined by this law because of its subjective constitution . . . Therefore no imperatives hold for the divine will, and in general for a holy will; the *ought* here is out of place, because the *would* is already of itself necessarily in agreement with the law.

Kant goes on:

> Consequently, imperatives are only formulas for expressing the relation of objective laws of willing in general to the subjective imperfection of the will of this or that rational being, e.g., the human will.[22]

In both Schiller and Kant, then, imperatives are reserved for situations in which contrary motivations are present. Such terms are needed only when the motivations of the self are divided.[23]

---

[21] Schiller 1967: Letter XXVII, secs. 11 and 10.

[22] Kant 1981: secs. 413–14. And speaking of the moral 'ought' later, Kant says (sec. 449):

> this *ought* is properly a *would* which is valid for every rational being, provided that reason is practical for such a being without hindrances. In the case of beings who, like ourselves, are also affected by sensibility, i.e., by incentives of a kind other than the purely rational, and who do not always act as reason by itself would act, this necessity of action is expressed only as an *ought*.

See also Kant 1956: 82–3.

[23] The same idea is contained in Kant's notion that in morality one 'legislates for oneself,' which is attacked by, for example, Anscombe 1958: 2–3.

Kant is not talking here about moral language alone. He is saying something quite general about the force of imperatival expressions, which is meant to show why moral discourse makes use of them in the ways that it does. The same claim is echoed by Sidgwick:

> [P]ossible conflict of motives seems to be connoted by the term 'dictate' or 'imperative', which describe the relation of reason to mere inclinations or non-rational impulses ... This conflict seems also to be implied in the terms 'ought', 'duty', 'moral obligation', as used in ordinary moral discourse: and hence these terms cannot be applied to the actions of rational beings to whom we cannot attribute impulses conflicting with reason.[24]

Sidgwick's conclusion, accordingly, is that even in Kant's view an imperative is appropriate only when conflicting motives exist, because these are what the imperative is called upon to counteract.

6. Imperatives and Attractives

Suppose it granted for the moment that imperative language is indeed linked in this way to conflict and discord, and that such expressions indicate that one part of a self is being commanded by another part or by something outside the self. Even so, that idea simply leaves us with further questions. Are there any alternatives available for articulating the relevant ethical judgements? If so, what are these alternatives? Are they in fact superior to the imperative terms that are under attack?

Some philosophers have been ready to propose, as I have said, that ethics would be better off if it simply gave up using imperative notions. Instead, according to these proposals, ethics should employ notions of a different kind. These notions are the ones that Sidgwick called 'attractive'. The pre-eminent attractive term is the word 'good'. Others are 'fine', 'flourishing', and 'beautiful'. A further group of attractive terms comprises those that stand for virtues. These terms include the word 'virtue' itself, as well as other terms for virtues, for example, 'just', 'truthful', 'courageous', and so on.[25]

---

[24] Sidgwick 1907: 34–5. Sidgwick also says that the word 'ought' 'implies at least the potential presence of motives prompting to wrong conduct; and is therefore not applicable to beings [such as God] to whom no such conflict of motives can be attributed'.

[25] The distinction between imperative and attractive notions is, it should be said, not easy to explain. There is even room to ask whether at bottom it is really a clear distinction at all. We want to count as imperatives terms those, like 'ought', that are not actually used in what are grammatically commmands, but still convey a sense of being commanded. And we want to contrast these terms with terms which, like 'good', give a sense of being attracted but not, it seems, any sense of being commanded. What is it, though, to give a command? That is not fully clear. That there is a difference between being commanded and being attracted, however, seems plain enough even in the absence of an explanation of it, and so does the difference between terms that give a sense of a command and those that do not.

On one view of commands, which is advanced by John Austin and can be loosely traced back to Suarez and Locke, a command is an expression of a desire that a person do a particular action, combined with an

Philosophers who object to imperative language in ethics think that attractive notions, including notions of the virtues, do not have the defects associated with imperatives. Attractive terms do not mislead us, these philosophers say, by purporting to lend a bogus air of authority to the statements in which they appear. These terms also do not suggest the conceptual oddity that supposedly attaches to the idea of a command without a commander.

II. The Ethics of Duty and the Ethics of Virtue

1. The Ethics of Virtue as a Way of Avoiding Imperatives

One of the manifestations of philosophical antipathy to imperative notions has been a preference for what is called the *ethics of virtue* over the *ethics of duty*. Virtue is to be classified as an attractive rather than imperative notion. So too, arguably, are most of the several notions of particular virtues, such as bravery, temperance, and so forth. Conscientiousness might be an exception, since it seems to designate a disposition to do one's duty. Still, the common notions of virtue are by and large attractive rather than imperative in nature.

As a rough first approximation, I have said that an ethics of virtue is an ethical out-look, or view, or doctrine in which terms designating virtues, or the term 'virtue' itself, are especially prominent, and in which terms like 'duty' are less so.[26] An ethics of duty puts it the other way around. This will do as a way of gesturing at the type of distinction we need to have in mind. However, there are other, more precise ways of drawing the distinction than simply by degree of 'prominence', and occasionally I shall make use of some of them. Many philosophers, however, deploy the distinction in a very loose way, so it is useful at this juncture to think of the contrast, as I have done

---

indication that the person will suffer in some way if he does not comply. Along these lines one might hope to reduce a command to a presentation of a choice: either you do this or (I will bring it about that) some evil will befall you.

Against this explanation of commands, however, Hart objects as follows (1961: 19–20): 'To command is characteristically to exercise authority over men, not power to inflict harm, and though it may be com-bined with threats of harm a command is primarily an appeal not to fear but to respect for authority.' In a similar spirit, Adam Smith holds that what motivates us to abide by rules of duty is not the threat of a sanc-tion, even a divine sanction, but rather a 'natural sense of duty', consisting in a 'regard' or 'reverence' towards general rules of a certain sort (1976: 159–65, 171–4). And of course Kant's notion of 'respect for the moral law' is similar to this and descended from it.

Hart is right, perhaps, that commands 'characteristically' invoke authority. It is not clear, though, that for something to be a command, authority has to be invoked. Sometimes, it would seem, mere fear of some bad outcome is enough.

[26] See Chapter 2, sec. V. 1.

just now, simply as a matter of the relative prominence of one or the other type of notion.[27]

Accordingly, a good way to avoid imperative notions, particularly the notion of duty, would seem to be to adopt an ethics of virtue. That is exactly the line of thought that a good many recent writers on ethics have followed. This is not to say that the notion of duty is excluded from an ethics of virtue, or vice versa. Virtues can, for instance, be thought of as 'requiring' or 'demanding' particular actions.[28] The point is merely that an ethics 'of' virtue is normally thought of mainly as one that relies especially on virtue-related notions, and correspondingly less on the obvious alternative, namely, the notion of duty. By the same token, the chief motivation to adopt an ethics of virtue is often to avoid the notion of duty, or at least a heavy reliance on it.

Rarely, in fact, does one find a philosophical defence of the ethics of virtue that does not take its start from a criticism of notions like duty and obligation, and from a rejection, too, of the practice of placing duty at the centre of ethical theories and discussions—a practice that has been common during much of this century.[29]

Certainly the recent revival of the ethics of virtue has been closely associated with a simultaneous reaction against the ethics of Kant, and especially against his way of understanding morality as centred on the Categorical Imperative. But the same revival has also been directed against classical forms of Utilitarianism, and also against the kind of intuitionist ethics which, as in A. C. Ewing or W. D. Ross, places heavy stress on the notion of duty.[30] Kant is the most prominent target, because of his salient use of the notion of an 'imperative', but he is by no means the only one.

It seems fair to say, furthermore, that among the various considerations that have led some philosophers to reject an ethics of duty in favour of an ethics of virtue, the principal stimulus is the desire to avoid the imperative notions that are the focus of the former, or at least to minimize their importance. The goal of such philosophers is not always to escape from the idea or institution of morality. For one thing, some defences of the ethics of virtue have nothing bad to say about morality itself.[31] Moreover, there is no reason why an ethics of virtue may not be a morality in a fairly standard sense.

[27] For instance, an ethics of duty can be thought of as an ethics in which the notion of duty is definitionally basic and notions of virtue are defined in terms of it, whereas an ethics of virtue would be an ethics in which the order of definition is reversed. Thus, in an ethics of duty the actions that are duties would be specified in terms of a rule or rules of duty, and then a virtuous person would be defined as someone who usually does his duty. On this notion of the contrast between an ethics of virtue and an ethics of duty, see further Frankena 1973a: 63–8, and 1976b: 1–17, repr. in 1976a: 148–60, along with Larmore 1990.

[28] See e.g. Foot 1978b: 53, 54.

[29] Geach 1977; Foot 1978e; Wallace 1978; Baier 1985. A partial exception is Dent 1984. One account of virtue ethics that is less hostile to the notion of duty is Moravcsik 1990.

[30] It is easy to see to what a great extent the revival of interest in the ethics of virtue is generated by a reaction against Kant just by considering Anscombe 1958, which was instrumental in starting the revival, and by perusing a recent collection of essays that continues it, namely, French, Uehling, and Wettstein 1988.

[31] Slote 1990: e.g. at 429–30.

Rather, regardless of what is to be said about morality, the aim is simply to avoid, either wholly or to some extent, the imperative formulations of norms.[32]

The issues of imperativity and morality, though they are distinct, find themselves closely linked in recent discussions. For example, Bernard Williams writes: 'The reasons for [the unjustified] neglect [of the virtues] chiefly lie in a narrow view of ethical concerns and a concentration on the preoccupations of morality.'[33] One of the main motivations for objecting to morality, in the sense of that term that Williams has in mind, is itself a desire to avoid the particular moral notion of duty and to achieve its replacement by a different sort of notion of virtue. Similar motivations can be seen in works of Anscombe, Richard Taylor, and Charles Taylor, among others.[34] If the prevailing line of criticism of the concept of morality did not arise in some degree from opposition to imperativity in ethics, then one would expect to find, among suggested alternatives to morality, some that made free use of imperative but *non*-moral notions. But the tendency of virtue ethics—to react to the notion of duty by looking instead to notions of virtue—bespeaks an opposition to imperatives themselves, as does the frequency with which proponents of the ethics of virtue focus their criticism on imperative terms like 'duty', 'obligation', and 'law'.

2. Other Considerations Supporting the Ethics of Virtue

It would be a mistake to contend, however, that objections to imperative notions constitute the only consideration motivating the idea that the ethics of virtue is superior to the ethics of duty. It may be argued that other advantages attach to the ethics of virtue besides simply its avoidance of imperativity. Some proponents of certain versions of the ethics of virtue, for instance, do not contend that notions like duty are misconceived per se, but only that they do not cover the full range of ethical or even moral phenomena, and that they therefore need to be supplemented, not replaced, by virtue notions.[35]

In this vein, it is commonly held that the ethics of duty focuses too much on the evaluation of actions and not enough on the assessment of other kinds of things. In particular, the claim is, the ethics of duty neglects important matters concerning the assessment of individuals, their traits, and their overall characters.[36] Nietzsche gave

---

[32] Moreover, it is clear that not all terms that figure in morality are imperatives; see e.g. the distinction in Gert 1988: ch. 8 between moral requirements and moral ideals, along with Sinnott-Armstrong 1988: 11–15.   [33] See Williams 1985: 205.

[34] See Anscombe 1958; R. Taylor 1988; C. Taylor 1989: 79–80, 89–90.

[35] See esp. Baier 1988.

[36] It is also sometimes held that the evaluation of whole lives needs to be allowed for, and it is sometimes suggested that here, too, concepts of virtue are of use. For the idea of assessing a 'whole life', see Williams 1985: 4–5 and Nussbaum 1986: 1–10, 87, 292–4. For one way of connecting the assessments of traits and lives, see Burnyeat 1971.

voice to this thought. 'It is obvious', he says, 'that moral designations were everywhere first and foremost applied to *human beings* and only later, derivatively, to actions. Therefore it is a gross mistake when historians of morality start from such questions as: why was the compassionate act praised?'[37] Some philosophers who adopt this type of view think that attention to the notion of duty merely needs to be supplemented by due attention and respect to the notion of virtue as well. More common in recent times, however, is the idea that the notion of duty ought to be accorded much less importance than it has been, or even put aside altogether in favor of the notion of virtue.[38]

Whether actions or characters ought to be the primary objects of ethical evaluation is a genuine question. However, accepting the latter alternative does not force us to accept an ethics of virtue, since we can speak of how a person *must* be or *ought* to be, without employing, let alone stressing, attractive terms like 'good' or the virtue terms. That fact itself shows that the rejection of imperativity is not the only idea supporting the ethics of virtue. Nevertheless, the rejection of imperativity plays an important role even in areas where it does not initially appear to be the principal consideration. Think, for instance, of the idea that when someone does a kindness to somone else— such as visiting a sick friend in the hospital—but does so simply because he takes it to be his duty, he might seem to fail to show the kind of benevolent personal concern that we hope to receive from, and praise in, our friends and associates.[39] To describe the situation in imperative terms alone seems to omit something that an ethics of virtue might be well suited to make us attend to.

There is an additional reason for asserting that a sense of duty is not, or is not entirely, the appropriate sort of motivation in such cases. The conscientious visitor makes his rounds because he thinks he *ought* to, 'because he thought it his duty'. If that is so, the thought seems to be, then something is *telling* him to do it, and moreover that that something is distinct from himself. So, it is felt, the stimulus does not fully come from *him*. This feeling may be accompanied by the thought that in such a case, the considerations supporting the imperative do not take sufficient account of the well-being of the person to whom it is addressed, and that an ethics of virtue may be superior in this regard.[40]

I think that this sense—that one's duty is done in response to an imperative—is a crucial part of what motivates the idea that the ethics of virtue has something to offer that the ethics of duty fails to supply. There may even exist a yet more general sense

[37] Nietzsche 1966b: sec. 260.

[38] See, for instance, Stocker 1976, Dent 1984. For discussion of and reservations about this strategy, see Frankena 1973a: 65–7 and 1973b; Baier 1988; Conly 1988.

[39] See Stocker 1990. For a defence of Kant's views on this score see also Baier 1988.

[40] See e.g. Slote 1990: 435–7, where he associates Hume also with this view (cf. Hume 1975: Bk. 4, sec. 262).

that the notion of virtue is somehow always less closely associated with deliberative conflict in general than the notion of duty is.[41] At any rate, the idea of imperativity and the desire to escape from it are the important things to focus on.

III. The Nostalgic Flight from Imperativity

To thinkers who have objected to imperative notions in ethics, and especially to those who have attacked the modern notion of morality for relying on such notions, Greek ethics has been an indispensable source of ideas. These thinkers have looked to the Greeks both for ideas about how to avoid imperative notions and for a supply of attractive concepts to take their place.

The idea that Greek ethics contains such a supply is an old and well established one. Sidgwick, for instance, speaks of 'the old Greek view of ethics, in which the notions of Good and Virtue were taken as fundamental' by contrast with 'the modern view in which ethics is conceived as primarily a study of the "moral code"'.[42] More fully, he explains the contrast this way. It is possible, he says,

to take a view of virtuous action in which . . . [the] notion of rule or dictate is at any rate only latent or implicit, the moral ideal being presented as attractive rather than imperative . . . This . . . was the fundamental ethical conception in the Greek schools of Moral Philosophy generally.[43]

Sidgwick himself does not praise Greek ethics for its neglect of imperative notions. He thinks that these notions form an essential part of a reasonable ethical view. Sidgwick's account, however, concurs with the account of Greek ethics that has been offered by both kantian and hegelian interpreters, and in general with those interpreters—philosophers and others as well—who have been nostalgic for Greek ethical thought. This account fits with a picture of 'the Greeks' as purveyors of a homogenous intellectual culture that can be easily idealized and set off against the ills of modernity.

This same spirit can be felt in the way in which Matthew Arnold described the Greek view in contrast to the Jewish one: 'The uppermost idea with Hellenism is to see things as they really are; the uppermost idea with Hebraism is conduct and obedience.'[44] And much earlier, David Hume had compared his own emphasis on the virtues to the prominence given them by the ancients. He contrasts both the ancients and himself with 'modern philosophers', who treat 'all morals [as] on a like footing with civil laws, guarded by the sanctions of reward and punishment'. This is due,

---

[41] On the idea that virtue is not subject to conflict, and for some difficulties lying in the way of justifying that idea, see Becker 1990–1.

[42] Sidgwick 1931: 97.

[43] Sidgwick 1907: 105–6.

[44] Arnold 1971: 88.

Hume says, to the fact that '[i]n later times, philosophy of all kinds, especially ethics, have been more closely united with theology than ever they were observed to be among the heathens'.[45] Like Anscombe, Hume has in mind the thought that the modern view of ethics is derived historically from a conception of ethics as expounding divine laws and is wholly dependent on that conception.

On the basis of this tradition of interpretation, it is now standard in modern treatments to hold that ancient ethics is far less concerned with imperative ethical notions than is modern ethics, and that the Greeks concentrate far more heavily on concepts like goodness and virtue. Greek ethical writings are claimed to be much more concerned to inculcate virtuous traits rather than to propound rules of obligation. Anscombe thinks of herself as going back to a position more like Aristotle's when she rejects phrases like 'morally ought' and 'morally wrong' and makes use instead of concepts like 'human flourishing', which is roughly equivalent to the Greek term *eudaimonia* (often translated also as 'happiness').[46] Similarly for MacIntyre in *After Virtue*, Aristotelian ethics is, among other things, an ethics in which the notion of virtue plays a central role.[47] And 'the key question' is 'can Aristotelian ethics, or something very like it, after all be vindicated?'.[48]

IV. Imperatives, Attractives, and Repulsives

1. The Search for an Attractive Ancient Ethics

There is of course far more that gives rise to the idealization of Greek ethics than merely the belief that it eschewed imperativity. The contention that Greek thinking was based on attractive notions is tied to the very general view of it that is typified by Matthew Arnold's characterization of it as a region of 'sweetness and light'.[49] This description is even broader than the thought that Greek ethics does without the moti-

---

[45] Hume 1975: App. IV, sec. 268.

[46] Anscombe 1958: 8, 17–19.

[47] One might also argue a link between this view and the idea that Greek culture was, in the terms of Ruth Benedict, a 'shame culture' rather than a 'guilt culture'. (See her 1946: ch. 10.) If there is a link, it would arise from the idea that guilt is tied to transgressing a *law or command*, whereas shame involves a failure to be *good* enough (cf. Williams 1985: 223). Dodds 1951: ch. 2 holds that between the time of the Homeric poems and the Classical period, Greek culture shifted from the former to the latter. Here he is no doubt influenced by Nietzsche's idea that Archaic Greek heroes were free of 'slave morality', and instead tried to live up to standards of excellence (Nietzsche 1966b: sec. 260, paras. 3–4). Lloyd-Jones 1983: 26, on the other hand, says that Greek culture remained a shame culture 'until well after the fifth century'. It seems to me that he is right, though, to stress that it is hard to classify a culture in one way or the other. In view of the evidence that I give in the text, the best thing to say is, in broad outline, that Greek culture was all along a cross between the two types.

[48] MacIntyre 1981: 111.

[49] Cf. Chapter 1, sec. II. 5.

vational dualism implicit in the use of imperative notions. The description suggests that Greek ethics does its work entirely on the basis of positive, attractive motivational force, and has no dark, negative side of the sort that might be used to counteract conflicting motivations.

This view of Greek ethics, however, is straightforwardly wrong. Indeed, no one can adequately understand what the Greeks wrote about ethical matters without being aware of its incompleteness. For it conveys the impression that Greek ethics postulated, in a good man, a single motivation, attraction to the good, to which no other motivation could stand in opposition. On such an account, the only reason why a person might fail to seek the good would be ignorance of what it is or where it lies—the paradigm of this way of thinking being the Socratic thesis that no one willingly does what is bad. Once one discovered what the good is, then, one would be motivated solely by one's attraction to it. There would be no need to counteract any other opposing motivation.

In addition to notions like 'good' and 'fine'—and quite aside from imperative notions like 'ought' and 'duty'—Greek thinkers often employ notions of another important sort: what I shall call *repulsive* notions such as 'bad' and 'ugly'.[50] Analogously to attractive notions, which convey an idea of being attracted by something, repulsive notions convey an idea of being repelled by something.

Being repelled by a thing does not require or imply being attracted by something else. Likewise, the force of repulsive concepts is not captured by any definition in terms of attractive concepts alone. In the first place, for example, to say that spitefulness is bad is to say more than just that the absence or the contrary of spitefulness is good. There are things whose absence or contrary is good, but which are themselves not bad, but rather are only so-so and are to be regarded with indifference. Nor is the idea that spitefulness is bad captured by saying that the avoidance of spitefulness is good, or even by saying that it is very, very good. This may even be false, even though spitefulness is bad. In the second place, the force of saying that spitefulness is bad is not captured by saying simply that spitefulness lacks goodness. For that is compatible, once again, with spitefulness's being simply so-so or neutral.

To be sure, some philosophers have held that there is a property of badness which is merely the total absence or lack of goodness. This view is often attributed to Plato and often also to philosophers like Augustine who were influenced directly or indirectly by him.[51] Nevertheless, I do not think that this idea touches the point at issue here. Perhaps some metaphysical thesis tells us that the property of badness (if there is

---

[50] It might be argued that in addition to imperative notions we also need *permissive* ones. I take it that being permitted to X is for relevant purposes equivalent to not being commanded not to X (and being commanded to X is equivalent to not being permitted not to X), so that permissive force can be explained in terms of imperative force.

[51] See e.g. Cherniss 1971 and Augustine, *Confessions* III. 7.

such a thing) is nothing but the property of lacking goodness (if there is such a thing). But regardless of that, it seems clearly false to say that our *concept* or notion of badness is just our *concept* or notion of the absence of goodness.[52] Whether by a metaphysical mistake or not, we all use a concept of 'affirmative' badness that is not at all simply the concept of a lack. The thesis at the word 'evil' expresses an affirmative notion in this sense has often been upheld. The same, however, seems just as clearly true of the word 'bad'.[53] In that sense, one can say that our set of evaluative concepts has what we might call a 'Manichaean' structure.

The root cause of the irreducibility of repulsive to attractive notions seems to be this. As I have said, being repelled by a thing is, so to speak, an affirmative rejection of it, not merely a reaction to something else that draws one away from it. Repulsion in this sense is what terms like 'bad', as well as 'ugly', 'disgusting', and so forth, often are called on to signal.[54]

2. Repulsives and Affirmative Badness in Greek Ethics

Greek popular morality uses repulsive terms liberally. The word for 'bad', *kakos*, frequently appears as contrary to the standard word for 'good', *agathos*. Even more striking is the word *aischros*, customarily translated as 'ugly' or 'shameful' but also used in the sense of 'disgraceful', 'scandalous', 'base', or even just 'nasty'. In standard Greek, *kakos* does not simply express a thing's lack of being *agathos*. Even more clearly, *aischros* does not simply express a thing's failure to be *kalos*. *Kalos*, too, can be translated in various ways: 'beautiful', 'fine', 'splendid', 'admirable', 'creditable', 'honourable' are all possibilities. To say that a thing is *aischros* is to say more than that it simply fails to be one of these things.[55]

There is a reason why. To say that a thing is *kalos* is to suggest that it is the appropriate object of any of a range of attitudes, such as attraction, awe, admiration, respect. The word *aischros*, on the other hand, is linked not to the mere absence of these responses, but to affirmative responses of another sort: shame, disgust, and so forth— the impulse to hide oneself, and the impulse to avoid looking at a thing. The term

---

[52] Likewise, there seems to me no reason to accept Nietzsche's contention that 'bad', in the sense of 'low' or 'common', was invented in any sense subsequently to the invention of 'good' in the sense of 'noble' (even if, for the sake of argument, one accepts other parts of his view about these notions). See Nietzsche 1966e: Essay 1, sec. 10.

[53] This holds true even when 'bad' is not taken as equivalent to 'evil', since 'evil' has, for example, theological overtones that 'bad' can lack completely.

[54] This is not to say, of course, that repulsion is all that they express. It is also why to say that one thing is good and another is bad is not just to say that the former is preferred, or preferable, to the latter—even though it may suit philosophical argumentation to replace the notions of good and bad with notions like that of preference.

[55] See Dover 1974: 69–73, 236–42.

kakos, although it is nominally a more general word, is closely associated both with the word *aischros* (to which it is often equivalent) and with those same responses. Each member of each pair of contraries is connected to a distinct type of affect and response. Neither indicates merely the absence of one.

Once we notice that repulsive notions are in this way separate from attractive ones, we can easily see that Greek philosophers make substantial use of the former as well as the latter. Plato and Aristotle freely use *kakon* as well as *aischron* to express the opposites of *agathon* and *kalon*. Both philosophers also use 'badness' or 'bad characteristic' (*kakia*, sometimes misleadingly translated 'vice') as the opposite of 'excellence' (*arete*), and they do so in a way that clearly conveys an affirmatively unfavourable reaction, so to speak, rather than simply the absence of a favourable one. Plato also makes room for a class of things that can be regarded as neutral, neither affirmatively good nor affirmatively bad (*Rep.* 583–7), which shows that 'bad' for him does not mean simply 'failing to be good'.

Any description of the Greeks as simply the purveyors of sweetness and light must largely ignore their use of these repulsive notions, which figure in their thinking in no merely marginal way. Aristotle's doctrine in *Nicomachean Ethics* II–V, for example, is that virtue is a mean or intermediate state between excess on the one hand and deficiency on the other. This doctrine describes badness of character in patently affirmative terms. Badness is not merely a lack. It is the possession of certain traits in *either* deficiency *or* excess. According to Aristotle's parallel, 'the master of any art avoids excess and deficiency, but seeks the intermediate and chooses this'.[56] The extremes as such are to be affirmatively avoided, just as the mean is to be affirmatively sought.

No more than Aristotle does Plato dispense with the concept of affirmative badness, nor does Aristotle's account depict the bad man as simply lacking the goodness that characterizes his opposite. The descriptions of various sorts of injustice of the soul in *Republic* VIII–IX are cases in point. The tyrant in Book IX, for instance, experiences affirmative discomfort and pain in his life, and is affirmatively vicious, not merely someone with deficient consciousness and deficient impact on what goes on around him. His motivation is characterized not primarily by a failure to be attracted by the Good, but by the strength of a countervailing desire, namely lust, which takes control of him and his actions (572b–573c). In less extreme form, the same is true of each of the other inferior personalities that Plato treats. Their inferiority is in each case constituted by an affirmative tendency to something other than the good. Thus the timocratic man aims at honour (548d–550c), the oligarchic personality aims at money (553a–e), and the democratic man is ruled by a disorganized plurality of appetites (559d–562a).[57]

---

[56] *Nic. Eth.* 1106b6–7, in Ross's translation (with 'deficiency' replacing Ross's 'defect').

[57] The point is reinforced by the fact that Plato pictures each desire that has its seat outside of reason as an attraction to something distinct from the good (437b–439b).

3. Greek Ethics and Greek Metaphysics

These facts are obvious enough once one thinks about the evidence. There is, though, a straightforward reason why they often go unstressed or even unnoticed. The reason is a striking lack of parallelism between Greek ethics, on the one hand, and, on the other, certain doctrines that are prominent in Greek metaphysics. Greek metaphysics tends not to reflect the role that repulsive notions have in Greek ethics. Greek metaphysical philosophy tends to treat attractive notions as though they were metaphysically fundamental, and neglects what one might call the metaphysics of the repulsive notions. If we concentrate too much on the structure of Greek metaphysics, then, we can easily lose sight of the facts about the ethics.[58]

This is the way things are, for instance, in Plato's description, at *Republic* 505–11, of the Form of the Good. The role of the Good is not balanced by any role for a Form of the Bad.[59] That fact has made it look as though Plato accepts the Augustinian idea that badness is nothing at all beyond the absence of goodness, even though there is plenty of reason to reject that interpretation of Plato's metaphysical position itself.[60] Moreover, as I have said, repulsive evaluations play an essential role in Plato's characterization of the various degrees of injustice to which a person may be subject.

Aristotle's metaphysics likewise fails to give a clear picture of the extent to which repulsive notions figure in his ethics. In his metaphysics, the Prime Mover functions as a cause of all change. It is unopposed by any Prime Stopper, or by any other contrary metaphysical force such as an affirmative impetus producing what is bad.[61] That fact, however, does not prevent Aristotle from using repulsive notions in his description of the vices.

In view of these facts about Greek metaphysics, it is not difficult to understand why historical accounts neglect the role of repulsive notions in Greek ethics. Once we focus our attention away from metaphysics, however, the facts about Greek ethics come much more clearly into view. We then lose the temptation to suppose that all Greek ethical judgements convey a sense of being *drawn towards* something good or beautiful or otherwise attractive, and never a sense of being repelled by something. Then we can escape from Arnold's picture of Greek thought as pervaded by sweetness and light, and can start to see the full complexity of Greek ethical discourse in all of its various aspects.

---

[58] Gauthier and Jolif point out that a philosopher's metaphysical treatment of a notion may diverge from his treatment of it within ethical discussions (1970: i. 285).

[59] In fact it is not clear whether indeed Plato believed in such a thing; the evidence is ambiguous enough to make the point controversial. For evidence that he did, see Vlastos 1965: 5–9.

[60] See Cherniss 1971.

[61] See *Met.* XII. 7, 9–10 as well as the treatment of the good in *Nic. Eth.* I. The point is not affected by what Aristotle says about matter. He does not as a rule think of it as resisting the forces that form, moving cause, and purpose bring to bear on it, and he certainly does not think of it as resisting those forces in the way in which an opposing force would.

Facts about Greek metaphysical views also help us understand why observers of Greek ethics have not expected to find it using imperatives, and have therefore tended to minimize the role of such notions in it. The metaphysical doctrines of the Greeks contain few of the elements that we would expect to be associated with imperativity. In modern theological ethics, in particular, we are accustomed to views that hypostatize a deity who issues commands, which are taken in turn as the basis of ethical standards. For us, this idea is often taken as the paradigm that gives rise to imperative ethical norms.

When we turn to Greek thought, however, we see a different picture. The metaphysical theologies of Plato and Aristotle do not by and large present us with gods who act through imperatives. No dictates are issued by Aristotle's unmoved mover in *Metaphysics* XII and *Physics* VIII. Instead, the Aristotelian unmoved mover causes motion in the world, not by commanding it nor by decreeing that it occur, but rather by the fact that the perfection of its state *draws* things on, by functioning as in some sense a goal of what they do. Plato's view is similar, though less consistent. In the *Timaeus*, the so-called demiurge or divine craftsman mainly moulds or forms things in the physical world, though he is also sometimes pictured as issuing commands.[62] When we move to Greek philosophy of the Hellenistic period, we see that Epicurus explicitly rejects the idea that there are gods who command us or threaten us with punishments. So when we think of these three particular Greek philosophers, we can easily gain the impression that commanders and commands have little place in Greek metaphysics.

No doubt these facts are much of the cause of the widespread notion that imperative notions do not play a role in Greek ethical thought. But as in the case of repulsives, Greek metaphysics is not a good guide to the structure of Greek ethics. For in fact the Greeks use imperative terms a great deal in their ethics, in both philosophical contexts and non-philosophical ones.

V. Uses of Imperativity in Greek Literature

1. Imperatives in Early Greek Literature

In order to comprehend the true state of Greek ethics, then, rather than expecting that Greek metaphysics will faithfully represent it, we have to look at the shape of Greek ethical thinking itself. Moreover, we should examine not just the ethical doctrines of the philosophers, but also, at the start, the way in which ethical ideas are presented more broadly in the culture as it is represented in its literature. Then we can turn to the working out of these ideas by the philosophers.

---

[62] See, however, the use of imperatives at 41c ff.

Outside philosophy, the facts about Greek culture in general are perfectly clear. So far from avoiding the feeling or concept of imperativity, the Greeks are thoroughly familiar with ethical norms framed as imperatives. It does not take more than a few prominent examples to make the point evident. From the *Iliad* and the *Odyssey* onward, humans are accustomed to thinking of certain courses of action as enjoined by the gods. Punishments for violating those plans are the most prominent feature of the Greek religious outlook.

Illustrations are easy to come by. The *Odyssey* begins with the discussion and formulation of a plan by Athena and Zeus, which they wish to communicate to Odysseus (1.85–6), so as to allow him to return to his home on the island of Ithaca. Athena then goes to Ithaca to approach Odysseus' son, Telemachus, and, disguised as Mentes, gives him directives about what to do to secure his father's return (e.g., 1.269 ff.). When she leaves by flying away in the shape of a bird, Telemachus recognizes that it is a goddess who has enjoined him.[63]

The *Iliad* also is dominated not only by divine plans but also by the dictates that result from them. In the beginning, Apollo causes a struggle between Achilles and Agamemnon (1.8 ff.). The most overarching plan, though, comes from Zeus. First its existence is announced to the other gods and goddesses, along with a threat of punishment for disobedience (8.5–14):

Hearken unto me, all ye gods and goddesses, that I may speak what the heart in my breast biddeth me. Let not any goddess nor yet any god essay this thing, to thwart my word, but do you all alike assent thereto, that with all speed I may bring these deeds to pass. Whomsoever I shall mark minded apart from the gods to go and bear aid either to Trojans or Danaans, smitten in no seemly wise shall he come back to Olympus, or I shall take and hurl him into murky Tartarus, far, far away.[64]

This passage conveys the general tone associated with the relations between gods, or gods like Zeus, and humans in the Homeric poems: do what I say or I'll hurl you into Tartarus. That tone did not change much during the next generations, into the Classical period of the late fifth century BCE. The use of the notions of law and dictate are common—just as common as they are in modern ethical discourse. The justice of Zeus, the king and most powerful of the gods, is a justice of dictates and sanctions. Some of his dictates are individual and ad hoc, such as the one just cited from the *Iliad*—but a command need not be general, or be part of a code, in order to be a command. Moreover, other dictates of Zeus are indeed general. Prominent among the general dictates are ones saying that oaths are not to be broken, and that strangers,

---

[63] Athena's injunction coincides with a wish that Telemachus already has, to find his father; the directive tells him how to do that (being thus something like a kantian 'hypothetical imperative'). It is thus all the more striking – in the context of the thesis that Greek thinking tended away from the use of imperatives – that the imperative mood is employed here, even though it need not have been.

[64] Trans. A. T. Murray. The plan itself is given in 8.469ff. See Lloyd-Jones 1983.

guests, and suppliants are not to be harmed.[65] The imperativity of Zeus' injunctions is evident. His arsenal of punishments includes, notably, the thunderbolt—a phenomenon scarcely calculated to motivate human beings by its attractiveness.

Hesiod, writing probably not long after the time of the Homeric poems, says that 'for those who practise violence and cruel deeds far-seeing Zeus, the son of Cronos, ordains a punishment (*dike*). Often even a whole city suffers for a bad man who sins and devises presumptuous deeds', and 'whoever deliberately lies in his witness and forswears himself and so hurts justice (*dike*) and sins beyond repair, that man's generation is left obscure thereafter'.[66] According to Pindar, quoted in Plato's *Gorgias*: 'Law is king over all, mortals and immortals; he governs everything, making just what is most violent with arm supreme'.[67] Likewise, a famous passage in Sophocles' *Antigone* speaks of both laws (*nomoi*) and what is in accord with unwritten law (*agrapha nomima*):

> CREON. And you had the gall to break this law?
> ANTIGONE. Of course I did. It wasn't Zeus, not in the least,
>   who made this proclamation—not to me.
>   Nor did that Justice, dwelling with the gods
>   beneath the earth, ordain such laws (*nomoi*) for men.
>   Nor did I think your edict had such force
>   that you, a mere mortal, could override the gods,
>   the great unwritten, unshakable traditions (*nomima*).[68]

These passages are far from being exceptional. The whole of Greek literature in the Classical period is full of an association of justice with law. It is full, too, of the thought that the laws of justice are to be obeyed, that they are dictates that humans must follow even when they do not wish to.[69] The point here is not that these dictates are *moral* ones in some specific sense. That is a quite different issue. The present point is that in this period of Greek thought, ethical norms are often felt and presented as imperatives, and that attractive terms are far from bearing the whole weight of promulgating standards.[70]

---

[65] See Lloyd-Jones 1983: 5.

[66] Hesiod, *Works and Days*, ll. 238–41, 282–4.

[67] Pindar, frag. 169, at Plato, *Gorg.* 484b.

[68] Sophocles, *Antigone*, trans. Fagles, ll. 499–505. See also e.g. ll. 396, 410, 825, and *Oedipus Rex* 957–63.

[69] See, for example, Lloyd-Jones 1983: esp. 5ff., 49–51, 79–85, 94–5. Passages like these show the deficiency of the view (expressed e.g. by Brochard 1901: 7–8) that *nomos* always means merely 'custom' rather than anything imperatival.

[70] Lloyd-Jones is clearly right, I think, that the Greeks believed that the gods act justly, and that they took this concept of justice seriously. Lloyd-Jones also believes that the notion of justice in question is a 'moral' one. On that issue, see Chapter 2, sec. IV.

2. Imperatives and Codes: Reasons for the Neglect of Imperatives in the Historiography of Greek Ethics

That imperatives are present in these passages is clear enough. Why has it therefore been possible for readers to take so little notice of this fact, and think that imperativity is unimportant in Greek thinking in general? To this question one answer readily comes to mind. It has to do not with whether imperatives are used, but with the form in which they are organized and presented in Greek literary writings. Even though Greek literature and mythology contains imperatively formulated norms arising from commands issued by gods, there is little or no tendency to *systematize* or *codify* them.

This is the element of truth in Sidgwick's contrast, already cited, between Greek ethics and 'the modern view in which ethics is conceived as primarily a study of the "moral code"'.[71] The Greeks do put imperatives into the mouths of their gods. But when the Greek gods express their will, they do so mainly in an ad hoc and piecemeal manner, not in a systematic or even a compact format, such as the Ten Commandments of the Hebrew Bible. They do not promulgate a code. From the things that the Greek gods tend to punish, we can often extract generalizations about what they approve or disapprove of. A case in point is the injunction of Zeus against harming suppliants. In instances of this sort, a god indicates displeasure and the human being infers what the god was displeased about. These generalizations are then articulated as, for example, a general norm against harming suppliants or guests. Even then, however, the norms are not organized or related to each other in any systematic way.

A second fact likewise contributes to the tendency in modern times to overlook the role of imperatives in Greek ethics. We usually think of laws and commands as promulgated explicitly and publicly, so that an opportunity is available to examine them and understand their formulation exactly. In Greek literature, however, the commands of the gods do not follow this pattern. By and large, the gods do not express their plans through overt statements, let alone explicit codes. They do not, for instance, tell a mortal that they are about to issue commands which are to be written down on tablets and conveyed to human beings at large. Instead, as Hugh Lloyd-Jones stresses, the gods mainly work through the thoughts and other mental states of individuals. The reservations that a person might feel about a proposed course of action are interpreted as a god's warning to him which is inserted into his thoughts. This procedure is pervasive in the *Iliad* and the *Odyssey*. We also see it in the case of Socrates, who often spoke—for example, in Plato's *Apology*—of the spirit, the *daimonion*. It would come to him and silently warn him away from particular plans, but it did not give him a rationale, let alone a system of injunctions or even prohibitions.

[71] Sidgwick 1931: 97

It is of course true that notions other than imperative ones—both attractive and repulsive—are very important in Greek ethics. It may well be true to say, too, that Greek ethics, especially in the Classical period, gives imperative notions a less important role than does modern ethics. However, it is wrong to think that Greek philosophers came close to doing without imperatives. It is equally wrong to think that they made any effort to dispense with or avoid them.

It is also wrong in this regard, as in so many others, to think that Greek ethical thought and Greek culture in general fit any simple pattern. We find it all too easy, especially after two hundred years of somewhat stereotyped ideas about the style and tendencies of Greek culture, to think that Greek culture and art set the tone for Greek philosophy, and the Greek philosophers simply developed or elaborated, with perhaps some superficial disagreements among themselves, what the culture presented them with. When we look, however, at the role of imperative and attractive notions in Greek literature and philosophy, we find a clear illustration of how misleading this picture is. Greek philosophical thought is not a straightforward mirror of the outlook that Greek literature exhibits. And Greek philosophical thinking is itself far from uniform.

VI. The Alleged 'Transition' to Roman Christianity: Imperativity in Greek Ethics after Aristotle

1. Against Sidgwick's Account of the Transition: Early Stoic Imperatives

An especially tenacious myth about Greek ethics runs as follows. From thinkers as different as Hegel and Sidgwick we hear that the Greeks of the Classical period preferred attractive norms.[72] But the closer in time we come to the juridical Romans, it continues, the more 'jural or quasi-jural' Greek philosophy becomes. A look at Stoic and Epicurean formulations shows how inadequate this account is.

Let us begin with the Stoics. It is widely known that they used imperative notions. Indeed, it is sometimes said that their thinking led directly to the modern concept of natural law. For example, the early Stoic Chrysippus wrote the following:

Law is king of everything both divine and human . . . and must preside over what is honorable (*kalon*) and what is despicable as ruler and leader. Accordingly, it must be the standard of what is just and unjust, and prescribe (*prostaktikon*) what naturally political animals *must do* (*poieteon*) and prohibiting them from what they *must not do* (*ou poieteon*).[73]

---

[72] Hegel 1991: 251–2, 293; Sidgwick 1931: 105–6.

[73] *SVF* iii. 314; cf. on Zeno i. 262, with Long and Sedley 1987: i. 435 and the texts referred to there, as well as Inwood 1985: 60–3, 160. As noted just below in sec. 2, however, the Stoics also employ attractive notions, as Chrysippus does in this very passage, where he uses the concept of the *kalon*. For an explanation of why the Stoics employ both kinds of notions together, see Chapter 7, sec. IV, esp. IV. 5 and 8.

This is about as clear a use of imperative language as one could ask for.[74]

Sidgwick was not oblivious to the fact that evidence like this makes difficulty for his generalization about the contrast between the ancient use of attractives and the modern use of imperatives. He responded to the problem by describing the Stoics as a 'transitional link' between ancient and modern thinking.[75]

This simple account fits well with another popular story, which I have already mentioned, of the history of Greek culture. That is the story—whose survival I noted in connection with Dodds's views on the role of the irrational in Greek thought—of the Greek cultural decline after the Classical period, ending with the subjugation of Greece by Rome.[76] If one sees something in Greek thought that one wishes to regard as atypical of a truly Greek cast of mind, this story provides the opportunity to try to think of it as late, and thus as indicative of the subsiding of Greece into subordination to Rome.

The Stoics often play a role in this sort of account. Historians of thought, including Sidgwick, tend to regard them as standing closer to modern styles of thinking than other ancient philosophical schools, and as being intermediaries between Greek and Roman culture. Scholars often associate the Stoics closely with the Romans, partly because Stoic philosophy seems to have influenced some Roman thinkers and statesmen.[77] Sometimes, in particular, the Stoics are felt to have anticipated certain Christian views.[78] It is often maintained that the Romans by temperament had a predilection for legal institutions and that this influenced their normative ideas. Hegel thought that Roman interest in the concept of individuals' legal rights anticipated modern individualism.[79] Insofar as Roman legal notions affected western Christianity, scholars can feel free to detect Stoic influence if they wish to. Thus it might appear to make sense to regard the Stoics as transitional, and therefore perhaps an insignificant exception to any generalization about Greek ethics.

This appearance is thoroughly deceptive, however, if it is taken to suggest that the Stoics' ideas were in some way not a genuinely Greek phenomenon.[80] If that

---

[74] Cooper 1996: 276 maintains that, according to the Stoics, even the virtuous man or sage will experience 'virtuous action as something imposed on them'. The evidence that he cites, however, does not seem to me to support this conclusion. See further Chapter 7, sec. VI.

[75] Sidgwick 1907: 105 and 1931: 97. Brochard on the other hand (1901: 3–4, 11–12), who wanted to establish a sharper contrast between ancient and modern ethical notions, thought that the relevant Stoic terminology contains only an 'optative' rather than an 'imperative' element. I do not see good grounds for that claim.

[76] See Chapter 1, sec. III. 2.

[77] Sidgwick expresses this view, 1907: 105 and 1931: 97.

[78] See Pohlenz 1959: i. 400–65.   [79] See Hegel 1991: 253, 268–9, and Wood 1991: 22–3.

[80] Pohlenz suggests that Stoic views had a Semitic origin, largely on the basis merely of the facts that the founder of Stoicism, Zeno, came from Cytium in Cyprus, and that Cyprus had a substantial Semitic population. The evidence for this connection is very weak and the hypothesis seems to be needless, and to be weakened by the evidence exhibited in the present chapter.

suggestion were right, one would expect in the present instance that the strength of imperative notions, and especially of law, would be weaker in the earlier period of the third century BCE, and stronger from the first century BCE onwards, as Roman influence becomes more clearly demonstrable.

This expectation, however, is not fulfilled. Stoic use of the idea of dictates and laws does not only arise in the later period of the school's activity. It flourishes vigorously much earlier, well before Roman intellectual influence had made itself felt. The Stoics' use of the idea of law is not attributable to the influence of Roman juridical notions. I quoted just now a passage by Chrysippus, one of the earlier Stoics, who wrote in the third century BCE. That places the quotation in the 'Hellenistic' period of Greek philosophy—after the 'Classical' period of Plato and Aristotle (whose end is traditionally set at around 322, the date of Aristotle's death), but well before the period of Roman influence. If we tried to think of the Stoics as transitional, the alleged transition would accordingly need to have taken place in the Hellenistic period.

Rather than postulate such a transition at all, it is better to question the generalization that led to it. The whole idea of a Greek neglect of imperative ethical notions is far less convincing than its status as an established historical commonplace makes it seem.

2. Attractive Stoic Formulations

At the same time, however, an examination of Stoic philosophy shows us even more of the complexity of Greek ethical thinking. It would not be correct to picture the Stoics as relying exclusively on the imperative notions of law and dictate. The passage from Chrysippus that I quoted prominently employs the imperative notion of law and dictate. There is more to Stoic ethics, however, than that. Much of it, morever, deals with attractive notions as well as imperative ones.[81]

For one thing, the Stoics say that every human being aims for his own end or *telos*. Accordingly, they spend a great deal of philosophical effort trying to explain what that *telos* is. Their position is that it is 'life in accordance with nature (*physis*)'. This claim then leads them to try to explain what such a life consists in, and what the notion of nature involved in this idea comes to. Moreover, the Stoics concern themselves extensively with the question what the good (*agathon*) is. Here their fundamental doctrine is the well-known thesis that 'the only good is virtue'. It follows, they maintain, that the rational, or wise, human being will aim at virtue.[82] All of these notions—*telos*, good, and virtue—fall squarely within the category of attractive concepts.

It is by putting these passages alongside passages about law like the one that I quoted earlier that we can get a balanced picture of Stoic thinking on these matters. Rather

---

[81] For an explanation of the Stoic use of both types of notion, see Chapter 7, sec. IV, and esp. IV. 9.

[82] *SVF* i. 187–90; Cicero, *De Finibus* III. 21–2, 26–31; *Paradoxa Stoicorum* 6–15.

than focusing exclusively on attractive or imperative concepts, Stoic specifications of the good and of the *telos* introduce an interesting mixture of imperative and attractive language. On the one hand there are formulations like Chrysippus's, which present conformity to nature as a matter of abiding by a certain kind of *law* which *dictates* certain things. At the same time this conformity is treated as the *end* of human life, and as tantamount to virtue, which is *good*.

Confronted with this pair of ideas, what should we think? Is there any tension between them? Someone might wish to expend a great deal of effort to determine which of these two sorts of evaluation the Stoics regard as the more basic or more apt as an expression of their position. Such effort would be misspent. In my opinion, there is no evidence of any Stoic formulation that firmly settles the question one way or the other. The Stoics themselves have no objection to *either* sort of formulation. That means, at the least, that they were not concerned to exclude one kind of evaluative language in favour of the other, nor to exalt one at the other's expense. As the Stoics saw things, a person can certainly have a sense of being attracted to an end. That end is life in accord with nature and with the good, which is virtue. But the idea of a life in accord with nature can without strain also be regarded as consisting in conformity to the law that nature lays down.

The Stoics thus show no sign of treating imperative and attractive formulations as mutually exclusive or inconsistent with each other. As I shall explain later, there is a reason for this indifference on their part.[83] That reason has to do with the particular way in which they try to deal with the apparent facts of deliberative conflict as manifested in ordinary ethical thought. For the present, however, the notable fact is that the Stoics employ both imperative and attractive notions side by side. That should make us less inclined to regard a lack of imperativity as an important feature of Greek ethics.

3. Epicurean Attractives

From Sidgwick's claim that the Stoics' use of imperatives is a symptom of their 'transitional' status, and a similar suggestion of Hegel that the tone of ethics becomes more 'jural' as one moves closer to Roman times,[84] one might suppose that the other great Hellenistic ethical doctrine, Epicureanism, would make some use of the same kind of notion. This, however, is not the case. Indeed, Epicurus is the thinker who, oddly enough, best fits the historical stereotype of the attraction-minded Greek philosopher.

Epicurus is a hedonist in at least two senses. First, he has often been interpreted as a psychological hedonist, that is, as someone who believes that everyone always in fact aims at pleasure as his ultimate end. This interpretation is open to serious question.[85]

---

[83] See Chapter 6, esp. sec. 9.   [84] Hegel 1991: 284–5, 289–91.
[85] See Cooper 1999a.

Second and far more clearly, Epicurus is a hedonist about the human good, or what it is rational for a human being to aim at. That is, he holds that everyone *rationally should* aim at pleasure alone, and that a person's true well-being consists in attaining a pleasant state to the highest degree possible.[86] 'Pleasure' in his sense turns out to be an absence of pain and anxiety. Epicurus takes that to mean that there is a theoretical maximum state of pleasure, that is, the state in which all pain and anxiety are removed.[87]

Social customs and things such as justice, Epicurus believes, have the point of enabling people to pursue their well-being. He pays little attention to the possibilities of conflict between justice and an individual's pursuit of his own greatest good. Indeed, he seems to believe that not much conflict, if any, is in the offing. Clearly, though, social strictures can for him exert no rational force on a person's deliberations, except insofar as obeying them is conducive—as he thinks it quite generally is—to attaining the most pleasant condition one can.[88]

Epicurus has little or no use for imperatives. The Roman poet Lucretius celebrates him for having dispelled people's fear of the gods and of their threats against people who disobey them. When we are free from these fears, Lucretius says, we can appreciate what well-being really is.[89] The Romans may have been legal-minded, as Sidgwick and many others say, but Lucretius could as an Epicurean take a stand directly against formulating an ethical doctrine as a set of commands.

So far, we might still think that the vacillation between imperatives and attractives that the Stoics exhibit, together with Epicurus's reliance on attractive notions, need not shake our faith in Sidgwick's account completely. For we might still retain the feeling that in the Classical period, that is, in the work of Plato and Aristotle, the predominant manner of expressing norms—and thus the way that may be thought of as typical of Greek ethics in its paradigmatic form—relied mainly on attraction and eschewed imperativity.

VII. Imperativity in Aristotle

1. The Prominence of Goodness in Aristotle's Ethics

When we move back to Aristotle we are squarely within the Classical period, the period that has traditionally been regarded as paradigmatically Hellenic. Accordingly, those who have thought that the Greeks avoid imperative notions normally treat

---

[86] For discussion and defence of the ascription of this sort of hedonism to Epicurus, see Chapter 7, sec. III.

[87] See the passages and discussion in Long and Sedley 1987: 112–25.

[88] Long and Sedley 1987: 117–18, 138.

[89] *De Rerum Natura* II. 1–61.

Aristotle as an exemplary case in point. At first sight this attitude seems readily under-standable. Right from the first sentence of his *Nicomachean Ethics*, the emphasis rests on the notion of the good—which is non-imperative if any notion is—and on the kin-dred concept of *eudaimonia* or happiness. The emphasis then quickly passes, from *Nicomachean Ethics* I. 7 onwards, to the concept of virtue (or excellence, *arete*) and the various virtues—which are likewise attractive notions. Subsequently, the explanation of virtue of character (*ethike arete*) takes up all of Books II–V. Then in Book VI, Aristotle turns to the virtues (or excellences) of intellect (*dianoêtikai aretai*).

In the light of such a summary, one would be inclined to say that the notions of good and virtue dominate Aristotle's outlook. The summary scheme of Aristotle's *Ethics* makes us expect a doctrine that has little to do with obligation or imperativity and much to do with goodness and attractiveness, and also a doctrine that places its emphasis entirely on the notion of virtue. That is in fact the normal picture of Aristotle's ethics. However, it is by no means the whole story.

2. Aristotle's Imperative Formulations

In addition to the general scheme of Aristotle's exposition, there is another and deep-er reason why his modern readers often suppose that he must have little use for imper-ativity. This reason has its basis in a general interpretation of his ethics and ethical psychology, and raises issues that I shall deal with in later chapters.[90] The leading idea is that Aristotle does not believe that virtue involves the kind of motivational conflict, in particular a conflict between one's own happiness and broader considerations, that would lead him to formulate ethical norms in imperative terms. If the point of imper-atives is to combat resistance to following ethical norms, this interpretation says, and if Aristotle does not think that a virtuous person encounters any such internal resis-tance, then there would be no occasion in Aristotle's view for the use of imperative language. According to this account, Aristotle would advocate precisely the kind of harmony of motivation that Schiller and others have looked for in Greek ethics.

This interpretation says that because Aristotle adopts a certain general position concerning ethics and motivation, he has no need for imperativity. I shall have a good deal to say within the present chapter about this line of thought, though it extends also, as I have noted, to matters that I shall deal with further when I come to treat Aristotle in his own right.[91] In the present section, however, I want to shift away from this question, namely, 'Which notions does Aristotle *need* to use?' and concentrate for the time being mostly on the question, 'Which notions *does* he actually use?'

In fact, Aristotle's ethical language is substantially different in two ways from what the common impression of it leads one to expect. In the first place, his view is in

---

[90] See esp. Chapter 6, sec. V.   [91] See Chapter 6, secs. II, IV–V, and IX.

an important sense not an ethics of virtue, even though it gives a great deal of attention
to the virtues. For his account of the virtues makes essential use of an imperative
notion of what a person 'ought' to do (*dei*), which he makes no effort to avoid or dis-
guise, but which would be out of place in an ethics of virtue. Secondly, as a general
matter concerning his ethics as a whole, Aristotle neither makes any attempt to eliminate imperative notions from his ethics nor even gives any sign of having made an
effort to circumscribe their role. He gives no indication that he hopes to make attractive notions bear the whole weight of formulating his view, or that he has any particular antipathy to imperativity. Indeed, when we look closely at Aristotle's language at
crucial points, we find no reason to think that he accords preference to attractive
formulations over imperative ones.

Early in the *Ethics*, Aristotle defines happiness, which he identifies with the human
good, as 'activity of the soul in accordance with virtue (or excellence, *arete*)'.[92] That,
however, is not the whole of his definition. To complete the definition, he needs to
specify what virtue is. He begins by indicating that virtue comes in two types, virtue
of character and virtue of intellect.[93] Next, starting at the beginning of Book II, he
undertakes an explanation of virtue of character. This is the point at which he introduces his famous 'doctrine of the mean'. According to this doctrine, activity in accordance with virtue of character is to be defined in terms of the notion of a mean or middle
between extremes.

Formulated in this manner, however, the doctrine merely raises another question:
how is 'the mean' to be specified? Aristotle's answer to this question is complex. His
first step is to examine actions (*praxeis*), since these determine or control character
(1103b29–31). The notion of the mean, he thinks, can be applied to actions, in the sense
that in the sphere of actions there can be excess, deficiency, and a mean (1106b16–18).
The question then is, how does Aristotle specify the mean for actions?

It needs to be stressed that Aristotle is indeed talking here about actions. He
believes, that is, that he needs to discover which actions lie in an intermediate position
between excess and deficiency. The reason why emphasis on this fact is necessary is
that it runs counter to one prominent interpretation of Aristotle's ethics, namely, one
taking him to be advancing a pure ethics of virtue.

Those who adopt such an interpretation believe that, on Aristotle's view, what is
good or excellent about the activities that constitute happiness is simply the fact that
they proceed from certain dispositions, namely, the virtues. According to such an
interpretation, value attaches to an action not simply as an action of a certain extern-

[92] *Nic. Eth.* I. 7, 1098a16–18. Aristotle goes on to say, 'and if there is more than one virtue, in accord with
the best and most complete'. See below, Chapter 6, esp. secs. II and IX.
[93] *Nic. Eth.* I. 13, 1102a5–6, 1103a3–6, 14. 'Virtue of character' is sometimes translated 'moral virtue'.
However, since I am postponing the question of the relation of Greek ethics to what we call morality, I need
to avoid this translation.

ally describable type, but rather simply because it expresses or exhibits or arises from a virtue. Such an idea is of a piece with the kind of ethics of virtue that holds that the fundamental kind of goodness attaches to traits of character, not to actions as such.[94] That is what Aristotle would have to hold if he indeed advanced an ethics of virtue of this sort.[95]

From what Aristotle says, however, it is clear that he does not advocate this view.[96] In the first place, he never says that what makes an action good is solely its relation to a virtue that it manifests. Moreover, he denies that virtue itself is the good, and his reason is that

[virtue] appears somewhat incomplete; for possession of virtue seems actually compatible with being asleep, or with lifelong activity, and further with the greatest sufferings and misfortunes; but the man who was living so no one would call happy, unless he were maintaining a thesis at all costs.[97]

Rather, the activities are the 'actualization' (energeia) of the virtues.[98] Furthermore, as I have already said, Aristotle speaks explicitly of the need to specify what the mean is in action, and, as I shall show shortly, tries to give such a specification.

3. Actions and Traits in Aristotle

One must be careful, however, not to fall into a mistake opposite to the one that is made by those who ascribe to Aristotle a pure ethics of virtue. That would be the mistake of thinking that, in his view, the evaluation of action is basic to all other evaluations, including those of traits of character. Even though Aristotle does not attach value to actions *solely* through their relation to the dispositions that give rise to them, neither does he seem to wish to maintain, on the other hand, that goodness attaches purely to the action as such and not to anything else. On the contrary, Aristotle maintains something that involves attributions of goodness that are not attributions to actions in and of themselves. He thinks that in addition to the value that can attach to an action itself, there is *also* a kind of value that attaches to it because it arises from a virtuous disposition. He says:

Actions, then, are called just and temperate when they are such as the just or temperate man would do; but it is not the man who does these that is just and temperate, but the man who does them *as* just and temperate men do them.[99]

This passage explicitly allows *actions* to be called just or temperate even when they are *not* done 'as' the just or temperate man would do them—that is, even when they are

---

[94] See above, secs. I–II.   [95] See e.g. Urmson 1988: 28–9, 36–7.

[96] Here I think Broadie has the matter right; see her 1991: 83, 87.

[97] Nic. Eth. 1095b30–1096a3.

[98] Nic. Eth. 1103a29–b3.   [99] Nic. Eth. 1105b5–9; cf, 1105a27–b4.

not done out of the virtuous dispositions of justice or temperance. On the other hand, the passage at the same time implies that value is to be attached to being just and temperate as such. In other words, merely doing the just or temperate action is not as fully good as doing them out of the corresponding traits of character.[100]

The right conclusion to draw is that Aristotle attaches goodness independently *both* to virtuous actions *and* to the traits that are exhibited in them. The value of the virtue is incomplete if it is not manifested in the action that is its actualization. Likewise, however, there is value in being virtuous that is additional to and independent of the value merely of the actions themselves.[101]

4. The Mean in Actions and Traits

Since Aristotle does not attach value to actions alone, it should be no surprise that, when he defines the mean, he does not try to define the mean for actions only. In addition, he indicates that there is a mean in the sphere of certain things that manifest the disposition—the virtue or vice—out of which the action arises. Thus he says that to understand virtue we must investigate pleasure and pain, because we measure our actions by these and because they are revelatory of the choices that a person makes, and thus also of his character.[102] Accordingly, moreover, he says that virtue involves hitting a mean in regard to pleasure and pain.

Aristotle also regards himself as called upon to discuss what he calls 'passions' (*pathe*), for example 'appetite, anger, fear, confidence, envy, joy, friendly feeling, hatred, longing, emulation, pity'. For virtues and vices are 'the things in virtue of which we stand well or badly with reference to the passions'. And so he likewise undertakes to explain what it is to hit the mean with regard to passions as well. For passions are like pleasure and pain, in that they 'may be felt both too much and too little, and in both cases not well'.[103]

Thus Aristotle's account of virtue requires him to explain what the mean is with regard to actions, and also with regard to pleasure and pain and the passions. Actions are the actualization of virtue, and happiness consists in this actualization. And pleasure, pain, and the passions are things whose occurrence is indicative of whether the actions are done out of a virtuous disposition or not.

Once it is clear that Aristotle thinks that we can talk about the mean with regard to

---

[100] Moreover, Aristotle never suggests that the *only* reason why the traits themselves have value is that they make the doing of the corresponding actions more likely. See Broadie 1991: 83, 87.

[101] As I shall explain below (Chapter 7, sec. IV. 4), Aristotle believes that a thing can be good both for its own sake and for the sake of something else that it is related to. In the present case, that means, for instance, that a virtue is good both for itself but also for the sake of the action that actualizes it.

[102] *Nic. Eth.* 1104b30–1105a7, 1106b18–19.

[103] *Nic. Eth.* 1106b15–20. Cf. 1107a3–6, where Aristotle applies the notion of the mean jointly to passions and actions.

actions and not only with regard to traits of character, we also need to see how he thinks that the mean is to be specified. Imperatives here play an essential role, in a way that contradicts the idea that he straightforwardly advocates an ethics of virtue and eschews the use of imperative concepts.

When Aristotle explains the mean with regard to pleasures and pains, he says that it involves feeling them

at the times when one *ought* (*dei*), with reference to objects one *ought*, towards the people one *ought*, for the sake of things one *ought*, and in the way one *ought*.[104]

I translate *dei* here by the imperative word 'ought', thus bringing out what I think, as I shall argue below, the force of the Greek word clearly is. Parallel explanations are given of the mean with regard to both passions and actions. For instance he says, concerning the virtue of liberality, that

the liberal man will both give and spend the amounts one ought on the objects one ought . . ., and he will also take the amounts one ought from the sources one ought.[105]

And more generally he maintains,

For the bad man, what he does clashes with what he ought to, but what the good man ought to do he does.[106]

It would be a serious mistake to try to minimize the bearing of these uses of 'ought' on questions about imperative language in Aristotle.[107] They appear at many important junctures in his accounts of the virtues of character.[108] They should not be ignored or brushed aside, as they frequently are. Aristotle's word is the impersonal verb *dei*, 'it is necessary' or 'it ought (sc. to be the case)'. This word does not express attraction. Far from it. It is as directly imperatival a term as one could ask for and as the Greek language contains. It conveys the idea of what *must* be the case, not of something whose being the case would be good or attractive.

5. Imperative Formulations of the Mean

So ingrained is the modern idea that Aristotle treats attractive notions as fundamental and has little use for imperativity that many interpreters pass over these passages

---

[104] *Nic. Eth.* 1106b21–2.   [105] *Nic. Eth.* 1120b20–21, 24, 29–31.

[106] *Nic. Eth.* 1169a16–17. The application of the idea to passions appears at 1106b15–23, 1109a26–9.

[107] See Gauthier and Jolif 1970: i. 284–99 and ii. 568–75. They fully recognize the importance of imperative notions in Aristotle's ethics. They add a further point, however, about which I have reservations: they believe that the imperative in question is 'moral' (ii. 569, 573–5); see Chapter 2, sec. IV. 2. (Williams 1993: 181 n. 43 seems to me to mistake the import of what they say, since he takes them to support his view that Aristotle does not employ a notion of moral imperativity.)

[108] Thus see as examples *Nic. Eth.* 1104b20ff., 1107a4–1120b30ff., 1118b20, 1121a21–b8, 12, 1122a1–7, b11–12, 29f., 1123a20, 1169a15–16.

without noticing their force. Some translators even go so far as frequently to render them in a way that completely masks the occurrence of the imperatival idea. In W. D. Ross's translation, for instance, which has long been the standard for readers of English, the word *dei* is rendered by 'right'; and more recently Terence Irwin translates it in the same way.[109] For most purposes this translation will do well enough. Indeed, the word 'right' itself has a somewhat imperatival flavour, especially by virtue of its legalistic overtones. The phrase 'not right', like 'wrong', certainly conveys the negatively imperatival suggestion of something out of bounds or forbidden. Still, the word *dei* has an even more strongly imperatival character, which the rendering 'right' tends to obscure.[110]

Not only does Aristotle employ this notion freely, he uses the imperatival term here to frame his very *definition* of virtue and thus, indirectly, his definition of happiness—that is, the human good—itself. For when we unpack the whole series of definitions that Aristotle presents in the *Nicomachean Ethics* up to this point, happiness turns out to be defined as activity in accordance with virtue of character, that is, with activity that falls in the mean, that is, with activity that consists in doing 'what one ought, when one ought, with reference to the objects one ought, with regard to the people one ought', and so on.[111] So far, then, Aristotle in effect holds that our understanding of what *virtue* and *happiness* consist in is based on an understanding of facts about what one *ought* to do—that is, on a straightforwardly imperative concept. The notion of 'ought' is thus an essential component of his definition of virtue.

This use of imperative language here is not an isolated aberration on Aristotle's part. It also occurs elsewhere in his discussion of virtue of character. Early in the discussion of justice (*dikaiosyne*) in Book V, Aristotle says that the law *commands* us (*prostattei*) to do the works of human beings covered by all the special virtues (1129b19–24). Immediately after (at 1129b25–1130a13), he identifies general justice (as opposed to special justice) both with the whole of virtue, and equally with law (*nomos*):

[I]n one sense we call those acts just that tend to produce and preserve happiness and its components for the political society. And *the law commands* (*prostattei*) us do both the acts of a brave man . . ., and those of a temperate man . . ., and those of a good-tempered man, and sim-

---

[109] Ross's Oxford translation (Aristotle 1925), and Irwin's (Aristotle 1985). Sometimes, however, Ross does use the translation 'ought', as at 1122b12. Irwin (Aristotle 1985: 423–4) is correct that 'ought' here is not specifically moral (in our sense); but it is nonetheless imperative. Sherman's translation, 'appropriate', seems much too weak, though notice that 'inappropriate' has the force of a prohibition, and perhaps 'appropriate' does have imperative overtones (Sherman 1989: 114).

[110] Moreover, Aristotle uses another term, *orthos*, which is less straightforwardly imperative, and more accurately translated by 'right' than *dei* is (e.g. at 1120a25).

[111] Later, in *Nic. Eth.* X. 6–8, Aristotle perhaps holds that happiness is actually activity in accordance with *intellectual* virtue, rather than excellence of character. The present argument holds, however, insofar as Aristotle takes virtue of character a part of happiness. Cf. below, Chapter 6, esp. secs. VI and IX.

ilarly with regard to the other virtues, commanding some acts and forbidding others ... This form of justice, then, is compete virtue, not absolutely but in relation to our neighbour.[112]

He says nothing whatsoever to dissociate the notion of virtue from the imperative connotations that this discussion introduces. Indeed in another connection he also says generally of practical wisdom (*phronêsis*) that it 'issues commands' (*epitaktikê estin*).[113] We are permitted without reservation to conceive of the standards of virtue to be expressed by the imperatives.

6. *The* Phronimos: *Attractive Formulations Again*

In spite of the passages that I have cited, however, the essential place of imperativity in Aristotle's account of virtue is still not guaranteed. There remains room to doubt whether he really does end up treating the imperative notion that is expressed by the word *dei* as a fundamental one in terms of which virtue and happiness are ultimately to be defined.

The reason why this point is not yet fully established by the foregoing passages alone is that elsewhere in the *Nicomachean Ethics* he seems to explain the notion of the mean in other ways.[114] Thus the term *dei* is not consistently and unambiguously made to bear the full weight of his explanation of virtue. Shortly after the first passage that I cited, Aristotle says (1106b36–1107a2):

Therefore virtue is a state concerned with choice, lying in a mean relative to us, determined by reason (*logos*), namely by that principle by which the man of practical wisdom (the *phronimos*) would determine it.

This passage makes it possible to hold that, rather than explaining the mean in terms of what one 'ought' to do, Aristotle instead ultimately specifies it in terms of 'what the man of practical wisdom would determine'. If that is so, then determining the actions that one is to do would be a matter not of finding out which things one 'ought' to do, but rather of discovering who the man of practical wisdom is. That, however, does not seem, at least explicitly, to involve imperatival notions. Aristotle's phrase 'the *phronimos*' is perhaps not obviously an attractive term; but neither is it straightforwardly an imperative one. Accordingly, there seems to be room to hold that the imperative notion conveyed by 'ought' is not the basic one in Aristotle's account.

---

[112] See *Nic. Eth.* 1129b19–26; cf. 1129b27–1130a13 and also *Rhetoric* 1366b8–22, where Aristotle says: 'Justice is the virtue through which everybody enjoys his own possessions in accordance with the law ... Courage in the virtue that disposes men to do noble deeds in situations of danger, in accordance with the law and in *obedience* to its *commands* ... Temperance is the virtue that disposes us to *obey* the law where physical pleasures are concerned' (8–15). On the imperativity that attaches to *tattein* and *prostattein* in Aristotle, see Gauthier and Jolif 1970: ii. 572–3.

[113] *Nic. Eth.* 1143a8.   [114] See Frankena 1965: 27–37.

Perhaps, then, one might hope to interpret Aristotle so as to minimize the importance of the passages that involve imperativity, namely by specifying the mean, and thus virtuous activity, ultimately without recourse to imperative notions.

If we wish to follow this line of interpretation, so as to specify the Aristotelian mean without recourse to imperative notions, the various things that Aristotle says offer us possibilities for doing so—too many, in fact, for us to be sure which one, if any, he might conceivably have preferred to the imperatival specification that I have focused on.

For one thing, he holds that the ultimate end of all human action is a person's own good, which is his happiness or *eudaimonia*. Perhaps, then, a person who is trying to determine what to do should not, after all, think of what he 'ought' to do, nor use imperatival notions. Perhaps he should instead specify, and justify, activity in accordance with the mean simply as that which is conducive to his own *good*—which seems not at all to be an imperatival concept.

Alternatively, some passages in Aristotle point to the idea that one should do what produces good not just for oneself, but for one's community or perhaps even mankind as a whole. Aristotle says in another ethical treatise, the *Eudemian Ethics*, that the promotion of the contemplation of God is the standard that we should use for making choices.[115] Further, at another point Aristotle introduces the idea that the people with practical wisdom are those who aim at 'what is good for themselves or for men in general'.[116]

These specifications are of the type that is nowadays called 'consequentialist'. They tell us to choose actions by reference to the good or bad results that they cause. If Aristotle ultimately specified virtuous actions as those that cause or bring about the good, then he would not have any need to introduce imperative notions into his account. The imperative specifications that I have quoted above could then be taken as informal and unofficial—as mere asides, that is, which do not accord any special role to imperativity in his account of happiness. These consequentialist specifications raise other problems.[117] But they might at least be held to allow us to accept a reading of Aristotle in which attractive notions held decisive conceptual priority over imperative ones.

---

[115] *Eud. Eth.* 1249b18–24.   [116] *Nic. Eth.* 1140b4–11, 20–1.

[117] In particular, there is a danger of circularity pointed out by Frankena 1965: 34–5. If one simply said that the good is activity in accordance with virtue, and then defined this activity as activity that promotes the good, the definition would be circular. (Note that on these terms the circularity would hold no matter whether the good in the definiens is supposed to be one's own good, the good of one's community, or the good of people in general.) The problem would be avoided if one specified virtuous activity as activity promoting the contemplation of God, for instance, or simply philosophical thought in general (this is the interpretation favoured by Ackrill 1981: 139–41), or in some other specific way. (Notice that the danger of circularity here is distinct from the similar danger that worried Sidgwick about Socrates' views; see his 1907: Bk. III, chs. 13–14.)

7. Vacillation between Imperative and Attractive Formulations

Some of Aristotle's remarks, on the other hand, are suggestive of non-consequentialist formulations. For instance, he says that virtuous activity is done 'for the sake of the noble (*to kalon*)' and 'for its own sake' (1115b12–13, 1120a23–4, 1122b6–7, and 1105a32). Perhaps, then, the mean could be defined as the most noble act, or the most noble amount of pleasure or of pain or of some other passion. As stated, and apart from any further explanation that it might need or receive, this formulation in and of itself plainly involves the language of attraction rather than that of command.

Possibly this idea might be amplified by means of something else that Aristotle says. In one well-known passage, he holds that when it comes to determining what to do in particular instances, 'the decision rests with perception (*aisthesis*)'.[118] This famous dictum seems to indicate that in any particular case the mean, construed perhaps as 'the noble', is to be discovered by the use of a perceptual faculty of some sort. In one terminology this kind of faculty is designated 'intuition'. (Strictly, however, this English word would be misleading, because in spite of its etymology, which connotes vision, it is now standardly used for an intellectual faculty, not a perceptual one.)

Aristotle does not indicate, however, what the content is of the deliverances of this faculty. Therefore we cannot tell whether he thinks of the faculty as addressing us, so to speak, in attractive terms, or in imperative terms, or indeed in any terms at all. As most interpreters understand the passage, it indicates that the faculty comes into play only in particular situations and that it does not rely on any general rules of action. (Elsewhere, however, Aristotle certainly writes, as is well known, as though general rules play an important role in deliberation.)[119] But that fact, if it is a fact, would not settle the present question either way. The 'perception' in question might tell us that a given particular action *ought* to be performed, or give us a sense of being enjoined to do it; or equally it might make us see that the action is good, or present it to us in an attractive light.[120]

8. Aristotle's Hospitability towards Both Moods

So we may still wonder whether to take Aristotle as focusing mainly on imperative notions or on attractive notions. So far, our effort has been based on the working assumption that one or the other of these two types of terms must be in some sense basic or fundamental to his position. This assumption, however, must be called into

---

[118] *Nic. Eth.* 1109b23.

[119] See Frankena 1965 and Cooper 1975: esp. ch. 1.

[120] It is true that Aristotle sometimes seems to hold that the conclusion of a practical syllogism is an *action*. However, that view, whatever exactly it comes to, would not preclude him from saying that a certain form of words is more suitable than another for 'accompanying' the action that is the conclusion. Cf. Anscombe 1963: sec. 33.

question. It arose, of course, from the idea that as a representative of Greek ethics, Aristotle can be taken as providing an alternative to the modern emphasis on imperativity. And this idea in turn involves the thought that Aristotle must at least believe in a strong contrast between the two sorts of notions, imperative and attractive, and that he is likely to have definite opinions about which sort ought to be treated as in some sense primary.

Let us reconsider this idea, however. At 1120a23–9, Aristotle says:

Actions in accordance with virtue are noble and for the sake of the noble. So the liberal person will give *rightly* (*orthôs*) and for the sake of the *noble* (*to kalon*); since he will give to those to whom he *ought* (*dei*), and as much as and when he *ought*, and in all the other ways that are entailed by right giving, and he will do this *with enjoyment and without pain* . . . But he who gives to people to whom he *ought not* to give, or not for the sake of the noble but for some other cause, is not said to be liberal but rather some other kind of person.

This passage, I would say, gives us strong reason to doubt the assumptions that I articulated just now. The passage conveys the impression that, according to Aristotle, the virtuous person will think of himself as *both* doing things as he ought, *and* doing them for the sake of the noble. That is, he will think of his action in *both* imperative *and* attractive terms, and will not focus especially on either the one type or the other.[121]

The rest of the chapter, *Nicomachean Ethics* IV. 1, contains similar remarks, including this one (1121a1–4):

But if [the liberal man] happens to spend in a manner *contrary to what he ought and to what is noble* (*para to deon kai to kalos echon*), he will be pained, but moderately and as he ought; for it is the mark of virtue both to be pleased and to be pained with things that one ought and as one ought.

One might here be tempted to ask just what Aristotle means when he says 'contrary to what he ought and to what is noble'. Are these two phrases meant to stand for the same notion, or are they different? Someone might propose that they show Aristotle here explaining the mean in terms of what is *kalon* or noble, and not in imperative terms. That seems to me dubious. What they seem to indicate, instead, is that he is willing to place the two explanations—'what he ought' and 'what is noble'—on a par with each other, and to use *both* of them equally. Neither one takes precedence over the other. Let us consider what the consequence of this reading is.

The right conclusion to draw, I suggest, is that Aristotle is simply not concerned to pronounce decisively on whether the specification of the mean, or of virtuous action, is to be thought of as couched in imperative terms or in attractive ones. At some points

---

[121] I am deliberately ignoring the distinction between how Aristotle thinks the *criterion* of virtuous action ought to be framed, how he thinks its *justification* ought to be formulated, and how he thinks a person's *motivation* to perform it ought to be expressed. It is difficult to make his texts bear the full weight of these distinctions. Fortunately for present purposes it is unnecessary.

he seems to go in the one direction, and at other times in the other one, and in these passages he goes both ways at once. That need not be taken as a sign of indecision, nor as a contradiction. The point is just that he is not focusing especially on *either* attractive *or* imperative notions; nor is he insisting that one must have priority over the other. Certainly he is not aiming to exclude imperative terms. To be sure, the beginning of the *Nicomachean Ethics* gives a dominant role to the notion of the good, and the rest of the work plainly focuses on the virtues. However, Aristotle does not behave at all like someone to whom it is important to show that ethics can be done without notions like 'ought' or that a practically wise agent would dispense with such concepts.

The significance of the idea that Aristotle eschews imperatives has seemed to many interpreters to lie in the thought that his views are in fundamental ways unlike Kant's and other modern, supposedly command-centred ones. If Aristotle avoided imperatives in favour of attractives, that would be a symptom of this ostensible difference, as I shall explain later, when I turn to the general issue of conflict in Greek ethics.[122] As to the symptom, the conclusion must be that Aristotle saw no special antagonism between the two sorts of formulations, imperative and attractive. He was quite capable of attending chiefly to discussion of what the good for a human being is, while at the same time making ample room within that project for imperative notions.

Earlier I mentioned a general reason that interpreters have for thinking that by rights Aristotle *should* avoid imperative notions, a reason that is rooted in what is normally held to be his overall ethical psychology. According to this account, Aristotle does not believe that if a person is acting out of virtue, there is any opposing motivational force that interferes or generates conflict. This idea has been put by saying that in the relevant sorts of cases there is no 'internal friction', as there is in someone who, out of 'strength of will' resists a desire that runs counter to what he has decided is best to do.[123] If there is no such friction, however, then it seems that there should be no occasion for a person who acts out of virtue to command some part of himself to do what he has decided is best; and therefore there should be no occasion for imperatives.

Still confining ourselves for now to matters of usage, consider how Aristotle's manner of speaking compares with Kant's, which would customarily be said to rely more fully on imperatives than Aristotle's does. As I remarked earlier, Kant held that an 'ought' is not appropriate except when the 'law of reason' is addressed to a will that is not necessarily determined by it, but can be led in a different direction by inclination.[124] Thus a Kantian divine or perfect will would not present norms to itself in imperative form. Surprisingly enough, Aristotle turns out to be in a substantial way more hospitable to imperative formulations of norms than was Kant. In the passages that I just cited, Aristotle is describing not the strong-willed man who has to resist irrational impulses, but the good man, the man of virtue. Aristotle's description of

---

[122] See Chapters 5–6, and esp., with regard to Aristotle, Chapter 6.
[123] Urmson 1988: 66.   [124] See sec. I. 5.

such a man does not exclude imperative formulations. As Aristotle puts things, the virtuous man regards his actions *both* as the actions that he 'ought' to do, *and* at the same time as actions that he enjoys doing.[125]

VIII. Imperativity in Plato

1. The Attractive Good and the Imperative Just

In Plato, almost as much as in Aristotle, one would expect to find a stereotypically Hellenic preference for attractives over imperatives exemplified. The Form of the Good, which seems in the *Republic* to represent a paradigmatically attractive notion, is the coping-stone of Plato's metaphysics as well as his ethics and politics. Although we have seen that Greek metaphysics does not always run fully parallel to Greek views about value, we might still be strongly tempted to think that the pre-eminence of the good in Plato's philosophy must embody a general predilection for attractive concepts.

Indeed, Plato seems to have granted a general prominence both to the notion of good (*agathon*) and sometimes, too, to the notion of beauty (*kalon*). Books VI–VII of the *Republic* seem to tell us that the Form of the Good is the cause of not only the goodness but also the being of all other things (509b). The *Symposium*, for its part, gives the impression that the Form of Beauty has a quite similar status (209–11). Nowhere is an imperative notion, or even the notion of justice or right (*dikaiosyne*), said to have such a role in his ethics, let alone his metaphysics.

As in the case of Aristotle, however, the situation in Plato is much more complicated than it at first appears, and it militates against a simple imputation to him of a preference for attractive notions. His formulation of his position by no means dispenses with imperatives. His account of justice, for one thing, contains a straightforwardly imperative element. He holds that justice involves a kind of 'necessity', which is linked to commands, law, and compulsion.[126] In particular, the rulers of Plato's ideal city are enjoined to govern the city rather than spending all their time philosophizing. Thus:

And when they have reached fifty years, those who have lasted and are still the best . . . must be led (*akteon*) to the finish. They *must be necessitated* (*anagkasteon*) to raise the gaze of their soul upwards and look to the very thing that casts light on everything, to see the good itself, and to use it as a paradigm and to arrange the city and its citizens and themselves . . . And when their turn comes they must labour in the city's affairs and govern for the sake of the city, doing so not as something splendid, but as something *necessary* (*anagkaion*). (*Rep.* 540a–b)

---

[125] See Urmson 1973 and 1988: 27–8.
[126] *Rep.* 519e, 520d–e, 521b, 540a–b, d–e.

Plato says that even when considerations of justice arise, the guide that the rulers ultimately use is the good (540a–b; cf. 519c–d). He does not treat justice as a guide to deliberation independent of goodness. Unlike Aristotle, moreover, Plato does not evince the thought that the notion of virtue might be explicable in terms of an imperative term like *dei*. Instead he explains the justice of an action as a tendency in the action to promote or preserve the virtue of justice in the soul of the person who performs it (443e–444a). Definitionally, then, the virtue of justice in a person is prior to justice, or indeed any feature, in an action.

In addition, Plato gives another kind of prominence to the notion of good. In the *Republic* the good, as Sidgwick notes,[127] appears to be something like a genus under which justice falls. What makes justice something that is imperatively *to be* pursued, he appears to believe, is the fact that it is good (541a–b). This fact should perhaps make us think that, in his view, the attractive notion of good is granted a kind of priority over the (to him) partially imperative notion of justice.

In spite of this special pre-eminence that is accorded to goodness, however, the imperative formulations associated with justice persist undiluted: 'we shall be giving just orders to just people; each of them will certainly go to rule as to something that is necessary—the opposite way to that of those who rule in every city now' (520e). Attractive as the good may be, the things that the rulers do in its name are done also with the sense of obeying an explicit imperative.

2. A Neutral Concept of Good

The resulting conception of the relation in Plato between goodness and justice might appear to be paradoxical, or at least to be in need of explanation. Perhaps goodness is, for instance, a kind of genus under which justice falls. But that idea might well seem problematical, if goodness is an attractive notion while justice is an imperative one. For example, that idea might seem tantamount to the idea that being commanded to be a certain way could be, as it were, a way of being attracted to being that way. But that does not seem to make sense if being commanded to do something in fact involves being also pulled towards its contrary, so that the command is necessary in order to induce one to do it. This is one of the problems that might appear to arise from Plato's way of relating justice and goodness to each other.

Plato does not indicate how such a problem might be solved—supposing indeed that it does actually arise within his view. One reason for thinking that it does not arise there is the possibility that in treating his notion of goodness as if it were purely attractive we are looking at it too narrowly. Perhaps the good is not attractive in a sense that contrasts with its being imperative. Perhaps instead Plato's goodness is designed to be a notion of value that is so very general that it must taken to include *both* the attractive

[127] Sidgwick 1907: 105–6.

and the imperative.[128] In that case, Plato's pre-eminent normative notion, *to agathon*, would be neither simply imperative nor simply attractive. Rather, it would be a still more general notion, a fused notion of evaluative normativity, or a notion of general normative force, under which both the imperative and the attractive would be subsumed.[129] We could try to think of a general normative force, for instance, as a norm which a person followed either against some resistance within himself *or* without there being such resistance.

Put this possibility aside, however, and the most important point remains. It is still clear from what Plato says that he does not intend the pre-eminence of the Form of the Good to obviate the partial imperativity of the notion of justice. The notion of the good is metaphysically pre-eminent, according to his scheme. Plato's making it so, however, is no part of a programme to eliminate either imperative notions in general or the imperative character of justice in particular. As in the cases both of the Stoics and of Aristotle, the special importance that Plato accords attractive notions leaves room for imperative notions to operate along with them.

IX. Imperatives in Ethics and their Philosophical Examination

That there is a difference between ancient and modern ethics with regard to the treatment of imperative notions vis-à-vis attractive ones has been felt by many observers. A feeling that is so widespread is not to be passed over without explanation. It seems to me, moreover, that ancient ethics does indeed attach a special prominence to attractive concepts that goes beyond anything that it accords to imperative ones. In this respect, the standard account is not only understandable but correct. The mistake has come, however, in the attempt to say just what this prominence consists in. The result of this mistake has been to lend credence to a misguided picture of the character of Greek ethics—a picture that I shall be trying to combat in the following chapters.

The mistake has been to think that imperativity plays only a minor role within Greek normative ethical discourse itself. In reality, however, the Greeks were not averse to employing imperative terms in the formulation of norms, whether these were the norms employed in ordinary discourse or in the discourse of philosophers. Whereas attractive terminology is more saliently employed in certain of the contexts of Greek ethics whose modern counterparts might use imperative notions, the difference is far from being great enough to justify the idea of a fundamental conceptual

---

[128] In line with this suggestion, it may be that *to kalon* represents its attractive genus. That would seem compatible with much of what Plato says in *Symp.* 199–212.

[129] I believe that some such fused notion figures in Gauthier and Jolif, 1970: i. 289, and, somewhat less unequivocally, in the thinking of Sertillanges 1901: 320–1; at i. 294, Gauthier and Jolif also in effect raise the question whether Aquinas may not also employ such a fused notion.

difference between the two periods of ethics. Moreover, there is no good reason to hold that the tendency to use imperatives increased as Greek ethics developed.

There is, however, a real contrast to be drawn between ancient and modern ethics with regard to the issue of imperativity—not in the *use* of such notions in normative ethical discourse itself, but rather in the manner and degree to which such notions are subjected to *philosophical scrutiny*. Sidgwick makes a remark that is à propos here:

[The Greek thinkers'] speculations can scarcely be understood by us unless with a certain effort we throw the quasi-jural notions of modern ethics aside, and ask (as they did not) not 'What is Duty and what is its ground?' but 'Which of the objects that men think good is truly Good or the Highest Good?' or in the more specialized form . . . 'What is the relation of the kind of Good we call Virtue, the qualities of conduct and character which men commend and admire, to other good things?'[130]

The important difference between modern and ancient ethics, as Sidgwick's observation distantly suggests, is *not*, I would maintain, the difference between use and the neglect of these concepts. It is rather that, as Hans Reiner insists, modern philosophers *discuss*, *analyse*, and *try to understand* the nature of ethical imperativity.[131] In contrast, ancient ethics by and large makes no such attempt.[132] Instead, it turns its analytical gaze on the notions of happiness and good.[133] That is the important difference. It is quite compatible with the recognition, which we have no choice but to admit, that imperative notions—like Aristotle's 'ought' and Plato's 'necessity'— played an indispensable role in Greek ethics.

---

[130] Sidgwick 1907: 106.

[131] Reiner 1964 and 1977 take it that the Greeks had the notion of *moral* obligation. That can be doubted, but is in any case not the issue here. Cf. Chapter 2, sec. IV.

[132] One might argue that partial exceptions are constituted by the discussions of justice in the *Republic* and *Nic. Eth.* V, insofar as they convey something about why laws and other edicts are to be obeyed; but it still remains true that the idea of imperativity itself receives little or no elucidation there.

[133] Reiner 1964: 15–16, 92.

Chapter 4

THE CITY-STATE IN GREEK ETHICS

I. The Hegelian Conception of the Polis

1. The Polis *as the Source of Norms*

In the previous chapter I discussed a matter having to do with the formulation of Greek ethical thinking. Here I move to a more substantive matter.

Within the hegelian response to Greek thought, there has been no more potent force sustaining nostalgia for harmony in Greek ethics than the *polis* or city-state. This force was exerted through the notion that both in idea and in fact, the *polis* manifested a unique consistency of rational aims, both in society at large and within the deliberations of the individual. On the one hand, the *polis* has been taken to be a political institution that was capable of reconciling actual conflicts among individuals to an unparalleled degree. Even more important, it has been believed that the concept of the *polis* itself, when properly understood, can be used to demonstrate that apparent conflicts within a good society are to a considerable extent unreal. Along with other factors already discussed, thoughts about the *polis* have encouraged a pervasive pattern of generalizations about 'the Greeks'. Greece is the *polis*, and the *polis* is the harmony of the community. As such, the *polis* often presents itself as a model for nostalgia and emulation.

At work here is another fundamental idea: that according to the Greek outlook, the *polis* is the source of all of the norms and standards that govern the life of an individual in it. In outline, the thought is that any practical questions that arise can be answered by somehow consulting the concept of social activity that the *polis* embodies.

Under the hegelian response, this way of thinking about the *polis* dovetails with a eudaimonist account of Greek ethics as a whole. Eudaimonism says that each person, insofar as he is rational, makes his own happiness his ultimate end. On hegelian views, however, the individual's happiness and the good of the community are not regarded as separate aims. The former either includes the latter, according to the Inclusivist form of the view, or, according to the Fusionist version, is identical with it. If the community is then equated to the *polis*, there is held to be no inconsistency between saying, on the one side, that the individual's sole ultimate aim is his own well-being, and holding, on the other side, that the notion of the *polis* somehow generates all answers to practical questions.

Such an approach to Greek thought is of course quite different from the kantian response.[1] That response agrees that according to what the Greeks assumed, each individual would rationally pursue his own happiness; but the response also takes this assumption to entail conflicts between the individual's good, on the one hand, and considerations of ethics, altruism, and the good of the community, on the other. From the kantian perspective, the *polis* could well be a notable institution. It could also be the source of man-made or 'positive' law. It could not, however, be the sole source of the individual's norms and aims, and it could not be guaranteed to be reconcilable with the individual's happiness.

To explore this idea more fully, we need to distinguish several matters. One of these has to do with sources of practical considerations and norms that might rival those that arise from the *polis*. In particular, to regard the norms or the good of the *polis* as exhaustive of the norms that an individual need observe is to deny independent normative status to two other potential rival sources, some being wider than the *polis* and some being narrower. Examples of the former would be norms that are designed for, or are taken as binding on, all humans or all rational beings or on the whole world or *kosmos*. Narrower norms, on the other hand, would pertain to groups smaller than the *polis*, including the clan or family and also the individual. In each case, the norm can be thought of either as somehow determined by examining the unit in question; for instance, by the individual for himself or by the family for its members. (Often, though not necessarily, these two things are thought to coincide.) The idea of centring all valid practical considerations and norms on the *polis* is tantamount to declaring that none of these other standards has independent force of its own.

There are two main ways in which the concept of the *polis* can be claimed to generate norms, each of which corresponds to important strands in Greek thinking. One has to do with the *good* of the *polis*; the other concerns the norms that it lays down for its citizens. Along the former lines, one thinks of the individual's actions as being guided by determining what will *benefit* his *polis*. According to the latter way of thinking, the individual conforms to the *norms* or *standards* that the *polis* enunciates for him, which may be variously conceived and formulated. As will emerge, these two ways of thinking about the matter are ordinarily understood to coincide. We should bear in mind, however, that they are, at the very least, conceptually distinct.

---

[1] See Chapter 1, sec. V.

In some such way as this, at any rate, the *polis* could appear to serve as a focus and guide for all of the individual's aims. It would serve to define an individual's *eudaimonia*, and through that concept it would dictate a plan of life through which all rational deliberative considerations could be organized into a fully consistent structure. To the degree to which the *polis* could be expected to achieve consistency among its own standards—which cannot be automatically taken for granted—the possibility would be precluded that the individual might be rationally required to take any other, independent considerations into account. The norms of the *polis* would be expected to generate and harmonize the individual's own good and other valid standards. By this line of thought, the *polis* acquires central importance in the hegelian construal of Greek ethical thought.

No one would deny that the *polis* is a phenomenon of the first importance, both historically and intellectually. The Greeks were extremely proud of it and of the developments that led to its increasing importance from the Archaic period into Classical times. They took it to be an important factor that set them off from, and made them superior to, all other peoples.[2] In recent times, too, admirers of Hellenism have been proud of the *polis* on the Greeks' behalf. Moderns who have looked to the Greeks to show us how to counteract the ills of contemporary society have found in the *polis* the main cause of the unity that they contrasted with the fragmentation of modern society including, in the eyes of some, the excesses of individualism.[3]

2. *The* Polis *as Reconciler of Aims*

Without denying the importance of the *polis*, however, we must face two questions. One is whether the concept of the *polis* yields the philosophical dividends that have been claimed for it. The other question, on which I concentrate, is whether as a historical matter the *polis* actually possessed the capacity for harmony with which it is so regularly associated in the historiography of ideas.

The role that the *polis* plays in the hegelian account depends on the linking to each other of two elements. The unifying force that has been ascribed to the *polis* has several aspects, of which two need to be highlighted here. One has to do with the particular mechanism by which the *polis* has been seen as supplying norms and standards by which its citizens could guide their actions. Just how is the *polis* supposed to have created norms and communicated them, and the motivations for adhering to them, to its citizens? The second aspect concerns its role of reconciling or mitigating potential conflicts over well-being. These include potential conflicts between the happiness of one citizen and that of another, and also potential clashes of the well-being of each citi-

---

[2] For general treatments, see e.g. Ehrenberg 1969: 24–7, 102; Kitto 1957: 71–2.
[3] Wood 1993: 201, 216; Gray 1941: 40, 53.

zen with the happiness of the *polis* as a whole. On the plausible supposition that the *polis* did supply norms, how do these eliminate or mitigate conflict?

The core of the hegelian interpretation in this connection is its view that the mechanism by which the notion of the *polis* generated practical norms was such as to diminish oppositions among considerations that threaten to clash. If the *polis* supplied the *unrivalled* norms by which an individual was willing to regulate *all* of his significant actions, the view says, that was in large part because no conflict was believed to be possible between his own happiness and the smooth functioning of his *polis*. Conversely, the importance ascribed to obeying the standards laid down by the *polis* tended, it is said, to eliminate or reduce any conflicts of happiness that might seem to threaten, either among individuals or between any one of them and the *polis* itself.[4]

The particular manner in which this interpretation of Greek political thought and history has normally been worked out turns on the notion of the *function* or *role* of an individual within the structure of his *polis*. This is to ignore slaves, of whom there were many; but slaves did not figure in the story of the *polis* that has been most influential in modern thought. It seems to me that one reason why slavery is often neglected is precisely because it would have introduced obvious difficulties into the picture of the *polis* as a harmonious organism. However, I shall carry out the discussion independently of that point.[5]

At any rate according to this standard hegelian account, the increasing importance of the *polis* in Greek life brought it about that in the Classical period, a Greek citizen could think of his own identity, in some sense of that term, and also his well-being as fully defined by his role in the existence and activity of his *polis*. Some interpretations of this type go so far as to maintain that in the Greek view, an individual regarded his very existence and identity, in quite literal senses, as wholly dependent on his *polis*, so that his life without his *polis* would be strictly inconceivable to him. The individual *is*, this idea has it, his function as a citizen.[6]

Evidently this is the kind of strategy for dealing with oppositions that I have labelled *eliminative* or at least strongly *mitigative*; it is not a kind of adjudication between two deliberative considerations that are acknowledged to exist and to have independent weight. The question asked is not, 'Given that there are conflicts among citizens, how can we make decisions that will, though not satisfying everyone completely, preserve their willingness to cooperate?' Instead the question is seen as being, 'How can we make the citizens realize, and realize ourselves, that conflicts among them are only apparent or largely so?'

---

[4] See Hegel 1991: 252; cf. 253, 255, and other passages cited in Chapter 1, sec. VII.

[5] This is largely because the topic of Greek slavery introduces enormous historical difficulties on its own account. It should be borne in mind, however, that Greek slavery was not on the whole organized along ethnic or racial lines.

[6] For this idea in recent discussions, see e.g. Sandel 1982: 11.

The strategy has two prongs. First, it says that the norms governing the individual were thought of as defined by his function. If a person was a guard at the city's gate, that meant that he was to do the things that are a guard's function. Likewise for a statesman, and so on. But the role of a guard was also held to determine, in addition to the norms governing him, also what constituted his good or well-being. Harking back to a well-known passage in Book I of Aristotle's *Nicomachean Ethics*, interpreters of this type have suggested that for a guard at the gate to perform his function in the *polis* well is the same thing as his being happy.[7]

In this fashion, we see a combination of the two ways in which, as I mentioned, the *polis* can be thought of as generating practical considerations governing an individual's deliberation. These were, first, the well-being of the *polis* and, second, the norms that it lays down for its citizens. Straightforwardly enough, the norms are thought of as prescribing an activity for each citizen, consisting of the performance of his role in civic life. On the other side, the well-being of the *polis* is held to be possible when, and only when, each citizen performs his function. In this way, it is thought, obedience to the norms of the *polis* and the furthering of its good are equivalent.

With relatively little further ado it would then seem to follow that the well-being of the city and the well-being of the individual are inseparable. If the well-being of the city consists in the fulfilment by each individual of his role, and if the fulfilment by an individual of his role is identified with his well-being, and if this is how a Greek saw things, then he would regard his own well-being as necessarily coincident and even identical with that happiness of the *polis* as a whole. Thus no conflict would arise, and the norms of the *polis* would supply a standard with which no others could compete for the individual's attention. The individual's standards would therefore be simply those of the *polis*.

3. Hegelian Reflections

As things have developed, the best-known exponent of this idea is Hegel. However, he was by no means the first to conceive it. Herder, for instance, had already said that in ancient Greece, 'splendour and greatness were not dispersed, as in modern times; rather they were fused as the concern of the state'. Schiller and others had written in the same vein.[8] Hegel, however, gave the idea a philosophical impetus that has won it a long-lasting place in the general understanding of Greek thought.

Hegel believed that the Greeks regarded the individual as by his very essence inseparable from the *polis*:

[T]he consideration of the state in the abstract—which to our understanding is the essential point—was alien to them. Their grand object was their country in its living and real aspect;

---

[7] *Nic. Eth.* I. 7, 1098a16–18.
[8] Herder 1989: III. 13. iii, and Schiller 1967: Letter VI, sec. 7; cf. Chapter 1, secs. II and VI.

this actual Athens, this Sparta, these temples, these altars, this form of social life, this union of fellow citizens, these manners and customs. To the Greek his country was a necessity of life, without which existence was impossible.[9]

Hegel's statement reflects the influence of the Aristotelian idea that the individual is essentially just a part of the *polis*, and as a part of a whole depends on it for being the thing that he is.[10]

This dependence might appear to entail a complete submersion of the individual, a totalitarian suppression and sacrifice of each person's happiness in favour of the collective good of the state. Many of Hegel's critics have accused him of precisely that.[11] Much of the hegelian tradition of thought, however, has struggled to reject this way of thinking, especially in its account of Greek ethics. The citizen of a *polis* was not, it is maintained, merely a cog in a machine (to recall Schiller's condemnation of the modern state).[12] Rather, a Greek would supposedly have a conception of himself arising from his activity in the city; a conception which, according to Hegel, would seem to him entirely satisfactory, even though it was wholly relational. As one writer describes Hegel's view, 'true individuality consists in fulfilling in one's own way a determinate function, having a specific job or profession'.[13] It was this kind of individuality, according to Hegel, that the Greek *polis* lent to its citizens. It is the same kind of individuality that many modern communitarians hope to defend from charges of totalitarianism.

From this claim—that the identity of the individual was in Classical Greek thinking wholly bound up with the *polis*—Hegel appears to draw a conclusion that is both enormously important and enormously problematical. It is the thesis that during the Classical period there prevailed an identification of one's own good with both the norms of one's *polis* and its good:

Of the Greeks in the first and genuine form of their freedom, we may assert, that they had no conscience; *the habit of living for their country without further reflection, was the principle dominant among them*.[14]

---

[9] Hegel 1991: 253. Cf. Wood 1993: 201. Cf. also Charles Taylor, describing Hegel's view of the Greeks (1979: 383; also 383, 385, 388); and Gray 1941: 58:

The happiest, unalienated life for man, which the Greeks enjoyed, is where the norms and ends expressed in the public life of a society are the most important ones by which its members define their identity as human beings. For them the human matrix in which they cannot help living is not felt to be foreign. Rather, it is the essence, the 'substance' of the self.

[10] Aristotle, *Pol.* I. 2, 1253a19–33.

[11] Thus famously, thought not uniquely, Popper in his 1950.

[12] Cf. Chapter 1, secs. II. 7 and VI. 1.

[13] Wood 1993: 200–2.

[14] Hegel 1991: 253. Hegel did not think that the Greeks had reached the point of perfectly embodying the highest political condition, because they did not fully possess the idea of the autonomous individual.

If my existence depends on that of my *polis*, the thought seems to run, then the well-being of my *polis* and my own well-being must coincide. Such inferences are far from secure. It is not at all to be taken for granted that the dependence entails the coincidence of goods.[15] Nevertheless, Hegel took it that the coincidence was accepted without question by the Greeks of the Classical period.

Not only without question, but 'without reflection', too. As already noted, Hegel believed that the Hellenic identification of an individual's happiness with that of his *polis* was, in the Periclean period, an unarticulated, unselfconscious one.[16] Later it was articulated to some extent by Plato and Aristotle, but only after it had come under attack from the Sophists and Socrates. Before that, the conception was simply taken for granted without being made explicit.[17]

II. Some Assumptions of the Hegelian Account

1. The Good of the Individual and the Good of the Polis

To bring the historical facts to bear in assessing this account of Greek ethics, we need to take note of a number of assumptions that it embodies. All of these assumptions are designed to support the idea that when a Greek of the Classical period asked himself what to do, he could answer unambiguously by looking to and following the standards of action that his *polis* laid down and, simultaneously, to the happiness of the *polis* in which they operated. If the individual did that, there would be no call for him to consult any other potentially competing standard. All valid norms would be related to the *polis*, and would win their claim on his attention by that very fact.

Closely linked with this thesis are two ancillary theses, each bearing on the coordination of roles of the individuals within a *polis*. One of these theses says that the goods of individual citizens are mutually non-competitive. That is, the reasonable individual will conceive of his well-being as something that does not, either in theory or in the actual circumstances, require competition with other individuals in the *polis*.

This point is easily illustrated. Suppose—to the contrary of the idea now under discussion—that citizens conceived of their happiness as consisting, for example, either in being the wealthiest person in the city, or as simply being very wealthy. In both cases, these aspirations would be, respectively, certain or highly likely to bring the individuals into competition with each other. Someone interpreting Greek society as Hegel does must hold that individual citizens of a well-functioning Greek *polis* did

[15] See Chapter 5, sec. II. 5.

[16] Chapter 1, sec. VII. 6–8.

[17] Hegel did not believe that the coincidence was ever articulated fully in antiquity, either in philosophy or in political activity. Rather, he thought that the beginning of full articulation had to await the coming of the modern state.

not in fact regard their well-being as depending in this way on goods over which competition must or usually does arise. That is one reason why Hegel insists that it is characteristic of a Classical Greek democracy to be a place where 'the citizens are still unconscious of their particular interests'.[18]

The second ancillary thesis has to do with the whole collection of functions that the citizens together are to perform. It must be supposed that once we find a group of roles whose fulfilment we can reasonably accept as constituting the citizens' well-being, the joint fulfilment of these must both be posssible and be conducive to the well-being of the *polis*. Not everyone can be a plumber or a barber, for instance, just as there cannot be a city wholly made up of a population of natural-born arsonists. We must accordingly presuppose the existence of some harmonious coordination of the tasks that are available to each citizen, and also their effectiveness in meeting the basic needs of the community.

2. The Role of the Individual in the Polis

This whole line of thought finds its main inspiration in Plato's *Republic*. As the hegelian account interprets Plato, his central contention is that when people perform their roles in the *polis* well, their doing so cannot result in conflict over their well-being.[19]

In due course I shall argue that this interpretation of Plato mistakes a crucial element of his intention.[20] For the present moment, however, I let this mistake pass, and examine simply the manner in which it plays itself out in the hegelian response to Greek thought.

Taken as the hegelian account interprets him, Plato achieves this harmony within the *polis* by conceiving of the roles of its citizens in a very particular way. He takes those roles to be necessarily non-competitive, in the sense that one person's excellent performance cannot lead to another's failure to perform excellently. This requires Plato to exclude certain types of roles. There are no such roles, for instance, as that of

---

[18] Hegel 1991: 252; cf. Hegel 1965: sec. 148. MacIntyre advocates a somewhat similar view, but he acknowledges much more clearly than Hegel did that the *polis* was also expected to regulate the distribution of what he calls 'goods of effectiveness' (1988: 33–4). Hegel is aware of the pressure exerted by the concept of these goods, which was articulated by the Sophists, but gives little explanation of how the concept arose; MacIntyre traces it back more explicitly to Homeric times (1988: ch. 3); cf. n. 21.

[19] For the community to function here means for it to continue to exist in such a way that people can go on doing the things that they regard as constituting their well-being. When Plato, for instance, talks in the *Republic* about the good of the city, what he primarily means is its stability and continued existence. See *Rep.* 422e–423a, 546a, and White 1979b: 39–43. However, Plato makes an important exception to this claim, and thus shows his view to be in an important respect quite different from what the hegelian interpretation makes it out to be; see Chapter 5, secs. VI–VII.

[20] See below, Chapter 5, secs. VI–VII.

working to outdo others in the magnificence of one's contributions to the city. There can of course be localized competition among citizens, in athletics, for instance, but it is carefully circumscribed so as to take place only insofar as it is, as a whole, conducive to concord within society. This assumption of wholly non-competitive excellence supplies Plato with his main ground for contending that harmony within the *polis* would come more easily if people aimed to fulfil their 'functions' well than if they, for instance, aimed at becoming rich.[21]

In the ideal *polis* that Plato sketches in the *Republic*, each citizen is to have one and only one role. Under Plato's arrangement,

each must be directed to the one task for which each is naturally fitted, so that he should pursue that one task which is his own and be himself one person and not many, and the city itself be a unity and not a plurality.

The harmony and stability of the city is the chief aim of this arrangement:

—Is there any greater evil that we can mention for a city than whatever tears it apart into many communities instead of one? —There is not.[22]

Since happiness consists in the fulfilment of one's function, and since fulfilment of all of the functions together is both non-competitive and sufficient for the well-being of the *polis*, Plato believes that his scheme guarantees that conflict among individuals over happiness will not arise.[23]

Plato's city is of course an idealization, but the hegelian tradition believes that the harmony of the *polis* was more than that. Hegel believed that the exemplification of this idea in actual Greek politics was described in the famous funeral oration of Pericles in Book II of Thucydides' *History of the Peloponnesian War*. Any idea of a cleavage between the good of the individual and the flourishing of his *polis*, according to Hegel's account, is a departure from the original and genuine Hellenic spirit that actually was embodied in the politics of that place and time.[24]

3. Explaining Away Rival Norms

The idea that the *polis* supplies all valid deliberative norms and considerations, as I earlier pointed out, encounters resistance from two types of rivals, one wider and one narrower. On the narrower side we find an individualist thesis that standards are provided by the individual, or by some other unit smaller than the *polis*, such as the family.

---

[21] Following Hegel, MacIntyre assumes throughout his discussion (1988: 323–46) that the 'goods of excellence' do not introduce competition, or do not introduce it to anything like the degree to which the 'goods of effectiveness' do. On the other side, someone who believes that the operation of the free market constitutes the basis of society is rather likely to adhere to a contrary view.

[22] *Rep.* 423d and 461a–b.   [23] See further Chapter 5, sec. VI.

[24] Hegel 1991: 269–71; Gray 1941: 59–64.

On the wider side there is the universalist contention that a person is to do what makes sense from some broader perspective than that of the *polis*—that of a human being, for example, or a rational being as such.

Hegel could hardly deny that such rival standards were ever considered in Classical Greece. He recognized that present among them were emphatic representatives of an individualist type of opposition to the norms of the *polis*. He well knew also that the ideal city of the *Republic* was not the Athens of Plato's own day. Hegel knew, too, that during the Classical period some individuals, including notably Thrasymachus in *Republic* I, are portrayed by Plato himself as expressing attitudes that are quite contrary to his. There was therefore no way in which Hegel could maintain that in Plato's time, at any rate, no other source of norms than the *polis* had ever been heard or dreamed of. Rather, he had to cast his view in a different fashion.

His way out was to say that these non-*polis*-centred attitudes resulted from a contamination of the pure stream of Hellenic thought. They were introduced into Greek consciousness, he held, by Socrates and the Sophists. Thereafter they went on ultimately to break down the concord of Greek *Sittlichkeit*. The Sophists, Hegel asserted, were the first to broach the idea of 'subjective reflection'.[25] They thus engendered the *polis*-centred notion of individual good and thereby anticipated the modern emergence of competitive individualism.[26] But they did not exemplify, he believed, a truly Greek style of thought.

Whereas Hegel was aware of individualist thinking in ancient Greece—though he endeavoured to discount it—he tended to treat the universalist outlook, for its part, as though it were wholly absent. As he interpreted the Greeks of this period, they did not seriously entertain the possibility of valid standards wider than those of one's own *polis*—such as, for example, norms binding on all city-states or on all human beings. Hegel did not think that Greek philosophy had yet developed anything like the universalist stance that Kant espoused. The cults of the Greek gods, Hegel supposed, were all tied to the local practices of individual communities. He drew the conclusion that norms extending beyond the city walls did not come within the ken of the Hellenic mind. Accordingly, it appeared, thinkers like Plato and Aristotle did not need to, and so did not, worry about dissent from any such wider quarter. Unencumbered by such worries, they could unreservedly uphold the idea—which in their time had lost some of its grip on Greek politics itself—that what makes sense for a person to do always arises from and depends upon his own actual community in its own local setting.[27]

The concept of the *polis* that Hegel did so much to disseminate has not disappeared. It still lives a vigorous life, as already noted, in the works of thinkers of the

---

[25] Hegel 1991: 261–2; for the same idea, see MacIntyre 1988: ch. 4 and pp. 77, 392.
[26] Hegel 1991: 253, 267–9.   [27] See Taylor 1979: 375–6.

present day such as Charles Taylor, Michael Sandel, and Alasdair MacIntyre.[28] On MacIntyre's account, in particular, the harmonizing capacities of the Greek conception of the *polis* are especially robust. As he describes it, the Periclean *polis* provides a pattern for an even more inclusive harmony than the one that Plato's *Republic* suggests. According to MacIntyre, the Periclean city allowed all excellences to be realized, and it also—as Plato's city did not attempt to do—coordinated the demands of people struggling over competitive goods:

> Every citizen is free not only to participate in the life of the city but also to pursue his own ends, and each will be able to do so all the more successfully by reason of that participation. Those ends may be those of excellence, of wealth, or of power. There is on the Periclean view nothing in the pursuit of any one of these that needs to be destructive of the good of the city or of any other individual citizen.[29]

Here we are still in the tradition of, for instance, Herder's earlier-cited view that in ancient Greece, 'splendour and greatness were not dispersed, as in modern times; rather they were fused as the concern of the state'.[30]

III. Norms Independent of the Polis

1. Ground-Clearing

Powerful and suggestive as this image of the *polis* is, it is radically oversimplified and deeply misleading. It fosters a distorted impression of both the historical state of affairs in Classical Greece and of the overall character of Greek ethical thinking.

First of all and most straightforwardly, it is not true that, for the Greeks, all standards arise from the city-state. In fact the Greeks believed that some of the things that a person might rationally do are based on quite different grounds than their conduciveness to the good of the *polis* or their conformity to its norms. Some of these grounds, for one thing, are narrower than the *polis*. They have to do with smaller groups like families. Others concern a person's individual good. These cannot be discounted as somehow aberrant or foreign to Greek thought. In the other direction, too, there are broader considerations that are taken seriously by Greek thinkers, and treated as having force independently of either the *polis* or the individual's own good. Some of these, moreover, have a quite straightforwardly universalist character.

In the present chapter, my main concern is not to show the full range of norms that Greek thinkers recognized, nor the kinds of basis that they took those norms to rest

---

[28] See Chapter 2, sec. III.

[29] MacIntyre 1988: 51; cf. esp. pp. 34, 37–9, 53–4, and (with regard to Plato and Aristotle) 98, 102, 122–3, 133, 141.

[30] Herder 1989: III. 13. iii. 3, quoted in Chapter 1, sec. II. 9.

on. I limit myself here primarily to demonstrating a negative point: that not all of the grounds for decision that the Greeks take seriously are derived from the *polis*. At the moment I am not concerned directly with the possibility of conflict between different norms or considerations. I am not, for instance, contending at this juncture that *polis*-related and non-*polis*-related considerations necessarily clash with each other in the actual world, in the sense of recommending incompatible courses of action (though some of the passages that I cite do refer to such conflicts). I turn to questions of actual conflict later.[31] Rather, I confine myself here to simply preparing the ground for that idea, by showing how norms that are not centred on the *polis* play an important role in Greek practical philosophy from an early time onwards.

2. *From Homer to Sophocles and Socrates*

In the first place, it needs to be stressed that the *polis* did not spring full-blown from the soil of Greece, and that the Greeks were vividly aware of this fact. The *polis* arose by a process of development that extended well into the Classical period. The social world of Homer is not the world of the developed *polis* at the end of the fifth century. The Homeric world does not contain things that are recognizably *poleis*. As we progress through Greek history down into the fifth century BCE, the *polis* becomes progressively stronger and more effective in governing people's actions. The Greeks were aware of this development. It is recorded explicitly in their literature, for instance, in Thucydides' *History*, Aeschylus's *Eumenides*, Sophocles' *Oedipus at Colonus*, and other works. Any genuine understanding of Greek ethics must take account of this fact.[32]

Far more important than the facts of earlier Greek history, however, is the following point. The Greeks of the Classical period did not think of the city-state as the only institution to possess a claim to their loyalty. They were able to see that other considerations could compete, within practical decision-making, against the well-being and the standards of an individual's own city-state. The chief rival of the *polis*, as Greek society developed, was the clan or extended network of a person's family members and other close associates. The force of these attachments is evident in the Homeric *Iliad* and *Odyssey*. As is widely accepted, Thucydides likewise illustrates the point:

It appears . . . that the country now called Hellas had no settled population in ancient times; instead there was a series of migrations, as the various tribes, being under the constant pressure of invaders who were stronger than they were, were always prepared to abandon their own territory.

---

[31] In Chapters 5 and 6, that is.

[32] See esp. Adkins 1960. Notice that one can readily accept Adkins's story of the development of the importance of the *polis* without buying into his more controversial theses about Greek ethics.

The difference between clan attachments, such as one finds in Homer, and the ones on which the *polis* relies has increasingly come to be recognized—far more so than during much of the past two hundred years. It is indispensable to a comprehension of the role of the *polis* in Greek ethics.[33]

It was not only in Archaic times that the *polis* was required to compete with other sources of practical deliberative considerations. Plato's *Crito* supplies a striking illustration of the persistence of this state of affairs well into the Classical period. Socrates is urged by his friend Crito—who plainly represents, not a purely Sophistic outlook, but rather a more old-fashioned family- or clan-oriented viewpoint—to escape from the jail in which he is waiting to be executed for offences against the city, and to flee from Athens. Socrates refuses to do this, and explains why.

The issue on which Socrates' explanation turns shows something important, namely, that he assumes that his readers will not take the pre-eminence of the claims of the laws of the *polis* for granted. Obedience to the laws is important, he expects them to think, but other claims, too, have to be weighed in the deliberative balance. Some of these claims—which Crito exploits as he tries to convince Socrates to escape—arise from loyalty to Socrates' friends and his own family.[34] We therefore cannot take it as a foregone conclusion that these rival claims will fail to determine the action of a reasonable person. If loyalty to the laws of the city is to prevail over them, the laws have to be supported by a powerful argument, which Socrates endeavours to supply.[35]

The same kind of argument needs to be mounted by Plato on behalf of the strict cohesiveness that he demands for the ideal *polis* in the *Republic*.[36] His discussion of the arrangements that he plans for producing and rearing children, especially in Book V, are a self-conscious assault against the claims of the family on behalf of the *polis*. These claims did not originate with Socrates or the Sophists. It was by no means only with them that claims first arose that could compete with the *polis*. Such claims stem from a much older time, and represent the traditional clan loyalties that one can see at work in Homer's *Iliad* and *Odyssey*.

Many tragic dramas of the period, especially the ones written by Sophocles, explicitly and self-consciously manifest the same kind of clash of other claims with those of the city-state. One of the best-known exemplifications of this type appears in Sophocles' *Antigone*. The action takes place in the city of Thebes. Antigone wishes to bury her brother Polynices. Her uncle Creon opposes her, because Polynices has died in an attack against Thebes, fighting against his brother Eteocles, who has died defending the *polis*; Creon does not, for that very reason, wish to permit Polynices' burial. Against Antigone, Creon urges the prestige of the *polis* thus:

[33] See Adkins 1960.
[35] This fact is rightly emphasized by Adkins 1960.
[36] See *Rep.* 423d, 453b–c, 457b–461e, 462a–464a.

[34] See esp. *Crito* 44b–c, 45c–46a.

whoever places a friend
above the good of his own country, he is nothing;

and

Remember this:
our country is our safety.
Only while she voyages true on course
can we establish friendships, truer than blood itself.
Such are my standards. They make our city great.[37]

These words are spoken not because they express a commonplace accepted on all sides, but precisely because their appeal to the city does not go unchallenged. In Antigone's own eyes, allegiance to her brother, though quixotic, has decisive force.[38]

Hegel himself was of course not at all unaware of the appearance of these conflicts in Greek tragic dramas. He recognized them, for instance, in *Antigone* and *Oedipus Rex*.[39] However, he believed that in the plays themselves Sophocles manifested the view that the conflict is in the end unreal. In *Antigone*, for instance, there is a collision between the family and the state. Both considerations 'have their value'. The mistake of Antigone and Creon is, respectively, to uphold each value as absolute. As a result, each of them exhibits one-sidedness. In the end, however, Sophocles brings about a reconciliation:

The removal of this state of collision consists in this, that the moral powers which are in collision, in virtue of their one-sidedness, divest themselves of the one-sidedness attaching to the assertion of independent validity, and this discarding of the one-sidedness reveals itself outwardly in the fact that the individuals who have aimed at the realization in themselves of a single separate moral power, perish.[40]

It is hard not to react to this idea, as an interpretation of the play, by saying that Hegel seems not to allow enough room for a distinction between, on the one hand, a drama depicting the reconciliation or elimination of a conflict and, on the other hand, a work that shows how a conflict may lead to the destruction of the people who are caught up in it. Hegel's metaphysics perhaps encourages this assimilation. At any rate, one must adopt an especially rigid philosophical preconception, such as Hegel's, if one is to read *Antigone*, in particular, as a play in which conflicts are resolved, or by which the viewer or reader is shown that such a resolution is possible.[41] Greek dramas of this kind

---

[37] Sophocles, *Antigone*, trans. Fagles, ll. 203–4, 210–14. The word translated 'friend' here is *philos*, which can designate any attachment, including family attachments, as here.

[38] As Hegel recognized; see Taylor 1979: 502.

[39] See Hegel 1962: ii. 264–7. According to Hegel, the conflict in the former is between state and family, whereas in the latter it is between 'consciousness' and 'unconsciousness'.

[40] Hegel 1962: ii. 263–4.

[41] See Gellrich 1988: ch. 1.

show how much damage these conflicts can ultimately do, not how unreal they ulti-mately are.

Moreover, there is no reason at all to think that it was only because of the Sophists that the Greeks recognized the possibility of struggle among different loyalties, in particular a struggle between the *polis* and other sources of norms. All along the Greeks were fully capable of recognizing such states of affairs, without automatically supposing that the considerations deriving from the *polis* inevitably had to prevail.

The Greeks themselves regarded these other, potentially rival sources of norms as ancient. Aristophanes and other conservatives sometimes complain that pristine virtues have been eroded by new-fangled Sophistic thinking. Some of the opposition to Socrates arose from attitudes of this kind, as manifested for instance by Aristophanes in his *Clouds* and Anytus in Plato's *Meno*.[42] Other writers, however, demonstrate that this account of existing threats to loyalty to the *polis* was by no means universal. As I have just noted, the *Crito* is only one manifestation of another consid-eration that rivals that loyalty, namely, allegiance to family. No one regards this alle-giance as created by Sophistic influence. The idea of norms and considerations not generated by the *polis* did not present itself, even to the Athenians of the late fifth cen-tury, as a new or superficial phenomenon that had been somehow artificially generat-ed by Socratic or Sophistic activity. The phenomenon was rightly regarded as being every bit as much a part of the culture that gave rise to Greek philosophical ethics as any other factor that produced it.

When we turn to the other side of the matter, namely, the question whether the Greeks were also susceptible to considerations broader than those deriving from a single *polis*, the situation is much the same, and the answer is once again that they were. This is true not merely in later, Hellenistic times—when it is generally held that the power of the *polis* had declined[43]—but also prior to the Classical period as well. The world beyond the confines of the *polis* also gave rise to norms that were capable of rivalling the standards laid down by the city-state. It would be mistaken to accept the widespread idea that all fundamental allegiances of pre-Hellenistic periods were con-sistently local. Sometimes the Greeks appeal to considerations that plainly are thought of as having force not because of any link either to city-state or even to family, but wholly because of someone's status as being a human being. And at other times, furthermore, considerations of justice are introduced to assess, from some *independent* perspective, the justifiability, and even the validity, of the laws of one's own city-state.

This point can be illustrated by evidence concerning general obligations that the Greeks accepted from early in their recorded history. These obligations include the requirement that one not harm a stranger, guest, or suppliant.[44] Moreover, the whole situation in the *Iliad* requires that at least some standards be available to deal with dis-

---

[42] *Meno* 90b–94e.   [43] See e.g. Ehrenberg 1969: 97–8.
[44] See Lloyd-Jones 1983: 5–6.

putes that affect the coalition encompassing the whole Greek army that besieges Troy.[45] Another case in point has already been given above. Here again is Antigone, defending her actions against Creon's appeal to the interests and laws of the *polis*:

> Of course I did. It wasn't Zeus, not in the least,
> who made this proclamation—not to me.
> Nor did that Justice, dwelling with the gods
> beneath the earth, ordain such laws (*nomoi*) for men.
> Nor did I think your edict had such force
> that you, a mere mortal, could override the gods,
> the great unwritten, unshakable traditions (*nomima*).[46]

There is nothing at all aberrant, by standards of Greek thought, about this effort to seek a broad standpoint from which a person might judge her own city's norms. As a general matter, the Greeks were quite capable of appealing to extremely general considerations of justice against laws of their own city.[47] The standards of the *polis* have weight, but they by no means possess the unquestioned overriding force that some writers on Greek culture have claimed for them.

3. Trans-Political Norms in Thucydides

In Thucydides' *History of the Peloponnesian War*, too, we encounter appeals to norms and considerations broader than those of the *polis*—though for reasons that I shall mention shortly the fact is often overlooked. These appeals have to do with disputes of two types. In the first, the well-being of one city-state is irreconcilably pitted against the well-being of another. In the second, there are disputes between cities in which neither side can claim that the case is governed by its own laws rather than the laws of the other city.

In cases like this, standards of justice are invoked which clearly are based in neither the good of one *polis* nor its laws. These standards are invoked to govern relations between different city-states—indeed, it could hardly be otherwise, if cities come into conflict and if there is to be any expectation of an orderly way of settling matters. Thucydides, as well as the people whom he portrays, are usually cynical about the *effectiveness* of these inter-city standards, that is to say, about whether or not people will actually adhere to them very much. However, that is largely a different issue from the question whether the standards are deemed to exist, that is, to be there to be appealed to, on the chance that a hearer might find them to have some weight.

---

[45] Not, of course, that the coalition is made up of city-states; it is made up instead of something more like clans (cf. Adkins 1960: e.g. 156–63). As a whole, however, it is broader than a city, and requires coordination of groups that come from widely disparate parts of Greece.

[46] Sophocles, *Antigone*, trans. Fagles, ll. 499–505.

[47] For more examples, see Dover 1974: 186–7.

Perhaps it makes no sense to say that a standard exists if it is *never* observed; but even if it is often flouted, it may reasonably be said to exist, and may play a role in argument and deliberation.

The speakers in Thucydides, as will be evident shortly, do not deny that inter-city standards exist. Everyone is fully aware that cities generally try to act in their own interest, and that a city's own norms will usually have that tendency. That does not, however, gainsay the fact that standards more general than those of a particular *polis* are often referred to and invoked in defending a claim or offering a justification. The existence and relevance of the standards are acknowledged, even when it is not expected that they will be obeyed.

Consider a speech that Thucydides wrote as a part of the so-called Mytilenian Debate in Book III of his *History*. In this debate, the Athenians are deliberating about whether to punish the people of Mytilene harshly for their disloyalty to the Athenian empire. In a speech that is a part of that debate, the Athenian politician Cleon is made to say the following:

> Let me sum the whole thing up. I say that, if you follow my advice, you will be doing the right thing (*dikaia*) as far as Mytilene is concerned and at the same time you will be acting in your own interests (*xympheron*); if you decide differently, you will not win them over, but you will be passing judgement on yourselves. For if they were justified in revolting, you must be wrong in holding power. If, however, whatever the rights or wrongs of it may be, you propose to hold power all the same, then your interest demands that these too, rightly or wrongly, must be punished. The only alternative is to surrender your empire, so that you can afford to go in for philanthropy.[48]

Cleon here treats what is right or just (*ta dikaia*) and what is in the Athenians' interests (*to xympheron*) as two distinguishable considerations, which happen in the present case to coincide. Nothing in the passage, furthermore, suggests that the considerations of justice arise from anything to do with a particular *polis*, rather than from considerations involving *poleis* in general. Nor is it suggested that there is anything remarkable about that fact. Even when the notion of justice that is introduced is not expected to carry decisive weight, its relevance and point is acknowledged.

Arguing against Cleon a little later, then, Diodotus makes the same distinction:

> If we are sensible people, we shall see that the question is not so much whether they are guilty as whether we are making the right decision for ourselves. I might prove that they are the most guilty people in the world, but it does not follow that I shall propose the death penalty, unless that is in your interests; I might argue that they deserve to be forgiven, but should not recommend forgiveness unless that seemed to me the best thing for the state. (III. 44. 1)

Diodotus stresses that he is advising the Athenians to spare the Mytilenians not because that is just—though he thinks it is—but because it is advantageous to them:

---

[48] Thucydides, *History* III. 40. 4 (trans. Warner, with minor changes).

'this is not a law-court, where we have to consider what is fit and just; it is a political assembly, and the question is how Mytilene can be most useful to Athens' (III. 44. 4). The justice in question here is clearly not a product of the *polis*. Diodotus of course knows that the Athenians will not in fact do what is just if that conflicts with the good of their city; and he certainly does not appeal to laws of Athens itself. That fact, however, does not prevent him from thinking that it makes perfectly good sense to refer to it as a consideration that merits attention.

The same distinction, between justice and the interest of a city-state, is even more emphatically stressed in the so-called Melian Dialogue in Book V of Thucydides' history. This dialogue arises from a situation roughly analogous to that of the Mytilenian Debate, involving Athenian policy towards the island of Melos. Once again, a notion of justice is invoked that cannot be defined by the customs or well-being of some particular *polis*. Both the Melians and the Athenians equally agree that the paths of justice and the good of one's city may diverge (V. 107, 104). They also agree that the motivations respectively associated with them may also lead to different actions (V. 90, 106).[49]

The norms that are appealed to in the Melian Dialogue, then, are not the customs of any particular city-state. They govern relations among city-states, and are treated as the common possession of all. This is so even though the parties see that the norms may be disregarded when there is no agency powerful enough to put them into effect.

4. Some Causes of the Misunderstanding of Thucydides

Thucydides' readers, as I mentioned, are sometimes misled on this point. They fall victim to the mistaken impression that according to him, or to the speakers whose voices are heard in his writings, the only thing that creates an ethical standard at all is the power to enforce it, so that if that power does not exist, then the standard could not play any serious justificatory role. At one point in the Melian Dialogue, indeed, it does begin to look as though a notion of justice is being advanced according to which ethical standards are created solely by someone's power to enforce them, and can hold only relatively to the possession of such power.[50] The Athenians say:

[W]e on our side will use no fine phrases saying, for example, that we have a right to our empire because we defeated the Persians, or that we have come against you now because of the injuries you have done us—a great mass of words that nobody would believe . . . [Y]ou know as well as we do that, when these matters are discussed by practical people, *the standard*

---

[49] For similar examples from writers after Thucydides, see Dover 1974: 311–12.

[50] I take this view to be antithetical to morality as it is standardly conceived. If that is not so, then the present argument is not necessary to the case against dissociating Greek standards from modern moral notions.

of justice depends on the equality of power to compel and that in fact the strong do what they have the power to do and the weak accept what they have to accept.

When the Athenians utter the sentence, '[T]he standard of justice depends on the equality of power to compel', they are sometimes taken to mean that unless some actual city has the power to put a standard of justice into effect, it does not exist at all. This, however, is not the meaning of the sentence. That fact is shown by the fact that the Melians reply immediately as follows:

> Then in our view (since *you force us to leave justice out of account* and to *confine ourselves to self-interest*)—in our view it is at any rate useful that you should not destroy a principle that is to the general good of all men, namely that . . . there should be such a thing as fair play and just dealing.[51]

The Athenians do not here claim that justice exists only by virtue of the power that someone may have to enforce it. Nor are they saying that considerations of justice have rational weight only in so far as justice is conducive to someone's interests. Rather, they question whether considerations—which are *agreed* to *exist* in an articulable form—actually do *motivate* people strongly enough to override strong considerations of self-interest.

The Athenians' contention, that is, is that expecting people actually to *do* what is just is realistic only when they are willing so to act, and that such a thing usually happens only when acting justly is not sharply contrary to their interest. But the Athenians do not deny that the standards of justice exist when the willingness to abide by them is absent. On the contrary, the Athenians' words *presuppose* that the standards *do* exist even then.[52] For this reason the Melians rely on their existence in their argument. They do not simply say, 'Oh well, since no one will enforce it, no such standard exists and there is no point in referring to it.' Rather, they overtly and explicitly use the standard as the basis of their reproach to what they fear the Athenians will do.

In fact, the very cynicism that is sometimes exhibited towards standards of justice between city-states shows that even when those standards are unlikely to be obeyed, the concept of the existence of such standards was clearly apprehended.

Here we must guard against a common error that arises when issues concerned with one's own good arise in Greek ethics. We often find accusations to the effect that someone is speciously bringing forward a claim of justice as a mere pretext for advancing his own interest. The fact of this accusation does indicate, on the one hand,

---

[51] Thucydides, *History* V. 89–90. The Melians are appealing not to fair play as such, but to its usefulness to the Athenians, which is a special case of its usefulness to 'all men'.

[52] See Gomez-Lobo 1989: esp. 190, 198–9, 201. (I demur, however, at his wording at 184, where it is suggested that the description of the contemplated Athenian actions as 'wrong' is rejected. As Gomez-Lobo shows concerning the other pages that I have cited, the point is that such a description is allowable; for what is naive is the idea that it will actually cause the Athenians to change their minds about what they will do.)

that the person is perceived as motivated by consideration of his own good, and as thinking that matters of justice in and of themselves carry little or no weight. At the same time, however, it also demonstrates that he thinks that, as a matter of strategy, the notion of justice is worth deploying in his own cause. He wants to make people believe that he will do certain things precisely *because* they are just—*even as* those same people believe it obvious that he will thereby be acting against his own good. But that means, in turn, that he supposes that his audience *does* treat justice as carrying at least some weight. If the notion of justice were unknown, or were thought to have no force at all, then appeals to it would be useless, even as a way of making an action that is actually motivated by self-interest look respectable.

Precisely this sort of phenomenon, however, is what we see occurring in relations between Greek city-states. A further passage from the Melian Dialogue shows that considerations of justice are thought of as fully distinct from considerations of benefit to a given *polis*. There Thucydides makes the Athenians speak to the Melians as follows:

[O]f all people we know the Spartans are most conspicuous for believing that what they like doing is honourable and what suits their interests is just. And this kind of attitude is not going to be of much help to you in your absurd quest for safety at the moment. (V. 105)

The Athenians are accusing the Spartans of presenting their pursuit of the interests of Sparta under the cover of justice. But the very possibility of making this accusation manifests consciousness of norms that are distinct from the good of a given *polis* and can conflict with them.

For consider what the accusation means. In order that this bit of deception be even possible, the notions of justice must be regarded as distinct from that of the interest or norms of a particular *polis*. For if that were not taken for granted, then there could be no point in a city-state's pretending that it was following a just course of action and not simply trying to further its own interest, as Thucydides' Athenians describe the Spartans as doing. For everyone would know, and would know that everyone else knew, that the pretext was meaningless. I shall have occasion to return to this point in the discussion of Plato's *Republic*.[53]

IV. The Golden Rule

I now move on to examine the Greeks' employment of a principle which, even more clearly than the considerations that I have just described, is far more general in its scope than any *polis*-centred norm and is in fact quite unconnected with the *polis*, namely, what we now call the 'Golden Rule'.

---

[53] See Chapter 5, sec. III.

The Golden Rule has over its long history been framed in various ways, many of them not equivalent to each other.[54] In one of its forms it is close to the sort of principle of universalization that Kant uses in his Categorical Imperative, 'Act only on that maxim that you can will to be a universal law'. For example, the principle that a person should not do anything that he would blame someone else for doing—this being one of the dicta that goes under the heading of the Golden Rule—has an import that is close to that of Kant's dictum. For this principle suggests that a person is to permit himself only those actions that he regards as falling under a rule that he would extend to *all* others as well as to himself.

Not every form of the Golden Rule has this character. Some formulations can be taken as simple rules of self-regarding prudence. Take, for instance, the maxims, 'Do unto others as you *would have* them do unto you', and '*Don't* do unto other what you *would not have* them do unto you'. Both can easily be understood in a purely prudential self-interested sense. That is, they might be based simply on the observation that if you act (or refrain from acting) towards others as you wish them to act (or refrain from acting) towards you, then you will have a better chance of being treated as you would like to be treated.[55] If it were construed in some such way, the Golden Rule would turn out to be simply a prudential and possibly even an egoistic maxim.

However, the injunction not to act towards others as you would *blame* them for acting towards you must be taken in a quite different fashion. This injunction is not a rule of prudence. It does not warn you off all behaviour that you would not like to have directed at yourself, but only off the type that you would *blame* if it were so directed. It enjoins a person to generalize or even universalize the attitude of blame that he might adopt towards certain acts performed vis-à-vis himself, so that the attitude would inhibit acts of his own towards others. This is not the same as Kant's imperative, but it is not far from it. It does not tell us to act only on universalizable maxims. It does, however, enjoin us to treat ourselves just as we treat others in a certain respect, by telling us not to exempt ourselves from blame for actions for which we would blame others.

There is a long-standing propensity—which I have already criticized—to suppose that signs of modern-seeming ethical views in antiquity tend to occur in the later part of the period, chronologically close to the rise of Christianity and as a 'transition' to it. This is what Sidgwick maintained, as I have said, about the Stoics' use of imperatives and laws.[56] The same is often contended to apply to the concept of universally applied norms, as opposed to those that are merely local or community-bound.

This idea, however, is mistaken. Lest there be any suspicion that the appearance of

---

[54] On these issues, both philosophical and historical, see Sidgwick 1907: 379–80 and esp. Reiner 1983: 269–70, as well as Reiner 1977.

[55] In this connection, note that Kant did not choose to acknowledge any debt to the Golden Rule for his ideas; see Kant 1981: 68–9 and Reiner 1977.   [56] See Chapter 3, sec. I. 2.

the non-prudential form of the Golden Rule is a late phenomenon, it is worth stress-
ing that the non-prudential form of the Golden Rule appears early in Greek thought.
For instance, such a form can be found before the late fifth century, and so before the
Sophistic period, in the historian Herodotus. Herodotus recounts the following story.
After the dictator Polycrates of Samos dies, the man to whom his power falls,
Maeandrius, speaks as follows:

You know as well as I do that the sceptre of Polycrates, and the power it represents, have
passed into my hands, so that I may, if I wish, become your absolute master. So far as I am
able, however, I shall refrain from doing myself what should rebuke (*epipleessein*) in another.
I did not approve of the conduct of Polycrates (*ou ... moi ... eereske*), nor should I that of any
other man who sought power over people as good as himself; therefore, now that Polycrates
has met his end, I intend to surrender power, and to proclaim you equal before the law
(*isonomiee*).[57]

Although subsequently Maeandrius chooses not to conform his actions to this noble
thought, nonetheless the point of the thought itself is clear. It does not arise from the
norms of any *polis*—Maeandrius is after all in a position to determine those norms as
he pleases—and its content represents a generalization that goes beyond any such
limited group.[58]

Nor is this appeal isolated. In another place, Herodotus describes the Persian
emperor Xerxes as adopting the following attitude:

that he would not behave like the Spartans, who by murdering the ambassadors of a foreign
power had broken the law which all the world holds sacred. He had no intention of doing the
very thing for which he blamed them, or, by taking reprisals, of freeing the Spartans from the
burden of their crime.[59]

There is nothing either late or un-Greek about this sort of universalization in ethical
thinking.[60]

---

[57] Herodotus, *History* III. 142. The word *epiplêssein* stands for an attitude of disapproval, not merely
dislike, so the statement is not merely that Maeandrius will not do to other people what he *would not want*
them to do to him.

[58] The same type of sentiment is also attributed to Thales and to one of the so-called Seven Wise Men,
Pittacus. In the latter case, the saying comes in the form, 'Don't do what you would blame another person
for'. See Stobaeus III. 1. 174 (*hosa nemesaais tooi pleesion, autos mee poiei*). The attribution to Thales occurs
in Diogenes Laertius I. 36. Thales flourished around 590 BCE, but the genuineness of the attributions to him
and Pittacus (ca. 650–570) cannot be relied on in the way in which the occurrence of the idea in Herodotus
can be.   [59] *History* VII. 136.

[60] A number of writers have discussed a form of 'generalization argument' in the *Crito*. It is a mistake
to think that this is the first occurrence of such an argument in Greek ethics, as we can see. Nor does it even,
strictly, involve 'universalization', because it has to do only with the citizens of a particular *polis*. (Kraut
1984: 42ff., 126–40 seems to me not to attend sufficiently to this point, though he notes that the generalization at work in the *Crito* applies only to private citizens.) By contrast, the examples that I have cited involve
no such restrictions.

V. On Some Sources of Confusion about Greek Norms

I have till now left unmentioned two important facts about Greek thought. When they are not properly understood, these facts contribute to the mistaken impression that the Greeks conceived of no norms that are broader than those of the *polis*. One of these facts has to do with the absence in Greece of an established system of 'international' or, better, inter-*polis* law. The other concerns the Greeks' attitudes, especially during the Classical period, towards peoples who were not Greek.

I take up the former fact first. It is often observed that a system of laws governing the relations between city-states was not at all well developed. Indeed, Greek cities often behaved towards each other with extreme untrustworthiness, as any reader of Herodotus or Thucydides is well aware. It certainly often appears, as we might say today, that the 'default' relation between two city-states, in the absence of a specific treaty of peace on which they had agreed, was one of hostility. Thus Plato simply takes for granted in his *Republic* that cities will constantly be on the point of war with each other. Moreover, he does not envisage any stable cooperative institution into which a plurality of cities might be organized.[61] As to the second fact, it is often stated that only later in their history—during Hellenistic times at the earliest—did the Greeks come to regard all human beings as in some important sense equal and akin to each other. In particular, they tended earlier on to think of non-Greeks as notably inferior to themselves, and as deserving less consideration.[62] From these two facts it is inferred that the Greeks could not have conceived of obligations that, in any important sense, extended beyond the scope of an individual *polis*.

The first point is exhibited both by Thucydides himself and by the people whom he describes in the passages discussed above. As I have already remarked in passing, however, the implications of such passages are not what they are often taken to be. They do not show us that the Greeks did not conceive of norms and standards arising from some source beyond the *polis*. What the passages do show is actually to the contrary. They tell us that even while recognizing the high likelihood that a city will often, in order to protect its interests, transgress norms of behaviour among city-states, nevertheless those who negotiate on behalf of cities still believe both that such norms exist, and also that they are worth citing to justify one's actions. People can recognize the existence and even the force of norms that are seen to be usually flouted. By the same token, people make points for the record even when they think that those points may well not be heeded. Insofar as we are discussing the history of concepts and ideas, as we are here, rather than political history, it behoves us to recognize such points.

Plato's own discussion of the relations among cities suggests the same conclusion.

---

[61] *Rep.* 373d–374e, 469b–471c.   [62] See Baldry 1965: 8ff., 16ff.

Plato thinks that there is a natural 'kinship' among Greeks, even when they live in different city-states. Though he does not set up an institution to enforce or strengthen that kinship, he nevertheless recommends norms whereby Greeks will refrain from enslaving each other and from ravaging each other's lands. Hostilities between Greek cities are to be described, he says, as 'civil dissension' (*stasis*), by explicit contrast with 'war' (*polemos*).[63] Moreover, Plato does not recommend these norms on the basis of any advantage that might accrue to the particular ideal *polis* that he is describing. Rather, the norms are put forth as standards that are presumed reasonable independent of the *polis* itself.

The second fact that I have mentioned just now concerns the Greeks' views about non-Greek peoples. This calls for a two-part response. First we need to guard against a confusion of two distinct issues. There is an undeniable inegalitarianism, or even sometimes anti-egalitarianism, that is present in much Greek ethical thought.[64] One can accept many forms of inegalitarianism, however, and at the same time believe that there exist norms that apply to all human beings and that do not arise merely from local institutions such as the *polis*. Someone can consistently hold, on the one hand, that a certain norm applies to all people—in the sense of saying that the same treatment should be accorded to everyone who comes up to a certain standard, regardless of his *polis*—while at the same time holding, on the other hand, that not all people *do* come up to that standard.

In brief, universal applicability of norms does not of itself imply an egalitarian view about the *value* or *deserts* of all people.[65] Therefore the Greeks' tendency to regard non-Greeks as unequal in value to themselves does not show that Greek thought could not conceive of principles that apply to all people, even to non-Greeks. Nor a fortiori does this tendency necessarily betoken any propensity to think that standards of behaviour hold only within the relationships defined by a single *polis*.[66]

Nor indeed was it the unanimous opinion of the Greeks that they were fundamentally different in relevant respects from other people. It is perfectly true that by and large, in their early history, the Greeks did not regard all human beings as equal or even akin. Plato says, for example, that Greeks and non-Greeks, or 'barbarians', are 'natural enemies' of each other.[67] On the other hand, this attitude was not universally

---

[63] *Rep.* 469b–471c.   [64] On this point, see Chapter 8, sec. III.

[65] In a related vein we see that, as is often pointed out, Mill was mistaken in maintaining (1871: ch. 5) that a substantive principle of equality is contained in his view that in the Utilitarian calculus a quantity of happiness counts for the same no matter whose happiness it is.

[66] Indeed, quite the contrary. The belief that people outside one's own city are inferior to those within it, and that the city is *justified* in having a law providing for better treatment of the former than of the latter, is an acknowledgement of a standard that is itself not dependent on the laws of the city themselves. In fact, however, the Greeks did, as I have indicated, accept norms governing behaviour towards suppliants and other outsiders, and thought that they ought to apply to everyone, regardless of the city from which they came.   [67] *Rep.* 470c.

accepted. Gradually, in the Hellenistic period, the Greeks did develop the idea of the kinship of humanity. But, as H. C. Baldry has shown, there also were signs of this idea earlier in Greek thought, for instance in the medical writers.[68] Thus we read in *On Breaths*:

Epidemic fever is of this character because *all men* inhale the same wind, and when a similar wind has mingled with the body in a similar way, similar fevers result . . . So whenever the air is infected with pollutions inimical to the human constitution, *men* become sick; but when the air becomes ill-suited to some *other species of animals*, these fall sick.[69]

The lesson to be drawn here is that although many Greeks took a dim view of non-Greeks as a group, there is evidence enough to show that a conception of universal human features was not on that account excluded from the Greek mind, even if it was not as vigorously developed as it was later to become.

VI. The Kosmos

1. Types of Universality

In any case, moreover, the tendency to suppose that the Greeks entertained no ethical norms of universal scope or applicability is engendered on the whole by a failure to appreciate the variety of forms that normative universality may take, and a consequent unjustified concentration on universality of a particular sort. If we bear the variety of notions of universality in mind, we shall be unlikely to deny flatly that the Greeks were attentive to universal norms.

There is a general tendency nowadays to suppose that the only ethically important kind of universality is a kind just discussed. This kind involves the applicability of norms to, or their validity for, all persons, or rational beings, or human beings or, still more broadly, sentient creatures. This kind of universality is in brief, a *universality of applicability*. A stress on this kind of universality is certainly a characteristic of much modern ethical philosophy, as manifested for instance in Kant—in his notion of universalization in particular—and in Mill. It constitutes a movement in the direction of a kind of egalitarianism (even though, as just noted, it does not in and of itself amount to any substantive egalitarianism).

It would be much too restrictive, however, to suppose that this kind of universality

---

[68] See Baldry 1965: 48–51, 57–9, and 16.

[69] C. 6, quoted from Baldry 1965: 49. Baldry also cited a number of fragments attributed to Democritus. Here we find such dicta as, 'Since we are human, we should sorrow over the misfortunes of human beings, not laugh at them' (DK 107a: 57) and 'To a wise man every land is open; for the whole world is the native country of a good soul' (DK 247: 58). However, the authenticity and the dating of these fragments is often questioned, so they do not serve here as sound evidence.

is the only important kind of universality that there is, or to think that anyone who does not focus on it must *eo ipso* adopt a normative perspective that is focused on local institutions such as the *polis*. To accept such a supposition would be to neglect another important way in which norms may be non-local, and may fully deserve to be called universal. The kind of universality that I have in mind here plays a role both in Greek ethics and also in some important ethical doctrines espoused in more recent times.

2. *Norms of the* Kosmos

The kind of universal consideration that the Greeks certainly did take into account emerges in the notion of the *all-embracing order or pattern or structure* of the universe as a whole. To employ such a notion in formulating or justifying norms is to suppose, for example, that a person or character or action is to be evaluated or judged by reference to the role that it plays within such an all-embracing structure.

Although in Greek thought the pattern of the whole *kosmos* is sometimes compared with various smaller patterns within it, such as the *polis*, nevertheless the importance that is accorded to the structure of the *kosmos* is its own, and it does not amount simply to loyalty to the *polis* itself. This fact can be seen in conception of justice expressed in a number of places by Pindar, for example in the following lines from *Isthmian* V:

> Now again in war the city of Aias could testify
> That it has been set upright by its sailors,
> Salamis, in the murderous storm of Zeus,
> In the hail of blood of men past counting.
> Nevertheless drench your boast in a rain of silence.
> Zeus disposes this and that,
> Zeus the master of everything.[70]

The same Pindaric outlook was well known to Plato, who records it in the *Gorgias* this way:

> Law, which is king of all,
> Both moral men and immortals,
> ... Conducts the uttermost violence
> With the hand of power
> Making it just.[71]

Hugh Lloyd-Jones describes Pindar's thinking in this way:

---

[70] Pindar, *Isthmian Odes* V. 47–53 (trans. Bowra).
[71] Plato, *Gorgias* 484a–b, in the translation given by Dodds in his commentary, p. 270. I have omitted the question mark that Dodds places after 'conducts' to indicate his (understandable) uncertainty about the meaning at that point; on the overall meaning of the passage see his discussion on pp. 270–2.

Justice in Pindar does not simply mean justice in one's dealings with other men. When Bellerophontes tries to fly up to heaven on Pegasus, his action is contrary to justice. It is an infringement of the order maintained by Zeus within the universe, a failure to heed the warnings so constantly repeated that mortals must remember that they are mortal.[72]

Here the ethical idea has a religious component, but that is irrelevant to the present issue. The essential point here is that something is thought of as having or lacking a certain value by virtue of its relation to an order that is seen as embodied in the *kosmos* as a whole—and not because of some relation in which it stands to a *polis*. The same idea is exhibited in philosophical writings as well, especially in Plato and the Stoics. In both philosophical positions, ideals are often described in terms of a pattern, which may embrace some or all of the *kosmos* or universe. This fact is hardly unfamiliar. What is often not noticed, however, is its bearing on issues about the nature of Greek evaluative thinking.

For it goes without saying, of course, that many of the evaluations that Plato expresses in his *Republic* are based on facts about the *polis* and the relationships of people to it. For instance, one sort of justice has to do with whether or not a person performs the task to which he is naturally suited within the *polis*; and the goodness of the city is a matter of the relations of its parts to each other and the city as a whole.[73] Ascriptions of this kind of value dominate the *Republic*.[74]

These *polis*-centred evaluations, however, should not mislead us into thinking that all of Plato's evaluations are of this type. These *polis*-centred judgements are by no means the only evaluations that Plato makes or takes seriously. The subject of the *Republic* extends only to the organization of the *polis*, and the evaluative issues that arise there are, for the most part, related to that institution. The *Timaeus*, however, shows that Plato's evaluative concerns are broader. This work describes the structure of the *kosmos*. Plato recounts the creation of the physical world this way:

Let me tell you then why the creator made this world of generation. He was good, and the good can never have any jealousy of anything. And being free from jealousy, he desired that all things should be as like himself as they could be. This is in the truest sense the origin of creation and of the world . . . God desired that all things should be good and nothing bad, so far as this was attainable. Wherefore also finding the whole visible sphere not at rest, but moving in an irregular and disorderly fashion, out of disorder he brought order, considering that the latter was in every way better than the other.[75]

---

[72] Lloyd-Jones 1983: 50; he traces this notion of justice back to Homer.

[73] *Rep.* 419a–421c, 422e–423d, 427e–428a.

[74] Not exclusively, however. Some of the evaluations of individuals have merely to do with whether they perform their functions within the city. However, others have to do with whether the parts of one's soul, or personality, stand in appropriate relations to each other and to the soul as a whole. The connection between these two types of evaluation is, notoriously, a problem for Plato. See esp. Vlastos 1971a.

[75] Plato, *Timaeus* 29d–30a (trans. Jowett).

Writers who are interested in Plato's ethics ordinarily are not attentive to passages like this one. The main reason for this is perhaps that these passages involve metaphysical views that are uncongenial to modern philosophy, and that are widely held either not to have important ethical implications or to be simply untrue or unfounded. But however that may be, as a historical matter passages like these are every bit as indicative of Plato's overall doctrine about value as anything that he says in the *Republic*.

Such passages also exhibit a component of Greek philosophical thinking that goes back to its earliest recorded beginnings. Since the time of Anaximander at the latest (*c.* 610–540 BCE), the Greeks had long regarded the *kosmos* as an entity that is possessed of structure, and even as subject to a kind of evaluation. According to our sources, Anaximander said that

the principle and element of existing things is neither water nor any other of the so-called elements, but some other *apeiron* ['indefinite' or 'infinite'] nature, from which came into being all the heavens and the worlds in them. And the source of coming-to-be for existing things is that into which destruction, too, happens, 'according to necessity; for they pay penalty and retribution to each other *for their injustice* [*adikia*] according to the assessment of time.[76]

Let us put aside the question what exactly Anaximander meant by 'injustice'—about this matter there is room for doubt and debate. There is no doubt, however, that injustice is here an evaluative notion of some kind, that it plays a significant role in Anaximander's thought, and that it is not here defined by reference to a city-state or anything like it.[77] Justice here represents a cosmic normative perspective.

Plato took over this perspective and gave it an explicit place in his account of the nature of value. According to the *Timaeus*, the overall structure of the *kosmos* exemplifies a good that is all-embracing. The god or 'craftsman' who organizes the *kosmos* models it after the intelligible world as a whole. He does this in order to make the physical world as good as possible.

This attribution of value to the *kosmos*, irrespective of any relation to the *polis*, is not merely something that Plato touches on in passing. The whole of the *Timaeus* is an elaboration of this idea into a theory of the structure of the physical universe. Into this structure Plato then fits, in the *Critias*, an account of how human society is organized into the *polis*. There is a sense, to be sure, in which this idea is marginal to Plato's views about deliberation by specifically human beings. For as the *Republic* pictures matters, the widest scope for a human being's action is the *polis*. Plato does not suggest that people have much opportunity to plan on any larger scale, much less to put such plans

---

[76] Kirk, Raven, and Schofield 1983: chs. 1 and 2 and pp. 106–7, 117–18, from which this translation is taken. Cf. Baldry's remark that in Hesiod *dike* might better be translated by 'good order' than by 'justice' (1965: 16).

[77] See esp. the account given by Kahn 1960.

into action.[78] Nonetheless, the notion that the *kosmos* is good falls squarely within Plato's thinking about value. Accordingly, even though it is uncongenial and largely irrelevant to many modern views, it is thoroughly germane to an understanding of the historical facts about Greek notions of value, and is a useful corrective to the misconception that all Greek thinking about evaluative issues revolves solely around the *polis* and involves no wider considerations.

The Stoics subsequently carried this kind of *kosmos*-centred evaluation further. The only perfectly good thing, they hold, is the *kosmos* as a whole. The good of an individual human being consists simply in living 'in agreement with nature', that is, within the structure of the *kosmos*. Their view is expressed in this way:

[L]iving in agreement with nature comes to be the end, which is in accordance with the nature of oneself that of the whole, engaging in no activity wont to be forbidden by the universal law, which is the right reason pervading everything and identical to Zeus, who is this director of the administration of existing things.[79]

Stoicism is far from clear or unanimous about what this 'agreement' or 'accord' should be taken to amount to. Some Stoics feel the need to specify it more plainly, but they disagree about how to do it.[80] They believe, however, that a 'sage', who is the model of the perfect human condition, would know what this accord consists in. They hold, furthermore, that the sage's effort to pursue his own end will always be consistent with his effort to fit into the pattern of the nature of the *kosmos*. There will never be an incompatibility between his happiness and the good. The only thing that is perfect, however, is the all-inclusive structure of the world.[81]

3. The Diversity of Greek Attitudes

Once again let me return to the old idea that there is some single ethical outlook that is characteristic of 'the Greeks'. When we look at the kinds of evaluations that Greek thinkers bring into play, what is most striking about these evaluations is their variety, not their conformity to any simple pattern. For example, Plato accords comparable degrees of importance to both *kosmos*-based and *polis*-centred values. In the Stoics, on the other hand, it seems fair to say that the *kosmos* comes more distinctly into the foreground and the *polis* tends to recede.

At the same time, it must be noted that some later Greek thinkers attach little or no importance to values that involve a relation to the *kosmos*. Such values find no signifi-

[78] Although Plato never suggests that an individual will be able to exert much influence on a broader part of the *kosmos* than his own *polis*, he does indicate at a couple of points, in the *Republic* and the *Laws*, that one may take wider features of the *kosmos* into account in thinking about one's own actions. See Chapter 5, secs. V. 3–4, and Chapter 7, sec. IV.

[79] Diogenes Laertius VII. 88, trans. in Long and Sedley 1987: i. 395.

[80] White 1985b: 70–2.   [81] *SVF* ii. 550, 549, 641, 1178.

cant place, for instance, in Epicurus's scheme. According to it, value consists in or derives from the pleasure that is experienced by an individual. The universe is infinitely extended, he maintains, and is ordered by no pattern except the regularities obeyed by its atoms. To atoms and their motions *per se*, however, he ascribes no value of any kind. He does believe that individuals can avoid anxiety and discomfort by gaining knowledge of the workings of the universe and the atoms in it. Here, however, the value attaches in the first instance to freedom from discomfort, not to the knowledge in and of itself.

On the other hand, eschewing the idea of *kosmos*-based value does not bring Epicurus any closer to thinking that all value derives from the *polis*. According to his hedonist theory, the value of the *polis* itself is derived solely from the pleasure that it generates for individuals in it. He recognizes, of course, that social institutions and practices, including also friendship, can bring about pleasure for individuals. But the idea that conduciveness to the functioning of the *polis* confers value on the life of a human being directly, rather than conferring value on his life merely in virtue of causing him pleasure or freedom from pain, is foreign to Epicurus's thought.[82] In sum, it can be said that neither *polis* nor *kosmos* plays a central role in his thinking about value.

In Aristotle, on the other hand, we find a view of a different type. He places little or no stress on the idea that value might arise from some relation to the overall scheme of the *kosmos*, but for whom the *polis* plays a very substantial part in some—though not all—evaluations. Aristotle makes a great deal of use of the notion of the end (*telos*) or function (*ergon*) of a thing, and he brings this idea into play extensively throughout his biology and metaphysics. Some of his readers think that they find a link between his ethical views and ideas about the overall *telos* of the universe. It does not appear to me, however, that this kind of consideration enters into his view at all. And even if it does, it does not seem to play a role in his ethics, that is, his thinking about the value of human actions and human lives.[83]

On the other hand, Aristotle does, as is well known and as I have just observed, place a heavy emphasis on the role of the *polis* in the lives of individuals. Here it is enough to cite his famous statement in Book I of the *Politics* that 'man is a political animal'.[84] By this he means that it is essential to human beings to live their lives within the

---

[82] There has been some tendency recently to try to argue that Epicurus attaches value to social arrangements in a way that does not derive directly and solely from bringing about pleasure. See for example, Annas 1993: ch. 16, esp. p. 343. It does not seem to me, however, that the case for this interpretation has been made convincingly; see Chapter 7, sec. III below.

[83] See esp. the arguments of Balme 1972: 93–8; see below, Chapter 6, sec. VIII. 4. This is not to deny a connection in Aristotle between a biological notion of an end and the notion of a *telos* that figures in his ethics, although even here the link is very far from being explicit enough to allow confidence that he intended to rest much weight on it. The present point, however, is that the end for man is not, in Aristotle's scheme, derived from any thesis about the relation of man to a structure or goal of the universe as a whole, as it arguably is in Stoicism. See further Chapter 7, sec. IV.   [84] *Pol.* 1253a2–3.

organization of the *polis*. This one pithy sentence has been as influential as any in Aristotle, and perhaps in all Greek literature, in promoting the standard conceptions of Greek ethics. It tends to overshadow, in many minds, the many other passages that point in different directions. At any rate on the hegelian interpretation of Aristotle's doctrine, the good of the individual is inseparable from the good of the *polis*, as I have indicated, and the norms of the *polis* themselves determine what an individual should aim at.[85] Later I shall lay out reasons for thinking that this account of Aristotle's position is one-sided, and that the fact that man is for him a 'political' animal does not by any means imply that the individual's good always derives from or coincides with that of his *polis*.[86]

---

[85] See Chapter 1, sec. VII. 7.   [86] See Chapter 6, secs. VII. 1–2.

Chapter 5

INDIVIDUAL GOOD AND DELIBERATIVE CONFLICT THROUGH THE TIME OF PLATO

I. Homogeneity and Variety in Classical Greek Ethics

Once the idea of the *polis* is placed in its proper perspective as an important source and focus of Greek norms but by no means the only one, and once we have brought to mind the fact that Greek evaluative language is not designed to avoid imperative expressions with their overtones of conflict and motivational ambivalence, we are left with the task of determining what sorts of considerations are taken by Greek thinkers to play a role in rational deliberation, how those considerations are related to each other, and what sorts of oppositions and conflicts they admit.

It will be important to observe what our results show about the concept of *eudaimonia*. We must ask whether, as hegelian-style interpretations suggest, Greek thinkers unselfconsciously assumed, or alternatively wished to demonstrate, that *eudaimonia* is a harmonious notion, in the sense of including within it a consistent set of aims, all of which (or, if there be only one aim, which) can be embraced without conflict, or nearly enough, by rational deliberation. Now that we are about to discuss the deliberative conflicts that Greek ethics admits, this matter will become directly pertinent.

The main potential conflict to keep in mind is the one between self-regarding aims and aims of an ostensibly broader sort.[1] Historians like Sidgwick find this dualism among modern thinkers only, and hold that ancient ethics is untouched by it. The kantian response to ancient ethics maintains that Greek eudaimonism ignores such oppositions, whereas the hegelian says that the eudaimonist monism of ancient ethics

---

[1] See Chapter 2, sec. VII.

offers at least some prospect of mitigation of or even freedom from dualism of ulti-mate aims.

In the next two chapters, I shall argue for a different account. In the first place, I shall stress the variety of Greek views on this topic. Second, I shall maintain that not all Greek ethics is eudaimonist in the sense in which I have argued that we should use the term. For one thing, much Greek thought is not so completely crystallized that it either affirms eudaimonism or denies it. This state of affairs, I argue, is exemplified by Socrates among others.

More important, however, some Greek thinkers explicitly acknowledge that an individual may rationally aim at something that is independent of his own happiness and that can clash with it. Contrary to the view that the Greeks entertained no notion of goodness except the self-referential and self-regarding goodness consisting in *one's own* well-being, they were quite capable not only of conceiving this notion but also of maintaining that it could, under some conditions, rationally outweigh or override one's own happiness as a deliberative aim.

One such thinker is Plato. He is normally portrayed as trying to show that 'there is no conflict between duty and interest'.[2] Widespread though this interpretation is, it seems to me mistaken. Plato recognizes an opposition between an individual's good and the good of the *polis* which, though it has a different shape from most modern conflicts between moral obligation and self-interest, for example, is nevertheless in some ways similar to the kind of dualism that we find in Kant and other contempo-rary philosophers. For Plato thereby allows that there is a consideration distinct from one's well-being that can not only conflict with it but can also outweigh it in reason-able deliberation.

Thus far the present chapter. In the following chapter, on Aristotle, I shall discuss a different way in which deliberative conflict can break out, this time within a eudai-monist framework.

II. Before Plato's Time

1. Varieties of Conflict in Tragedy

I have already spoken of some of the conflicts that we encounter in Greek tragedies. They set before us both individuals and groups that are torn apart. The tensions thus exhibited often obtain between the groups themselves or their members, on the one hand, and the city-states with which they are associated, on the other.

Though tragedy arises in the time of the rise of the *polis*, the plots that appear there—like those described in the *Iliad* and the *Odyssey*, when clans or tribes were the

---

[2] Irwin 1995: 301; cf. White 1999a.

most salient units of social organization[3]—are intended to be interpreted within the contexts of fifth-century city-states. These stories frequently bring to the fore the oppositions that were felt by the Greeks to have arisen historically between the *polis* and older units of family or clan.[4]

Every bit as important as the opposition that tragedies exhibit between family and *polis*, however, is the way in which they also show that families themselves can be deeply divided. These divisions can present the individual with a conflict that seems utterly without resolution.[5] Often such clashes amount to 'tragic dilemmas', in which nothing that the protagonist can do seems right or even defensible, and which, according to some interpretations, simply cannot be resolved without its still being the case that some wrong has been done.[6] Dramatists allow a plurality of considerations to come into play, without insisting on or, usually, even hinting at any overarching way of unifying them.

I will adduce just three examples, all well known. In Aeschylus's *Agamemnon*, Agamemnon kills his daughter Iphigeneia to gain the gods' favour for the military expedition to Troy, which aims to recapture the wife of his brother Menelaus. In Sophocles' *Oedipus Rex*, Oedipus kills his father and marries his mother, then discovers what he has done, blinds himself, and wanders the world with his two daughters. In the *Antigone*, Antigone of Thebes buries one brother who has died killing another brother, even as the latter was fighting for Thebes and the former was attacking it along with the army of Argos. Before Antigone commits suicide, she engages in a struggle over the action with her uncle, Creon, who holds that the security of the *polis* forbids any aid or comfort to the brother who has attacked it. However, Creon's son, Haemon, is in love with Antigone, and when he learns of her suicide he kills himself.

These are certainly not tales of harmony.[7] More important, they do not demonstrate, or encourage us to console ourselves with the prospect of, any fundamental unity of deliberative rationality that might have led to a way out. On the contrary, they show conflicts of many sorts, each of which affects the others. We can focus on the struggle between *polis* and family, or the struggle within the family itself, or the war between the two cities, Thebes and Argos, and the struggles between Antigone and Creon and between Creon and his son. The important thing is the way in which these many struggles are intertwined with each other, and the fact that they present the individuals who are caught up in them with incompatible considerations, all of which those individuals must take into account.

---

[3] See esp. Adkins 1960: 49–57, 156–63.

[4] See e.g. Knox 1982: 24–5.

[5] On the importance of conflicts within families in Greek tragedy, see Knox 1979: 20–3.

[6] See above, Chapter 2, sec. VII, as well as Sinnott-Armstrong 1988, the essays in Gowans 1987, and Calabresi and Bobbitt 1978.

[7] See further Most 1993 and Williams 1993.

Hegel's own interpretation of *Antigone* does small justice to the depth of the conflicts that the play presents. He supposes that Creon, as the explicit spokesman for the
interests of the *polis*, cannot be in the wrong when he opposes Antigone's effort to bury
her brother.[8] However, it seems quite plainly incorrect to suppose that the play
straightforwardly endorses one of the various different motivations and considerations that are portrayed in it. Antigone, Creon, the chorus, and Haemon all show different lines of thought, but Sophocles formulates no way of summing them to a single
vector, no overriding consideration in terms of which they can all be taken into
account. In opposition to Creon, as already noted, Antigone obeys laws that she thinks
are immutable:

> Nor did I think your edict had such force
> that you, a mere mortal, could override the gods,
> the great unwritten, unshakable traditions.
> They are alive, not just today or yesterday:
> they live forever, from the first of time,
> and no one knows when they first saw the light.[9]

But Creon, for his part, is equally uncompromising in his adherence to the laws of the
city. It seems plain that the audience is meant to feel the force of *both* viewpoints
strongly. Indeed, at the end of the play Creon recognizes the force of the considerations that motivate Antigone. This fact, however, does not reduce the importance of
the good of the *polis*, since Creon has already betrayed its interests before his recognition takes place.[10] The conclusion yields neither a guiding aim nor any overriding
deliberative criterion.[11]

2. Aristophanes' Canniness

We cannot cite the conflicts in *Antigone* as evidence of conflicts between the good of
the individual and considerations of a broader kind. The reason is that although individuals figure there, they can easily be taken as representatives of certain groups or
types. Thus, for instance, it seems more natural to say that the play deals with such

---

[8] Hegel 1962: ii. 265. For some of the limitations of Hegel's interpretation, see Knox 1982: 41;
Nussbaum 1986: 59–63, 82, 353; and Gellrich 1988: ch. 1, esp. pp. 46–56, 61–2, 67–71. Nussbaum holds that
the tendency of the play runs mainly against Creon and more or less for Antigone, but it seems to me all of
the positions presented, including Creon's, are part of the conflict, which is not resolved in favour of any of
them.

[9] Sophocles, Antigone, trans. Fagles, ll. 503–8 (cf. sec. III. 2 above). Hegel cites these lines in a different
connection in the *Phenomenology of Spirit*: Hegel 1977: 261; cf. 275.

[10] The point is clearly made by Knox 1982: 423 with 37.

[11] Gellrich 1988 argues convincingly, to my mind, that the fragmentation of the ethical issues in
Antigone, and in other tragedies too, is even more thorough than this, but what I have said is sufficient to
establish my main point here.

clashes as the one between loyalty to city-state and loyalty to family, and not between either and the good of the individual per se.

When we turn away from the tortured aristocratic hothouse of Athenian tragedy, however, and examine the familiar scenes from more ordinary lives that are presented by comedy, we observe straightforward cases of this latter sort of opposition. The comic plays of Aristophanes provide plenty of evidence of a robust belief in the possibility of conflict between an individual and both the *polis* and its norms. In the *Acharnians*, for example, various politicians are lampooned for benefiting themselves at public expense. At one point, the main character, Dikaiopolis, speaks with a public ambassador to Persia who has done just that:

AMBASSADOR. Gentlemen, you will remember that you sent [the three of] us to the Great King, fixing our expenses at two drachmas per person per day, in the year when Euthymenes was archon.

DIKAIOPOLIS (*aside*). Six a day for eleven years—oh, God!

AMBASSADOR. And, I may add, we had a very hard time of it. We processed very slowly up the Caÿster valley in covered coaches, and we actually had to lie down in them. We endured tremendous privations.

DIKAIOPOLIS. And all the time here was I in the lap of luxury, sleeping among the rubbish on the city walls! Unfair world, isn't it?[12]

Aristophanes ought to be required reading for people who believe that Greek culture standardly regarded an individual's good as identical with the good of his *polis* and consonant with all of his obligations to it. That certainly is not what we are supposed to think about this ambassador, nor what we are to suppose he himself thinks. He is blunt about people's concern for their own individual good, and he knows how it can lead them away from obedience to ordinary norms. Here is something from the *Clouds*:

STREPSIADES. They say they have two Arguments in there—Right and Wrong, they call them—and one of them, Wrong, can always win any case, however bad. Well, if you can learn this Argument or whatever it is, don't you see, all those debts I've run into because of you, I needn't pay anyone an obol of them ever.[13]

Strepsiades is watching out for himself. Moreover, watching out for himself means, among other things, trying to make sure that his own son does not get the better of him.

In these scenes from Aristophanes, the concept of the individual's good is not developed philosophically. By relying on common sense we can regard the Ambassador's monetary gain and Strepsiades' hypothetical non-repayment of his

---

[12] Aristophanes, *Acharnians*, ll. 65ff. (trans. Sommerstein).

[13] *Clouds* 112–18; see also, for example, *Acharnians* 141–50, 496–525, 566–605; *Clouds* 1067–82.

debts as conducive to their own good. It seems absurd to envisage Aristophanes as focused only on the notion that from some more pious perspective, the agent's and the city's good will coincide—for instance, because returning the *per diem* or repaying the debts will turn out really to be good for the agent.

The sly canniness about individuals' interests that permeates Aristophanes' plays helps to break through the cloud of professorial high-mindedness that envelops many writings about Greek thought. Aristophanes represents a side of life in which there are few lofty illusions about harmony and serenity. Not only does Aristophanes show us yet again that the *polis* is not the sourse of all important deliberative considerations.[14] In addition, he knows what it is for people to consider doing what they think they should not do, and what it is to look out for one's own good against the good of both one's fellow citizens and one's nearest relatives. Such oppositions are entirely familiar to moderns, both philosophers and others. Self-interest is tangible, mainly monetary, and it is opposed by obligations that are real even if they are also the object of cynicism, much like the ones that we observed in Thucydides.[15]

Aristophanes is, to be sure, nostalgic for an earlier time when citizens in general and politicians in particular were, he is convinced, less acquisitive and more public-spirited than in his time. It would, however, be a mistake to regard this nostalgia as support for the hegelian contention that he identifies, or suggests that the Greeks identified, their own good with that of the *polis*. His nostalgic description of earlier times is a description of people who 'joined in the toil of the city', that is, who *cooperated with* the city, not of people who identified its good with theirs. Indeed, they see the distinction between the two well enough to 'blame' the city as they see it now.[16]

A striking tendency, in Hegel and others who share his perspective on Greek ethics, is to try to discount evidence of the kind that we see in Aristophanes by saying that it does not represent a truly Hellenic way of thinking. Hegel himself tried to do this by detaching certain sentiments expressed in Greek literature from the putative mainstream of Greek thought, and associating them with the activity, which took place in the later part of the fifth century BCE, of those teachers and intellectuals known as the Sophists.[17] In this way he believed it possible to attribute to the original and genuine Greek spirit an innocence of any sharp sense of dissonance between individual and communal well-being. According to such a resolutely harmonizing account, any awareness of such a clash would *eo ipso* be a sign of Sophistic thinking at work.

There is of course a temptation to read Aristophanes quite differently. Aristophanes sometimes harks back nostalgically to the good old days, when Athenian

---

[14] See Chapter 4, sec. III. 2.   [15] See Chapter 4, sec. III. 3–4.

[16] *Acharnians* 694, *polla dê xymponsanta*; cf. 676–8, e.g. esp. *memphometha*.

[17] Hegel 1991: 261–2; cf. MacIntyre 1988: ch. 4 and pp. 77, 392. Against this tendency it is well to remember that the Sophists were a broad and varied group; see esp. Kerferd 1981.

citizens were hardworking and the city prospered through their homely uprightness. One might hope to see in such passages indications of a belief on his part in the kind of original harmony that hegelian readers see as the fundamental Hellenic condition. We could then believe that the newfangled vices against which Aristophanes rails were, just as Hegel said, creations of the subjectivity introduced by Socrates and the Sophists.

This reading, however, seems implausible. Aristophanes himself does not blame the decline of virtue on the Sophists. He believes that the finagling around him arises mainly from the cupidity of politicians and the gullibility of ordinary people. The Sophists, among whom he ranges Socrates, appear to him merely to be some of those who exploit the new vices, not their originators. What is more, his perception of many individuals as willing to cheat the *polis* in order to help themselves is offered as his own observation, not something that is derived from Sophistic concepts.

3. Archaic Conflicts

Lest it be supposed that in this latter respect Aristophanes had absorbed Sophistic thinking in spite of himself, or was merely reporting it, the same cannot be said of earlier signs of the same conflict. Long before the Sophistic period Greek literature was full of conflicts between individuals and the groups of which they are parts. Nietzsche was right about that. In the *Iliad*, the opposed interests of Achilles and Agamemnon openly strain the cooperative enterprise of the Greeks besieging Troy. Their concern with both their own honour and their own possessions stand in conflict with each other and with the other Greek chieftains. In the *Odyssey*, the suitors who waste Odysseus' substance in Ithaca during his wanderings represent a patent disruption of unanimity, even among themselves, and also a great deal of self-serving at the expense of what is pictured as the common well-being.[18]

Hesiod's *Works and Days*, too, contains a rich supply of complaints against selfish and grasping behaviour:

[D]o not let that strife who delights in mischief hold your heart back from work, while you peep and peer and listen to the wrangles of the court-house.

He might well have complained. Addressing his brother, Perses, he says that they

had already divided our inheritance, but you seized the greater share and carried it off, greatly swelling the glory of our bribe-swallowing lords who love to judge a cause such as this—fools![19]

---

[18] In 1991: 230, Hegel tries to soften this claim by saying that the suitors' loyalty is to Odysseus, not Telemachus. That seems to ignore the straightforwardly self-seeking character of their behaviour, which is plainly directed against Odysseus' house and against Odysseus himself (as the events ensuing on his return to Ithaca show). [19] *Works and Days*, ll. 27–9, 37–4; cf. 174–382 *passim*.

One might conceivably question the relevance of these observations. After all, they date from a time before the institution of the *polis* had established itself as firmly as it had by the fifth century. Thus the conflict in the *Iliad*, for instance, would be a clash not between an individual and a city-state, but between a chieftain and a larger military expedition that he had agreed to participate in.[20]

Even so, however, these conflicts make plain to us, as they did to the Greeks who heard and read about them, how someone's well-being could fail to accord, and also be perceived to fail to accord, with the good of a cooperative enterprise in which he is engaged, or with the legal institutions to which Hesiod alludes. When we read Homer, Hesiod, Aristophanes, and Sophocles together, as well as the passages of Thucydides that I have already discussed,[21] it seems exceedingly artificial to attribute the later texts to a different cast of mind from the earlier ones, or to say that the later manifestations of conflict were the product of a newly formed Sophistic state of mind, as contrasted with some other, more distinctly and originally Hellenic outlook.

Far better to say that all along Greek thought was fully alive to the possibility of conflicts between individuals and social institutions. On this score, the contrast between what the Sophists said and what had gone before should not be exaggerated by an arbitrary partitioning of Greek intellectual history.[22]

4. The Canniness of Pericles

On any interpretation, the figure of Pericles occupies an important position in the history of Greek politics and political thought. He has played an especially significant role in the hegelian response to Greek ethics. Thucydides' account of his funeral oration has been treated as a *locus classicus* of descriptions of the *polis* and the individual's relation to it, as seen from the hegelian perspective. Hegel himself believed that in the funeral oration that Thucydides puts into his mouth in Book II of his *History*, Pericles enunciates the nature of the *polis* as both an ideal of harmony and an actually functioning institution. The spirit expressed was the one that Hegel pointed to in a passage that I have already quoted:

[20] MacIntyre urges that in Homer a person's interests and responsibilities are defined by his social role (1988: 20). The problem about the dispute between Achilles and Agamemnon in the *Iliad*, however, is that although Agamemnon is the leader of the expedition, the roles defined by that enterprise are not determinate enough to settle what they may and may not do vis-à-vis each other. Therefore their deliberations about what to do vis-a-vis each other (particularly those of Achilles, who is not accidentally pictured as the more solitary sort of person) cannot be pictured as being fully role-defined. Moreover, even so, there is a clear conflict between what they respectively are aiming for and the success of the cooperative venture that they are engaged on. That is a conflict that Greeks thenceforth could not be unaware of.

[21] See Chapter 4, sec. III.

[22] George Grote (1888: ch. 67) criticized the Hegelian account on this and other grounds. One does not have to accept Grote's view of the Sophists and Socrates to recognize the power of his arguments against Hegel's rather artificial schematization of the periods of Greek thought.

Of the Greeks in the first and genuine form of their freedom, we may assert, that they had no conscience; the habit of living for their country without further reflection, was the principle dominant among them.[23]

But in spite of Hegel's reliance on Pericles' oration—or rather, Thucydides' account of it—as evidence for his interpretation of Greek thought, it fails to provide the support that the hegelian account seeks from it. Pericles does indeed say that all citizens can pursue their goods within the framework of the Athenian *polis*. No one, though, could exhibit a livelier awareness than Pericles does, not merely that conflicts can break out within a *polis*, but in particular that an individual citizen's good and the well-being of the Athenian *polis* are two different ideas, and that many people believe that they can be at odds with each other.

Here [i. e. in Athens] each individual is interested not only in his own affairs but in the affairs of state as well: even those who are mostly occupied with their own business are extremely well-informed on general politics—this is a peculiarity of ours: we do not say that a man who takes no interest in politics is a man who minds his own business; we say that he has no business here at all.[24]

This is a far cry from a claim that all citizens' goods are consistent with that of the city (let alone of each other).[25] Nor could anyone be more self-conscious than Pericles is when he urges that those who have died for Athens in the war have not always strived for its good alone:

Some of them, no doubt, had their faults; but what we ought to remember first is their gallant conduct against the enemy in defence of their native land. They have blotted out evil with good, and done more service to the commonwealth than they ever did harm in their private lives.[26]

---

[23] Hegel 1991: 253. Hegel thought that the Greeks did not perfectly embody the highest political condition because they did not fully possess the idea of the autonomous individual. MacIntyre's account of Pericles' role is essentially the same as Hegel's, though much more fully expounded (1988: 50–1, 54).

[24] Thucydides, *History* II. 40 (trans. Warner).

[25] On p. 54 of his 1988, MacIntyre maintains (emphasis added) that

[c]entral to Periclean rhetoric is the unargued and *never wholly spelled out* claim that all the goods which Athenians pursue can be pursued in harmony with one another and above all that the individual citizen may pursue his own good, whether that of excellence or power, in also pursuing the good of the city.

It seems to me that, just like Hegel's account and in just the same way, this goes very far beyond what is even implied in Pericles' speech. On the contrary, the speech seems to me to take for granted that there is no such harmony among Athenian citizens, but that in spite of that they are capable of cooperating to a substantial degree. Even Ehrenberg seems to me to overestimate the extent to which Pericles' speech expresses the idea of a harmony between the good of the individual and that of the *polis* (1969: 91).

[26] Thucydides, *History* II. 42 (trans. Warner).

These are not the words of someone who presumes that his audience makes no sharp distinction between individual and social good, or thinks without reflection that their own good must coincide with that of their country. Private action that injures the public good is explicitly envisaged. Pericles knows that the people whom he is addressing see that the two sorts of well-being do not always coincide.

5. *The Fallacy of Communal Identification*

The foregoing passages cast serious doubt on traditional accounts of Greek ethics. The fact that many readers tend to place less than due emphasis on them, however, is not impossible to explain. Once one has the idea firmly in mind that the Greeks were harmony-minded eudaimonists, it becomes all too easy to focus less on expressions of different attitudes or to treat them as simple aberrations. I wish to urge, however, that such methods of accommodation are not plausible, and that the force of passages like these becomes evident once one suspends this interpretative preconception.

No one can deny that the bonds among citizens that constituted Greek political life were often strong. (We must always remember, as already noted, that a large number of slaves were living enclosed within this system; they are usually left entirely out of account by standard interpretations, because in their writings the Greeks treated them as for the most part invisible.) At the same time, however, a tempting confusion on this point can encourage a mistaken assessment of both Pericles' speech in particular and the body of the evidence in general.

It is easy to think, mistakenly, that if a citizen felt his whole life and everything valuable in it to be in some sense defined by his relation to his *polis*, then it follows that he saw his good and that of the *polis* as identical or coincident.[27] This inference is fallacious, and might be called the Fallacy of Communal Identification. It may be impossible for a citizen to have existed without his *polis*, or to continue to exist in detachment from it. From this it does not follow, however, that his well-being and its must always coincide. It could perfectly well be the case, for instance, that an Athenian citizen could not imagine a worthwhile life without the existence of his *polis* and his own presence in it. But it could nonetheless be the case that he saw all sorts of conflicts in particular cases between the city's good and his own.[28]

In spite of being fallacious, this line of thought has been used to bolster the view that, according to the Greek supposition, an individual's well-being and that of his *polis* must coincide with each other. The claim is frequently advanced that a Greek could not conceive of existing in isolation from his *polis*, or at the least from some *polis*

---

[27] See Chapter 1, sec. VII, and Chapter 4, sec. II.

[28] This is one reason why in the *Crito*, Plato has the Athenian laws presuppose that if Socrates disobeys them then he must destroy them (50a–b).

or other, and this claim is then used to support some thesis to the effect that the Greeks regarded the happiness of the latter as fully consonant with that of the former.[29]

6. *Socrates and the Imaginability of Life without the* Polis

Even more striking than the Fallacy of Communal Identification, however, is the widespread exaggeration of the idea that a Greek citizen could not imagine a life without his *polis*. Greeks were far from being as footloose as modern cosmopolitans—that much is clear. Nevertheless there were well-known cases of people who, though often notorious in the eyes of their fellow citizens, lived quite imaginable and even successful lives without the benefit of close ties to their community. In the first place, citizenship was always a rare commodity in most city-states, where various restrictions excluded most people. Even at Athens, where it was more widespread, people who were not citizens, such as metics and freed slaves, were able, in spite of being socially stigmatized by aristocrats, to occupy an essential and important place in the economy.[30] Moreover, although a figure like Alcibiades was regarded as a traitor by those Athenians who were politically opposed to him, he certainly managed a highly flamboyant and successful career through successive allegiances to Athens, Sparta, Persia, and then Athens and Persia again. He was murdered at the end, but at that period so were many whose civic attachments were not at all so mercurial. He is not typical, but he does not have to be in order to show that life was possible without a fixed *polis*.

The well-known figure of Socrates is often invoked to illustrate how completely a Greek predicated the possibility of worthwhile life on his link to his *polis*. It is said, for instance, that in the *Crito*, Socrates pictures life in exile as not worth living, and indeed that he preferred to die rather than to leave Athens.

This way of viewing the matter is deeply misleading.[31] For one thing, the disadvantage to Socrates of going into exile is said in the dialogue said to be that in any new home that he chose, he would be unable to pursue not life itself, but philosophy. This is said to be so not because of any general impossibility of life in another city, but because of the suspicion that would be directed against him as a well-known

---

[29] See e.g. Green 1883: secs. 235, 239. How deeply rooted the fallacy is in much hegelian thought can be seen from the terminology employed by Bernard Williams. He speaks of an 'illusion, hidden in the seductively phrased Hegelian claim that human beings are "constituted" by society: the idea that the relations of human beings to society and to each other, if properly understood and properly enacted, can realise a harmonious identity that involves no real loss' (1883: 162). Not that Williams commits the fallacy—quite the contrary. The point is that the fallacy is reflected in the terminology that he cites, which runs together two things that are different and non-equivalent, namely, being 'constituted' by one's society and having one's good coincide with society's good.

[30] See Finley 1973: esp. chs. 2–3.

[31] As I have already indicated, to some extent, in Chapter 4.

iconoclast, and because such pursuits were not in general freely allowed in Greek city-states.[32] Furthermore, the interlocutor in the dialogue, Socrates' friend Crito—a thoroughly conventional personality, and much more closely representative of ordinary thought than Socrates is—thinks that Socrates *should* go into exile. How could there be plainer evidence that entirely respectable Greeks did not regard their identity as preserved or their lives as worth living only within the context of their own *polis*?

There are therefore two reasons on this front not to accept the idea that ordinary Greek thinking posited an identity of interest between individual and *polis*. First, even if it is true that attachments to the *polis* were more important to the Greeks than analogous attachments are to moderns, the Greeks did not in general believe that life outside one's *polis* was unthinkable. Second, even if they had so believed, it would not have followed that a complete coincidence of good between individual and *polis* must hold.

III. Plato's Milieu: Thrasymachus

1. Plato's Eudaimonist Opponents

Many interpreters take it as a given that Plato's entire argument in the *Republic* is predicated on these two harmonizing eudaimonist assumptions together with a recognition by all parties that they share it as common ground.[33] Unquestionably there were in Plato's time people who espoused a straightforwardly eudaimonist position—even, sometimes, an out-and-out egoist view—according to which one's own well-being is a condition narrowly confined to one's own self and has little or nothing to do with the good of others around one. One such character in Plato's works is Callicles in the *Gorgias*. His conception of human good focuses on states that are quite private to the individual—a fact that is taken up by Socrates' illustration of the pleasure of scratching an itch.[34] This is an extreme case of the type of view that Hegel called 'subjectivist', and that he associated with the Sophistic movement and also with Socrates—with the latter because of his urging, for instance, that the most important aim is to make one's own soul as good as possible.[35]

Another such person is Plato's main adversary in the *Republic*, Thrasymachus. In Book I he scornfully calls justice 'another's good', and he makes it plain that he sees no reason whatsoever to adhere to such standards, since he assumes that in benefiting 'another' person one is harming oneself, that is, that one's own good includes neither

---

[32] See Kraut 1984: 14–17, 89 n. 48, 228–9 n. 67.

[33] Sidgwick 1931: 198; see also Sidgwick 1907: 91–2.

[34] For Callicles, see *Gorg.* 494c–e. Likewise the tyrant of *Rep.* IX, who seems to be designed to mirror the attitudes of Thrasymachus, clearly aims at a good that is confined to himself.

[35] *Apol.* 29e, 30b, and Hegel 1991: 269–70.

the good of others nor adherence to norms that justice embodies. At the same time, he says that those 'who give injustice a bad name do so because they are afraid, not of practising but of suffering injustice'.[36] This theme is taken up in Book II by the characters Glaucon and Adeimantus. Claiming to 'renew' (though not to endorse) Thrasymachus's argument,[37] they suggest that 'those who practise justice do so against their will because they lack the power to do wrong', and that if they could act unjustly without being caught, they would eagerly do that instead.[38]

The underlying presupposition here plainly is that everyone aims only at his own good, in a quite restricted, self-confined sense, and will pursue it as far as he can. Apparent exceptions to this regularity arise because people who are weak have decided that, in view of their weakness, the best way of maintaining their well-being is to submit to norms of justice. For if they attempted to act unjustly, as the strong do, they would be punished and thus would lose rather than gain from the attempt. Indeed, Glaucon contends, this is the 'origin and essence' of justice: laws are established by convention to allow weak individuals to protect themselves against the strong, and thus constitute a strategy for pursuing their own good as effectively as they can.[39]

Given this much as stage-setting for Plato's argument, it is then supposed that his whole aim in the *Republic* is to reply to Thrasymachus's position by showing that a person gains rather than loses by being just. This is Plato's strategy, the interpretation runs, because, like Thrasymachus, Glaucon, Adeimantus, and all present company, he assumes that the only way in which he could rationally persuade anyone to be just is by showing that, once the notions of justice and of one's well-being are correctly understood, the former in fact contributes to the latter.[40]

2. Plato's Non-Eudaimonist Allies

Although such an interpretation of the *Republic* would capture a signficant portion of its meaning, it would also omit much that is essential to a full understanding of the work, that is, both of Plato's own position and of the range of views with which he was familiar and to which he was obliged to attend. Part of his purpose there (though not,

---

[36] *Rep.* 344c.   [37] *Rep.* 358bc, 361de.
[38] *Rep.* 359b–360d.   [39] *Rep.* 358e–359b.
[40] A prima facie objection to such an interpretation arises from *Rep.* II. 357–68. There Plato indicates that it will be argued that justice is good 'for itself' and not merely 'for its consequences'. It can be argued, however, that by 'for itself' Plato does not only mean that justice is to be valued without consideration of the happiness that it brings to the individual who is just but also means to be praising it for the happiness that the just person possesses solely on account of being just and without the intervention of any other factor. As a result, this passage does not by itself refute a eudaimonist interpretation of the *Republic*, even though, as I shall make clear below, such an interpretation is in a fundamental way mistaken. See *Rep.* 358a, 366e–367a.

as I shall show, his only purpose) is indeed to argue against Thrasymachus on his own terms or on terms very like them.[41]

Plato does indeed hope to demonstrate to Thrasymachus, and to many others who think roughly as he does, that a *completely* just person is far happier than the person whom Thrasymachus claims to be the happiest of all, namely, the *completely* unjust person.[42] On the other hand, however, to focus merely on Plato's reply to Thrasymachus (as I shall indicate when I come to treat the *Republic* in its own right) is to leave an essential part of his project out of account. In addition, moreover, it is to misjudge the context within which Plato addresses the issue of justice. For it neglects the existence of another view, quite distinct from the one that Thrasymachus espouses, which Plato could not possibly ignore.

For Plato supposed neither that everyone accepted Thrasymachus's rational egoism, nor that rational egoism in general was the only view that merited his attention. Nor did Plato assume—nor think that everyone else assumed—that a person's own well-being is the only ultimate, independent consideration that he must rationally take into account in practical deliberation. Accordingly he did not assume that the only reason that he could offer for being just is merely that being just is conducive to one's happiness.

To the contrary, the position that Plato puts into the mouth of Thrasymachus in *Republic* I makes it evident that both of them recognize the existence of people who take their own well-being not to be their sole end. They both acknowledge, furthermore, that some of those people cultivate justice without thinking that it is valuable solely for its contribution to their happiness. So far from presupposing that everyone takes his own happiness as his ultimate aim, Plato's discussion exhibits a very different outlook.

In order to understand this state of affairs, it is necessary to think through the implications of everything that Thrasymachus says about his attitude towards people who act justly. Although he states that most just people act only out of the fear of punishment, he also acknowledges, and ridicules, the notion that considerations of justice

---

[41] MacIntyre holds that Plato does not think that there is enough common ground between himself and Thrasymachus to allow an argument that Thrasymachus must accept to be mounted (1988: 73–4). I do not see evidence for this view. Whereas Thrasymachus defends the life of the tyrant as paradigmatically happy, Plato says that by looking inside the tyrant's own soul one can tell that he is not happy, even though he appears to be so from outside (576e–577a, 577e–578b). He also gives an argument that attempts to show the objective basis for devaluing the goods that the tyrant favours (580d–583b). It is true that Plato's argument involves introducing notions of justice and happiness that are not the same as the ones that Thrasymachus employed in stating his thesis. Nevertheless, Plato thinks that the correctness of his notions can be demonstrated. (See White 1979b: 119–22.) It may be that he is wrong about this (indeed, I think that he is). Nevertheless, *he* believes that he is advancing an argument that should be convincing even to Thrasymachus. Cf. Adkins 1960: 282–3.

[42] See *Rep.* 360e, 361d.

have a force independent of conduciveness to one's own well-being—a notion that he thinks some people take seriously. What he himself thinks is so foolish about these people is precisely that they *do* value justice, 'another's good', and think that it should be acted on in spite of the damage it can do to their own well-being. This fact can be seen in the following way.

The point is that Thrasymachus takes himself to be *unmasking* a naive view about justice. This view is entertained by people who are foolish enough to try to be just. According to the standard type of eudaimonist interpretation advocated by Sidgwick, as we have seen, this naive view accepts that being just is advisable, but does so only because it accepts the belief that it is ultimately in one's own interest to be just.

That interpretation, however, cannot be sustained. It would make nonsense of Thrasymachus's desire to bring to light the following fact: that rulers aiming at self-aggrandizement try to *conceal* their true intentions by presenting their own interests under the fine-sounding guise of the word 'justice'.[43] Thrasymachus contends that rulers use this word only to hide their pursuit of their own advantage. They pretend, that is, that it stands for an objective property of justice, which the other interlocutors in the dialogue have been trying to define. Thrasymachus denies that there is any such thing.[44] But what could the point be of Thrasymachus's accusation of pretence, if it were presumed all around that everyone acts for the sake of his own self-confined good anyway?[45]

If it were in fact assumed 'on all sides' that each person makes his own happiness his sole ultimate aim, Thrasymachus's view could not possibly be the revelation that he presents it as being. If everyone assumed that each person pursued his own good, what Thrasymachus is claiming to unmask would already be out in the open. His declaration that rulers make laws for their own advantage would be no news to anyone at all, because everyone would assume, as a matter of course, that everyone does everything for his own advantage. Indeed, his chief thesis, that justice is the interest of the stronger, would not need to be made at all, and he could not possibly be portrayed, as he is, as thinking that he exhibits a perspicacity for which he should be applauded.[46]

3. *What Thrasymachus Aims to Unmask*

What Thrasymachus intends to unmask, I have urged, is what he supposes is the irrationality—the 'high-minded foolishness', as he calls it[47]—of sacrificing one's own

---

[43] See *Rep.* 338e, 343c.   [44] See *Rep.* 338c–339a.
[45] Might each consider the good of others, or adherence to norms of justice, to be included somehow in his own good? Such an inclusive concept of justice, and perhaps even a fusionist one, can be found elsewhere in the *Republic* (see sec. VI. 6 below), but it is not in play in the debate with Thrasymachus, and cannot be attributed to all parties to the discussion (cf. sec. III. 4 below).
[46] *Rep.* 338bc. On the philosophical point, cf. Foot 1978c: 128–9.   [47] *Rep.* 348c.

good for the sake of doing what is just. The implication of this fact is that, as Thrasymachus and therefore Plato both recognize, there exist people who take justice as itself a sufficient reason to act even at the price of sacrificing their good. This fact shows, in turn, that such people recognize being just as an aim that has rational force independent, in a significant sense, of their own well-being. (What sort of independence this is is, of course, a further question.) Against this viewpoint, Thrasymachus maintains the irrationality of sacrificing one's good, on this or any other ground, at all.

Or could Thrasymachus be unmasking not this but something else? Could he be presuming that it is common knowledge that everyone pursues only his own well-being, and unmasking merely the falsity of the belief that acting justly is conducive thereto? Could he, that is, be telling people, 'You think that by being just you enhance your happiness, but I wish you to realize that the actions that are often called just are actually damaging to it'? I do not see how he could be saying this.

In the first place, this reading does not seem to make sense of the reproach of 'high-minded foolishness'. If the 'foolishness' were simply a mistake about what would be most conducive to one's own happiness, which itself was nevertheless one's ultimate goal, wherein would lie the 'high-mindedness'? Whence would the thought of high-mindedness even arise, if we were dealing here with a simple strategic or tactical error about what one's happiness might result from?

There is another reason, moreover, why this suggestion cannot be sustained. It makes nonsense of Thrasymachus's contention that rulers label actions just in order to help persuade other people to do them. If the suggestion were true, there would be no need at all for him to think of the stratagems of rulers as cloaked under the word 'justice', as he explicitly does. All that the rulers would need to do would be to issue explicit threats against disobedience. However, one of Thrasymachus's most salient claims is that rulers try to provide *additional* motivation by cleverly pinning the word 'justice' on their edicts, because they think that people will be further motivated by *it* to obey them. This is why he thinks the notion of justice was introduced in the first place. But that means, precisely, that some people *think* that the word designates something that is genuinely a consideration for them.[48]

Injustice . . . exercises its power over those who are truly naive and just, and those over whom it rules do what is of advantage to the other, the stronger, and, by obeying him, they make him happy, but themselves not in the least.[49]

---

[48] See the similar point that was made in Chapter 4, sec. III. 3–4, concerning Thucydides' Melian Dialogue. There an attempt at deception showed that justice was regarded as a consideration distinct from the norms or the interest of a particular city-state. The present issue has to do with the good of an individual. Taken together, however, the passages manifest a conceptual distinction between the notion of justice and that of benefit to something or someone.

[49] *Rep.* 343c–d.

Moreover, this is why Thrasymachus castigates Socrates for his illusions about the motivations of stock breeders:

You think ... that shepherds and cowherds seek the good of their sheep or cattle, whereas the sole purpose of fattening them and looking after them is their own good and that of their master. Moreover, you believe that rulers in the cities . . . have a different attitude towards their subjects . . ., and that they think of anything else, night and day, than their own advantage.[50]

That there are such high-minded people is, to repeat, perfectly compatible with Thrasymachus's observation that *most* people who act justly have no such attachment to justice per se and are merely trying to make the best of their own weak position. These people presumably ascribe to the rulers, who establish the laws, the motivation of benefiting themselves, just as Thrasymachus does. Nevertheless, this cannot be the attitude of the people to whom Thrasymachus ascribes justice as 'high-minded foolishness'.[51] Recognizing that one is too weak to disobey would in Thrasymachus's terms be neither foolish nor high-minded, but only a prudent strategy in a bad situation. Thrasymachus could despise them for their weakness, but not for their naivety.[52]

Thrasymachus should therefore be read exactly as he is most naturally read. The challenge that he poses is this: why does it make any sense to follow the belief, which many people in fact hold, that one rationally should do certain things because they are 'just', even though one sees that they are inimical to one's own good? That is a question that the Greeks were perfectly capable of raising. But they could not raise it if a straightforwardly eudaimonist interpretation such as Sidgwick's represented the whole of Greek thinking.

What Thrasymachus's line of thought shows us about how Plato gauged Greek attitudes towards justice is, therefore, largely the opposite of what Sidgwick and similar interpreters take it to be. The Greeks recognize the existence of two types of people (though Thrasymachus does not always take care to distinguish them). Some are weak, but pursue their good as best they can by conforming to standards of justice because they fear punishment. There are also the naive and high-minded, who—foolishly, in Thrasymachus's view—adhere to justice in spite of thereby plainly diminishing their well-being. Those whom Thrasymachus laughs at for being taken in by unjust rulers and other strongmen are precisely people who think, first, that there is such a thing as justice, and, second, that something's being just is itself a reason to favour it. Here we should recall the passage from Thucydides that I mentioned just now. The latter group, whom Thrasymachus mocks, are people from whom the unjust cloak their pursuit of self-interest under the word 'justice'. If all Greeks were acknowledged and self-acknowledged rational egoists, there would be nothing to cloak.

[50] *Rep.* 343b.   [51] See *gennaia euetheia* in 348d–e.   [52] *Rep.* 343c; cf. nn. 47–9 above.

4. The Non-Eudaimonist Outlook of Glaucon and Adeimantus

When the role of interlocutor passes in Book II from Thrasymachus to the more sympathetic Glaucon and Adeimantus, the same impression of the dialectical situation presupposed by Plato is confirmed. In particular, there is corroboration of the fact that some people, though not all, regard an action's being just as a reason in its favour whose force is not derived simply from its contribution to one's well-being.

At the beginning of Book II, Glaucon and Adeimantus issue a challenge to Socrates. They ask him to show that being just is advantageous to the just person.[53] As I have indicated, this fact by itself can be misinterpreted so as to support the idea that Plato is assuming that the only possible ground on which a person could reasonably decide to be just would be the belief that he will thereby benefit. Such an impression, however, would be as mistaken in Book II as in Book I.

First of all, Glaucon and Adeimantus dissociate their own view from Thrasymachus's position. They say explicitly that in issuing their challenge to Socrates they are not expressing what they think, but rather speaking on Thrasymachus's behalf.[54] 'I will renew the argument of Thrasymachus', says Glaucon, with its claim 'that those who practise justice do so unwillingly': 'It is not that I think this, Socrates, but I am puzzled and my ears are deafened from listening to Thrasymachus and countless other speakers.' Since the enunciation of Thrasymachus's position by Glaucon and Adeimantus does not show that they accept it, it cannot show that everyone else does so either.

More tellingly, Glaucon and Adeimantus say that everyone values a reputation for justice (361a–b). Here again it is necessary to think about how such a reputation could be worth having. If everyone were presumed to accept rational egoism, as I have noted, a reputation for justice would do no good at all. It would be plain that all professions of justice were ultimately aimed merely at one's own advantage. Everyone would expect that in any situation in which one person's gain could be another's loss— a type of situation that is presumed here to be common—the ostensibly just person would depart from justice if and when that could be seen to further his well-being. The same point emerges when Glaucon says,

The man who did not wish to do wrong [when given the] opportunity, and did not touch other people's property, would be thought by those who knew it to be very foolish and miserable. *They would praise him in public, thus deceiving one another*, for fear of being wronged.[55]

Clearly people are presumed here to believe that the deception has a chance of working.

As in Book I, Plato does not deny that most people—'the many'—believe that it is

---

[53] They challenge Socrates to show that justice is 'to be welcomed both for itself and for its consequences' (358a). See above, n. 39.

[54] *Rep.* 358a–c, 361e, 362d, 365e.   [55] *Rep.* 360d.

irrational to forgo a benefit for the sake of justice. Their view is highlighted by the story of the ring of Gyges, which causes its wearer to be invisible and thus enables him to practise injustice without being detected. It is held, Glaucon says, that everyone would behave unjustly if he had such a ring. Plato presents this view, however, as the opinion of 'these people', the people whom Glaucon is trying to answer, not as the position that everyone adopts. On the contrary, Plato explicitly recognizes exceptions: men 'of godlike character', he says, are disgusted by injustice and avoid it, and some people say that justice is 'beautiful' (*kalon*) even though difficult and toilsome.[56]

The situation that Glaucon and Adeimantus present us with is evident. It is not one in which everyone claims to be just only in order to further his own well-being. Rather, two distinct attitudes prevail. Some people find justice attractive and injustice repulsive, and engage in just action without reckoning on advantages to themselves. Many others profess to be like these people, but they do so merely in order to reap the benefits of a reputation for justice. What they profess, however, is not that they are just for their own advantage, but rather that they think justice beautiful and injustice ugly.

IV. Plato's Milieu: Socrates

1. Evidence about Socrates

We do not know what the historical Socrates believed. Therefore when we read Plato's earlier works, which are usually supposed to have been written under more direct influence of Socrates than later ones, we do not know whether Plato is describing the Socratic background of his thinking or his own early thoughts. In either case, however, we can take the ideas expressed in those works to be part of the atmosphere in which he wrote the *Republic*, which is the main work bearing on the issues with which we are dealing.

In recent times a fragile consensus has arisen about the historical Socrates that seems to me reasonable. According to it, Plato's *Apology* and the *Crito*, though by no means verbatim reports of things that Socrates said, come the closest of any Platonic works to conveying a sense of Socrates' own intellectual activity, though they are no doubt also influenced by Plato's own views as of the time when they were written. The *Protagoras* and the *Gorgias*, on the other hand, seem to have been more deeply affected by Plato's thinking, to a degree that probably takes them quite far from the sort of positions that Socrates himself adopted.

The *Republic*, it would seem, represents (along the with the *Meno* and the *Phaedo* in particular) yet a further and substantial step, to the point where we can think of it

---

[56] These quotations occur, respectively, at *Rep.* 358a, 360b, 366c, and 364a.

as exclusively Plato's work, except that *Republic* I is intended partly to convey some rough impression of Socrates' style of conversation and preoccupations, along with, principally, Plato's own way of framing the issues to be dealt with in the *Republic* as a whole.[57]

This at any rate is the scheme that I shall presuppose. I stress, however, that the main issue is not about what Socrates actually thought. Concerning that issue, we may simply have to plead unavoidable and permanent ignorance. What concerns me is rather the views about ethics that are actually recorded, whether those be held by Socrates, by Plato, or by whoever is recorded in the several Platonic works that I shall discuss. In particular, I shall deal with whatever ethical ideas were prevalent in the period leading up to the *Republic*.[58]

2. *Socrates and the Unity of Practical Reason*

It is ironic that although Hegel took Socrates to be an apostle of the 'subjectivism' that caused the fragmentation of the *polis*, some of the things that Plato puts into Socrates' mouth suggest a line of thought that was congenial to Hegel and subsequent hegelian thinkers. For one thing, many interpreters take it as a matter of course that in Socrates' view, everyone takes his ultimate goal to be his own happiness.[59] In addition, two respects are commonly noted in which Socrates appears to have stressed the harmony of human motivations, and thus to have minimized the likelihood of deliberative conflict. One of these two is his thesis of the so-called Unity of the Virtues. The other is his denial of the possibility of *akrasia* or, as it is also called, 'weakness of will'. In view of how widespread these ways of thinking are, it is at the least worth re-examining the evidence—which seems to me surprisingly weak, too weak to support the eudaimonist, and indeed harmonizing eudaimonist, interpretation that is often founded on it.

Although the thesis of the unity of the virtues, as it appears in the *Protagoras,* for example, does not by itself entail that there can be no conflict among rational deliberative considerations, it goes some distance in that direction. If all virtues are in some sense one (or, for that matter, if they are plural but always accompany each other), then one virtue cannot recommend an action that is incompatible with the action that is recommended by another virtue. We could not, for instance, encounter a situation in

---

[57] I here leave aside the *Phaedrus*, which has sometimes been thought to be an early work but also bears some signs of having been written after the *Republic*. Its position is too controversial to allow it to be helpful to cite here.

[58] I take most of what goes on in Plato's dialogues, including the *Republic*, to indicate, when suitably interpreted with a view to the qualifications and warnings that are given, the thinking and sometimes the convictions and conclusions of Plato himself. I have no time for the argument that because the works never ascribe views to Plato by name, it is therefore risky to suppose that they show, in a fairly straightforward way, what his thinking was.   [59] Thus for instance Vlastos 1991: 177, 203, and Irwin 1995: 201.

which it would be truly courageous to do a certain thing but truly just not to do it. The impossibility of rational conflict would follow if it were assumed, in addition, that all rational considerations that exist are implicated in the operation of the virtues. This Socrates is never made to state, but it is something that he might plausibly be taken to have believed.

Socrates' denial of the possibility of *akrasia* has a different character. It does not have to do with whether or not rational considerations can conflict with each other. Rather, to deny that akratic action can occur is to assert that a person can never act against his own belief about what is best. That means that (except in cases of coercion or compulsion) a person who holds that a particular course of action is best, all things considered, can never be led by a desire or emotion to do something else instead. The kind of conflict that this Socratic view rejects is not that between different parts of reason, but that between reason and non-rational emotion or desire.[60]

There is in addition a further way in which Socrates' thinking—or at least the thinking that appears in Plato's *Protagoras*—appears to rule out the possibility of any fundamental deliberative dualism. In that work, Plato puts into Socrates' mouth a general procedure for an agent to use in deciding what to do. Socrates is made to describe deliberation as simply a matter of determining how to gain for himself the greatest amount of future pleasure (see esp. *Prot.* 350–61). This hedonistic calculus would provide a way of resolving any deliberative quandaries that threatened to arise. The model of deliberation suggested in the *Protagoras* involves a single, homogenous type of consideration, and precludes any deliberative dualism.

3. Uncertain Signs of Socratic Eudaimonism

So far we have seen evidence linking Socrates with a tendency towards a belief in a single aim that governs practical reasoning. These indications, however, are not all homogenous. In particular, the *Protagoras* presents a straightforward, seemingly egoistic hedonism, which is not present, or at least very far from prominent, in most of the works that seem to be written under substantial Socratic influence.[61] The question is whether Socrates is fully committed to such a eudaimonist position.

In spite of a widespread tendency to take it as a matter of course that the answer must be affirmative, the matter is problematic. The main difficulty arises from two Platonic works that are normally taken to be the most directly indicative of Socrates' own thinking, namely, the *Apology* and the *Crito*. It is wrong to think, he says in the *Apology*,

---

[60] On Socrates' tendencies in this direction, see e.g. Santas 1971 and Price 1995: 27.

[61] See Nussbaum 1986: ch. 4 on the importance of deliberative monism in the *Protagoras*. For present purposes it is unimportant whether Plato there accepts that view (as is argued by Irwin 1995) or whether it is simply put into Socrates' mouth for the sake of some argument.

that a man who is worth anything will take into account the odds of living or dying, or will, when he does something, consider *anything besides whether he is doing things that are just or unjust*, or the acts of a good or a bad man.

In the *Crito*, furthermore, Socrates is made to say that

we should not regard living as the most important thing, but living well . . . and living well is the same thing as living nobly and justly.[62]

Taken by themselves and at face value, what these passages say might well be supposed to be patently incompatible with the thesis that a reasonable person's sole ultimate end is his own happiness. For on the surface at least, it might appear that one's happiness is indeed something 'besides whether one is doing things that are just or unjust'. Thus we would seem to lack any guarantee that all human aims fall under the rubric of one's happiness, or that they must be consistent with one another.

Furthermore, this impression is not disarmed by reading these passages within the contexts of the works in which they occur. It is a striking fact that neither in the *Apology* nor in the *Crito* does Socrates make any reference whatsoever to well-being or *eudaimonia*. Most notably, he simply does not say that happiness is a person's ultimate rational goal. Nor does he say that it is the basis of his own commitment to acting justly. Socrates surely thinks that one's aim in life is a state of *oneself* or, as he sometimes says, a state of one's own soul. He also says that this state consists in one's 'living well' (*eu zein*). Our question, however, is what state Socrates takes that to involve. Does 'doing well' automatically include all of one's aims, in such a way that even when doing just acts works against one's other aims, one must nevertheless be counted as advancing one's own overall happiness? Or does 'doing well' perhaps include performing actions that can, on occasion, damage one's overall well-being? The *Crito* gives no unambiguous indication how we are to answer these questions.

It seems to me quite clear, however, that Socrates' statement that we should not 'consider *anything besides whether he is doing things that are just or unjust*, or the acts of a good or a bad man' is hardly the language that one would choose if one wished to say, let alone make it plain, that this aim falls under one's own happiness. After all, Socrates was operating, as we have seen, within a milieu in which it had been seriously suggested that being just is foolish and damaging to one's well-being. A prior assumption that Socrates accepted eudaimonism would certainly incline us to read works like the *Apology* and the *Crito* as embodying such an unarticulated axiom. But surely we should not accept such an assumption without question. And when we see how many passages we have to read, not as actually stating this assumption, but as at

---

[62] *Apol.* 28b and *Crito* 48b; cf. *Gorg.* 512d–e. Note that one cannot assume that 'living well' (*eu zein*) at this point is intended to mean nothing but 'be happy'. Likewise the roughly equivalent 'doing well' (*eu prattein*). Whether it does is precisely the thing that is left open; see below.

best leaving it unspoken in a context in which it could only seem somewhat tendentious, the strength of the assumption dwindles very substantially.

It seems to me, then, that we should not without further ado assume that Socrates simply must have accepted a eudaimonist position. Rather, we should recognize that if we had only these works to go on, it might not occur to us that the Socrates who figures in them was a eudaimonist at all. We would not doubt that Socrates attached importance to an individual's own good. But we would not feel pressure to conclude that he regarded it as the ultimate aim, much less the sole ultimate aim, were it not for the standard presumption that all Greek philosophers are eudaimonists.[63] Once we free ourselves from the thought of such pressure, it seems to me, we are in a position to take seriously the evidence both that Socrates and Plato were operating, as I have already started to try to show, in a milieu in which eudaimonism was not taken for granted, and that they may not have accepted it themselves. Let me then proceed to discuss that evidence.

4. The Weakness of those Signs

It is reasonable to examine this question in the light of what emerged earlier about *Republic* I–II. If it were there universally and openly taken for granted, as Sidgwick and others maintain, that everyone seeks his own happiness as his ultimate aim and recognizes no potentially competing considerations, then we would be well advised to conclude that the same must be true of the *Apology* and the *Crito*. But since *Republic* I–II attest the existence of people who acknowledge justice as a consideration in its own

---

[63] Vlastos 1991: 230–1 says that happiness is one's final end and virtue is the 'supreme nonfinal' good, 'both necessary and sufficient for happiness', but he says this there on the basis of *Gorg.* 499e and *Lysis* 330b. However one cannot assume that the sayings of these two works are to be read as presupposed in interpreting the *Apology* and *Crito*. Vlastos (302) notes that these two works make no reference to happiness. He thinks, however, that eudaimonism or rational egoism (in his terminology, 'the Eudaimonist Axiom', 203; cf. 230–1) is nevertheless taken for granted here. To deny this on the ground that no eudaimonist thesis is expressed here would, he says (302), be to assume that Plato must always voice all major assumptions that are in force in a given dialogue. Not so. The question is whether it *is* an assumption in these two works. The relevant passages make the weight of the argument rest merely on the conviction that one is to act justly, *without any appeal's being made to happiness.* It seems to me likely that Vlastos has been influenced by a general presumption that all Greek ethics is eudaimonist. But that presumption needs to be tested against the texts, rather than assumed as a principle for interpreting them (cf. n. 68 below).

In a similar way, C. C. W. Taylor takes Socrates to have adopted a similar eudaimonist position (1998: 59). Taylor also maintains that the view that 'the moral life is the best life *for the agent*' (his emphasis) has a 'central role' in Socrates' thinking. 'Given that centrality,' Taylor says, 'it is surprising how little argumentative support it receives.' But Taylor finds no argumentative support at all until the time of the *Gorgias* (1998: 61). The right thing to do is to doubt that Socrates adopted a clear-cut eudaimonism at all, and to conclude that he also attached an independent value to moral action without exploring fully the relation between the two. This is not to say that Socrates was not concerned to work out a 'broadly coherent position' (Taylor 1998: 40), but only to deny that he had gone as far in that direction as eudaimonist interpreters suppose.

right, which can even lead them to act in ways not conducive to their own well-being, we must seriously entertain the idea that the *Apology* and the *Crito* might perfectly well express the same thought, too. Certainly it is striking that the injunction to act justly is there presented as bolstered neither by a relation between virtue and happiness, nor by a claim that the value of the former is based on its contribution to the latter. Equally striking is the absence from those works of any statement at all of a eudaimonist position.

It can hardly be said in general that the notion of well-being plays much of a role in either the *Apology* or the *Crito*. The *Apology* in particular gives it hardly any role at all. Socrates insists that his activities have always been conducive to the good of Athens.[64] When we wonder, however, about his reasons for having thus benefited his city, his answer is not that doing so will contribute to his own well-being, but instead that he is obedient to 'the god' and must do what is commanded. (It is not always easy to tell which deity Socrates is referring to at a given point; sometimes it is Apollo, the god of Delphi whose oracle said that no man was wiser than he, and sometimes it is his 'spirit' or *daimonion*, which turns him aside from inadvisable courses of action.)[65] Indeed, the language attributed to Socrates' 'god' here is consistently imperative rather than attractive.[66] Socrates introduces notions of benefit and well-being principally in order to express the idea that death is not to be regarded as bad for a person, and to indicate that the defence that he has chosen is better for himself than any other would be.[67] Of a general claim, however, that practical deliberation is focused on one's happiness there seems to me to be no sign.

Socrates is made to say, it must be observed, that nothing can harm a man who is good. From this it follows that being just cannot harm a virtuous person either.[68] This idea is not, however, developed very far in the Platonic works that seem to reflect Socrates' influence most strongly. For one thing, no explanation is offered of why a good man cannot be harmed. Moreover, there is lacking here any account of the relation between well-being and justice (such as Plato was later to supply in the *Republic*) which might show why such harm cannot occur.[69]

---

[64] See esp. *Apol.* 30a–31a.   [65] See e.g. *Apol.* 21e–22a, 28d, 37e.

[66] See *Apol.* 21e–22a, 23b, 28d, 29b and d, 30a, 31d, 33c, 37e, and cf. Chapter 3, secs. V and VIII.

[67] e.g. *Apol.* 28a–b, 30c–d, 35a, 36c–d, 40e.

[68] See *Apol.* 41c–d. Irwin adduces *Euthyd.* 278e–80a and *Lysis* 219–20 to construct, in conjunction with this passage from the *Apology*, an argument for saying that Socrates is committed to a eudaimonist position (1995: 52–5 with 32–3 and 87–8). What seems most striking about the argument, however, is that it is so ingenious and unobvious, and that it must make such heavy use of premises from passages that are widely separated both from each other and from the *Apology*. The supposition that a reader would be likely to put these passages together to see the reasoning leading to eudaimonism seems to me to gain much of its plausibility from the prior assumption that Greek thought was imbued with eudaimonism.

[69] This fact is pointed out by Irwin (1995: 45; cf. 47). Irwin says that Socrates 'implies that what is fine and just must be beneficial for the agent', on the ground that it 'is such an important good that it is not worth living with an unjust soul'. This does not, of course, by itself imply that happiness is the ultimate aim.

In addition and more importantly, the statement that a virtuous person cannot be harmed, or that he cannot be harmed by justice, neither amounts to nor entails eudaimonism. It does not entail either that happiness is the only ultimate rational aim, nor that conduciveness to happiness is all that makes virtue worth pursuing. In view of these facts, the idea that the *Apology* is in any substantial degree a eudaimonist document is hard to sustain, except against the background presupposition that it must be one.

Sidgwick proposes a way of dealing with the combination of eudaimonist and non-eudaimonist thinking that appears in Plato's portrayals of Socrates. Socrates' thinking, he says, 'depends upon an inseparable union of the conceptions of Virtue and Interest in the single notion of Good'.[70] Something about this seems right. Something about this may be right, although it is not clear precisely what Sidgwick has in mind under the phrase 'inseparable union'. Perhaps he means that Socrates took virtue and well-being to be identical, or else to be related as part to whole.[71] (These are respectively what I earlier called the fusionist and the inclusivist conceptions.)[72] Or perhaps he meant something less systematic, such as that Socrates did not sharply separate the two aims, without specifying exactly what he thought their relation to each other is.

As an interpretation of Socrates, this last option seems the most promising. There is a strong tendency on the part of interpreters of Plato's early works to picture Socrates as a systematic philosopher with a well-worked-out position—after some modern pattern of a philosopher working out a theory or doctrine.[73] Nevertheless, the variety of thoughts exhibited in those works makes that project look in many ways unpromising. As matters stand, it is hard to justify any confident assertion that Socrates espoused any very definite position about the relation of virtue and happiness.[74]

[70] Sidgwick 1931: 26. He goes on to say, 'This union Socrates did not of course, invent—he found it, as the sophists did, in the common thought of his age.' This is a somewhat surprising thing to find Sidgwick saying. For the most part, at least in his 1907, he adopts a kantian interpretation of Greek ethics (see above, Chapter 1, sec. V and Chapter 2, sec. I). This passage from his 1931 might conceivably be taken in that way, as noted, but it sounds more like a hegelian way of reading the Greeks, of either the fusionist or the inclusivist variety. Cf. MacIntyre 1981: 131.

[71] In opposition to Irwin (see above, nn. 68–9), Vlastos argues for a type of inclusivist interpretation of Socrates, though Vlastos also considers the possibility of a fusionist interpretation. See his 1991: ch. 8, esp. 204–6, 214–31.

[72] See Chapter 1, sec. VII. 4.

[73] This tendency is manifested, for instance throughout Vlastos 1991, cf. my review (White 1995b) for reservations. A more reasonable attitude towards the possibility of ascribing a worked-out view to Socrates with regard to a particular issue can be found in Cooper 1999b: 89–90, reprinted from Cooper 1998.

[74] It seems to me that this is the real upshot of Santas 1994 and many other studies that show how Plato tried to work out various unclarities in Socrates' thinking.

5. Indications against Socratic Eudaimonism

An additional fact seems to support a reluctance to ascribe too definite a position to Socrates. This is the fact of Socrates' own philosophical activity, and his attempt to persuade the Athenian citizens that his own stance in ethical matters was the one for them to adopt. No one reading the *Apology*, for instance, can fail to be struck by the tone of almost proselytizing zeal that pervades it. Moreover, Socrates there makes more than one reference to his own efforts in this regard:

> It is literally true, even if it sounds rather comical, that the god has specifically appointed me to this city, as though it were a large thoroughbred horse which because of its great size is inclined to be lazy and needs the stimulation of some stinging fly. It seems to me that the god has attached me to this city to perform the office of such a fly, and all day long I never cease to settle here, there, and everywhere, rousing, persuading, reproving every one of you.[75]

Not only does Socrates make such efforts. They plainly dominate his life, and he spends little energy on anything else.

There is a problem to be raised here. How might Socrates' own proselytizing activity fit into his conception of his own happiness? Are we to take it that that activity furthers his happiness or is a part of it, or are we, on the contrary, to believe that the goal of helping other Athenians is an aim that is independent of his own well-being, and that it is adopted in some fashion for its own sake? Socrates says that he has been commanded to engage in this activity. But that merely pushes the question back a step. How are we to conceive of his reason for obeying the command? It of course seems inconceivable that he might have disobeyed. That fact, however, does not answer the question. We must still ask whether the reason for obedience is, say, simply that disobedience would be *wrong*, or whether it would contribute to unhappiness, or whether it is some combination of the two motivations.

We cannot of course jump to the second, straightforwardly eudaimonist conclusion merely on the basis of the fact that Socrates presents himself as giving up his life rather than cease discussing ethical issues publicly. For he stresses continually that death may not in and of itself be something to be avoided. Moreover, there are certainly ways in which we might flesh out Socrates' statements so as to exhibit teaching as a component or consequence of his efforts to improve his own soul and thus secure his own well-being. For example, he regards himself as obliged to determine whether the oracle of Delphi, which said that no one was wiser than he, was speaking the truth, and much of his examination of the Athenians was a by-product of this activity.

On the other hand, when we look to his own actual words for an account of why he makes such efforts to improve his fellow citizens' thinking, we find little to clarify

---

[75] *Apol.* 30e (trans. Tredennick, with minor alterations).

what their place in his own *eudaimonia* might be. Suppose he were confronted with this question: 'Are you better off by virtue of your educative activities, and is that the reason why you engage in them, or do you pursue them partly or wholly for themselves?' It does not seem to me—suspending the automatic unargued presumption that Socrates accepted a straightforwardly eudaimonist view—that Plato's early works really give us a basis for saying how he would answer. Indeed, it seems to me extremely unlikely that Socrates had a fully worked-out position on the matter.[76]

6. The Unlikelihood that Socrates Took a Position on Eudaimonism

As I have stressed, however, my chief concern here is not to reconstruct the position of the historical Socrates, but to take note of the ideas that were available for expression at this period. The *Apology* and the *Crito* make clear that it was possible to say that justice should be treated as paramount, and to say this without citing its contribution to happiness. If this idea is present in those works, it could only be as a suppressed enthymeme, which we are led to find by a prior general supposition about the eudaimonist nature of Greek ethics as a whole.

When we look at these works in conjunction with *Republic* I–II, on the other hand, we can see the same fluidity of thought in all of them. Moreover, when we bear in mind the similar indications in Thucydides and other earlier writers, the same impression is strengthened. It seems best to conclude that this was, overall, a period in which the relation between people's concern for justice and their attachment to their own well-being is not at all fully worked out. The thought was certainly in the air that one's happiness is one's paramount aim that must somehow subsume all others. But this thought was also accompanied, sometimes within the same minds, by the idea that justice was a consideration that carried independent weight. There is no good reason to think that the Greeks simply took eudaimonism for granted.

V. Some Platonic Passages outside the Republic

1. The Structure of the Argument

The main body of evidence concerning Plato's overall position in ethics is to be found in the *Republic*. The exposition there is systematic and touches on virtually everything

---

[76] Kahn 1996: 237–8 notes a tendency in the *Protagoras* to switch between a prudential/hedonist and a moral viewpoint. Kahn takes this to be calculated on Plato's part. Calculated it may indeed be, but I think it is more plausibly interpreted as, in addition, a reflection of Plato's recognition that the distinction had not fully crystallized in Socrates' thinking. Likewise, Santas 1994 seems to me to show Socrates not to be a philosopher who strove for a fully systematic view; and I am inclined to say, too, that the considerations offered by Nehamas 1999: 99–104 also demonstrate complexity in Socrates' value judgements.

that is relevant to questions about eudaimonism and deliberative conflict.[77] Never-theless, passages in other Platonic writings are also relevant to these issues. Moreover, it is possible to think that when the correct interpretation of the *Republic* seems doubt-ful, it makes sense to take the other works as guides for one's reading of it.

Eudaimonist interpreters of Greek ethics sometimes tend to think that the eudaimonist tendency of other works is so plain that they virtually force us to read the *Republic* as a eudaimonist document. I think they are right to appeal to other works, but wrong to think that the thinking shown by those works is in fact eudai-monist.

Let me here adopt a bipartite strategy to show this. First, I shall discuss a number of passages from the *Euthydemus*, the *Symposium*, and the *Philebus* that might seem to evince a eudaimonist outlook and have been taken to do so. When the words of these passages are closely examined, they turn out to be straightforwardly restricted, so as not to be support for an ascription to Plato of any generally eudaimonist thinking. (Here it is well to remember that Plato often uses arguments based on the premise that it makes sense to seek one's own happiness; he does indeed believe that one's happiness is a rational ultimate aim, without, however, believing—and this is my point—that it is the *only* ultimate rational aim.)

Second, I shall turn to some other passages in the *Timaeus*, the *Laws*, and *Republic* X. In these places Plato deploys a notion of non-self-referential goodness—of a thing's being good 'absolutely' and not 'for me' or indeed 'for' anyone. Plato's use of this notion shows without doubt that his concept of goodness was not restricted to the con-cept of a thing's being good for oneself. Therefore he was in a position to express the idea that something might be commended on grounds not related to one's own well-being.

That he deploys such an idea in the *Republic* is what I shall argue subsequently. The purpose of the present section is to prepare the way for that argument, by show-ing that we are not well advised to read the *Republic* against the background of an assumption that a eudaimonist interpretation must be presumed antecedently.

2. The Euthydemus, the Symposium, and the Philebus: The Weakness of their Evidence for Eudaimonism in Plato

A revealing example of the kind of passage that we should not too hastily suppose advocates eudaimonism, at least in the sense relevant here, is *Euthydemus* 278e–282a. Here Plato repeatedly says that everyone wishes 'to do well' (*eu prattein*) and 'to be

---

[77] The *Laws* is the only other work that provides the scope for a systematic presentation of an ethical position, but it is largely taken up with other matters, and in any case, as Aristotle notes (*Pol.* 1265a1–2), more taken up with institutional issues than with general matters of ethical doctrine.

happy' (*eudaimonein* or *eudaimon einai*), and draws conclusions from that claim.[78] This is certainly not to say, however, that there are no independent considerations that could rival happiness in a person's deliberations.

It is doubtful in any case that Plato here tries to achieve a degree of precision that would be needed for propounding a strict thesis of this kind. He says with some emphasis in the middle of the passage that people have 'forgotten the greatest good of all', and then states that this good is 'good fortune' (*eutychia*), which is then said to be best provided by wisdom.[79] One is reminded here of Socrates as he appears in the *Apology* and *Crito*. There, I argued, there is no indication that Socrates either assumes or propounds eudaimonism in any clear-cut way. Rather, his style of investigation is much too relaxed to make it reasonable to suppose that he had such a fixed thesis in mind.

Similarly in the *Meno*, Plato says that everyone desires to be happy, and that no one desires to be unhappy or to have what is bad—none of which assertions imply eudaimonism in the present sense.[80] Just before that passage, Plato makes Socrates ask Meno, his interlocutor, whether anyone knowingly 'desires things that are bad'. When Meno replies, 'Of course', Socrates asks, 'What do you mean by "desire"? "Desire to possess them"?' 'Yes, what else?' Meno replies, and Socrates then responds to Meno on that basis.[81]

Should we take this exchange to mean that according to Socrates, or according to Plato as he describes Socrates, 'desire' means or is tantamount to 'desires to possess' or 'desires that one oneself possess', so that there would be no desires with non-self-referential content? Aside from a presupposition that Plato must take eudaimonism for granted, this idea has little to support it.

Surely what is at issue *in the passage* indeed involves self-referential matters: the question is whether anyone desires to acquire or possess what he judges to be bad for himself. However, it does not seem justified or plausible to take this exchange as an indication that Plato can *in general* attach no sense to the idea of desiring except desiring to possess something, or that he means to exclude non-self-referential desires. Rather, Plato is interested here in the particular issue of what one desires to possess. The reason for this focus lies close to hand. The topic that is here up for discussion is Meno's suggested definition of virtue—which Socrates, it should be noted, does *not* accept—namely, that virtue is the desire for fine things (*kala*) and the ability to get (*porizesthai*) them. The rest of the relevant conversation is governed by this suggestion, not by any theme of Socrates' own. There is therefore no reason at all to take the passage as evidence that in Socrates' view, or in Plato's, the only admissible desires or goods concern oneself and one's own happiness.

Other passages in other works likewise speak of desires and aims that are possessed

---

[78] *Euthyd.* 278e–279a, 282a.
[80] See, for instance, *Meno* 78a

[79] *Euthyd.* 279c–d, e–280a, 281b.
[81] *Meno* 77c.

by particular people or in particular circumstances, but do not make blanket claims
that exclude non-eudaimonist or non-self-regarding motivations. For instance, one
passage in the *Symposium* that is often cited in a favour of an across-the-board eudaimonist reading of Plato does not uphold any such sweeping claim. *Symposium* 204d
says that a lover wishes that what is beautiful 'be one's own' (*genesthai hautoi*). In 204c,
however, Plato has already made it explicit that Plato here is talking about *lovers* and
their motivation as such, without any indication that he is attempting to state a general fact about *all* human desires. The passage runs as follows:

> So much, then [Diotima says], for the nature and the origin of love. You were right in think-
> ing that he was the love of what is beautiful ... But what do you mean by the love of what is
> beautiful? Or to put the question more precisely, what is it that the lover of the beautiful is
> longing for? —He is longing to make the beautiful his own, I [Socrates] said ... Well then,
> she went on, suppose that, instead of the beautiful, you were being asked about the good. I
> put it to you, Socrates? What is it that *the lover of the good* is longing for?[82] —To make the
> good his own. —Then what will he gain by making it his own? —... He'll gain happiness.

The passage does not say that the only aim that is possible concerning the good is to
'make it one's own'. Neither does the sequel say that the only ultimate aim is one's own
happiness, although it does say that 'there is no need to ask why men should want to
be happy', that 'we all long to make the good our own', that 'everybody is in love', and
that 'Love ... includes every kind of desire (*epithymia*) for goods and for happiness'.[83]

People who take this passage to express a eudaimonist thesis make a mistake. The
passage does not claim to be a catalogue of all human aims and motivations. It only
tells us about the desires of lovers, and says that love as such and lovers as such desire
to have the good belong to them, and that everyone desires goods and happiness. The
passage does not rule out aims that are not directed at one's own well-being.[84]

The *Philebus* contains two passages that might also be thought to be pertinent to
the matter at hand.[85] At one of them, Plato says that because no one would choose
pleasure without the recognition that he had it, or would choose to have reason with-

---

[82] *Symp.* 204e2–3: 'erai ho erôn tôn agathôn. ti erai? —Genesthai ... hautôi.'

[83] *Symp.* 205d, and in general 204e–205d. See likewise 206a, e–205a, c–d, which make the same claims.
The *epithymia* for good things and for happiness (*he tôn agathon epithymia kai tou eudaimonein*) mentioned
in 205d1–3 does not cover all motivation; ('*epithymia* for something' is not on its own naturally taken as cov-
ering all aims, unless of course one takes it for granted already that all motivations that Plato recognizes are
in some way self-regarding). Price 1989: 56 seems to presume this, though at p. 99 he introduces a complication that seems to me to cut in favour of the present interpretation of Plato's overall meaning.

[84] Irwin discusses this passage on pp. 306–8 of his 1995. He does not seem to me to give reason to believe
that it applies generally to human motivation. In addition, he seems to me to introduce a non-eudaimonist
and non-self-referential consideration when he says that the kind of 'self-propagation' mentioned in the
Symposium is a matter of preserving what I 'value' in myself (see also 309); see White 1999a.

[85] Annas cites *Phileb.* 20–3 and 60–1, along with *Euthyd.* 278–9 and *Symp.* 204–5, as showing that 'for
the ancients, but not for us, it is trivially true that we all seek happiness as our final end' (1998: 71).

out any pleasure, 'neither of these two would be perfect, choiceworthy for all, or the completely good'.[86] This might seem to evince an assumption that 'the completely good' must be good *for* someone, though the implication is far from explicit. The second passage says the following:

Now, this point, I take it, is most necessary to assert of the good: that everything that has any notion of it hunts for it (*thêreuei*) and desires to get hold of it and secure it for its very own, caring nothing for anything else except for things that are realized at the same time as good things are.[87]

This passage comes the closest of any to saying that the good is something that one can aim only to possess.

The force of these passages as signs of eudaimonism is completely blunted, however, by their context within the problem that the dialogue officially poses. From the very start, the *Philebus* announces itself as asking 'what is good *for all creatures*': whether it is enjoying oneself or knowing things, or which 'possession or state of the soul is the one that can render life happy for all human beings'.[88]

One can hardly fail to be struck by how difficult it is to find a statement in these works of any straightforwardly eudaimonist thesis. If these passages are indeed the best that can be adduced, the ascription of that thesis to him is in serious jeopardy.[89]

We might always fall back, of course, on the bare *postulate* that because Greek ethics uniformly presupposed eudaimonism there was no need for anyone to enunciate it.[90] Once that strategy has been called into question, however, and we actually

---

[86] *Phileb.* 61a1–2, where 'completely good' translated *to pantapasin agathon*. The passage is to be compared with *Rep.* 504e–6a. Here Plato also denies that particular things, pleasure and knowledge, are the good. But although he says that the good is what is required to make anything that one possesses beneficial, he does not say that to be good is to be something that one possesses (505d–506a). And as I will argue, *Rep.* VII shows that he deploys a notion of non-self-regarding goodness (secs. V. 3–4 below).

[87] *Phileb.* 20d, in D. Frede's translation, with the exception of 'things that are *realized* . . . good things are'. Frede has here 'what is connected with the *acquisition* of some good', while Hackforth translates 'such things as involve this or that good in the course of their *realization*'. The verb in question is *apoteloumenôn*, whose meaning is 'realized' or 'completed' rather than 'acquired'. My 'at the same time as' renders *hama* more literally than Frede's 'connected' or than Hackforth's 'in the course of'; the link signified by *hama* is, strictly, merely temporal. [88] *Phileb.* 11b, d.

[89] Perhaps there are other passages that could be cited in this cause, but I doubt it. Irwin maintains (1995: 310–11) that when the *Phaedrus* speaks of a lover educating and moulding a beloved (252d–e), this must be done out of the lovers' self-interest rather than in the interest of the beloved. This does not seem convincing. Irwin cites a passage in which Aristotle seems to indicate that when a sculptor loves a statue, that cannot be a case of concern for the interests of the wood of which it is made, and then asks, 'Why should attitudes to persons be any different, from Plato's point of view?' One reply would be to cite *Rep.* 342–3, where Plato first says that a good horseman does his work for the good of his horses, and then says the analogous thing about ruling, in spite of Thrasymachus's objection. Perhaps, of course, Plato does mean that in the present case the lover acts for his own benefit. But however that may be, this passage of the *Phaedrus* is certainly no direct evidence for saying that Plato subscribes to a general eudaimonist thesis.

[90] Recall Vlastos's 'Eudaimonist Axiom' as applied to Socrates; see above, n. 61.

look at the putative evidence for it, the case is seen to lose most of its force. Self-referential notions of desiring and the like figure in particular discussions, but there is no suggestion that there is no other kind of desiring. When Socrates speaks as he does in the *Crito* of justice as something that we should follow under all conditions, then, we have no grounds for assuming that he takes eudaimonism for granted. And when he opens the door, as we shall see he does in the *Republic*, to an explicit discussion of actions that may give up one's own good for the sake of some other consideration, such as justice, we are not entitled to interpret such passages as if a non-eudaimonist reading were ruled out by some firmly established eudaimonist background assumption.

The passages treated in this section, then, do not indicate that Plato espoused eudaimonism in the sense that bears on the really serious ethical issues concerning conflict. Rather, they merely show—what no one would deny—that questions about what is good for a human being and what produces happiness were central to his ethical investigations, and that he took them to be central considerations governing practical deliberation. The importance of these issues to him, and to Greek thinkers generally, is not to be doubted. It is quite another thing to say, however, that he regarded an individual's happiness as his *only* rational aim, or ignored or excluded all others, or especially that he did any of these things in order to eliminate deliberative conflict. Such a conclusion cannot be drawn from the passages thus far examined.

3. Non-Self-Regarding Goodness in Plato's Timaeus

Now let us turn to the task of showing that Plato employed a notion of what might be called 'absolute' goodness or goodness *simpliciter* a notion that is not self-referential. The point is this. When Plato expresses the idea that something is good, he does not always mean that it is good *for* someone, let alone that it is good *for me* or for *oneself*. Sometimes he intends to say that it is good in a way that is not relational, and is in particular not *self*-referential. This means that he is in a position to express the idea that although a thing is good for me, or for someone in particular, it nevertheless is not good in an absolute way. And this in turn allows him to express the idea of a conflict between something's being good and its being good for me.

In much of the *Republic*, as we shall see, Plato imagines a ruler trying to achieve the good of his or her *polis*—or what a given ruler might express as the good of '*my*' polis. The idea of what is good for my city is in a relevant sense partly self-referential. For although (under most understandings) my city is not identical with myself, I single out 'my' city by reference to myself. As I have noted,[91] C. D. Broad classified this kind

[91] Chapter 2, sec. VII. 4, and Broad 1942. Brink 1999: 271 argues against ascribing self-referential altruism in Broad's sense to either Plato or Aristotle, and also against ascribing to them an 'impersonal' conception of love and friendship (on the latter point he seems to me to be right).

of idea under the rubric 'self-referential altruism'. It involves concern for something that is not oneself, but for which one has a concern in virtue of a relation that it bears to oneself. It is thus not narrowly egoistic or self-confined, but it is self-referential.

For the most part, the good of the *polis* is the broadest kind of good that Plato ever discusses. That fact might make us think that the broadest concept of goodness that he can entertain, and the broadest sort of aim also, would be self-referential, namely, the well-being of *one's own* city-state. If that were the case, it would show that he pays attention to non-self-confined considerations. It would not, however, give us reason to think that he approached the idea of an aim detached from oneself, let alone the idea of a universal aim such as figures in modern thinkers like Kant or, in a different way, Mill. It might also lead us to believe that his position really is what fusionist inter-preters have maintained: namely, a way of saying that all worthwhile aims are includ-ed in one's good. For it seems a relatively small step—though conceptually not an insignificant one—from picturing all aims as defined by some relation or other to one-self to treating them as parts of one's own good.

Plato does not neglect, however, to attend to goods and considerations broader than one's *polis*, or, indeed, to those that are universal in a substantial sense. For one thing, as I have pointed out, he also holds that the structure of the whole *kosmos* is good.[92] Thus recall that in the *Timaeus* he writes:

God desired that all things should be good and nothing bad, so far as this was attainable. Wherefore also finding the whole visible sphere not at rest, but moving in an irregular and disorderly fashion, out of disorder he brought order, considering that the latter was in every way better than the other.[93]

The concept of goodness that figures here certainly is not one of what is good *for* any-one, not even for the demiurge. The demiurge's aim is plainly not that the *kosmos* be good *for him*. He plainly does not think either 'I shall make *my* universe as good as pos-sible', nor 'I shall do what is *best for my* universe'. Passages like this one put it beyond doubt that Plato's notion of goodness does embrace applications beyond the self-ref-erential.

4. Non-Self-Regarding Goodness in Platonic Practical Deliberation in the Laws and Republic X

It is perfectly true that normally Plato does not expect judgements about the goodness of the *kosmos*, or other such evaluations, to play a dominant role in the deliberations of human beings. The demiurge may need to consider such matters, but human beings, it seems, rarely or never do. As I earlier noted, Plato's horizon of effective human

---

[92] Sec. V. 3.
[93] Plato, *Tim.* 29e–30a (trans. Jowett). Cf. Chapter 4, sec. VI.

political activity is the boundary of the *polis*, along with the forging of alliances with neighbouring city-states to help ensure its preservation.

From this fact one might conclude that even though Plato does have a concept of non-self-referential goodness, he does not suppose that it is relevant to deliberation by human beings or to ethics in the sense in which that term is normally used in the present day. Should that be so, the case for saying that in ethics Plato attends only to self-referential considerations, and even the case for the fusionist interpretation just described, would still stand. All *human* practical thinking would have to do with a self-referential good.

Still it remains to observe that we also find Plato sometimes intimating that a person should adopt a broader perspective, even for the purpose of deliberating about his own action. In *Republic* X, he says that someone who has suffered some great calamity should recognize

that the best thing is to remain as quiet as possible in misfortune and not to resent it because it is not clear whether such events are good or bad, [and] also because to take it hard makes the future no better, because no human experience is worth taking very seriously.[94]

At first sight one might presume that Plato merely means that a person should be concerned about what will happen to him after death or in the long run, rather than about what befalls him in this life. If this were so, this passage would involve merely a self-referential and indeed self-regarding consideration.

However, there is more to Plato's point than that. In the *Laws*, expanding on what seems evidently to be the same thought, he says:

Of course, the affairs of human beings are not worthy of great seriousness; yet it is necessary to be serious about them. And this is not a fortunate thing. But since we're here, if somehow we would carry out the business in some appropriate way it would perhaps be a well-measured thing for us to do so.

He then continues:

I assert that what is serious should be treated seriously, and what is not serious should not, and that by nature god is worthy of a complete, blessed seriousness, but that what is human . . . has been devised as a certain plaything of god, and that this is really the best thing about it. Every man and woman should spend life in this way, playing the noblest possible games.[95]

It is hard not to take Plato here to be indicating that as a person guides his actions, he should evaluate his life by attending to a larger context. The issue will not then be

---

[94] *Rep.* 604b–c.

[95] *Laws* 803b–c; cf. 644d–645c. One cannot rule out the possibility that the thought expressed in the *Laws* is different from the one at work in the *Republic*. In any case, however, the occurrence of the idea in the *Laws* is enough to establish the point that I am making.

what is good for oneself, nor even what is good for one's community. Rather, it will be what is good in a yet broader and universal, non-self-referential way.[96] The cognizance that a human being takes of this kind of goodness would thus have a bearing on his attitudes and actions. Plato's treatment of this idea is not extensive—not nearly as extensive as it is in the Stoics in the following century. Nevertheless, the presence of the idea in his thinking, and even his strictly ethical thinking, seems impossible to deny.

I have argued, then, that Plato can entertain not only a non-self-referential notion of goodness, but also the thought that a person might deploy such a notion in his deliberations. This latter is what we shall later see in the *Republic*. However, there remains a loose end. I have contrasted the notion of 'absolute' goodness with a notion of what is good for 'my' city that is not identical, I have said, with the notion of what is good 'for me'. We should ask how these notions are related, and I shall return to this question later.[97]

VI. The Republic: Plato's Project

1. On Questioning the Assumption of Eudaimonism in the Republic

The *Republic* is largely taken up with an argument for the proposition that 'justice pays', that is, that being just is conducive to the well-being of the just person. That much fits with a eudaimonist interpretation, and is uncontroversial. It is, however, compatible with the contention that in addition Plato also allows, non-eudaimonistically, for a rational consideration that can oppose one's well-being and even possibly override it. In the present section, I discuss the eudaimonist element of the *Republic*, the argument that justice pays, showing that it is so formulated as to make room for the non-eudaimonist consideration to be taken up subsequently.[98]

As I have said, if we start with the presupposition that the *Republic* was written in an atmosphere of unquestioned eudaimonist monism, we can easily find passages that make the work appear to be an elaborate development of it. If Socrates, Thrasymachus, Glaucon, and Adeimantus really all took it for granted that a rational person aims ultimately at his own well-being, and if that idea truly governed the stage-setting that takes place in *Republic* I–II, then it would seem, after all, highly unlikely that the rest of the work might depart from it. However, the lines of thought that lead up to Plato's own examination of the nature of justice and its relation to the good produce a result that is more complex than straightforward eudaimonism.

In the first half of Book II, Plato makes it plain that he must clarify the subject of his discussion before he can improve upon the argument of Book I for the advisability

[96] See Chapter 4, sec. VI.   [97] In sec. VII.   [98] In sec. VII.

of being a just. The rest of the work then undertakes to 'praise justice', and at the same time to explain what that praise consists in and what the grounds are on which it is based.

Part of this explanation, as Plato makes explicit in Book II, involves a specification of the different ways in which justice might be held to be good. Book I had left this matter unspecified. Only in Book II, at 367a–368b, does Plato formulate the issue explicitly. He distinguishes three kinds of goodness that might be attributed to justice. Justice might be said to be good either for its own sake, or for its rewards, or for both together. Plato states that justice belongs in the third, and best, category. By drawing this tripartite distinction only at this late juncture, rather than in Book I, he intends to suggest that it had not been drawn clearly by Socrates.[99] That suggestion appears to be correct, so far as we can tell, and it fits with Plato's tendency, already noted, to picture Socrates' position as not fully worked out.[100]

2. The Eudaimonist Component

Plato's way of framing his project in *Republic* II, I have argued, already marks a difference between two attitudes towards justice, one eudaimonist and one not.[101] The first is manifested by people who think that just action is worth engaging in only when

[99] It seems to me that this is compatible with the evidence of *Lysis* 219e–220b and *Gorg.* 467c–468d. According to Irwin 1979: 141–6, what Plato had said there committed him to rejecting, at that time, all possibility of wanting (*boulesthai*) something both as a means and as an end—which is very close to what this passage of the *Republic* maintains that we do to things in the third category of goods. Whether or not Irwin is right about this, both passages show that Plato, and perhaps Socrates, had earlier entertained some thoughts pertinent to the distinction described at *Rep.* 367a–368b. They do not show, however, that he had earlier thought through the matter as fully as he did in the *Republic*. (I do not believe, however, that Irwin is right about this. Both passages seem to me to operate under a particular presupposition. It is that when Plato talks about wanting *A* for the sake of *B*, the scope of his discussion is confined to cases in which *A* is wanted for no other reason. I do not think that Plato intends to deny that in other sorts of cases than the ones that concern him here, *A* might be wanted both for itself and for something else. As Irwin notes (p. 141), Plato's argument here does not establish that denial. Nor does the denial play any essential role in the conclusions that Plato ultimately wishes to reach there.)

[100] It is widely believed that Book I (perhaps along with a part of Book II) is either an earlier work of Plato that he has incorporated into the *Republic*, or else was composed as an introduction to the whole work, with the intention that it portray the kind of discussion that his earlier works had engaged in, but which he now regards as preliminary and superseded by the sort of investigation that the rest of the *Republic* pursues. I see no reason to think that *Rep.* I was written much earlier than the rest of the work. It is clear, however, that even if it was, Plato's intention in the act of *incorporating* it into the rest of the work can only have been to show how its earlier sort of effort now has to be regarded as incomplete. For that reason, the emphatic drawing of the distinctions among kinds of goods at 357–8 must be taken as a deliberate and explicit supplementation of the apparatus deployed in earlier discussions, with the pointed suggestion that those discussions could not be adequate until those distinctions have been heeded.

[101] See sec. III.

one is not strong or clever enough to avoid the harm that results from being detected and punished. This is plainly Thrasymachus's stance. Glaucon and Adeimantus, on the other hand, distance themselves from Thrasymachus even as they present his case. They wish to hear Socrates praise justice rather than merely the appearance of justice. They make this request, however, on behalf of the very people whom Thrasymachus especially disdains, namely, the 'naive' and 'high-minded' people who take justice seriously.

From the end of Book I on, the *Republic* mounts an extended and complex argument that is designed to explain what justice is and why it is worth having. By the time he completes it, he has carried his discussion far beyond that point at which Books I–II had left it. Synoptically viewed, his treatment contains two main elements. First, he shows a way in which justice can be argued, against Thrasymachus and others who share his outlook, to be conducive in some way to the well-being of the person who possesses it. In addition, however, he also presents a view of the value of justice that does not appeal to its benefit to its possessor.

The former element is quite straightforwardly eudaimonist. For that reason, most interpreters focus on it exclusively. The latter element, however, is also crucial to Plato's project. It responds to the attitude of the naive and high-minded admirers of justice already discussed.[102] It also articulates, in terms of Plato's metaphysics and epistemology, their intuition that justice is to be pursued even if it can involve some sacrifice of their well-being. In addition, however, this same idea has the function of explaining the true motivation, as Plato understands it, out of which a good ruler will try to pursue the good of the *polis*. For although Plato is convinced that a just person lives a far happier life than an unjust person does, as we shall see, he makes it explicit that when a ruler endeavours to ensure that his *polis* is happy and good, he must do so not simply for his own well-being but for the sake of a broader aim.

3. The Content of the Eudaimonist Component

Plato's thesis in the *Republic*, as is widely recognized, has to do not with actions but with the 'soul', or, in other words, with personality or states of character. When he tells us that 'justice pays', he is not saying that each just action brings a corresponding increment of happiness. Rather, he is saying something in the first instance about justice 'in the soul'.

And justice . . . does not lie in a man's external actions, but in the way in which he acts within himself, really concerned with himself and his inner parts. He does not allow each part of himself to perform the work of another, or the sections of his soul to meddle with one another . . . Being thus moderate and harmonious, he now performs any action . . . [H]e

---

[102] In sec. III.

thinks the just and beautiful action . . . to be that which preserves this inner harmony and indeed helps to achieve it.[103]

But Plato's thesis about justice in the soul is likewise not a statement of exact proportionality. He does not say, in this sphere either, that each increment of justice in the soul brings a corresponding increment of happiness. Instead his thesis is cast in terms of the extremes of justice and injustice. Thus he argues that a person who is *fully* just is happier than a person who is *fully* unjust:

As for the choice between the two lives that we are discussing, we shall be able to make a correct judgment about it only if we put the *most* just man and the *most* unjust man face to face; otherwise we cannot do so. By face to face I mean this: let us grant to the unjust the *fullest* degree of injustice and to the just the *fullest* justice, each being perfect in his own pursuit . . . [Thus] our two men may reach the *extremes*, one of justice, the other of injustice, and let them be judged as to which of the two is happier.[104]

This thesis is a direct response to Thrasymachus's contention in Book I that in order to reap the benefits of injustice, a person must possess 'the most complete form of injustice', and must stick at nothing in order to avoid punishment and support his self-seeking in a grand style.[105] What Plato undertakes is thus a comparison between the extreme and, in his view, paradigmatic forms of justice and injustice.[106] His stated thesis is simply that the most just is the happiest and vice versa.

Plato accordingly focuses on two extreme characters, the philosopher and the tyrant. It is these extreme degrees of well-being that are compared in Book IX. 'The

[103] *Rep.* 443c–e; cf. Sidgwick 1907: 171 and Sachs 1963. Thus Plato here defines just action as action that establishes and maintains a just condition of soul. Thus the use of 'just' in application to the soul or personality is definitionally primary. Contrary to the impression that some interpreters give, Plato does *not* define a just action as an action that *results from* or *expresses* a just soul, but as an action that *brings about* or *maintains* a soul's justice. I suspect that this mistake is due largely to the influence of Kant, who leads many modern philosophers to tend to think of a right action as an action that is done 'from' a sense of duty.

[104] *Rep.* 360e, 361d. Compare 472c–d. Here Socrates says that he has been describing justice and the perfectly just man not in order to show that such a man is possible, but to give a paradigm (*paradeigma*) to show, about 'us', that the man who is 'most like' (*homoiotatos*) the paradigm has a lot (*moira*) that is 'most like' (*homoiotatên*) its lot. Here, too, Plato speaks of the extreme cases. He does not say that '*the more* someone is like the perfectly just man, *the more* his lot is like its lot'. Naturally he wants his claims about the extremes of justice and injustice to be applicable to actual people; but that does not require a strict proportionality of well-being to each increment of justice, and he does not assert one.

[105] See *Rep.* 344a, with 343c–e, 344c, 345a, 351b, 352b–c, 361c, 366b, 360e–361d, 367b–d, and White 1979b: 67, 77–8.

[106] Plato's interest in the extreme cases is related to a methodological view that he holds, concerning how to see what a property or condition brings about. He believes that we see what justice brings about in the soul by examining the paradigm cases of its complete presence and its complete absence. This view arises from his conception of the Forms, as paradigm cases of concepts or properties, and of the way in which they are 'causes'. See Vlastos 1965 and 1969, and White 1984.

most happy' is 'the most just', and 'the most miserable' is 'the most unjust'. Fancifully arithmeticized, his conclusion is that the former is 729 times as happy as the latter.[107]

4. The Balance of Motivations

Plato's conception of justice, as a conception of the just personality rather than primarily of just action,[108] is based on the idea that for some purposes, a person's soul can be thought of as a complex of motivations. He famously divides the soul into three parts: the reason (*to logistikon*), the so-called spirit (*thymos*), and the appetites (*epithymiai*). In a just personality, reason rules and thus orders the motivations of all of the parts, including itself. That is, reason determines (in a manner that Plato does not succeed in fully clarifying) the degrees and manners in which the desires, needs, and impulses of the three parts of the soul (and their subparts) will express themselves in action. Reason also directs the overall training and long-term regulation of the personality, and thus, when it is fully effective, determines the strength of a person's various desires throughout life.

Plato believes that each motivational element of the personality has a unique function that is assigned to it by nature.[109] That is, each desire has a purpose in the maintenance of the person's life and activity. Justice in a person, he says, is a condition in which each such element performs its natural function, and does not encroach on the function of any other element. For instance, the function of the appetite for food is to provide nourishment; it is not to dominate or organize all of the activities of a person, as it would in a glutton. When reason rules a person, all of his motivations operate at a level, and with a scope, that allows them to perform its natural task, or 'do what is its own'. This condition, Plato holds, is what the term 'justice' primarily signifies. Injustice, by contrast, is a condition of disorganization in which the various motivations within the soul do not operate in balance with each other.[110]

Among the motivations included in the soul are those associated with reason itself. As is widely recognized, reason is not in Plato a mere calculator of means to the

---

[107] *Rep.* 580b–c, 587d–e.

[108] As is well known, this fact engenders a serious problem for Plato's position. For it is not plain how he can be confident—if indeed he needs to be—that there is an adequate connection between a person's having a just soul and his engaging in actions that are by ordinary standards just. On this problem, see Grote 1888: iv. 99–106, Adkins 1960: 286–9, and Sachs 1963. Both Grote and Sachs maintain that this shift in the senses of the words is damaging to Plato's argument. I believe, however, that in Plato's view the new senses can be justified, as constituting the idea that we are, as it were, trying to get at in our ordinary uses of the words (see White 1979b: 120–2, 131–3, 236–8).

[109] This is, of course, the analogue of the idea, as it appears in both Plato and Hegel, that each person fulfils a natural function within the community. (Plato himself does not use the word *telos* in this connection in the *Republic*. His word is usually *ergon*, and sometimes he also employs, in connection with inanimate things, *chreia* or 'use'.)

[110] See *Rep.* 443b–444e.

satisfaction of desires, as it is on the view of Hume and others, but is itself pictured as having desires of its own. One of these desires is the desire to engage in philosophical thinking; another is the desire to regulate desires, both of itself and of the other parts of the soul. This latter desire can often, and perhaps even always, be interpreted as a special case of the desire to introduce order or structure into the world, where and when that is possible. Plato sometimes thinks of its aim, in the case of oneself and one's personality, as a kind of balance or harmony or concord of the parts of the soul.[111]

These two sorts of desires might seem to be associated with two distinct functions of the reason: philosophizing and regulating or governing. As we shall see, that turns out to be the case in an important respect. That fact does not, however, lead Plato to divide the reason into two distinct 'parts' of the soul. Rather, the reason itself has two functions.[112]

Plato tends strongly towards the view that the most salient case of imbalance among human motivations occurs when sexual desire is excessive in both strength and scope.[113] When this happens, motivations associated with sex determine too much of what a person does, and leave insufficient scope for the manifestation of other desires. The result, Plato believes, is that the overall health of the person is damaged, both physically and psychologically, because the other desires are denied their natural tendency to contribute to the maintenance of healthy human life.[114] Similar results would be associated with an analogous hypertrophy of other desires, such as those for food or drink.

5. The Kantian Hedonist Interpretation

What kind of interpretation best reflects Plato's thinking in the eudaimonist part of his argument? Let us consider our traditional candidates, the kantian reading, and the two hegelian readings, fusionist and inclusivist.[115] There are texts that support each of them. Plato's thinking seems to contain elements of them all.

The kantian reading pictures Plato's position as a form of self-regarding conse-quentialist hedonism. The benefit of justice, that is, would be the pleasure that justice causes in one's soul. Sometimes, indeed, Plato does describe the condition of a harmo-nious soul as one of 'pleasure' (*hedone*), and thus maintains that the life of the philoso-pher is the 'most pleasant' life. At other points, however, he uses the less specific word 'happiness' (*eudaimonia*). Surprisingly, he at times switches from one word to the other without warning or explanation.[116] This formulation tends to encourage the

---

[111] See *Rep.* 443f.

[112] See Cooper 1999b: 122 (reprinted from Cooper 1984); White 1986.

[113] See the portrait of the tyrant in 572b–576b.

[114] In this connection Plato relies on a distinction between necessary and unnecessary pleasures and desires: *Rep.* 561a, 572c, 581d–e.

[115] See Chapter 1, secs. V and VII.   [116] This happens notably in Book IX, at 580b–d.

kantian interpretation. When Plato speaks in this way, he appears to suggest that in a disorderly soul, the desires of some parts of it will be inhibited or curtailed, and that those parts will therefore lose the pleasure that they would otherwise gain. The consequence of the harmony of soul in which justice consists, he would be maintaining, is a greater amount of pleasure than is possible when the soul is unjust.

A position of this kind would be indeed a narrowly egoist basis on which to argue for the advisability of being just. The 'benefit of the very possession of justice' would simply be a gain in pleasure to the individual.[117] On this way of looking at Plato, he would readily come under the criticism that kantian-minded readers have levelled against him. His eudaimonism would be narrowly confined to states of the individual himself. External considerations, including here conformity to ethical standards or concern for the well-being of others, could play only an instrumental role, as a way of achieving one's own hedonistically construed happiness. This state of affairs would justify the claim that is characteristic of the kantian response to Greek ethics, namely, that it grants no independent force to genuinely non-self-regarding deliberative considerations.

6. The Hegelian Fusionist and Inclusivist Interpretations

There are, however, alternative ways of reading Plato's argument, which bring it far closer to the hegelian interpretation of Greek ethics in general. This account admits of two main types of development. The support that both of them receive from the text makes it difficult to believe that the kantian reading reflects the whole of Plato's view of the matter.

As already remarked, Plato's understanding of the notion of happiness is not by any means consistently hedonist. In fact, much of his treatment of human well-being suggests that it is itself a balance among the parts of the soul, rather than the pleasure that results from it.[118] In both Book IV and Book IX, Plato often writes so as to suggest that the link between justice and happiness is somehow more than a merely causal one in our sense.[119] His thought seems to be that happiness is not a mere causal result of justice, and that it is scarcely even thinkable, once we realize what the two things are, that the one should be present without the other. Rather, he appears to regard the link between them as closer than a logically contingent causal connection.

Some readers have followed this line of interpretation far enough to offer a fusionist reading, that is, to claim that on Plato's view, justice and happiness are identical.

---

[117] *Rep.* 368d.

[118] This construal is strongly suggested both by Book IV, 441b–445e, and by much of the argument in Book IX up until 580c (see White 1979b: 223–4).

[119] Nevertheless, in a more Platonic sense of the word 'causal'—associated with his use of the terms *aitia* and *aition*—the relation could be said to be causal; on these notions of *aitia* in Plato see White 1984.

The basis of this claim is that, as his explanation of the matter emerges, both justice and happiness turn out to be the very same balance among the soul's parts.[120] On this reading, his thesis that justice is a benefit to its possessor turns out, once we correctly judge what justice and well-being really are, to amount simply to an identification of what ordinary language labels 'justice' with what ordinary language labels 'happiness'.

The inclusivist interpretation, on the other hand, ascribes to Plato a less radical strategy: to argue that even though justice and happiness are not completely indistinguishable, they are nevertheless so intimately connected as to exclude the possibility that anyone who knows what each of them is might aim at the one without aiming at the other. Within the context of Plato's view of the personality, we can think of the matter as follows. Happiness is a harmony of the parts of the soul. It is a state of the soul in which each of its components is in every respect in the condition that is appropriate to it. Justice, then, is the state of affairs in which each part of the soul performs the task or function to which it is naturally suited. This state can be thought of as an aspect of overall psychic harmony, but not as exhausting it. The overall balance would also include, in addition, the capacity of each part to receive the kind and degree of satisfaction that is appropriate to it. When we say, then, that a particular soul is happy, we say more than simply that each constituent performs its function. We also indicate that each part is, therefore, in a condition to receive the satisfaction that comes from fulfilling its function. Nevertheless, although justice is only thus an aspect of happiness and not the whole of it, the inclusivist view holds that a soul will be happy if, and only if, it is just.[121]

7. The Inadequacies of these Interpretations: The Two Harmonies of the Soul

I shall now argue that none of these interpretations adequately captures Plato's views about the way in which 'justice pays', though all of them point to aspects of the complex idea that Plato favours.

It is easy, first of all, to find objections to the kantian interpretation. Chief among them is the fact that in the *Republic* Plato explicitly denies that pleasure is the good.[122] There seems to be no chance that Plato would say that the reason to be just is simply that one gains pleasure thereby.[123]

A straightforwardly fusionist interpretation seems equally to be ruled out. For one thing, Plato never says that justice and happiness are identical. Moreover, that is a sufficiently counterintuitive claim, from the Greek point of view, that one can hardly

---

[120] Mabbott 1971 with Wood 1991: 57.

[121] The logic and metaphysics of 'aspects' and 'constituents' is of course not at all clear, but the basic idea of inclusivism seems, for all that, clear enough for present purposes.

[122] *Rep.* 505c.   [123] See Kraut 1993a: 312–14.

suppose that he would have advocated it without expressly enunciating it and trying to confront, with arguments, the consequences of its counterintuitiveness. In addition, we shall see below a further reason for rejecting a fusionist account of Plato's position.[124]

An inclusivist interpretation seems more attractive than either of these two readings. Much of Plato's account of justice in the last few pages of *Republic* IV strongly suggests that justice and well-being are not identical, but that they are tied to each other in some non-contingent way. We might thus express that point by saying that they are both aspects, in some sense, of what Plato regards as fundamentally the same order or harmony of the personality. Equally in Book IX, although he points to the same kind of intimate, non-contingent connection between them, he never says that they are really just the same thing, nor that we gain anything by identifying them with each other.[125]

On the other hand, this connection seems unlikely to be the straightforwardly part–whole relation that the inclusivist reading needs. For one thing, Plato never uses the language of part and whole or inclusion to describe it. For another thing, as noted, he shows no objection to formulating his claim, that the most just person is the happiest person, by means of the statement that that person has the most pleasant life, as though pleasure is what the goodness of a human life is measured by.[126]

We must also do justice to the fact that if we examine Book IX carefully, we find that Plato refers not to one harmony but to two, which are easy to distinguish conceptually once we attend to them.

The difference between them is the difference between, briefly put, a harmony of performance of *functions*—which is justice—and a harmony of the *satisfactions* that arises therefrom—which is happiness or well-being. This distinction emerges from a comparison of Book IV, and its explanation of psychic justice, with the arguments in Book IX for Plato's conclusion that the fully just person is far happier than the perfectly unjust person. In Book IV, Plato shows us how a just soul is organized so that each part performs its own function without interference with the other parts. But Plato does not conclude, yet, that the soul endowed with this harmony is the happiest, though he certainly does say that he *will* reach this conclusion in the end. It is only in Book IX that he announces that the conclusion has been reached.[127] What he has added by then to what he had said in Book IV is a detailed account of how, by contrast

[124] See below, sec. VI. 6–7.

[125] In fact it seems to me that the inclusivist interpretation, as opposed to the fusionist one, is supported by all those passages that support a hegelian-style account, that is, by 441b–445e and the argument in Book IX to 580c.

[126] Once again, the abrupt casualness of the shift at 580b–d cannot be overestimated (cf. also 588a, 591d).

[127] Some readers think that the conclusion is reached already in Book IV; against this see White 1984 and 1979b: 137.

with various other souls, the just soul gains, from the performance by each part of its function, a balance of satisfactions.

The disharmony of function suffered by the tyrant is described by Plato as being a condition in which 'the best parts are enslaved' and 'the most wicked' part 'is master'. But this condition is not the end of the story. Just as 'the enslaved and dictator-ruled city *is least likely to do what it wants*', so likewise 'the dictator-ruled soul will also be the least likely to do what it may want', and such a person will be 'by far the most miserable of men'.[128] Such a person thus lacks not only a harmony of function but also, correspondingly, a harmony of satisfactions. Plato's meaning seems clear. The relevant satisfactions are the conditions of the various parts of the soul as they do what they are naturally motivated to do, namely, to perform their functions. A satisfaction must be, roughly, the awareness that one of one's natural aims has been realized. Attention to this pair of harmonies in Book IX provides an obvious explanation of Plato's refusal to identify justice and happiness, and thus of the fusionist interpretation. The relation between justice and happiness is in Plato's view indeed close, but it is not identity.

Plato's idea in Book IX is not to be confused with, nor does it entail, the hedonism that he had rejected earlier in the *Republic*. For there is a clear difference between the two theses. The thesis that Plato espouses in Book IX is a claim that happiness is a *balance* of certain satisfactions. The notion of a balance or structure here is essential, and makes this a different idea from the idea that pleasure is flatly the good or flatly happiness. If pleasure were flatly the good, or the good for a human being, that would in Plato's view mean, quite simply, that more pleasure makes for a better life. But that is clearly not the point of Book IX, which insists that satisfactions be ranged in a certain structure.[129] Throughout Book IX Plato attempts to do justice to the role of pleasure in happiness, while at the same refusing to identify them.[130]

VII. The Republic: The Rulers' Choice

1. Non-Self-Regarding Goodness as Part of the Interpretation of the Republic

In spite of the importance of the eudaimonist aspect of the *Republic*, the thinking that the work contains extends beyond eudaimonism.[131] Eager as Plato is to praise justice

---

[128] *Rep.* 577d–578a.

[129] Plato's formulations in *Rep.* 580–7 involve, I think, a mixture of quantitative and qualitative considerations; certainly he expresses himself in quantitative terms at 587d–e.

[130] Plainly this is the line of thought that leads to the *Philebus*, however exactly we interpret that dialogue.

[131] The interpretation for which I am arguing seems to fit with some contemporary German interpretations of Plato that treat Aristotle's criticism of his ethics as in some ways analogous to Hegel's criticism of

on the ground that it is conducive to happiness, in that the most just person is the happiest, he does not believe that the only ground for being just is its conduciveness to happiness, nor that conduciveness to one's own happiness is the only ultimate rational aim. I have shown evidence of this fact in the challenge to Socrates raised by Glaucon and Adeimantus, and also in a passage of Book X.[132] Now I want to show the role that it plays in Plato's own argument later in the *Republic*, specifically in Book VII.

I have argued that when we approach the interpretation of the *Republic*, we should from the very start bear in mind an important fact. As the *Timaeus* and the *Laws* show, Plato does indeed possess a notion of what is good *simpliciter*, and he allows this notion to figure in human deliberation.[133] When we read the *Republic* with this fact in mind, we must refrain from presuming on conceptual grounds alone that Plato operates only with a notion of self-referential good, and must for that reason necessarily adopt a eudaimonist stance towards human rational deliberation.

For one thing, there seems to me to exist no signficant room to doubt that the notion that is represented in *Republic* VI and VII as 'the Good itself' or the Form of the Good is the notion of non-self-referential goodness that, as I have said, figures in

Kant, and see a resemblance between Plato and Kant, in that both appear to accept absolute principles that are not tailored to empirical circumstances. See e.g. Schnädelbach 1986: 42, Apel 1986: 217–22. It is on the whole customary in the English-speaking world to class Plato and Aristotle together as eudaimonists.

There are exceptions to the normal Anglo-American pattern of interpretation of this point. One is Julia Annas: she earlier attributed to Plato a notion of 'impersonal' good that seems to me to belong to a non-eudaimonist account of his outlook, though I would say that she attached insufficient importance to his use of this notion; see her 1981: 258–71, 331–4, along with other references at pp. 195–6 of White 1979b, esp. to Cooper 1977b, who appears to me similarly torn between a recognition of the non-eudaimonist elements of Plato's thinking and the sense that, nevertheless, it must be eudaimonist through and through. An earlier case of what appears to be a non-eudaimonist account can be found in Demos 1963; and sort of a non-self-regarding motivation is ascribed to the rulers by Price 1995: 58–9, 108 (though cf. 185).

Something similar can be said about Kraut's account in his 1993a. He, too, recognizes the anti-eudaimonist implications of the rulers' situation (327, 'this example seems to show that justice does not always pay'), though he does not give what I think is due weight to the passages that show that Plato recognizes these implications emphatically. Kraut then suggests that the rulers' motivation to govern is that otherwise they would 'create a certain disharmony in the world', i.e. in the *polis*. That is indeed the point. But one must then ask why the rulers are motivated to avoid doing that, even at the cost of a life of governing that is less good for themselves than a life of philosophizing would be. Kraut's answer is that one must imitate the Forms. This is true, in that the rulers are to try to make their *polis* instantiate the Good. But again, this comes at a cost to them, as noted. Not so, Kraut maintains, because in governing the *polis* one is serving 'one's highest good'. The phrase 'highest good' does not occur in this passage. One serves *the good of the polis* in this way, indeed, and one also causes *the* Good to be instantiated in it. But Plato does not say that doing this serves 'one's' good. The passage makes clear, I believe, that we are not to think of it is in this way. The use of the phrase 'one's highest good' in this way seems to me, once again, to obscure the explicitly anti-eudaimonist implications of the passage. What is 'highest' about the good of the *polis* is that it outweighs an individual ruler's *own* good; it is, precisely, not *his* or *her* good.

[132] See above, sec. V. 4.
[133] Sec. V. 4.

the *Timaeus* and the *Laws*.[134] Moreover this is the Form which, Plato believes, is grasped by the philosopher-rulers whom he puts in charge of his ideal *polis*, and which they are to use to guide their actions in the city. Plato holds, in addition, that this conception of goodness can be grasped only by people who have reached a mature age and have been carefully educated so to lead them to this understanding. It is precisely the non-relative, non-perspectival character of this conception of goodness that, according to Plato, makes the understanding of it such a long and laborious process.

Justice, according to Plato, is a virtue (*arete*)—that is, a way in which a person is good (*agathos*)—and it is itself a good thing (*agathon*). There is no reason to think that when Plato holds that a virtue, such as justice, is a good, he means thereby merely that it is good *for* anyone (though of course it may be that too). When a philosopher or a ruler is guided in his choices by a recognition of what is just, he is therein guided by a recognition of what is good *simpliciter*, as distinct from what is good for himself. Determination of what is just is in this sense a non-perspectival matter. So, too, are deliberating and choosing on the basis of judgements about what is just.

Further, I shall argue, there can be cases in which what is good for oneself is different from what is good non-relationally or non-perspectivally, that is, good *simpliciter*. The most salient such case involves what is good for the *polis*. What is good for one's *polis* is not in the full sense non-perspectivally good—as we shall see—because it is, after all, good for *one's polis*. Nonetheless, it is as close to being non-perspectivally good, Plato thinks, as many things that most people, even philosopher-kings, are normally in a position to deliberate about. Plato believes that yet more global judgements about what is good are possible, and can conceivably be acted upon by such beings as the Demiurge in the *Timaeus*. Human beings can to a degree act upon them too—an example would be the man who, in *Republic* X, has lost his son—but only in a limited way. An exception, however, is presented by the rulers in the ideal *polis*, whose situation is described in Book VII.

2. *The Motivations of the Philosopher-Rulers in* Republic *I and IV*

Early in the *Republic*, Plato begins to set the stage for a conflict between justice and individual well-being. In Book I, he presses a general diagnosis of the deficiency of existing political constitutions. Rulers in the true sense, he says, are concerned for the advantage of those whom they rule, not for their own benefit. For that reason, cities must reward rulers either with money or with honour, or else must compel them to rule. Good men are not willing to be rulers for money or honour. Therefore they must be compelled by punishment. But the greatest punishment for someone of good

---

[134] See Hare 1965 and Santas 1980 and 1985 for interpretations that are close to each other, and, I think, are naturally linked to and supportive of the present account, in that they both seem to me to ascribe to Plato a non-self-referential notion of goodness.

character 'is to be ruled by a worse man than oneself'. This is the only reason why such people consent to participate in governing their city-states:

They approach office not as something good or something to be enjoyed, but as something necessary because they cannot trust it to men better than, or even equal to, themselves.

However, Plato continues,

In a city of good men, if there were such, they would probably vie with each other in order not to rule, not, as now, in order to be rulers. There it would be quite clear that the *nature of the true ruler* is *not to seek his own advantage but that of his subjects*, and everyone, knowing this, would prefer to receive benefits rather than take the trouble to benefit others.[135]

As Plato proceeds in Books II–VII through his long description of his ideal *polis*,[136] he is occupied mainly with the character and education of the 'guardians' who are to rule it. Ruling over the *polis* is in his view analogous to the rule of the individual personality by reason. Reason regulates the various motivations, including its own, in order to provide for the good of the whole. It is not pictured as aiming in any sense simply for its own good, in contrast to the sexual desire that characterizes the tyrannical personality, which dominates, Plato says, in such a way as to provide for its own satisfaction at the expense of the satisfactions of all other parts of the soul.

Likewise, the rulers in the ideal *polis* regulate the desires and activities of both themselves and of all the other groups of people who inhabit it, so as to benefit the city as a whole. Most of this central part of the *Republic* is devoted to describing the character and education that is necessary for those who are to perform this task. This description issues in Plato's famous thesis that such rulers must be philosophers, because only philosophers are capable of grasping what the good is, so as to order the city in accordance with it.[137]

Throughout Plato's description, his picture of the advantages and disadvantages of ruling in a *polis* remains constant. In Book IV, he says, 'in establishing our city, we are not aiming to make any one group outstandingly happy, but to make the whole city so, as far as possible'. The aim, Plato says, is the good of the city; it is not to make any group as happy as we can. He does not say that these two aims coincide. Insofar as the rulers share his outlook, through sharing his understanding of what the city and its purpose are, their aim must be the same.

But how is the good of the city related to the rulers' own good? Will achieving the greatest happiness of the city require any sacrifice of the happiness of any group, in particular that of the rulers? What Plato says opens up that possibility:

[135] *Rep.* 347a–e; cf. 420b–c, 421b–c, 520e–521a, 345e–346a.
[136] Its status as an ideal is made clear at the end of Book VII, at 592a–b.
[137] See esp. *Rep.* 519–21, 540a–b, 590c–592a.

We should examine then, with this in mind, whether our aim in establishing our guardians should be to give them the greatest happiness, or whether we should in this matter look to the whole city and see how its greatest happiness can be secured. We must compel and persuade the auxiliaries and the guardians to be excellent performers of their own task, and so with all the others. As the whole city grows and is well governed, we must leave it to nature to provide each group with its share of happiness.[138]

It is now up to 'nature' to determine whether the greatest happiness of the city requires less than the greatest happiness for anyone else. We can think of subsequent passages as explaining what nature will do.

First, however, Plato focuses on how to educate the rulers about the good of the city. They must be able, he says, to care for the city. But one cares for something most, he says, 'when one believes that what is good for it is good for oneself'. He goes on:

We must therefore select from among our guardians those who, as we test them, are throughout their lives willing in all eagerness to do what they think to be to the advantage of the city, and are in no way willing to do what they think is not to its advantage.[139]

So the rulers will be trained to be willing to pursue the good of the city. At this point there seems little room to doubt what Plato thinks the basis of the rulers' willingness must be. One expects him to say that the good of the city coincides with the good of the rulers, and that that is what their education should teach them.

However, what Plato actually says is very significantly different. We must educate the rulers so that 'they cannot be tempted or forced to discard or forget the belief that they must do what is best for the city'. This belief, says Plato, is the truth. And a moment later he formulates the point in almost exactly the same terms: 'the belief that they *must* always do whatever they think to be in the best interest of the city'.[140] Instead of the belief that what is best for the city is 'best for them', the rulers are to hold onto the belief that what is best for the city is what they *must* do.[141] I shall explain a bit later what I take the significance of this imperative formulation to be, in light of what Plato says in Book VII.[142]

---

[138] *Rep.* 420b–c, 421b–c.

[139] Here I depart from Grube's translation, even though my interpretation would be very slightly strengthened if it (or Reeve's revision of it) were correct. According to Grube, the rulers will 'hold ... to *the belief that it is right* to pursue' the advantage of the city. (According to Reeve, the rulers 'believe that they *must*' pursue the city's advantage.) The Greek contains nothing corresponding either to 'right' or to 'must'). Some translators have missed the fact that *poiein* must depend on *ethelein*. Shorey's translation has the point right.

[140] The whole passage is *Rep.* 412c–413c.

[141] Both of the quoted formulations—*dein* (412e8) and *poieteon* (413c6)—are straightforwardly imperative, and both are properly translated by 'must'.

[142] Below, sec. VIII. 4.

3. The Conflict of Motivations of the Philosopher-Rulers in Republic VII

The crucial point in Plato's exposition—where the deliberative conflict comes explicitly to light—occurs in Book VII, when the rulers' dedication to the good of the city is tested. This is the point at which they finish their philosophical education. Through it they have at length come to understand what the good is. Now, Plato says, we must not allow such people to do 'what they are allowed to do today', namely, to continue to study philosophy rather than ruling the city. He then reminds us of the purpose of establishing the ideal *polis*:

[I]t is not the law's concern to make some one group in the city outstandingly happy but to contrive to spread happiness throughout the city, by bringing the citizens into harmony with each other by persuasion or compulsion, and to make them share with each other the benefits which each group can confer upon the community. The law has *not made men* of this kind in the city in order *to allow each to turn in any direction they might wish* but to make use of them to bind the city together.[143]

Accordingly, the philosophers whom the city has trained will be required to rule it, and not be allowed simply to philosophize. They will be persuaded that this requirement is just, he says, because they owe their education to the city, and because they are best suited to rule.

Plato recalls the diagnosis of the deficiencies of existing cities that he gave in Book I:

For this is the truth: a city in which *the prospective rulers are least keen (prothymoi) to rule* must of necessity be governed best and be most free from civil strife, whereas a city with the opposite kind of rulers is governed in the opposite way.[144]

And he continues the reiteration of his diagnosis:

Do you think that those we have nurtured will disobey us and be unwilling to share the labours of the city in turn, and that they will wish [instead] to spend a greater part of their time dwelling with each other in a pure atmosphere? —They cannot, he said, for we shall be giving *just orders to just men*, but each of them will certainly go to rule *as to something that must be done*, the opposite attitude from that of the present rulers in every city.[145]

So the philosophers will be required to rule, even though they would prefer to do something else.

It does not seem possible to mistake Plato's explanation of the motivation that the

---

[143] *Rep.* 519d–520a.   [144] *Rep.* 520d.

[145] *Rep.* 520d–521a. Here the imperative 'must' in Grube's translation renders the word *anagkaion*, 'necessary'. At 519c3 we have *dei*, and at e1 we find *nomoi*, 'by law'. (I have departed from Grube's translation of 520d7–8. *Oikein* at d8 depends on an *ethelesousin* understood from *ouk ethelesousin* at d7. Grube and Shorey both insert, with different implications, a notion of permission that is not present in the Greek. Reeve is much closer to the right idea.)

philosophers would have for choosing the activity of philosophizing over that of ruling. It is that such a life is better and happier. What Plato says precludes our saying
that their decision is based on a consideration of their own happiness or what is good
for them. 'Are we', he asks, 'to do them an injustice by *making them live a worse life
when they could live a better one?*' It is not an injustice to require them to rule the city,
he replies, but he continues to insist that the other life would be better for them.
'Better' here must mean 'better *for them*', as this passage shows:

> If you can find a way of life which is *better* than governing *for the prospective governors*, then a
> well-governed city can exist for you. Only in that city will the truly rich rule, not rich in gold
> but in the wealth *which a happy man must have*, a life with goodness and intelligence.

And he concludes:

> What other men will you compel to become guardians of the city rather than those who have
> the best knowledge of the principles that make for the best government of a city and who also
> know honours of a different kind, *and a better life than the political*. —No one else.[146]

4. Goodness, Justice, and Individual Well-Being in the Philosopher-Rulers' Deliberations

Here, I maintain, we have a straightforward conflict between the good of an individual ruler and what justice requires. Plato provides the conceptual resources for
describing this conflict—resources which we have already seen in the *Timaeus* and
elsewhere.[147]

If these philosophers consent to rule even though they could have a better life for
themselves, then there must an explanation of their reason for doing so.[148] That

---

[146] *Rep.* 519d, 521a–b.

[147] Note that the issue here is not adequately described by saying, as some do, that in Plato's view, the
good to be sought is a non-competitive good, as opposed to the competitive goods aimed at by the Sophists.
Kantian-minded readers like A. W. H. Adkins (1960: 277–8) have also taken Plato in this way, and have
criticized him on the ground, which is quite correct, that competition can arise over the exercise of even
intrinsically non-competitive goods too. In a similar way, Alasdair MacIntyre (1981: 74, 84) thinks that
Plato focuses on a contrast between 'goods of excellence' and 'goods of effectiveness', and tried to obviate
conflict by having his rulers, unlike the Sophists, strive for the former rather than the latter. But as Adkins
points out, the pursuit of *technai* in the sense of *Republic* I, for instance, can be subject to competitive situations, since two doctors, say, can normally not amputate the same limb, even if surgical skill is an excellence
and not intrinsically competitive. The present matter, however, involves a quite different sort of problem,
namely, a kind of conflict that is not generated by the pursuit of the (arguably) intrinsically competitive
kinds of things, like money and power, that Thrasymachus is after.

[148] Cooper 1977b recognizes that 'Plato's philosophers will settle for a less flourishing existence than
they might have had', and that 'Plato's just man is no egoist' (see Cooper 1999b: 147). What keeps me from
thinking that Cooper would accept the interpretation offered here is his insistence, nonetheless, that 'any
philosopher who ever opts for the mixed life will actually be more *eudaimon* than who opts for the purely

reason, Plato says, is that it is just for them to rule, and that if they do so, then the city will be well governed.[149] When we put this to them they will accept it, because 'we shall be giving just orders to just men', but they 'will go to rule as to something that must be done'.[150] It make sense for Plato to describe their evaluation of ruling in imperative terms. It is something that they are obliged to do, even though it is neither the best thing *for them* nor what they would prefer to do if their own good were the only consideration that they took into account.

The imperative formulation that Plato employs here harks back to the imperative formulation that he earlier employed, when he said that the future rulers should be taught 'that they *must* always do whatever they think to be in the best interest of the city'. The imperative registers the resistance felt by a ruler, stemming from the consideration of his or her own greatest well-being, to the course of action that is just— the very resistance that the imperative mode so often registers.[151] We could regard this formulation as mere stylistic variation on Plato's part, but there is no reason to do so, when the context and the course of the argument provides a natural rationale for it.

Some interpreters have thought that the imperatives in Book VII literally indicate compulsion, as if an individual ruler were to be somehow dragooned into governing the city. There is no evidence for such a reading and much against it. Ruling the city is a course that Plato explicitly says these philosophers could avoid. Their consent to obey the injunction to rule amounts, he says, to a decision to 'live a worse life *when they could live a better one*'.[152] The compulsion and necessity that Plato speaks of is explicitly said to be one that 'we' impose on them, by pointing out their obligation, not one that is imposed by their fellow rulers. The requirement is one that the rulers acknowledge, and which they follow.[153]

Nor do the rulers choose to rule in order to secure their own greater well-being in the face of some alternative that would make them less happy. Plato simply does not say, contrary to what many interpreters assume, that the rulers must govern because otherwise the city would collapse and the opportunity to philosophize would vanish, nor is there any ground for assuming that this is what he must intend. On the contrary, he asserts that the rulers govern the city instead of 'wish[ing] to spend a greater part of their time dwelling with each other in a pure atmosphere'.[154] This is not a choice

---

intellectual life' (1999b: 147). It seems to me that Plato's text explicitly denies this; and moreover, if the philosophers of Plato's *polis* thought this, Plato's way of describing the advantages for the *polis* of their motivation would fall apart. It is true, as Cooper says, that 'any philosopher would always prefer the mixed life'; however, that 'preference' is based, not on a consideration of his or her happiness, but, I maintain, on a non-self-regarding consideration.

[149] *Rep.* 520a, c–d, e, 521b   [150] *Rep.* 520e.
[151] See Chapter 3, sec. I.
[152] *Rep.* 519d (*dynaton autois on ameinon*), and cf. Gerhardt 1997: 46–7, 49–52.
[153] *Rep.* 519d, 520a, e.   [154] *Rep.* 520d.

between leaving philosophy aside in order to rule the city and, on the other hand, being forced to break off philosophizing anyway because of the collapse of the city.

Indeed, it is not at all true that in Plato's view, the only way to be able to philosophize is to live in the ideal *polis*. Earlier in the *Republic*, he asserts that a person can engage in philosophy if he withdraws from public affairs. Moreover, in the passage that I have just examined, he says that the rulers of the ideal *polis* must be obliged to govern it, and that we 'must not allow them to do what they are allowed to do today', namely, to refuse to govern and engage in philosophy instead.[155] This statement would make no sense at all if he supposed that only by consenting to rule can the rulers preserve their opportunity to philosophize.

It is striking that when Plato treats justice here as an imperative, and depicts it as opposing the consideration of the rulers' greatest happiness, he turns away from opportunities, which certainly are not lacking, to argue that governing the city is in fact the way for the rulers to maximize their own well-being. Since ruling the city is just, he might have reasoned, failing to rule would be unjust. Moreover, because failing to rule would be unjust, he might have inferred that it must therefore cause disorder in a philosopher-ruler's soul. Plato would be obliged, indeed, to draw this inference. In Book IV, it may be recalled, he defined unjust action as action that destroys psychic harmony.[156] Accordingly, he *could* have asserted that philosophizing would not benefit the ruler after all, on the ground that failing to govern would destroy psychic harmony, which he has said is present only in the soul of someone who is happy, whereas ruling would preserve that harmony. One might suppose, then, that by following this argument, he could have combined his contention that the philosopher-rulers must consent to rule the city with a straightforwardly eudaimonist position according to which philosophizing would be deleterious to the ruler's well-being because it would damage his soul.

This line of argument, however, would have been inconsistent with Plato's express purpose in this passage. It would have completely subverted his explicit effort to depict the rulers as consenting to rule *in spite of* having available to themselves *a greater source of happiness*—which is the feature that chiefly distinguishes them from the actual rulers of his day, whom he says wish to rule.[157] If Plato thought that the rulers' life would be made better by governing the city, or even that a life of ruling would be

---

[155] *Rep.* 496a–497a and 519d, with White 1979b: 169–70 and 1986.

[156] *Rep.* 443e–444a; see above, sec. VI. 2. What seems to me to be essentially the same line of argument is suggested by Reeve 1988: 255–6.

[157] It seems impossible to maintain that in Plato's view, the course of philosophizing, though better in some general or abstract way for some beings, would not be better for the rulers in the particular circumstances in which they actually find themselves. For as we have seen, Plato explicitly says that they 'live a worse life when they *could* live a better one (*dynaton autois on ameinon*)' (519d). Moreover, for there to be any force in Plato's point—which is that ruling must be for the good *of the ruled*—the superior alternative must actually be available to the rulers, not merely to other beings in some other situation.

as good as one of philosophizing, he could not have said that in consenting to rule they were consenting 'to live a worse life when they could live a better'.

The ground for Plato's contention, that it is just for the philosopher-rulers to govern the city, is the idea that this is the only way in which the city can be well governed. The rulers' procedure, he says, must be to 'lift up the eyes of their soul to what itself provides light to all and, as they look upon *the Good itself* and *taking it as their model*, they must put in order the city and its citizens as well as themselves for the remainder of their life'.[158] Their actions in governing are determined by what they recognize to be good, in the light of their understanding of what the Good itself is. Plato's ground cannot be the claim that the rulers must repay the city for their education; he has said explicitly that the repayment of debts is not always just.[159] For the value of justice is based on its being good or a kind of goodness: '[T]he form of the Good . . . must be reckoned to be the cause of all that is right and beautiful . . . and he who is to act intelligently in public or in private must see it.'[160]

It can hardly be supposed, it seems to me, that in Plato's view the Good can represent a notion of what is good for oneself. When the rulers comprehend what the Good is and take it as a model for their governing, they must be considering what is good from a broader perspective than their own.[161] The judgement that governing the city is just, therefore, is based on a recognition that what is just is good from this broader perspective. The action that results from this deliberation is an attempt to see to it that the good is exemplified as broadly as possible, not merely within one's own soul.

The purport of the foregoing passages should not be misjudged. For one thing, Plato is not denying that the life of the rulers who govern is extremely happy. He believes that it is happier than any other life except that of philosophizing, and far happier than any life of a person who is completely unjust or close to it—recall that it is this comparison of extremes to which Plato is explicitly committed.[162] Secondly, Plato is not denying that reason will tell the rulers to act unjustly. Precisely what

---

[158] *Rep.* 540a–b.

[159] *Rep.* 331e–332a.

[160] *Rep.* 517c. See also *Rep.* 517b–c, 518c, 519b–d, 534b–e, 540a–b. Although it seems to me clear from these passages of the *Republic* itself that the notion of goodness employed there is a non-relative and non-perspectival one, the point is supported also by considerations arising from Plato's general metaphysical and epistemological doctrine. His general view about the Form of F—where F is a predicate—is that the Form represents the notion of a thing's being F not *to* a particular person or from a particular perspective, but F in some sense apart from perspectives and qualifications. For example, the Form of the Beautiful in the *Symposium* represents the notion of a thing's being beautiful without regard to any particular perspective (211a–b). See Owen 1957 and White 1993: 287–9.

[161] As I have remarked (sec. V. 3–4), Plato acknowledges a still broader perspective, which encompasses the entire *kosmos*. What is fundamentally correct about G. E. Moore's interpretation of Plato (see Chapter 2, sec. II above) is his recognition that for Plato the ultimate notion of value is thus a non-relative and non-self-referential one.

[162] See above, sec. VI. 2–3.

reason tells them is that they must govern the city because that is the just thing to do. Nor is he denying that justice is in some sense a pre-eminent part or aspect of their happiness, even though in this case there is some measure of conflict between the two.[163]

Finally, Plato is not denying that one's own happiness is a good and fully rational ground on which to base one's action and planning, when that is appropriate. His point is not to say that the rulers are in all instances guided by justice and the good, and never by their own good. He does not cast aspersions, as Kant sometimes seems to do, on the legitimacy of one's happiness as a rational consideration. Rather, he maintains that the rulers' own good is in the overwhelming majority of instances the relevant manifestation of the Good, insofar as it is relevant to one's actions. Only in this unusual circumstance do the two diverge, when the benefit to one's life of philosophizing is at odds with the governing of the city.

5. Good, Good for One's City, and Good for Oneself

There remain, however, further questions about how Plato conceives of this deliberative conflict. The conflict arises from what Plato believes to be the impossibility of engaging fully in two activities, philosophizing and governing, in both of which the rulers realize their own unique capacities.[164] The philosopher-rulers, Plato contends, will choose the latter alternative.

But how is this conflict to be articulated? I have pictured it both as a conflict between what is 'good for me' (as a ruler would put it) and what is 'good for my city', and also as a conflict between what is 'good for me' and what is 'good *simpliciter*'. Clearly, however, these conflicts are not the same. Nevertheless, Plato describes the rulers' governing of the city both as what is good for it and as taking place under the guidance of the Good, which is also what guides the thinking of, for instance, the demiurge in the *Timaeus*.[165] We need to say something about the relationship between these two ideas.

A full treatment of this issue would take us into the central parts of Plato's theory of metaphysics and the philosophy of thought and language for which we have no space here. We must content ourselves with saying briefly why, according to Plato, a

[163] As Joseph Butler saw, there can be a conflict between any part of happiness and happiness itself, unless of course one tries to fix it by *stipulation* that no conflict is to be thus labelled—which Plato never does (see Butler 1726: Sermon XI and White 1999a).

[164] One can ask whether Plato attributes this impossibility to the mere lack of time and energy for an individual to do both, or to some more intrinsic opposition between the simultaneous pursuit of both activities (cf. Chapter 2, sec. VII). *Republic* VII seems to me to contain bits of evidence pointing in both directions, but no clear sign that Plato had addressed the question. The same issue will arise in connection with Aristotle; see Chapter 6, sec. VI.

[165] *Rep.* 540–1 and 520–1.

concern for what is 'good for *my* city' is any closer to a concern that involves goodness *simpliciter*, given that the former notion is just as self-referential as the notion of what is 'good for my soul'. We have already seen that for a ruler, what is 'best for me' and 'what is best for my city' can diverge. But why is what is 'best for my city' more a matter of what is 'best *simpliciter*' than what is 'best for me' is?

Very briefly, I take Plato's answer to involve the following idea: a city is a more comprehensive thing than an individual soul. A concern for a city is, so to speak, closer to being an all-embracing concern than is a concern for one's soul. Causing goodness to be exemplified in a city, accordingly, is causing a more inclusive exemplification than causing it to be exemplified in an individual soul. This last point is best put not by saying merely that this concern is simply broader, nor by saying that it simply contains more. Rather, the point is that it comes closer to embracing the *whole*, which is what the demiurge's concern for the goodness of the whole physical *kosmos* does fully. A full treatment of this issue would need to explore Plato's theory further, but this will do for present purposes.[166]

The main issue for Plato is the following. Those who understand what the good is, according to Plato, will regard the aim of achieving what is good as rationally over-riding the aim of one's own well-being. In other words, one might say, doing what is good from one's own standpoint is not as rationally 'important' as trying to bring

---

[166] We might be tempted to think that when Plato speaks of what is 'good for X', he simply means what is 'good and is in X'. In that case, what is 'good for me' simply means what is 'good and is in me' or what is 'good and is in my soul'. In that case, he would not be suggesting that there is any relational notion of goodness at all, but merely the 'absolute', non-relational notion, supplemented by a relational notion expressed by 'in', which merely gives a kind of location. This idea was advocated, for instance, by G. E. Moore, and has been defended recently by Donald H. Regan. Some Platonic passages, to be sure, might suggest such a reading. For instance, in the *Symposium* it looks as though the Form of Beauty, *to kalon*, is 'the same everywhere', except merely for the fact that it is instantiated *in* different kinds of things. It is also natural to take various geometrical Forms in this way.

For various reasons, however, I do not think this interpretation can be correct. The correct interpretation, however, is not easy to arrive at, and here I shall have to be content with merely gesturing in what I think is the most fruitful direction. One reason why this interpretation cannot be correct can be gained from a consideration of some of Plato's examples. When Plato talks of pleasantness in *Republic* IX, for example, and distinguishes (surprisingly, to some) between what is pleasant *simpliciter* and what is pleasant to a particular kind of person, an issue arises that seems to be more than that of location. What is pleasant to you, that is, does not seem simply to be what is pleasant and is in you, at least inasmuch as something might on Plato's terms be pleasant simpliciter and in you but not pleasant to you, because you are not in the right condition to recognize or appreciate its pleasantness. I see no way of remedying this problem by excogitating some special sense of 'in' or the like.

The reason for such phenomena, according to Plato, seems to be something like the following (see White 1993). The exemplification of a Form in the physical world, according to Plato, is a kind of embedding of it that involves not merely location but also, at the least, a kind of *perspective*. Thus a physical thing that is large is large from a certain standpoint and in view of a certain comparison. Plato even says the same thing about beauty in the *Hippias Major*, and, I take it, about equality in the *Phaedo*.

about the broadest possible exemplification of the good.[167] A full account of why this is so would require a lengthy discussion of Plato's metaphysics. Roughly, however, the point is this. According to Plato, what is judged to be thus and so from a particular perspective is less 'truly' or 'really' so than what is judged to be thus and so in a way that is independent of perspective. What is good merely for a particular person, on this view, counts as less truly good than what is good for a city as a whole.[168]

The rulers are thus confronted by a choice between two perspectives, one focused on the individual's own well-being and the other focused on a more inclusive good. In that way it amounts to a dualism of practical reason. In this situation a ruler must do either what is good for himself, or what is just and good. The dualism is formulated and is shown to involve a conflict. Plato's strategy is to adjudicate it, not to eliminate it. He confronts it directly, as a choice between the better life for oneself and the course that is just.

The fact that Plato confronts the problem rather than eliminating it or explaining it away shows that his repertoire of concepts does not differ significantly from the modern one that creates the distinction between self-regarding and broader aims. If Plato could conceive of no goodness except goodness for oneself, explicable only in a self-regarding way, then he could not have formulated the options for the rulers in the way that he does. Moreover, the fact that he settles it as he does, in favour of the broader, non-self-regarding good, shows that he is capable of conceiving of an aim that overrides that of one's own well-being.

Plato does not believe, however, that the dilemma is irresoluble. He does not merely oppose self-regarding and the broader considerations to each other and leave it at that, claiming an irresoluble dualism as Sidgwick does.[169] But neither does he maintain that the conflict is unreal. Rather, as soon as the dualism is formulated and presented, Plato tries to adjudicate the conflict that it generates. The framing of the dualism thus gives way immediately to a settling of the conflict. This resolution is based on the dualist view that both sides to the conflict are significant, so that neither can be eliminated, but that the clash between them can be adjudicated through the

---

[167] See Owen 1957, Vlastos 1965, and White 1993. One of the main problems confronting this view is the need to make sense of the equation of what is good for so-and-so with what is good from the perspective or standpoint of so-and-so.

[168] There seems to me to be no ground for claiming, as is often done, that in discovering what is good, the rulers are discovering what is 'really good for themselves'. This is not what Plato says. Rather, in discovering what is really good (in particular, governing the city), the rulers are discovering that what is good only for themselves is not 'really good'. In Plato's metaphysical scheme, what is really (*ontos*) good is what is good without regard to any particular perspective. See further White 1993. Likewise, I do not believe that there is any good evidence for taking Plato's notion of the Good to be that of the good *for a human being* (as is done by e.g. Reiner 1964: 50).

[169] At the end of his 1907.

contention that what is good takes deliberative precedence over what would produce the happiest life for oneself.

6. An Objection: Plato's Psychology in Republic IV

Probably the greatest source of puzzlement about Plato's view, and one of the strongest motivations to suppose that he must, in spite of what he says in *Republic* VII and its link to his non-self-referential notion of good in other works, nevertheless advocate a eudaimonist position, arises from the psychology that is expounded in *Republic* IV and developed further in Books VIII and IX. One might easily suppose that that psychology is designed for a eudaimonist idea of human aims and deliberation, and that it forces us to read Book VII so as to conform to it.[170] This, however, is not the case.

This line of thought runs as follows. It says that according to Book IV, an unjust action is one that weakens or destroys justice in the soul.[171] This justice, however, is a harmony of the soul. According to Plato's arguments in Books IV and VIII–IX, the harmony of the parts of the soul in which justice consists is coextensive, in some strong sense, with the order in the soul in which happiness or well-being consists.[172] It follows that if a ruler acts unjustly in declining to rule the city, he must thereby lessen the psychic harmony in which his justice consists. Accordingly, he must *pari passu* lessen the psychic harmony in which his happiness consists. This would imply that the suggested conflict between justice and happiness that we seem to find in Book VII must be an illusion.[173]

However, as an objection to the non-eudaimonist interpretation of Book VII this argument is not sufficient. It rests on the claim that doing something unjust—and Plato says explicitly that a refusal to govern would be unjust—diminishes the well-being of one's soul, since that, indeed, is his *definition* of an unjust action. But the question relevant to Book VII is not simply whether failing to rule would diminish the order in the soul. Rather the issue is whether it would do so *sufficiently* to render the ruler *less* happy than he would be made to be *if* he continued to philosophize instead.

Let us articulate the objection more fully. According to it, a ruler should reason thus:

(1) My failing to govern, according to Plato's *Republic* VII, would be unjust.

---

[170] For the general thesis that the psychology offered in the *Republic* should play a special role in the interpretation of the work, see Cooper 1984, at Cooper 1999: 120.

[171] Book IV, 443e–444b.

[172] Book IV, 443ff. and Book VIII, 586d–e.

[173] Note that it is unclear that someone advocating Irwin's sort of 'inclusivist' interpretation could take advantage of this objection, since it makes quite unclear how the well-being of others could be 'included' in an individual's happiness.

(2) By the definition of just action in *Republic* IV (that is, by inferring the definiens from the definiendum), that implies that my failing to govern would damage the harmony of my soul.

(3) But to damage the harmony of my soul is to diminish my well-being.

Therefore,

(4) My failing to govern would diminish my well-being.

From this it would seem to follow, contrary to what Plato appears to suggest in Book VII, that the ruler's continuing to philosophize rather than governing simply cannot be 'better for him than the political life'. In effect this line of argument relies on a version of the fusionist interpretation. If justice and happiness are both one and the same harmony or order within the soul, then to damage the one is *eo ipso* to damage the other.

However, this argument cannot go through on Plato's terms, for reasons related to the fact that, as I have said earlier, the fusionist interpretation is implausible, since Plato simply does not identify justice and happiness, and moreover treats them as distinct.[174] This fact emerges when we examine premise (3) of the proffered argument, and recall the point made earlier, about the difference, which emerges in Book IX, between the harmony of the soul that Plato identifies with justice and the harmony that he identifies with happiness. The difficulty in (3) accordingly lies in the implication of uniqueness in the phrase '*the* harmony of my soul' in (2). For in fact Plato's argument in the *Republic* invokes at least two psychic harmonies. Justice is one and happiness is another. The difference between the two is the difference between, once again, a harmony of performance of *functions*—justice—and a harmony of the *satisfactions* that arises therefrom—happiness or well-being, that is, the 'ability to do what it wants'.

The soul that philosophizes, according to Plato, is indeed in a position 'to do what it wants'. This activity, moreover, should not be pictured as simply the indulgence of a whim. Philosophizing is a part of reason's *function*. According to Plato, the performance of a thing's function in the economy of the structure of which it is a part is what is just for that thing. Accordingly, philosophizing is also in general something that is just for a soul, and in particular for a philosopher, to do. Accordingly, in the very act of philosophizing, the ruling part of the soul manifests its proper order. The benefit to the soul of philosophizing is therefore not separate from the order in which justice consists.

There is therefore no lack of room in Plato's psychology for the proposition that the philosopher philosophizing is happier than the philosopher governing, even though

---

[174] See sec. VII. 7.

[175] It obviously follows from this interpretation that Plato cannot accept an account of happiness that makes it simply equivalent to desire-satisfaction in the most general sense. For the ruler who chooses to

the philosopher in the ideal *polis* will choose to govern on grounds of justice and of good *simpliciter*.[175]

7. Platonic Dualism and Kantian Dualism Contrasted

The effort to show that Plato recognizes both other rational considerations besides one's own well-being and also conflicts between one's own well-being and broader considerations should not be construed as an effort fully to assimilate his views to modern ethical thinking. Plato's use of non-self-referential and non-self-regarding considerations differs substantially from what is typical of modern ethics. I do not wish to let that fact fall from view.

Whereas in modern views non-self-regarding considerations are often portrayed as both overriding and pervasively present to consciousness of good persons, in Plato they play an in some ways restricted role. The usual situation, Plato indicates, is one in which a person may, rationally and without qualm, aim at his own happiness. This is true not merely of the overwhelming majority of people—for whom the comprehension of the Form of the Good and the non-self-referential notion that it represents are out of reach—but also of philosopher-rulers at most stages of their lives. Only when the crucial question arises whether or not such a person will actually govern the city does the question arise of doing anything else.

Moreover, Plato does not seem to show the propensity, which some philosophers think of as characteristic of modern ethics, to be suspicious of the value, or the respectability, of self-regarding motivations and considerations. Perhaps in order to strengthen ethical motivation, many modern philosophers attach a stigma, however vague, to the whole idea of pursuing one's own good, and some philosophers, such as Kant at times, hold that the whole notion of happiness is too obscure to serve as a guide.

Nothing like this tendency appears in Plato. If you like, you can think of him as having a healthy enthusiasm for aiming at one's own happiness, and, if you like, you can also contrast that enthusiasm with certain modern moral or puritanical inhibitions about such an aim. In contexts in which no conflict with the good of the city arises, Plato holds that a philosopher will without qualm pursue his own well-being. He expects that his philosophers-in-training will be persuaded that the good of their city coincides with their own good. Until the conflict arises, he makes no objection to allowing the philosophers to seek their own happiness, and to do so under precisely

govern, and in that sense does what he chooses, is according to Plato not, for all that, the happiest. What such a ruler 'wants to do' is, in effect, what he wants for himself. But nothing in Plato encourages us to think that he accepts a general desire-satisfaction account of well-being, which in general is incompatible with the possibility of self-sacrifice (see Brandt 1993).

[176] See *Rep.* 412c–413d.

that very description.[176] Nor does he ever expect the philosophers to regard as unimportant the fact that their life is far happier than the life of someone who is unjust. Indeed, they are to regard that fact as a good reason for preferring the former life to the latter. In *Republic* IX, in particular, when Plato compares the life of the just and the unjust person, he extols the happiness of the former's life, and gives us every reason to believe that the just person will regard this superior happiness as a reason not to be like someone who is unjust. These facts are all the more striking in view of his capacity, vis-à-vis certain kinds of pleasures, to exhibit a vehemently puritanical attitude. For self-regard as such, however, he shows no aversion.

In another way, too, Plato's thinking differs from its modern counterparts. The considerations that he opposes to the non-self-regarding ones are, in the important cases, quite different from the ones that we usually notice in modern ethics. In the latter, it is worldly and bodily goods and enjoyments that are the main adversaries of virtue. The same is true in Hesiod and Aristophanes, we saw, since they are concerned with ordinary self-seeking and acquisitiveness. That fact, indeed, demonstrates that the ordinary Greek outlook was by no means totally different from the one with which we are familiar among most people today. In Plato, however, things of that sort are in large part excluded from an individual's happiness. For since an individual's happiness consists, according to Plato, in a balance of satisfactions, and since bodily and other such satisfactions are granted only a subsidiary role, the normal modern type of opposition of duty and narrow self-interest or acquisitiveness is already put to one side. Instead, the conflict for Plato's rulers is between civic duty, as we can call it, and the rarefied activity of Platonic philosophizing.

Nevertheless, the rulers face a conflict, and it is right to insist on the structural similarity that it bears to the modern idea of an opposition of one's own happiness and broader aims. Even though the broader consideration that is here in question is the self-referential good of something related to oneself, namely one's own *polis*, the emphasis in *Republic* VII falls squarely on the idea that one's own best life is not identical with the life of civic activity. This is a matter of a dualism of considerations, and of a clash between them, that belongs to much the same structural type that we often think of as characteristic of modern rather than ancient ethics; and here we find Plato claiming that in such cases, the broader and more universal considerations have priority.

Chapter 6

INDIVIDUAL GOOD AND DELIBERATIVE CONFLICT IN ARISTOTLE

I. The Periods of Greek Ethics

1. The Highlighting of the 'Classical' Period

For most writers on the history of Greek ethics and for most philosophers who have been influenced by it, Aristotle is the pre-eminently 'Classical' Greek philosopher. In both the kantian and the hegelian interpretative traditions he is held up as the paradigm of Classical thought. It will be helpful to begin the discussion of Aristotle by asking what this label 'Classical' signifies in this context.

It is traditional and still entirely normal to think of Greek ethics, in parallel with Greek literature and Greek history, as divided into three periods. The most prominent of them is chronologically the central one, the 'Classical' period. Its chief philosophical representatives are Plato and Aristotle, though it also includes what can be gleaned about Socrates from the works of Plato and others. Prior to the Classical period stands the Archaic, often labelled simply the 'Presocratic period', the time 'before Socrates'. The last of the three, often called 'Hellenistic', is also very often characterized also as 'post-Aristotelian'. There is nothing accidental about the fact that the Classical period is the only one that is consistently granted its own designation. It is never 'post-Archaic', let alone 'pre-Hellenistic'. The other two periods are often designated not in their own right but by their relations to Classical times.

By long-standing habit, people nowadays regard the Classical period as the era during which Greek philosophical thinking reached its peak. No coincidence, then, that we tend to regard Classical thinking as also the most typically *Hellenic*. The two periods adjacent to it fore and aft have traditionally seemed, so to speak, less Greek. To this way of viewing the matter Archaic Greek thinking looks primitive, less fully developed, unrefined. Hellenistic thought, at the later end of the Classical era, has been felt to have an air of decadence, and of either vulgarity or scholasticism or both.

The great revival of interest in Greek thought which began in Germany in the eighteenth century, and which gave rise to the kantian and hegelian responses to Greek ethics, adopted this sort of focus. To both the detractors and the admirers of the Classical period, its philosophers—the Athenians Socrates and Plato, and the Athenianized Aristotle—were the quintessential philosophical representatives and articulators of Hellenic culture. In the view of readers of both kantian and hegelian styles, Greek ethics was the ethics of the Classical period—as these readers interpreted it. In particular, this period seemed to be the time of the most characteristically Greek ideas concerning virtue and happiness, *aretê* and *eudaimonia*, in their most characteristically Greek form.

This picture of Greek philosophy mirrored a largely isomorphic picture of Greek social and political history. The Classical period is, not coincidentally, regarded also as primarily the heyday of the political institution, the *polis*. Correspondingly in philosophy, the *polis* plays a leading role in the writings of Plato and Aristotle which is matched in neither of the other two periods. Hegel recognized that in Archaic times the *polis* was less prominent in Greek thought, and believed that after its heyday it had weakened somewhat even by the time Plato and Aristotle wrote about it. Even so, however, the Classical period seemed to him to be the time during which philosophers expounded the reasons why the *polis* was the most characteristic manifestation of Greek life. Earlier thinkers seemingly had not yet been fully aware of its importance; according to Hegel, they lived in it 'unselfconsciously'. By Hellenistic times, however, it had lost its robustness, having been submerged under the broader political currents generated by the imperial conquests of Philip of Macedon and his son, Alexander the Great.

The customary division of Greek ethics into these three periods has been felt to reinforce the significance that is conventionally attributed to the thinking of 'the Greeks'. This tripartition reinforces the sense, already conveyed by both kantian and hegelian responses to Greek thought, that there is a fundamental difference between ancient and modern ethics. Hellenistic ethics seems to some to come fairly close to possessing Christian features associated with modern positions, especially Kant's. Presocratic thinking, on the other hand—even though Nietzsche was to invoke it for the articulation of his own attack on morality—looked to kantian and hegelian readers to be too undeveloped to constitute either an anticipation of modern ethics or a counterweight to it. The Classical period, then, occupies centre stage; it is the representative of Greek ethics in general, as it is contrasted with the ethics of modernity.

2. Exceptions: Hume and Nietzsche

Not all modern philosophers have adopted this perspective on the Greeks, but the exceptions have done little to alter the general impression that the Classical period of ethics is the most Greek, and that Aristotle is the most Classical. Consider Hume. He in many ways already found the main themes of Kantian ethics every bit as discordant as many later thinkers in the hegelian tradition were to do. Even though Hume is hostile to the idea of duty and is sympathetic to the notion of virtue, nonetheless he is on the whole relatively uninterested in Plato and Aristotle. He pays far more attention to the schools of the Hellenistic period—Stoics, Epicureans, and Sceptics.[1] One would never know from reading Hume that Plato and Aristotle are the 'Classical' philosophers of Greece, nor would one be aware of the tripartition of the chronology of Greek thought that places them at its centre. But by the modern period of interpretation that concerns me, Hume was very much an exception, and his outlook had little or no influence.

Another exception to the rule is, as usual, Nietzsche. Unlike Hume, however, he wrote in a period during which it was widely believed that Plato and especially Aristotle exhibited the best of Greek philosophy. Nietzsche had to fight against this assessment, and he did so eagerly. Even if we had never read the modern thinkers whom he attacks, we could tell by reading him alone that his opponents esteem Socrates, Plato, and Aristotle as the most valuable of Hellenic philosophers, and, just as clearly, that he rejects their estimate. In Nietzsche's opinion the truly worthwhile part of Greek philosophy extends up to, but does not include, Socrates. From Socrates onward there is no especially significant line to be drawn in Nietzsche's taxonomy between the Classical period and the Hellenistic.[2] They were both, he thinks, equally inadequate.

Nevertheless, Nietzsche does in one respect discriminate among Classical philosophers. He regards Socrates and Plato as both forces to be reckoned with, that is, as philosophical personalities whom he had to confront directly and openly. Aristotle, on the other hand, seems to hold little interest for him.[3] Evidently he thought that in Aristotle, the tendencies that he deplored in Socrates and Plato had become petrified into academic dogma, enunciated by a personality whom he found simply boring. But by this very neglect, Nietzsche backhandedly confirms Aristotle's position as the definitive, if not the most vigorous, spokesman for Classical Greek ethics.

3. The Conception of the Classical Period and its Impact on the Interpretation of Aristotle

In the context of a discussion of Aristotle, a fresh view of Greek ethics in its full variety means two things, one having to do with the idea of the Classical period and the other with Aristotle's own doctrine. On the former side, it means trying to disentangle

---

[1] Note which ancient philosophers are given the most attention in Hume's *Essays*.

[2] See Chapter 1, sec. VIII. 1–2.

[3] The tone of the reference to Aristotle in sec. 80 of Nietzsche 1966d seems to me to be typical.

oneself from the customary chronological tripartition of Greek thought, and thus from the usual kantian and hegelian responses that are closely connected with it. Let us not, then, take that tripartition, or the assignment of Aristotle to the middle period of it, for granted. Far better to try moving away from fixed presuppositions by avoiding the chronological divisions with which they are linked.

This is why I here begin a new chapter with Aristotle. I do not say that Aristotle belongs with the Hellenistic thinkers rather than with Plato. Indeed, on matters concerning deliberative conflict, as we shall see, Aristotle continues many of Plato's lines of thought directly enough.[4] Rather, my aim is to weaken the grip of the tendency of the tripartition to highlight a single way of thinking as pre-eminently Hellenic. The right thing to emphasize is not a uniform picture of 'the Greeks', or a common fixed outlook that they allegedly share, but rather the diversity of their ways of thinking as responses to recognized unsolved problems.

Secondly, as an application of the point that I have just made, I want to combat the account of Aristotle that is normally given by those who regard him as the quintessentially Classical writer on ethics. That is, I wish to urge that although he is a eudaimonist, he is not the Classically *harmonizing* eudaimonist that he is normally presented as being. A 'harmonizing eudaimonist' is, once again, someone who espouses, in addition to the *eudaimonist thesis* that a rational person makes his own well-being his sole ultimate aim, the further *harmonizing thesis* that if well-being consists of a plurality of aims or goods, then they can all be pretty fully achieved consistently with one another.

Many times Aristotle scholars slide from the idea that Aristotle is a eudaimonist, which is true, to the false supposition that he is a harmonizing eudaimonist and that his chief aim as a eudaimonist was to advocate harmonizing eudaimonism. Some writers who would, I think, reject the idea that Aristotle is a harmonizing eudaimonist if it were explicitly presented to them, nevertheless pass silently from the former to the latter attribution when the issue is not explicitly raised—which it seldom is. More thought needs to be given, therefore, to the ways in which a given version of eudaimonism can fail to be a harmonizing version. Thinking about this matter, it seems to me, yields both historical and also philosophical dividends.

The view that Aristotle is a harmonizing eudaimonist is enshrined in the many interpretations of his ethics that say that according to him, human beings can aspire to a life in which all genuine values are fully realized, and that a person's happiness consists in a balanced combination of activities or states in which each aim is granted a fully adequate place, so that all worthwhile capacities receive their due. Thus John

---

[4] This is one reason why I disagree with Annas's procedure in her 1993, which tries to present Greek eudaimonism by starting with Aristotle. Aristotle's idea of a conflict between *theôria* and ethically virtuous activity plainly continues, as is often noted, Plato's presentation of the choice that his rulers must make between governing and philosophizing (see Chapter 5, sec. VI).

Cooper takes Aristotle to maintain that 'the virtuous person's desires and interests would constitute a coherent whole', in which

[a]*ll* the different types of desires and interests can be harmoniously satisfied, in such a way as to allow for the full realization, in the best life as defined by [the] end [which is *eudaimonia*], of many different interests and many different kinds of good things.[5]

The same picture of Aristotle's thinking is suggested by the title of a recent book by Anthony Kenny, *Aristotle on the Perfect Life*. The word 'perfect' in this title conveys the impression that according to Aristotle, human beings can live a life in which no genuine value is less than fully realized. Many interpreters have the same impression. Although this fact is not surprising in view of some of Aristotle's own remarks, it is nevertheless based, as we shall see, on a mistaken reading of them. Fortunately not all scholars accept a harmonizing interpretation of Aristotle. One exception is Nussbaum, who insists that conflict has a place in Aristotle's ethics.[6] Nevertheless, in spite of such occasional exceptions, the idea that Aristotle believes in a harmony of all worthwhile human aims still remains firmly rooted in the main interpretative tradition, and continues to be for most people the standard, default account of his position.

This harmonizing interpretation, I say, is mistaken. Aristotle's position is a form of eudaimonism, indeed, but not a harmonizing eudaimonism. He neither denies the reality and importance of deliberative conflict, nor claims to use eudaimonism to establish, or even to any great extent to promote, consistency of practical reason. When he tells us to organize our lives around *eudaimonia*, and to devote ourselves mainly to a single activity, he is not thereby promising us that we can, even in theory, eliminate deliberative oppositions, nor saying that a method for doing so exists.

In asserting the foregoing I do not necessarily reject the type of interpretation commonly called 'inclusivist'. An *inclusivist*, or 'inclusive-end', interpretation says that according to Aristotle, happiness consists in a structure of various aims, not in one 'dominant' aim.[7] To deny that Aristotle is a harmonizing eudaimonist is not in itself to deny that he takes happiness to be an inclusive aim consisting of a plurality of parts

---

[5] Cooper 1975: 131–2 (emphasis added).

[6] I shall argue in sec. V. 3, however, that her description in her 1986 of deliberative conflict in Aristotle mislocates it, and does not allow for the close connection of the conflicts that Aristotle recognizes to the modern conflicts between wellbeing and ethical norms. (At p. 480 of her 1994, she speaks of 'the Aristotelian, who so wants all of life to fit harmoniously together'—which seems to run against the tendency of most of her interpretation of Aristotle in her 1986.)

[7] The verbal distinction is due to Hardie 1965. I would point out, by the way, that in spite of a persistent tendency on the part of interpreters to think that dominant-end and inclusive-end interpretations of Aristotle must exclude each other, it is perfectly possible to maintain both that happiness consists in a plurality of ends (or achievement of aims, when these could be activities) *and* that that plurality is so structured that one end is dominant in the standard sense.

or included aims. You can hold that happiness consists of a plurality of components without holding that they all are consistent. In denying that Aristotle is a harmonizing eudaimonist, I am simply denying that he regards all worthwhile human aims as fully or substantially consistent with each other, or capable of being fully or substantially coordinated without loss. In that sense, I shall urge, he is not an apostle of Classical harmony.

It is accordingly important to look at Aristotle against the background not of the standard picture of Greek ethics, but rather of what has been exhibited in the previous chapter about the period extending from the earliest Greek ethical reflections through the work of Plato. The thinking that goes on in that period is not homogeneous. Rather, it generates a variety of ideas about the relation between an individual's good and other deliberative considerations, not a thoroughgoing, uniform eudaimonist monism. Eudaimonism is strong and dominates some thinkers. It is not, however, the only force at work. Other ideas, too, show themselves, as does an awareness of potential opposition between self-regarding and non-self-regarding aims. Consciousness of this issue is vivid in the period leading up to Plato. It pushes him in the direction of a position in which not only eudaimonist ideas but also some distinctly non-eudaimonist thoughts have significant roles to play.

4. Detaching Aristotle from the Standard Conception of the Classical Harmonizing Philosopher

Aristotle fits into this picture in a distinctive way, both because of the place that he occupies in traditional accounts and also because of his own approach to the relevant issues. I now briefly summarize the conclusions of my treatment of him.

The two main interpretative traditions, as I have said, cut Aristotle to fit their respective patterns of the stereotypical Greek writer on ethics. Kantian-style interpreters have thought it easy enough to portray him as conforming to their thesis that Greek ethics is not only eudaimonist but also egoist in a pejorative sense.[8] Hegelian readers, for their part, have found him much more congenial. He was the Greek philosopher whom Hegel himself most admired,[9] and is repeatedly invoked by modern philosophers searching in Greek ethics for a harmony of rational human aims. It

---

[8] Recently there have been efforts to interpret Aristotle as himself subscribing to a position much like that of Kant himself, but this is of course not what I have meant by 'the kantian interpretation', which is, rather (cf. Chapter 1, sec. V), the very different interpretation of Aristotle normally offered by those advocating a kantian ethical view. For instances of these more recent attempts to read Aristotle as himself a kantian in ethics, see e.g. Korsgaard 1996. It seems to me that this account of Aristotle, while suggestive philosophically, is too far from Aristotle's texts to have much chance of representing his views, for reasons given by Schneewind 1996 and Meyer 1998: esp. 88.

[9] See Gray 1941: 77, 83ff.

is no accident that recent hegelian and quasi-hegelian impulses to return to Greek ways of thinking are often styled, quite simply, 'neo-Aristotelianism'.[10]

Aristotle's works, however, are treacherous ground for those who defend these interpretations. Readings that seem at first sight to find a footing in his language end up slipping away. Although he says some of what these interpreters expect him to, he does not try to support his views on the basis that they expect. As a result, the lay of the land in his ethical view turns out to be different from what the kantian and hegelian responses are fundamentally designed to depict.

This is quite easy to show, as we shall see, in the case of the kantian interpretation. For that very reason, it has in recent years been largely abandoned. Starting from Aristotle's statement that each of us aims at his own *eudaimonia* or happiness, kantian readers take his doctrine to be a form of hedonist egoism. That reading collapses under the realization, now widespread, that for Aristotle, 'happiness' does not mean pleasure or anything much like it and does not signify a straightforwardly egoist notion.

The hegelian reading is more subtle, but its description of Aristotle's grounds for his claims encounters difficulties just as great as those that confront the kantian interpretation. The point of Aristotle's eudaimonism, according to the hegelian response, is to exhibit and support a harmony of rational human considerations. Aristotelian ethical virtue (*êthikê aretê*), on this account, does not need to compete against countervailing considerations concerning an individual's own good. Instead, it harmonizes with them and is even included within them.

But this account of Aristotle's purpose cannot be sustained any more successfully than can the kantian reading. Aristotle's reason for espousing a eudaimonist position is not that he thinks that eudaimonism serves up deliberative harmony or freedom from conflict. Aristotle's eudaimonism is eudaimonism indeed, but eudaimonism *without* any thoroughgoing harmony. That is, it is a eudaimonism that admits sharp internal deliberative conflicts that he does not try to hide. Rather than using his eudaimonism to argue for a consistency of rational aims, I shall maintain, he makes clear that he takes some fully rational human aims to collide with each other. As a result, his ethical works take on a shape that they never could have had if the hegelian account of them had been correct.

In particular, I shall also argue, Aristotle admits a disharmony of the special type that mostly concerns me here: an opposition, of the sort that is familiar in modern ethics, between an individual's well-being and broader considerations.

Nevertheless, Aristotle's position is formulated in a type of eudaimonist language that obscures the oppositions that lie within it. Earlier I distinguished two ways of thinking about conflicts involving an individual's good. One was the opposition of one's well-being to 'broader' aims which are conceived of as lying outside of it. This

---

[10] See Schnädelbach 1986. Sandel 1982 seems to me to exhibit much the same tendency.

type of opposition is exemplified in modern terminology by the idea of a clash between one's duty and one's happiness. The other contrast sets off a person's 'self-confined' aims against aims that have to do with what is external to him.[11] As inclusivist interpreters have urged, however, the two poles of this contrast can easily be described as both lying within a person's well-being.

The point is this. In some cases, one can simply *relabel* a conflict that some see as occurring between happiness and broader aims, so that it remains as much present as it ever was, but comes to be formulated as a clash between two parts of happiness, namely, a part that is self-confined and a part that is external.

Essentially this is what we find in Aristotle's writings. He makes it clear that self-confined aims and external aims may clash in a serious way. He presents this as a clash, however, between two components of happiness, or between two ways of conceiving of happiness as excellent activity, rather than as a conflict between one's happiness and something outside it. That fact easily leads hegelian-minded readers to conclude that he is attempting to portray worthwhile aims as consistent with each other. In fact, however, this is not the case.

For—and this is the crucial point—Aristotle does not *pretend* to be eliminating conflict. When he fails actually to show that deliberative conflict can be obviated, he is not breaking any promise that he has made. Rather, as we shall see, he is both above board and consistent in conceding that deliberative conflict occurs and that it is extremely important and problematic. Moreover, he recognizes and acknowledges that some oppositions confront aims that are more closely self-confined with aims that are less so. In this regard, he seems to me to be far more clearsighted than some subsequent inclusivist thinkers and than many of his inclusivist interpreters. As a result, we should believe neither that his eudaimonism successfully supports a deliberative harmony, nor that it is even an attempt to do so.

II. Aristotle, the Harmonizing Eudaimonist

1. Aristotle's Eudaimonist Starting Point

Many features of the *Nicomachean Ethics* make it unsurprising that Aristotle is so often taken to be the paradigm of the eudaimonist philosopher. We should keep these features firmly in view in order to understand how they fit into Aristotle's overall scheme, and in particular why they do not demonstrate that his eudaimonism is of the harmonizing variety.

In the first place, of all Greek thinkers Aristotle made the most sustained attempt

---

[11] On these two distinctions and the terminology associated with them see Chapter 1, sec. VII. 2–3, and Chapter 2, sec. VII.

to focus his own thinking, and also his readers' attention, on the notion of *eudaimonia*. The opening of the *Nicomachean Ethics* shows how he did this. Plato had begun his *Republic* by bluntly asking why a person should bother to be just when justice seems to conflict with his own well-being. By contrast, Aristotle opens the *Nicomachean Ethics* blithely with no open reference at all to any problems of conflict.[12] Instead, he starts with a declaration that everyone seeks *eudaimonia*, and he also states that people aim at every other worthwhile thing for the sake of *eudaimonia*. Then he adds that *eudaimonia* is the only thing that everyone seeks for its own sake and its own sake *alone*. That seems like a fitting introduction to a eudaimonist treatise. And it is. In the system of human aims, one's *eudaimonia* certainly has a very special position.

Having said that happiness is the only thing that is sought for its own sake alone, Aristotle accepts the obligation to explain what happiness is. After some further argumentation, he arrives at the view that happiness is, as he puts it, 'activity of the soul in accordance with virtue [*aretê*, also translatable as "excellence"], and if there are more than one virtue, in accordance with the best and most complete'.[13] He follows this explanation with a division of virtue into two kinds: virtue of character or ethical virtue (also misleadingly translated as 'moral virtue') and virtue of intellect.[14] In Books II–V, he discusses the former kind at length. Justice, which Plato had placed at the very centre of the argument of the *Republic*, appears as only one among these virtues, and the last one to be treated. Nowhere does Aristotle highlight the problem of the potential conflict of justice and happiness. Quite to the contrary, he appears to have eliminated it from notice.

By the end of *Ethics* V, then, Aristotle has asserted that happiness is the end which everyone ultimately seeks, and that it is activity in accordance with virtue, including justice. It appears to follow without further ado that activity in accordance with justice is, like other kinds of virtuous activity, a part or constituent of human well-being, rather than something that ever comes into competition with it.

In addition to all this, the beginning of the *Nicomachean Ethics* has given rise to the further impression that its eudaimonism is specifically designed to exclude rational deliberative conflict altogether. Human well-being has been so defined as to include activity in accordance with justice. Therefore the reader might well suppose it to follow that any question of an opposition between it and justice has been definitionally ruled out. For how could happiness, one might ask, possibly conflict with a part of

---

[12] The point holds not only for the *Nicomachean Ethics* but also for his other ethical treatise, the *Eudemian Ethics*—and for the *Magna Moralia* as well, which in any case I, like most scholars, believe not to be Aristotle's work. Again like most scholars, I take the *Nicomachean Ethics* to be Aristotle's best-thought-out presentation of his views.

[13] *Nic. Eth.* I. 7, trans. Ross.

[14] The reasons why 'moral virtue' is nowadays misleading arise from the largely kantian flavour that often attaches itself to the word 'moral'; cf. Chapter 2, sec. IV.

itself? The idea is thus encouraged that a harmonization of the opposition treated by the *Republic* is in the works.

This same impression might be strengthened by an additional fact. Although Aristotle acknowledges the existence of many virtues of character, he never suggests explicitly that they, or the activities associated with them, can clash with each other. Because of the absence of any systematic account of how this could happen, the reader is easily led to assume that activity in accordance with virtue is a seamless whole, a state in which no conflicts can arise between one type of virtuous activity and another—between courageous activity, for instance, and activity in accordance with justice. If this is so, one might readily presume, then the person who aims at *eudaimonia* must *eo ipso* pursue justice, and the person whose actions are in accordance with justice must necessarily achieve *eudaimonia*. This conclusion turns out to be entirely premature, as will emerge. If we consider only the virtues of character, however, and ignore what Aristotle says about certain other topics, especially *theôria* and *philia*, the temptation to form the conclusion is strong.[15]

Small wonder, then, that Aristotle was so much admired by Hegel, and that he remains the Greek philosopher who is most consistently cited for evidence in support of the hegelian response to Greek ethics. For Aristotle's strategy in the *Ethics* seems at first blush to imply acceptance of both of the two main components of the hegelian interpretation, eudaimonism and a harmony of the parts of happiness which is guaranteed by its definition.

2. The Harmony of the Aristotelian Good Man

A further feature of Aristotle's doctrine has often seemed to lend additional support to the notion that he embraces a belief in the ultimate consistency of worthwhile aims. This feature attaches not simply to the overall architecture of his discussion of *eudaimonia*, but to the core of his account of ethical virtue.

Central to Aristotle's doctrine of virtue is his distinction between the person who is genuinely virtuous and the person who is not fully virtuous but merely self-controlled. Both types of person perform the same actions. They differ, however, in their motivations. The self-controlled person, the *enkratês*, is someone whose reason must struggle with his emotions in order to bring him, against their resistance, to perform virtuous actions.

The virtuous person, on the other hand, does not, as standard readings of the *Nicomachean Ethics* portray him, seem to experience this kind of struggle. His reason

---

[15] Nussbaum maintains that Aristotle's position on virtue of character leaves room for conflict (see below, sec. V), but agrees that *Nic. Eth.* 1100b33–1101a10 casts some doubt on this, and that 1199b36ff. of the *Magna Moralia* (which she believes is by Aristotle) insists that the virtues are 'mutually reinforcing' (1986: 333–5).

and his emotions, including his desires for pleasure and pain, are in tune with each other—so much so that performing the right action does not require him to suppress or counteract impulses or emotions that might cause his behaviour to be different.[16] The thought might be illustrated this way. We could compare the good man to someone who, instead of being either gluttonous or completely uninterested in food, finds his appetite adjusted perfectly to his own correct judgements about what he rationally ought to eat. Thus as he walks down the buffet table, he judges certain foods good for him and others not, and finds his appetite waxing and waning in glad unison with his judgements about nutrition.

It is easy to see where this line of thought appears to lead us. It induces us to think that a good man is subject to no conflict of any kind between considerations of virtue and other aims. Thus, for instance, commentators have said that in the case of Aristotle's good man the motivation to act virtuously is 'frictionless', or that considerations of virtue 'silence' all others.[17] The idea is that when virtue requires or recommends a certain particular thing, then in a good man there is simply no countervailing motivation or consideration. Such a person's action, that is, appears to be utterly wholehearted.

Certainly Aristotle does not in most contexts link virtue to the strenuous efforts at self-control that some modern views associate with it. Moreover, even the brave man as described in the foregoing passage, although he feels emotions that in some sense tend against the actions that he takes, is not pictured as regarding his own dismay at the thought of his death, for instance, as a sufficient basis for judging that perhaps he ought not to do the action after all. The brave man would not, that is, entertain two competing rational *considerations*—one favouring the action and the other opposing it.

Thus if the good man is indeed someone in whom the totality of rational aims is embodied, as appears to be Aristotle's view, then it might appear to follow that, within this sphere and subject to a few qualifications, a full harmony of rational considerations must be possible. This emphatically does not mean that people who embody this harmony are common. It might even be the case that 'the good man' is, in Aristotle's view, a sheer idealization which is never realized in any actual human being. Even so, however, Aristotle would still be acknowledging—this interpretation has it—that rational aims are ultimately consistent with each other in theory, so to speak, even if actual people find it difficult to exemplify the ideal. Considerations of this sort appear at first blush to supply a powerful argument for the proposition that Aristotle is motivated by the desire to demonstrate that in a good man, at least, there can be no fundamental deliberative conflict.

---

[16] See *Nic. Eth.* VI. 1–2 and III. 11, esp. 1118b28–1119a21.

[17] See Urmson 1988 and McDowell 1979 and 1980.

Finally, Aristotle's description of *eudaimonia* as *teleion*, and the common translation of this term by the English word 'perfect', encourages the idea that according to
him, all conflicts between aims must somehow be obviated and all of them must be
fully realized. Thus, for instance, as noted, Kenny's title. However, the translation is
problematic, as has often been recognized,[18] and in fact there is good reason not to
take the word *teleion* in Aristotle to connote either complete realization of aims or lack
of conflict among them.

III. The Kantian and Hegelian Interpretations of Aristotle

1. The Deficiencies of the Kantian Hedonist Interpretation

Nowadays hegelian interpretations of Aristotle are in the ascendant—especially
under the title 'neo-Aristotelianism'—and kantian readings are far less popular.[19]
The kantian interpretation, however, has in the past been so influential that we may
scarcely pass it by without seeing clearly why it is no longer so. Moreover, it will in the
end be seen to contain some important truth.[20]

Kantian-minded readers have generally construed Aristotle as espousing a
straightforwardly hedonist egoism, that is, as maintaining that an individual's ultimate rational aim is to experience pleasure.[21] The kantian reading of Greek ethics is,
of course, not normally offered as a way of defending it. On the contrary, those who
interpret Aristotle in this way usually attack him, suggesting that as a hedonist egoist,
he failed to acknowledge the independent weight of non-self-regarding considerations.[22]

To anyone who defends this reading it is of course natural to place heavy stress on
his statement that happiness is sought for its own sake, as well as on some of his treatment of the notion of pleasure. Advocates of this reading also appeal, in addition, to
his declarations in *Nicomachean Ethics* X. 6–8 that the best life for a human being is a
life of *theôria*, and that this activity is the most pleasant that there is.[23] Taken together

---

[18] By Kenny himself, for one (1992: 17, 19), adopting a point noted by White 1981 and Heinaman 1988.

[19] A different phenomenon from both of these is the appearance of interpretations that attempt in one
degree or another to assimilate Aristotle's position to Kant's. (Obviously the sense in which these are 'kantian interpretations' is quite different from the sense in which I use that phrase.) An example of this tendency is Korsgaard 1996. For reasons too involved to be registered here, I believe that such readings cannot
be sustained. For some of the reasons see Schneewind 1996, and for qualified resistance to the general
assimilation of Aristotle and Kant see Sherman 1997. Less fully assimilationist accounts of Aristotle can be
found in McDowell 1996 and Whiting 1996.

[20] See below, sec. IX. 4.

[21] Prichard 1968a advances a hedonist interpretation. Field 1932: chs. 6–9 gives a non-hedonist but
fairly straightforwardly egoist account.   [22] See Chapter 1, sec. V.

[23] See *Nic. Eth.* 1178a4–7, quoted below in sec. VI. 2.

and in isolation from some other things that he says, these passages might appear to give comfort to a hedonist account of his conception of the human good.

Nonetheless, it is clear enough—and nowadays very widely recognized—that in its standard, straightforwardly hedonist form, the kantian interpretation is open to insuperable objections. These appear immediately when we examine Aristotle's treatment of the notion of pleasure, together with the details of his definition of *eudaimonia*.

In the first place, Aristotle explicitly denies that pleasure is the good.[24] Certainly that is strong evidence against any straightforwardly hedonist interpretation. As scholars have repeatedly pointed out, moreover, he equates happiness with a kind of activity (*energeia*), namely, activity in accordance with virtue or, in other words, virtuous activity. He also says further things that seem irreconcilable with an out-and-out hedonist position—for instance, that it is impossible to be happy when one is asleep, even though in the sense that we normally associate with the word 'pleasure', it is plainly not possible to experience the pleasure when one is sleeping.[25]

Furthermore, there seems to be little room for doubt that when Aristotle talks as though pleasure is essential to a happy life, his understanding of the term 'pleasure' works directly against a standard hedonist construal of his overall position. He does not want to concede the standard hedonist's contention that we should be indifferent to what actions we do in order to obtain pleasure as long as our doing it does not lead to subsequent lessening of pleasure or increase of pain. Nor does he hold that something's being pleasant is enough, in and of itself, to make that thing choiceworthy. Rather, even if an activity is pleasant, what makes it choiceworthy is not its being pleasant *per se* but rather its being a good activity.[26]

At the end of the day, Aristotle propounds an account of pleasure that appears to be designed to allow him to say that we pursue pleasure as good in itself while at the same time holding that activity is what we should ultimately aim at. His thesis is that pleasure is actually *identical* with activity. Alternatively, he claims that activity and pleasure are so closely 'bound up together' as 'not to admit of separation'. He thus says that he will dismiss the question 'whether we choose life for the sake of pleasure or pleasure for the sake of life'.[27]

Although this idea is in some ways obscure and has struck many critics as flatly paradoxical, his motivation for putting matters this way is not hard to fathom. He does so in order to maintain two things simultaneously that might otherwise not be reconcilable.[28] The first is that we should sometimes seek pleasure for itself alone. The second is that virtuous activity is that for whose sake we ultimately value everything else, at least in part. But in insisting that we value activity for its own sake, he is directly

[24] *Nic. Eth.* I. 3.
[25] *Nic. Eth.* I. 3.
[26] See *Nic. Eth.* X. 2, 4, and Annas 1988.
[27] *Nic. Eth.* 1175a19–20, with Annas 1980.
[28] See Annas 1980.

contradicting the kantian account of his position, which says that he regards virtuous
action as merely an instrument for gaining happiness, and is leaving the door wide
open to an inclusivist interpretation.[29]

2. *The Superiority of the Inclusivist to the Fusionist Reading*

Nowadays, the hegelian type of interpretation is far more widely favoured than the
kantian type, and of the two main hegelian interpretations by far the more commonly accepted is the inclusivist one. Occasionally people have taken Aristotle to espouse
a fusionist position (or else, very commonly, they have failed to distinguish clearly
between inclusivist and fusionist accounts).[30] However, the inclusivist account of his
views has won far more extensive allegiance, especially in recent years.[31] Inclusivist
interpretations also play a significant role in recent neo-Aristotelian attempts to maintain that Aristotle's view is today still philosophically viable.

Certainly there is firmer textual evidence for an inclusivist than for a fusionist
interpretation of Aristotle's argument. According to a standard fusionist account,
a person's well-being must be flatly identified with adherence to ethical and social
norms. Aristotle, however, does not restrict happiness to activity in accordance with
the single virtue of justice, nor indeed with virtue of character alone. The relevant
type of virtuous activity is much broader than that. As I have observed, Aristotle also
embraces within the ambit of virtue what he calls *intellectual* virtue or excellence
(*dianoêtikê aretê*). Intellectual excellence is in his view many-faceted. Most notably, it
includes the capacity for what he calls *theôria*—philosophical thought or (perhaps)
contemplation. That all of these sorts of activities should be potentially included in

---

[29] See Gauthier and Jolif 1970: ii. 574.

[30] See Chapter 1, sec. VII. 4. On the whole, the distinction between the fusionist and the inclusivist
views has not been clearly drawn. Therefore it is sometime hard to tell which view a given philosopher or
interpreter wishes to adopt. T. H. Green sometimes says things that suggest the fusionist interpretation; see
esp. his 1883, e.g. secs. 235–6, 239. Other things that he says, though, indicate an inclusivist account. The
same is true of Hegel; see e.g. his 1955: ii. 98–9, 99–100, 114, with Taylor 1979: 79–90. In Irwin's version of
this type of argument, an individual's good is identified not immediately with the good of the *polis* but
rather, in the first instance, with the good of his friends (1988: 391–3). However, some of what Irwin says
seems to fit instead with an inclusivist interpretation; cf. also next note.

[31] Hardie 1965 and Ackrill 1980 formulated the interpretation in recent times, though without any evident dependence on Hegel. See also Cooper 1975: 122, 132–3; Sherman 1989: 6, 94–106, 128–9; Hursthouse
1999: ch. 9, where the 'aspects' discussed on 202–5 yield what is in effect an inclusivist view. See also Irwin's
complex argument in his 1988: esp. chs. 16–18, 21, for what seems to me to be a partly inclusivist and partly
fusionist interpretation. The statements of his interpretation on pp. 359–63, 397, 404–6, 430, 440, 442–4, for
example, seem best taken as inclusivist. For a more fusionist-sounding account, however, cf. Irwin's 1992,
esp. sec. 4, next-to-last paragraph. (It is not always easy to tell there when Irwin is interpreting Green and
when he is giving his own views. In any case, Irwin here points to some Hegelian features of his own interpretation.) The clearest statement of an inclusivist view in the Aristotelian corpus occurs in the *Magna
Moralia* (a work whose authenticity is debated, as previously mentioned), at 1184a25–30.

happiness speaks strongly against the kantian interpretation. So, too, do the reasons, given above, for refusing to think of Aristotle as a hedonist.

Likewise it is implausible to ascribe to him the fusionist thesis that adherence to justice, and in general to ethical and social norms, is the *whole* of an individual's well-being. (Rather, such a position might, as we shall see, more credibly be attributed to the Stoics.)[32] According to Aristotle, therefore, ethically virtuous activity can be, at best, something that well-being includes; it cannot be all there is to well-being. Henceforth, therefore, it makes sense for us to set the fusionist reading aside, and to treat the inclusivist reading as the contending hegelian interpretation.

One point of a hegelian inclusivist view is to insist that happiness is a compound of a plurality of parts. That being the case, aiming at happiness amounts in some sense to aiming at its parts as a group. As it stands, this idea is not yet fully or clearly formulated. Nevertheless, even without further ado the inclusivist idea can be seen to fit much of what Aristotle says about *eudaimonia*, and thus, in the respects thus far discussed, to be superior to the kantian reading. It makes ample room, as the kantian reading does not, for his claim that *eudaimonia* is activity, and his evident belief that it is potentially capable of comprising a plurality of activities. Henceforth, therefore, let us take the hegelian inclusivist interpretation to have the best chance, of the traditional accounts, of representing Aristotle's position though, to repeat, it will turn out later that the kantian reading also catches an important aspect of Aristotle's view.[33]

3. The Inclusivist Interpretation and the Charge of 'Egoism'

I turn for a moment to another aspect of the hegelian reading, which has won it considerable favour among interpreters sympathetic to Aristotle's approach. That is its defence against the charge that his position is indefensibly selfish or egoistic. As I have emphasized, the overall hegelian response to Aristotle's ethics is not simply a historical description. It also essentially involves a defence of his thinking by trying to show that it is a viable way of understanding certain central features of practical deliberation. An inclusivist strategy is often employed for this defence.

When Aristotle's views are interpreted in the kantian fashion, they seem wide open to the accusation that they recommend an attitude that is straightforwardly egoistic. Naturally those philosophers who defend egoism will not think of this as an accusation. Others, however, will believe that insofar as Aristotle's thinking fits such a description, it is *eo ipso* subject to criticism. At any rate, the tendency of most kantian-minded philosophers is to take Greek ethics to task on precisely this basis, namely, that it ignores—they assert—the non-self-regarding considerations involved in morality. A principal thrust of the hegelian interpretation, therefore, is its attempt to defend Aristotle against such an attack.

---

[32] See below, Chapter 7, sec. IV. 7.   [33] See below, sec. IX. 4.

The kantian charge that Aristotle's ethics is objectionably egoistic is to a significant extent based on supposing that it recommends an individual's own pleasure as his only ultimate rational aim.[34] On these terms, eudaimonism would not accord any importance to others' well-being, or the pursuit of ethical aims, for their own sake. At best, the kantian reading has it, a eudaimonist can ascribe only instrumental value to ethical activity, as conducive to a desirable state of one's own self in a narrow sense.

Being more sympathetic to Aristotle's position than is the kantian response, the hegelian inclusivist interpreter is inclined to try to find a reply to this criticism.[35] In the present case that is a relatively straightforward task.[36] Under the Greek concept of *eudaimonia*, the inclusivist says that among the parts of happiness we find not only states of the individual himself, but also states that are not self-confined. Rather, a person's happiness can include such external things as conformity to ethical standards and, in addition, the happiness of people other than oneself.[37]

The same idea can be expressed in another way as I have explained earlier. We can maintain that under an inclusivist interpretation, Aristotle's position is only—as Williams puts it—'formally' egoist, not 'substantively' so.[38] The position is formally egoistic, one could say, in that it represents one's ultimate aim linguistically as a state of oneself.[39] It says, that is, 'My ultimate rational aim is *my* well-being'. Nevertheless, Williams's idea continues, the view is not substantively egoist, because the connection of 'my' well-being in this sense with myself is in some sense arbitrary and purely linguistic. As the phrase '"my" well-being' is used here, it does not refer to any self-confined state—any state that really belongs to *me*—but embraces such things as the well-being of other people, the *polis*, and so on, so that good states of others are among the things that I am to seek as I pursue my own well-being.[40]

In parallel, we might then take Aristotle to be saying that a person cannot aim at his own *eudaimonia* without conforming to norms of virtue. Indeed, it appears that on this account, the pursuit of one's own *eudaimonia* simply is 'in part' the pursuit of virtue. If one views the matter in this fashion, one might well think that there can be no conflict between the two.

---

[34] See Chapter 1, sec. V.

[35] As always, the term 'hegelian' refers to a general tendency among interpreters of Greek philosophy, and not necessarily to doctrines propounded by Hegel himself. Nevertheless, there are points of contact with Hegel here. See above, Chapter 1, sec. VII; and Wood 1993: esp. 216–18, 224–9.

[36] See Chapter 1, sec. VII. 2.

[37] See Chapter 1, sec. VII. 2; cf. e.g. Brink 1992, 1997, and 1999 for philosophical development of this idea.

[38] See, for example, Williams 1985: 32, 49–52. In her 1988 and 1993: 127, 224–6, 322–5, Annas advocates a similar view; see also Irwin 1988: 441–2. See above, Chapter 2, sec. III. 2.

[39] See also Field 1932.

[40] A paradox might be thought to arise if it is true both that A's well-being includes B's and that B's includes A's. Various replies to this difficulty are available, however, and it seems to me mistaken to take it to constitute a serious difficulty for the inclusivist position.

Clearly this manner of speaking delivers up an inclusivist interpretation of Aristotle. Its point is to disarm the charge of egoism by showing that the state of oneself that one aims for, on Aristotle's view, is not a self-confined state that attaches merely to oneself, and therefore not a state of oneself that it is selfish to seek. Rather, the claim is, happiness is a state that it is virtuous for a person to be in. It contains parts that are themselves entirely non-selfish, because they are good states of others.

Equally clearly, this inclusivist interpretation has a harmonizing outcome.[41] It lends plausibility to the idea that the aim of one's own well-being is fully compatible with considerations involving the well-being of others and also adherence to the standards of virtue, as Aristotle understands them. A person can seek his own happiness, this view says, while paying due attention to broader norms and aims. Clashes between these two types of aims, it says, need not occur.

IV. The Need for a Non-Harmonizing Interpretation

1. The Controversial Nature of Aristotle's Ethics

In the first five books of the *Ethics*, Aristotle expounds his thinking with measured assurance, often as though no deep opposition to it were even thinkable. That is not all: he also repeatedly defends his views by appeal to the everyday thinking of ordinary people. Consequently it is easy to gain the impression that not only does he believe in a harmony between the standards of virtue and the individual's own good, but that he also takes this harmony to be built into the very concepts that he and his contemporaries employ. If we look at matters in this way, then he emerges as someone who not only believes in this harmony, but also is convinced that—as many hegelian-minded thinkers have supposed—Greek culture itself enshrines this harmony, unreflectively and unselfconsciously, as an integral part of its framework of concepts.

This impression, however, is misleading. In the first place, the *Ethics* is not a plant growing directly and naively from the soil of Greece. It is a meticulously cultivated fruit of self-conscious philosophical reflection, which was produced in a milieu dominated by sophisticated philosophical argument and debate. So also would it have been taken by Aristotle's readers at the time.

Aristotle defines the human good so as to include justice and the other virtues of character—along with, as will emerge soon, the virtues of intellect, too. He might thus seem to suggest that simply by investigating the generally accepted facts about what human well-being is, we can see immediately that ethical conduct is an essential part of it and meshes smoothly with all of its other constituents—in other words, that all of the constituents comprised within *eudaimonia*, including ethically virtuous

---

[41] See e.g. Irwin 1995: 301, 314, with Brink 1992 and White 1999a.

activity, are fully consonant with each other, *and* that Aristotle's contemporaries would acknowledge this state of affairs as guaranteed by the structure of their own ethical concepts.

But it takes only a little examination of the context of Aristotle's work to recognize that his line of thought could not have struck his contemporaries in this way. They knew far too much—just as we do—about the debates that had led up to his own philosophical activity. Any reader of his time would have been able to see instantly that Aristotle was not merely laying bare what could unproblematically be claimed to be the implicit content of Greek ethical concepts, but was rather taking a controversial position on hotly debated issues.

Such a reader would have been fully aware, in particular, of the controversy about the advisability of being just that had raged in the *Republic*. Not just that: in addition, such a reader would have been equally conscious of the issues that had been raised in numerous Sophistic discussions, about whether abiding by ethical standards was reasonable or, as Thrasymachus and others had contended, 'high-minded foolishness'. To a contemporary reader, it would have been immediately evident that the harmony of happiness with ethical activity, which Aristotle's definition seems designed to enshrine, is the very same thing that a lengthy portion of Plato's *Republic* had been devoted to arguing in the most laborious way. Aristotle constructs a powerful position, but he could never have supposed that even those who agreed with him would accept his view as nothing but an uncontroversial and naive articulation of the concepts of his culture or tradition.

Accordingly, no one who interprets Aristotle as believing in a harmony of rational aims should suppose that he treated that idea as a matter of course, or believed it inextricably woven into the concepts that he was using to frame his position. Rather, such an interpreter would have to show how he could have argued for such a position and have disarmed not only widespread doubts about its tenability, but also a propensity—like the one exhibited by Thrasymachus—to pooh-pooh any claim of a harmony between well-being and virtue. Opponents like Thrasymachus would be ready to point to notorious instances in which virtuous actions ostensibly detract from an individual's own good, and do not at all seem to be a part of it. Aristotle was in no position simply to ignore such sources of opposition.

If the hegelian response to Aristotle is correct, then, that cannot be so because of some harmonious conception of *eudaimonia* that he and other Greeks would have recognized as uncontroversially given to them by their culture or conceptual scheme. More than that, however, the hegelian interpretation of Aristotle ultimately does not succeed. It fails at precisely that point at which it sees in Aristotle's ethics an effort to advance the hegelian harmonizing project. For however much Aristotle's inclusivist position may seem to resemble the thinking that the hegelian response wishes to find in him, his view does not aim primarily at harmony and does not hold out a hope of achieving it. Aristotle does maintain, to be sure, that a bad man is subject to certain internal conflicts from which a good man is free.[42] But Aristotle's scheme, as will become clear in the rest of this chapter, expressly admits other conflicts among rational ends, even those pursued by the good man. On this point Aristotle is entirely candid.

2. Millian Inclusivism

One of the factors that helps sustain harmonizing interpretations is a particular way of understanding Aristotle's classification of goods, and thus his view of the relation between happiness and the parts that make it up. On this account, there is in a certain sense no distinction between a person's aiming at a given part of happiness and his aiming at the whole of it.

We can approach this matter by considering what might appear at first sight to be a contradiction in Aristotle's thinking. On the one hand he says that ethically virtuous action is done for its own sake. However, he also says that everything is done for the sake of happiness. How can these two statements be reconciled?

One way that suggests itself is to maintain that in a sense there is really no distinction between ethically virtuous action and happiness, and that therefore aiming at the one is the same as aiming at the other. This is much the same as Mill's idea, introduced earlier, that '[i]n being desired for its own sake [a thing] is . . . desired as a part of happiness. The person is made, or he thinks he would be made, happy by its mere possession; and is made unhappy by failure to obtain it.'[44] Mill takes this to imply that 'there is in reality *nothing desired except happiness*'.[44] That would answer the question raised in the previous paragraph: ethically virtuous action would be done for its own sake, and 'in' being so done, it would supposedly be done for the sake of one's happiness.

I observed that Mill appears to be taking for granted that there is no conflict between seeking to be virtuous and seeking to be happy, and that such an assumption, if left unargued, raises difficulty for his view. The same would be true of Aristotle, if his thinking were indeed the same as Mill's.

Aristotle's view, however, is different from Mill's and is not subject to the problems that afflict it.[45] The relation between parts of happiness and happiness, as aims, does not appear to be the one that Mill attempts to describe. Rather, I shall argue, Aristotle

---

[42] e.g. *Nic. Eth.* IX. 4, 1166a13–15, 26–8, b6–29; IX. 6, 1167b5–15.

[43] See Chapter 2, sec. I. 4.

[44] Mill 1871: ch. 4, with my emphasis. As noted in Chapter 2 above, a similar idea can be found in Joseph Butler's eleventh sermon. Irwin uses this idea extensively in both his interpretation of Aristotle (e.g. 1988: 392–3, 405–6). Irwin's thought is that this could not be so if acting virtuously merely led causally to well-being, or if the former is desired as a *means* to the latter rather than as a 'part' of it. A very similar interpretation of Aristotle is given by John McDowell, esp. in his 1996, but also in 1978, 1979, and 1980. Irwin also uses the same idea to interpret Plato, in his 1977: 254–9, 341.

[45] For further problems in Mill's idea, see White 1999b.

believes that some parts of an individual's happiness are aimed at both for their own sake and also for the sake of their contribution, whether causal or otherwise, to happiness. (Other subsidiary aims, on the other hand, are valued only contributively and not for themselves.) Thus there are two distinct ways in which such a thing can be valued, for itself and for its relation to another thing. Thus it is not a matter, as it is in Mill, of something's being valued for itself and 'therein' being valued for the sake of one's happiness.

3. The Notion of a Thing's Being both Good for Itself and for its Contribution to Happiness

We can begin to treat this matter by noting one thing that Aristotle does not say: he does not say that *eudaimonia* is the *only* thing that people seek for its own sake, full stop. Instead he says in *Nicomachean Ethics* I—and he repeats this formulation in *Nicomachean Ethics* X[46]—that *eudaimonia* is the only thing that people seek for its own sake *alone*. He thus leaves the way open to say, as he will later, that there are other things that people seek for their own sake *as well as* for the sake of *eudaimonia*. Such things are doubly worthwhile, as it were: they are valuable in themselves, but they are also valuable for the contribution that they make to, or the role that they play in, a person's overall well-being.[47] The fact that other things besides *eudaimonia* are in part worthwhile for themselves throws important light on Aristotle's eudaimonism. That light allows us to understand features of it that are lost to view in the normal harmonizing interpretations.

When he comes to describing the value of ethically virtuous action, then, Aristotle states that a person should engage in virtuous activity 'for itself' and also that one should do so 'for the sake of the noble (*to kalon*)'.[48] About virtuous acts, he says:

> if the acts that are in accordance with the virtues have themselves a certain character, it does not follow that they are done justly or temperately. The agent also must be in a certain condition when he does them; in the first place he must have knowledge, secondly he must choose the acts, and choose them *for their own sakes*, and thirdly his action must proceed from a firm and unchangeable character.[49]

---

[46] See *Nic. Eth.* X. 6, 1176b5.

[47] This point is recognized by e.g. Ackrill 1980: 23, Annas 1993: 372, and (by implication) Cooper 1980: 315–16; see also White 1981, Heinaman 1988: 53, and Kenny 1992: 91, 92. It is by now widely recognized that, as Allan, Ackrill, and others point out, we can think of this 'role' or 'contribution' as either a cause—in which case the thing in question is of the nature of a *means* to happiness—or else as a part (in some sense), in which case it is probably best not thought of as a means. See Allan 1953 and 1955, Ackrill 1980: 29. Aristotle's terminology has it that such a thing is *pros*, 'in relation to', a *telos* or end.

[48] Ross sometimes translates this phrase, 'for honour's sake,' which is extremely misleading in view of Aristotle's denial that honour is good for itself (1095b26–30).

[49] *Nic. Eth.* 1105a28–38.

He also says, about brave action in particular:

Now the brave man is as dauntless as man may be. Therefore, while he will fear even the things that are not beyond human strength, he will face them as he ought and as the rule directs, *for the sake of the noble (to kalon); for this is the end of virtue.*[50]

Aristotle also maintains something analogous to this about the most genuine kind of friendship. He says that when one does something for someone who is a friend in the strictest sense, one does it 'for his sake': 'those who wish well to their friends for their sake are most truly friends.' Aristotle takes this to be something that is generally believed: '[T]o a friend, people say, we ought to wish what is good for his sake.'[51]

Earlier I raised the question how these statements can be squared with Aristotle's assertion that we aim at everything for the sake of happiness. By far the simplest and most natural way is to deploy Aristotle's idea, which I have stressed above, that a thing can often be aimed at both for its own sake and for the sake of something else, partly for the one and partly for the other. During his discussion of the human good, he says:

Now we call that which is in itself worthy of pursuit more final than that which is worthy of pursuit for the sake of something else, and that which is never desirable for the sake of something else more final than the things that *are desirable both* in themselves *and* for the sake of that other thing.[52]

The word 'never' in the second line might make the reader suppose that in Aristotle's view a thing is, on each occasion, pursued either solely for itself or else solely for the sake of something else, but that we never aim at anything on both accounts. It seems to me that this would be a very strange thing for Aristotle to assume without argument, but at any rate the rest of the quotation indicates that such an interpretation would be mistaken. In a moment I shall explain some of what is at stake in this fact.

The rest of the passage then continues:

and therefore we call final without qualification that which is always desirable in itself and never for the sake of something else. Now such a thing happiness (*eudaimonia*), above all else, is held to be; for this we choose always for itself and never for the sake of something else.

What distinguishes the human good or happiness, therefore, is that it is aimed at *only* for its own sake, whereas other things can be aimed at for it *and* for themselves:

but honour, pleasure, reason, *and every virtue* we choose indeed *for themselves* (for if nothing resulted from them we should still choose each of them), but we choose them *also for the sake*

---

[50] *Nic. Eth.* 1105a28–38 and 1115b10–13. Compare also 1116b2–3, 1120a23–6, quoted in Chapter 3, sec. VII. 8, and 1122b6–7.

[51] *Nic. Eth.* 1156b9–10, 1155b31, 1168b3.

[52] *Nic. Eth.* 1097a30–4. Cf. Cooper 1975: 92, 106–10, and e.g. Heinaman 1988: 52–3, Stocker 1990: 70, and Kenny 1992: 8, 90.

of happiness, judging that *through them we shall be happy*. Happiness, on the other hand, no one chooses for the sake of these, nor, in general, for anything other than itself.[53]

Here, too, Aristotle evidently allows that in our reflections on virtue and the like, we see at one and the same time that they are choiceworthy on two counts: for themselves and because 'through these (*dia touton*) we shall be happy'.

It thus seems to me evident that in these passages, Aristotle maintains that as we think about these matters, we sometimes treat things as worth pursuing on two accounts at once: for themselves and for the sake of happiness. This point will emerge more fully as we proceed.[54]

A hegelian interpreter will tend to construe Aristotle differently. Taking a cue from the idea of Mill's cited above, such a reader might suppose Aristotle to be saying that when something other than happiness is aimed at for itself, it is *by that very fact* being aimed at for the sake of happiness—in Mill's words again, '*in being* desired for its own sake [a thing] is . . . desired as a part of happiness'. On this interpretation, we should think of pursuing happiness and pursuing each of its constituents as one and the same thing.[55] That would fit with the idea that, according to Aristotle, no conflict or inconsistency could arise among those constituents.

Aristotle's words, however, seem to me to point decisively away from the hegelian reading. Mill, in order to make his point, has to explain painstakingly and emphatically that although happiness is our ultimate end we can *still* seek virtue for its own sake, precisely because in spite of the verbal difference between them, these two aims are really in some sense the same. Aristotle, on the other hand, says simply that we pursue some thing, including virtue, '*both* for themselves . . . *and* for the sake of happiness (*kai . . . kai . . .*)'. That sounds to me too much like a way of giving two reasons, and too little like a way of saying with Mill that, appearances notwithstanding, there is really only one.

Aristotle holds, then, that morally virtuous activity and beneficent activity towards

---

[53] *Nic. Eth.* 1097a30–b6.

[54] Korsgaard 1986 proposes interpreting *teleion* as meaning 'unconditional'. This seems to me not to fit Aristotle's explanation of the matter, though what he said would have been interesting if that were what he meant. Korsgaard maintains that the usual interpretation 'makes what Aristotle says absurd' (490). She believes it absurd, that is, to maintain that what is aimed at only for its own sake is more desirable than what is aimed at both for itself and for something else. Perhaps. That depends, though, on what one means by 'desirable'. Aristotle's claim means, one might say, that such a final end is to be preferred to anything else. But what does 'preferred' mean? Not that the thing is to be chosen over other things in all circumstances. As we shall see, Aristotle does not believe that, since he is not claiming that *theôria* is to be maximized. Rather, he means that such a final end is to be chosen as the end of life, i.e. the thing to which one's life is to be 'devoted' in the sense that I shall develop (sec. VI). In that sense, however, it does not seem to me absurd to maintain that the most final thing is the most desirable. (Also relevant to this issue is the fact pointed up by Santas 1989: esp. 93–4, that there are substantial differences between two notions of goodness with which Aristotle operates, an orectic notion and a functional notion.)

[55] See Chapter 2, sec. I. 4, with its references to the use of Mill by Irwin 1977 and to McDowell 1996.

friends are each doubly worthwhile: both for themselves, and also for the fact that they contribute to one's happiness.[56] That, then, is why he says, not that happiness is the only thing aimed at for itself, but that it is the only thing aimed at for its own sake alone. These other, doubly worthwhile things count, therefore, as constituents of happiness that nevertheless also have value on their own account.

Within this framework, Aristotle expounds a view of what is worthwhile for a human being to aim at. According to this view, some goods must be sacrificed if others are to be fully realized. To explain the conceptual grounds that give rise to this situation is a philosophical matter of some intricacy. I shall say something about it in due course. The principal point, however, is Aristotle's acknowledgement of the fact of conflict among aims. His exposition of his position incorporates no attempt to conceal it or lessen its impact.

4. Uneliminated Conflicts in Aristotle

We are now in a position to recognize that neither Aristotle's conceptual apparatus in the *Nicomachean Ethics*, nor the expectations with which he could have expected his readers to approach it, are set up so as automatically to provide for a harmony or consistency of worthwhile human aims. On the basis of what we have seen so far, therefore, I take that we have ample basis for looking in his writings for evidence of conflicts, and specifically conflicts of the kind that would disconfirm harmonizing inclusivist interpretations.

The main forces that generate the Aristotelian conflicts that are most significant for the topic of this book centre on two points: *theôria*, or philosophical contemplation, and *philia*, friendship. The latter is treated in *Nicomachean Ethics* Books VIII–IX and the former is discussed in Book X. I shall consider *theôria* at some length and then turn to *philia*. The former conflict, as indeed it has often been interpreted, is a straightforward confrontation of what later came to be called the *vita contemplativa* and the *vita activa*. In some ways it resembles Plato's conflict in the *Republic* between philosophizing and ruling. The issue of *philia*, for its part, turns on whether one's goal in friendship is one's own good or the good of one's friend.

In both of these cases, Aristotle presents a pair of aims that a person cannot pursue completely, but he does not suggest that there is a harmonious way of combining them both so that no significant loss will result. The conflict must be *adjudicated* and settled by making a choice, not *eliminated* or shown to be illusory.[57]

---

[56] Aristotle does not offer a full account of what it means to aim at something partly for its own sake and partly for the sake of something else. On the other hand, he does give us a hint of what he means. A thing is valued partly for its own sake, he says, if we would seek it even if nothing else came from it. See further White 1988a and Reeve 1995: 116.

[57] For the distinction between settling a conflict and dissolving it, see Chapter 1, sec. VII. 5.

V. The Question of Conflict within Ethical Virtue

1. The Absence of the Issue from Aristotle's Agenda

Before I take up these two matters, however, it will be advisable to say something about another possible locus of deliberative conflict. The question at issue here is whether it is possible, according to Aristotle, for two considerations falling under the heading of ethical virtue to oppose each other, whether resolubly or irresolubly. There are indications in Aristotle's texts that point in the direction of both an affirmative and a negative answer.

This kind of conflict, it should be remarked, is not directly germane to the main subject of the present investigation. My concern in this chapter is focused chiefly on the question whether Aristotle's thinking allows for the possibility of conflicts between one's own good and non-self-regarding considerations, or between considerations that are self-confined and aims that are external, or some combination of these two types of conflict. Conflicts within ethical virtue, on the whole, have a different character. For the most part they would, should they occur, set broader or external considerations against other aims of the same kind.

The question, however, is whether Aristotle thinks they do occur. Here it appears to me that the evidence available to us does not allow a clear-cut answer. There are some indications that he admits such clashes of ethical considerations with each other. On the other hand, he also says things that seem to exclude them. The conclusion that I shall draw is that he does not settle the issue.

More strikingly, he does not pose it in any explicit way at all. This fact, and the inconclusiveness of the evidence that I have just mentioned, are together uncomfortable for those who have argued vigorously on both sides of the question and have clearly believed that it was of great moment to Aristotle to come down resoundingly on one side or the other.

More recently it has been argued by some that Aristotle does admit conflicts within ethical virtue. Two different such suggestions should be noted. One is the claim by Nussbaum that it is central to Aristotle's outlook to recognize such conflicts, and that this is a significant disagreement between him and Plato.[58] A different suggestion has been made by Stocker. According to it, Aristotle recognizes cases of what are sometimes called 'dirty hands', in which an obligatory or reasonable action can nevertheless be wrong or even worse than wrong.

Although I think that there is room for reasonable disagreement about whether one or both of these suggestions is correct, I do not think that we should ascribe a par-

---

[58] See Nussbaum 1986: chs. 11–12, and esp. pp. 335–6 and 353, and Sherman 1989: 30–1, 105–6. See, however, Nussbaum 1994: 480, where she speaks of 'the Aristotelian, who so wants all of life to fit harmoniously together'. See also Stocker 1990: 51ff.

ticularly important place to either of them in our reading of Aristotle. Regardless of whether they are right, there is no call whatever to think that Aristotle made a *special point* of either denying or asserting the existence of conflicts within ethical virtue. In the first place, some things that he says do bear on Nussbaum's interpretation, to be sure. But nowhere does he announce where he stands on the matter or say that it is something that concerns him. Most of the time, in fact, his attitude towards questions about conflicts among ethical virtues seems to be one of indifference. By contrast, as we shall see, he does raise questions about possible clashes between aims that are self-regarding, or *mutatis mutandis* self-confined, and aims that are not so.[59] As for Stocker's reading, it can be said that although Aristotle probably does raise the possibility of clashes of the sort that might be classified under the heading 'dirty hands', they are not a focus of his attention. Indeed, the whole drift of his treatment of ethical virtue, including his consistent tendency *not* to give more than very cursory attention to any questions at all about conflicts within ethical virtue, make it implausible to maintain, I contend, that it was central to his purposes either to assert or to deny the possibility of conflicts within this area.

2. The Question of Conflicts between Ethical Virtues

Let us briefly survey some of the evidence that is relevant to conflict among ethical considerations. I shall focus first on whether Aristotle admits conflicts between different virtues.

The strongest reason for supposing that Aristotle rejects the possibility of this sort of conflict consists in his assertion that the virtues are inseparable. He says:

It is clear, then, ... that it is not possible to be good in the strict sense without practical wisdom (*phronêsis*), not practically wise without ethical excellence. But in this way we may also refute the dialectical argument whereby it might be contended that the excellences exist in separation from each other; the same man, it might be said, is not best equipped by nature for all the excellences, so that he will already have acquired one when he has not yet acquired another. This is possible in respect of the natural excellences, but not in respect of those in respect of which a man is called without qualification good; for with the presence of the one quality, practical wisdom, will be given all the excellences.[60]

This passage tells us that although the 'natural' virtues—the not-yet-cultivated virtues of a young person—may not all be present together in one person, a *mature* virtue that is supported by practical wisdom does imply the presence of all of the other

---

[59] There is a way of straddling the line between saying that there are conflicts and that there are not (see Chapter 8, sec. V. 1 and its n. 25; and Annas 1993: 44–6, 445).

[60] *Nic. Eth.* 1144b30–1145a6. I have substituted 'ethical' for 'moral' in Ross's translation, for reasons given in Chapter 2, sec. IV. 2. See also 1130a8–13.

virtues. This in turn appears to imply that whenever practical wisdom takes into account the considerations relevant to one virtue, and reaches a conclusion about what to do in accordance with it, that conclusion will be consonant with the considerations bearing on all other virtues as well. For otherwise what Aristotle says here would seemingly have no tendency to show, as he takes it to, that the virtues are not separable.

There are passages that might be argued to indicate that Aristotle recognizes such conflicts in particular cases, and that appear to preclude us from saying that his conception of virtue involves no psychological conflict at all.[61] On the whole, Aristotle maintains that the virtue of moderation (*sôphrosynê*) involves experiencing only so much enjoyment of a given pleasure as fits the value attached to it by rational assessment.[62] His view of some other virtues, however, might be claimed to be different. For instance, speaking of bravery, he says: 'it is not the case ... with all the virtues that the exercise of them is pleasant, except in so far as it reaches its end'. The brave man, he says, will be pained at the thought of losing the things, in particular his life, that he may sacrifice in doing a brave action:

death and wounds will be painful to the brave man and against his will, but he will face them because it is noble to do so or because it is base not to do so. And the more he is possessed of virtue in its entirety and the happier he is, the more he will be pained at the thought of death; for life is best worth living for such a man, and he is knowingly losing the greatest of goods, and this is painful. But he is nonetheless brave.[63]

It would be inadvisable, however, to claim to find in these lines a clear conflict within virtue. The passage does not, to be sure, paint a portrait of complete serenity and satisfaction. It is less obvious, however, exactly what Aristotle takes the conflict or problem to be. Perhaps this is indeed a clash between the exercise of bravery and the person's happiness; that is in one way suggested by Aristotle's wording. On the other hand, Aristotle might just as well have in mind an opposition of bravery to 'virtue in its entirety', that is, to the rest of the virtues that a person might exhibit if bravery did not lead him to his death. Or perhaps Aristotle has both types of conflict in mind without taking the trouble to focus the reader on the difference between them. Or, finally, he might simply be claiming that it is disappointing, from the viewpoints of both happiness and virtue, that this sacrifice of his life was necessary. Given the situation he was

---

[61] *Top.* 105b19–26 mentions a case in which one's parents and the laws give conflicting injunctions. It is worth emphasizing how rarely such cases are explicitly presented in the ethical treatises themselves. Cf. Annas 1993: 28.

[62] See Urmson 1988: 28–8, 67–70.

[63] *Nic. Eth.* III. 9, 1117b7–16. Compare 1169a18–b2, which is cited by Nussbaum 1986: 336. It is not evident that this passage presents a situation which a good man experiences as a conflict; it may simply report what choices such a person would make. But in either case, the terms of the conflict are unclearly marked, just as they are in the passage quoted.

forced into, he is not ambivalent; but his virtue and his happiness would both have been better served if the situation had never arisen.[64]

What Aristotle says about voluntary action raises rather similar interpretative difficulties. Having defined such actions as those whose 'principle is in the agent', Aristotle goes on to add that in some cases a person would not choose such an action 'in itself' (*kath' hauto*). He continues:

For such actions men are sometimes even praised, when they endure something base or painful in return for great and noble objects gained . . . On some actions praise indeed is not bestowed, but pardon is, when one does what he ought not under pressure which overstrains human nature and which no one could withstand . . . It is difficult sometimes to determine what should be chosen and at what cost.[65]

Plainly there is some kind of motivational clash here. But what is said to clash with what? On the one side, clearly, is some kind of virtue. What is on the other side? Something that 'strains' a person (*hyperteinei*), and which raises in the agent the question what is worth enduring for what. Again we cannot tell whether it is a consideration arising from some other virtue.

What is in question here is not whether there is a conflict—for there is no question about that—but rather what sort of conflict Aristotle had in mind. Moreover, the mention of such oppositions fits well with an aspect of Aristotle's view that we have seen already. The occurrence of this kind of conflict of motivation, even in someone who is virtuous, is part of the reason why sometimes, as I have explained earlier, Aristotle allows norms of virtue to be expressed in imperative form.[66] Insofar as a virtuous action runs counter to an emotion, it meets resistance. To that extent, it makes sense for Aristotle to think of the recommendation to do the action as taking the form of a command—of being something that one 'ought' to do (*dei*), rather than merely an act whose performance is in Sidgwick's term 'attractive'. The 'ought' may not be an 'ought' of morality—that is a separate issue—but it is an imperative nevertheless.

3. *The Question of Conflicts between Virtuous Actions*

Although it appears from the foregoing discussion that Aristotle gives mixed signals about whether he believes in conflicts between distinct ethical virtues, the difficulty may be argued to be only a superficial one. Although Aristotle indicates that the ethical *virtues* are inseparable as dispositions—that is, that if a person has one then he has them all—it might be argued that such a view leaves open the possibility that sometimes the particular *actions* recommended by them might in some cases be

---

[64] Here I am indebted to a reader for Oxford University Press.
[65] *Nic. Eth.* III. 1, 1110a20–9.   [66] See Chapter 3, sec. VII.

incompatible.[67] For example, it might be contended, a person who is just must be brave and vice versa, but nevertheless bravery might in a particular case call for an action that justice rules out. Then doing the brave action might in some cases violate justice, but without calling into question the person's entitlement to be called just or to be said to have a just character.

Perhaps this is indeed how we should take Aristotle, but there is an obstacle to this interpretation in the passage, quoted earlier, that states the inseparability of the virtues. That passage explicitly calls attention to the role of practical wisdom in making genuine virtues inseparable. It suggests that although the 'natural' tendencies underlying virtue can be possessed in isolation, the intelligent reflection made possible by practical wisdom will join the mature virtues together, precisely by thinking through individual situations and seeing that what each virtue calls for fits with what is called for by each other virtue. Aristotle says nothing about the possibility that practical reason might ever end in a dilemma. Moreover, if he had, it would have cast his argument for the inseparability of the virtues into doubt, and would at the least have required him to explain why his conclusion held up nevertheless.

On balance, therefore, it seems unclear just what Aristotle's position is on the question whether conflicts really can, according to his view, arise within ethical virtue. If he allows them at all, it seems, it is only to mention them in passing, without commenting on their significance for his contention that the virtues are always exemplified together.

Certainly there is no evidence that within his ethics Aristotle believes that the existence of conflict among aims would be a good thing, or that he was exhilarated by such conflict in the way in which Nietzsche was.[68] He indicates that it is characteristic of the bad man to be subject to conflict, and never maintains that either a good man or a good man's life would be the better for being in such a condition.[69] It is plain that he regards the division into reason and appetite, for instance, as part of human nature, and thus as an inevitable aspect of human life.[70] However, the idea that it is a good thing or something to be welcomed about being human makes no appearance in his writings.

Accordingly it is unlikely that Aristotle saw any need to place much stress either on

---

[67] This point is made by Sherman 1989: 105–6; Nussbaum 1986 does not mention the passage quoted above, 1144b30–1145a6, nor acknowledge the problem raised for her thesis by its contention that the ethical virtues are inseparable.

[68] Something like this is claimed by Nussbaum 1986: 341, 353, but she seems to me to produce no evidence in suppport of it. What she does adduce is evidence that Aristotle allows that conflicts of some kinds do inevitably occur in human beings, but such evidence does support an ascription to him of the idea that it is valuable. Aristotle's treatment of tragic conflicts in the *Poetics* appears to me to have no such implication for his ethical views.

[69] *Nic. Eth.* IX. 4, 1166a13–15, 26–8, b6–29; IX. 6, 1167b5–15. The point applies especially to the akratic man (e.g. 1166b8), but also holds more generally of the bad man.   [70] *Nic. Eth.* X. 7

asserting the existence of such conflicts or on denying it. Perhaps we should conclude that he tended to assume as a theoretical matter that the virtues are inseparable, but recognized as an observed fact that sometimes they seem to oppose each other. The former thesis might naturally have seemed acceptable, in view of the fact that Socrates was well known to have advanced the claim that the virtues are not merely inseparable but are even in some sense all the same.[71] The counterexamples might have seemed unexceptionable, but not important enough to precipitate a full-scale examination of how the general thesis might be squared with them. The issue that they raise seems important to us, but to Aristotle—who after all maintains stoutly that we are not to expect precision in ethics, and that most ethical claims can be expected to admit of exceptions—it does not seem to have required a thorough treatment.

4. Aristotle's Indifference to the Issue

Though the cases of this type are multifarious, one illustrative sort of case involves actions which, though they are entirely justified under the circumstances (and which may even be necessary for *eudaimonia*), one should nevertheless regret doing *even in* those very circumstances.[72] Aristotle cites, for instance, the jettisoning of cargo, an action which is necessary for avoiding the foundering of the ship. Another is a case in which someone is forced to do something base because a tyrant has in his power the person's parents and children.[73]

One important point to notice here, in connection with the preceding section, is that Aristotle never describes such cases as those in which virtues clash, either in the sense that they would make it impossible to possess both of a pair of virtues, or in the sense that the cases might illustrate the impossibility of exhibiting two virtues at once. This may seem surprising, but it exhibits, at the least, a notable fact about Aristotle's tendencies in labelling conduct by means of virtue terminology.

Even more striking, however, is the fact that Aristotle does not introduce these cases under any such heading as 'conflicts of ethical conduct'.[74] Rather, they are brought to bear principally on the question which actions are *voluntary*, and Aristotle's point is that such actions need not be involuntary. This seems to me quite striking. For rather than raising the question, 'Can there be conflicts involving conduct relevant to ethical virtue?', let alone the question, 'Can there be conflicts between the virtues?', Aristotle simply makes no mention of such constellations of

---

[71] This view is ascribed to Socrates in e.g. Plato's *Protagoras*.

[72] Stocker 1990: 54–6, 66, though see also his 70, where he maintains, as I have here, that there may also be 'non-eudaimonic' values.

[73] *Nic. Eth.* 1109a9ff.

[74] I thus take it to be something of an exaggeration to say, as Stocker does (1990: 51), that 'the topic of dirty hands and conflicts of values ... [lies] at the heart of Aristotle's ethics'. That might be our considered view of the matter, but it was not Aristotle's.

problems, and introduces such cases within the context of a quite different discussion of quite different issues. Make of that what one may, the fact is that the issue of ethical conflict does not seem to have presented itself to him as a salient one.

There is yet a further point to be made, which will emerge most clearly after the discussion in the next section of how Aristotle treats the relation between *theôria* and ethical virtue. There we shall see a conflict that in some ways is structurally similar to cases of 'dirty hands' in the sense at issue here. As I shall argue, Aristotle maintains that although the life of *theôria* is better than the life of ethically virtuous activity, and is to be chosen over it and indeed over any other life, there is nevertheless still a sense in which the life of ethically virtuous activity is good in itself, and one's lack of an opportunity to engage in it is a real loss. This is a conflict of value, I take it, but not, however, a conflict within ethical virtue itself. Instead, it is a conflict between ethical and intellectual virtue. It is also, I shall further argue, a conflict between a fundamentally self-regarding sort of life and a sort of life that is, at least in substantial part, other-regarding.

VI. Theôria

1. The Emergence of the 'Best and Most Complete' Virtue

In *Nicomachean Ethics* I, Aristotle states that the human good is 'activity of the soul in accordance with virtue'. As it stands, this statement seems to presuppose that virtue can be treated as one single thing, free of internal division. Immediately afterwards, however, Aristotle cancels any such automatic presupposition when he adds, 'or if there is more than one virtue, in accordance with the best and most complete'. He is subsequently forced to exploit this latter option, and to try to discover just which of the virtues is indeed the 'best and most complete'. At the beginning of chapter 7 of Book X, the last book of the *Nicomachean Ethics*, he says: 'If happiness is activity in accordance with virtue, it is reasonable that it should be in accordance with the highest virtue; and this will be the best thing in us.' By the end of chapter 8 of Book X, then, happiness turns out not to be activity in accordance with virtue *simpliciter*, or with all of the virtues, but activity in accordance with one virtue.[75]

In the last chapter of Book I of *Nicomachean Ethics*, Aristotle says that there are two kinds of virtue, virtue of character and virtue of intellect. He treats the virtues of character in Books II–V. Then he turns in Book VI to virtue of intellect. So far, he has said nothing about whether there can be conflicts among the virtues or the corresponding activities. In *Nicomachean Ethics* X. 6–8, however, it emerges explicitly that there are two types of activity that are candidates for the title of happiness. One is the intellec-

---

[75] See Kenny 1992: 17–18, who says (rightly, in my view) that in Bk. I of the *Nicomachean Ethics* Aristotle leaves the way open for his conclusion in Bk. X that the life of *theôria* is the best life.

tual activity of *theôria* or philosophical thought. The other is practical activity in accordance with virtue of character, which he equates to civic activity and statesmanship having to do with the *polis*.

As Aristotle presents matters, the fundamental question in the final chapters of the *Ethics* is this: to which type of activity—*theôria* or ethically virtuous action—is the pre-eminently happy human life devoted, in whatever sense of 'devoted' may be relevant? The fundamental point to recognize is that Aristotle treats this state of affairs, not as manifesting a dualism that is to be *eliminated*, by showing that there really is no conflict between the two types of activity, but as a conflict to be *adjudicated*, by deciding which of the two rival claimants must be chosen.[76] The possibility of reconciling the two, or of combining the two types of activity into a life that harmonizes and fully realizes them both, as we shall see, does not come into the picture.[77]

2. Theôria *and Ethically Virtuous Activity*

In Aristotle's view, the best activity is *theôria*. It is superior to its only potential rival, practically virtuous activity or, in other words, activity in accordance with virtue of character. 'Perfect happiness', he says, 'is contemplative (*theoretikê*)'; 'complete happiness of a man', he repeats, is 'contemplative . . . activity of reason'; the human activity that is most akin to the 'contemplative activity' of a deity is the 'happiest'.[78]

Aristotle ranks ethically virtuous activity behind *theôria* on several counts. *Theôria* is more self-sufficient than practical activity, more leisurely, more continuous, and also valuable only for itself and not for the sake of anything else.[79] By contrast, practical activity is sometimes onerous and is tied to the seeking of further ends:

the action of the statesman is . . . unleisurely, and aims—beyond the political action itself—at despotic power and honours, or at all events happiness, for him and his fellow citizens—a happiness different from political action, and evidently sought as being different . . . But the activity of reason which is contemplative seems both to be superior in serious worth and to aim at no end beyond itself.[80]

Aristotle does not here cancel his earlier assertion, which I have stressed, that ethically virtuous activity is worthwhile partly for itself. He contends, however, that such activity is valuable not only for itself but also for the sake of other ends too, including

---

[76] Recall Chapter 2, sec. VII. 2.

[77] This point is stressed by Kenny 1992: esp. 29 with 23–6, 28, as against e.g. Ackrill 1981: 140–1, who argues for an interpretation according to which 'there cannot, at bottom, be any conflict between morality and philosophy'.

[78] See respectively 1177a17–8; 1177b19–20, 24–5; and 1178b21–3.

[79] See respectively 1177a27–b1, 21–2 (on *autarkeia* or self-sufficiency), b4–15, 17–18 (leisureliness), 1177a21–2 and b22 (continuousness), and 1177b13–14, 18–21 (being worthwhile for its own sake alone).

[80] *Nic. Eth.* 1177b12–15, 17–20.

power and honour and also happiness itself.[81] *Theôria*, by contrast, is worthwhile for its own sake alone:

[*Theôria*] alone would seem to be loved for its own sake; for nothing arises from it apart from the contemplating, while from practical activities we gain more or less apart from the action.[82]

Thus *theôria* can lay claim to the title of *eudaimonia* itself.

Aristotle's conclusion in *Nicomachean Ethics* X involves a comparison not only of two activities, but also of two lives that are given over respectively to them. He maintains not only that *theôria* is superior to ethically virtuous activity, but also that the life devoted to the former is superior to the life devoted to the latter:

that which is proper to each thing is by nature best and most pleasant for each thing; for man, therefore, the life according to theoretical reason (*nous*) is best and pleasantest, since reason more than anything else *is* man. This life, therefore, is also the happiest.[83]

3. Theôria *in Human Life*

Aristotle cannot be said to have made it entirely clear what he takes the life 'of' *theôria*—the *bios theôrêtikos* or 'theoretic life'—to be, and this fact has led some modern interpreters to think that he cannot have given *theôria* the pre-eminence in the best life that his words seem clearly to imply. There is a fear, for instance, that the life of *theôria* might involve refusing to lift a finger to help a drowning child if that effort would rob a few seconds from philosophic thought.[84] Such an implication would not merely violate what seems to be ethical common sense—not to mention the importance that kantian-minded readers accord to morality.[85] It also seems to make pointless the large amount of energy that the *Nicomachean Ethics* devotes to ethical virtue. For this reason, some interpreters have strived to read Aristotle in some other way, so as to make *theôria* less important in his account of human happiness—but to be

---

[81] *Nic. Eth.* 1177b4–15.

[82] See 1177b 2–4 and 20.

[83] *Nic. Eth.* 1178a4–7. Instead of 'theoretical reason', Ross's translation has only 'reason'. *Nous*, however, is the term that Aristotle uses in these chapters to designate the element of a human being that engages in *theôria*.

[84] On the imputation of this implication to certain such interpretation, see the discussion in Kenny 1992: 89–90 and Devereux 1977.

[85] For a discussion of Kant's reason for denying that contemplation is unconditionally valuable, see Korsgaard 1986: 503–4. Certainly the idea that if we interpret Aristotle as thinking that the life of *theôria* is the best life, we shall be taking him to undervalue morality, has been a strong stimulus to try to read him otherwise. However (as Morrison 1999: 159 rightly observes), Aristotle certainly holds that an apolitical life of *theôria* is a very good life indeed, good enough that he is likely to be subject to this charge under any plausible interpretation, so that we can do him relatively little charity after all—by *that* standard—if we refrain from ascribing to him the view that the life of *theôria* is the best life.

instead the focus of divine happiness—and ethically virtuous activity to be more weighty.

It does not appear, however, that the importance of *theôria* can be downplayed in this way. It bears reiterating, for one thing, that according to Aristotle, the life of *theôria* is better than the life of ethically virtuous activity not merely in some general way, but specifically for a human being. It is true that Aristotle introduces an objection to this contention, which takes the form of a claim that the life of *theôria* is 'too high for a man' and is more correctly regarded as the life of a deity.[86] But Aristotle responds to this objection immediately by arguing that in any case the part of a person that engages in *theôria* is, in an important sense, that person himself and furthermore the best part of him.[87] Plainly there is room to ask, as a philosophical matter, just how convincing Aristotle's response to the objection is, and in particular what the meaning is of his seeming identification of the human being with the theorizing part of him. Nevertheless it seems evident that he takes himself thereby to have rebutted the objection, and does not reintroduce it.

He does, to be sure, introduce two similar ideas, which he does not, however, take to contradict his claim that the life of *theôria* is the happiest life. One idea has it that 'the life in accordance with the other kind of virtue', virtue of character, is happy 'in a secondary way' (*deuterôs*).[88] The other is that the life of *theôria*, though declared to be the happiest life for a human being, will itself contain a certain amount of ethically virtuous activity: 'But, being a man, one will also need external prosperity; for our nature is not self-sufficient for the purpose of contemplation, but our body must also be healthy and have food and other attention.'[89] He goes on to say, however, that the activities necessitated by this fact require 'only moderate advantages'.[90] He then expatiates on this theme. He adduces arguments, and also the testimony of Solon and Anaxagoras, for saying that someone can act virtuously even with moderate means. At the end of his discussion, however, he makes it clear that he is still discussing the life devoted to *theôria* and the exercise of theoretical reason (*nous*), and he concludes that this is the life that 'will more than any other be happy'.[91]

What does it mean, though, to speak of a life 'devoted to' or 'given over to' *theôria*

---

[86] See *Nic. Eth.* 1177b26–31.

[87] The latter claim is made at 1177b33–1178a2; the former, at 1178a2–7. The argument based in the former claim is prepared for by 1177a13. See further Lawrence 1993: esp. 19–20.

[88] *Nic. Eth.* 1178a9. Ross translates this word 'in a secondary degree', but I think that 'way' is suitably vaguer than 'degree' here, even though it is plain that according to Aristotle, the life of practically virtuous activity is in the end less choiceworthy for a human being than the life of *theôria* is. See Kenny 1992: 29.

[89] *Nic. Eth.* 1178b33–5.

[90] See 1179a5 as well as 10–13.

[91] See 1179a23, 27, with *sophos* at 30, 32, and Lawrence 1993, whose conclusions seem to me to be, in the main, compatible with the interpretation that I am espousing, particularly concerning the main issue of conflict of goods.

or, in more closely Aristotelian terminology, a life 'of' *theôria*, or a life 'in accordance with' the virtue of which *theôria* is a manifestation? In the course of discussing Aristotle's views on *theôria* we shall have to answer this question.

Some commentators are dissuaded from believing that Aristotle could have attached so much importance to *theôria*, or that he could have held that the life devoted to it is the happy life, by a mistaken understanding of what he would have meant by that thesis. But the consequences of his treatment of *theôria* are not what they are usually feared to be. For example the life 'of' *theôria*, on his account, cannot be a life in which every moment is spent on *theôria*. In the first place, Aristotle could not consistently maintain that the life of *theôria* is to be lived according to a maxim such as, 'Engage in *theôria* on all occasions on which the opportunity to engage in it is open to you'. If Aristotle had said something like this, then he would have provided a fully general rule governing action, which he explicitly insists is not possible.[92] Aristotle does recommend a life of *theôria* as the best life for a *human* being, even though he says explicitly that only a deity could engage in *theôria* continuously, and that a deity's life would *eo ipso* be better than a human being's life.[93] That does not imply, however, that a human being who can contemplate should adopt the maximizing strategy of trying to do it as much as possible, or at the expense of everything else that he might do.[94] For Aristotle also makes clear, as I shall explain shortly, that his praise of the life of *theôria* is compatible with saying that other activities have their own intrinsic value.[95]

There must therefore be a more relaxed and a less precise sense, which does not implicate a rule of maximization, in which the life 'of' *theôria* is 'given over to' that activity. Indeed, because of Aristotle's denial that ethics permits exceptionless rules, there obviously cannot be a rule telling interpreters of Aristotle precisely how much theorizing the life of *theôria* will contain, or determining when the theorizing is to take place. Accordingly, we should think of the life of *theôria* loosely, as a life in which a person plans to devote himself as fully to *theôria* as is feasible, and possesses sufficient leisure to put that plan into effect. It is not a life in which *theôria* at every moment takes precedence over everything else,[96] or in which an imperative of maximizing one's philosophical contemplation strictly governs his thoughts and actions.[97]

---

[92] *Nic. Eth.* I. 3, 1094b19–22. In addition, such a rule would be a maximizing rule, whereas in general it seems that ancient ethical theories, with the possible exception of Epicureanism, did not make this sort of use of the idea of maximization; see Annas 1993: 84–6; White 1988a; Heinaman 1988; Kenny 1992: 89–90 vs. Devereux 1977 and 1981.

[93] Someone who thinks that a human being who only contemplates, and thereby fails to be ethically virtuous, should probably also be critical of Aristotle's idea that a deity who contemplates has the best form of existence.

[94] See Lawrence 1993: 32–3, and Reeve 1995: 184.   [95] See 1178b5–7, 25–7.

[96] Thus I think that the appropriate sense of 'devotion' is different even from Cooper's 'single-minded devotion', which so far as I can see does not seem to involve a fully strict rule; see his 1987, and what he says at 1999b: 232.

[97] Thus I think it is a mistake to think that if an interpretation attributes to Aristotle the view that the

This is a difficult conception for many modern philosophers and interpreters to digest—so strong is our impulse to think that a philosopher must show us how to settle all of the difficult ethical and other practical dilemmas that life throws at us, and to guide our actions at every turn.[98] We can perhaps, however, understand Aristotle's outlook by noting that his reason for fixing on any single dominant end, such as *theôria*, as a focus of life is not the *methodological* conviction that he must provide a rule or criterion for choice or action. Rather, it is more likely to be simply the *substantive* idea that a life is scattered if it does not mainly revolve around some one pursuit, and that a human being needs a focus if his pattern of activity is not to become unmanageably diffuse.[99] This is how I think we should interpret his statement in the *Eudemian Ethics* that

> we must enjoin everyone that has the power to live according to his own choice to set up for himself some object for the noble life to aim at (whether honour or reputation or wealth or culture), with reference to which he will do all his acts, since not to have one's life organized in view of some end is a mark of much folly.[100]

This appears much more like a piece of substantive advice rather than a remark about philosophical method. It helps us see why we should not take Aristotle's claim that the happiest life is devoted to *theôria* as a criterion or maximizing rule, but as something considerably looser.

4. Theôria *as an 'Imperfect Recommendation'*

A bit of the conceptual apparatus from contemporary ethics can help us frame this idea, and perhaps dispel the impression that the looseness of Aristotle's treatment of it is intolerable. Consider the notion of an 'imperfect duty'. An imperfect duty is, roughly, an action that is to be done, but for the doing of which no particular times, places, and circumstances are fully specified. For instance, some have said that there is an imperfect duty of charity. This can mean that one ought to give something to those who are unfortunate, but that there is no directive to be given that tells us how much, when, how, and to whom this is to be done. Perfect duties, by contrast, are held to be

---

best life is a life of *theôria*, it must be committed to any such maximizing interpretation (cf. Cooper 1975: 98, 108–10, 167; Kenny 1992: 91).

[98] For some reasons to reject this view of the task of ethics, see Millgram 1997: ch. 5.

[99] For the view that this issue plays an influential role in earlier Greek thinking, see Cooper 1999b: 78.

[100] *Eud. Eth.* 1214b6–11 (trans. Solomon, with 'noble' replacing 'beautiful'); see Kenny 1992 and esp. Cooper 1975: 94, though I disagree with Cooper's and Kenny's contention that the *Eudemian Ethics* is focused mainly on the idea of an inclusive end; note that the examples that Aristotle gives here are dominant ends, not inclusive ones. (Notice, too, that when Aristotle says here that all acts (*praxeis*) will be done by reference to (*pros*) the end, he does not imply that there will be a fixed rule of action, nor does he exclude the idea that things done by reference to the end will sometimes be good for themselves.)

fully determinate in all respects, and some ethical views aim towards specifying all duties fully. It is obvious that imperfect duties leave room on occasion for perfect duties to be done: an act of charity may have to be omitted in order that a stringent perfect obligation be fulfilled. Nevertheless, the thought is, imperfect duties cannot be omitted altogether, and the assumption is that life will contain enough time and resources for them as well as the others.

This concept of an imperfect duty can be adapted so as to elucidate Aristotle's view. Let us construct a distinction between goods that is roughly parallel to the distinction between 'perfect' and 'imperfect' duties (though in some ways the parallelism will fail). We may conceive the notion of an 'imperfect recommendation' corresponding to the notion of an 'imperfect duty'—a 'recommendation' here being an attractive notion, having to do with goods rather than with imperatives or obligations. Thus we imagine a recommendation to do some of a certain type of thing, sometimes and to some significant degree, but without much of a specification of how much or when. Then we can think of Aristotle's attitude towards *theôria* as constituting an imperfect recommendation to engage extensively in that activity, but not as a specification of just when, how, and so forth. Analogously to an imperfect duty, an imperfect recommendation allows for the possibility of obligations, and even for other recommendations, that on occasion may take priority over it.

5. The Life of Theôria as Containing Other Goods

Aristotle thus can be understood as painting a picture of a life that is, in the sense noted, devoted to *theôria*, but that also makes room for ethically virtuous activity. The place that is granted to the latter results from the fact that the nature of a human being is 'composite'. Such a person has a body to attend to, and also must live among other human beings, and so cannot spend all of his time on philosophical thinking. His circumstances make it incumbent on him to perform various actions. He must accordingly, Aristotle maintains, engage in them well, that is, in accordance with the virtues of character that govern that sort of activity. A deity would not, Aristotle insists, need to do that sort of thing, and would not do it.[101]

This picture does not necessitate that a human being living the life of *theôria* will engage in ethically virtuous activity only with grudging reluctance, or will always wish to avoid it or get it over with quickly in order to spend as much time as possible pursuing the activity of theoretical reason. As I have already said, Aristotle advocates no general rule of trying to maximize the time spent on *theôria*. Situations that call for ethically virtuous actions, however, exert demands of their own.[102] Occasions will

---

[101] *Nic. Eth.* 1178b8–18.

[102] Compare Chapter 3, sec. VII, where I have pointed out that in Aristotle's view, considerations associated with ethical virtue can take the form of imperatives. See also Foot 1978b: 53, 54.

arise on which certain things must be done if one is not to be cowardly or illiberal or unjust.[103] On such occasions, as Aristotle presents matters, someone living the life of *theôria* will not be in a position to beg off on the ground that he has more theorizing to do with which the proposed ethically virtuous action would interfere. In some degree the action will appear to the good man as an imperative, something that he 'must' do—this is why, as I have shown, Aristotle regularly uses the imperative word *dei* for ethically virtuous actions.

At the same time, it is to be emphasized that the notion of a 'mixed' life, as some have put it,[104] does not figure in Aristotle's thinking. He never says that in addition to the life of *theôria* and that of ethically good activity, there is a third life which combines in some optimal way the values of theorizing and of practical activity, so that a person's potentiality for both would be fully realized; and likewise Aristotle does not describe the life of *theôria* as itself a mixed life.[105] If we accept the enumeration that Aristotle gives, then we must say that only two lives figure in *Nicomachean Ethics* X. 6–8.

How, then, can we take account of both Aristotle's insistence that the best life will be a life devoted in a substantial sense to *theôria*, and his view that a person living such a life will also think that it is valuable to engage in some morally virtuous activity? Must we not say that happiness itself is an organized structure of various activities, in which *theôria* is somehow pre-eminent, and that in that sense Aristotle does advocate a 'mixed life' after all, in spite of his never saying so explicitly? If we accepted such a reading, the life of *theôria* would turn out to *be* a mixed life after all.

There is, however, another interpretation which fits Aristotle's words far better, and which I shall develop in the next sections. The leading idea of this reading is that the place in the best life of other activities besides *theôria* is generated, not by the idea that happiness *itself* is a structured combination of activities, but rather by the two-part idea that (a) a human being is incapable of engaging in *theôria* all the time, and so will necessarily spend some time doing other things, and (b) other activities besides *theôria*—such as morally virtuous activity, sight, and so on—are themselves good for their own sake, and not merely good because of their contribution, causal or otherwise, to happiness. Thus when one asks why a particular morally good activity has a place in the life of someone living the life of *theôria*, the answer is not, 'Because a

---

[103] Thus it seems to me that Cooper 1975: 155 is mistaken in saying that aside from excellent activity, a happy man engages 'in other pursuits only so far as they contribute to or are involved in' excellent activity. At times, that is, one will simply be unable to engage in *theôria*, because doing so is ruled out by one's human limitations; then other intrinsically good activities will be desirable apart from their contribution to *theôria*. See also Reeve 1995: 119–22.

[104] For instance, Cooper 1975: 145, 166–7, with Kenny 1992: 24, 29–30.

[105] See in general Kenny 1992: 5–9, 23–42 on grounds for accepting a 'dominant end' interpretation of the *Nicomachean Ethics* (though as noted in the next footnote, it is a terminological mistake to think of the 'dominant' and 'inclusive' interpretations as mutually exclusive).

specification of happiness allows a place for it', but rather, along with whatever considerations speak for the action itself, 'Because one cannot theorize all the time, and occasions arise for morally good activities, and because they are good for their own sake'.[106] To put the point another way, these other activities besides *theôria* are not *parts* of happiness, or of the happy life *as such*, but necessarily have a place, as independently valuable in the temporal span of such a life. The life of *theôria* as such is not *itself* the better for their occurrence; rather, its value derives entirely from the *theôria* that takes place in it. Thus *theôria* satisfies Aristotle's stipulation in *Nicomachean Ethics* I. 7 that happiness is not 'counted as one good thing among others', and that it is 'not made more desirable by the addition of' these other goods.[107]

The end result of Aristotle's view is indeed something that is extensionally much like what it would be if happiness were a structured combination of activities, but its rationale is different. The specification of its structure is exhausted by the claim that it is devoted to *theôria* in the loose sense already mentioned. Its value derives, moreover, from *theôria*. Other goods occur in it because of the incapacity of a human being to contemplate continuously. As a result, there need be no specification of the programme of a happy life, nor of how the various good activities are combined within it, and no claim is made that all of those activities are fully or optimally or harmoniously realized. This is all to the good, from the interpretative point of view, because, I have noted, Aristotle never offers such a specification, or even hints at a discussion of what it might be.

It is appropriate enough, we may say, to use the term 'inclusive' to describe Aristotle's view of *eudaimonia*, so long as the point of speaking in this way is clearly understood. Because Aristotle's view allows that a plurality of things are good in

---

[106] It is against this backdrop that I can best distinguish the present interpretation from the one that is espoused by Cooper 1987, repr. in Cooper 1999: esp. 234–5. Cooper takes the other activities to be part of the *eudaimonia* of the theorizer. They seem to me to be not that, though they are, or can be, part of a 'secondary' kind of *eudaimonia* in the life of someone leading a political life.

Cooper maintains that in Book I, Aristotle emphasizes 'the special need for the activity of the best virtue, *as a completion to the others*' (1999: 227). I find this dubious as an account of passages in Book I, but even if it is correct it does not conflict with the interpretation that I have offered. For Cooper's claim still allows that, as I think Aristotle holds, other activities, besides the one to which the good man's life is devoted, are not parts of *eudaimonia*, but rather are additional intrinsically good activities. Cooper's interpretation seems, in addition, to have the untoward consequence of ascribing to Aristotle the view that the value of the activity which is happiness consists partly in its completing of the other activities, which would appear to conflict with Aristotle's statement that it must be good *only* for itself. Similar considerations seem to me to militate against the interpretation of Charles 1999 (esp. p. 220). The present interpretation of the *Nicomachean Ethics*, as noted, sides rather with Heinaman 1988, Kenny 1992: 89–93, and Scott 1999: 237–8. (Scott 1999: 238 is right to raise the question which intrinsic goods ought to be chosen by someone who is happy; however, this can be treated as a problem to be solved by consulting particular situations or types of situations, not by specifying what *eudaimonia* is.)

[107] See *Nic. Eth.* 1097b15–21. See in this connection also Reeve 1995: 119–22.

themselves and independently of each other, his account is in that sense inclusive, even though it says that happiness consists in *theôria*.[108]

6. Theôria *and Ethically Virtuous Activity: Two Values that Cannot be Realized Fully Together*

The life that Aristotle describes as happiest does not, in his opinion, realize the value of ethically virtuous activity to the same full extent as the life that is devoted to that activity, for instance, the life of the statesman. According to Aristotle, the statesman's actions are directed towards procuring happiness for himself and his fellow citizens.[109] This latter aim is not mentioned in Aristotle's treatment of the life of *theôria* in chapter 8. Moreover, Aristotle acknowledges that greater and nobler practical actions require more external resources than do lesser actions.[110] The life of *theôria* is depicted as a life of less extensive virtuous activity, and less extensive benevolence towards others in one's community, than a person can engage in whose life is devoted to such pursuits themselves.

Conversely, too, the life of practical activity must plainly fail to realize fully the value of *theôria*—even if, as one may perhaps suppose, Aristotle thinks that the statesman might sometimes be able to reserve some amount of time for that activity. His account of the military and political lives makes it plain that they do not, in Aristotle's view, possess the requisite leisure for philosophical thought.[111]

The outcome of Aristotle's discussion of happiness in *Nicomachean Ethics* X is therefore a picture of two values that cannot be freely and fully realized together, and of the consequent necessity to choose a life focused on one rather than on the other, which must be to some extent sacrificed.[112] Full engagement in both *theôria* and practical activity, exemplified by politics, is out of the question. In order for one of them to be pursued so as to manifest its worth fully, the other must be less than fully realized.

---

[108] The terminology introduced by Hardie 1965, and employed by scholars since, suggests that there are 'dominant end' interpretations of Aristotle and 'inclusive end' interpretations, and that no interpretation can be both. There is nothing in itself wrong with such a terminological stipulation, but it obscures the availability of an interpretation that in another way both is inclusivist and recognizes the dominant position in Aristotle's scheme of one particular end.

[109] *Nic. Eth.* X. 7, 1177b14. The happiness in question must, as the subsequent lines indicate, be the happiness that is identified as *theôria* itself (1177a17–8).

[110] See 1178b2–3. Although he stresses, late in ch. 8, that someone with moderate possessions can do the noblest actions (1179a11), he does not thereby maintain that the life described there is as valuable, from the standpoint of virtue of character, as the life that is governed by it.

[111] *Nic. Eth.* 1177b4–18.

[112] The incompatibility of the two lives is noted by Wilkes 1980: esp. 351–2, but I think that she is incorrect in seeing this as an inconsistency in Aristotle's view rather than as something that he thinks of as a conflict of aims. Rorty 1980b presents a more reconciliationist interpretation which, however, acknowledges the conflict to some degree (392).

There is no such thing as a human life that completely develops the goodness in them both.

On this point, Aristotle is in agreement with Plato's position in the *Republic*. Plato, too, held that a philosopher-ruler must make a choice between philosophical thought and governing the *polis*. Although Aristotle's metaphysics is different from Plato's, he joins Plato in rejecting the possibility of the full pursuit of the value of both of the two activities.[113] Whichever activity one chooses, some value attaching to the other is lost.[114]

Aristotle's response to this state of affairs is not to say that the appearance of loss is only an illusion, or that in reality there is an optimum life that ideally realizes or maximizes the values of both activities together—a harmonious combination in which each activity receives all of its due, and nothing needs to be viewed as sacrificed for the sake of anything else. He gives us two pre-eminent rational ends, and tells us that they cannot both be attained completely. On the contrary, since we must choose one activity as the main focus of our life, a person must pick one or the other of these two as the main object of concern. As I have earlier put it,[115] Aristotle does not claim to eliminate the dilemma posed by the presence of two rational aims; instead, he adjudicates between the two alternatives that the dilemma presents. In this sense, his view possesses a dualist character, in the terms earlier explained, rather than the monist structure of harmonizing eudaimonism.

7. *The* Eudemian Ethics

In their different ways, both kantian and hegelian traditions of interpretation have had difficulty getting a clear view of these aspects of Aristotle's position. Accordingly, both have striven, as I have said, to find alternative ways of dealing with the text.

Representatives of both these traditions often find it incredible that Aristotle should have attached as much value as he does to philosophical contemplation, especially in contrast to ethical virtue. For one reason or another (and it is interesting to speculate about why), most contemporary philosophers seem inclined to scoff, for

---

[113] It would not, I think, be correct to say that in Aristotle's view the two values are 'incommensurable', still less that they are incomparable. The value of *theôria* is superior, on the scale that Aristotle thinks matters, to the value of practical activity. How much of one is worth how much of the other is not something that he specifies, concerned as he is here mainly to compare simply two kinds of whole lives, rather than to engage in casuistry concerning particular choices of actions.

[114] Recent controversies about Aristotle's views are couched largely in terms of the question whether in his account of *eudaimonia* he adopted a conception of it as an 'inclusive' or a 'dominant' end. As noted, I think of the main question for my purposes as a different one: whether Aristotle thinks that the pursuit of *eudaimonia* involves any sacrifice of one good for another, and whether all rational human aims can be fully pursued in consistency with one another.

[115] See Chapter 1, sec. VII. 5 and Chapter 2, sec. VII. 3

instance, at Aristotle's contention—which of course was Plato's belief too—that philosophical thought is the most pleasant and best activity.[116] Moreover, it has seemed almost shocking to many readers that Aristotle should not have regarded certain moral or social obligations as obviously strong enough to dislodge, or at least render highly doubtful, his view that *theôria* is the activity that someone who is wise should generally prefer.[117]

A different sort of reaction—and a more important one in the context of the present discussion—is often directed not at the particular choice that Aristotle makes as between the two alternatives, but at the fact that he presents them as competitors at all. Here I have in mind harmonizing interpreters who believe that Aristotle's guiding philosophical aim must be to try to reconcile seemingly conflicting practical considerations, and to show that they really do not ultimately come into conflict with each other. The thrust of this sort of interpretation is to insist that he must, in the end, have thought—as I have argued he did not—that the different values that his treatment of human reason and virtue reveals can be shown to be consonant with each other, and not really to have been alternatives at all.[118]

Some commentators have gone so far as to maintain that the passage that seems to present most of the difficulty, *Nicomachean Ethics* X. 6–8, either was not written by Aristotle at all or else was written by him at a period different from that of his mature thinking about ethics. On the whole, this suggestion has not won many adherents. There is no independent evidence for it, however, and it seems unappealingly ad hoc.[119]

But suppose that we set *Nicomachean Ethics* X. 6–8 to one side for the moment, and imagine that we are trying to interpret Aristotle's *Nicomachean Ethics* without it. Then it must be a difficulty for any harmonizing interpretation that nowhere in the *Ethics* prior to chapter 6 of Book X does Aristotle seriously explore the issue of how the various different virtuous activities might be combined together into a consistent whole. This fact is awkward for any reader who believes that it can have been one of Aristotle's main purposes to show that rational human aims must be consonant with each other. Aristotle and his readers knew well, from Plato's *Republic* and other sources too, that a lively controversy existed concerning whether considerations of justice, for instance, were compatible with the pursuit of individual aims, including the aim of philosophizing. It seems impossible to believe that the *Nicomachean Ethics*

---

[116] See e.g. 1177a18–21, 23–7.

[117] For a recent version of this type of interpretation, as against the more directly inclusivist readings cited in the next footnote, see Kraut 1989.

[118] This is a standard inclusivist interpretation. See Ackrill 1980; Cooper 1975: 131–2, 95–7; Irwin 1988: 359–63, 397, and 1992: secs. 6–11 passim.

[119] This idea is invoked by Cooper 1975 and by Nussbaum 1986: 377. Cooper, however, later rejects it, rightly, in his 1987.

could have been intended to address this issue in a serious way without pursuing it extensively.

At this point it is appropriate to bring the *Eudemian Ethics* into the discussion. Although some scholars have doubted the authenticity of this work, many believe that it is an early and less polished treatise on ethics by Aristotle himself, while a few hold that it is better, and perhaps later, than the *Nicomachean Ethics*.[120] I assume the *Eudemian Ethics* to be authentic, but I here waive questions about its date relative to the Nicomachean treatise, and also about its quality, though I think of the latter as a more fully definitive statement of Aristotle's views.

As commentators have noted, the *Eudemian Ethics* seems plainly to hold that happiness consists in activity in accordance with *all* of the virtues, both intellectual and moral, not merely some of them or some single one of them.[121] Thus the Eudemian treatise advocates, not a life of *theôria*, but rather what appears to be some form of 'mixed life', of the sort that I have maintained is not even brought up for discussion in the *Nicomachean Ethics*.[122] In the *Eudemian Ethics* Aristotle says,

> But since happiness is something complete, and living is either complete or incomplete, and virtue is too—one virtue being a whole and the other, a part—and the activity of something that is incomplete is itself incomplete, therefore happiness would be activity of a complete life in accordance with complete virtue.[123]

As is generally noted, 'life in accordance with complete virtue' pretty clearly means here, as it does not in the *Nicomachean Ethics*, all of the human virtues, both intellectual and moral. This is indicated by the fact that Aristotle lists several parts and virtues of the soul with which he is not concerned, notably the 'nutritive' part of the soul, in such a way to imply that he *is* interested in the parts and virtues that he does not exclude. Of these, he mentions explicitly the intellectual and moral virtues.[124] There seems no room for doubt, then, that according to the *Eudemian Ethics*, happiness includes the exercise of both of them.

How should we react to this idea in the *Eudemian Ethics*, and to the contrast between it and what we find in the *Nicomachean Ethics*? In particular, what does it show about Aristotle's attitude to conflict between different worthwhile aims?

In the first place, we ought to be impressed by something that it shows about Greek ethics. We would here be seeing a single philosopher advocating at one time an inclusive view which tries to incorporate a plurality of goods into a conception of happiness, and also a quite different view which allows for a conflict between different aims.

---

[120] See Kenny 1978 and especially, for clarification and revision of his 1978 view, his 1992: esp. App. 1.

[121] See *Eud. Eth.* 1219a35–9, b26–1220a12; see also Kenny 1992: 93–4.

[122] See Kenny 1965 and 1992: 19–22, 86ff.; Cooper 1975: 136–43 and 1999b: 213–14. Both Kenny and Cooper maintain, in my opinion rightly, that Aristotle adopts different positions on this matter in the two treatises.

[123] *Eud. Eth.* 1219a35–9.   [124] *Eud. Eth.* 1219b26–1220a13.

What we certainly would not see is a fixed assumption that all goods must harmonize with each other.

The contrast between the two treatises should also make us wonder which came first, and especially whether Aristotle had some particular reason to move from the one view to the other. An answer to this question might give us a hint as to the fundamental direction of his thinking.

One might, for instance, find it natural to suppose that he moved from the Nicomachean to the Eudemian position. This supposition would be tempting if one thought of harmonizing views as characteristic of Greek thought, that is, as the view that a Greek thinker would adopt if he had no pressing reason not to. Thus the Nicomachean position would appear as a way-station on the path to the harmonizing inclusivism of the *Eudemian Ethics*.[125]

But another account is also possible—one which I think is more plausible, though by no means certain. This account says that Aristotle felt himself pressed, by the thinking already in evidence in the *Eudemian Ethics*, to abandon the inclusivism of that treatise and to take up the position of the *Nicomachean Ethics* instead.

One should start this line of interpretation by reflecting on how much ground the *Eudemian Ethics* already has given up to the notion that there is conflict between worthwhile aims. As many commentators recognize, Aristotle states that if we adopt an inclusivist view of happiness, a good man needs to have a 'standard' (*horos*) by which to deliberate.[126] This statement is a reflection of the fact that thus far, he has given no account at all of how the claims of the various goods and virtues are to be coordinated with each other. The idea that they can all be included in happiness needs, as I have stressed, to be backed up by some account of how this is to be done.

The answer to this question that Aristotle gives in the *Eudemian Ethics* is striking.

One must ... live by reference to the ruling principle and the formed habit and activity of the ruling principle ... [E]ach of us should live in accordance with the governing element within himself—but this is ambiguous, since medical science governs in one sense and health in another. Likewise with the theoretical faculty (*to theôrêtikon*); God is not an imperative ruler, but is the end by reference to which practical reason issues its commands. What choice, then, or possession of natural goods ... will most produce the contemplation (*theôria*) of God, that choice or possession is best; this is the noblest standard; but any thing that by deficiency or excess hinders one from the contemplation and service of God is bad ... So much, then, for the standard of perfection and the object of the goods *simpliciter*.[127]

Now, it is not in all ways clear what this means, but whatever exactly it does mean, the passage certainly identifies the 'standard' of activity as the encouragement of a kind of contemplation.

---

[125] Kenny remains cautiously agnostic on this point—see his 1992: App. 1—but I think it is fair to say that he shows himself to be tempted by a story of this kind.

[126] *Eud. Eth.* 1249a22–b24.

[127] *Eud. Eth.* 1249b6–24.

Now, to take contemplation as the standard in this way is certainly not, as is often pointed out, to identify happiness with contemplation. For it is not in general true that to give the standard by which one decides whether to do something is to say what is good or worthwhile about that thing. Nevertheless, in a case like this it is a very short step from the former to the latter. For here the standard is incontrovertibly something, contemplation, that Aristotle *does* regard as very much worthwhile, and he makes plain here that he wishes to encourage it, and moreover to test other activities by their encouragement thereof. It could well have struck him that if the encouragement of an activity already judged worthwhile is the test for engaging in other worthwhile activities, then it is very plausibly said to be, itself, the rationale of those activities. For it is difficult to see why *theôria*, worthwhile as it is, would be the standard for activity if it were not what is worthwhile *about* it.[128] And if that was how he thought of the matter, that might easily have led him to the view of happiness that is endorsed by the *Nicomachean Ethics*.

Although I do not think it is as likely that Aristotle's thought shifted from the position of the *Nicomachean* to the position of the *Eudemian Ethics*, that possibility is certainly not to be ruled out. My point here, however, is rather that he could, for all the texts of the two treatises show us, have gone either way. My conclusion is therefore that there is no reason arising from the texts of Aristotle's ethical treatises to maintain that his thought was pressing in the direction of a harmoniously inclusive view of the relation of human aims to human happiness, rather than a view that gave special prominence to one activity, *theôria*.

The comparison of the *Eudemian Ethics* with the *Nicomachean Ethics* brings to light another striking fact. Whereas the latter treatise stresses the unavailability of hard and fast rules in ethics, as we have noticed, the former work seems to present us with something approaching just such a rule. For the passage that we have just seen tells us that the encouragement of a kind of *theôria* is a standard for our activities. This may not be just the sort of rule that Aristotle rejects in the *Nicomachean Ethics*, but it comes closer to one than anything else that Aristotle offers.

Just as Aristotle cannot in consistency regard the concept of *eudaimonia* as yielding a rule to coordinate its component aims with each other, likewise he cannot, at least in the *Nicomachean Ethics*, advocate a rule for determining when a particular worthwhile aim should be given priority and when it should be adjusted to a global scheme of *eudaimonia*. As I have pointed out, this is the inevitably unsystematic character that

---

[128] It seems to me that Ackrill 1980: 31 understates the problem that arises in this passage when he says: 'The test is only to determine when and within what limits natural goods should be chosen or acquired.' The word 'only' seems out of place. The question is why *this* test is appropriate. Ackrill goes on to say that contemplation is not put forward 'as the foundation of morality'. That is perhaps true; still, the role of contemplation as *horos* need have nothing to do with a 'foundation', but the question is, once again, why it is the appropriate test, or even *an* appropriate test, if not because it confers value.

attaches to the pluralist notion that a part of happiness may be both intrinsically and contributively valuable.[129] According to Aristotle, many things are valued for themselves, and even though all of them are also valued for the sake of *eudaimonia*, this latter fact does not eliminate their irreducible plurality, or provide any systematic way of deciding when to pursue one of them and when to adjust it to other considerations.[130]

To a philosopher looking for a more or less clear-cut method for deciding priorities and making choices, Aristotle's belief in a plurality of things worthwhile for their own sake must, as I have said, seem uncomfortably unspecific. We tend to expect that the concept of *eudaimonia* will serve to coordinate these aims. But although Aristotle thinks that devoting oneself to a single activity keeps life from becoming intolerably disorganized, nonetheless, as I have said, that concept is not intended to eliminate the irreducible plurality of intrinsically good components of a good life.

Earlier I suggested that we temporarily leave *Nicomachean Ethics* X. 6–8 out of consideration and focus on the evidence from the *Eudemian Ethics*. When we bring that passage back into consideration, a striking fact about it is surely that, unlike the end of the *Eudemian Ethics*, it contains no discussion whatsoever of a way in which the two activities there under examination might be combined into a harmonious composite.[131] In view of Aristotle's clear statement, for instance, that political activity is destructive of the leisure necessary for *theôria*, it would seem plain, to repeat once more, that if Aristotle had meant to advocate a 'mixed' life involving both activities, he would have been obliged to explain how, in such a life, this difficulty could be overcome.

More generally, these chapters contain no hint of any attempt at all even to sketch a plan or governing conception by which the activities might be coordinated. I do not see how it can be denied that the general drift of the chapters as a group, in addition to their explicit conclusion, suggests a pronounced opposition between the two aims rather than a confidence that they can both be somehow pursued adequately side by side or combined into a single plan of life. In this situation, then, Aristotle's response is not at all what a harmonizing inclusivism would insist that we expect, and cannot be turned into such a thing through any plausible interpretation or editing of his text. If he had indeed held an inclusivist position in the *Eudemian Ethics*, it is all the more striking, as I have said, that he gives a standard for activity there that focuses so strongly on *theôria*, and so completely neglects the possibility of a harmonizing inclusivism in the *Nicomachean Ethics*.

---

[129] See Chapter 1, sec. VI. 3.

[130] Thus it seems to me misleading, too, to speak of the 'unification' of ends, as Sherman does (1989: 58; cf. 77–8, 86).

[131] In this connection it is pertinent to cite the observation by Price 1989: 130, that 'By comparison with the *Eudemian Ethics*, the *Nicomachean* is less concerned to define a precise conclusion'. (It seems to me mistaken, however, to say that the *Nicomachean Ethics* is accordingly 'the more popular work'; it is rather a question of what Aristotle there thinks is possible to do in ethics.)

8. The Need for a Single Activity

There is considerably more to be said than I have space for here about why Aristotle believes that *theôria* and practical activity simply cannot be combined together into a single whole that is harmonious in the sense of fully realizing the goodness of both. I do not think that we could reach a complete explanation of Aristotle's position just from the text of *Nicomachean Ethics* X alone. Rather, we would have to discuss such additional passages as *Metaphysics* XII. Nevertheless, here are a few pertinent points about the *Ethics*.

One possibility is that Aristotle took the difficulty of combining the full pursuit of the two activities to be simply the inevitable limitation of time and energy that all human beings face. Humans simply do not have enough resources and enough of a lifespan to do all of the things that are worthwhile, including the pursuit of political and intellectual aims. In that case, it would seem that a being not subject to these limitations would be able to combine *theôria* and ethically virtuous activity into a single life, or in some sense to live both lives. Perhaps this is something that Aristotle believed.

Or perhaps he looked at the matter differently. In chapter 8 of *Nicomachean Ethics* X, he says that the gods would not engage in such activities as making contracts and keeping them, or the other kinds of things associated with virtue of character, and that actions of this kind are too trivial for such beings. But he does picture deities as engaging in *theôria*.[132] Perhaps, then, he believes that even beings without limitations of time and resources would not exhibit virtues of character even if they in some sense could—or at least would not be prevented from doing so by such limitations. Perhaps he thinks that something intrinsic to the nature of *theôria*, or of beings that engage in it, makes it unsuitable for combination with practical activity in a single life.

Or perhaps he believes that any good life must necessarily have a single focus, on pain of otherwise being scattered or disorganized. Plato's *Republic* contains a criticism of a life—characteristic, he thinks, of a 'democratic personality'—that is divided between one pursuit and another.[133] Aristotle too, in his *Eudemian Ethics* also seems, as we have just seen, to take the position that a life should be organized around some single principle or pursuit. Perhaps this contention arises from the sense that there is something intrinsically objectionable about living according to a pattern that is disunified (though, to reiterate, this sense does not push him so far as to search for a precise rule or method for deciding what to do). If so, then it might be all the more difficult for a harmonizing inclusivist reading to gain a foothold in Aristotle's texts. The same thing might be taken to be suggested by indications, in Book VIII of Aristotle's *Physics* and Book XII of the *Metaphysics*, that the life of the Prime Mover is superior because of being in some sense unitary and undivided. If that is so, then Aristotle might believe that any existence, even the existence of a being with no limita-

---

[132] See 1178b8–22.   [133] See *Rep.* VIII, 559d–562a.

tions such as restrict humans, must best be focused on one thing. If that is so, then the conflict in *Nicomachean Ethics* X is not caused merely by human limitations and incapacity for multiply adequate pursuits.

At the same time, however, Aristotle could still face the question whether a person who was like a human in being unable to engage continuously in *theôria*, but was nevertheless unlimited in time or resources, might engage fully in both *theôria* and ethically virtuous activity.[134] If the answer is affirmative, then the reason why an actual human being must choose one or the other would consist, after all is said, in human limitations. It seems to me most likely that this is indeed Aristotle's thought. That that is so is strongly suggested by his emphasis on the idea that practical activity permits so little leisure for *theôria*. It seems likely that this problem would be obviated by an ample supply of time and resources for both, and that Aristotle would acknowledge that fact.

9. *Self-Confined* Theôria *and Non-Self-Confined Ethically Virtuous Activity*

Before moving on to my discussion of Aristotle's treatment of *philia*, it will be helpful briefly to make a couple of further observations about the opposition between lives that Aristotle describes in *Nicomachean Ethics* X. This point has to do with the contrast between considerations that are self-regarding and those that are broader.

It seems to me beyond doubt that when Aristotle confronts the issue of deciding whether *eudaimonia* is to be associated with *theôria* or instead with ethically virtuous activity, he sees clearly that this question opposes two types of consideration, of which one is decidedly more narrowly self-confined than the other. Certain minor niceties aside, *theôria* is very plainly more self-confined than ethically virtuous activity, and practically virtuous activity is less self-confined and more other-regarding. The question whether to lead the life devoted to the one or the other, therefore, is in part a question about the extent one will be concerned, to a substantially greater or lesser degree, with the well-being of other people than oneself.

Moreover, Aristotle himself views the issue in just this way. For one thing, he emphasizes the degree to which ethically virtuous activity depends on other people, because it involves actions affecting them and their interests, whereas philosophical thinking is to a great extent 'self-sufficient'. Liberal actions, for instance, involve giving things to others, while justice requires the presence of other people to whom one will act justly.[135] Plainly Aristotle thinks of these virtues as tied up in some essential way with the well-being of others.

Moreover, in his argument for denying that the life of the statesman is the happiest life, Aristotle makes the point explicit. As I have already noted, Aristotle says that 'the

---

[134] On this issue in Aristotle see e.g. Cooper 1975: 95.

[135] See e.g. 1178b13–14, 1177a30–2

action of the statesman . . . is unleisurely, and aims—beyond the political action itself—. . . at all events at happiness, for him *and his fellow citizens*—a happiness different from political action, and evidently sought as being different'. Obviously, then, such activity is regarded by the agent as explicitly directed partly at the well-being of others in his *polis*. 'The activity of theoretical reason', by contrast, 'aim[s] at no end beyond itself'.[136]

It is true that Aristotle sometimes mentions a social aspect of *theôria*. This aspect lies in the fact that *theôria* can be promoted and enhanced by the common intellectual activity that goes along with the best kind of friendship.[137] On the other hand, he never says that cooperation with others is required for *theôria*, or even for the best *theôria*. In contrast to the just man, he says in *Nicomachean Ethics* X. 7, 'the philosopher, even when by himself, can contemplate truth, and the better the wiser he is; he can *perhaps* (*isôs*) do so better if he has fellow workers; but still he is the most self-sufficient'.[138] This is no declaration that the fellowship of others is essential to engaging in *theôria* itself, as distinguished from the providing of circumstances in which it may take place; nor is it an indication that such a thesis is required for Aristotle's argument. His treatment of friendship in *Nicomachean Ethics* VIII–IX, to be sure, contains statements that the best kind of friendship will involve common intellectual activity. For the most part, however, this activity consists of friends' mutual observation and appreciation of each other's ethically virtuous actions, not the kind of *theôria* that Book X identifies with happiness. None of these earlier passages maintains that *theôria* is an essentially social or sociable activity.

Indeed, Aristotle's thinking in *Nicomachean Ethics* X obviously runs in the opposite direction altogether. The stress falls entirely on the fact that both *theôria* and the person engaged in it are comparatively 'self-sufficient'. That is precisely why *theôria* has a better title than practical activity to be thought of as *eudaimonia*. One can hardly believe that Aristotle's purpose is to insist that *eudaimonia* is a fundamentally social or other-regarding condition, much less that it is so in the way in which a substantial part of ethical virtue is.[139]

---

[136] *Nic. Eth.* 1177b12–15, 19–20.

[137] See esp. 1169b33–4, 1170b12–13. The former clearly involves the contemplation of action. Although it has been suggested that this is what the *theôria* of Book X is about, that idea seems to me to be countered decisively by 1078b12–21, which indicates that practical activity is not a worthy object, not merely of divine participation, but of divine contemplation, too—and hence not of human contemplation either, which is said to imitate the divine version (23, 26–7). The latter passage has to do with *dianoia*, not *nous* or *theôrein*. On the other hand, 1172a4–5 deals with *philosophein*, and so could be what is involved in Book X (see 1177a25).

[138] *Nic. Eth.* 1177a32–b1.

[139] Nor, for that matter, does sociability seem to be involved in Aristotle's comparison of this activity with the condition of a divine being, especially when one takes into account his emphasis on the self-sufficiency of the Prime Mover as described in *Metaphysics* XII. 6–9, who is pictured as a divine being engaged in thought but dependent on no other being at all.

It is important to bear in mind also that in any case ethical virtue is other-regard-ing here in only a restricted way. It concerns the doing of actions that concern the well-being not of all other persons, but of one's fellow citizens. In fact, this group does not comprise even all of the people living in one's own *polis*, but only those who have the status of citizenship within it. At one point, Aristotle says, 'it is not proper to have the same care for intimates and for strangers, nor again is it the same conditions that make it right to give pain to them'.[140] This sentence would not be remarkable on its own. What makes it remarkable is that Aristotle never asserts the desirability of a like benevolence towards all of one's fellow citizens as such (even though he says that they are in a sense all one's *philoi*), let alone towards all human beings. Still, the chief fact here remains that in *Nicomachean Ethics* X, two sorts of concern confront each other, one of which is, in an unmistakable way, much more fully and directly self-confined than the other is.

10. The Persistence of Conflict

Early on in this chapter I asserted that Aristotle is a eudaimonist. His acknowledge-ment of conflict does not gainsay that fact. Notice, then, how this conflict arises with-in the context of a eudaimonist scheme. The capacity to theorize and the capacity to perform ethically virtuous actions can be thought of as two elements of the human capacity for well-being. Given the primacy of the former, moreover, the exercise of these capacities can be treated as parts of the happy life. Nevertheless, within this con-ception of happiness the realizations of two distinct components thereof tend to inter-fere with each other. We have eudaimonism, then, without a harmony of all practical aims.

Given the point that I have just made, we can describe the situation in the follow-ing way. According to Aristotle's scheme, the exercise of one quite thoroughly self-confined constituent of an individual's well-being, and another constituent, which has much to do with the well-being of others and is thus not self-confined to anything like the same degree, interfere with each other and prevent each other's full realization. We thus have a situation in which an individual must choose between the realization of a more and of a less other-regarding aspect of his own good.

Analogous situations are described rather differently within the context of more modern philosophical doctrines. As I have emphasized, for example, modern philosophers often speak of a conflict between an individual's happiness and moral considerations. Then we hear talk of a conflict between happiness and duty, or between one's good and one's obligations. In either way, modern ethics tends to speak of a clash between one's own happiness and some consideration taken as external to it.

Although it is possible to focus on the difference between these modern ways of

---

[140] *Nic. Eth.* 1126b27–8.

expressing matters and Aristotle's rather different formulations, the similarity in content often overshadows the terminological difference. We can talk of an opposition between one's well-being and considerations that threaten to interfere with it, or we can talk alternatively of a conflict within one's well-being between a part that is more strictly self-confined and a part that is less so. But a conflict is a conflict, after all, no matter how it is described. We can think of happiness as an aim against which some other independent aim can compete, or as an inclusive aim within which conflict can break out. Which way we think about the situation seems to be little more than a matter of labelling. Certainly this is so if our main question is whether or not there is a conflict. For it appears that there is a conflict either way, regardless of which way we think of it.

VII. Philia

1. The Types of Philia

One might suppose that the opposition that arises in Aristotle's treatment of *theôria* is the product of his division of virtue into two kinds, ethical and intellectual, and that if one considered ethical virtue on its own, one would find it to be an entirely consistent whole in which no conflicting aims appear. This impression is generated partly by the fact, which I have already noted, that in Aristotle's catalogue of the several ethical virtues in Books II–V, and in his account of practical wisdom (*phronêsis*) at VI. 5 and of related matters elsewhere, he does not mention the possibility of clashes between different virtues and the actions that manifest them. However, the impression is mistaken. It fails to take account of another point at which opposition within ethical virtue can arise, namely, his complex description of friendship in *Nicomachean Ethics* VIII–IX.

The meaning of the word *philia* is extremely broad. It is usually translated by 'friendship', and also often by 'love'. However, *philia* covers a broader range of relations than either of those English terms. Perhaps 'attachment' would be the best translation, though even that word connotes an emotional bond that is not always part of what *philia* conveys.[141] For the most part I shall here use the translation 'friendship', which in spite of its unsatisfactoriness is still the most widely accepted and least misleading rendering.

In spite of the breadth of the application of his word, Aristotle focuses mainly on what he takes to be its strictest sense. This is the sense in which it designates what he takes to be the best kind of the three types of *philia*. Contrasted with this kind of friendship, virtue friendship, are two other kinds: friendship for the sake of advan-

---

[141] I first heard the translation 'attachment' suggested by John Rawls, in lectures in 1973.

tage and friendship for the sake of pleasure.[142] According to Aristotle, one's aim in maintaining such a friendship is, respectively, one's own utility and one's own pleasure.

This feature of Aristotle's account has often led to its being charged with being egoistic or selfish in an indefensible way, though some also think that its self-regarding character is acceptable.[143] As I have already indicated, this criticism has often been levelled against his doctrines as a whole, especially by philosophers of a kantian or similar cast of mind, who believe that he neglects non-self-regarding ethical considerations. Much that he says in *Nicomachean Ethics* VIII–IX, indeed, lends itself to a baldly egoist construal, as if he openly took it that a person should always and without hesitation or even reflection aim pre-eminently for his own good, even in situations in which his own gain would be his friend's loss.

In the hope of counteracting this picture of Aristotle, other readers, including defenders of a hegelian response, point to Aristotle's description of what he calls the truest and best kind of friendship. He holds that if one has a friend in this strict sense, at least, then although one wishes good for oneself, one also wishes what is good for that friend 'for his sake'.[144] This most genuine kind of friendship, of which Aristotle believes only people who are good are capable, does not concern things like money. If one of a pair of friends owns some money, then the other friend does not own it. So Aristotle says that if someone takes things like money to himself he is rightly called grasping. However, the goods of strict friendship are not like that. If a person gains nobility (*to kalon*) through his actions, he is not called grasping. For the situation is not a competitive one, and the one friend's gain is not the other's loss. The interpretation and defence of Aristotle, then, consists in arguing that his view is not egoist in a significant way, because the benefit that the individual gains does not come at anyone else's expense, and indeed the benefit of acting nobly is one that both or all can share without loss or competition.

2. Philia *as Both for one's Well-Being and for one's Friend's Sake*

What Aristotle says about friendship, however, does not support this picture of his intentions.[145] In the first place, although he certainly maintains that a good person

---

[142] *Nic. Eth.* VIII. 3.

[143] So I take e.g. Ackrill 1980, and Price 1989: 113 ('the whole argument . . . is that notional self-sacrifice . . . in fact displays a higher possessiveness') with 130.

[144] See Cooper 1980.

[145] This is related to the fact that, as Kenny points out, Aristotle has some difficulty fitting all of what he says about *philia* into a eudaimonist scheme (1992: 52–3). What I take that to show, however, is that there is difficulty in thinking about Aristotle's scheme as in all ways eudaimonist, since he does, as I have argued, accept the existence of goods that are independent of their contribution to *eudaimonia*.

aims at the good of a friend for the friend's sake, this point is not intended to exclude the idea that part of the rationale for having friends is that that is conducive to one's own happiness. In the second place, Aristotle's account of *philia* explicitly allows for competitive situations in which conflict arises.

On this first point Aristotle's position seems to me to be quite clear. As I have stressed, Aristotle believes that some things are valuable both because they are conducive to well-being (either by being part of it or by leading causally to it) and also for themselves. His treatment of *philia* shows that he takes it to be a good of this type.

On the one hand, Aristotle makes clear that friendship can benefit a person. In the case of the *philiai* of usefulness and pleasure this is obvious. From such attachments one gains pleasure and other sorts of advantage. This is not to say, however, that such friendships are worthwhile only for their benefit to oneself. Rather, it is merely to say that one of the grounds for valuing them is the benefit that one gains thereby. Thus, when Aristotle discusses virtue *philia*, he stresses both the fact that it involves benefiting one's friend for his sake and also the fact that one gains a benefit from it, namely, the fact that one is better able to understand, appreciate, and foster one's own virtue.[146]

Aristotle maintains, as I have said, that it is true *both* that one wishes one's friends well for their sake *and* that one values having friends for the sake of one's own happiness. There is no contradiction or incoherence here. In a sense, it could be argued, one wishes well to one's friends in order to maintain their friendship, and aims at that in turn partly in order to secure one's well-being. In that sense, one wishes one's friends well both for their sake and for one's own. But so long as we notice that Aristotle acknowledges that things may be valuable in this twofold way, we can see that there is nothing problematic for him about such a view.[147]

In fact, however, the connection between these two kinds of valuing is complicated, in a way that easily leads readers into confusion. Reflect upon the fact that the benefit that a virtuous person gains from virtue friendship arises, according to Aristotle, *from the very fact that* he values the friend's well-being for the friend's sake. If one did not value one's friend's well-being in *that* way, one could not thereby be a party to a virtue friendship and thus could not gain the special benefit thereof. Accordingly, there is a sense in which wishing well to one's friend for his or her sake is, even if one does not think about the fact, for one's own sake.

---

[146] Cooper makes these points clear. In particular see his 1980: 303–5 for an argument that Aristotle does not hold that the former two types of friendship are merely self-serving.

[147] Indeed, this appears to be precisely the view that Cooper ends up attributing to Aristotle (1980: 333–4). Cooper recognizes that a thing may be valued both for its own sake and for something else, but for reasons that he does not make clear, he does not think that Aristotle separates these two lines of thought (332). It seems to me, however, that Aristotle does indeed separate them, both here and in the other contexts in which, I here argue, he makes use of the possibility of this type of twofold aim.

Some of Aristotle's readers have thought they find a paradox here.[148] There is, however, nothing paradoxical in what Aristotle holds. The benefit that one gains from virtue friendship depends on the fact that that friendship involves wishing well to one's friend for his sake. There is nothing incoherent in a person's recognizing this fact. To be sure, there is a *problem* for any person *if* it turns out that the part of his well-being deriving from his virtue, including his virtue friendship, conflicts in some way with his friend's well-being. But as we are about to see, Aristotle recognizes that such conflicts can arise, and has a response to the problem that they generate.

Conflicts between one's own well-being and the well-being of one's friend are not excluded by the fact that one can and does value both of them for their own sake. It can hold true of things that one values for themselves that they may clash with each other. And in fact in the case of many pairs of things that one values for themselves, the two aims may not in all circumstances be fully consistent. After all, one's own well-being (like that one of one's friends) contains a plurality of parts. The good of one's friends, therefore, can easily compete with one's aims.[149] Accordingly, we have here, in the case of friendship, another instance of the type of opposition among aims that I have stressed.

3. A Conflict within Friendship

Having seen that the basic outlines of Aristotle's treatment of friendship do not exclude the possibility of conflict between friends' good and one's own, let us now do justice to the fact that Aristotle takes this possibility to be realized and tries to deal with it.

In the first place, Aristotle discusses some fairly straightforward problems in which circumstances and available resources do not permit a person to benefit all of his friends. For example, he speaks of 'such questions as . . . whether one should render a service by preference to a friend or to a good man, and should show gratitude to a benefactor or oblige a friend, *if one cannot do both*'. Such questions, Aristotle says, are

---

[148] Cooper 1980: 309–10 and Kraut 1989: 137. Thus Kraut holds there that 'If one says, "I did it for his sake for my sake," the last three words undermine the claim made in the first part of the sentence'. This claim, however, wrongly assumes that 'for his/my sake' means 'for his/my sake *alone*', which it need not and does not, and the claim also neglects the further point that I am making here. Annas 1993: 259–60 seems to accept this point (though on 289 she seems to me to underestimate the degree to which conflict is generated by Aristotle's view).

[149] See again Cooper 1980: 332 and 338 n. 18. It seems to me that interpretations like Sherman's exaggerate the extent to which Aristotle postulates extensive cooperation between friends; see her phrases like 'coordinated planning between lives' (1989: 134; cf. 130–1). It appears, rather, that Aristotle supposes that friends of each of the three types will coordinate their activities in the particular area corresponding to that type (e.g. *Eud. Eth.* 1237a30–b2).

'hard to decide with precision', but we must decide them 'as best we can'.[150] Unfortunately, Aristotle does not explore the structure of these problems at length. What he says, however, is enough to show that the availability of resources can, according to him, be an important factor in generating deliberative conflicts. This fact will take on considerable importance shortly.

A second kind of case is more important in the present context. Aristotle believes that on some occasions there is an opposition between the best good of two friends, even of the best and most genuine type. In such cases, the outcome for one of them must be better than the outcome for the other. This state of affairs leads to a deliberative conflict, in which someone must determine whether to choose the outcome in which he is better off or, instead, the one in which his friend is so. Under these conditions, Aristotle says, even the good man will prefer the situation in which he is preeminently better off, in the sense of gaining the greatest nobility. This is, once again, part of the reason why Aristotle's view has been accused of being egoist.

At the moment, however, I wish to look away from the issue of egoism, and concentrate on the fact that Aristotle explicitly recognizes the existence of conflicts of both types just mentioned.

According to Aristotle, competition over well-being sometimes occurs even in true friendship. At *Nicomachean Ethics* IX. 8 he treats a situation, not hitherto broached, in which the goods of genuine friendship cannot be allocated to both friends alike. What one friend has, the other cannot have. The goods in question are the opportunities to engage in certain kinds of virtuous activities. Here Aristotle says:

[A friend] may even give up actions to his friend; it may be nobler to become the cause of his friend's acting than to act himself. In all actions, therefore, that men are praised for, the good man *is seen to assign to himself the greater share in what is noble. In this sense*, then, as has been said, *a man should be a lover of self*; but in the sense in which most men are so, he ought not.[151]

Here again a person's well-being—that is, acting in accordance with virtue—is pictured as containing two parts which are not fully compatible with each other. One part of one's good is to act virtuously in certain ways. Another part is to help or allow one's friend to act virtuously, in those same ways or in others. Aristotle indicates that it is even more virtuous to allow one's friend to act virtuously than it is to do that act oneself. Often these two parts of virtuous activity will be compatible. Sometimes, though, they will not be. Such are the cases that occupy Aristotle here.

---

[150] *Nic. Eth.* IX. 2, 1164b23–8, 29 and 1165a36. Cf. Nussbaum 1986: 35 with n. 29.

[151] *Nic. Eth.* 1169a32–b2. Irwin's translates as follows: 'It is also possible, however, to sacrifice actions to his friend, since it may be finer to be responsible for his friend's doing the action than to do it himself. In everything praiseworthy, then, the excellent person awards himself what is fine.' This version, however, leaves out an important point. Aristotle explicitly says that the good man will assign to himself the *greater* share in what is noble (*heautôi tou kalou* pleon *nemôn*). Irwin does not translate *pleon*, thus leaving unindicated the comparative nature of the good man's decision and thus its egoist tendency.

Many philosophers in recent times would recoil from this way of looking at the matter. They would find uncongenial not simply the fact that Aristotle's account seems to lend a selfish or egoistic character to even the truest friendship. Even more striking than that, however, is another point which I wish to stress here. It is the fact that Aristotle treats opportunities for virtuous action as potentially scarce, as not always present in abundance, as moderns are usually disposed to think that they are. That means that there might in some circumstances not be enough such opportunities to go around.[152] On most modern views, there is always, even within constrained circumstances, enough scope for virtuous activity that no one need ever be caught short.

Nevertheless, Aristotle unquestionably intends, it seems to me, to describe a situation of precisely this type, which poses the problem of how to allocate opportunities for virtuous action.[153] The best kind of friend does things 'for the friend's sake', Aristotle says. This can often happen when certain resources are scarce and not everyone can gain everything that is good for them:

[T]he good man too . . . does many acts for the sake of his friends and his country, and if necessary dies for them . . . They will throw away wealth, too, on condition that their friends will gain more, for while a man's friend gains wealth he himself achieves nobility; he is therefore *assigning the greater good to himself.* The same is true of honour and office; all these things he will sacrifice to his friend; for this is noble and laudable for himself.

Then, however, Aristotle applies the point to noble action. He presents a case in which it is plainly presupposed that both friends cannot engage in such action on an equal footing:

But he may even give up actions to his friend; it may be *nobler* to become the cause of his friend's acting than to act himself.[154]

Here the presupposition obviously runs: only one person can act, and only one can allow him to act.

Consider how easy it would have been for Aristotle, had he so wished, to deny that the relevant options are ever so limited. He could, for example, have simply *said* that in the long run there are ample opportunities for virtuous activity, and for allowing other people to perform them. Modern ethics simply does not raise the issue of allowing others to do virtuous actions; it takes the opportunities to be so common that there

---

[152] The point is made clear by Price 1989: 113–14, though as part of a complex overall interpretation that seems inconsistent, as far as I can tell, with the one offered here.

[153] Whiting 1996: 172–8 defines a sense of 'non-competitive' in which she then argues that Aristotle's view of friendship here may indeed count as non-competitive; but the price to be paid is that that claim no longer concerns the case that Aristotle is discussing in this passage. Aristotle is dealing here not with a case of 'essentially' comparative goods (Whiting 1996: 174), but he nevertheless is dealing with a case of competition.

[154] *Nic. Eth.* IX. 8, 1169a18–34.

is no question of that. We cannot, however, simply assume that Aristotle views things in the same way, and we need to take Aristotle's claims as we find them.

But Aristotle does not view the matter in that way. He allows his description of the situation to stand, without any protest or qualification, as a case in which the opportunity to perform virtuous action is limited.[155] It is impossible for both to help the other to do the act, so one person will come out of the situation better off. If you choose to do the act and your friend enables you to do it, the friend is better off by being nobler; if you allow the friend to do the act and the friend does it, then you are better off in the same way.[156] Not everyone can be as well off as possible in this regard, or even as well off as everyone else.[157]

4. Aristotle's Recognition of the Conflict

Like Aristotle's treatment of *theôria*, his description of this aspect of *philia* sets an individual's own good off against broader considerations which have substantially to do with the good of other people. No less plain is the fact that Aristotle regards the matter in just this way. He thinks of the problem in precisely these terms: 'Shall I assign the greater benefit to myself, or to my friend?' he wishes us to ask—where these are the only two options that he envisages as available.

Aristotle makes plain that both he and those with whom he is discussing the issue think of it in this way. He does not talk as though he were operating within a context where everyone assumes that harmony of friends' ultimate aims always prevails—though of course often it would. He is fully aware that his contemporaries believed that the matter gave rise to a conflict between one individual and others. His discussion in this chapter begins as follows:

---

[155] Here I agree with Kraut 1988 and 1989: ch. 2.

[156] Actually the situation can become more complicated: presumably it is possible for you to allow your friend to allow you to do the act, and indeed the 'allowings' might be iterated indefinitely. The basic point, however, remains if the series can be thought of as stopping at some finite point—which is what Aristotle presumes. It does not seem to me that Reeve's response to the problem at 1995: 178 is something of which Aristotle avails himself.

[157] On p. 441 of his 1988, Irwin holds that at 1117b7–15, Aristotle says that '[i]n seeking the common good the virtuous person . . . on some occasions has to sacrifice his own self-confined good to the fine and to the good of others'. It is not inconsistent with my interpretation, and it may be true, that Aristotle advocates the overall sacrifice of one's self-confined good in some cases. On the other hand, 1117b7–15 seems to construe the courageous sacrifice of one's life not principally as a 'loss of the greatest of goods' (12–13) but rather, as he then suggests we might better say, a gain in *to kalon* (14–15). If so, it is not clear whether this case counts as a sacrifice of one's own self-confined good to 'the good of others' or rather a sacrifice of one part of one's self-confined good to another part of it. At issue is whether *to kalon* here counts as *itself* the good of others, which seems to me doubtful, or instead as a part of one's self-confined good. The strength of the latter interpretation seems to me enhanced by the present passage, inasmuch as there is a clear contrast here between the *kalon* for oneself and the *kalon* for one's friend. That 1117b7–15 is a direct recommendation of *altruistic* self-sacrifice seems to me therefore dubious. Cf. n. 191 below.

The question is also debated, whether a man should love himself most, or some one else. People criticize those who love themselves most, and call them self-lovers, using this as an epithet of disgrace, and a bad man seems to do everything for his own sake, and the more so the more wicked he is ... while the good man acts for the noble, and the more so the better he is, and acts for his friend's sake, and gives up his own interest.

On the other hand, Aristotle also is aware of the opinion that approves of seeking one's own good. Just after this, he writes:

But the facts clash with these arguments, and this is not surprising. For men say that one ought to love best one's best friend, ... and these attributes are found most of all in a man's attitude towards himself; ... he is his own best friend and therefore ought to love himself best.

This situation, aside from being one in which the outcome can be best for only one friend, is acknowledged by Aristotle to generate a substantial deliberative question. Which outcome should a reasonable person choose? This is the practical question through which Aristotle leads his readers in this chapter.

Furthermore, Aristotle holds that each side of this question has its own independent force. Immediately following the passage just quoted, he says: 'It is therefore a reasonable question which of the two views we should follow; for both are plausible.' Aristotle grants the force of the idea that a person should benefit a friend for the friend's sake. We are not told that this force derives simply from thinking of the friend's good as part of one's own. Aristotle does not say that when people advocate acting for a friend's sake, they do so on the ground that one's own good includes that of one's friend. This regimentation of Aristotle's thinking is not one that he propounds.

The view to which Aristotle requires us to attend and to which he thinks himself obliged to react—much like the view of Glaucon and Adeimantus in *Republic* I—thus ascribes a weight to other-regarding considerations that is independent of one's own well-being, and is presented explicitly as potentially requiring sacrifice of it. In the end, Aristotle comes down on the other, self-regarding side. Nevertheless, he knows full well that according to one entirely respectable position, friendship makes a substantial claim on a person that is independent of its contribution to the person's own well-being.

Misunderstanding of Aristotle's position is sometimes caused by his statement that '[f]riendly relations with one's neighbours, and the marks by which friendships are defined, seem to have proceeded from a man's relations with himself', and by his use of such formulae as the proverbial statement that a friend is 'another self'.[158] These passages make some readers believe that in Aristotle's view, there is no real difference between one's attachment to a friend and one's attachment to oneself, and that one's

[158] *Nic. Eth.* IX. 4, 1166a1–2 and 9, 1170b6–7.

own good and one's friend's good are identical. Aristotle's words, however, stand in the way of such an inference. He says:

and if as the virtuous man is to himself, he is to his friend also (for his friend is another self)— if all this be true, as his own being is desirable for each man, so, or almost so (*paraplêsiôs*), is that of his friend.

'Almost so', indeed! What Aristotle says here is that friendship 'proceeds from' one's relation to oneself, not that the former relationship is the same as the latter.

Aristotle places another self-regarding constraint on the degree to which a person wishes his friend well. This type of case does not arise from a situation that most modern philosophers would regard as realistic or important. Nevertheless, it illustrates his willingness to acknowledge oppositions between independent self- and other-regarding considerations.

Philia, says Aristotle in *Nicomachean Ethics* VIII. 7, requires some degree of equality, though how much it requires 'is not possible to define exactly, for much can be taken away and friendship remain, but when one party is removed to a great distance, as God is, the possibility of friendship ceases'. He goes on to draw a conclusion:

This is in fact the origin of the question whether friends really wish for their friends the greatest of goods, e.g. that of being gods; since in that case their friends will no longer be friends to them, and therefore will not be good things for them.

Aristotle handles the case as follows:

The answer is that if we were right in saying that friend wishes good to friend for his sake, his friend must remain the sort of being he is, whatever that may be; therefore it is for him *only so long as he remains a man that he will wish the greatest goods*.

Finally he makes the restrict fully explicit:

But perhaps not *all* the greatest goods; *for it is for himself most of all that each man wishes what is good*.

Friendship, in Aristotle's view, places certain limitations on the ways in which competition over virtue manifests itself, but it does not eliminate the competition. Aristotle says:

[T]hose who are friends out of virtue are eager to do good to each other . . ., and when people are competing (*hamillômenôn*) in this there cannot be complaints (*egklêmata*) or fights (*machai*). No one is annoyed with someone who loves and benefits him; if he is gracious he retaliates by doing his friend good; and since the one who excels will have got what he aimed at, he will not complain about his friend.[159]

This passage does not say that since virtue and virtuous activity are never scarce,

---

[159] *Nic. Eth.* VIII. 13, 1162b6–13.

friends do not compete over them. It says that friends *do* compete over these things, and denies only that such competition issues in fights or reproaches.[160]

In these passages, then, Aristotle reveals several things. First, he recognizes—and presupposes a context in which it is generally recognized—that there may be conflicts of goods between different individuals. Moreover, in such contexts it is not assumed in advance that in some fundamental sense all people's, or even all friends', goods stand in harmony. Second, Aristotle shows that in his view this situation gives rise to a deliberative conflict over how an individual is to act. Third, such conflicts involve problems about the extent to which someone's actions should be guided by the aim of furthering his own good. It is acknowledged that the concept of an alternative to this self-regarding consideration is available. The question then arises which of the two options to choose. The passage exhibits a clearsighted awareness of a controversy between people who advocate a version of rational egoism and those who espouse the opinion that some kind or degree of self-sacrifice is required by friendship and virtue.

5. Conflicts Involving 'Non-Competitive' Goods

Sometimes modern writers suggest that in Aristotle's view, or for that matter in the Greek view in general, what gives rise to conflict among individuals is the pursuit only of certain obviously 'competitive' goods, such as money, fame, power, and the like.[161] On this account, the most important step towards avoiding the possibility of conflict is to think of choiceworthy goods in a different fashion, as excellences and virtues. This step, it is sometimes maintained, was taken by Aristotle, perhaps among other Greek thinkers. The assumption underlying this suggestion is that excellence and virtue are less prone to generate conflict—and perhaps even that they are intrinsically incapable of doing so.

Aristotle's treatments of *theôria* and *philia* do not support this suggestion. For one thing, although he is emphatic that a happy person will not have to worry himself much over practical affairs, he explicitly notes that such a person will have to be provided with external prosperity. It can hardly have escaped his notice that external prosperity is often the subject of competition. More important, although he insists that

---

[160] Accordingly I take Annas to be mistaken when she says that 'the language of competition has been completely reinterpreted' (1993: 258) on the ground that 'virtue is an inexhaustible good' (257). I cannot see here any reinterpretation at all, only a claim about what the competition does and does not cause. It seems to me significant, moreover, that when Annas wishes at this point (257) to capture explicitly the idea that 'virtue is an inexhaustible good', she needs to have recourse to a quotation from Shelley's *Epipsychidion* rather than Aristotle's *Ethics*.

[161] Cf. Chapter 4, sec. II. 1, and Chapter 5, sec. VIII. 4. There I noted (see Chapter 5, n. 147) that Hegel, and others like MacIntyre who follow the same line of thought, tend to suggest that if people only value excellence of activity, and do not think that other goods (like money) constitute their well-being, then conflict will *ipso facto* be diminished or eliminated. See e.g. MacIntyre 1988: 66–8.

good people do not compete over items like money or fame, which are not intrinsically worthy of pursuit,[162] he maintains that good people will vie with each other to do noble deeds. In *Nicomachean Ethics* IX. 8, we have seen, he presumes that competition over virtuous activity cannot always be transcended or eliminated, and advocates trying in such cases to win. It is not part of his plan to try to show that concord among individuals can be achieved if only we adjust our notion of what is good to focus on those items that are not subject to competition. Within an individual's deliberation about his own aims, the corollary is the point that I have just made: one cannot always aim conjointly at the best outcome both for oneself and for someone else, for example, one's friend. For sometimes it is clear, Aristotle urges, that those severally optimal outcomes are incompatible.

VIII. Politics, Biology, and Cosmology

1. The Effort to Absorb Aristotle's Ethics *into his* Politics

Next I wish to examine some considerations that have led Aristotle's readers, even those who are fully aware of the facts that I have laid out above, to think that these facts do not represent the whole of Aristotle's position on practical deliberation. According to this way of reading him, the ideas expressed in the *Nicomachean Ethics* should be to some extent discounted by being interpreted through the lens of other works. For although the *Ethics* is usually acknowledged to be Aristotle's main exposition of his ideas about ethics, there has been some tendency, especially among hegelian-minded interpreters, to devalue what it says, and to maintain that it must be construed in the light of material from other works. The result of thus understanding the *Ethics* in full context of Aristotle's œuvre, it is contended, is to show that its contents, and therefore Aristotle's doctrines as a whole, are best construed, overall, as an attempt to establish a harmony of rational aims.[163]

Of interpretative strategies that tend to minimize the importance of the *Nicomachean Ethics*, the most important ones rely on his *Politics*. The *Ethics*, it is urged, is preliminary and subsidiary to that work, and must be read in its light. Any apparent discrepancies between the works, this view says, are to be resolved in favour of the *Politics* and its contents, and passages in the *Ethics* must be construed accordingly.[164]

---

[162] *Nic. Eth.* IX. 8.

[163] I have already noted that, for reasons too involved to be discussed here, I do not take the *Eudemian Ethics* or the *Magna Moralia* to be factors that could modify or substantially supplement our picture of Aristotle's ethical views.

[164] This is true, for instance, of MacIntyre 1988: 102. It is not true of all other inclusivist accounts—not, for instance, the one given by Irwin in his 1988 (see e.g. 467).

The *Politics* contains some famous statements by Aristotle that might seem to cancel the indications in *Nicomachean Ethics* VIII–IX and X of conflicts between an individual and others in his community. In *Politics* I. 2, for instance, Aristotle says that 'man is a political animal', and explains as follows:

[T]he *polis* is by nature clearly prior to the family and to the individual, since the whole is of necessity prior to the part . . . The proof that the *polis* is a creation of nature and prior to the individual is that the individual, when isolated, is not self-sufficing; and therefore he is like a part in relation to the whole. But he who is unable to live in society, or who has no need because he is sufficient for himself, must be either a beast or a god; he is no part of the *polis*.

Some of the most insistently harmonizing interpretations are stimulated by passages like this one. Thus, for instance, we see in T. H. Green the fusionist-sounding explanation of 'an identification of [a man's] own and others' well-being' in Aristotle:

[T]he idea of a true good as for oneself . . . is ultimately or in principle an idea of satisfaction for a self that abides and contemplates itself as abiding, but which can only so contemplate itself in identification with some sort of society.[165]

A case for taking the thought expressed in *Politics* I. 2 to take precedence over what Aristotle says in *Nicomachean Ethics* X. 6–8 has often been derived from the last chapter of the *Ethics* itself. *Nicomachean Ethics* X. 9 is often called a 'transition to the *Politics*'.[166] In this chapter, Aristotle emphasizes the importance of legislation, and in general the administration of the *polis*, ending with some words that are obviously designed to lead the reader into the topics of *Politics* I. This emphasis has made it appear to some interpreters that the *Politics* is the governing work, and that statements in it supersede or dominate those in the *Ethics*. The same argument can seem to be bolstered by things that Aristotle says in *Nicomachean Ethics* I, especially his statements that politics is the authoritative study of the good for a human being, and that the end for a *polis* is 'greater and more complete' than the end for a single man.[167]

Some interpreters try to strengthen this connection with the *Politics* by the intermediary of Aristotle's views on *philia*. In outline, the strategy is to say that because a good man is just, and because a just person is linked by bonds of *philia* with the other citizens of the *polis*, and because *philia* brings a coincidence of goods, therefore the well-being of the individual and of the *polis* are likewise coincident. As a result, it is suggested, the claim in the *Politics* that human beings are 'political' can be taken to have the implication for Aristotle's ethics that I have just described.[168]

---

[165] See Green 1883: secs. 236, 235.

[166] To use Ross's phrase, from the summary headings that he inserts in his translation of the work.

[167] *Nic. Eth.* I. 2, 1094a26–b11. Cf. Adkins 1984.

[168] This strategy has been especially forcefully developed by Irwin in his 1988 and 1992.

2. The Inadequacy of this Effort

As a demonstration of an Aristotelian belief in a coincidence of rational human ends, however, these lines of argument are unsatisfactory in two respects. In the first place, Aristotle's remarks about politics do not license us to give precedence to the statements in the *Politics* over those in the *Ethics*. Second, his claims for the pre-eminence of politics and its ends do not contradict the statements in *Nicomachean Ethics* X. 6–8, nor obviate the conflicts to which they give rise. Third, the argumentative route through *philia* will likewise not reach the desired conclusion.

As a preliminary point, we should note that statements to the effect that the good of the city-state is greater than that of the individual, as Aristotle says in *Nicomachean Ethics* I, do not imply that there must be a harmony between the two. (In fact, they might be felt rather to carry the contrary suggestion.) The same point can be made about Aristotle's assertions that politics organizes and directs other pursuits. This idea is fully compatible with the view that those aims can come into conflict with each other. It is compatible also with the thought that one of those aims is more worthwhile than the activity of politics itself. Indeed, this is exactly what Aristotle holds in *Nicomachean Ethics* X. 7, as I have already indicated, when he says that one point against statesmanship is that it aims at other goals than itself. Even the assertion of man's essentially political nature does not imply that *theôria* is not human happiness or that the best life is not the life devoted thereto.

Precisely this point is made explicitly by Aristotle in the *Politics* itself. Whereas a life of activity is best, Aristotle says in *Politics* VII. 3, it is not true that 'a life of action must necessarily have relation to others, . . . nor are those ideas only to be regarded as practical which are pursued for the sake of practical results, but much more the thoughts and contemplations which are independent and complete in themselves'. As in *Nicomachean Ethics* X. 7–8, Aristotle tries to combat the idea that the contemplative life is isolated and therefore more characteristic of a god than a human being:

[A]cting well, and therefore a certain kind of action, is an end, and even in the case of external actions the directing mind is most truly said to act. Neither, again, is it necessary that states which are cut off from others and choose to live alone should be inactive . . . If this were otherwise, the gods and the universe, who have no external actions over and above their own proper actions, would be far enough from perfection.[169]

Nor does the political nature of human beings entail that there is some harmonious way for politics to reconcile all activities, including itself. In *Nicomachean Ethics* X. 8, Aristotle stresses the fact that human beings must live together in communities, but

---

[169] *Pol.* VII. 3, 1325b15–30.

this does not prevent him from continuing to declare, in that chapter, the superiority of *theôria* as a human activity.[170]

Green's reading exaggerates what Aristotle says in the *Politics* itself. Aristotle does not assert quite generally that the well-being of an individual is just the same as the good of his *polis*—let alone that the individual thinks of himself as identical with his *polis*. Aristotle also makes it clear that he regards the two goods as distinct. In a related vein, *Politics* III. 4 argues that 'the good citizen need not of necessity possess the virtue which makes a good man'. Aristotle does allow one exception to this statement. That is the case of the good ruler who is also a free subject, or, the citizen of the perfect state:

In the perfect state, the good man is absolutely the same as the good citizen; whereas in other states, the good citizen is only good relatively to his own form of government.[171]

But this is far from being a general statement of a coincidence of goods of citizen and *polis*. It applies only to a certain ideal sort of person in a certain ideal sort of city.[172] It shows that there are certain favourable circumstances in which rational considerations fail to clash, not that conflict among them is ruled out. Even more importantly, it is a long way from a cancellation or qualification of the statement in *Nicomachean Ethics* X that *the happiest* human life is the life of *theôria*. In the *Ethics* itself, someone who exhibits excellence in practical activity is in Aristotle's terms a good man and a good citizen.[171] Nevertheless, the happiest man is still the man whose life is devoted to *theôria*. The *Politics* does not deny this and even, in the passage quoted above, asserts it.

Nor does *Nicomachean Ethics* X. 9 indicate that the material in the preceding chapters of the *Ethics* is to be superseded by what Aristotle will have to say in the *Politics*. The point of this chapter is made clear at the start: we must not merely know what is good but must also put it into practice. This requires statesmanlike activity, and in particular legislation. Aristotle's claim is that politics is the activity by which human aims can be realized, not that it is the human aim itself.[174]

---

[170] In *Nic. Eth.* IX. 9, 1169b18–19, too, Aristotle does not fail to say, as he says also in the *Politics* (1253a2–3, 1278b19–20), that man is a political being who by nature lives with others of his kind.

[171] *Pol.* V. 7, 1293b5–7, trans. Jowett; see also *Nic. Eth.* 1130b28–9; *Pol.* 1278a40–b6, 1288a38–9, 1333a12–17.

[172] See Rapp 1997: 66, and in general against the descendent of Green's interpretation that is presented by MacIntyre 1981.

[173] *Nic. Eth.* 1179a9, 1178b5–7.

[174] Perhaps we should see the passage, then, as fitting with *Eud. Eth.* 1249a21–b23, but the interpretation of that passage is problematic (see Cooper 1975: 135–43).

3. The Weakness of Political Philia

What Aristotle says about *philia* among the citizens of a *polis* is likewise not designed to obviate conflict completely, though of course it is intended to lessen it.[175] At its most effective, such a bond would generate a complete coincidence of goods. For instance, if a friend is as much as 'another self', in Aristotle's phrase, and if one is bound by friendship to all of one's fellow citizens, then presumably a complete coincidence would be achieved.

It does not, however, seem possible to justify saying that Aristotle believes that the coincidence is as complete as this. No one would deny that in his view, the organization of the *polis* is such as to reconcile individuals' goods to a great degree under those types of constitution that are satisfactory, particularly by making sure that the rulers do not rule simply for their own benefit.[176] In addition, each individual citizen regards his fellow citizens as friends and wishes them well for their sake. To say that, however, is far from expressing the idea that Green attributes to Aristotle—the 'idea of satisfaction for a self . . . which can only so contemplate itself in identification with some sort of society'—if that is taken to mean that because the good of each citizen coincides with the good of the *polis*, the good of all citizens coincide.

The kind of bond that *philia* creates among citizens seems in any case to be insufficient to generate such a coincidence. Of the three types of friendship, it seems fairly clear that the citizens in general are joined by advantage friendship.[177] Aristotle does not give any indication that this kind of friendship is sufficient to establish a complete coincidence of goods for a virtuous person. The activity of such a person requires a sharing of virtue, and of the perception of each other's virtue, that is not possible with other sorts of friendship between other sorts of people. Indeed, Aristotle is explicit that there are limits to the number of people with whom one can be friends in this way:

> In the way proper to fellow citizens, indeed, it is possible to be the friend of many and yet not be obsequious but a genuinely good man; but one cannot have with many people the friendship based on virtue and on the character of our friends themselves, and we must be content if we find even a few such.[178]

---

[175] In *Pol.* III. 6–7, for instance, Aristotle holds that a good *polis* is ruled 'for the common good', and not simply for the good of the rulers, but the use of the phrase 'common good' is not intended to imply that there are no conflicts among the inhabitants' goods, let alone that there is no conceptual distinction among the various goods of the various people in the *polis* (see e.g. 1279a5–7 with II. 2, 1261a17–30.) Note that although the notion of 'common good' is freely used both by Aristotle and his commentators (see e.g. Morrison 1999), there is no tendency to think that that phrase itself connotes an absence of conflict of interests. Moreover, many of the provisions for justice in *Pol.* III. 9, for example, as well as in *Nic. Eth.* V. 6–7, presuppose potential conflicts of interest that need to be adjudicated; Aristotle does not suggest that these disputes are the result of some failure to recognize that the conflicts are illusory.

[176] *Pol.* III. 6.

[177] See Cooper 1977a: 645–6, and Rapp 1997: 72.

[178] *Nic. Eth.* IX. 10, 1171a17–21.

It therefore seems unjustified to think that Aristotle uses the notion of *philia* either to show that the life of *theôria* is not, after all, superior to a life devoted to the activity of a citizen or statesman, or to demonstrate that the good of all citizens is the same. That being so, a citizen who aims at both his own good and the good of his *polis*, and therein of his friends who are its citizens, seems bound to be subject to deliberative conflict in significant ways.

4. Telos *and* Kosmos

There is a further, quite different interpretative strategy for arguing that unharmonious aspects of the *Nicomachean Ethics* are unimportant. This strategy invokes biology and cosmology instead of politics. Sometimes Aristotle points to a connection between his doctrines in these areas and his views about human ends. That is, sometimes he indicates that the existence of certain ends of human beings, the pursuit of which constitutes virtuous or excellent activity, is determined in the same way as the kind of *telos*, or goal, that he ascribes to biological species and to other entities in the *kosmos* as well. Insofar as that is the case, excellent human activities are somewhat like instances of the biological flourishing of a species of plant or animal.[179]

On this basis it might seem possible to argue that on Aristotle's view, the ends of individual human beings ought to be coordinated with each other in such a way that someone who perceived the overall structure of natural ends could realize how his own end is subsumed in some way under it. In that case, it might be possible to argue in eliminativist fashion that, from the standpoint of such a person, the various conflicts among various aims ought to appear illusory.[180]

Although it is not obvious how this argument could be worked out within an Aristotelian context, that point does not in any event matter. This whole line of thought is simply not employed by Aristotle to support a harmony of human deliberative rationality. To be sure, Aristotle does believe that the *kosmos* is to some degree an organized whole, many—though by no means all—of whose components are coordinated with each other to produce a global pattern.[181] Nevertheless, he nowhere extends this idea to subsume the interrelations of all of the species of animals and plants. It is not part of his teleological account of the universe to maintain that each of these various species, nor the *telos* possessed by each one, is coordinated with all of the others, either in some global pattern or in such a way as to encourage the overall

---

[179] For discussion of issues pertinent to this connection, see e.g. Irwin 1988: esp. 296–8, 344–6, 362–72; Furth 1988: sec. 16. On the other side, see Adkins 1984.

[180] Such a position as this, or at least an approximation of it, was indeed a part of Stoic ethics. See below, Chapter 7, sec. IV. 8.

[181] See esp. *Met.* XII. 10; that not all parts of the universe are embraced by its overall organization is evident there.

flourishing of each. Aristotle does believe that the *kosmos* exhibits an overall structure, and that the *telos* of each species has a role in that structure.[182] He does not, however, contend that this structure is such as to harmonize the various different activities and ends that are played out within it.[183] Aristotle's teleology is not a global or even a highly coordinated teleology. It is not designed to rule out all conflicts among its elements.

Furthermore, even if Aristotle had urged such a coordinated teleology of species, that fact would not of itself imply that the rational ends of individual human beings are consistent. Still less, moreover, would a coordinated teleology be sufficient to guarantee that one and the same individual's aims would all stand in concord with each other. Aristotle's general idea that the universe is to some degree unified is not employed by him to establish, nor does it of itself imply, a harmony of the aims of a single individual, nor for that matter of all individual human beings with each other. The overall structure of Aristotle's teleological cosmology is accordingly irrelevant to the issues of practical reason that are at stake here.

IX. Eudaimonism without Harmony

1. Adjudicative, Non-Holist, Non-Harmonizing Eudaimonism

In the light of what we have seen so far, we can gain a clear overview of Aristotle's position with regard to issues about conflict and harmony. Let me summarize the main conclusions that I wish to draw.

Aristotle's view is a form of eudaimonism, but it is not a harmonizing eudaimonism. Aristotle neither designs his notion of *eudaimonia* to show that rationally worthwhile aims are consistent, nor does he attempt to show this in any other way. On the contrary, his eudaimonism allows for conflicts. These are not expressed as oppositions between a person's happiness and other considerations lying outside it, but rather as conflicts within *eudaimonia* itself, whose existence Aristotle does not endeavour to deny.

In particular, Aristotle does not attempt to deny the existence of these conflicts by upholding a holist conception of happiness. He does not, that is, contend that the parts of happiness are valuable only insofar as they, or certain amounts of them, fit with each other consistently within a human life, nor that their goodness is only contributive, arising from their role within an overall structure. On the contrary, their value is in his view intrinsic as well as contributive, and it is an inevitable loss that a person can engage in only one worthwhile activity fully within a human life. This point is worth

---

[182] Such is evidently the burden of *Met.* XII. 10.

[183] The import of 1075a18–23 lies in the contrary direction. Much of the universe has little bearing on the overall order. See also Balme 1972: 93–8, and above, Chapter 4, sec. VI. 2.

emphasizing because, as will emerge in the next chapter, the Stoics later adopted a view that is strongly holist in some respects.

In saying that Aristotle accepts the existence of conflicts among worthwhile aims, I am in effect denying that his strategy for dealing with those conflicts is eliminative in the sense explained earlier.[184] Rather, it is adjudicative. Aristotle examines the respective claims of the goods that he acknowledges, and tries to determine which is superior without asserting that there is no conflict between them, or that one can gain them all in a fully satisfactory way.

Modern philosophy has been actively concerned with problems about the dynamic ways in which people might rationally adjust aims to each other over time in the light of improved information, changed circumstances, and the like.[185] I remarked earlier that on the whole Greek ethics is inattentive to problems about action under imperfect information and to the diachronic adjustment of aims.[186] The same is true of Aristotle. He often stresses, for instance, that with the transition to maturity a person develops aims and an understanding of them that is absent in childhood.[187] He does not, on the other hand, present any dynamic account of deliberation that would suggest a way of adjusting aims to each other over time.[188] Instead, he pictures human beings as focused on an aim —which will normally not be defined in detail, but will rather be such a thing as 'money' or 'fame' or 'activity in accordance with virtue'— that remains constant. He does not attend at all systematically to the ways in which aims and plans must be filled in and adjusted dynamically, nor—and this is the main point here—suggest that such a process might produce deliberative harmony.

Not only does Aristotle resemble modern ethical thinkers in accepting the existence of such oppositions; in addition, the oppositions have a character very similar to the ones with which modern ethics occupies itself. That is, to put it neutrally, they are

[184] See Chapter 1, sec. VII. 5 and Chapter 2, sec. VII. 3.

[185] Interest in these issues has picked up especially in recent years, as shown by works such as Frankfurt 1988, Bratman 1987 and 1999, Hurley 1997, Gauthier 1994 (inter alia), and Millgram 1997. Looking at Aristotle and other ancient ethical writers in light of these works will be worthwhile. It accordingly seems to me inadvisable to characterize as Aristotelian the kind of harmonizing view espoused by Hursthouse 1999: 247–65. The conflict that Aristotle thinks he sees is too deep for us to think of it as simply an exception to a harmony that holds 'always or for the most part' (e.g. 203–4).

[186] See Chapter 2, sec. VII. 2.

[187] *Nic. Eth.* I. 3, and VI. 11, 1143b8–17.

[188] It seems to me that in her 1989, Sherman gives Aristotle far more credit than he deserves for attending to dynamic adjustment of aims, though she is right to emphasize that he acknowledges the existence of intentions that reach into the future; see her pp. 6, 66–8, 73–4, 190–1, and esp. 86–106, where the evidence presented does not seem to me to support an attribution to Aristotle of much awareness of the idea of revision of ends. I would say that it counts very heavily in favour of my contention here that Aristotle insists early in the *Nicomachean Ethics* that a person must approach philosophical lectures with an already well-formed character (1095a31–b13). This would have been the place, if any, for Aristotle to comment on the possibilities for revising aims.

conflicts between what are viewed as goods that belong closely to oneself and those that in some way or degree accrue to other people under circumstances in which not everyone is in a position to gain as much of them as would be optimal for him. This point has emerged clearly in the treatment of *theôria* and *philia*.

Aristotle's oppositions of goods, while they involve contrasts similar to the one that exists between one's own well-being and the well-being of others, are nevertheless different from the standard modern dualisms of morality and happiness, duty and inclination, and so forth. This difference is no doubt responsible for the widespread belief that Aristotle's ethics has a structure different from that of modern ethics. Nevertheless, the similarity of Aristotle's oppositions to modern ones is by and large more important philosophically than the difference. It cannot rightly be said that modern ethics lacks an important kind of deliberative harmony that Aristotle's view supplies.

Finally, when Aristotle comes to adjudicate the conflicts that his view involves, he comes down on the side that would be best labelled self-regarding or even egoist, not on the side of broader considerations. This is a disappointment to many of his modern readers, who have tried in all sorts of ways to rescue him from this position. Nevertheless, such rescue efforts seem to me to be vain.

2. Hegelian Holism and Aristotelian Anti-Holism

The significance of the facts that I have described about Aristotle's treatment of deliberative oppositions can be best seen when we bring to mind how far harmonizing interpretations of Greek ethics have been willing to go towards reading conflicts out of Greek ethics. As I explained earlier, a complete harmony of aims is gained by denying that the parts of an individual's well-being have value on their own, except to the extent that they fit into an overall coordinating system of aims. This is the type of position that I labelled 'holist'.[189] Just such a position is what Hegel ascribes to the Greeks.

Tragedy, according to Hegel, presents us with a 'collision' of values, each of which is represented somehow by a figure in the drama. By itself, each figure and each value is 'one-sided'. As the drama progresses, however, we are presented with what is in effect, according to Hegel, a reconciliation. Hegel's view of this reconciliation is holist in the sense explained:

> The removal of this state of collision consists in this, that the moral powers which are in collision, in virtue of their one-sidedness, *divest themselves of the one-sidedness attaching to the assertion of independent validity*, and this discarding of the one-sidedness reveals itself outwardly in the fact that the individuals who have aimed at the realization in themselves of a single separate moral power, perish.[190]

---

[189] See Chapter 1, sec. VII. 5, and Chapter 2, sec. VII. 3.
[190] Hegel 1984: ii. 263–4.

In the final synthesis, that is, it turns out that none of the several values possesses 'independent validity'. By itself, that is, such a value does not ultimately count, and the individual who represents it is annihilated. What value there really is emerges in the overall assessment, the synthesis, of the situation as a whole.

This is the type of interpretation of Aristotle that we arrive at if we ignore the fact that in his view, as R. A. Gauthier points out, whereas each good is valued for the sake of one's happiness, some things are valued also for their own sake.[191] This fact is what makes possible the conflicts that Aristotle finds within *eudaimonia* itself. If Aristotle had held that partial aims are valuable only for the sake of their role in happiness, then he would have no alternative but to embrace holism.

That Aristotle does not espouse a holist view is plain from the fact that when in *Nicomachean Ethics* X. 6–8 he raises questions about the values of *theôria* and ethically virtuous activity, these are framed as questions *neither* about their contribution to some resulting happiness to which they lead, *nor* about their role in some containing happiness of which they are constituents. Rather, Aristotle formulates them as questions about the values of these activities themselves. Aristotle's method there is to determine which activity is itself more valuable, and *then* to conclude that the happier and better life is the life that is devoted to the superior activity. The first step is the assessment of the activities; the assessment of the whole comprising them is based on that.

The same conclusion is indicated by his way of determining further features of the happiest life beyond the fact of which activity it is devoted to. Aristotle notes that a human being must live among his fellows, and will therefore need to engage in activities with them. Aristotle then passes from that to supposing that these activities will be 'noble' and 'virtuous', and so will require 'external prosperity'.[192] Aristotle's argument is not at all that such activities will go along with *theôria* to make up the best whole, and that they are to be engaged in for that reason. Rather, he supposes that noble and virtuous activities will be engaged in because they are good in themselves. In other words, the judgement that activities of this particular kind are good is made prior to the judgement that the life in which they figure is the happiest. Aristotle is accordingly not treating the assessment of the whole life as prior, and the assessment of the activities figuring in it as derivative simply from the value of the whole. Although the components are sought in part for the sake of *eudaimonia*, Aristotle insists, they also possess value on their own account.

---

[191] Cf. Chapter 2, sec. VII. 4. Gauthier and Jolif 1970 take note of Aristotle's use of the notion of a thing's being valuable both for its own sake and for the sake of something else (ii. 574). They are correct in saying that this notion is taken by Aristotle from Plato, and that it is not 'techniquement élaborée'. It does not at all follow from that, however, that the notion does not play an important role in Aristotle's thinking. On the contrary, it is presupposed throughout.

[192] *Nic. Eth.* X. 8, 1178b33–1179a6.

3. Harmonizing vs. Relabelling

It remains to describe the character of the oppositions that Aristotle acknowledges, to compare them with modern ones, and to indicate how Aristotle responds to them.

It seems evident, as I have said, that some of the most important conflicts with which Aristotle deals can be broadly described as bringing into confrontation aims that are more closely confined to oneself with those that are less so. It is no accident that one of the criticisms most frequently advanced against Aristotle's ethics, at least as a prima facie objection, has it that his view is egoist or selfish. Gregory Vlastos, for instance, has advanced this charge against Aristotle's account of *philia*, and although Aristotle has his defenders on this account, notably John Cooper, the evidence that can be adduced in support of the charge is at least some ground for saying that there are some signs in Aristotle of a contrast between the more and the less self-regarding, or alternatively self-confined, aims that a person might pursue.

Strikingly enough, this impression is not at all weakened by one of the most prominent recent defences of Aristotle against the overall accusation that his ethics is egoist in a pejorative sense. According to Bernard Williams, we should think of Aristotle's position as only 'formally' and not 'substantively' egoist. It is formally egoist, Williams admits, in that it depicts a person's ultimate goal as a state of himself. However, it is not substantively egoist, Williams maintains, because it allows a person's goal to include others' well-being as well as his own. This is pretty much equivalent to saying that it does not include merely self-confined aims, but admits others as well.

Williams's defence, however, cannot suffice by itself to rescue Aristotle from the accusation. Certainly Williams is right to point out that a position can be formally egoist without being substantively egoist. Thus the mere fact that Aristotle says that all aims are pursued for the sake of one's own happiness does not entail that his view is a form of substantive egoism. On the other hand, it is equally clear that being formally egoist does not *exclude* being substantively egoist, either. Moreover, to show positively that Aristotle's view is *not* substantively egoist would require something that Williams does not attempt.[193] That would be, as we have seen, to demonstrate that according to Aristotle there is no conflict between the more self-confined parts of an individual's happiness and the parts that are less so. For only if that is done can we safely suppose that someone who seeks his own happiness will not end up stinting on, or even excluding, the pursuit of other-regarding aims, because they are simply crowded out by the pressure of the need to focus on self-confined ones.

---

[193] I do not suppose that Williams is under any illusions on this score, or that he believed that by claiming that Aristotle's view was formally egoist, he was *eo ipso* demonstrating that it was not substantively egoist. Nevertheless, his formulation of his argument, which leaves out some crucial steps, makes it appear that he was reasoning in that way. Cf. Irwin 1988: 441, who allows that on Aristotle's view there are conflicts between one's self-confined good and other parts of one's good, but denies that in such a case one 'really sacrifices his own good'.

In other words, Williams's defence is subject to the same difficulty as any merely inclusivist interpretation: the fact that (on any view other than strict holism) conflicts can exist among the components of an individual's well-being, and a person's good can include non-self-confined aims. In that case, it will be not entirely egoist in a substantive sense. At the same time, however, it may also include powerful self-confined components. If those are given sufficient scope in determining how happy the person is, then it may easily turn out that he would count as happy even if his non-self-confined aims are scarcely attended to at all.

In fact, it seems to me that what is most salient in Aristotle's view is the fact that he does *not* claim to use his inclusivist eudaimonism to argue that self-regard is fully compatible with regard for others' well-being.[194] His treatment of *theôria* does not contain claims to this effect. And whereas his discussion of *philia* attempts to show ways in which concern for others can be accommodated, not only does he allow for some conflict between self- and other-regard, as I have indicated, he also omits to maintain that a complete reconciliation of the two is possible. It seems hard, therefore, to regard Williams's defence as something that Aristotle himself is advancing.[195]

What Aristotle's inclusivist eudaimonism does rule out, on the other hand, is a certain manner of *speaking*. If all worthwhile aims are fully included in well-being, then there is no way of formulating a deliberative opposition between two global, overarching aims, one's well-being and *something separate*, which is aimed at ultimately and wholly for itself. Oppositions between parts of happiness are presented, rather, as clashes between partial aims which are included in the overall aim of one's own well-being. By contrast a dualist scheme will say that we must decide in some cases whether to aim at one's happiness *or* at some rival ultimate goal, such as the performance of one's moral obligations. But if the eudaimonist merely *relabels* the latter thing so as to count it a 'part of well-being', and then declares that there can now be no rival aim for one's well-being to conflict with, then it will not be substantively different from dualism. The very same conflicts will arise. They will merely be described in a different way, as occurring between different parts of happiness rather than between happiness and something else.[196] And if the favoured side of the conflict is more fully

---

[194] This seems to me to be so even if one accepts Kenny's inclusivist interpretation of the *Eudemian Ethics* (Kenny 1978); cf. sec. VII. 7.

[195] As noted earlier (n. 157), Irwin holds that at 1117b7–15, we have a case in which a good person 'has to sacrifice his own self-confined good to the fine and to the good of others'. I there gave reason why we should probably take the passage otherwise. In any event, it seems far from being a clear attempt to rescue Aristotle from a charge of advocating an egoist view.

[196] Something analogous seems to me to occur within a harmonizing virtue ethics, such as the one espoused by Hursthouse 1999. Here one speaks of an 'overall, summing-up evaluation' (see her 203, 205, with Chapter 2, sec. V. 2 above), without an adequate indication, to my mind, of how the 'summing' is to be accomplished and of whether it is not really forced or artificial.

self-confined than the other, the result will be substantively egoist, even if it is given an inclusivist formulation.

4. Aristotelian and Modern Deliberative Conflicts Contrasted

Much of what I have said about Aristotle heretofore has tended to dissociate his views from the picture of them that is painted by those who most wish to say that Greek ethics is very different from its modern counterpart, and consequently to assimilate, to a degree, Aristotle's views to some modern ones. But one must not go too far in this direction. For just as we saw that it is a mistake to assimilate Plato's views about deliberative conflict to Kant's, there is likewise, in particular, something quite wrong about assimilating the conflicts that Aristotle discusses to those that are standard in modern ethics, and equally it is misleading to portray his view as egoist in the most usual modern sense. Deliberative conflicts in Aristotle do not take the same form as those that we observe in typical modern treatments.

Typical modern conflicts pit one's happiness against some universal good or obligation, such as Kant's Categorical Imperative or Utilitarian morality. I have argued that Plato's notion of the good of the *kosmos*, too, is not utterly dissimilar to these modern universalist notions, as is, likewise, the idea expressed in Greek writers' invocation of the Golden Rule.

The non-self-confined aims that appear in Aristotle, on the other hand, are like Plato's appeal to the good of the ideal *polis* in being non-universal. The aims of statesmanship in Aristotle's ethics and politics are oriented towards the *polis*. The aims of *philia* are mainly not even as broad as that—though sometimes Aristotle links *philia* with the *polis*[197]—because they mostly have to do with one's own friends, especially with a relatively narrow group of virtue friends of the good man.

Both of these types of considerations are non-universal in two ways. In the first place, they are narrower, as I have just said. They embrace neither every person nor the whole universe. In the second place, however, they are self-referential. The city in question is *one's* city, and the friends are *one's* friends. Thus the aims are instances of what Broad calls 'self-referential altruism', in being directed at the good of things that are specified in terms of a relation to oneself.[198] Aristotle has none of the kantian aversion to self-referential considerations as such, nor any belief that rationality must be expressed in an impersonal form.[199] Thus we have, in the cases of both friends and city, an opposition between one's good taken in a narrow way and a consideration that is in one straightforward way broader. In particular, both cases exhibit pairs or groups of aims that are not fully compatible with each other. But the oppositions are not the

---

[197] See esp. Irwin 1982 and 1988: ch. 18.

[198] See Chapter 2, sec. VII. 4 and Broad 1952.

[199] Note that a statesman aims at his own good as well as that of his *polis* (see above, sec. VI. 10).

conflicts of self vis-à-vis morality or self vis-à-vis humanity that present themselves in most modern writings.

Moreover, there is another way in which modern treatments of such conflicts differ from Aristotle's. These are arguably a matter of mere difference of formulation rather than anything substantive, but they help explain why modern readers often think of Aristotle as following different lines of thought from their own.

In the first place, Aristotle's way of putting matters does not encourage him to draw a clear and explicit line between what belongs to one's well-being in a self-confined sense and what lies to the outside of it. There is no question that Aristotle recognizes the existence of such a distinction. His account of *philia* shows that, and he never advances the hegelian-sounding thesis that such contrasts are unreal. Nevertheless, he does not explain the distinction or in any other way make it the object of direct philosophical investigation.

The historical import of this point is that Aristotle does not interest himself in such a project, any more than he concerns himself with the task of explaining how to distinguish more and less self-confined parts of a person's *eudaimonia*. When he discusses the broader goods of one's *polis* and one's friends, he does not focus on their being non-self-regarding aims *as such*, but merely on the fact of their being opposed in *particular* ways to one's own narrowest good. He does not ask the standard modern dualist's question, 'How is my well-being to be weighed overall, in general, against the aggregate of aims that lie outside it?'—which question then normally leads to an effort at adjudication between the two sides of the dualism. And if he had asked this question, his response would probably have been based on his general methodological belief that ethical questions are not to be settled by any fixed rule or method.

Nevertheless, Aristotle's eudaimonism contains, in spite of what I have said, important disharmonies between aims that are central to an individual and those that lie some palpable distance from them. The respective differences between *theôria* and political activity, and between one's own best good and that of one's friend, are not classified or aggregated by Aristotle in the way that one often sees done in modern ethics. In modern ethics, it is standard to see certain aims, for example, *classified* as self-regarding or the like. This is not true in Aristotle. Likewise, modern ethics often asks questions about how one's satisfactions might be *aggregated* into one's overall self-interest or well-being. Aristotle does not do this either. Certainly he recognizes and acknowledges the relevant contrast. That is shown by his raising of the question whether someone will be self-seeking in relation to his friends. But recognizing the contrast and thinking systematically about it are two different things. If we want to put the matter loosely in something like our own manner, we can regard Aristotle as treating cases in which a 'more' self-confined consideration is confronted with a 'less' self-confined one, and raising questions about what to do in each such case, taken separately. Theorizing is 'more' self-confined than is much ethically virtuous action. And some virtuous actions are 'more' self-confined than others.

Where does this leave us, then, with regard to the question whether or not Aristotle's position is 'egoist' in the sense that has worried interpreters like Williams? The answer to this question needs to be somewhat complicated.

First, we have seen that on the two main occasions when Aristotle is faced with conflicts of more and less self-confined aims, that is, on the occasions involving *theôria* and *philia*, he recommends that a person seek the more self-confined ones. This is an adjudicative, not an eliminative, stance, and there seems to me to be no way of interpreting Aristotle otherwise than as forthrightly taking it. To say that *theôria* involves greater happiness than statesmanship, and that the good man will wish the most noble option of all for himself, is to forego both a harmonizing eliminativism and self-sacrifice.

On the other side, we should not lose sight of the fact that Aristotle's scheme makes room for the recommendations that he gives to possess a distinctly non-self-regarding aspect. Certain things, including morally virtuous activity and actions for one's friends' well-being, are, according to Aristotle, to be sought not only for one's *eudaimonia* but all for themselves. This aspect of Aristotle's view is a not inconsiderable move away from egoism and any other strictly self-regarding position. And although it is not the same as saying, with some modern moralists, that such activities are to be valued *only* for themselves, or that self-regard should be no part of them, it certainly is to say that an important facet of their goodness is non-self-regarding.

Apart from what I regard as the excessively self-regarding nature of Aristotle's thought, he nevertheless appears in a good light from a philosophical point of view. He seems to me considerably more clearsighted than Mill, and possibly also even than Butler, about the situation in which his arguments leave him. Although his overall position is inclusivist, and therefore must reckon with the possibility of conflicts among parts of well-being, he does not attempt to evade this fact, nor to claim for his scheme a harmonious consistency that it does not possess. His discussions of *philia* and *theôria* are entirely candid on this point. Mill, by contrast, and even to some extent Butler, tend to gloss over this difficulty—Mill far more so in that he, unlike Aristotle and Butler, tries to claim a greater degree of harmony of aims than his arguments fully entitle him to.

5. Platonic and Aristotelian Conflicts Contrasted

I conclude with a very brief comparison of Aristotle's position to Plato's. In one way the two are similar, though in another way they are importantly unlike. Both acknowledge an irreducible rational attachment to one's own well-being, as distinct from the well-being of others. For both philosophers, for instance, it can count in favour of some proposed action that it benefits oneself. Neither exhibits any kantian tendency to link rationality in deliberation with universality. Neither, in other words, comes close to thinking it essential to either rationality or goodness of character that one refrain from assigning to one's own happiness a special place in one's deliberations.

On the other hand, both Plato and Aristotle acknowledge that other considerations, distinct from one's well-being, can carry rational weight. Both, moreover, envisage the possibility that the considerations of these two kinds may oppose one another. In Plato, the opposition crops up only at one isolated and well-defined point, the rulers' choice about whether to govern or to philosophize. Most ordinary ethical deliberation is insulated from the special considerations that it involves. In Aristotle, on the other hand, the occasions are scattered more diffusely. Plato's reaction to the conflict, on the one occasion when it arises, is to say that pursuing the good, and thus the good of the *polis*, takes precedence, for a person who comprehends it, over the pursuit of the good for oneself. In Aristotle, there is a stronger urge, it is fair to say, to give preference to the individual's own substantive, self-confined good, though, again, Aristotle offers no method or rule to decide all cases. Nevertheless, the most important fact about both Plato and Aristotle is that they resist any pressure to claim to eliminate the problem by denying that oppositions between one's own good and other considerations ever really arise.

Chapter 7

CONFLICT AND
INDIVIDUAL GOOD
IN HELLENISTIC ETHICS

I. The Traditional Picture of Hellenistic Ethics

1. On the Supposed Inferiority of Hellenistic Philosophy

The main movements in ethical thought beginning during the third century BCE were Epicureanism and Stoicism.[1] In recent times their reputations have followed an interesting course. In eighteenth-century England, for example, both of these movements were by and large more influential, and were felt to be more congenial, than the thinking of Plato and Aristotle. On the other hand, by the nineteenth century Hellenistic philosophy, as it is called, was in eclipse and the Classical period dominated the thoughts of most people who thought about Greek philosophy. Since the start of the twentieth century, opinion has for the most part followed that of the nineteenth. Under this assessment, Hellenistic ethics is weak and decadent. It fails where Classical ethics succeeded, or came close to doing so. It provides, this account says, no coherent picture of human practical rationality.

Hellenistic ethics fell victim in the nineteenth century to the attack that kantians launched against Greek ethics as a whole, and hegelian admirers of Classical thought did not defend it. The chief ammunition for Kant's attack had been the charge of egoism and a disregard for the importance of non-self-regarding deliberative considerations, notably moral ones. While hegelian readers thought that this charge was unfairly brought against Plato and Aristotle, they showed no inclination to try to pro-

---

[1] Scepticism was important, too, to be sure. The Sceptics' work on ethics, however, although it has some interesting points (see Annas 1993: chs. 8 and 17), does not seem to me to have possessed genuine philosophical importance, and moreover its influence on subsequent conceptions of Greek ethics has been minimal. Another school, the Cyrenaics, deserves mention; see below, sec. III. 2, 4.

tect Hellenistic ethics from it. Hegel's reaction is typical. As he saw it, Hellenistic philosophy was characterized by what he called 'subjectivity'. It encouraged the individual to strive for little more than his own private imperturbability. Imperturbability, Hegel believed, was an appropriate aim for those subject to the power of Rome, with its drive towards what he thought was the generalized abstraction exhibited in Roman law. Hellenistic philosophy was accordingly 'Greek philosophy, but transferred into the Roman world'.

Hegel held that what was important about Greek philosophy had belonged to the Classical era, and was gone from both this Hellenistic, proto-Roman world and the philosophy that arose within it: 'This concrete *Sittlichkeit*, this drive toward the introduction of the Principle into the world, through the constitution of a state as in Plato, this concrete knowledge, as in Aristotle, disappears here.'[2] The *polis* was gone, Hegel believed. It had been destroyed by the imperial march of Alexander the Great, who died in 323, and was to be definitively replaced by the Roman Empire. Gone, too, was the independent but community-minded spirit of Greek citizenship—until, Hegel supposed, it could eventually re-emerge, embodied in more self-conscious form within the modern state. In Hellenistic ethics, however, the disappearance of the *polis*, it seemed, had left merely a cramped egoism that focused only on an individual's narrowly self-confined aims. It has taken a long time for the idea to wear off that because the *polis* supposedly ceased to function as an institution after the Classical period, efforts to establish some consistency of practical considerations must likewise have been absent from post-Classical ethics.

The stigma of inferiority that was attached to post-Classical Greek philosophy has still not fully vanished. Even though in the last three decades Hellenistic thought has been much more closely studied than it was before, Plato and Aristotle are still regarded by philosophers as much greater and more important figures than Epicurus, Zeno, and Chrysippus. Through the last two hundred years, the picture of Hellenistic philosophy as the enfeebled offspring of genuine philosophy of the Classical era has persisted in many people's minds, even though the scholarly study of Hellenistic and later Greek philosophy has in the last three decades enjoyed a vigorous revival.

2. *The Self-Conscious Rejection of 'Classical' Thinking by Hellenistic Philosophers*

No longer encumbered by the idea that Classical Greek ethics believed itself to have tried to articulate a harmony of rational aims, we are free also to dispense with the old portrait of the stereotypical Hellenistic philosopher as someone who had lost his grip on this idea. Suppose we look at matters from the standpoint of the Hellenistic philosopher himself. Such a philosopher, we may now suppose, need not have looked

---

[2] Hegel 1955: i. 2, 'Dogmatismus und Skeptizismus', last para. For an even more dismissive treatment, see Hegel 1991: Pt. II, sec. iii, 'The Fall of the Greek Spirit'.

back on his Classical predecessors as thinkers aiming at, much less possessed of, a consistent scheme of rational deliberation. Instead, he would have seen that earlier thinkers had been sorely troubled by deliberative conflicts that they could not ignore or eliminate, and which they were sometimes hard put even to adjudicate. He might well have asked himself, then, how he might deal with those difficulties. In that frame of mind, indeed, he could well think that his predecessors' efforts to resolve practical conflicts had faltered. He would then aspire to do better. Rather than regarding earlier philosophers as giants whose achievements he could not match—this is in fact a rare attitude for philosophers to adopt towards their forebears, even when it is justified—he could well think of himself as called upon to respond to their failures by finding better solutions of his own. And there would be no reason for him not to try a new approach. This, I believe, is in fact what happened.

3. Against an Over-Simple Picture of the Connection between Philosophy and the Surrounding Culture

Reaching a better understanding of Hellenistic ethical thought requires correcting mistakes on a number of fronts. One type of mistake concerns historical facts about the *polis* which I have already mentioned. On one side, the *polis* was by no means as cohesive an institution in Classical times as the stereotype would lead us to believe. Conversely, the same stereotype pictures the post-Classical *polis* as far more decayed and ineffectual than it actually was. The *polis* still remained the focus of most people's lives.

A second type of mistake exhibited by the traditional accounts has to do with their oversimplified idea of the relationship between philosophical thinking and social conditions that surround it. Some responses to Greek ethics take for granted that these two phenomena are joined by a simple regularity: 'If the surrounding conditions exhibit cohesiveness, then the ethical thought will be harmonious; if not, not.' This idea is a by-product of the view that philosophical thought springs automatically from the soil of its culture. Historians of philosophy who think along these lines expect to find freedom from deliberative conflict when—as they believe—society is cohesive, and equally they expect 'subjectivity' in philosophy when—as they again believe—that cohesiveness breaks down. But such connections are rarely so simple. The characterisics of the philosophical doctrines of the Hellenistic world cannot be read off so directly from the social history of the period. No doubt there are important connections between the two—indeed, I shall tentatively suggest one or two myself—but the traditional historiographical story of what they are does not have much to support it.

4. 'Egoism' and Hellenistic Ethics

On more directly philosophical issues there are also misapprehensions that need to be removed, and which I shall explore in what follows. Some pertinent issues have to do, first, with the question whether Hellenistic ethics is in fact 'subjectivist' or narrowly egoist. Others concern a second idea, that Hellenistic positions do not exhibit a harmony of practical reason, but show instead a high degree of deliberative conflict.

On the first front, the aforementioned tendency to think of Hellenistic ethics as uniform, and to ignore the variety within it and the complexity of some of its doctrines, has had a deleterious effect. Indications of egoist views in some Hellenistic doctrines have led to the hasty conclusion that all ethical views of the period must be egoist. Epicureanism, to take it first, may well be correctly labelled an egoist position, even though some scholars are inclined against so interpreting it.

Stoicism, on the other hand, can only through the gravest misunderstanding be treated as a form of egoism. Indeed, one of the principal features of Stoic ethics is that it endeavours to view questions about egoism in an entirely new light—new for ancient Greece, and highly unusual in modern philosophy, too (though there are parallels with Spinoza). In its purest form, Stoicism attempts to obliterate the distinction between points of view that gives rise to the whole idea of egoism as a way of discounting other-regarding considerations. According to the Stoics, that is, the attempt to distinguish between what is valuable from my point of view and what is valuable from some broader perspective rests on a mistake about how evaluations can be made. As a result, Stoicism attempts to offer a form of judgement about value that is neither self-regarding nor the contrary. Stoic philosophers do not always carry out this idea in full consistency. Some of them offer advice to individuals that speaks to a narrowly egoistic outlook.[3] The more careful Stoics, on the other hand, try to develop a style of thought that leads away both from self-regarding aims and from considerations that are thought of as competing with self-regarding ones.

5. Limits of the Present Account

The second issue—whether Hellenistic ethics exhibits stronger tendencies towards deliberative conflict and a correspondingly lesser degree of consistency or harmony within practical reason—is a bit more complex to lay out. It will be helpful to sketch some of the main relevant points.

I shall start from a general observation, and then apply it to the ethical doctrines that were developed in the Hellenistic period. I use the phrase 'that were developed' in that period. It should always be borne in mind that these ideas lived on vigorously for centuries after the period in which they originated. As a result, we tend to think of them as philosophies of, in addition, the late Roman republic, of various periods of imperial Rome, and of the development of Christianity and pagan interaction with it.

---

[3] Certain such aspects of Hellenistic ethics in general are highlighted by Nussbaum 1994; for a partial corrective, see Osborne 1996.

Over this span of centuries, these philosophies underwent many changes. I do not propose here to take account of all of the resulting variations. Much less do I attempt to provide a complete account of Hellenistic ethics as a whole. Rather, I present merely the outlines of the features—some of which persisted, some of which did not—that are relevant to my main themes.

II. Systematic Monism in Hellenistic Ethics

1. The Systematic Character of Hellenistic Ethics

To understand Hellenistic ethics and its relation to its Classical predecessors, the crucial fact is this. First, both Stoicism and Epicureanism are far more systematic, and more systematically expounded, than the ethical doctrines that came before them. Second, by their systematic character itself Stoicism and Epicureanism try to make good what could be seen as the failures of those earlier doctrines to develop a consistent picture of deliberative aims. As a result, both strove for a far higher degree of unity in their treatment of ethical problems of all sorts.

If you try to explain the practical relevance of Greek ethical doctrines to someone who is unfamiliar with them, you quickly discover that it is incomparably easier to do this for Epicurean and Stoic ideas than for those of Aristotle and Plato. Stoic and Epicurean ethics can be encapsulated in a few principles which, for all their generality, have allowed these doctrines to become lay philosophies of everyday life. Each incorporates, without much distortion, broad maxims that non-philosophers have thought they could try to live by. Plato's and Aristotle's ideas never popularized themselves in this comparatively easy way. In some quarters this feature of Hellenistic ethics has diminished its reputation among historians of thought, by making it look to be nothing more than a cracker-barrel philosophy, designed to provide simple guidance to simple people.

However, the source of this ready applicability—or, better, the appearance of it— should not be mistaken, and is directly related to the issues of deliberative harmony and conflict that I have been treating here. That source is not simplemindedness, but rather a considerable theoretical sophistication, and in particular a strong tendency, which can be seen in both of the major Hellenistic doctrines, towards theoretical unity and systematicity. Hellenistic ethical positions are far more tightly organized than the more diffuse structures of Platonic and Aristotelian ethics.

Indeed, Stoicism and Epicureanism are far more like what present-day philosophers often call 'theories' than virtually any ethical view that was produced before them. Both of these Hellenistic schools attempted to systematize their thoughts into tightly organized collections of theses, with clear-cut arguments for them and straightforward consequences derived from them. Epicureanism is built around the idea that pleasure is the good, and around the rule that all action should be directed towards obtaining it. The central thesis of Stoicism, on the other hand, is that 'virtue is the only good', and that a person should try to live in accordance with nature. Each of these can be taken both as a fundamental theoretical tenet, and simultaneously as a criterion for determining what to do. To opponents of their theses, whether philosophers or lay people, both schools responded by trying to explain their disagreement as based on mistakes about the fundamental nature of human motivation and well-being.

In comparison, both Plato's and Aristotle's doctrines, or at the very least the expositions of them that we possess, are more loosely organized. Likewise and as a result, their concrete practical recommendations are a good deal less susceptible of concise formulation. Plato might be thought of as telling us straightforwardly to aim at the good, but his explanation of what that amounts to yields no simple formula, and in the important case of the rulers, as I have stressed, it even issues in a practical conflict for the rulers. Aristotle, for his part, says that the good or happiness of a human being is activity in accordance with virtue. That statement, however, is immediately complicated by the fact that there are according to his account two types of virtue, each containing a plurality of virtues, which are not in all cases reconcilable with each other. In addition, although the thoughts located at the respective cores of Platonic and Aristotelian ethics can be identified easily enough, the doctrines as wholes contain, in addition, many more extensive regions that seem less definite, more exploratory, and also not so directly linked to their central areas. By contrast, Stoics and Epicureans are always intent on showing vividly how their views on any topic spring from their most basic ideas.

2. *The Comparatively Unsystematic Character of Plato's and Aristotle's Ethics*

The effects of this contrast can be observed in some of the history of the respective schools. Testimony to the comparatively unsystematic nature of pre-Hellenistic philosophy is the fact that for several centuries from the Hellenistic era onwards, the positions of Plato and Aristotle appeared to most people to be rather indistinct. Compared with the comparatively crisp outlines of Stoic and Epicurean thinking, the earlier ethical views appear to have struck most people—understandably, I have implied—as diffuse.

Two historical developments illustrate this reaction. First, consider the fact that during the third century BCE, Plato's Academy was taken over by Scepticism and ceased, as far as we can see, to be a centre of what we recognize as Platonic thinking. What is striking about this development is not just that it occurred. Any institution can be taken over by dissidents, heretics, or outsiders. What is truly notable is that when this shift occurred, the reaction was not immediately to perceive a gap that had to be refilled. That is to say, the Greek intellectual world did not react by bringing

forth thinkers who would try to establish a place or school in which Plato's true thinking could be represented or continued.

Even more striking, to the extent that any regeneration of Platonic thought did
take place over the next few centuries, Plato's ideas were regularly confused and
mixed not only with Aristotle's—indeed their respective thoughts came to be regarded as almost indistinguishable from each other—but also with those of the Stoics.
This process can be seen in Cicero's work, *De Finibus Bonorum et Malorum* (*On the
Limits of Good and Bad*), where the lines between Plato and Aristotle, on the one hand,
and Stoicism, on the other, come to appear partially blurred.[4] The factors responsible
for this state of affairs are complex, but one of them is the indistinctness of Plato's and
Aristotle's ideas as they were viewed by those living in this period. That is in large part
a consequence of the fact that Plato's and Aristotle's doctrines were less systematically unified than what was expected in this later time.

3. Systematic Unity and General Principles

However that may be, a direct result of the greater unity of the Hellenistic doctrines is
the fact that each of them attempts much more aggressively to develop a systematic
approach to ethical issues. Each school, the Stoic and the Epicurean, attempts to
develop a single principle, embracing all practical considerations, which is directed at
definitively settling questions about what to do, how to be, and what kind of life to
lead. Both doctrines press towards their own forms of deliberative monism—
Stoicism being focused on a concept of virtue, Epicureanism on its own special conception of pleasure.

Given this drive towards systematic unification, through a single well-defined way
of determining what course of action a person should rationally follow in any given
situation, it is not surprising at all that each doctrine offers less scope for deliberative
conflict than do the views of Plato and Aristotle. The whole project of constructing an
ethical position in this systematic way often consists in framing an exceptionless principle governing action. There are to be no auxiliary considerations that rival it or create unclarities or exceptions. Each individual decision is to be handled by one and the
same test—the aim of pleasure in the Epicurean theory, and of virtue in the Stoic.
Within each of the doctrines itself we find no room for opposition between different
considerations. Each view presents a single standard of practical rationality. No other
consideration is accorded rational weight.

To be sure, this monism can appear to be far too cheaply won. A cut and dried doctrine, which attaches weight only to certain considerations, might seem able to
achieve a consistency of aims more easily than a position that takes many varied con-

---

[4] Not, however, completely blurred: see White 1979a.

siderations into account too, particularly by riding roughshod over people's ordinary ethical judgements.[5] On the other hand, the idea of a systematic unification of deliberation is not to be regarded as trivial. There are plenty of occasions, some of them already discussed, in which conflicts within even a single type of aim create oppositions with which philosophers feel hard put to cope. Even from this point of view, therefore, the systematizing efforts of Hellenistic philosophers need to be taken seriously, as a move in the direction of a kind of harmony of practical reason.

4. Systematic Deliberative Monism: Normative and Psychological Aspects

The deliberative monism of Hellenistic ethical doctrines has a companion in the monism that each of them also adopts in the sphere of psychology. The side of psychology dealing with aims and motivation was important to both Stoics' and Epicureans' ways of dealing with opponents. Stoics and Epicureans reacted to criticism of their ethical positions chiefly by constructing accounts of human motivation, including motivational development from childhood to adulthood. These accounts, they hoped, would demonstrate that their respective opponents were mistaken about what people truly aim for and thus about what their good consists in. All of these accounts are also monist. Epicureans seek to show that human behaviour can be explained by a fundamental effort to gain pleasure. Stoics dispute this claim, and respond with an elaborate story according to which everyone is governed by the aim of conforming virtuously in a certain way to nature.[6] Both of these views strongly discourage any fundamental dualism, or pluralism, of human motivational psychology and of the deliberative considerations that are based on them.

Once again there is a contrast to be drawn with the views of the Classical thinkers. Plato and Aristotle of course developed accounts of human motivation. Both of these, however, are far less unified and compact than the Hellenistic theories. Neither Plato nor Aristotle, moreover, attempts in Hellenistic fashion to reduce matters to one aim or type of aim. Plato's story in the *Republic* of the tripartite soul and its several aims and impulses is an obvious instance of this point. Aristotle's psychology is in this respect even less systematic than Plato's. It is true that Socrates seems to have maintained a kind of monistic account of human action, at least to the extent of holding that a person always does what he believes to be best. Plainly, however, he did not elaborate a full-scale account of motivation.

Insofar as a systematic deliberative monism may be regarded as contributing to

---

[5] See Annas 1993: 78–9, 443–4.

[6] Likewise the Stoic doctrine concerning the part of the soul known as the *hêgemonikon*; see Inwood 1985: chs. 2 and 3, esp. pp. 28–41. Because Epicurean and Stoic doctrines have in large part come down to us in fragmentary reports, I shall often in this chapter refer the reader to secondary sources in which their views are expounded.

harmony within practical reasoning, Hellenistic ethics is harmonious to a far greater degree than its Classical predecessors, and goes much further in trying to close off avenues towards deliberative conflict. According to both Stoicism and Epicureanism, all practical questions, rightly understood, are susceptible of only one answer, and that answer is given unambiguously, they contend, by their own respective doctrines. Moreover, each of these doctrines is expressly designed to achieve this unambiguous monism, to settle ethical issues without remainder or ambivalence.

5. Different Types of Harmonious Monism

Nevertheless, as I shall go on to explain, the kind of harmony that we find in Hellenistic ethics is not the kind that admirers of Greek thought have looked for. Here I briefly list two main factors that come into play.

For one thing, as I have said, these interpreters took Hellenistic views to be narrowly egoist. That meant that non-self-regarding aims appeared to be excluded, more or less, from rational deliberation. From this exclusion a kind of harmony of practical reason might easily result, of course, since self-regarding considerations would not have to compete with any others. However, that seemed much too high a price to pay for freedom from deliberative conflict, not only for kantian- but also for hegelian-minded thinkers. This holds especially for what they took to be the purely hedonist egoism that they ascribed to Epicureanism. To both of these traditions it seemed that whatever systematic unity these doctrines possessed came only by virtue of their simply having ignored or gerrymandered away whatever aims might conflict with a restrictively self-confined and egoist outlook. This picture of Hellenistic ethics is not accurate, but it has often been taken to be so.

Here, as I have already said, those who championed Classical ethics against the kantian accusation of egoism were not tempted to bring Hellenistic thought within the perimeter of their defences. They believed that Epicurean and Stoic views really were, unlike their Classical predecessors, every bit as objectionably egoist as Kant himself had charged all Greek ethics with being.

Not only that: from the standpoint of hegelian interpreters, Hellenistic thinkers appeared in addition to have accepted precisely the philosophical error for which hegelians themselves criticized kantians and other deliberative dualists. This was the error of thinking that an individual's own good really does oppose and exclude broader ethical, social, and altruistic considerations. The Hellenistic thinkers, so the impression was, had been able to be egoists only because they had begun to mark off the sphere of the self-confined from the broader range of practical aims. They had lost the sense, previously possessed by Classical thinkers, that self-regarding and broader aims are compatible with each other by virtue of being included under the capacious concept of *eudaimonia*.

6. Universalization and the Intended Audience of an Ethical View

An important cause of the appearance of out-and-out egoism conveyed by Hellenistic doctrines is the way in which they are often expounded, especially in the writings that survive. Many of these are exhortations, efforts to win converts to the writer's view. These are normally directed at individuals. A particular person is urged to adopt Stoicism, for instance. Sometimes—though by no means always—these appeals are based, explicitly or implicitly, on the claim that he will be happier if he does so.

But although such writings are formally addressed to a single person, they are of course available in some sense to all and sundry. Anyone who broadcasts self-regarding advice to a plurality of people, however, runs a notorious risk of difficulty. If you advise several people each to pursue his own well-being, then there is substantial chance that the aim that you are recommending to each of them will turn out to be incompatible with what you are urging on all of the others (not to mention the policy that you might be following yourself). If so, then your advice cannot be successfully followed by your whole audience. That might seem already to generate a kind of practical conflict. The Hellenistic philosopher, for instance, might seemingly be making persuasive efforts to bring people all to follow a path that plainly was not large enough to accommodate them all. Both Stoicism and Epicureanism might appear to run into difficulty in this way. Perhaps the world is not set up so that everyone may gain the kind of pleasure that Epicurus championed. The same may hold for the Stoic goal of conformity to nature.

By way of contrast, we might suppose that Classical writings are addressed to groups rather than to individuals, and that they therefore do not encounter the same kind of difficulty about universalizing or at least generalizing their prescriptions. It is natural to believe, for instance, that this holds true for Plato's *Republic*, which is a prescription for the planning of an entire *polis*, and one might think the same of Pericles' Funeral Oration in Thucydides' *History*. In this way one might think—unjustifiably, I shall argue—that one could justify Hegel's idea that Hellenistic is more properly characterized as 'subjectivist'.[7]

7. Systematic Ethics and Deviations from Ordinary Opinions

In a second way, too, Hellenistic impulses towards monism struck these interpretative traditions as unacceptable. To start with, notice that one result of the cohesive systematicity of the two Hellenistic positions is their dogmatic character: a strong tendency to oppose or even ride roughshod over some of the beliefs towards which people are strongly inclined in their prereflective or prephilosophical thinking. The drive towards systematic unification is so strong that it often leaves little place for the

---

[7] Hegel 1955: i. 2; (cf. also his 1991: 253, 267, where he describes certain Sophists in the same way).

qualifications and ambiguities that seem to be required by common sense and ordinary opinion.[8] To these complexities of unreflective ethical opinion, as is often noted, Aristotle seems especially attentive. Moreover, even Plato does not ignore them completely, even though he is much more willing to flout them on theoretical grounds. Stoics and Epicureans went considerably farther than Plato in this latter respect. For this reason the doctrines of both schools were often greeted with incredulity, and were often felt to be paradoxical and even shocking. Their proponents often needed to spend considerable energy to try to show that they were not so outrageous as they seemed.[9]

Once again, if we want to understand Hellenistic ethics, we must also attend to, and compensate for, distorting influences present in our sources of information concerning it. First, our sources include many writings by thinkers hostile to these schools. The prime examples are Cicero and Plutarch. These writers rarely leave room for sympathetic presentation of Epicurean and Stoic doctrines. Moreover, even when they do, they constantly make their own unfriendly presence on the sidelines palpable.

As a result, the modern reader can scarcely escape the feeling that the atmosphere in which Hellenistic philosophizing was done was one of controversy and even squabbling, in which most people believed that both Stoics and Epicureans were hopelessly wrong. Furthermore, some defenders of both doctrines themselves write in an intensely controversial style. Lucretius's exposition of Epicureanism in his *De Rerum Natura* (*On the Nature of Things*) illustrates the point. No one believes that Classical times were strangers to controversy. Far from it, as we can see especially from Plato's writings—though Aristotle by contrast usually tries to present himself as taking opponents' views duly and irenically into account, even when he is not really doing so. Nevertheless, as any reader of Cicero's *De Finibus Bonorum et Malorum* can see, the mood that is conveyed by our sources on Hellenistic doctrines is on the whole perceptibly more controversy laden, and therefore harder to associate with any harmony of opinion about ethics, than the one that dominates many works of the Classical period.

Nevertheless, many Stoic and Epicurean theses did indeed go against the grain of prereflective opinion, and at best required extensive argumentation to make them seem less intensely paradoxical. That means, however, that neither doctrine could easily appear to be the natural outgrowth of the culture around it, nor to correspond smoothly to most people's firmly held ethical judgements. Contrast Hellenistic philosophers in this respect with Classical thinkers, whom hegelian interpreters

---

[8] Cf. Annas 1993: 384, 391, 426–35, 442–6 (esp. 446), though she thinks of Hellenistic accounts as less determinedly systematizing than I do.

[9] Epicureanism can be interpreted as taking a less rigidly systematic form (as by Annas 1993: e.g. 85–7), but not, in my opinion, without distorting its basic character. See Chapter 7, sec. III. 3, below.

believed—falsely, as I have argued—to have reflected the harmonious outlook of the culture of their time or a slightly earlier one. Subjected to this comparison, Hellenistic thinkers often appear to be out of tune with their surroundings.

III. Epicureanism

1. Epicurean Psychology and Epicurean Norms

As he is normally interpreted, Epicurus fits the kantian stereotype of a eudaimonist Greek philosopher neatly. He believes that it is rational for an individual to aim at pleasure—that is, his own pleasure. This is both a theoretical thesis and also a guide to action. This is the kind of hedonist eudaimonism that Kant thought was characteristic of Greek ethics as a whole.

This description of Epicureanism, which reflects the traditional and standard conception of it, seems to me essentially correct, in spite of recent efforts to picture Epicureanism as being more similar to Classical views. In what follows, I shall say some things in defence of the traditional interpretation, which ascribes to Epicurus a position that is systematic in the way that I have said is characteristic of Hellenistic ethics. This is the feature of it that I shall highlight.

First, however, to sketch in some background. Analysed a bit more finely, Epicurus's thinking evidently contains two relevant parts, one descriptive and the other normative. The descriptive part explains how human motivations in fact operate, and in particular what it is which human beings by nature aim at. The normative or evaluative part tells us what it is rational to do and how it is rational to be. This part makes overt recommendations. Epicurus plainly thinks of it as in some sense supported by the descriptive part, and as drawing its recommendatory force from it. He does not make fully clear how he takes this process to work—in what way, that is, judgements about how motivations actually function will support judgements about how it is rational for people to be motivated. Naturally this unclarity provokes the sort of question that Hume is famous for having broached, about how an 'is' can support an 'ought'. Here, however, it is unnecessary to enter into these matters.

Under the traditional interpretation, the descriptive part of Epicurus' view is what is nowadays known as 'psychological egoism'. This thesis says that each human being always aims (in some sense) to act for the ultimate end of what he thinks to be his own good. Epicurus takes this good that he thinks everyone pursues to be pleasure. That means that his view is the particular variety of psychological egoism known as *hedonist* psychological egoism, which says that each human being always acts for the ultimate end of his own pleasure. So far, this sounds like the view that is nowadays associated with the name of Jeremy Bentham. It maintains that when a person decides what to do, he calculates which course of action (or way of life) will bring him the greatest quantity of pleasure. This view is properly known as *quantitative* hedonist psychological egoism.[10]

The ascription to Epicurus of psychological hedonism, and a fortiori of hedonist psychological hedonism, is open to challenge.[11] But whether or not Epicurus is indeed a psychological hedonist, it is clear enough that his position is not quite the same as this straightforwardly quantitative version of hedonist psychological egoism, but— depending on which interpretation one adopts—something fairly close to it.

But apart from whether Epicurus espoused such a psychological theory of what human motivation actually is as a matter of fact, he can be fairly securely said to defend a normative view about what it is *rational* for a human being to aim at. His contention seems to have been, that is, that pleasure is the only thing that is rational to pursue as an intrinsic and ultimate end. This thesis can properly be called hedonist rational egoism.[12] That being so, it becomes crucial for him to explain what pleasure is.

2. *Epicurean Systematic Hedonism*

Probably the most thoroughly systematic form of rational hedonism is quantitative rational hedonism, in the form proposed by Bentham, which pictures the rational thing to do as the action that will bring one the greatest quantity of pleasure. Epicurus's hedonism, however, seems to depart at least somewhat from this quantitive model, as I shall now explain. In spite of this fact, however, the Epicurean position is a highly systematic one.

Bentham took the quantity of an episode of pleasure to be measured as a function of its intensity and its duration. On this basis, he thought that we can calculate the quantity of prospective pleasures and pains and then proceed to choose actions on the basis of determining which action is likely (in some terms) to cause the greatest balance of the former over the latter. It does not seem, however, that we can interpret Epicurus in quite this way, or in any of the quantitative ways that are most usual among modern quantitative theorists.[13]

It is true that Epicurus sometimes writes in a manner strongly reminiscent of such thinking. He explains that we do and must attend to whether a given prospective pleasure may not cause 'greater annoyance' later, and whether a present pleasure may

---

[10] In terms of the classification given in Chapter 2, sec. VII. 3, I would call this an eliminative strategy. However, there is room for some disagreement about this classification, as there is in the case of many Utilitarian theories, for instance, and the theory of Hare 1981 (see esp. his ch. 2).

[11] See Cooper 1999a.

[12] See Long and Sedley 1987: i. 121–5.

[13] What are now called 'preference theories' do not seem to have been part of the ancient debate, though there are hints of such ideas in e.g. Plato's *Philebus*.

not properly be eschewed so as to gain a 'greater pleasure' afterwards. And he goes on, '[O]ne should judge all these matters by *measuring together* [*symmetrêsei*] and looking at the advantages and disadvantages'.[14] But in spite of passages of this sort, an interpretation invoking Bentham's style of measurement does not really fit what Epicurus says.

As to duration, we are confronted with the striking fact that according to Epicurus, the duration of a pleasure does not seem to be a factor in determining its value or choiceworthiness, or even its quantity. Thus Cicero reports on his view as follows:

Epicurus . . . denies that duration of time adds anything to living happily, and says that no less pleasure is experienced in a short period of time than if it were everlasting.[15]

When we turn to the notion of intensity of pleasure, moreover, we also find a further complication. Epicurus's account of what pleasure is does not permit us to think of its intensity as freely and indefinitely variable, especially in the positive direction. According to Epicurus, pleasure in the proper sense is what he calls *ataraxia*. This he understands to mean freedom from pain and anxiety. Once pain and anxiety are gone, he thinks that there is nothing further in the way of pleasure to be gained.

Many of Epicurus's ancient critics found his identification of pleasure with *ataraxia* implausible and even absurd. A few of these were themselves hedonists, such as Aristippus of Cyrene and his followers the so-called Cyrenaics, who believed that the ultimate rational goal was pleasure but insisted on a more full-blooded variety of it than *ataraxia* could be. Most opponents of Epicurus, however, were not hedonists. These opponents sometimes granted some credibility to the idea that we often seek pleasure, but they found that this credibility was diminished rather than increased by the identification of pleasure with mere freedom from pain and anxiety.[16]

The main opponents of Epicurus's hedonism were naturally those who denied that it was compatible with the view, which they accepted, that people might rationally aim at virtue. The opponents would also include thinkers who shared the worry, alluded to above, that the pursuit of pleasure by everyone, or even by very many people, would inevitably lead to conflicts among them, so that Epicurus's advice could not be successfully followed by all of his putative audience. His identification of pleasure with such a seemingly modest and quiet condition as *ataraxia* seems in large part to have been used to reply to these latter opponents. His thought must have been—to judge by the use that he makes of this idea in his argumentation[17]—that *ataraxia* was far less likely than more boisterous forms of pleasure to lead to competition. A byproduct of this view might then allow Epicurus to respond to those who worried that

---

[14] Epicurus, *Letter to Menoeceus* 130 (trans. Annas 1993: 334).
[15] *De Fin.* II. 87 (trans. Annas 1993: 344).
[16] See e.g. Cicero, *De Fin.* II. 87–8, and Annas 1993: 21–2, 227–36, 343.
[17] See e.g. Long and Sedley 1987: i. 122–3.

hedonism was inimical to the pursuit of virtue. If efforts to attain *ataraxia* were unlikely to lead to competition among people, they might be relatively easy to reconcile with the cooperative aspects of virtue as ordinarily conceived, and with attainment of that goal by all who were capable of it. Virtue would not thus be sought on its own account, but at least the pursuit of pleasure would not seem as damaging to it as might at first appear.

Epicurus's conception of pleasure as *ataraxia* seems to leave us with a notion of pleasure that is still susceptible of some quantitative treatment. This accounts for Epicurus's undeniable and unfailing willingness to talk of 'greater' pleasures and to speak of 'measurement', even if of a somewhat restricted kind. Variations in quantity of pleasure involve only the degrees of *approximation to* a condition of *ataraxia*, which can be greater or lesser. And Epicurus plainly believed that it mattered how close to complete *ataraxia* a person was, even if the complete absence of pain and anxiety is a theoretical maximum that cannot be exceeded.[18] One's rational aim, then, is to come as close as one can to that condition, that is, to be as little subject to pains and anxieties as one can. The exact method of measuring this condition is not obvious, but whatever it is, it is obviously a matter of determining a more and a less.

Plainly Epicurus's view, even as described only to this partial extent, is systematic enough, insofar as it strives for a single measure to be used in deliberation. In this sense it is straightforwardly monist. Beyond aiming at pleasure in the sense of *ataraxia*, there is no other consideration for a reasonable person to take into account, either in theory or in practice. This monist normative view and its accompanying rule of action is supported by a descriptive psychological theory that is equally systematic and equally monist. Indeed, Epicurus insists on a strict congruence of one's ethical theses with one's practical maxims:

If you do not on every suitable occasion refer each of your actions to the end given by nature, but stop short and make your avoidance or choice with reference to something else, your actions will not be consistent with your theories.[19]

---

[18]   Annas 1993 says that on Epicurus's view pleasure—i.e. katastematic or static pleasure, which is what he thinks happiness is a function of—is 'something not amenable to quantitative measurement' (335). This seems to me mistaken. The evidence that she adduces shows that complete *ataraxia* is a purely theoretical maximum, but not that there is no measuring possible short of that point. On the other hand there is a sense in which she seems to me right in saying that Epicureanism is not a 'maximizing' view, if that term is reserved for theories that say that some value should be 'maximized' indefinitely, in the absence of any theoretical limit (see her pp. 84–7). Striker 1996 ascribes, at least verbally, some sort of maximizing view to Epicurus (see her pp. 198, 201), but she seems to have a different notion of 'greatest' in mind from the one for which Annas uses the term 'maximizing'. It is not clear to me how Striker's interpretation fits into the discussion of the present issue.

[19]   *Kyriai Doxai* 25 (trans. Annas 1993: 342).

3. Interpretative Controversies

Some interpreters, however, have doubted that Epicurus's position really is as systematic as I have portrayed it as being. They have thought that his thinking involves something more like the informal weighing of considerations, without a single way of organizing them, that is reminiscent of what we find in Classical philosophers. Let me consider some of the evidence for this way of construing him.

The intention of such interpreters is to rescue Epicurus from the crudity, as it is supposed, of the hedonist monism that has normally been ascribed to him, in much the same way as hegelian interpreters hoped to rescue Aristotle from the egoist hedonism that kantian interpreters attributed to him. In antiquity, Epicurus was roundly attacked for recommending friendship and the ethical virtues, including justice, as mere means to one's own pleasure. That thought has given rise, especially in recent times, to an attempt to construe him as attaching to virtue and friendship a value that is independent of their bringing about some enjoyable state of oneself. The upshot of this type of reading is to give us not only a less egoist Epicurus, but also a more pluralistic, less systematic one, who does not make pleasure out to be the sole ultimate aim guiding practical deliberation.[20]

The evidence for this type of interpretation can be summarized quite briefly. In the first place, Epicurus maintains that we are best off conforming to ordinary ethical standards, cultivating virtues, maintaining friendships, and the like. Some have found it quite implausible that *ataraxia* might reliably be attained by such a strategy. They have therefore doubted that Epicurus could be using that test as the basis of this recommendation. Moreover, it is possible to find remarks that suggest that in his view, people do or should value virtue as merely an instrument for the acquisition of *ataraxia*. Thus he says:

[P]rudence (*phronêsis*) is the natural source of all the remaining virtues: it teaches the impossibility of living pleasurably without living prudently, honourably and justly, <and the impossibility of living prudently, honestly and justly> without living pleasurably. For the virtues are naturally linked with (*sympephykasi*) living pleasurably, and living pleasurably is inseparable (*achôriston*) from them.[21]

This passage might be understood to indicate that Epicurus does not regard *ataraxia* as the only thing that is valuable per se, but thinks that we should pursue a plurality of things for their own sake.

A different sort of evidence that might incline us in somewhat the same direction is the way in which Epicurus talks about justice. He seems to offer a quasi-Utilitarian ground for being just. In his *Principal Doctrines*, Epicurus says:

---

[20] See e.g. Annas 1993 and Mitsis 1988.

[21] Epicurus, *Letter to Menoeceus*, at Diogenes Laertius 10.132 (trans. Long and Sedley 1987: i. 114, 21 A).

Justice was never anything per se, but a contract, regularly arising at some place or other in people's dealings with one another, over not harming or being harmed . . .

What is legally deemed to be just has its existence in the domain of justice whenever it is attested to be useful in the requirements of social relationships, whether or not it turns out to be the same for all. But if someone makes a law and it does not happen to accord with the utility of social relationships, it no longer has the nature of justice.[22]

One might suppose that this passage provides a recommendation of justice that is not, after all, addressed solely to a given individual, but rather to people in general. It would accordingly be telling you not that your own individual pleasure would be secured by being just, but that justice would increase the pleasure enjoyed by your fellow citizens collectively. That might be taken to indicate that an individual ought to be concerned not only with his own well-being but also, independently, with that of others as well.[23]

One could even bring forward some facts about Epicurus' concern with the establishment of communities of people who would live together and depend on each other for well-being. It is true, one might argue, that Epicurus does not place much stock in the *polis*, and therefore does not have quite the same view of social organization as had Plato and Aristotle. Nevertheless, he placed a great deal of emphasis on another type of association, the relatively small philosophical community of people represented by his own 'Garden'.[24] On this account, therefore, it would be misleading to interpret him as believing that individuals are isolated and that their goods are not bound up with one another.

Suppose that we infer from this evidence that Epicurus did not, after all, espouse simply a systematic hedonist egoism. Suppose that instead we impute to him the belief that certain things—such things as virtues, including justice, and friendship—are to be taken as valuable in and of themselves. And suppose we also take him to be offering some advice collectively to groups of people, not merely to individuals one by one. How then could we understand his view about the relation between these things and an individual's happiness or pleasure?

One possibility is to interpret him as saying—rather as Mill did—that we can seek a thing, such as virtue, for its own sake when we seek it 'as a part of happiness'.[25]

---

[22] *Principal Doctrines* 33, 37 (trans. Long and Sedley 1987: i. 125, 22 A–B); cf. Cicero, *De Fin.* II. 71. For this type of way of taking the passage—though in a more elaborate form—see Annas 1993: 293–302, esp. 301.

[23] For a fuller development of this idea, see Annas 1993: 293–302; and for the similar problem about friendship see her 236–44, esp. 240–1. Notice that there seems to be no good evidence for the attribution to Epicureans of a belief in the existence in individuals of a generalized benevolence directed at all humanity—although perhaps Lucretius's paean to Epicurus as a benefactor of the whole world is an exception (see *De Rerum Natura* VI. 1–42.   [24] See Annas 1993: 243–4.

[25] This seems to be the interpretation given by Annas 1993: 341, which is as she acknowledges 'influenced by Mill's solution to his analogous problem' (n. 26); cf. Chapter 2, sec. I. 4, and Chapter 6, sec. IV. 3, above.

Similarly, as I have noted in passing, Epicurus might have maintained that some intrinsic value attaches to the happiness of an individual's friends. À propos this possibility, we find evidence that in the opinion of some Epicureans, 'friends are loved for their own sake', and that 'people can love their friends no less than themselves'.[26]

If we did indeed interpret Epicurus along these lines, then his position would turn out to be far less plainly a form of deliberative monism than the more traditional and usual description of it makes it appear. On such a non-monist interpretation, our ultimate aims emerge as plural, comprising the well-being of friends and also the several virtues, including justice. We would thus end up with a picture of an inclusivist eudaimonist Epicurus, not unlike the portrait of Aristotle examined earlier.[27]

The foregoing evidence, however, seems to me insufficient to persuade us that Epicurus rejected the idea that a person's choices should be explicitly and systematically governed in the same uniform way by the overall aim of *ataraxia*. After all, we do have his seemingly forthright insistence, quoted earlier, that you should refer 'each of your actions' to a single end. Numerous passages, moreover, appear to manifest a tendency on his part to do precisely that. The question is whether this evidence can be overturned or qualified by passages suggesting that he also believed that people should in some contexts attach intrinsic value to friendship and virtue. I doubt that it can.

Support for this doubt can be found in several places. For one thing, there is evidence that some Epicureans recommend to an individual the practice of cultivating virtue and friendship purely on the ground of its conduciveness to his own pleasure.[28] In the *De Finibus*, Cicero writes the following about friendship:

Some Epicureans, *however* (*Sunt autem quidam Epicurei timidiores*) . . . are a little more timid in facing the criticisms . . .; they are afraid that if we regard friendship as desirable just for our own pleasure, it will seem to be completely crippled, as it were. In their view, then, the first associations and unions and wishes to form relationships occur for the sake of pleasure; but when advancing familiarity has produced intimacy, affection blossoms to such an extent that friends come to be loved just for their own sake even if no advantage accrues from the friendship.

The most striking thing about this passage, it seems to me, is that it ascribes the idea that friendship is sought for its own sake only to *some* Epicureans. Furthermore, it states that these are people who have been swayed by strenuous opposition to the implications of the Epicurean stance. Thereby it gives us to understand that this idea

---

[26] Here see Long and Sedley 1987: i. 138. The passage that they cite is Cicero, *De Fin.* I. 69–70 (text 21 O, in Long and Sedley 1987). Long and Sedley (rightly, in my view) refrain from interpreting the passage as showing that Epicurus wavered from his straightforwardly egoistic hedonism.

[27] That this is Annas's tendency is indicated by her 1993: 350.

[28] See Long and Sedley 1987: i. 122–3.

is not standard Epicureanism. Furthermore, Cicero asserts firmly that Epicurean views about the value of friendship and the value of virtue run parallel to each other. The upshot of these facts fits with the general run of the evidence about what Epicurus and his orthodox followers maintained about both virtue and friendship, and also with what Cicero has indicated just before. That is, virtue and friendship are valuable on fundamentally instrumental grounds, and not in the strict sense for their own sake.[29]

Not that Epicurus himself ignored the objections of people who believed that his straightforward hedonism was shockingly unacceptable. Certainly he seems to have been willing sometimes to offer assurances that the policy of cleaving to the ethical standards of one's city will make it as likely as any policy can that one will attain *ataraxia*.[30] Likewise, he seems to have insisted that cheats and bullies will always be so afraid of detection and punishment that their anxiety will outweigh the gains that they could reap.[31] These arguments sound like a direct attempt to persuade us that justice is instrumentally valuable because it will probably lead to tranquillity. Unconvincing as such arguments may be in our eyes, they are unquestionably an important component of Epicurus's position.

Annas argues vigorously for the contention that Epicurus adopted something very like the idea of Mill's, anticipated by Butler, that virtue and friendship are parts of happiness, and that in aiming for it one is thereby aiming for them, so that they are valued for themselves and not for a relation that they bear to it.[32] This seems to me extremely hard to accept, in view of Epicurus's identification of well-being with *ataraxia*. Being virtuous, for instance, is not the same thing as being in a state of freedom from desire and anxiety. Perhaps such a state might *ensue* on being virtuous, if indeed one had a desire for virtue which was satisfied by the recognition of one's virtue. It does not seem to me possible to maintain, however, nor to believe that Epicurus himself could have thought, that any of these items—virtue, friends' well-being, and the like—either are identical with or are parts of *ataraxia*.[33]

Still, we need somehow to account for the indications that in Epicurus's opinion, we do have some kind of intrinsic desire for these other items. This it is not easy to do. Perhaps his thought is what Annas calls a 'two-level' view, which is much the same as the view that Butler adopted. It states that if a person is to be able actually to gain the

[29] The long quoted passage is from Cicero, *De Fin.* I. 69 (also at Long and Sedley 1987: 22 O). The parallelism between virtue and friendship is asserted at I. 66 and 68, and I. 66–8 describes two views about them which I take Cicero plainly to regard as more orthodox than the one described in I. 69.

[30] See Long and Sedley 1987: i. 125–37.

[31] Epicurus, *Principal Doctrines* 17, 35.

[32] See the references to Annas in the previous notes.

[33] See Armstrong 1997 for what I think is a plausible reading of the evidence for Epicurus's account of justice. For related reasons, it appears to me that Annas's translation (1993: 341 n. 26) of *sympephykasi* in the *Letter to Menoeceus* is unlikely to be right (see n. 21 above).

pleasure that it is rational to aim at, it is necessary that, as he is deliberating, he *not* think of the happiness of others as desired merely for the sake of his own pleasure. If one did think of the happiness of others in that way, Epicurus might reason, then the pleasure that one could gain from it would be either diminished or eliminated.[34] Therefore, although considered from a rational reflective standpoint, the only ultimately worthwhile end is indeed one's own pleasure, nevertheless in order to attain it—Epicurus might be saying—one must be directly seeking other things, at least when one is caught up in one's thoughts of it, and is not reflecting philosophically on the justification of that attachment.[35] Unfortunately we lack solid evidence that might show whether this is in fact what Epicurus, or Epicureans, had in mind.

4. Systematic Hedonist Thinking in the Hellenistic Period

In spite of these questions about what Epicurus's doctrine was, it does not seem to me that they alter the fundamental facts about the systematic character of at least much Epicurean thinking on these matters. In the first place, suppose that he did espouse a two-level view. Suppose he held, that is, that an actual agent would not think of himself as aiming at merely the single end of *ataraxia*, but would instead regard himself as weighing against each other a plurality of distinct considerations, all of which he treated as intrinsically valuable. Nevertheless, Epicurus would on this interpretation still be maintaining that there in another point of view, on the other 'level', that would aim systematically to reach a single goal, namely, the closest possible approximation to the state of *ataraxia*. Moreover, there is a sense in which this monist standpoint is primary, and the pluralist standpoint is justified merely as a way of helping ensure that the single goal, *ataraxia*, will be reached or closely approached.[36]

However, beyond what Epicurus himself may have advocated there is a broader point about Hellenistic ethics to be made here, which is crucial for understanding the general shape of the history of Greek ethics as a whole. Leave aside whether or not Epicurus's own position was as systematically monist, as I have contended it is. Indeed, suppose for the sake of argument that it was not. Still it is obvious that *some* philosophers in the Hellenistic period expressly conceived the idea, taken very

---

[34] Alternatively, Epicurus might conceivably have anticipated the argument that Butler later made famous in his eleventh sermon, by supposing that the desire for *ataraxia* would be empty if we could not specify other 'primary' desires that *ataraxia* would be identified as freedom *from*. I see no evidence for this conjecture. I also find it doubtful, on the following ground: there is no reason to think that *ataraxia* in fact *is* empty without such further specification. *Ataraxia* is freedom from *any* desires (and anxieties). To make sense of this idea, there is no reason to identify which desires one thereby lacks.

[35] This sort of view distinguishes between the attitude towards a thing that philosophical reflection recommends and the possibly quite different attitude towards it that we are recommended to adopt when we are not engaged in reflection. See Annas 1993: 190, 196–7, 200.

[36] At least this seems to me to be the import of Annas's interpretation.

generally and abstractly, of developing a monist position that followed hedonist lines. It is also fairly clear, from the passage of Cicero quoted just now, that some of them were *Epicureans*, whether orthodox (as I think they were) or not, and whether Epicurus was among them (as I think he was) or not. Certainly, moreover, some opponents of Epicurus took him to be espousing a straightforwardly hedonist monism. We know that because they attacked him for it, unfairly or not.

We may thus conclude firmly that the idea of such a thoroughgoing monism was in the intellectual air in Hellenistic times, to a greater extent than it had been earlier, at least so far as we can judge from the evidence that remains to us.[37] Indeed, it is as certain as these things can be that other hedonists—the Cyrenaics, led by Aristippus—actually advanced it straightforwardly.[38]

We should see the availability of this sort of idea in the Hellenistic period as a response to the problem of rational deliberation, which remained a problem because the Classical period had plainly failed to solve it, *not* because Hellenistic philosophy somehow lost its grip on something that earlier thinkers had grasped. To say this is not to denigrate the work of Plato and Aristotle nor to glorify post-Aristotelian thought. The project of harmonizing an individual's good with broader aims has exercised (and, in my opinion, defeated) philosophers ever since.

The present point is not that Classical philosophy failed. It is that Classical philosophers did not take themselves to have solved the problem, nor did Hellenistic philosophers think that they had either. Hellenistic philosophers tried a different type of attack on a common problem, by arguing for a single, systematic standard that would unify practical rationality. They were striving, in some respects more singlemindedly and systematically than Plato and Aristotle had done, to articulate an idea of practical reason with features for which Platonic and Aristotelian views are often praised as typically Hellenic.

The Epicurean resolution could of course not be congenial either to those hegelian interpreters who looked to Classical philosophy nostalgically, nor to kantian readers who believed that Greek ethics was egoist and ignored moral considerations. Epicurean ethics, as it is traditionally interpreted and as I interpret it here, is indeed straightforwardly egoist. Its fundamental goal is a state of oneself that is self-confined: one's own tranquillity. Deliberative consistency is won by taking the value of non-self-regarding or ethical aims to depend on whatever capacity they may have to promote

---

[37] There are hints of it in Plato's *Protagoras*, of course, and perhaps in the position of Eudoxus reported by Aristotle in *Nic. Eth.* X. 1–5. But we do not have evidence that this view was more widely shared or even discussed, except in a somewhat oblique form in the *Philebus*.

[38] See Annas 1993: e.g. 227–36, 338–9. Her p. 236, in particular, acknowledges the way in which the Cyrenaics were willing to flout the complications introduced into ethics by the feeling that it must cleave fairly closely to certain ordinary ethical beliefs.

ataraxia.[39] This strategy is as straightforwardly eliminativist as any strategy of the Classical period could possibly be taken to be. It completely removes the possibility of conflict by removing any dualism of practical reason. There is only one rationally compelling aim, one's own tranquillity or approximation thereto. Everything else derives value from that. But this is the very position that kantian-minded critics of Greek ethics have found so repugnant, and it is hardly the kind of harmony of practical reason that hegelian harmonizing eudaimonists could tolerate either.

IV. The Stoics

1. The Stoic Assimilation of Self-Referential and Non-Self-Referential Viewpoints

When we shift our attention to the Stoics, we find even stronger reason to think that the idea of deliberative monism was in significant respects more lively in Hellenistic ethics than it had been in Classical times. The Stoics exhibit what is probably the most thorough attempt in the history of Greek philosophy to conceive of rational aims as unified, and to reconcile the idea of the rational aim of an individual, as seen from his own point of view, with a universal good as judged from a completely global and indeed impersonal standpoint. In that sense, the Stoics fulfil to a high degree the description of Greek ethics as an effort to establish a harmony of ends.[40]

Nevertheless, the Stoics' efforts in this area go largely unrecognized. Their doctrines are often expounded in a form that gives them the look of a vulgarly inspirational ascetic prudentialism, which tries merely to buck people up so that they can cope with whatever bad situation they happen to be in. Some Stoic thinking undoubtedly deserves to be described in this way. However, the most serious and least popularizing Stoic thinkers developed a position of great subtlety which, even where it cannot be reconciled with ordinary prereflective ethical opinion and seems sometimes even perverse, is for all that a sustained and cohesive response to problems about deliberative conflict.

The crucial and most striking element of Stoicism is the unusual, complex, and problematic interrelation that it posits between two evaluative points of view, one self-regarding and the other not. When Stoicism is fully developed, it results in an assimilation of these two standpoints to each other. The opposition of what is good for me and what is good from a non-self-regarding or even non-self-referential standpoint is made to disappear.

For an individual to adopt his own perspective on questions about what is good,

---

[39] As indicated already, this is so even on a 'two-level' interpretation. An agent will value virtue and friendship intrinsically, but that is because doing so is the way to approach *ataraxia* as closely as possible.

[40] Among recent treatments of the importance of unity and freedom from conflict among aims in Stoic ethics, see e.g. Striker 1996: 223 and Cooper 1996: 263–5.

according to this position, is nothing other than for him to adopt a global perspective, from which he makes judgements about what is good from the point of view, extravagantly enough, of the universe as a whole. There is therefore no longer any question either of discovering that what is good for oneself is not good by the standard of some independently important broader consideration, or of encountering a conflict within deliberative rationality. According to Stoicism, there are no such two distinct kinds of evaluation that could yield divergent or conflicting recommendations. There is only one evaluative standpoint, the global one. To adopt it is—paradoxical as that may seem, and to many in antiquity did seem—precisely to adopt the standpoint that is one's own.

2. *The Stoic* Kosmos

The Stoics maintain that the only thing that is perfectly good is the structure of the universe or *kosmos* as a whole. Its perfection is a value that is to be described not by its relation to a particular person who apprehends it or stands in any sense to benefit from it, but in terms that are impersonal and in particular non-self-referential. That is, they are to be described without any reference to oneself at all.[41] Moreover, the perfection of the *kosmos* is not a function of the values of each of its parts taken separately, not even the part that is one's own life, but has to be grasped as a whole.[42]

Grasping the goodness of the *kosmos* is essential, the Stoics maintain, for an understanding of the value of anything whatsoever. The person who is in the ideal human condition, the so-called 'Sage', reaches an understanding of what is valuable for any man by knowing the structure of the *kosmos* and the pattern and regularities by which it is governed.[43] 'No one', says Cicero's account in Book III of his *De Finibus*, 'can judge truly about good things and bad except by knowing the whole plan of nature

---

[41] On the perfection of the *kosmos* see e.g. *SVF* ii. 641 (= Cicero, *De Natura Deorum* II. 38–9, with explicit attribution to the early Stoic, Chrysippus), 549, 550, 1009. There seems to me no reason to question that the ideas expressed here concerning the good are essential parts of the Stoic position. This conclusion is confirmed by the place of the non-self-referential, non-relational notion of goodness in Cicero, *De Fin.* III. 20ff., discussed below. The Stoics maintain that 'what is good benefits' (e.g. Seneca at Long and Sedley 1987: i. 374 (60 S). That is to say that non-self-referential and self-referential goodness coincide, when one takes them as conceptually distinct; it is not to say that all there is to goodness is self-referential or relational goodness. (See also Long and Sedley 1987: i. 368–9 (60 A), though on the whole they confine their quotations concerning the concept to passages focusing on self-referential goodness.)

[42] See e.g. *SVF* ii. 550.

[43] *De Fin.* III. 21, 'summum illud *hominis* per se laudandum et expetendum bonum'. See *De Fin.* III. 73, 29, 31. This idea is sometimes associated by commentators only with later Stoicism, perhaps because of the emphasis placed on it by Marcus Aurelius, but the evidence clearly assigns it to the earlier Stoics as well, including notably Cleanthes in his *Hymn to Zeus*. See Kerferd 1978: 135–6, and White 1979a: 165–70 and 1985b. On the part that logic played in the Stoics' efforts to regard the *kosmos* as coherent, see Long 1971a and 1978, and for a general account of the place of cosmology in Stoic philosophy, see Long 1974.

and also of the life of the gods, and by knowing whether the nature of man conforms to universal nature or not.'[44]

Here the Stoics describe a transition, which a person makes as he matures, from one motivational stage through a second and finally to a third. At the first stage, one 'naturally' and without thought selects and strives for certain goals. One's selecting and striving are determined by nature, whose patterns are manifested in them. These are the first 'duties' or 'appropriate acts' (the Greek is *kathêkonta*, which Cicero translates by the Latin *officia*). These strivings are conceived of as self-referential: one aims for certain states of oneself, such as the consuming of food by oneself.

The second stage, on the other hand, consists of the conception of a general pattern, to which, when one becomes aware of it, the label 'good' is applied. The only thing that is strictly good and is the end (*telos* or *finis*) is a man's living in agreement and accord (*homologia* or, in Latin, *congruentia* or *convenientia*) with nature.[45] From the perspective of this awareness, one realizes that this agreement is more properly to be sought than any of the conditions for which one previously strived. Indeed, one now regards those things as not possessing any value of their own; the only thing that one regards as strictly valuable or good is the pattern of conformity of nature itself.[46] Once a person starts to comprehend this notion of goodness, the Stoics think, he is on the way to becoming aware that the things that he used to seek because they preserved his nature are not valuable but instead 'indifferent', neither good nor bad.

This second stage, however, leads to a third stage, which the Stoics clearly think is fully reached only by someone who understands their overall position. At this third stage a person may conceive of the relationship between what has happened and been grasped at the first two stages. This third stage embraces a conception according to which the things valued at the first stage are regarded as having a derivative sort of value. This value attaches to them by virtue of their exhibiting the pattern or agreement of which one has now become aware.[47] Here a person notices that the regularities exhibited by his earlier strivings fall under the pattern of agreement of which he has become aware at the second stage, and can be valued, derivatively, by virtue of their so doing.[48]

The third stage does not, however, simply involve a straightforward application, to the strivings of the first stage, of the notion of 'agreement' that has been conceived at the second stage. For it can sometimes be a manifestation of that 'agreement', which one conceives of at the second stage, even to act against that self-preservation to which one is impelled by nature at the first stage. This idea lies at the basis of the Stoic

[44] *De Fin.* III.73.
[45] 'Congruenter naturae convenienterque vivere', *De Fin.* III. 26.
[46] *De Fin.* III. 20: 'tamen id solum vi sua et dignitate expetendum est'. Cf. cc. 50–1 and below, sec. IV. 5.
[47] *De Fin.* III. 21: 'eorum autem, quae sunt prima naturae, propter se nihil est expetendum'.
[48] *De Fin.* III. 21: 'ut recte dici possit omnia officia eo referri, ut adipiscamur principia naturae'.

doctrine concerning suicide: even though the first regularities of nature dictate self-preservation, nevertheless in some circumstances an understanding of the pattern of events can recommend the destruction of oneself. In either case, however, the ultimate aim is not preservation of oneself, but conformity to the overall order or pattern of nature, which is what is good in the fundamental sense.

Such, in outline, is the Stoic story about how we acquire our fundamental evaluative concepts as we mature. In the present context, however, the point to be noted is the following. Whereas the first stage involves exclusively self-referential aims, in that one aims to put oneself in certain states or conditions vis-à-vis the world around one, the second stage, by contrast, brings with it aims that are not conceived as thus self-referential. Rather, one sees a general pattern which applies 'to human beings' in general and to nature as a whole.[49] The pattern is observed not merely in one's own actions and strivings, but in nature as a whole.

For our purposes the crucial point is this. When one has reached the third stage, and has accordingly mastered evaluative concepts as the Stoics conceive them, one does not simply recognize how one's own strivings serve the maintenance of one's own life and satisfy one's own needs, and see simply how to gain one's own good. Rather, one values one's good *as* a component of the good or *bonum* as exhibited globally in nature as a whole, as one has grasped it at the second stage.[50]

This global concept of goodness also receives an explicitly ethical interpretation within Stoicism.[51] The Stoics maintain that their position can also be expressed by the slogan, 'Virtue is the only good'. In this formula, the term 'virtue' is as equivalent to 'living in accord with nature' or 'conformity to the plan or organization of the *kosmos*'. This 'accord' (*homologia* or, in Cicero's Latin, *congruentia*) is generally taken to be a state of the intellectual part of the soul, the understanding (the so-called 'leading part' or *hêgemonikon*). This might seem not to have anything to do with ethics proper nor with virtue in the ordinary sense of the term. For the understanding or knowledge in question might appear to have merely to do with the structure of the *kosmos* as it is described in physics. And indeed most Stoics do in fact contend that someone who

[49] *De Fin.* III. 21: 'of a man', 'illud hominis . . . bonum'; cf. III. 73.

[50] Thus it seems to me impossible to regard the notion that Cicero is expounding in this passage as purely a self-referential one, or to think that the Stoics treated the result of the process described there as simply a self-referential aim. Rather, the point is that at the end, one aims for, as one might put it, one's own good as exhibiting the (non-self-referential) goodness of the structure of nature as a whole. This is the kind of fusing of self-referential and non-self-referential aims that, as I shall continue to expound it, the Stoics were trying to articulate (see sec. IV. 9). (Whether it can in the end be made out to be coherent is a question that I shall not attack here.)

[51] See e.g. *De Fin.* III. 64–6, with White 1979a and 1985b, and Long and Sedley 1987: i. 352–3, along with Striker 1996: 230–1. Note that the systematization that the Stoics aimed for in ethics had as a by-product a simplification, and by many lights an impoverishment, of their view of beauty (see Most 1992).

lives fully in accord with nature must possess a detailed understanding of nature in physical terms. The Stoics developed their own physical doctrines to that end.[52]

3. The Global Normative Outlook of Stoicism

An understanding of nature, however, turns out to have a social dimension that links it to ethics and political philosophy.[53] We are born for society and natural partnership with each other, the Stoics hold, and are linked together by nature in such a way as to be fellow citizens of each other. It is also fitting for a person's native land to be dearer to him than he is himself, they contend, and one should think about the interests of people who will survive one 'for their own sake'.[54]

Nevertheless, our attachments are not limited to people who in fact live within our own political community. The fact that the *kosmos* is governed by divinity and that each of us is a part of it is said to yield by nature the result that we aim for the common advantage, and we are said to be motivated by nature to benefit as many people as possible, just as Hercules and Bacchus were motivated by nature to protect the human race. These last statements make explicit that anyone who correctly looks at practical issues from the perspective that fully comprehends the good, and therefore understands the goodness of virtue, relies on judgements that are not restricted to his own good or the good of any particular individuals to whom he is related in some special way.

Stoic universalism also retains a further conceptual connection with the *polis*. Like the Epicureans, the Stoics do not consistently pay attention to the workings of actual city-states. They maintain, however, that the whole world could be compared to a city-state:

The world is also called the habitation of gods and men, and the structure (*systema*) consisting of gods and men and the things created for their sake. For just as there are two meanings of city (*polis*), one as habitation and two as the stucture of its inhabitants along with its citizens, so the world is like a city consisting of gods and men, with gods serving as rulers and men as their subjects.[55]

The Stoics thus believe that the global outlook embodied in their evaluative holism is an extension of and attachment to the organized structure of the *polis*.

---

[52] It is, however, a matter of considerable uncertainty just what the terms are in which one's knowledge of physics ought to be expressed; see White 1985b.

[53] See White 1979a and 1985b, along with Striker 1996: 248–61

[54] See below, sec. VI. 6–7, and also Cicero, *De Off.* I. 31.

[55] Long and Sedley 1987: i. 431 (67 L); cf. p. 435.

4. The Development of the Global Outlook in the Individual

Although the Stoics say that the only truly good thing is the *kosmos* as a whole, and that other things are judged good by reference to their relation of fitting into its structure, they do not maintain that human beings begin their lives in possession of this global concept of goodness. Indeed, one of the Stoics' main projects in philosophical psychology is to try to explain how the notion of goodness required for global impersonal evaluation develops, in a human being, out of the self-regarding outlook that they say is characteristic of infants.

According to Stoicism, an individual begins life with a set of impulses, implanted by nature, to seek what tends to preserve his life and to avoid what tends to destroy it.[56] These impulses, it must be noted, are self-referential: they aim to achieve certain states of oneself. The same is true of all of the various impulses (*hormai*) that remain with us throughout life.

As a human being matures, however, he outgrows this exclusively self-regarding perspective. Once this initial pattern of behaviour becomes firmly established, the Stoics say, a person starts to become attached to the an 'order and harmony of conduct'. Having once conceived of this order, one values it more than the things to which we were attached previously, when one viewed matters only from one's own perspective. It is this appreciation of order, once we extend it to the entire *kosmos*, that constitutes our understanding of what the good consists in. The first step of the process occurs as follows:

> The initial principle being thus established that things in accordance with nature are 'things to be taken' for their own sake, and their opposites similarly 'things to be rejected', the first 'appropriate act' . . . is to preserve one's natural constitution; the next is to repel those that are the contrary.

The process is further extended:

> [T]hen when this principle of choice and of rejection has been discovered, there follows next in order choice conditioned by 'appropriate action'; then, such choice become a fixed habit; and finally, choice fully rationalized and in harmony with nature.

But only at the end of the process just described does the notion of good begin to appear:

> It is at *this final stage* that the *Good* properly so called first emerges and comes to be understood in its true nature. Man's first attraction is towards the things in accordance with nature

---

[56] The most important passage for understanding this aspect of Stoic views is III. 20–2 of Cicero's *De Finibus*. This passage gives the clearest picture we have of the Stoic view about the development of motivation, including their doctrine of what they called *oikeiosis*, the process by which animals and human beings first deal with the world. See White 1979a and Striker 1983.

[with this Cicero has recapitulated the first step]; *but* as soon as he has understanding ... and has discerned the order and so to speak harmony that governs conduct, he thereupon *esteems this harmony far more highly than all the things for which he orginally felt an affection*, and by exercise of intelligence and reason infers the conclusion that *herein* resides the chief *Good* of man, the thing that is *praiseworthy and desirable for its own sake*, ... whereas none of the primary objects of nature is desirable for its own sake.[57]

This notion of good lies beyond the self-referential notion of what preserves one's own nature intact. It emerges with an understanding, but not of the particular things towards which nature urges one for the sake of self-preservation. Rather, the notion of goodness lies in the comprehension of the *general structure* ('ordo et concordia') by which nature has organized things so that *any* being is urged towards what preserves itself. This notion of goodness, since it is a notion of a general structure by which everything is organized, is not self-referential. It does not involve the concept of oneself, nor the ability to evaluate things by their connection to some state of oneself. Nor does the appreciation of what is good consist in the valuing of a certain condition of oneself, nor of something as related to oneself. Instead, evaluation of something as good takes place from an impersonal point of view.

5. The 'Indifferents'

This universalist way of thinking is closely linked to the notorious and problematic Stoic doctrine of 'indifferents'. The general purport of this doctrine appears to be that nothing that affects an individual human being is, as such, of any value, good or bad. This line of thought seems to lead, in Stoic thinking, to a complete obliteration of any self-regarding, or even any self-referential, evaluative perspective that an individual might have on himself.

Stoicism was a source of scandal among philosophers for insisting that value in the genuine sense—that is, goodness and badness—can be attributed neither to the actions that a person performs, nor to whether or not he undergoes pleasure, pains, and other experiences of that kind. Rather all of these things are indifferent (*adiaphora*), strictly neither good nor bad. Stoicism does concede that certain actions are 'appropriate' or 'fitting', and that certain states are 'preferable' for an individual to be in. Despite this, however, the Stoic position is that in the correct and privileged sense

---

[57] *De Fin.* III. 20–1. Cicero's phrase is 'rerum agendarum ordinem et ... concordia'. In my 1979a, I stressed the difference between the first stage and the final stage, noting that as is made plain by Cicero, what is gained at the latter stage is obviously not a grasp of the concept of what will preserve one's own natural state, but rather a grasp of the universalization of that concept, i.e. the organization of the *kosmos* under which *each thing* acts in that way. It is this universalization to which the term 'good' is applied, not its self-referential instantiation.

of evaluation, these actions and states are without value, positive or negative.[58] The sense in which Stoics reject the standard assessment of such things as good or bad is no trivial one. The Stoics regard themselves expressly as working against the kinds of evaluations that they believed most people make when they call things good or bad, not as rephrasing them. To call things 'preferable' or 'fitting' was not, they insisted, merely a way of smuggling in such evaluations through the back door—though their opponents accused them of doing precisely that.

The effect of this view seems to be to nullify the force of any judgements that a person might make about what presents itself to his ordinary point of view as his own well-being. If all of the things that I can either do or feel are declared to be indifferent, then it seems to follow that there is nothing about myself to which I can attach any evaluative or deliberative importance. The importance of all self-referential judgements of value seems to have been obliterated. In their place, it would appear, are left only the judgements that one makes about the perfection of the *kosmos* as a whole. Here we see the beginning of the way in which Stoicism adopts an eliminative stance towards the dualism of individual good and broader considerations. Their whole position is designed to obliterate the possibility of an opposition between these two things.

But not wholly obliterated. The Stoics register and keep in view the fact that ordinary people do not abandon their own self-referential evaluations. Such people continue to react to indifferents as if they exhibited genuine positive or negative value, that is, goodness and badness. Recall here the fact, discussed earlier, that Chrysippus and other Stoics employ imperatives in formulating norms.[59] It is the lack of fit between what the Stoics hold to be the correct mode of evaluation and the kinds of evaluations that people ordinarily make that accounts for these imperative formulations. In ordinary people, at least, correct norms are resisted by the irrational impulses, which are responsible for our mistakes about what to do. To a sage, on the other hand, or even to someone who simply recognizes the point that the Stoics try to make, imperatives might seem to be unnecessary. This fact accounts for the Stoic willingness to employ formulations of both kinds.

When I spoke earlier of Aristotle's treatment of the clash in *Nicomachean Ethics* X. 6–8 between the life of political activity and the life given over to *theôria*, I observed that the way to avoid all possibility of conflict between distinct goods is to adopt a holist standpoint of evaluation. This consists in denying that individual constituents of a good are subject to assessment on their own. Rather, one says that the whole of

---

[58] See Long and Sedley 1987: i. 357–9; Cicero, *De Fin.* III. 50–1. It is this lack of fit between what the Stoics think is the correct mode of evaluation and the kinds of evaluations that people ordinarily make that accounts for the fact, discussed in Chapter 3, that the Stoics often cast norms in imperative terms. These norms are resisted by the irrational impulses that are responsible for our mistakes about what to do.

[59] See Chapter 3, sec. VI. 1–2.

which they are constituents is what is intrinsically good, and the parts have value only by virtue of their contribution to the whole.[60] It was Aristotle's willingness to evaluate particular activities on their own, rather than insisting that a good life is the only thing that is intrinsically good, that produced the possibility of conflict at the end of the *Nicomachean Ethics* and the need for Aristotle to adjudicate it.

The Stoic theory of value carries out the holist policy in a way in which Aristotle did not. The doctrine of indifferents is in effect a way of denying intrinsic value to parts of the *kosmos*, namely, those parts that are intimately connected with oneself. The Stoics are thus in effect insistent that the only value that matters is the value that one apprehends and appreciates from a holist point of view.

6. Stoic Self-Regard

However, the Stoics take a yet further and indeed quite radical step in the direction of eliminating this dualism. They do not believe that once a human being becomes mature enough to comprehend the global pattern of goodness embodied in the *kosmos*, he ceases to make judgements about local states of affairs or to make self-referential evaluations of his own condition. Rather, local self-regarding judgements persist, manifested in two principal features of Stoic doctrine.

For one thing, the Stoics do not appear in general to maintain that individuals somehow 'lose themselves' in the *kosmos*, or abandon their sense of their own identity or individuality. Perhaps some Stoics constitute exceptions to this statement. For example, some passages of Marcus Aurelius may express such a phenomenon. For the most part, however, the Stoic aim of living in accord with nature (*homologia têi physei*) is indeed construed self-referentially. What *I* am to aim at is that *I* conform to nature. It is *not* merely that, impersonally, nature *be conformed to*, even though according to Stoic doctrine that will in fact happen, quite regardless of what I think or prefer.[61]

This conformity to nature, moreover, is closely tied in Stoic doctrine to a kind of 'accord' that is thought of in a fully self-referential fashion as an aim that one has *for oneself*. This 'accord' (*homologia*, full stop) is a kind of self-consistency, or consistency within oneself. It evidently consists in a freedom from any sort of internal conflict of impulses, desires, or aims. This is plainly a state of a localized part of the *kosmos*, not of the *kosmos* as a whole. Moreover, it is regularly presented as something that a person reasonably aims at for himself.

The mode in which the Stoics expound their doctrines reinforces the sense that they are speaking, just as the Epicureans do, to individuals who view themselves as individuals, and wish to make the best of their own individual lives. Stoic texts seem

---

[60] See Chapter 6, sec. IX. 1–2, with Chapter 1, sec. VII. 4 and Chapter 2, sec. VII. 3.

[61] Consider in this connection the Stoic slogan (in the Latin of Seneca), 'Ducunt volentem fata; nolentem trahunt' *(SVF* i. 527; cf. ii. 1000).

to tell you how to treat your life. They presume that the members of their audience, as they receive the Stoic message, will view themselves as individuals attempting to live well. It is true that, as is traditionally said, the propensity of Stoicism to focus on its own value to individuals increased in later antiquity and was weaker in its earlier period. Non-writing teachers like Epictetus are more characteristic of Roman times than of the third century BCE. Nevertheless, this tendency was not absent earlier on, as for example Cleanthes' *Hymn to Zeus* shows:

> Nothing occurs on the earth apart from you, O God.
> . . . .
> And so you have wrought together into one all things that are
>   good and bad,
> So that there arises one eternal *logos* of all things,
> Which all bad mortals shun and ignore,
> Unhappy wretches, ever seeking the possession of good things
> They neither see nor hear the universal law of God,
> By obeying which they might enjoy a happy life.[62]

This is not a direct preachment, such as the ones that were common in later Stoicism, but it makes clear to the reader that he would be better off accepting the Stoic outlook than not.

Understandably, this mode of address can encourage an interpretation which construes Stoicism in a very narrow, self-confined, egoist fashion. Not only do the Stoics often give the impression of sermonizing; they convey the sense that they are sermonizing to people one by one. It seems difficult to regard this kind of writing as the manifestation of a doctrine that holds that an individual should not take self-regarding evaluations seriously, and should not be concerned with his own good but only with the fact that the *kosmos* as a whole is perfect.

7. Stoic Fusionism

Stoicism thus seems at first sight to present two contradictory faces. On the one hand, it seems to insist that the only thing of value is the *kosmos* as a whole and the structure embodied in it. On the other hand, it seems to address this insistence to individuals, as though it were a message by which each of them may assure his own individual well-being. The Stoics have sometimes been attacked both in antiquity and in modern times for just this sort of seeming incoherence.[63]

In these circumstances, one general strategy that the Stoics certainly followed was

---

[62] *SVF* i. 537, trans. Long 1974: 181.

[63] See Cicero, *De Fin.* IV. 14–20, where, I would argue, the line of criticism is generated by the point in question.

to deny that their doctrine generates any recommendations that conflicted *in fact*. They held, for instance, that the injunction to live in accord with nature 'as a whole' could not fail to coincide exactly with the injunction to live consistently with oneself.[64] These two injunctions, some of them further maintained, are also fully consistent with the additional injunctions to live both 'in accord with human nature' and also, certain Stoics say, in accord with the requirements of one's own station in life whatever it might happen to be.[65] Moreover, they certainly did not think that there could be any inconsistency in, on the one hand, judging that the structure of nature is perfect and, on the other, aiming at having one's own life be in accord with it.

By itself, this idea is already enough to imply that there can be no deliberative conflicts, and thus to assert a harmony of practical reason, notably as between self-regarding and broader considerations. On this view, the only rational aim is to stand in accord with the global order of nature, with human nature, with one's own position in life, and to maintain consistency within oneself. These things are all declared to coincide with each other. Every other aim that might conceivably clash with these—such as the performance of certain actions, or the experiencing or avoidance of certain pleasures and pains, and the like—is said to possess no value but instead to be merely indifferent. There is thus no scope, according to standard Stoic doctrine, for what is good for oneself and what is good in an impersonal, non-self-referential way to diverge. Moreover, since everyone's aims consist likewise in conformity to nature, one's own aims cannot conflict with theirs. For this reason, Stoic teaching would claim to generate none of the problems of coordination that arise from Epicureanism in this regard.[66] The Stoic outlook is thus as clearcut an exemplification of an attempt to espouse deliberative monism as one could expect to find—certainly more clearcut than any in the Classical period.

A closely related point can be framed by means of some terminology that I introduced much earlier, when I spoke of the view that I have called 'fusionism'.[67] A number of the positions that I have examined, particularly those of Plato and Aristotle, can be described as inclusivist. They take a person's well-being to be broad enough to include the important non-self-confined considerations but not to be exhausted by them. The thesis of fusionism, on the other hand, is that (in a sense that is often obscure) an individual's well-being is *identical* with the good of others and conformity to ethical standards. Given the Stoics' view of this latter dualism—that conformity to ethical standards and the good of others are to be sought within the framework of con-

---

[64] On the necessity of this coincidence, see Long 1970–1 and Inwood 1985: 105–6. See e.g. Hahm 1977: 163–5 and Inwood 1985: 21 on the Stoic view that the pervasiveness of the *pneuma* in the *kosmos* is somehow responsible for the connection of these two levels.

[65] This last-mentioned notion is especially closely associated with Panaetius, whose views are normally taken to be the ones mainly expressed in Cicero's *De Officiis* (as indicated in III. 7).

[66] See above, sec. III. 4.

[67] See Chapter 1, sec. VII. 4.

formity to nature and natural social arrangements—their view turns out straightforwardly to be a fusionist one.[68] Thus it purports to eliminate the deliberative dualism altogether.

8. The Eliminative Strategy of Stoicism

None of this is to deny that the Stoics paid no heed to the idea of conflicts between an
individual's good and broader considerations.[69] On the contrary, this was a much discussed topic among them, and was treated in a multi-faceted way by a number of Stoic
philosophers. Cicero's *De Officiis* is our most informative record of this fact. Cicero
makes clear that according to standard Stoic doctrine, as I have said, what he calls
'rectitude' (*honestas*) and 'utility' or 'expedience' (*utilitas*) are necessarily equivalent.[70]
(Likewise, as I have said, the Stoics employ both imperative and attractive formulations of norms; the former register the existence, in most people, of diverging evaluations that correspond to seeming motivational conflicts, which occasion the
imperative formulations.)[71] There may have been some disagreement on this point
within the Stoic school. But even if there was not, the possibility of non-equivalence
and conflict was certainly discussed, and is the main topic of *De Officiis* III.

What disagreement there may have been on this point is attested in the form of a
dispute between two heads of the school, Diogenes of Babylon, a student of
Chrysippus, and his own student, Antipater of Tarsus. In one passage of *De Officiis* III,
Cicero reports the dispute.[72] The case has to do with a grain merchant and the question whether he should fully disclose to his buyer the facts surrounding the proposed
transaction. Diogenes is reported to have maintained that he need not do so, Antipater
that he should. It is clear from Cicero's discussion that Antipater's position is the
orthodox Stoic one.[73] What Antipater is made to say brings out important facts about
Stoic ethics.

First of all, Cicero presents the case not as one in which rectitude and expedience
do conflict, but as one in which they 'appear' (*videatur*) to conflict. Thus he prepares
the way for Antipater's contention that a person should follow the principles of
nature, so that 'your utility be the common utility and conversely that the common
utility be yours'.[74] Thus the standard Stoic response to the problem is not to contend
that one must adjudicate between expedience and rectitude, nor that the latter over-

---

[68] Essentially the same point is made by Slote 1992: xviii.

[69] See Irwin 1996: 91.   [70] *De Off.* II. 9–10.

[71] See above, sec. IV. 5, and Chapter 3, sec. VI. 1–2.   [72] *De Off.* III. 50–7.

[73] See Annas 1989: esp. 158, 172–3. Annas translates *honestas* and *utilitas* respectively by 'being moral'
and 'advantage'.

[74] The quoted words appear in cc. 50 and 52, respectively.

rides the former and must be chosen instead of it.[75] Rather, the Stoics eliminate the conflict by maintaining that the two alleged sides to it do not diverge from each other at all.[76]

9. The Fusion of Individual and Global Perspectives in Stoicism

With the conclusion that Stoicism is a version of fusionism, however, we put ourselves in a position to raise a further question—which can in fact be raised concerning fusionism in any form. Is Stoicism in fact a eudaimonist view at all? Although the prudentialist-seeming side of Stoic ethics ordinarily makes historians of philosophy presume that it is, the matter is by no means obvious. Here we see the further step that Stoicism takes in the direction of eliminating the deliberative dualism.

The source of the uncertainty is the fact the Stoicism appears to be equally an attempt to speak simultaneously, and indeed in the same breath, to what we naturally take to be two distinct issues. One is the question, 'What is *my* well-being, and how can I attain it?' The other, however, is the question, 'What is non-self-referentially good, or ultimately valuable?' A eudaimonist view will typically address the former question, and will suppose that the answer to it provides a rational individual with his ultimate aim. A view that tries to respond to the latter question, however, and that takes what is good, rather than happiness for oneself, as the ultimate focus of practical deliberation, will appear, under ordinary circumstances, to be a doctrine of a quite different, broadly universalist type.

Perhaps the most distinctive feature of Stoicism is that it attempts in some substantial degree to fuse both these two issues and the responses to them, into one. It also tries to provide an account, recorded in Book III of Cicero's *De Finibus* and discussed above, of how human beings come to grasp this fusion.[77]

In opposition to this interpretation someone might hope to argue that in the Stoic view, one of these matters is prior to the other, and interpreters of Stoicism often tend

---

[75] There remains the question what Diogenes' position comes to, and whether it is seriously unorthodox. Annas's solution is to say that Cicero has misunderstood the issue. Diogenes, she suggests, maintained only that the merchant was not legally obligated to make full disclosure of the facts. Whatever his position may be, it is clear from c. 53 that the question that he is pressing is whether the kinship of all people excludes the possibility of private property—a much-discussed problem ever since the time of early Stoicism and their Cynic forebears.

[76] Thus Annas 1993: 172–3, where she notes that the money that rides on the decision in the case is by Stoic standards an 'indifferent', and therefore 'cannot conflict' with it. (I would say that Annas misstates the view slightly here, when she says that virtue 'overrides'; but she also says that Antipater's point, as c. 52 shows, is that *honestas* and *utilitas* coincide, not that they diverge nor that the former is to be chosen *over* the latter.)

[77] See sec. IV. 2.

to focus on one of these issues as basic.[78] For instance, it might be maintained that a person aims for his own happiness because that consists in the conformity to nature that is his ultimate aim. Or conversely, the Stoics might be taken to hold that the reason for aiming to conform to nature is that so doing will bring about or constitute one's own well-being.

There is no good ground, however, for thinking that the Stoics intend us to take matters *either* in the one way *or* in the other. On the contrary, it appears that they grant equal status to *both* ways of looking at normative issues, the self-regarding way and the impersonal way.[79] The Stoics maintain that the only fully good thing is the *kosmos*, which is comprehended from a global perspective. They also deliver advice to each individual about how to achieve this perspective. Interpreters tend to assume that one of these two thoughts must be primary. There is no good reason to think, however, that the Stoics as a body shared such a tendency (even if some of them might have).[80]

Stoicism thus in one way can be treated as a form of eudaimonism. It admits no norms or recommendations that could lead one to work against one's well-being. On the other hand, one cannot say that it is a form of eudaimonism and simply leave it at that. For at the same time Stoicism gives equal status to a non-self-regarding standard of rational evaluation. On the other hand, it can also count as a universalist position, which maintains that the proper perspective for making judgements about value is

---

[78]   Thus it seems fair to say, for instance, that in her 1993 Annas's treatment tends to put the issue of the individual's happiness in the foreground.

[79]   It is possible to offer a conjecture as to why the Stoics fuse these two points of view. According to the Stoic view, the grounds on which a person would rationally embrace the aim of his *own* conformity to the structure of nature can come only from comprehending the universal fact that *everything* must conform to nature. It is only one's understanding of the all-embracing fact that everything takes place according to the order of nature that provides one with a reason, under Stoicism, for accepting one's own conformity to that order as one's end. The Stoics believe that the universe is governed by a complete causal determinism, to which there are no exceptions (see esp. Cicero, *De Fato*). Taken entirely by itself, the adoption of one's own conformity to nature as an end would be groundless and irrational. What is nature, after all, that one should aim to conform to it? The only answer to this question that the Stoics give is the fact that like everything else, one's own states are already determined by the pattern itself. Conversely, the latter understanding immediately makes the willingness to conform rationally inescapable. In this way it turns out that the two aims are inseparable, in the sense that there is no way in which a person could rationally adopt one without the other, or treat the one as prior and the other as merely derivative.

According to one interpretation, the Stoics do exempt certain mental states of human beings from their determinism; see Kidd 1978. However, the weight of the evidence appears to me to indicate that the Stoics did not exempt any events or states from their determinism. The general argument of Cicero's *De Fato*, in particular, evidently is that what distinguishes human actions that we call free is merely that the causal chains that determine them pass through certain events in the souls of the people who do them.

[80]   It may be true (as is maintained by Inwood 1985: 118, 125–6) that according to the Stoics *orexis* is 'the pursuit of the good properly understood' (125). The issue, however, is what 'pursuit' or *orexis* actually *is*. Inwood may well be right that there was some variation among the Stoics on this point. But overall it seems to me best to conclude that on the Stoic view, no real distinction is to be recognized between the 'pursuit' of the good *for oneself* and the 'pursuit' of it in the sense of an aim *that it be exemplified*.

one that does not accord to oneself or one's well-being any special position within the scheme of things.

On the same ground, Stoicism can be seen to illustrate a point made earlier about eudaimonism, when I suggested that *eudaimonia* need not be the only concept that one might use to try to demonstrate a harmony of all rational aims. According to harmonizing eudaimonist thinkers, the concept of an individual's well-being or *eudaimonia* is uniquely serviceable for showing how distinct deliberative considerations can be coordinated in such a way as not to interfere with each other. I remarked, however, that there is no reason why such a coordination might not be established, if it can be established at all, without any focus on, or even reference to, the notion of one's own happiness.[81] Taken in one way, Stoicism illustrates this remark. It plainly contends that all rational aims are consistent with each other. The basis of this claim is the idea that for any aim to be genuinely worthwhile, it must conform to the pattern that is supposedly exhibited by nature. An aim is thus not to be evaluated by itself, but must be assessed in combination with all others. This combination of aims, however, is not based merely on the hypothesis that it must constitute the well-being of an individual. Rather, the thought is that it will also form the rational structure of the universe as a whole.

10. The Uncongeniality of Stoic Ethics to the Main Interpretative Traditions

The Stoics are willing to pay a high, and in most people's opinion exorbitant, price for their fusionism. For one thing, their conception of the good of the individual is from the ordinary standpoint highly counterintuitive. It was widely regarded in antiquity as simply perverse. The idea that a person's good consists simply in living in accord with nature or the pattern of the *kosmos* seems in many ways eccentric. It required the Stoics to declare that a great many things that people are concerned with, including most of the events that affect their minds and bodies, are neither good nor bad but merely indifferent.[82] Towards these things one was to take an attitude much like the one that we popularly call 'stoical', namely, not to be concerned with them and to regard them as 'unimportant'.[83] This aspect of Stoicism naturally causes it to lose plausibility in the judgement of many.

For much the same reason, Stoicism seems ill suited to satisfy the demand for deliberative harmony that has motivated many harmonizing admirers of Greek ethics. Even if the charge that Stoicism is egoist is set aside as based on a one-sided interpretation, Stoicism seems even on ancient terms so intensely paradoxical as to

---

[81] See Chapter 2, sec. VII.

[82] See the texts in Long and Sedley 1987: i. 354–7.

[83] For a popular and compact statement of this aspect of the Stoic view, see Epictetus's *Encheiridion* or *Handbook*.

resist the stream of Greek thought rather than to flow from it. Moreover, the way in which Stoicism avoids egoism is itself peculiar from most standpoints. It regards as indifferent many of the things that an individual is likely to think matter most to himself, and attempts to assimilate one's own well-being to something so impersonal as to seem wholly unrelated to one's well-being in any normal sense.

It is also signficant that Stoic norms are universalist in a way that is uncongenial to the hegelian thinking that is characteristic of most admirers of Greek ethics. The Stoics did not believe in the importance of the actual historical community. The *kosmos* was *polis* enough for them. In this loose way their thinking can be said to be closer to the universalist outlook of Kant than to Hegel's community-oriented position. In fact, they were to have a real influence on Kant's own ethical views.[84] There are, furthermore, some points of real, if vague, similarity between his thinking and theirs, not only in their belief in universal, impartial norms, but also their anti-hedonism. But there is also much that divides them from Kant, especially the appearance that they give of advocating egoist prudentialism. They therefore had no wholehearted champions within the two main interpretative traditions.

Nevertheless, when the Stoics are considered carefully they illustrate, to a higher degree than any other Greek ethical thinkers, some features that have been most insistently characterized as Hellenic. Neither the Stoics nor the Epicureans believe that the everyday beliefs of ordinary people express rational aims that are all in harmony with each other. Both schools contend that in order to articulate a single consistent system of rational deliberation, one must undertake a large amount of sophisticated philosophical thinking, or else receive the fruits of that thinking from philosophers such as themselves. Thus they do not maintain that the *polis* manifests an inarticulate consistency of human aims, of the sort that eighteenth- and nineteenth-century thinkers could think of as Classically Hellenic. But once that picture of Classical thought is seen to be misguided, we are left with the conclusion that the two main Hellenistic attempts at the regimentation of practical deliberation, even if they were unsuccessful, exhibited the most determined drive towards the unity of practical reason that is to be found in Greek philosophy.

---

[84] See Reich 1939 and Pohlenz 1959: i. 472.

Chapter 8

TOWARDS AN UNDERSTANDING OF THE HISTORY OF GREEK ETHICS

I. On Some Ideas about Differences between Ancient and Modern Ethics

1. A Brief Prolegomenon to a History of Greek Ethics

It is almost inevitable that curiosity about ancient ethics should express itself partly through an interest in asking to what extent ancient and modern ethics differ from each other. Certainly insofar as we are concerned with using information about ancient ethics in order to arrive either at well-founded judgements about ethical issues, we seem obliged to find out how the concepts of the two periods are related to each other. In particular, we need to know whether ancient ethics employed concepts, or involves an overall outlook, widely divergent from more recent ones. If it does, then presumably we should like to know whether they are better or worse, and whether we should try to adopt them ourselves, or adapt them somehow to a modern context. But if the contrary is true, it would be a good idea at least to understand why the differences exist, in case that should yield facts that possess some ethical importance.

Hardly anyone who is acquainted with ethical writings from both ancient Greek and modern times will fail to sense some general difference between them. One 'senses' this difference, as I have put it. Although there are numerous quite specific differences that are perhaps easy enough to describe, there is also an overall difference that is hard to articulate, but that nevertheless strikes one quite forcibly. One senses it not just as one reads ancient writings, but also after periods of time during which one reflects on works from both periods. One has the feeling that a kind of partition has crystallized, so to speak, which is permeable but which nevertheless separates the one from the other.

Nevertheless, in most of this book I have said a great deal that runs against the idea of such a separation. I have denied that the main interpretative traditions seeking to establish it are well founded, and have asserted that the main difference that they jointly see—between an ancient eudaimonist and a modern non-eudaimonist outlook—does not exist. I have also stressed the differences that are to be found among distinct Greek ethical views, and have insisted that concerning central issues that usually figure in philosophers' contrasts between the ancient and the modern, Greek thinkers were often as far apart from each other as most modern authors are from them.

For example, I stressed an important (though not complete) similarity between Plato and Kant with respect to certain issues concerning deliberative dualism. I also focused attention on the fact that Aristotle assigns a decided priority to certain self-regarding considerations, in a fashion that separates him from Plato. In addition, I urged that although much Greek thought exhibits a full awareness of the kind of deliberative conflicts usually regarded as characteristic of modern times, nevertheless we also find a concerted attempt to transcend these conflicts in the ethics of the Stoics, in spite of the fact that they are often declared to mark a transition to modern ways of thinking.

In these and other ways, I may seem to have discouraged any attempt to sort out characteristically ancient ways of thinking from modern ones. And indeed it does seem to me that overall, ancient ethics is less far removed from modern ethics than many writers suggest. What justice, then, can I do to the feeling that there is a genuine difference between them?

2. On Some Reasons for the Seeming Remoteness of Greek Ethics

Some of the important differences between ancient and modern ethics can perhaps be described vaguely as matters of style and mood. I shall describe a few of them in outline. Then I shall move on to sum up the main points that I have made in the body of this book.

Although Hegel was wrong to believe that the *polis* delivered the solution to problems of deliberative dualism, he was not wrong to hold that it was a central feature of the Greek ethical landscape. Certainly one crucial fact about Classical Greek ethics is its setting, the relatively restricted society that a *polis* contains. Its importance lies as much as anything in the fact that by our standards it is small and compact. That fact often allows ethical problems to be manifested simply, directly, and vividly.

The problems that come to the fore in a modern society have a very different texture for just the corresponding reason. Immediately one is swamped by their size and complexity, by the fact that the forces that are at work in them are not easily surveyable, and by the large amount of detailed knowledge that one would have to bring to bear in order even to begin to approach mastery of them. This has been true for a long time. As I have remarked, Schiller and many others noted it already, two hundred years ago.[1]

Another significant fact about Greek ethical issues is that they were *Greek*. This is not the truism that it might seem. The point is that most problems that concerned Greek thinkers arose in contexts in which all of the actors were Greek. However at odds with each other they might be, they shared a sense that they were different from the rest of the world and that their affairs stood apart from it. We cannot, of course, generalize this point too far. The Greeks came into contact with other cultures and sometimes had to deal with them. Moreover, some Greeks, such as Plato, even respected or admired some other peoples and what they had to say.[2] After Herodotus, indeed, Greek thinkers were fully aware that they lived in a world that was full of other kinds of human beings, and this awareness increased steadily through the Hellenistic period.

Nevertheless, Greek thinkers did not feel constant pressure to dwell on issues that arise from that sort of contact.[3] Sometimes, to be sure, they did feel pressure urging them in that direction. Consider, just for example, Euripides' *Medea*, with its self-conscious portrayal of an exotic woman from the faraway Black Sea. But this pressure was intermittent, and usually it was weak. It was nothing like the analogous pressure that exerted itself constantly within Europe after the Roman Empire. Through the period that I have discussed, the Greeks lacked any experience comparable to, say, the consciousness that the English and the French have had of each other for more than a thousand years, to say nothing of the mutual awareness of Catholics and Protestants over Europe for about half that stretch of time.

By themselves, these features of Greek life and intellectual activity—its localism as fixed by the *polis*, and its focus on the Hellenic—contribute in often imponderable ways to the general tenor of Greek ethical discussions. Hardly a page of any Greek ethical writing fails to exhibit some effect of these features—as any reader can easily verify, by picking one at random and asking himself how it might differ if things had been different in these respects.

These are some of the reasons, it seems to me, why the someone nowadays is likely to be struck by a sense of remoteness when reading Greek texts on ethics. When one brings these factors to mind, I think that one is more ready to think that they, rather than the features that have standardly been said to attach to Greek ethics, produce our impression that the Greeks thought about these matters in a radically different manner from our own. At any rate, I have argued throughout that they looked at ethical issues in much the same ways as we do, and often in very different ways from each other. Now I shall briefly review what I take to be, in the areas that I have examined, the most important comparisons that can be made.

---

[1] See Chapter 1, sec. II. 1.   [2] See notably the *Timaeus* and the *Critias*.
[3] See Momigliano 1975.

II. Greek Eudaimonism

That Greek ethics is in a significant way eudaimonist is not to be denied. What is mistaken in the usual view of Greek eudaimonism is rather the character and role that standard accounts assign to it within Greek ethical thought.

All Greek ethical outlooks make an important place for the aim of one's own happiness. In some doctrines, it is the single ultimate aim, the single thing that is taken to be worth seeking for itself. This is true of Epicureanism under the traditional interpretation, which I have argued is correct.

It is not true, however, of either Aristotle's view or of Plato's or, in a sense, of Stoicism. Aristotle holds that one's happiness is the ultimate aim of all other aims, the only thing that is sought for its own sake alone. But one's happiness is not the only thing that is sought for its own sake. Other things are, too, though they are also aimed at for the sake of happiness. This fact makes it wrong to regard Aristotle's position as straightforwardly a form of egoism—a charge that can be levelled with more justice against that of Epicurus.

Both Plato and the Stoics acknowledge the existence of aims that are non-self-referential and non-self-regarding. Thus Plato believes that the instantiation of the Good can be approved of even when the instantiation is not located in oneself but instead in something broader, such as a city-state or even the *kosmos*. Most important, he acknowledges the intelligibility and significance of an evaluative consideration that is neither self-regarding nor self-referential. The Stoics believe this, too, but with a difference. The Stoics believe in the coincidence, and even—perhaps paradoxically—in the identity, of the ultimate non-self-referential aim, conformity on the part of everything to the perfect pattern of the *kosmos*, and the ultimate self-referential aim, one's own conformity to that plan. They thus try to obviate, in a sense, the very difference between these two types of aims. However, they cannot be said in the least to be unaware or neglectful of the notion of aims other than one's own well-being.

Equally important is the fact that the Greeks never disapproved in any way of the general idea of seeking one's own good as an ultimate and crucially important aim. The recognition of the importance of other aims, that is, never led them to cast any doubt on the reasonableness or propriety of seeking one's happiness.

Contrast this outlook with Kant's. The recognition of the significance of an overriding moral consideration, given to us by the Categorical Imperative, seems to bring about in him a feeling that there is something wrong with aiming at one's own well-being. He does not say, for instance, 'Aiming at one's own happiness is acceptable, or even a fine thing, so long as it does not conflict with acting in accordance with moral duty'. Rather, he seems—at least at some times, even if not by any means always—to suggest that some kind of disapprobation ought to be directed at happiness as an end. At the very least, he regards it as a far more obscure notion than that of moral duty, and far less entitled to fall within the province of reason.[4] Moreover, he also appears to regard self-referential aims as such to lie outside of the sphere of reason, which he conceives of as operating with universally formulated, non-self-referential considerations.

Plato's attitude is quite different. Even though he grasps and employs the notion of non-self-referential goodness, he does not hesitate to say at the same time that one's own well-being, thought of precisely as *one's own*, is emphatically to be sought. Indeed, he bases much of the *Republic* on this presupposition. The only exception that he enters to this policy—though it is highly significant—arises when a conflict with a broader good appears in Book VII. On other questions he is content with a straightforwardly eudaimonist stance. Nor do Aristotle, the Stoics, or the Epicureans ever cast doubt on the general propriety of happiness as a rational aim, or indicate that anyone else does so.

Here we see much of the true basis of the idea that Greek ethics is eudaimonist. Most Greek thinkers allow that there are other significant considerations besides one's happiness, and even that the former can sometimes override the latter in reasonable deliberation. What they do not do is to denigrate eudaimonist aims as such, or try to thrust them away from rational thought.

A second part of the reason for the attribution of pure eudaimonism to the Greeks has to do not just with their ethical outlook, but with the focus of their philosophical investigations into it. As scholars repeatedly point out, they usually take the notion of *eudaimonia* as the first topic to broach in almost any ethical discussion, though sometimes virtue leads the way. By contrast, although a non-self-referential notion of good—and even a notion of what one ought to do that has the imperative character of a duty—appear in their writings, such concepts are never made the focus of philosophical investigation. The Greeks ask again and again, 'What is happiness?' but they do not ask 'What is it for it to be the case that someone "ought" to (*dei*) do such-and-such?' Plato and the Stoics say something about non-self-referential notions of goodness, but Plato dwells mainly on the difficulty of explaining it, in spite of its importance. The Stoics say more about it, especially in its relation to the structure of the *kosmos*—on which Plato had already touched in the *Timaeus*—but they do not give it the amount of attention that moderns have paid to the concepts of duty and morality.

This certainly constitutes an important difference between ancient and modern ethics, but it is a difference between their respective focuses of philosophical reflection, not between the content of their doctrines or outlooks. Or in other words, there is more of a difference between the philosophical questions that they ask about their views than between the sets of concepts that those views respectively employ.

---

[4] I have in mind here the passages from Kant 1981 (esp. secs 50–1), quoted to this effect in Chapter 1, sec. V.

III. Self-Referential, Partly Self-Referential, and Universal Aims

1. Kinds of Universalizability

It seems clear that although Greek ethics resembles modern ethics in entertaining the possibility of deliberative conflict, nevertheless the particular types of conflict that appear in Greek ethics are different from the ones that we find in the more egalitarian ethical views of the modern period. In modern ethics, an individual is called upon to take into account, over against his own well-being, considerations that in one way or another treat all people alike, and that place him on a par with everyone else. Although there are exceptions, Greek conflicts are not normally of this kind. In many cases, they are conflicts between the individual's well-being and some institution or collection of people, such as the *polis* and its citizens, that is not all-inclusive. This fact does not make them any the less conflicts, but they are nevertheless notably different from clashes between the individual and some universal good or obligation.

Moreover, even when Greek ethical doctrines do bring to bear considerations that are in an important sense universal, the type of universality involved in them is usually different from the potentially more egalitarian way of conceiving universality that dominates modern ethics. This difference seems to me to contribute substantially to the general sense, some of whose causes I have been exploring in this chapter, of a discontinuity between the two periods.

In modern ethical doctrines, as I have noted, it is frequently held that deliberation must at some point introduce considerations that are universal. More particularly, it appears that these considerations can weigh against matters that involve the individual's well-being. The prominence of universal considerations manifests itself, for instance, in the fact that a notion of *impartiality*, in the sense of impartiality among individuals, figures essentially in many modern notions of morality.[5] According to most moral doctrines, an individual's good must compete for attention against considerations or aims that are all-embracing, in the sense that they take proper account of all individuals.[6]

Two different ways of conceiving this universality seem to be especially common in modern ethics, especially over the last two hundred years. One of them can be illustrated through Kant. On his view, every person must be respected as an autonomous agent, and must always be treated as an end and never only as a means. In this connection, Kant holds that when someone acts on a maxim, to use Kant's word, it must

[5] There are of course exceptions—for example in the views of those who maintain that even egoism is a form of morality.

[6] Most commonly 'all individuals' is equivalent to 'all individual human beings', though some philosophers conceive the universality differently.

be one that the person can 'will to be a universal law'.[7] This requirement entails that
in some manner or other, the maxim must apply in the same way to everyone. Many
other modern writers of ethics join Kant in requiring that ethical norms be thus in
some sense universalizable.

The other main type of universality is illustrated by Utilitarianism, also aptly
called Universalist Utilitarianism. The fundamental principle embodied in this view
is one of universal beneficence, that is, the principle of maximizing the total happiness
of all persons (or all sentient creatures) taken together. The motivation that is expected to support obedience to such a principle is benevolence, which is directed towards
all persons.[8]

It seems undeniable that both kantianism and Utilitarianism contain an important
egalitarian element, even if it is less than some philosophers demand. Utilitarianism,
for example, standardly requires that in deciding what action to perform, we must
reckon the happiness provided to one person as neither more nor less important than
the happiness provided to another, even oneself. In this respect, at any rate, equal
treatment is to be accorded to all people.[9] According to Kant's view, for his part, the
main thought is that moral norms must in some sense apply in the same way to everyone. This, too, is a universalist and egalitarian idea, even though its universalism consists not in a concern for the happiness of everyone, but in an equal respect for—to put
it roughly—everyone's status as a person. The aim of a utilitarian ethical view based
on benevolence is that people collectively be as happy as possible. The point of an
ethics based on respect is that everyone alike be treated as a rational agent and as an
end.

Thus in both of these doctrines, the individual is asked to take into account, in one
fashion or the other, not only himself or his own well-being, but something having to
do with all people alike. This means that the individual is in a certain way to treat himself, as well as people who are closely related to him, as simply one person among all
others, without assigning himself or those close to him any special status. It is in this
sense that a marked egalitarian tendency is at work in these doctrines.

---

[7] Kant 1981: e.g. sec. 52.

[8] Mill 1871: chs. 2, 3.

[9] Mill, for instance, does not require that happiness be distributed equally (1871: ch. 5). He merely
insists that everyone's happiness shall count equally in the utilitarian calculation. The Kantian idea of
respect for personhood, too, may not imply very much in the way of any kind of substantive or even proce-
dural equality. Moreover, it is not clear that Kant's idea about how the Categorical Imperative is to be used
needs to result in equality of any significant sort, nor that it was intended to. Still, it is a short step, psychologically at least, from thinking in the Kantian way that a person should act only on universalizable maxims to holding that everyone ought to be treated in some sense equally. And Mill's view is more egalitarian
than a view that *denies* that everyone's happiness should count in determining the rightness or wrongness
of an action—as ancient views by implication do.

2. Restricted Universality

When we shift to Greek ethics, we see a picture that is noticeably different in some but not all respects. In the first place, many of the considerations that Greek philosophers consider weighing against an individual's happiness do not possess universal scope in the sense of a scope that embraces all human beings. Instead they centre on some smaller unit, such as the *polis*, rather than, for example, the good of all humankind or another such aim. This is a kind of universality, if one likes, insofar as it involves an application to all members of a given class. But it does not have to do with all of humanity.

As cases in point, take two important instances of conflict that appear in Greek philosophy. Plato and Aristotle, as I have explained in the previous two chapters, supply us with closely related illustrations. In Plato, on the one hand, we have an opposition, in a particular sort of circumstance, between justice and an individual philosopher-ruler's greatest happiness. In Aristotle, on the other side, we find a very similar opposition, based on the presumption that it is impossible to realize both practical wisdom and the capacity for *theôria* equally and adequately Although both of these cases involve genuine conflicts between an individual's own happiness and broader aims, and are in that respect similar to the dilemmas that regularly appear on the modern ethical landscape, nevertheless they both introduce oppositions between the individual's good and activity engaged in for the sake of his *polis*, rather than an opposition between individual good and what is done for the sake of all human beings or humanity as such.

Nevertheless, Greek ethics adduces considerations that are in an obvious way *all-embracing* and in *that* sense universal. For instance, various Greek doctrines make ample room for policies or principles that are not tied to one's own *polis*, but instead apply to all people from all city-states. One salient case in point is supplied by the formulations of the Golden Rule that appear early in Greek ethics. A second sort of case emerges in the manner in which some Greek philosophers sometimes appeal to the order of the whole *kosmos* in making or explaining evaluative judgements.[10]

3. The Whole Kosmos

Of these two kinds of instances, the former remind us more of modern universal considerations, whereas the latter are of an obviously different type, though they too, as I shall explain, can be assimilated in some degree to characteristically modern ways of thinking.

The Greek formulations of the Golden Rule are in spirit fairly close to modern egalitarian viewpoints. They enjoin us not to do what we ourselves would reproach if

---

[10] See Chapter 4, sec. VI; Chapter 5, sec. V; and Chapter 6, sec. VIII.

we saw them done by another. Thus they come close to requiring us, in assessing our own actions, to adopt the standpoint of an arbitrary other person. They amount to requirements that an agent must take all people equally into consideration in deciding what to do himself. This is hardly a full-scale egalitarianism, but it plainly moves towards it.

Something similar can be said of Aristotle's contention that all human beings are friends to each other.[11] As is well known, Aristotle applies this idea in a distinctly inegalitarian fashion. His distinction among three types of friendship—for pleasure, for profit, and for excellence—permits us to regard different people as possessing very different degrees of merit, and thus to treat them as deserving of radically different kinds of treatment. At the same time, however, it expressly provides for the possibility of deeming everyone a friend in some way or other—something that is emphatically not done by all Greek views of friendship.[12]

More smoothly illustrative of the way in which universality can enter into Greek ethics are cases of the second type that I just mentioned, in which the order of the *kosmos* is invoked. Unlike the type of universality implicated in the Golden Rule, or even in Aristotle's remark about friendship, universality of this sort exerts no pressure at all in an egalitarian direction. According to this latter outlook, a person may be expected to evaluate himself and what he does as somehow fitting into a broader pattern. The pattern may even include the entire *kosmos*. The pattern itself will be valued as a whole, in abstraction from the individual's own place in it. The individual's action or role can then be assessed by its place within or contribution to the whole. The value thereby ascribed to a person's life or deeds will in this way be derivative and relational, not primary or intrinsic.

Under such a method of assessment, there is no necessity for equal value to be attached to the actions or life of each individual. The overall pattern of the *kosmos* itself need entail no equality among the elements that are ordered by it. Indeed, it may be as inegalitarian or hierarchical as you like, even as it embraces all things in the universe. Different people may therefore be assigned roles of widely differing degrees of importance within the whole. And if different people fit differently into the structure thus conceived, then they may be assigned quite disparate values.

As I have already observed, this way of thinking is far from being entirely alien to Greek ethics. We find incipient expressions of it, for instance, in Anaximander. Plato, too, gives voice to assessments of just this type, both in the *Laws* and the *Republic*, when he holds 'no human experience is worth taking very seriously', and expands this idea by declaring that people should consider themselves 'playthings of the gods'.[13]

---

[11] *Nic. Eth.* 1155a19–23.

[12] Recall, for instance, Polemarchus's definition of justice in *Rep.* I as 'helping one's friends and harming one's enemies'.

[13] See Chapter 4, sec. VI, and Chapter 5, sec. V.

The same idea is even stronger in Stoicism. Stoicism urges the individual to deny that the particularities of his own situation possess any positive or negative value, but to assess his condition solely as a part of the overall course of events of the universe. According to Stoic doctrine, the end of a human being is to live in accord with nature.[14] Stoic views about human social activity are derived from this fundamental notion. Stoic norms that call on human beings to help other human beings, like those norms that require cooperation within a society, are presented as dependent on the general principle that enjoins each individual to be in accord with nature as a whole.[15] The Stoics do not fail to prize beneficence, cooperation, and justice. Nonetheless, it is striking that these are all conceived of as ways of conforming to the pattern that organizes the universe. The value of cooperation, on the Stoic view, is constituted by the goodness of this pattern, not by benevolence as such, nor by a universal regard for each individual human being per se.

4. Structure vs. Benevolence

The ideas of universal benevolence and universal respect for persons play only a marginal role in Greek ethics. The notion of a kinship of all human beings developed quite late, in the Hellenistic period. Even then it did not often yield the thought that all people are on a par from an ethical point of view.[16] The occasional appearance of the notion of the friendship or kinship of all humanity did not add up to any active employment in ethical theorizing of a sentiment of universal benevolence or the idea of respect for all humanity as such.

Such ideas do not play a significant role in either Plato or Aristotle. Aristotle's brief allusion to the natural friendship of all human beings receives no development in his accounts of either friendship or justice, nor in any other place in his ethical doctrines. Aristotle makes no place for universal and indiscriminate wellwishing towards all other people, or even, it seems quite clear, indiscriminate wellwishing towards all other people in one's own *polis*.[17] In Hellenistic times, Epicurus advances a notion of justice that is fleetingly reminiscent of Utilitarianism, by virtue of holding that justice arises out a general sense of its usefulness for each person. However, this idea turns out not to constitute anything like a normative principle of universal beneficence nor a generalized attitude of benevolence. Instead, it is merely a descriptive generaliza-

---

[14] Chapter 7, sec. IV.1–3.

[15] See Cicero, *De Fin.* III. 62–3, 64, 67.

[16] See Baldry 1965: ch. 4, and esp. 118ff., 143ff.; Long and Sedley 1987: i. 434–7.

[17] See esp. *Nic. Eth.* 1126b27–8. The casual directness of this remark makes clear not that Aristotle was at all inclined to espouse universal benevolence, but rather how little argument he thought he needed to supply against it.

tion to the effect that at any given time people set up standards of justice to benefit themselves in the particular conditions under which they are then living.[18]

As we recognize that the idea of universal benevolence does not play much of a role in Greek thought, we should at the same time not lose sight of the fact, just now touched on briefly in connection with Aristotle, that it is rare for Greek thinkers to generalize an attitude of benevolence even within a narrower context, such as one's own *polis*. Although the fact is not much remarked upon, there is little doubt that when Greek writers think about what binds the *polis* together and makes it cohesive, their main thought is not that each citizen wishes well equally to each of his fellow citizens individually. Aristotle does hold that citizens of a good *polis* are friends to each other. However, as noted, this statement is qualified by his careful distinction among kinds of friendship and the different and circumscribed benefits that they implicate.[19] There can be no thought that in his view, the city is based on general egalitarian benevolence of each citizen for each other citizen.

Even more plainly in Plato's thinking about the *polis*, the emphasis falls on its structure rather than the sum of the happiness of each of its citizens. Correspondingly the motivation that is invoked is not benevolence, but admiration for the overall pattern of political organization. Plato's illustration runs as follows:

If someone came to us while we were painting a statue and objected because we did not apply the finest colours to the finest parts of the body, for the eyes are the most beautiful part, and they are not made purple but black, we should appear to offer a reasonable defence if we said: 'My good sir, do not think that we must make the eyes so beautiful that they no longer appear to be eyes at all, and so with the other parts, but look to see whether by dealing with each part *appropriately* we are making the whole statue beautiful.'[20]

What Plato stresses about the well-being of the city is that it consists in the exemplification of a unified structure by the *polis* as a whole.[21]

Stoicism presents a mixed picture in this regard. On the one hand, Stoics advocate something that looks like a certain kind of impartiality among all individuals.[22] In their writings we see the idea that one should be concerned in some way or degree with the well-being of 'the remotest Mysian'— that is, of simply anyone.[23] On the other hand, as already noted, this idea is presented in close connection with the notion

---

[18] Epicurus, *Principal Doctrines* 32, 36–7.   [19] See Chapter 6, sec. VII. 1.

[20] *Rep.* 420b–d.

[21] *Rep.* 420–3, 462–3, 519–20. This is of course the idea that is often attributed to Plato under the label 'organicism' and the like.

[22] See Annas 1993: 289–90, 302–5, 319. Annas maintains that later Aristotelians 'caved in' to the Stoics on this issue (290) without thinking through how to integrate the notion of impartiality into their Aristotelian outlook, which, however, she thinks contained some element of impartiality in Aristotle himself (316).

[23] See Annas 1993: 269, 288–90.

of the fitting together of everything within the global plan of the *kosmos*, and does not seem to have a basis independent of that notion. Is the remotest Mysian to be of concern to one because he is, like oneself, a human being with human capacities and the like? Or is he to be of concern because he is a part—though perhaps a very different part from oneself—of an all-embracing cosmic structure? The former answer, shorn of links to or dependence on the latter answer, is characteristic of a more fully egalitarian view, whereas this does not seem to be what one finds in Stoic thought.[24]

5. Sidgwick: Some Similarities and Some Differences between Ancient and Modern Ethics

What are we to make of this overall picture? Much modern ethics is characterized by concern for the total well-being of all people or for the worth of each person as such. Greek ethics shows some hints of this somewhat egalitarian line of thought, but its tendencies towards universality normally express themselves in the idea that the individual is a part of an overall pattern of the *kosmos*, in which the notion of equality among people may play no role at all. These facts make it easy enough to say that what tendencies there are in Greek ethics to adopt a universal perspective set it apart, on the whole, from characteristic modern ways of thinking about ethics.

If we choose to look at matters differently, however, we can easily see a similarity between ancient and modern ethics within this sphere of ideas. Differences and similarities being both important, let me now stress one of the latter.

In both ancient and modern times, thinkers are capable of asking the individual to be aware that his own well-being is merely a component of a wider and, in a sense, all-embracing sort of value. In the case of Greek ethics, this state of affairs is fairly straightforwardly exemplified by the Platonic and Stoic thoughts that I have just described, according to which local values may be assessed by their contributions to the primary overall value of the whole. Among modern ethical doctrines, on their side, illustrations are provided by the kantian and Utilitarian positions. Here the picture is that of oneself as simply one person among many.

In spite of their differences, these ideas bear a similarity that can be conveyed by something that Sidgwick says about what he takes to be an inadequacy of the egoistic outlook:

And certainly one's happiness is, in many respects, an unsatisfactory mark for one's supreme aim, apart from any direct collision into which the exclusive pursuit of it may bring us with rational or sympathetic benevolence. It does not possess the characteristics which, as Aristotle says, we 'divine' to belong to the ultimate good: being (so far, at least, as it can be

---

[24] Thus I have reservations about Annas's term 'other-concern' (1993: 262–90, 302–3), which tends, I think, to suggest the more modern, egalitarian concept.

empirically foreseen) so narrow and limited, of such necessarily brief duration, and so shifting and insecure while it lasts.

Sidgwick then goes on to draw a contrast between this egoistic view and another standpoint, which he ascribes to Universalist Utilitarianism, but which can also, I think, be associated with a broad type of universalist outlook:

But universal happiness, desirable consciousness or feeling for the innumerable multitude of sentient beings, present and to come, seems an end that satisfies our imagination by its vastness.[25]

What Sidgwick shows us here is a way of subsuming the conceptions of universality that figure in modern ethics under the one that Greek ethics employs. Under the Utilitarian view, for instance, we can think of the individual's happiness as just one element of an aggregate that is the general happiness; and we can regard the individual's worth, under kantianism, as an element of the structure that he calls the 'kingdom of ends', the class of beings to which moral rules apply and that are respected by them. In this way, we can to some degree assimilate these conceptions to the ancient idea of local goods as merely parts of the overall good. This is not to say that we must on philosophical grounds thus assimilate ancient and modern views, nor even that we should. It is simply to point out a respect in which a modern picture can be seen as resembling an ancient one.

Seeing the resemblance allows us to notice a continuity as well, that is, a way in which modern ethical views can be seen as having developed out of ancient ones. Only late and gradually did modern ethics come to adopt a universal standpoint from which each individual could be regarded as, most important, one among many equally human beings. In an account of ethics in the seventeenth and eighteenth centuries, J. B. Schneewind describes a gradual movement away from what he calls the 'Divine Corporation' view of morality.[26] The transition was completed, or nearly so, in the works of Bentham and Kant. Before them, morality was to a substantial degree regarded as a large and complex venture carried on under a wise and benevolent divine director. Within this venture, different people are seen as having different roles. The point of the venture could involve some result to be produced, or simply the activities engaged in themselves, or both.

The Divine Corporation view is universalist in much the same sense as are ancient ethical doctrines. That is, the value of an individual's actions, apart from their conduciveness to his own self-interest, can be thought of as closely related to the overall structure of the universe of which he is a part. Benevolence and respect for all persons

---

[25] Sidgwick 1907: 403–4. (Sidgwick ends this paragraph with the words, 'and sustains our resolution by its comparative security', which seem to me false, but in any case not germane to the present point.)

[26] Schneewind 1984.

are not accorded value independently, but rather as a part of that structure. In the Divine Corporation, this arises from the Christian idea that all value derives ultimately from God and his love for his creation. In ancient views, on the other hand, it results from a direct concern with the overall structure of the *kosmos*. But likewise, if Sidgwick is at all correct, modern ethics too thinks of an individual as a part of a different sort of pattern, one constituted as an aggregate or association of human beings.

IV. Eudaimonism and Egoism

Admirers of Greek ethics have always been torn between a desire to think of it as advocating a powerful form of eudaimonism and an aversion to regarding it as egoist. Obviously there is danger inherent in eudaimonism that it may turn out to be egoist. Within the context of modern ethics, with its tendency to focus on concepts of morality, this is a powerful accusation. Interpreters of Greek ethical views have gone to great lengths to defend them against it.

Greek writers were much less preoccupied with this issue than their modern admirers, even though the Greeks were aware of it, and recognized that the good of others and ethical norms are important considerations, as I have stressed. Nevertheless, the Greek thinkers who advocated positions that are either egoist or close to being so do not show great anxiety about this fact. One does not find any Greek writer acknowledging that an egoist position is *eo ipso* refuted, or saying that he must take care to avoid egoist views as such.

It is perhaps an oddity that the two Greek philosophers who come closest to advancing egoist positions are generally treated by moderns as falling into rather different categories. Aristotle is perhaps the paradigm of the Classical philosopher. Epicurus is a characteristic figure of the Hellenistic period. A parallel observation is that Plato and the Stoics share important similarities with each other in this same regard, though Plato belongs to the Classical period and the Stoics to Hellenistic times. This is a count against an uncritical use of chronological categorizations in characterizing philosophers' outlooks.[27]

Nevertheless, Aristotle and Epicurus are rather different from each other in respect of the types of egoism that they might be claimed to represent. As Epicurus is traditionally and (in my opinion) correctly interpreted, he is a straightforward hedonist egoist. On this interpretation, he takes it that one's own happiness is the only thing that one is to treat as an ultimate aim or good for its own sake. Other aims may be presented to one as valuable, but in the final analysis their value is only extrinsic and depends on their capacity to serve one's own well-being.

Aristotle, on the other hand, is a pluralist inclusivist who recognizes the existence

---

[27] See Chapter 6, sec. I, and below, sec. VI.

of conflicts, but tends to adjudicate them in favour of self-confined considerations rather than other-regarding ones. In that sense he seems to be classifiable as egoist. In addition, the other-regarding aims that he treats as worthwhile are instances of self-referential altruism. That is, another's good is treated as valuable by virtue of a special relation that he bears to oneself, by being either one's friend or a fellow citizen of one's *polis*. That is a kind of egoism, one might say, but a kind of non-egoism, too. Moreover, Aristotle does not think that one's own well-being is the only thing good for its own sake, but allows that other things, including ethically virtuous activity and actions done for the sake of friends' happiness, are good partly for themselves and not merely by virtue of their contributions to one's own good. Thus the picture is mixed. In some ways Aristotle's view is indeed an egoist one, but in other ways it is not so.

Plato and the Stoics regard one's own happiness as an important and appropriate aim, but as I have explained earlier in this chapter, both leave a place open for aims that are not self-regarding or self-referential.[28] Certainly their views come less close than Epicurus's or Aristotle's to being classifiable as egoist.

To repeat, however, this question of classification attracts far less importance within Greek ethics itself than from modern writers attempting to describe it. Insofar as we are concerned with the Greeks' own ways of thinking about their positions—though of course we need not confine ourselves to that—we should not accord this question disproportionate significance, or think that it was a major factor motivating their thoughts.

V. Eudaimonism and Harmony

Of the points that I have pressed, the most important philosophically is that Greek eudaimonism is not designed for the purpose of reconciling rational aims. Greek philosophers do not maintain or presuppose that an examination of the concept of *eudaimonia* will have that result. I have pursued this point so assiduously in the foregoing pages that it is scarcely necessary, or even permissible, for me to make any more of it here. Some of its corollaries, however, are worth reviewing.

From the fact that the Greeks do not as a group deny the existence of deliberative conflicts, it obviously follows that when they encounter a putative conflict, they do not always deny that it is unreal. That is to say, they do not always maintain that it can be eliminated, as I have put it. Instead, they sometimes treat it as something to be adjudicated: one is to assume that the conflict exists, and some argument or other is adduced to decide which side should be followed and which side should, at some loss, be given up. Or to put the point another way, Greek ethical thinkers do not always simply

[28] See above, sec. III.

assume that worthwhile things can invariably be demonstrated to be compatible with each other.

This means that, as I urged especially in the case of Aristotle, the Greeks do not generally believe, in holist style, that values must be assigned to a plurality of things only insofar as they contribute to the value of some whole to which they contribute. Rather, things can have values of their own. *Then* the question can arise whether they can all be adequately pursued within the constraints of some whole, such as a human life. In this sense it would be mistaken to say, as is sometimes done, that the Greeks always consider a human life as a whole, though of course there is considerable truth in this dictum, provided that it is not pushed too far.[29]

Likewise it would be mistaken to contend that the Greeks avoid imperative formulations of norms, much less that they exhibit any desire to eliminate them in favour of formulations that rely on attractive notions. Obviously attractive terms like *eudaimonia* and *aretê* figure extensively and importantly in Greek ethics. Nevertheless, the Greeks use imperatives without hesitation, though without giving such notions the philosophical scrutiny that they receive in modern ethics, and they do so in contexts that involve deliberative conflict.

Perhaps it would be fair to say that Greek ethics is not as preoccupied with deliberative conflict as modern ethics is, or as much concerned to make ethical inquiry into a vehicle for solving concrete ethical questions, dealing with hard cases, and settling ethical dilemmas.[30] It is unclear whether this is correct or not, and indeed whether it is possible to support any firm generalization on the matter. The *Republic* is evidently devoted to answering some hard ethical questions, though most of them are not posed in the form of dilemmas. I noted earlier that Aristotle does not seem much concerned with whether there are conflicts within ethical virtue or not. On the other hand, he is interested in deciding between the life of ethical virtue and the life of *theôria*, and in certain dilemmas involved in *philia*. Hellenistic innovations in ethics, I have argued, tend by and large in the direction of systematization. This fact leads Hellenistic philosophers, especially Epicureans, in the direction of a decision procedure for deciding what to do.

I have already argued that there is no sign in Aristotle of a positive or welcoming

---

[29] See e.g. Annas 1993: 38. It is unclear to me to what extent Annas takes the view that she ascribes to most Greek ethics to be holist. When she says later, at p. 444, that '[a]ncient theories . . . are based on the assumption that ethical beliefs can in fact be unified', I am not sure whether, in my terms, she is contending that according to the ancients our aims exhibit no real conflicts (i.e. that conflicts can be eliminated), or that they do but the conflicts can be adjudicated. She maintains that ancient views allowed for some filling in and adjustment of our ordinary beliefs about what happiness is (e.g. pp. 44–6, 445). Given enough flexibility in this notion, one can regard a given way of dealing with a conflict indifferently either as an elimination or as an adjudication of it. To say that would be to regard conflicts not as unreal, but only as *capable of being regarded as* unreal.

[30] See Annas 1993: 442–6.

attitude towards irresoluble ethical dilemmas or deliberative conflict per se.[31] Indeed, although Bernard Williams has argued that Thucydides and Aeschylus firmly believe that such dilemmas arise, I do not believe that Williams or anyone else has produced evidence that any Greek thinker was exhilarated about them in the way in which Nietzsche sometimes seems to have been.[32] It seems to me that Greek thinkers uniformly believed that if there are putative conflicts that can be neither eliminated nor reasonably adjudicated—and here Williams is probably right that Aeschylus and Thucydides maintained that there are—then that is a bad thing, however unavoidable it may be.

VI. Greek Ethics: Development and Variety

1. Deliberative Monism and Systematic Consistency

Perhaps the greatest irony in the historiography of Greek ethical thought is that the very feature that its hegelian-minded admirers have most prized as 'Classical', namely, its supposed harmonization of human goods, is to be found most fully developed philosophically not in the Classical period but in Hellenistic times instead. Plato and Aristotle are not mainly apostles of deliberative harmony. They are also acute observers of deliberative conflict.

The most forceful ancient efforts to show how deliberation might be unified so as to settle conflicts systematically are due, I have argued, to the Epicureans and the Stoics. These efforts were so forceful, indeed, that they influenced later adherents of Platonic and Aristotelian views, and led them into more systematic ways of thinking than Plato and Aristotle had adopted.[33] Plato's reservations about whether actions in the sensible world could ever be lucidly rationalized, and the care with which Aristotle noted and attempted to accommodate ordinary ethical judgements, give way to theories with much cleaner and simpler outlines, which try to present comparatively unambiguous norms and criteria for assessing actions.

Moreover, insofar as philosophers of the Classical period did hope to deal with conflicts, it seems fair to suppose that it was the perpetuation of this hope that motivated the two major Hellenistic doctrines towards the systematization of ethics that they attempted. Both schools try principally to settle ethical questions, and not—or at least not nearly so much—to reflect the ethical leanings of the ordinary person. Thus their strategies are eliminative rather than adjudicative: they regard the conflicts that arise

---

[31] Chapter 6, sec. V.

[32] See Williams 1993 and White 1994b with Nussbaum 1986: 341, 353, and above, Chapter 6, n. 62.

[33] It seems to me that this is the chief lesson to be drawn from Book V of Cicero's *De Finibus*, with its assimilation of Platonic-Aristotelian ethics (here treated as essentially a single view) to Stoic. The push is in the direction of greater systematicity.

in ordinary ethical thinking as illusory. In the view of many philosophers, however, the price of system, in the loss of faithfulness to our ordinary ethical 'intuitions', is too great, though other modern philosophers—here Mill and, even more, Sidgwick come to mind—regard it as a price that we must pay for any adequate rationalization of ethics.

This tendency towards system worked itself out differently in the two Hellenistic schools of thought. The Epicureans accepted a straightforwardly eudaimonist framework of a substantially egoist type, and developed it as consistently as they could, into a view which, though it was not a strictly quantitative maximizing hedonist calculus, moved further in that direction than any other major Greek ethical doctrine. The Stoics, on the other hand, carried this unifying tendency to the point of insisting that all serious deliberative considerations must fit together, and of almost obliterating the distinction between universal and self-referential aims.

Modern thinkers who have traditionally adopted the role of admirers of Greek ethics, however, have not been impressed by these ways of thinking, nor taken them to exemplify the kind of deliberative or motivational harmony for which they strove. On the whole, these moderns have been hostile to the streamlining of ethics by simple rules. They liked their harmony spontaneous, not schooled or systematic. This and other causes have prevented Hellenistic ethics from being regarded as an exemplar of Hellenic harmony. As a result, the attribution to various Greek philosophers of efforts towards deliberative consistency has been displaced and distorted.

2. The Variety of Greek Ethical Positions

To counteract these ways of thinking, the best first step is to keep in view a picture of Greek ethics as heterogeneous, as not conforming to a single pattern, and as approaching ethical issues in a multitude of different ways. To reiterate: there is no such thing as the outlook of 'the Greeks'. Some tendencies are stronger in Greek ethics than in modern, but in general the preoccupations have remained fairly constant from then until now.

It is well to remember that the Greeks themselves never regarded certain of their philosophical movements as typically Hellenic, or take others to represent barbarian or otherwise deviant tendencies. That whole conception is a creation of thinkers like Hegel, who projected it onto the historiography of Greece. No Greek thinker ever voices the idea, for instance, that Socrates or the Sophists, for instance, are somehow un-Greek, though of course many Athenians regarded them as disruptive of their own political well-being. For the most part, the Greeks did not set their ethical views off against non-Greek ones—to which they paid, after all, very little attention.[34] They

---

[34] See again Momigliano 1975.

remarked on the distinctiveness of the institution of the *polis*, but that observation did not extend itself into a general identification of a certain ethical doctrine as properly Greek.

Accordingly, when we drop the whole idea of 'the Greek way' of thinking about ethics, and consider the philosophical problems themselves and the possible responses to them, we can gain a far clearer and more accurate picture both of what those problems actually are, and of the various ways in which Greek thinkers, both philosophers and others, tried to meet them.

Bibliography

A. Ancient Sources

Most of the listings here are translations (where they exist), chosen largely by availability to the reader, not necessarily by whether they have been used in this book (since I have often made my own translations).

Aristophanes. *Acharnians*, trans. Alan H. Sommerstein. Warminster: Aris & Phillips, 1980.

—— *Clouds*, trans. A. H. Sommerstein. Warminster: Aris & Phillips, 1982.

Aristotle. *The Complete Works of Aristotle*, ed. Jonathan Barnes. 2 vols. Princeton, N.J.: Princeton University Press, 1984.

—— *Eudemian Ethics*, trans. J. Solomon. Oxford: Clarendon Press, 1915.

—— *Eudemian Ethics*, Books I, II, and VIII, trans. Michael Woods, 2nd ed. Oxford: Clarendon Press, 1992.

—— *De Generatione Animalium I and De Partibus Animalium I*, trans. D. M. Balme. Oxford: Clarendon Press, 1972.

—— *Nicomachean Ethics*, trans. W. D. Ross. Oxford: Clarendon Press, 1925.

—— *Physics*, trans. R. P. Hardie and R. K. Gaye, in *The Complete Works of Aristotle*, ed. Barnes.

—— *Poetics*, trans. I. Bywater, in *The Complete Works of Aristotle*, ed. Barnes.

—— *Politics*, trans. B. Jowett. Oxford: Clarendon Press, 1920.

—— *Rhetoric*, trans. W. Rhys Roberts, in *The Complete Works of Aristotle*, ed. Barnes.

—— *Topics*, trans. W. A. Pickard-Cambridge, in *The Complete Works of Aristotle*, ed. Barnes.

[Aristotle]. *Magna Moralia*, trans. G. C. Armstrong, rev. ed. London: Heinemann, 1936.

Augustine. *Confessions*, trans. R. S. Pine-Coffin. Harmondsworth: Penguin, 1961.

Cicero. *De Fato*, trans. H. Rackham. Cambridge, Mass.: Harvard University Press, 1942.

—— *De Finibus Bonorum et Malorum*, trans. H. Rackham. Cambridge, Mass.: Harvard University Press, 1914.

—— *De Natura Deorum*, trans. H. Rackham. Cambridge, Mass.: Harvard University Press, 1933.

—— *De Officiis*, trans. Walter Miller. Cambridge, Mass.: Harvard University Press, 1913.

Cicero (cont.)

—— *Paradoxa Stoicorum*, trans. H. Rackham. Cambridge, Mass.: Harvard University Press, 1942.

Diels, Hermann, and Kranz, Walther, eds. *Fragmente der Vorsokratiker*, 8th ed. Berlin: Weidmann, 1956.

Diogenes Laertius. *Lives of the Philosophers*, trans. R. D. Hicks. Cambridge, Mass.: Harvard University Press, 1925.

DK, *see* Diels and Kranz.

Epictetus. *Handbook* (*Encheiridion*), trans. Nicholas White. Indianapolis: Hackett, 1983.

Epicurus. *Principal Doctrines*, in *The Epicurus Reader*, trans. Brad Inwood and L. P. Gerson. Indianapolis: Hackett, 1994.

Euripides. *Medea*, in *Medea and Other Plays*, trans. Philip Vellacott. Harmondsworth: Penguin, 1963.

Herodotus. *The Histories*, trans. A. de Selincourt, rev. J. Marincola. Harmondsworth: Penguin, 1996.

Hesiod. *Works and Days*, trans. H. G. Evelyn-White. London: Heinemann, 1943.

[Hippocrates]. *On Breaths*, in *Hippocratic Writings*, trans. J. Chadwick. Harmondsworth: Penguin, 1984.

Homer. *Iliad*, trans. A. T. Murray. Cambridge, Mass.: Harvard University Press, 1924.

Lucretius. *De Rerum Natura*, trans. H. A. J. Munro, 4th ed. London: Bell, 1886.

Pindar. *The Odes of Pindar*, trans. Maurice Bowra. Harmondsworth: Penguin, 1969.

Plato. *The Collected Dialogues*, ed. E. Hamilton and H. Cairns. Princeton, N.J.: Princeton University Press, 1961.

—— *Complete Works*, ed. John M. Cooper with D. S. Hutchinson. Indianapolis: Hackett, 1997.

—— *Apology*, trans. Hugh Tredennick. Harmondsworth: Penguin, 1954.

—— *Critias*, trans. H. D. P. Lee. Harmondsworth: Penguin, 1965.

—— *Crito*, in *Trial and Death of Socrates*, trans. G. M. A. Grube, rev. John M. Cooper. Indianapolis: Hackett, 2001.

—— *Euthydemus*, trans. Rosamond Kent Sprague. Indianapolis: Hackett, 1993.

—— *Hippias Major*, trans. Paul Woodruff. Indianapolis: Hackett, 1983.

—— *Laws*, trans. T. J. Saunders. Harmondsworth: Penguin, 1970.

—— *Lysis*, in *Early Socratic Dialogues*, trans. F. Burney. Harmondsworth: Penguin, 1987.

—— *Meno*, trans. W. K. C. Guthrie. Harmondsworth: Penguin, 1956.

—— *Phaedo*, trans. R. Hackforth. London: Cambridge University Press, 1972.

—— *Phaedrus*, trans. R. Hackforth. Indianapolis: Bobbs-Merrill, 1952.

—— *Philebus*, trans. R. Hackforth. London: Cambridge University Press, 1972.

—— *Protagoras*, trans. M. Ostwald. Indianapolis: Bobbs-Merrill, 1956.

—— *Republic*, trans. G. M. A. Grube. Indianapolis: Hackett, 1974.

—— *Republic*, trans. G. M. A. Grube, rev. C. D. C. Reeve. Indianapolis: Hackett, 1992.

—— *Republic*, trans. Paul Shorey. Cambridge, Mass.: Harvard University Press, 1930.

—— *Timaeus*, trans. H. D. P. Lee. Harmondsworth: Penguin, 1965.

Sophocles. *Antigone*, trans. R. Fagles. Harmondsworth: Penguin, 1982.

—— *Oedipus Rex*, trans. R. Fagles. Harmondsworth: Penguin, 1982.

Stobaeus, Joannes. *Anthologium*, ed. C. Wachsmuth. Berlin: Weidmann, 1958.

SVF, *see* von Arnim.

Thucydides. *History of the Peloponnesian War*, trans. Rex Warner. London: Penguin, 1954.

Von Arnim, Johannes. *Stoicorum Veterum Fragmenta*, 4 vols. Leipzig: Teubner, 1921–4.

B. Modern Sources

Ackrill, J. L. 1974, 'Aristotle on *Eudaimonia*.' In Rorty 1980a: 15–33. First published in *Proceedings of the British Academy*, 60 (1974): 339–59.

—— 1981. *Aristotle the Philosopher*. Oxford: Clarendon Press.

Adkins, A. W. H. 1960. *Merit and Responsibility*. Oxford: Clarendon Press.

—— 1984. 'The Connection between Aristotle's *Ethics* and *Politics*.' *Political Theory*, 12: 29–49.

Allan, D. J. 1953. 'Aristotle's Account of the Origin of Moral Principles.' *Proceedings of the XIth International Congress of Philosophy, Brussels*, 12: 120–7. Amsterdam: North-Holland.

—— 1955. 'The Practical Syllogism.' *Autour d'Aristote: Recueil offert à Mgr A. Mansion*. Louvain: Publications Universitaires de Louvain.

Annas, Julia. 1980. 'Aristotle on Pleasure and Goodness.' In Rorty 1980a: 285–99.

—— 1981. *An Introduction to Plato's Republic*. Oxford: Clarendon Press.

—— 1988. 'Self-Love in Aristotle.' Spindel Conference 1988. *Southern Journal of Philosophy*, 27: 1–18.

—— 1989. 'Cicero on Stoic Moral Philosophy and Private Property.' In Miriam Griffin and Jonathan Barnes, eds., *Philosophia Togata: Essays on Philosophy and Roman Society*, 151–73. Oxford: Clarendon Press.

—— 1992a. 'Ancient Ethics and Modern Morality.' *Philosophical Perspectives*, 6: 119–36.

—— 1992b. 'The Good Life and the Good Lives of Others.' In E. Paul, F. D. Miller, and J. Paul, eds., *The Good Life and the Human Good*, 133–48. Cambridge: Cambridge University Press, 1992.

—— 1993. *The Morality of Happiness*. New York: Oxford University Press.

—— 1996. 'Aristotle and Kant on Practical Reasoning.' In Engstrom and Whiting 1996: 237–58.

—— 1998. 'From Nature to Happiness.' *Apeiron*, 31: 59–73.

Anscombe, G. E. M. 1958. 'Modern Moral Philosophy.' *Philosophy*, 33: 1–19.

—— 1963. *Intention*, 2nd ed. Oxford : Blackwell.

Apel, Karl-Otto. 1986. 'Kann der postkantische Standpunkt der Moralität noch einmal in substantielle Sittlichkeit "aufgehoben" werden?' In Kuhlmann 1986a: 217–64.

Armstrong, John M. 1997, 'Epicurean Justice.' *Phronesis*, 92: 324–34.

Arnold, Matthew. 1994. *Culture and Anarchy* (1869), ed. Samuel Lipman. New Haven, Conn.: Yale University Press.

Aschheim, Steven E. 1992. *The Nietzsche Legacy in Germany, 1890–1990*. Berkeley: University of California Press.

Ashford, Elizabeth. 2000. 'Utilitarianism, Integrity, and Partiality.' *Journal of Philosophy*, 97: 421–39.

Austin, J. L. 1979. *Philosophical Papers*, ed. G. J. Warnock and J. O. Urmson, 3rd ed. Oxford: Clarendon Press.

Baier, Annette 1985, 'Knowing our Place in the Animal World.' *Postures of the Mind*, 149–55. Minneapolis: University of Minnesota Press.

Baier, Kurt. 1988. 'Radical Virtue Ethics.' *Midwest Studies in Philosophy*, 13: 126–35.

Baldry, H. C. 1965. *The Unity of Mankind in Greek Thought*. Cambridge: Cambridge University Press.

Balme, D. M. 1972. *Aristotle: De Generatione Animalium I and De Partibus Animalium I*. Oxford: Clarendon Press.

Bambrough, Renford, ed. 1965. *New Essays on Plato and Aristotle*. New York: Humanities Press.

Becker, Lawrence C. 1990–1. 'Unity, Coincidence, and Conflict in the Virtues.' *Philosophia*, 20: 127–43.

Beiser, Frederick C., ed. 1993. *The Cambridge Companion to Hegel*. Cambridge: Cambridge University Press.

Benedict, Ruth, 1946. *The Chrysanthemum and the Sword*. Boston, Mass.: Houghton Mifflin.

Benjamin, Walter. 1928. *Ursprung des deutschen Trauerspiels*. Berlin: Rowohlt.

Berlin, Isaiah. 1969. *Four Essays on Liberty*. Oxford: Oxford University Press.

—— 1980a. *Against the Current*. New York: Viking.

—— 1980b. 'The Originality of Macchiavelli.' In Berlin 1980a: 25–79. First published in Myron Gilmore, ed., *Studies on Macchiavelli*. Florence: Sansoni, 1972.

—— 1991a. *The Crooked Timber of Humanity*. New York: Knopf.

—— 1991b. 'The Decline of Utopian Ideas in the West.' In Berlin 1991a: 20–48. First published Tokyo: Japan Foundation, 1978.

—— 1991c. 'The Pursuit of the Ideal.' In Berlin 1991a: 1–19. First published in *New York Review of Books*, 17 March 1988.

Bowersock, G. W. 1965. *Augustus and the Greek World*. Oxford: Clarendon Press.

Boyle, Nicholas. 1991. *Goethe: The Poet and the Age*, vol. i. Oxford: Clarendon Press.

Bradley, F. H. 1927. *Ethical Studies*, 2nd ed. Oxford: Oxford University Press.

Brandt, Richard. 1993. 'Overvold on Self-Interest and Self-Sacrifice.' In Heil 1993: 221–31.

Bratman, Michael. 1987. *Intention, Plans, and Practical Reason*. Cambridge, Mass.: Harvard University Press.

—— 1999. *The Faces of Intention*. Cambridge: Cambridge University Press.

Brink, David O. 1992. 'Sidgwick and the Rationale for Rational Egoism.' In Schultz 1992: 199–240.

—— 1997. 'Self-Love and Altruism.' *Social Philosophy and Policy*, 14: 122–57.

—— 1999. 'Eudaimonism, Love and Friendship, and Political Community.' *Social Philosophy and Policy*, 16: 252–89.

Broad, C. D. 1930. *Five Types of Ethical Theory*. London: Routledge.

—— 1942. 'Certain Features in Moore's Ethical Doctrines.' In P. A. Schilpp, ed., *The Philosophy of G. E. Moore*, 43–67. La Salle, Ill.: Open Court.

—— 1952. 'Egoism as a Theory of Human Motives.' *Ethics and the History of Philosophy*, 218–31. London: Routledge & Kegan Paul.

Broadie, Sarah. 1991. *Ethics with Aristotle*. Oxford: Oxford University Press.

Brochard, Victor. 1901. 'La Morale ancienne et la morale moderne.' *Revue Philosophique*, 51: 1–12.

Bubner, Rüdiger. 1986. 'Moralität und Sittlichkeit: Die Herkunft eines Gegensatzes.' In Kuhlmann 1986a: 64–84.

Burnyeat, M. F. 1971. 'Virtues in Action.' In Vlastos 1971b: 209–35.

Bury, R. G., ed. 1897. *The Philebus of Plato*. Cambridge: Cambridge University Press.

Butler, Eliza M. 1935. *The Tyranny of Greece over Germany*. London: Macmillan.

Butler, Joseph. 1726. *Fifteen Sermons Preached at the Rolls Chapel*. London.

Calabresi, Guido, and Bobbitt, Philip. 1978. *Tragic Choices*. New York: Norton.

Chang, Ruth, ed. 1997. *Incommensurability, Incompatibility, and Practical Reason*. Cambridge, Mass.: Harvard University Press.

Charles, David. 1999. 'Aristotle on Well-Being and Intellectual Contemplation.' *Proceedings of the Aristotelian Society*, 73: 205–23.

Cherniss, Harold. 1971. 'The Sources of Evil According to Plato.' In Vlastos 1971c: 244–58. First published in *Proceedings of the American Philosophical Society*, 98 (1954): 23–30.

Conly, Sarah. 1988. 'Flourishing and the Failure of the Ethics of Virtue.' *Midwest Studies in Philosophy*, 13: 83–96.

Cooper, John M. 1975. *Reason and Human Good in Aristotle*. Cambridge, Mass.: Harvard University Press.

Cooper, John M. (cont.)

—— 1977a. 'Aristotle on the Forms of Friendship.' *Review of Metaphysics*, 30 (4): 619–48. Repr. in Cooper 1999b: 312–35.

—— 1977b. 'The Psychology of Justice in Plato.' *American Philosophical Quarterly*, 14: 151–7. Repr. in Cooper 1999b: 138–49.

—— 1980. 'Aristotle on Friendship.' In Rorty 1980a: 301–40.

—— 1984. 'Plato's Theory of Human Motivation.' *History of Philosophy Quarterly*, 1: 3–21. Repr. in Cooper 1999b: 118–37.

—— 1987. 'Contemplation and Happiness: A Reconsideration.' *Synthese*, 72: 187–216. Repr. in Cooper 1999b: 212–36.

—— 1996. 'Eudaimonism, the Appeal to Nature, and "Moral Duty" in Stoicism.' In Engstrom and Whiting 1996: 261–84.

—— 1998. 'The Unity of Virtue.' *Social Philosophy and Policy*, 15 (1): 233–74. Repr. in Cooper 1999b: 76–117.

—— 1999a. 'Pleasure and Desire in Epicurus.' In Cooper 1999b: 485–514.

—— 1999b. *Reason and Emotion*. Princeton, N.J.: Princeton University Press.

Cottingham, John. 1991. 'The Ethics of Self-Concern.' *Ethics*, 101: 798–817.

Craig, John. 1996. *Isaiah Berlin*. Princeton, N.J.: Princeton University Press.

Darwall, Stephen. 1995. *The British Moralists and the Internal 'Ought', 1640–1740*. Cambridge: Cambridge University Press.

Demos, Raphael. 1963. 'A Fallacy in Plato's *Republic*?' *Philosophical Review*, 72: 141–158. Repr. in Vlastos 1971c.

Dent, N. J. H. 1984. *The Moral Psychology of the Virtues*. Cambridge: Cambridge University Press.

Devereux, Daniel. 1977. 'Aristotle on the Active and Contemplative Lives.' *Philosophy Research Archives*, 3: 834–44.

—— 1981. 'Aristotle on the Essence of Happiness.' In O'Meara 1981: 247–60.

Dodds, E. R. 1951. *The Greeks and the Irrational*. Berkeley: University of California Press.

—— ed. 1959. *Plato: Gorgias*. Oxford: Clarendon Press.

Dover, Kenneth J. 1974. *Greek Popular Morality in the Time of Plato and Aristotle*. Berkeley: University of California Press.

Ehrenberg, Victor. 1969. *The Greek State*, 2nd ed. London: Methuen.

Engstrom, Stephen, and Whiting, Jennifer, eds. 1996. *Aristotle, Kant and the Stoics: Rethinking Happiness and Duty*. Cambridge: Cambridge University Press.

Ewen, Frederic. 1932. *The Prestige of Schiller in England, 1788–1859*. New York: Columbia University Press.

Feinberg, Joel. 1970. 'The Nature and Value of Rights.' *Journal of Value Inquiry*, 4: 243–57.

Ferguson, W. S. 1954. 'The Leading Ideas of the New Period.' *Cambridge Ancient History*, vii: 1–40.

Field, G. C. 1932. *Moral Theory: An Introduction to Ethics*, 2nd ed. London: Methuen.

Finley, M. I. 1973. *The Ancient Economy*. Berkeley: University of California Press.

Foot, Philippa. 1978a. 'Are Moral Considerations Overriding?' In Foot 1978e: 181–8.

—— 1978b. 'Euthanasia.' In Foot 1978c: 33–61. First published in *Philosophy and Public Affairs*, 6 (1977): 85–112.

—— 1978c. 'Moral Beliefs.' In Foot 1978e: 110–31. First published in *Proceedings of the Aristotelian Society*, 59 (1958): 83–104.

—— 1978d. 'Morality as a System of Hypothetical Imperatives.' In Foot 1978e: 157–73. First published in *Philosophical Review*, 81 (1972): 305–16.

—— 1978e. *Virtues and Vices*. Berkeley: University of California Press.

Foster, M. B. 1935. *The Political Philosophies of Plato and Hegel* (Oxford: Clarendon Press).

—— 1937. 'A Mistake in Plato's *Republic*.' *Mind*, n.s. 46: 386–93.

Frankena, William K. 1965. *Three Historical Philosophies of Education*. Glenview, Ill.: Scott Foresman.

—— 1970. 'Prichard and the Ethics of Virtue.' *Monist*, 54: 1–17. Repr. in Frankena 1976: 148–60.

—— 1973a. *Ethics*, 2nd ed. Englewood Cliffs, N.J.: Prentice-Hall.

—— 1973b. 'The Ethics of Love Conceived as an Ethics of Virtue.' *Journal of Religious Ethics*, 1: 21–36.

—— 1976. *Perspectives on Morality*, ed. K. E. Goodpaster. Notre Dame, Ind.: Notre Dame University Press.

—— 1980a. *Thinking about Morality*. Ann Arbor: University of Michigan Press.

—— 1980b. 'Three Questions about Morality.' *Monist*, 63: 1–128.

—— 1992. 'Sidgwick and the History of Ethical Dualism.' In Schultz 1992: 175–98.

—— 1993. 'Sidgwick's *Methods of Ethics*, Edition 7, Page 92, Note 1.' In Heil 1993: 257–69.

Frankfurt, Harry. 1988. *The Importance of What We Care About*. Cambridge: Cambridge University Press.

French, Peter A., Uehling, Theodore E., and Wettstein, Howard K., eds. 1988. *Ethical Theory: Character and Virtue. Midwest Studies in Philosophy*, 13. Notre Dame, Ind.: University of Notre Dame Press.

Furth, Montgomery. 1988. *Substance, Form and Psyche*. Cambridge: Cambridge University Press.

Gauthier, David. 1994. 'Assure and Threaten.' *Ethics*, 104: 690–721.

Gauthier, R. A., and Jolif, J. Y. 1970. *Aristote: L'Étique à Nicomaque*. Louvain: Publications Universitaires de Louvain.

Geach, P. T. 1977. *The Virtues*. The Stanton Lectures, 1973–4. New York: Cambridge University Press.

Gellrich, Michelle. 1988. *Tragedy and Theory*. Princeton, N.J.: Princeton University Press.

Gerhardt, Volker. 1997. 'Der groß geschriebene Mensch.' *Internationale Zeitschrift für Philosophie*, 40–56.

Gert, Bernard. 1988. *Morality*. New York: Oxford University Press.

Gibbard, Allan. 1973. 'Doing No More Harm than Good.' *Philosophical Studies*, 24: 158–73.

Gomez-Lobo, Alfonso. 1989. 'Philosophical Remarks on Thucydides' Melian Dialogue.' *Proceedings of the Boston Area Colloquium in Ancient Philosophy*, 5: 181–203.

Gowans, Christopher W., ed. 1987. *Moral Dilemmas*. Oxford: Oxford University Press.

Gray, J. Glenn. 1941. *Hegel's Hellenic Ideal*. New York: King's Crown Press.

Gray, John. 1996. *Isaiah Berlin*. Princeton, N.J.: Princeton University Press.

Green, T. H. 1883. *Prolegomena to Ethics*. Oxford: Clarendon Press.

Grote, George. 1846–56. *History of Greece*. London: John Murray.

—— 1888. *Plato and the Other Companions of Socrates*, new ed. London: John Murray.

Guthrie, W. K. C. 1975. *A History of Greek Philosophy*, vol. iv. Cambridge: Cambridge University Press.

Habermas, J. 1986. 'Moralität und Sittlichkeit.' In Kuhlmann 1986a: 16–37.

Hackforth, Reginald. 1945. *Plato's Examination of Pleasure*. Cambridge: Cambridge University Press.

—— 1955. *Plato's Phaedo*. Cambridge: Cambridge University Press.

Hahm, David. 1977. *The Origins of Stoics Cosmology*. Columbus: Ohio State University Press.

Hardie, W. F. R. 1965. 'The Final Good in Aristotle's *Ethics*.' *Philosophy*, 40: 277–95.

Hare, R. M. 1965. 'Plato and the Mathematicians.' In Bambrough 1965: 21–38.

—— 1981. *Moral Thinking*. Oxford: Clarendon Press.

Harrison, A. R. W. 1968. *The Law of Athens: The Family and Property*. Oxford: Clarendon Press.

Hart, H. L. A. 1961. *The Concept of Law*. Oxford: Clarendon Press.

Hatfield, Henry. 1964. *Aesthetic Paganism in German Literature*. Cambridge, Mass.: Harvard University Press.

Havelock, E. A. 1957. *The Liberal Temper in Greek Politics*. New Haven, Conn.: Yale University Press.

Hegel, G. W. F. 1955. *Lectures on the History of Philosophy*, trans. E. S. Haldane and Frances H. Simson. New York: Humanities Press.

—— 1962. *Lectures on the Philosophy of Religion*, trans. E. B. Speirs and J. Burdon Sanderson. Humanities Press: New York.

—— 1965. *Philosophy of Right*, trans. T M. Knox. Oxford: Clarendon Press.

—— 1977. *Phenomenology of Spirit*, trans. A. V. Miller. Oxford: Oxford University Press.

—— 1984. *Lectures on the Philosophy of Religion*, trans. R. F. Brown, P. C. Hodgson, and J. M. Stewart. Berkeley: University of California Press.

—— 1991. *The Philosophy of History*, trans. J. Sibree. Buffalo, N.Y.: Prometheus.

Heil, John, ed. 1993. *Rationality, Morality, and Self-Interest: Essays Honoring Mark Overvold*. Lanham, Md.: Rowman & Littlefield.

Heinaman, Robert. 1988. 'Eudaimonia and Self-Sufficiency in the *Nicomachean Ethics*.' *Phronesis*, 33: 31–53.

Herder, Johann Gottfried von. 1989. *Ideen zur Philosophie der Geschichte der Menschheit*, ed. Martin Bollacher. Frankfurt am Main: Deutscher Klassiker Verlag.

Hill, Thomas E., Jr. 1993. 'Beneficence and Self-Love: A Kantian Perspective.' In Paul, Miller, and Paul 1993: 1–23.

Hölderlin, Friedrich. 1994. *Poems and Fragments*, trans. Michael Hamburger. London: Anvil Press.

—— 1999. *Sämtliche Gedichte und Hyperion*. Frankfurt am Main: Insel.

Humboldt, Alexander von. 1961. 'Über das Studium des Alterthums, und des griechischen Insbesondere' (1793). *Werke*, ii. 1–24. Darmstadt: Wissenschaftliche Buchgesellschaft, 1961.

Hume, David. 1965 *Essays: Moral, Political and Literary*. Oxford: Oxford University Press.

—— 1975. *An Enquiry Concerning the Principles of Morals* (1777), ed. L. A. Selby-Bigge, rev. P. H. Nidditch. Oxford: Clarendon Press.

Hurley, Susan L. 1989. *Natural Reasons*. New York: Oxford University Press.

Hursthouse, Rosalind. 1999. *On Virtue Ethics*. Oxford: Oxford University Press.

Inwood, Brad. 1985. *Ethics and Human Action in Early Stoicism*. Oxford: Clarendon Press.

Irwin, Terence. 1977. *Plato's Moral Theory*. Oxford: Clarendon Press.

—— 1979. *Plato: Gorgias, Translated with Notes*. Oxford: Clarendon Press.

—— 1985. *Aristotle: Nicomachean Ethics*. Indianapolis: Hackett.

—— 1988. *Aristotle's First Principles*. Oxford: Clarendon Press.

—— 1992. 'Eminent Victorians and Greek Ethics: Sidgwick, Green and Aristotle.' In Schulz 1992: 279–310.

—— 1995. *Plato's Ethics*. Oxford: Oxford University Press.

—— 1996. 'Kant's Criticisms of Eudaimonism.' In Engstrom and Whiting 1996: 63–101.

Irwin, Terence, and Nussbaum, Martha, eds. 1994. *Virtue, Love and Form*. Edmonton, Alberta: Academic Printing and Publishing.

Jenkyns, Richard. 1980. *The Victorians and Ancient Greece*. Cambridge, Mass.: Harvard University Press.

Kahn, Charles. 1960. *Anaximander and the Origins of Greek Cosmology*. New York: Columbia University Press.

—— 1996. *Plato and the Socratic Dialogue*. Cambridge: Cambridge University Press.

Kain, Philip J. 1982. *Schiller, Hegel, and Marx: State, Society, and the Aesthetic Ideal of Ancient Greece*. Kingston, Ontario: McGill–Queen's University Press.

Kant, Immanuel. 1934. *Religion within the Limits of Reason Alone*, trans. T. H. Green and H. H. Hudson. Chicago: Open Court, 1934.

—— 1956. *Critique of Practical Reason*, trans. Lewis White Beck. Indianapolis: Bobbs-Merrill.

—— 1981. *Grounding for the Metaphysics of Morals*, trans. James W. Ellington. Indianapolis: Hackett, 1981.

—— 1983. 'What is Enlightenment?' *Perpetual Peace and Other Essays*, trans. Ted Humphrey, 41–6. Indianapolis: Hackett.

Kenny, Anthony. 1965. 'Happiness.' *Proceedings of the Aristotelian Society*, 66: 93–102.

—— 1978. *The Aristotelian Ethics*. Oxford: Oxford University Press.

—— 1992. *Aristotle on the Perfect Life*. Oxford: Oxford University Press.

Kerferd, G. B. 1978. 'What Does the Wise Man Know?' In Rist 1978: 125–36.

—— 1981. *The Sophistic Movement*. Cambridge: Cambridge University Press.

Kidd, I. G. 1978. 'Moral Actions and Rules in Stoic Ethics.' In Rist 1978: 247–58.

Kirk, G. S., Raven, J. E., and Schofield, M. 1983. *The Presocratic Philosophers*, 2nd ed. Cambridge: Cambridge University Press.

Kitto, H. D. F. 1957. *The Greeks*, rev. ed. Harmondsworth: Penguin.

Knox, Bernard. 1979. *Word and Action*. Baltimore, Md.: Johns Hopkins University Press.

—— 1982. 'Greece and the Theatre.' In Robert Fagles, trans., *Sophocles: The Three Theban Plays*. London: Allen Lane.

Korsgaard, Christine. 1986. 'Aristotle and Kant on the Source of Value.' *Ethics*, 96: 486–505.

—— 1996. 'From Duty and for the Sake of the Noble: Kant and Aristotle on Morally Good Action.' In Engstrom and Whiting 1996: 203–36.

Kraut, Richard. 1979. 'Two Conceptions of Happiness.' *Philosophical Review*, 88: 167–97.

—— 1984. *Socrates and the State*. Princeton, N.J.: Princeton University Press.

—— 1988. 'Comments on Julia Annas' "Self-Love in Aristotle".' Spindel Conference 1988. *Southern Journal of Philosophy*, 27: 19–23.

—— 1989. *Aristotle on the Human Good*. Princeton, N.J.: Princeton University Press.

—— ed. 1993a. *Cambridge Companion to Plato*. Cambridge: Cambridge University Press.

—— 1993b. 'The Defense of Justice in Plato's *Republic*.' In Kraut 1993a: 311–37.

Kuhlmann, Wolfgang, ed. 1986a. *Moralität und Sittlichkeit*. Frankfurt am Main: Suhrkamp.

—— 1986b. 'Moralität und Sittlichkeit: Ist die Idee einer letztbegründeten normativen Ethik überhaupt sinnvoll?' In Kuhlmann 1986a: 194–216.

Larmore, Charles E. 1987. *Patterns of Moral Complexity*. Cambridge: Cambridge University Press.

—— 1990. 'The Right and the Good.' *Philosophia*, 20: 15–32; repr. in revised form in Larmore 1996: 19–40.

—— 1996. *The Morals of Modernity*. Cambridge: Cambridge University Press.

Lawrence, Gavin. 1993. 'Aristotle and the Ideal Life.' *Philosophical Review*, 102: 1–34.

Lewis, C. I. 1946. *An Analysis of Knowledge and Valuation*. LaSalle, Ill.: Open Court.

Lloyd-Jones, Hugh. 1983. *The Justice of Zeus*, 2nd ed. Berkeley: University of California Press.

Long, A. A. 1970–1. 'The Logical Basis of Stoic Ethics.' *Proceedings of the Aristotelian Society*, 71: 85–104.

—— 1971a. 'Language and Thought in Stoicism.' In Long 1971b: 75–113.

—— ed. 1971b. *Problems in Stoicism*. London: Athlone Press.

—— 1974. *Hellenistic Philosophy*. London: Duckworth.

—— 1978. 'Dialectic and the Stoic Sage.' In Rist 1978: 101–24.

Long, A. A., and Sedley, D. N. 1987. *The Hellenistic Philosophers*, 2 vols. Cambridge: Cambridge University Press.

Lovejoy, A. O. 1948a. *Essays in the History of Ideas*. Baltimore, Md.: Johns Hopkins University Press.

—— 1948b. 'On the Discrimination of Romanticism.' In Lovejoy 1948a: 228–53.

—— 1948c. 'The Parallel of Deism and Classicism.' In Lovejoy 1948a: 78–98.

—— 1948d. 'The Meaning of the Term "Romantic" in Early Greek Romanticism.' In Lovejoy 1948a: 183–206.

Mabbott, J. D. 1971. 'Is Plato's *Republic* Utilitarian?' In Vlastos 1971c: 57–65. (A revised version of a paper of the same title first published in *Mind*, 46 (1937): 468–74.)

MacCormick, Neil. 1978. *Legal Reasoning and Legal Theory*. Oxford: Clarendon Press.

MacIntyre, Alasdair. 1981. *After Virtue*. Notre Dame, Ind.: University of Notre Dame Press.

—— 1988. *Whose Justice? Which Rationality?* Notre Dame, Ind.: University of Notre Dame Press.

Mackie, John. 1977. *Ethics: Inventing Right and Wrong*. Harmondsworth: Penguin.

MacNeice, Louis. 1939. *Autumn Journal* (1939). London: Faber & Faber, 1946.

McDowell, John. 1978. 'Are Moral Requirements Hypothetical Imperatives?' *Proceedings of the Aristotelian Society*, suppl. vol. 52: 13–29.

—— 1979. 'Virtue and Reason.' *Monist*, 62: 331–50.

—— 1980. 'The Role of *Eudaimonia* in Aristotle's Ethics.' In Rorty 1980a: 359–76.

—— 1996. 'Deliberation and Moral Development.' In Engstrom and Whiting 1996: 19–35.

Meyer, Susan Sauvé. 1998. 'Ethics and the History of Philosophy.' *Apeiron*, 21: 75–89.

Mill, John Stuart. 1871. *Utilitarianism*, 4th ed. London.

—— 1965a. 'Comments on Plato's *Gorgias*.' In Mill 1965b: 75–7. First published in *Monthly Repository*, 1834.

—— 1965b. *Mill's Ethical Writings*, ed. J. B. Schneewind. New York: Collier.

Miller, Richard W. 1992. *Moral Differences*. Princeton, N.J.: Princeton University Press.

Millgram, Elijah. 1997. *Practical Induction*. Cambridge, Mass.: Harvard University Press.

Mitsis, Phillip. 1988. *Epicurus' Ethical Theory*. Ithaca, N.Y.: Cornell University Press.

Momigliano, Arnaldo. 1975. *Alien Wisdom*. Cambridge: Cambridge University Press.

Moore, G. E. 1903. *Principia Ethica*. Cambridge: Cambridge University Press.

Moravcsik, Julius M. 1990. 'The Role of Virtue in Alternatives to Kantian and Utilitarian Ethics.' *Philosophia*, 20: 33– 48.

Morrison, Donald. 1999. 'Aristotle's Definition of Citizenship.' *History of Philosophy Quarterly*, 16: 143–61.

Most, Glenn W. 1992. 'Schöne, das.' In J. Ritter and K. Gründer, eds., *Historisches Wörterbuch der Philosophie*. Basel: Schwabe.

—— 1993. 'Schlegel, Schlegel und die Geburt eines Tragödienparadigmas.' *Poetica*, 25: 155–75.

Nagel, Thomas. 1970. *The Possibility of Altruism*. Oxford: Clarendon Press.

—— 1979a. 'The Fragmentation of Value.' In Nagel 1979b: 128–41.

—— 1979b. *Mortal Questions*. Cambridge: Cambridge University Press.

—— 1986. *The View From Nowhere*. New York: Oxford University Press.

Nehamas, Alexander. 1985. *Nietzsche: Life as Literature*. Cambridge, Mass.: Harvard University Press.

—— 1994. 'Before Virtue.' Review of Bernard Williams, *Shame and Necessity*. *The New Republic*, 24 October: 40–5.

—— 1999. *Virtues of Authenticity*. Princeton, N.J.: Princeton University Press.

Nietzsche, Friedrich. 1962. *Philosophy in the Tragic Age of the Greeks*, trans. Marianne Cowan. Washington, D.C.: Regnery Gateway.

—— 1966a. *The Basic Writings of Nietzsche*, trans. Walter Kaufmann. New York: Random House.

—— 1966b. *Beyond Good and Evil*. In Nietzsche 1966a: 191–435.

—— 1966c. *The Birth of Tragedy*. In Nietzsche 1966a: 31–145.

—— 1966d. *The Gay Science*, trans. Walter Kaufmann. New York: Vintage, 1974.

—— 1966e. *The Genealogy of Morals*. In Nietzsche 1966a: 449–599.

Novalis (Friedrich Philipp von Hardenberg). 1960. *Hymns to the Night and Other Selected Writings*, trans. Charles E. Passage. Indianapolis: Bobbs-Merrill.

Nussbaum, Martha. 1986. *The Fragility of Goodness*. Cambridge: Cambridge University Press.

—— 1994. *The Therapy of Desire*. Princeton, N.J.: Princeton University Press.

O'Meara, Dominic J., ed. 1981. *Studies in Aristotle*. Washington, D.C.: Catholic University of America Press.

—— ed. 1985. *Platonic Investigations*. Washington, D.C.: Catholic University of America Press.

Osborne, Catherine. 1996. 'Love's Bitter Fruits.' *Philosophical Investigations*, 19: 318–28.

Owen, G. E. L. 1957. 'A Proof in the *Peri Ideon*.' *Journal of Hellenic Studies*, 77: 103–11. Repr. in Owen 1986: 165–79.

—— 1961. '*Tithenai ta Phainomena*.' In S. Mansion, ed., *Aristote et les problèmes de méthode*, 83–103. Louvain: Béatrice-Nauwelaerts. Repr. in Owen 1986: 239–51.

—— 1986. *Logic, Science and Dialectic*, ed. Martha Nussbaum. Ithaca, N.Y.: Cornell University Press.

Parfit, Derek. 1984. *Reasons and Persons*. Oxford: Clarendon Press.

Pater, Walter. *The Renaissance* (1873), ed. Donald L. Hill. Berkeley: University of California Press.

Paton, H. J. 1947. *The Categorical Imperative*. London: Hutchinson.

Paul, Ellen Frankel, Miller, Fred D., Jr., and Paul, Jeffrey, eds. 1993. *Altruism*. Cambridge: Cambridge University Press.

Penner, Terry. 1973. 'The Unity of Virtue.' *Philosophical Review*, 82: 35–68.

Pohlenz, Max. 1966. *Freedom in Greek Life and Thought*, trans. Carl Lofmark. Dordrecht: Reidel. First published as *Griechische Freiheit: Wesen und Werden eines Lebensideals*. Heidelberg: Quelle & Meyer, 1954.

Pohlenz, Max. 1959. *Die Stoa*, 2nd ed. 2 vols. Göttingen: Vandenhoeck & Ruprecht.

Popper, Karl. 1950. *The Open Society and Its Enemies*. Princeton, N.J.: Princeton University Press.

Price, A. W. 1989. *Love and Friendship in Plato and Aristotle*. Oxford: Clarendon Press.

—— 1995. *Mental Conflict*. London: Routledge.

Prichard, Henry. 1968a. 'Duty and Interest.' In Prichard 1968d: 201–38. First published separately as an inaugural lecture, Oxford: Oxford University Press, 1928.

—— 1968b. 'The Meaning of Agathon in the Ethics of Aristotle.' In Prichard 1968d: 40–53. First published in *Philosophy*, 10 (1935): 27–39.

—— 1968c. *Moral Obligation*. In Prichard 1968d. First published Oxford: Oxford University Press, 1949.

—— 1968d. *Moral Obligation and Duty and Interest*. Oxford: Oxford University Press.

Quammen, David. 1998. 'Karl's Sense of Snow.' In *Wild Thoughts from Wild Places*, 155–64. New York: Scribner.

Rapp, Christoph. 1997. 'War Aristoteles ein Kommunitarist?' *Internationale Zeitschrift für Philosophie*, 57–75.

Rawls, John. 1971. *A Theory of Justice*. Cambridge, Mass.: Harvard University Press.

Reeve, C. D. C. 1988. *Philosopher Kings*. Princeton, N.J.: Princeton University Press.

—— 1995. *Practices of Reason*. Oxford: Clarendon Press.

Regan, Donald H. Unpublished. 'The Incoherence of "Good For".'

Reich, Klaus. 1939. 'Kant and Greek Ethics.' *Mind*, 48: 338–54, 446–63.

Reiner, Hans. 1964. *Die Philosophische Ethik*. Heidelberg: Quelle & Meyer.

—— 1974. *Die Grundlagen der Sittlichkeit*. Meisenheim: Hain.

—— 1977. 'Die Goldene Regel und das Naturrecht.' *Studia Leibnitiana*, 9: 231–54.

—— 1983. *Duty and Inclination*, trans. Mark Santos. The Hague: Nijhoff. (A translation of the first four chapters of Reiner 1974.)

Rist, John M., ed. 1978. *The Stoics*. Berkeley: University of California Press.

Roche, Timothy D. 1988. 'ERGON and EUDAIMONIA in *Nicomachean Ethics* I.' *Journal of the History of Philosophy*, 26: 175–94.

Rorty, A. O., ed. 1976. *The Identities of Persons*. Berkeley: University of California Press.

—— ed. 1980a. *Essays on Aristotle's Ethics*. Berkeley: University of California Press.

—— 1980b. 'The Place of Contemplation in Aristotle's *Nicomachean Ethics*.' In Rorty 1980a: 377–94.

Rorty, R., Schneewind, J., and Skinner, Q., eds. 1984. *Philosophy in History*. Cambridge: Cambridge University Press.

Sachs, David. 1963. 'A Fallacy in Plato's *Republic*.' *Philosophical Review*, 72: 141–58.

Ste Croix, G. E. M. de. 1981. *The Class Struggle in the Ancient Greek World*. Ithaca, N.Y.: Cornell University Press.

Sandel, Michael. 1982. *Liberalism and the Limits of Justice*. Cambridge: Cambridge University Press.

Santas, Gerasimos. 1971. 'Plato's *Protagoras* and Explanations of Weakness.' In Vlastos 1971c: 264–98.

—— 1979. *Socrates' Philosophy in Plato's Early Dialogues*. London: Routledge & Kegan Paul.

—— 1980. 'The Form of the Good in Plato's *Republic*.' *Philosophical Inquiry*, 2: 374–403.

—— 1985. 'Two Theories of Good in Plato's *Republic*.' *Archiv für Geschichte der Philosophie*, 67: 223–45.

—— 1994. 'Socratic Goods and Socratic Happiness.' In Irwin and Nussbaum 1994: 37–52.

—— 1989. 'Desire and Perfection in Aristotle's Theory of the Good.' *Apeiron*, 22: 75–99.

Sayre-McCord, Geoffrey, ed. 1988. *Essays on Moral Realism*. Ithaca, N.Y.: Cornell University Press.

Schiller, Friedrich. 1902. *The Works of Friedrich Schiller*, trans. E. P. Arnold Forster and Percy E. Pinkerton, ed. Nathan Haskell Dole. Boston, Mass.: Wyman-Fogg.

—— 1961. 'Über Anmut und Würde.' *Sämtliche Werke*, 2nd ed., v. 433–88. Munich: Hanser, 1961. First published in *Neue Thalia*, iii. 2 (1793).

—— 1967. *Letters On the Aesthetic Education of Man*, trans. Elizabeth M. Wilkinson and L. A. Willoughby. Oxford: Clarendon Press, 1967. (A translation of Schiller's revised edition of 1801.)

—— 1979. *The Robbers*, trans. F. J. Lamport. Harmondsworth: Penguin.

Schlegel, August Wilhelm. 1966. *Vorlesungen über dramatische Kunst und Literatur* (1809–11). Stuttgart: Kohlhammer.

Schnädelbach, Herbert. 1986. 'Was ist Neuaristotelismus?' In Kuhlmann 1986a: 38–63.

Schneewind, J. B. 1984. 'The Divine Corporation and the History of Ethics.' In Rorty, Schneewind, and Skinner 1984: 173–91.

—— 1996. 'Kant and Stoic Ethics.' In Engstrom and Whiting 1996: 285–301.

Schultz, Bart, ed. 1992. *Essays on Sidgwick*. Cambridge: Cambridge University Press.

Scott, Dominic. 1999. 'Aristotle on Well-Being and Intellectual Contemplation.' *Proceedings of the Aristotelian Society*, 73: 225–41.

Sertillanges, A.-D. 1901. 'La Morale ancienne et la morale moderne.' *Revue Philosophique*, 51: 280–92.

Sherman, Nancy. 1989. *The Fabric of Character: Aristotle's Theory of Virtue*. Oxford: Clarendon Press.

—— 1997. *Making a Necessity of Virtue: Aristotle and Kant on Virtue*. Cambridge: Cambridge University Press.

Sidgwick, Henry. 1907. *The Methods of Ethics*, 7th ed. London: Macmillan.

—— 1931. *Outlines of the History of Ethics*, 6th ed. Boston, Mass.: Beacon Press.

Sinnott-Armstrong, Walter. 1988. *Moral Dilemmas*. Oxford: Blackwell.

Slote, Michael. 1990. 'Some Advantages of Virtue Ethics.' In Owen Flanagan and Amelie Oksenberg Rorty, eds., *Identity, Character, and Morality*, 429–48. Cambridge, Mass.: MIT Press.

—— 1992. *From Morality to Virtue*. Oxford: Oxford University Press.

Smith, Adam. 1976. *The Theory of the Moral Sentiments*, ed. D. D. Raphael and A. L. Macfie. Oxford: Clarendon Press.

Stocker, Michael. 1976. 'The Schizophrenia of Modern Ethical Theories.' *Journal of Philosophy*, 73: 453–66.

—— 1990. *Plural and Conflicting Values*. Oxford: Clarendon Press.

Striker, Gisela. 1983. 'The Role of *Oikeiosis* in Stoic Ethics.' *Oxford Studies in Ancient Philosophy*, 1: 145–67.

—— 1996. *Essays on Hellenistic Epistemology and Ethics*. Cambridge: Cambridge University Press.

Swinburne, Algernon Charles. 1970. *Poems and Ballads*. Indianapolis: Bobbs-Merrill.

Taylor, C. C. W. 1998. *Socrates*. Oxford: Oxford University Press.

Taylor, Charles. 1979. *Hegel*. Cambridge: Cambridge University Press.

—— 1985. 'The Diversity of Goods.' *Human Agency and Language*. Cambridge: Cambridge University Press.

—— 1989. *Sources of the Self*. Cambridge, Mass.: Harvard University Press.

Taylor, Richard. 1988. 'Ancient Wisdom and Modern Folly.' In French, Uehling, and Wettstein 1988: 54–63.

Trianosky, Gregory. 1990. 'What Is Virtue Ethics All About?' *American Philosophical Quarterly*, 27: 335–44.

Tugendhat, Ernst. 1992. 'Zum Begriff und zur Begründung der Moral.' *Philosophische Aufsätze*, 315–33. Frankfurt am Main: Suhrkamp.

Turner, Frank M. 1981. *The Greek Heritage in Victorian Britain*. New Haven, Conn.: Yale University Press.

Urmson, J. O. 1973. 'Aristotle's Doctrine of the Mean.' *American Philosophical Quarterly*, 10: 223–30. Repr. in Rorty 1980a: 157–70.

—— 1988. *Aristotle's Ethics*. Oxford: Blackwell.

Vlastos, Gregory. 1965. 'Degrees of Reality in Plato.' In Bambrough 1965: 1–19.

Vlastos, Gregory. 1969. 'Reasons and Causes in the *Phaedo*.' *Philosophical Review*, 78: 291–325.

—— 1971a. 'Justice and Happiness in the *Republic*.' In Vlastos 1971c: 66–95.

—— ed. 1971b. *The Philosophy of Socrates*. Garden City, N.Y.: Anchor.

—— ed. 1971c. *Plato II*. Garden City, N.Y.: Anchor.

—— 1991. *Socrates: Ironist and Moral Philosopher*. Cambridge: Cambridge University Press.

Wallace, James D. 1978. *Virtues and Vices*. Ithaca. N.Y.: Cornell University Press.

White, Nicholas. 1979a. 'The Basis of Stoic Ethics.' *Harvard Studies in Classical Philology*, 83: 143–78.

—— 1979b. *Companion to Plato's Republic*. Indianapolis: Hackett.

—— 1981. 'Goodness and Human Aims in Aristotle.' In O'Meara 1981: 225–46.

—— 1984. 'The Classification of Goods in Plato's *Republic*.' *Journal of the History of Philosophy*, 22: 393–421.

—— 1985a. 'Rational Prudence in Plato's *Gorgias*.' In O'Meara 1985: 139–62.

—— 1985b. 'The Role of Physics in Stoic Ethics.' Spindel Conference 1985. *Southern Journal of Philosophy*, 23: 57–74.

—— 1986. 'The Rulers' Choice.' *Archiv für Geschichte der Philosophie*, 68: 22–46.

—— 1988a. 'Good as Goal.' Spindel Conference 1988. *Southern Journal of Philosophy*, 27: 169–93.

—— 1988b. 'Rational Self-Sufficiency in Greek Ethics.' Review of Martha Nussbaum, *The Fragility of Goodness*. *Ethics*, 99: 136–46.

—— 1993. 'Plato's Metaphysical Epistemology.' In Kraut 1993a: 277–310.

—— 1994a. 'Neoaristotelian Inclusivist Eudaimonism: Some of Its Problems.' *Internationale Zeitschrift für Philosophie*, Pt. 1: 57–72.

—— 1994b. Review of Bernard Williams, *Shame and Necessity*. *Journal of Philosophy*, 91: 619–22.

—— 1995a. 'Conflicting Parts of Happiness in Aristotle's Ethics.' *Ethics*, 105: 258–83.

—— 1995b. Review of Gregory Vlastos, *Socrates: Ironist and Moral Philosopher*. *Philosophy and Phenomenological Research*, 55: 237–42.

—— 1999a. 'Harmonizing Plato.' *Philosophy and Phenomenological Research*, 59: 497–512.

—— 1999b. 'Intrinsically Valued Parts of Happiness: Aristotle, Butler, and Mill.' In U. Meixner and A. Newen, eds., *Philosophiegeschichte und Logische Analyse/Logical Analysis and History of Philosophy*, 149–56. Paderborn: Mentis.

White, Stephen A. 1990. 'Is Aristotelian Happiness a Good Life or the Best Life?' *Oxford Studies in Ancient Philosophy*, 8: 103–43.

Whiting, Jennifer. 1996. 'Self-Love and Authoritative Virtue.' In Engstrom and Whiting 1996: 162–99.

Wilamowitz-Moellendorf, Ulrich von. 1913. *Reden und Vorträge*, 3rd ed. Berlin: Weidemann.

Wilkes, Kathleen. 1980. 'The Good Man and the Good for Man in Aristotle's Ethics.' In Rorty 1980a: 341–57.

Williams, Bernard. 1973a. 'Ethical Consistency.' In Williams 1973b: 166–86. First published in *Proceedings of the Aristotelian Society*, supp. vol. 40 (1965): 1–22.

—— 1973b. *Problems of the Self*. Cambridge: Cambridge University Press.

—— 1981a. 'Conflict of Values.' In Williams 1981c: 71–82. First published in Alan Ryan, ed., *The Idea of Freedom*. Oxford: Oxford University Press, 1979.

—— 1981b. 'Moral Luck.' In Williams 1981c: 20–39. First published in *Proceedings of the Aristotelian Society*, supp. vol. 50: 115–35.

—— 1981c. *Moral Luck*. Cambridge: Cambridge University Press.

—— 1981d. 'Persons, Character and Morality.' In Williams 1981c: 1–19. First published in Rorty 1976: 197–216.

—— 1981e. 'Philosophy.' In M. I. Finley, ed., *The Legacy of Greece: A New Appraisal*, 201–55. Oxford: Clarendon Press.

—— 1985. *Ethics and the Limits of Philosophy*. Cambridge, Mass.: Harvard University Press.

—— 1993. *Shame and Necessity*. Berkeley: University of California Press.

Winckelmann, Johann Joachim. 1960. 'Thoughts on the Imitation of Greek Works in Painting and Sculpture' (1755). *Kleine Schriften und Briefe*, 44–6. Weimar: Hermann Boehlaus Nachfolger. Selections translated in Butler 1935: 46–8.

Wood, Alan. 1991. *Hegel's Ethical Thought*. Cambridge: Cambridge University Press.

—— 1993. 'Hegel's Ethics.' In Beiser 1993: 211–33.

Woods, Michael, ed. 1992. *Aristotle: Eudemian Ethics, Books I, II, and VIII*, 2nd ed. Oxford: Clarendon Press.

Index